1998

PRESIDENTIAL POWER

IN THE UNITED STATES

PRESIDENTIAL POWER

IN THE UNITED STATES

Raymond Tatalovich
Loyola University of Chicago

Byron W. Daynes
DePauw University

Brooks/Cole Publishing Company
Monterey, California

Brooks/Cole Publishing Company
A Division of Wadsworth, Inc.

Printed in the United States of America

10 9 8 7 6 5 4 3 2 1

Library of Congress Cataloging in Publication Data

Tatalovich, Raymond.
   Presidential power in the United States.

   Bibliography: p.
   Includes index.
   1. Executive power—United States.   2. Presidents—
United States.   I. Daynes, Byron W.   II. Title.
JK516.T39   1983   353.03′22   83–7490
ISBN 0-534-02737-7

Subject Editor: Marquita Flemming
Production Editors: Jane Stanley and Gay L. Orr
Manuscript Editor: Adrienne Mayor
Permissions Editor: Carline Haga
Interior Design: Victoria A. Van Deventer
Cover Design: Debbie Wunsch
Art Coordinator: Judy Macdonald
Interior Illustration: Ryan Cooper
Typesetting: Graphic Typesetting Service, Los Angeles, California

To Anne, my wife, and to my Mother and Teti Mary—
three pillars of my life.

R.T.

To Dr. Byron Woodruff and Maxine Gaddie Daynes, my parents,
who unselfishly gave me moral and financial support, enthusiastic
encouragement in my endeavors, and enduring love and confidence.

B.W.D.

Acknowledgments

Our thinking about the nature of presidential power has matured over several years and culminates in this volume. Many students and faculty members at various universities, including Professor Thomas Engeman of Loyola University of Chicago and Professor Richard Bloss of Chicago State University, have provided valuable insights regarding our formulation of the empirical underpinnings of the president's power. We were especially fortunate to get insightful criticisms of our work by four reviewers, many of whose suggestions are incorporated in this manuscript. We are indebted to Professors Michael Mezey of DePaul University; Melvin J. Dubnick of the University of Kansas; Harry A. Bailey, Jr. of Temple University; and John W. Wood of the University of Oklahoma. In particular, we would like to give special thanks for the intellectual encouragement offered by Professor Harry A. Bailey, Jr. whose own research acknowledged the importance of our framework of analysis. We would like to also acknowledge our research assistants, Kevin Armstrong and Mary Stumpp, for their helpful and diligent work. Finally, we were most fortunate to receive strong endorsement for our project and much needed editorial assistance from our publisher, Brooks/Cole, and especially its Political Science editor, Marquita Flemming. Most importantly, we are eternally grateful to our wives, Anne Tatalovich and Kathryn Daynes, for their support, patience, and editorial criticisms throughout this project.

R.T.

B.W.D.

This book was written during a period of personal trauma, and I owe an emotional debt to many good people. To my wife, Anne, I am so grateful for her love, strength, and understanding, and to my mother and Teti Mary for their unflinching faith. I was also fortunate to be surrounded by a singular group of colleagues at Loyola University of Chicago who provided needed support and comfort at critical moments, particularly Sam C. Sarkesian and Father Joseph F. Small. The task of completing this manuscript was greatly eased by the labors of Bill Daynes, my good friend and a fine scholar. My recovery I attribute to the excellent medical care provided by the University of Chicago hospitals and clinics, where I was blessed to be under the care of extraordinarily talented physicians, Dr. Charles M. Johnson III, Dr. Eric P. Lester, and Dr. Barbara Hull. To these individuals, and my friends, relatives, and neighbors, please accept my heartfelt thanks.

R.T.

Preface

Since the United States has had only forty presidents, one might think that it is a relatively simple task to write a textbook on this subject. But the literature on the presidency is immense, and growing each year; it is a very comprehensive collection, ranging from statistical analyses of presidential elections to case studies of foreign policy decisions. The immensity of the literature may make it difficult for the undergraduate student to understand how each facet contributes to the functioning of the president in the American political system. Scholars who write on the presidency, moreover, use different approaches—historical, institutional, and behavioral—and each evaluates the presidency according to different criteria. This means that although seminal works exist on particular topics, there are few texts that give a comprehensive and systematic overview of the presidency.

As our overriding purpose, therefore, we want to supply a framework that synthesizes this wide-ranging literature in terms of a theory of presidential power. We also want to be somewhat detached from the ideological debate over presidential power—whether the president is too strong or too weak—by reformulating that question. In our view, presidential power is defined by presidential roles. For example, as a commander-in-chief a president's power is great; as opinion/party leader, however, his power potential is much less. We concentrate primarily on the empirical variables that underlie presidential power and suggest the conditions under which it is maximized. To illustrate our argument, we rely heavily on the contemporary presidents (since Franklin D. Roosevelt), and draw numerous case studies from the Carter and Reagan administrations. However, the student should also appreciate how political, legal, and institutional developments over time have shaped the contemporary presidency. In fundamental ways the modern presidency is a novelty, but in other ways it is the cumulation of long-standing historical forces.

The introduction surveys the major intellectual traditions about presidential power in the United States. We discuss the "textbook presidency," a concept that dominated scholarly analysis from the 1930s until the mid-1960s; this image of a strong, activist, and liberal president was promoted by many political scientists and historians during that era. We also explain what historical forces gave rise to increased presidential power in America. After Vietnam and Watergate, a "revisionist" argument surfaces in the literature, suggesting that a healthy skepticism—if not cynicism—regarding the president's power is warranted; we analyze the political conditions that promoted this reassessment of the president's role in our governmental system.

Chapter one outlines the broad contours of our theory of presidential power. Five roles are most important to understanding the presidency: commander-in-chief, chief diplomat, chief executive, legislative leader, and opinion/party leader. The power of a president in each role is largely determined by the workings of five variables: authority, decision-making, public inputs, expertise, and crisis. Explanation of the meaning of these five variables and their impact follows.

Chapter two focuses on the recruitment-nomination-election process. The selection of a president defines in large measure the democratic potential of the office for our system of government. What kind of person is generally elected to the presidency? To what extent do elections guide public policy during a president's term of office? We argue that the recruitment-nomination-election process sets the political agenda for a president and supplies cues by which his performance in office is judged by the electorate. The selection process, therefore, has a special relationship to the president's role as opinion/party leader.

Chapters three through seven discuss the five presidential roles, beginning with the weakest role, opinion/party leader, and concluding with the strongest, commander-in-chief. These five chapters follow a parallel organization: each role is analyzed in terms of the same five variables that underlie presidential power. These comparisons help the student perceive and understand the variables of presidential power. For example, whereas a president acting as commander-in-chief enjoys substantial legal authority to pursue his ends, the amount of legal authority available to an opinion/party leader is meagre indeed. The five variables inventory the major political and legal resources that political scientists usually cite when trying to account for the power potential of the modern president.

Chapter eight concludes our study by introducing the student to a relatively new approach that focuses on the president's personality. The seminal work in this field is by James David Barber, but political scientists before him were equally concerned about whether a president's "active" or "passive" style affected his use of political power. Since our volume is mainly concerned with defining the legal and political resources underlying presidential power, this chapter asks to what extent personality determines whether a president will become a leader. Given the contradictory evidence in this body of research, no entirely satisfactory answer to that question can be given.

Presidential Power in the United States addresses both normative and empirical considerations, studies the contemporary president in terms of historical trends, and synthesizes the legal and political factors that underlie presidential power. While the use of role analysis is not new to the literature, we hope that our novel interpretation will stimulate the student seeking a general knowledge of the presidency and will challenge the upper-level political science major and graduate student.

Raymond Tatalovich
Byron W. Daynes

Foreword

The problem of presidential power has continued to trouble president watchers since the beginning of the Republic. What is presidential power? Where is it located? How much is there when one finds it and under what circumstances can it be used? Professors Tatalovich and Daynes seek to answer those questions in this book.

The authors make use of role analysis to explore and plumb the depths of presidential power. What emerges is a fascinating theory and study.

Professors Tatalovich and Daynes organize five presidential roles hierarchically to reflect their relative power contributions. Each role is then examined in terms of five major variables which, the authors note, are used by political scientists to inventory the major political and legal resources available to a president. Each of these variables witholds from or grants to each role a specific amount of power. Thus, this book confronts the issue of the scope and limits of presidential power.

Importantly, the theory the authors develop here begins to close the gap between the two faces of presidential power: the notion that it is either a function of office and the prerogatives of that office a la Edward Corwin or a function of persuasion a la Richard Neustadt. In this book Professors Tatalovich and Daynes show that presidential power is truly a function of both. Such a book is long overdue.

Each chapter in *Presidential Power in the United States* addresses a major role of the modern presidency—from opinion/party leader to commander-in-chief. In this exposition president watchers, inside and outside of the classroom, can learn why a president is likely to be very powerful under some circumstances and relatively weak under others. The reality of presidential power is brightly illuminated by this theory and approach. All who value understanding the American presidency should welcome this significant addition to the literature of presidential studies.

Harry A. Bailey, Jr.
Temple University
Philadelphia, PA
April 11, 1983

Contents

CHAPTER SEVEN
Commander-in-Chief: Can the Constitutional Dictator be Checked? 321

CHAPTER EIGHT
The Man or the Office: What Makes the President a Leader? 374

Introduction

The central focus of scholars who study the presidency is the question of power, its definition and scope. In addressing this issue, however, political scientists in the past were guided by an ideology regarding the use of presidential power. Over the past century historians and scholars endorsed the concept of a strong president who would exert leadership in a variety of roles, and this tendency became doctrine after the era of Franklin D. Roosevelt's New Deal. The defense of a strong president was affirmed, moreover, by the actions of Harry Truman, John F. Kennedy, and Lyndon B. Johnson—that is, until President Johnson began the Vietnam War. The commitment of political scientists to the "heroic" president, to borrow Erwin Hargrove's term,[1] has been characterized by Thomas Cronin as the "textbook presidency."[2]

TEXTBOOK PRESIDENCY

The "textbook presidency" was a romantic, idealized view that glorified the office and especially the man. Americans grew up, Cronin argues, expecting the president to be a storehouse of power, wisdom, and goodness, able to win wars and cure the nation's socioeconomic ills. The president was pictured as being the most important and indispensable official in the country, and we came to expect his powers to grow commensurate with the expanding scope of the federal government. In addition, the "textbook presidency" contended that because of his access to expert opinion and advisers, a president knows what is best for us. James MacGregor Burns, for one, even suggested that the advisory network—not the separation of powers—is the essential check against a president's blunders. "The only protection possible is the one the White House already affords: a group of men closely related to the president who can restrain him if need be. If power and decision making in the White House are collective, prudence is collective too."[3] This argument was buttressed by the "textbook presidency" view of the president as a moral leader who boldly confronts problems, expands his powers, and inspires public confidence. Ultimately, this conception of the president implied all would be well if the right person is chosen for that job.

"Textbook presidency" is a powerful example of political "socialization," because political scientists and historians to a large extent define political reality by writing the books used in high school and college. As a child matures into a citizen he or she comes to expect certain behaviors from the president. The image of the forceful but benevolent president was cultivated by such writers as Clinton Rossiter, James MacGregor Burns, and Richard Neustadt, but similar themes can be found as early as 1940 in the writing of Harold Laski, an Englishman who was very impressed by the accomplishments of Franklin D. Roosevelt.[4] Writing at the end of the Great Depression, Laski argued that the president must necessarily be the "essential keystone of the political arch." The president, he said, could mobilize public opinion behind "positive" government and thereby confront Congress and entrenched business interests. Laski's argument reflected the dominant themes of the post–Franklin D. Roosevelt period: a strong president was desirable, he would counteract a leaderless Congress, and presidential power could advance progressive domestic legislation and enlightened foreign policies in behalf of the ordinary citizen.

Similar thinking affected the historians who evaluate America's presidents. Arthur Schlesinger, Jr. was among those influential scholars who encouraged the vision of a strong but good president. Polls showing how historians rank the presidents have remarkably similar results, and they indicate that few presidents are perceived as having extraordinary impact on American politics (see boxed material).[5] The historians taking the polls were not entirely unbiased in studying our presidents; for example, the questions asked by Schlesinger Sr.'s 1962 poll indicate an assumption as James MacGregor Burns observes, "that Presidents *can* influence history significantly, and that they *should* do so in a generally liberal, humanitarian, egalitarian, reformist direction."[6] Thus, conservative (and Republican) presidents tended to be ranked "average," "below average," or "failure" in Schlesinger's 1948 and 1962 polls. Only five presidents were considered "great" by the historians polled in 1948 and 1962: Lincoln, Washington, Franklin D. Roosevelt, Wilson, and Jefferson. In 1970 a more extensive survey by Maranell and Dodder found that the presidents classified as "great" or "near-great" in the earlier polls also ranked among the top twelve presidents in 1970. The major addition was John F. Kennedy's ranking ninth in the 1970 standings.

GROWTH OF PRESIDENTIAL POWER

In a sense the "textbook presidency" merely rationalized the fact that our presidency had grown in importance. The expansion of that office was due to historic forces rather than conspiratorial design. To reverse this development, therefore, requires more than a change in intellectual disposition;

Rankings of U.S. presidents by historians*

1948 Schlesinger Poll (N = 55)	1962 Schlesinger Poll (N = 75)	1970 Maranell/Dodder Survey (N = 571)
"Great"		
1. Lincoln	1. Lincoln	1. Lincoln
2. Washington	2. Washington	2. Washington
3. FDR	3. FDR	3. FDR
4. Wilson	4. Wilson	4. Jefferson
5. Jefferson	5. Jefferson	5. T. Roosevelt
6. Jackson		6. Wilson
		7. Truman
"Near-Great"		8. Jackson
7. T. Roosevelt	6. Jackson	9. Kennedy
8. Cleveland	7. T. Roosevelt	10. John Adams
9. John Adams	8. Polk	11. Polk
10. Polk	9. Truman	12. Cleveland
	10. John Adams	13. Madison
	11. Cleveland	14. Monroe
		15. J. Q. Adams
"Average"		16. L. Johnson
		17. Taft
11. J. Q. Adams	12. Madison	18. Hoover
12. Monroe	13. J. Q. Adams	19. Eisenhower
13. Hayes	14. Hayes	20. A. Johnson
14. Madison	15. McKinley	21. Van Buren
15. Van Buren	16. Taft	22. McKinley
16. Taft	17. Van Buren	23. Arthur
17. Arthur	18. Monroe	24. Hayes
18. McKinley	19. Hoover	25. Tyler
19. A. Johnson	20. B. Harrison	26. B. Harrison
20. Hoover	21. Arthur	27. Taylor
21. B. Harrison	22. Eisenhower	28. Coolidge
	23. A. Johnson	29. Fillmore
		30. Buchanan
		31. Pierce
"Below Average"		32. Grant
22. Tyler	24. Taylor	33. Harding
23. Coolidge	25. Tyler	
24. Fillmore	26. Fillmore	
25. Taylor	27. Coolidge	
26. Buchanan	28. Pierce	
27. Pierce	29. Buchanan	
"Failure"		
28. Grant	30. Grant	
29. Harding	31. Harding	

*In all three surveys William Henry Harrison and James Garfield were excluded from consideration.

it calls for modification of fundamental political processes. Four factors (social responsibility, economics, executive authority, and crisis politics) explain the growth of presidential power in the United States. They are discussed in the following sections.

Positive government

America evolved from a rural, agrarian society able to function efficiently with a small government into a highly urbanized, industrialized, and interdependent nation. The view of society held by the Founding Fathers who wrote the Constitution was that "limited" government was a virtue. Accordingly, separation of powers, checks and balances, and the protection of property rights were intended more to restrain government than to facilitate its governing. Our faith in the individual, buttressed by the "frontier" spirit, minimized class tensions and perpetuated the myth of equal opportunity in America. This assumption of equality further delayed the growth of what might be termed "positive" government in the United States. But the "welfare state" did eventually arrive, carrying with it increased responsibilities for the executive branch.

The great reform eras in American history include the Populist Era of the 1890s, the Progressive Era of the early twentieth century, the New Deal of the 1930s, and Lyndon Johnson's Great Society of the 1960s. The Populists represented the small farmer, forgotten in the post–Civil War era of massive industrialization, whose agitation ultimately resulted in the enactment of the Interstate Commerce Act (1887) and the Sherman Anti-Trust Act of 1890. The Progressive Era is associated with the presidencies of Theodore Roosevelt and Woodrow Wilson. Roosevelt, the "trust-buster" who mounted a legal challenge to the nation's monopolies, is also credited with promoting the Pure Food and Drug Act. During Wilson's term reform legislation established the income tax (Sixteenth Amendment), the Federal Reserve System, the Clayton Anti-Trust Act, and the Federal Trade Commission.

But government's scope remained relatively small until the 1930s. The Great Depression called into question the assumptions of "laissez-faire" capitalism, but President Herbert Hoover was unable to deviate from his deep commitment to individualism and capitalism. Hoover's efforts to revive the economy came too late and were too modest, setting the stage for Franklin D. Roosevelt's promise of a New Deal for the American people.

Building upon a new political coalition—the working classes, the immigrants, residents of big cities, blacks, Southerners—Franklin D. Roosevelt became the major exponent of welfarism. His administration enacted landmark policies in many social areas: Social Security, unemployment compensation, public assistance, aid to the blind and disabled, the Tennessee Valley Authority, the Wagner Act (to legalize unionization), and the Fair Labor Standards Act (to set minimum wage/maximum hours). Moreover, Roosevelt strengthened the regulatory arm of government by establishing various "independent" commissions and agencies, including the Federal Power Commission (1930), Federal Communications Commission (1934), the Securities and Exchange Commission (1934), and Civil Aeronautics Board (1938).

Roosevelt's commitment to improving the lot of the ordinary citizen was sustained by Harry Truman's Fair Deal and John F. Kennedy's New Frontier. The legislative achievements of Lyndon B. Johnson, however, perhaps exceed those of Franklin D. Roosevelt. During Johnson's term Congress passed major legislation in civil rights, medical care for the aged, federal aid to elementary and secondary schools, job training, preschool programs for disadvantaged children, and subsidized housing for the poor.

The cumulative effects of these massive waves of domestic reform resulted in a federal government employing about 2.8 million civilian workers and spending in excess of $695 billion by 1982. The federal government's responsibilities have expanded so much, especially since World War II, that many scholars argue that the president's authority as chief executive is inadequate to the task of supervising the burgeoning bureaucracy.

The economy

A second reason for broadening executive power is the economy. Although throughout our history presidents have intervened in labor–management disputes that threaten the nation's well-being, much more is involved in managing the economy today. We now expect the president to manage the economy in such a way that our collective prosperity is enhanced. Presidents, particularly those of the twentieth century, have been very supportive of private enterprise and the market economy. Even Franklin D. Roosevelt, who championed government regulation of business, believed that his actions would save capitalism during an era when many people lost faith in traditional economics. Again, it may be argued that expectations about presidential power may exceed the president's ability to assure economic vitality in view of overwhelming world economic ills.

The view that government should actively intervene in the marketplace to assure economic goals dates back to the influential writings of the British economist John Maynard Keynes. Keynes tried to convince Franklin D. Roosevelt of the validity of his argument that deficit spending was necessary for economic recovery, but Roosevelt's policies during the Depression were guided more by a practical sense than by a commitment to any theory. Later, during World War II the nation enjoyed a "full employment" economy, but afterwards suffered the pains of having to readjust to a peacetime economy. In reaction, Congress enacted the Employment Act of 1946 which charged the president with carrying out various economic goals. In part the act stated, "It is the continuing policy and responsibility of the Federal Government to use all practicable means . . . to promote maximum employment, production and purchasing power." It also noted the government's responsibility to foster "free competitive enterprise," but the thrust of this document was toward the formulation of economic policy. It directed the president to submit an annual economic report to Congress, it created a Council of Economic Advisors, and it established a Joint Economic Committee, composed of senators and representatives, to study the president's plan of action.

Congress' worries about responsible presidential economic planning were unfounded in the case of Eisenhower, whose orthodox views on economics affirmed the need for a balanced budget. Eisenhower balanced the budget twice during his term. In contrast, the Keynesian "new economics" was fully accepted by Presidents Kennedy and Johnson, whose advisers advocated use of fiscal policy (taxes and spending) to stimulate economic growth and to alleviate inflationary pressures. But Lyndon Johnson's commitment to "guns *and* butter"—that is, spending for both domestic social welfare programs and the Vietnam War—fueled the economy to the point that inflation became a more serious problem. During the terms of Nixon, Ford, and Carter, inflation was the major fiscal problem facing governmental decision makers. Moreover, during Jimmy Carter's term of office, we suffered "stagflation," a combination of double-digit inflation and economic decline, a dilemma Keynes had never anticipated. We are now in the "post-Keynesian" era, meaning that economists are postulating new economic theories to deal with today's economic problems. For example, early in his term, Ronald Reagan was influenced by the so-called supply-side economists who emphasized the need for investment coupled with a tight money supply, rather than the Keynesian stress on manipulating consumer demand.

Because economics is an imprecise science, a president's ability to fine-tune the nation's economy is severely limited. Yet we as a people hold him responsible for the health of our economic system.

Presidential advantages

Increased executive power is also related to the president's inherent advantages in decision making, compared with Congress' organizational weaknesses. Advocates of the "heroic" president point to Congress' unwillingness or inability to meet the challenges of modern society; they argue that executive power has increased by default. Related to this argument is the view that a strong president is needed to counterbalance Congress' conservatism and attachment to the status quo. The rise of executive authority at the expense of Congress, therefore, is often legitimized by the claim that the president more directly "represents" the people because only he and the vice-president are elected by the entire nation. Thus, whereas members of congress are responsive to their districts and senators to their states, the president is said to more truly embody the national interest. In evaluating this issue in 1960, Willmoore Kendall found that intellectuals and professors usually sided with the president against Congress. He concluded

> . . . The Executive tends . . . to have the nation's ministers and publicists with it on "peace," the nation's professors and moralizers with it on desegregation, the nation's economists with it on fiscal policy and redistribution, the nation's political scientists with it on political reform and civil rights, etc. To put it otherwise, Congress at least *appears* . . . to be holding out for either the repudiation or evasion of the moral imperatives that the nation's proper teachers urge upon us, or the assertion of an invincibly ignorant "layman's" opinion on topics that are demonstrably "professional" or "expert" in character, or both.[7]

In support of the idea that advances in the human condition are linked to aggressive leadership by the president is the assertion that the executive is better equipped than Congress to govern. For example, in *Federalist #70,* Alexander Hamilton argued that in regard to foreign affairs the president enjoys the advantages of secrecy, activity, decision, and speed. By its nature the workings of Congress are more public, slow, and directed toward compromise. Furthermore, constituents are usually ill-informed or uncaring about foreign affairs, leading many legislators to doubt that any serious electoral consequences result from their involvement or noninvolvement in the area.

Although most scholars acknowledge the president's predominant role in foreign policy, even in domestic policymaking much power remains in the executive branch by default. Critic Theodore Lowi and others contend that in the past Congress delegated broad, discretionary authority to the president because its members lacked the expertise and information needed to formulate public policy for our complex society, which is affected by a multitude of social, political, and economic forces.[8] To regain a measure of control over decision making, therefore, Congress must strengthen its fact-finding and intelligence capabilities. An example is the enactment of the Budget and Impoundment Act of 1974 in response to Nixon's abuse of budgetary authority. The legislation not only increased Congress' formal authority over budget making but also established the Congressional Budget Office as a staff counterpart to the president's Office of Management and Budget.

Wars and crises

International crises and wars provide extraordinary opportunities for any president to expand his authority. Each new executive draws upon certain precedents established by predecessors to justify his own war making. In an era of "total" war, as experienced during World Wars I and II, all domestic resources must be mobilized in the war effort. As a result, the president often assumes vast powers to regulate the economy and even to curtail civil rights and liberties. America's rise as a superpower in the post–World War II period, coupled with our perception that the Soviet Union constitutes a threat to peace, and the resultant Cold War, has precipitated innumerable crises and international incidents. The Berlin Blockade, the Suez crisis, the U-2 incident, the Bay of Pigs fiasco, and the Cuban missile crisis are but a few in the long series.

Nuclear arms proliferation and our defense treaty alliances, such as NATO, further consolidate the president's war-making power, because these situations allow little time for legislative debate. During our history, presidents have committed American troops to a military action about two-hundred times without a declaration of war by Congress. Today's wars and crises seem to demand the executive advantages of decisiveness and speed noted by Alexander Hamilton. The contemporary movement in political science to reassess the presidency stems in large part from our apprehension about the president's single-handed ability to make war.

THE REVISIONIST ARGUMENT

Besides describing academia's traditional admiration of the strong president, Cronin's criticism of "textbook presidency" also stimulated a reexamination of assumptions about presidential power. The abuses of power by Presidents Lyndon Johnson and Richard Nixon provoked a scholarly reaction against them as intense as that exhibited by the body politic. It became fashionable for some to characterize the president as an elected monarch, and an entirely new rationale was developed to legitimize this "revisionist" argument.[9] The turnabout in academic opinion is reflected, for example, in the admission made by Erwin Hargrove. Hargrove noted his own willingness—which was shared by many political scientists—to excuse the misuse of power by our strong presidents because they apparently did so much good for the nation. He explains that this common rationalization was based on the assumption that

> Presidents were guided by moral purpose and it was frankly biased in the direction of the liberal, power-maximizing Presidents. It was assumed that purpose would purify power. To be fair to oneself the argument was made that such power-striving, if rooted in personal needs, could lead to self-defeating eruptions of personality such as Theodore Roosevelt's in 1912, Wilson's rigidity in the League [of Nations] fight, and FDR's plan to pack the Supreme Court. However, it was assumed that institutional checks and balances were sufficient to control such behavior. The price was worth paying because strong political leadership was required.[10]

Thus, the revisionist argument that surfaced during the mid-1960s was not championed by conservatives but mainly by disillusioned liberals. Three causes for heightened concern about unchecked presidential power, the Vietnam War, Watergate, and neoconservatism, are discussed below.

Vietnam

The Vietnam War was perhaps the main reason for the revisionist thinking about presidential power. Unlike our actions in World War I, World War II, and the Korean War, the war in Vietnam was more controversial, prompting massive public demonstrations by anti-war groups. Dissidents were joined by liberal reformers, civil rights leaders, including Dr. Martin Luther King, and academics. For the many intellectuals who opposed our involvement in Southeast Asia the Vietnam War taught a fundamental lesson: it is nearly impossible for public opinion, the Supreme Court, or even Congress to stop a president who is determined to wage war. Writing in 1972, for example, Philippa Strum declared: ". . . the American presence in Vietnam and Cambodia should lead even the most diehard proponents of increased presidential power to question their assumption that expansion of power is always a good thing."[11] Although our involvement in Southeast Asia can be traced to John F. Kennedy's decision to send military advisers there, and even further to the Eisenhower administration, it was Lyndon Johnson who ordered the massive buildup by sending over 500,000 American troops into battle. Johnson viewed the matter simply as communist aggression by North Vietnam against South Vietnam, while many intellectuals, journalists, and others doubted that our national interest required such massive military involvement. Many skeptics, moreover, disliked the idea of our supporting the authoritarian regime that ruled South Vietnam.

Johnson's high-handed and secretive methods of engaging in war were another reason for academic disillusionment with the Vietnam War. Eventually his machinations led to a serious credibility gap between the president and the American people. In retrospect, we learned that the events leading to Congress' 1964 enactment of the Gulf of Tonkin Resolution, giving Lyndon Johnson carte-blanche authority to wage the war, were not accurately reported to the lawmakers, the media, or the public. Exposés by journalists such as David Halberstam[12] and disclosures by Daniel Ellsberg in the Pentagon Papers[13] revealed how both Johnson and Nixon deceived the American people into blindly supporting the war. After years of fighting, however, with outlays in the billions, great loss of life, and increased social tensions at home, the public tired of the administration's assurances that "victory" was just around the corner. The presidential abuses and deception surrounding the Vietnam War brought unchecked warmaking under congressional scrutiny. In 1970 Congress revoked the Gulf of Tonkin Resolution, and in 1973 it enacted the War Powers Act. This legislation required the president to obtain congressional approval in order to engage in warmaking beyond a period of sixty days. The War Powers Act also provided that the president consult with Congress before committing American forces abroad.

Watergate

Watergate has become a code word for a multitude of political sins committed by Richard Nixon and his associates. The Watergate break-in was the burglary and attempted wiretap of the headquarters of the Democratic National Committee, and was part of a widespread effort to harass the president's political opponents. During 1972, the White House supervised various "dirty tricks" against Democratic presidential contenders. Their clandestine activities included planting embarrassing letters and disrupting opponents' campaign appearances. The details of what a Nixon aide dismissed as a "third-rate burglary" were publicized by two *Washington Post* reporters, and the media coverage led to public outrage and legislative inquiries.[14]

Nixon had his aides order the CIA to block the FBI's investigation of the break-in, and approved efforts to pay "hush money" to the Watergate defendants. Consequently, the Senate refused to confirm Nixon's nominee for attorney general, Elliott Richardson, until a special prosecutor was named to study these charges. Nixon refused to cooperate and fired the first Special Prosecutor, Archibald Cox. He would not release his personal tapes and related documents to Cox's successor, Leon Jaworski. The special prosecutor asked a federal district court to subpoena President Nixon's tape recordings and other documents pertaining to his conversations with White House aides. The Supreme Court in *U.S. v. Nixon* (1974)[15] supported the subpoena request by the district court and denied the president's claim of absolute "executive privilege," thus directly calling into question Richard Nixon's unchecked authority.

In addition to the Watergate scandals, Nixon abused his powers in other ways. He ordered compiled a list of political enemies to be investigated by the IRS. He granted favors to milk producers and had an antitrust suit settled with International Telephone and Telegraph Company (ITT) in exchange for campaign donations. He established a secret police unit, the so-called plumbers, to engage in domestic surveillance and to prevent leaks of information to the press. The "plumbers" group burglarized the office of Daniel Ellsberg's psychiatrist in an effort to discredit his disclosures on Vietnam in the Pentagon Papers. Moreover, Nixon impounded (that is, refused to spend) about $40 billion already appropriated by Congress for public works programs, actions later declared by the courts to be illegal.

This series of incidents led the House of Representatives to consider Nixon's impeachment, thereby bringing Nixon closer to removal from office than any other president except Andrew Johnson. (Andrew Johnson, who became president upon Lincoln's assassination, had been "impeached" by the House of Representative but escaped conviction in the Senate by one vote.) Nixon's impeachment did not proceed beyond the Judiciary Committee before he felt compelled to resign from office. The Judiciary Committee of the House of Representatives brought three articles of impeachment against Nixon. Article I argued that Nixon engaged in a plan to obstruct the investigations of Watergate. Article II further accused him of violating his oath of office to execute the laws and of abusing his power in misusing the Internal Revenue Service, imposing illegal wiretaps, and in establishing a "secret investigative unit" in the White House. Article III charged the president with conduct "subversive of constitutional government"; here reference was made to his refusal to comply with the committee's subpoenas for 147 tapes and records.

Watergate had a profound impact on our view of presidential power. Not only did it undermine the public's support for the office but even the idealistic faith of children in the nation's highest leader was shaken. It is doubtful that political scientists could ever again write textbooks on the presidency without taking account of the excesses of Richard Nixon. In the 1975 edition of *The Chief Executive*, for example, Louis Koenig illustrates the impact of "revisionist" thinking by his differentiation between "high-democracy" and "low-democracy" presidents.[16] The former reflects the values of the "heroic" or "textbook" president while the latter was prompted by revelations that presidential power can be abused. Both tendencies may be found in any president, but clearly the attributes of a "low-democracy" milieu helped to wreck the Nixon presidency. According to Koenig's description, the "low-democracy" president is a force for divisiveness, is indifferent to civil liberties, is willing to encroach on the authority of the other branches of government, and is accessible mainly to the economically powerful. The "low-democracy" president, in addition, is manipulative and secretive in his dealings and exhibits a weak commitment to democratic values.

Neoconservatism

A third underpinning of the revisionist argument is the so-called neoconservative critique of social welfarism. Neoconservatism is not an ideology but rather a collection of ideas identified with a certain group of social scientists, intellectuals, and journalists. It is reflected, for example, in Edward Banfield's *The Unheavenly City*, in Daniel Moynihan's works on community control and black family structure, and in James Coleman's research on the impact of racial integration on the achievement patterns of minorities.[17]

The neoconservative movement reached its fullest development in the 1970s and extends into the 1980s. But its origins are in President Lyndon Johnson's Great Society, which promised to uplift disadvantaged groups in our country. Racial integration was promoted by Johnson's ability to get Congress to enact the Civil Rights Acts of 1964 (public accommodations), 1965 (voting rights), and 1968 (open housing). Other programs were aimed at helping the poor. To assist school children trapped in poverty, Project Head Start was launched, and Congress finally approved federal aid to elementary and secondary education—a program stalled in the legislature for over a decade. To provide training for the hard-core unemployed, the Job Corps was created, while public housing rent subsidies and Model Cities were designed to improve life in the inner cities.

In many instances, however, the grandiose objectives envisioned by these programs were not achieved during the 1960s, or since. One reason for their limited impact was that President Johnson stressed legislative victories at the expense of administration, with the result that some programs were poorly conceived and implemented. In addition, the liberal activists who championed these programs viewed them as a method of aiding the poor not just economically but also politically; they wanted to give the poor more power over the decision making that affected their lives. As might be expected, however, these attempts to give the poor and minorities "community control" over educational policy, urban renewal plans, and the distribution of social services alienated state and local political leaders who traditionally controlled these kinds of programs.

Beyond these difficulties, Great Society programs assumed that long-standing social problems could be successfully eradicated. One strong intellectual strain in the neoconservative position is that human nature is much too complex to be easily modified by even the best of government efforts. Behavior patterns are affected by a multitude of forces, including family, peer groups, personal values, and cultural mores. Neoconservatives doubt, therefore, that poverty can be effectively eliminated because too little is known about its causes to mount a comprehensive campaign against it.

This view is often summarized by the phrase, "we cannot solve problems merely by throwing money at them." Moreover, a concern arose that the philosophy behind the Great Society undermined certain social values that were important to America. Neoconservatives do not favor "equality of condition" but rather stress "equality of opportunity"; they are not convinced that government is always more effective than private institutions or the marketplace in allocating needed goods and services. They came to believe that disproportionate burdens were being placed on the middle and working classes, who themselves have to struggle to educate their children, pay taxes, and cope with inflation. The rhetoric of the Great Society, for example in Lyndon Johnson's reference to his "War" on poverty, was seen as raising the expectations of disadvantaged groups far beyond the government's capabilities. The critics argued that this gap between rising expectations and reality was one cause of the urban rioting and social unrest that accompanied Lyndon Johnson's Great Society in the 1960s.

Summary

The "revisionist" argument developed as an antidote to the image of the "heroic" president which dominated political science literature since Franklin D. Roosevelt. The new attitude stressed the need to restrain presidential power, to reassert the constitutional role of Congress, and to question the long-standing assumption that executive leadership inevitably aids morally right causes. Revisionists now pictured the president as mortal, with all the needs, insecurities, and fears common to the ordinary person. To give this official, or anybody for that matter, life-and-death power over thousands of citizens is a very serious proposition. Thus, the revisionist position reaffirmed the validity of constitutional separation of powers as the best mechanism for keeping political leaders, especially the president, responsible.

In the wake of our disillusionment over Vietnam and Watergate, therefore, we have become uncertain about how to view the president or to judge his effect on society. Critical instincts have obviously matured greatly from the time when such questions were resolved according to the tenets of the "textbook presidency." But how long will the revisionist arguments be persuasive? Given that such skepticism was stimulated by Presidents Lyndon Johnson and Richard Nixon, the saliency of those arguments against presidential power may fade in the future. A 1979 Gallup Poll, for example, found that only 8 percent of its respondents believed that the president had "too much power," whereas 38 percent thought he had "too little power." Moreover, 63 percent agreed that "what this country needs is some really strong leadership that would try to solve problems directly without worrying how Congress and the Supreme Court might feel."[18] No doubt this public sentiment reflected the widespread belief that Jimmy Carter was largely ineffectual as president, a judgment also held by many political scientists and historians. Therefore, as Hargrove contends, our society may cry out again in the future for a strong, heroic president to deal with pressing social issues and international crises.[19]

Various commentators suggest that we translate our concerns about presidential power to another level. In reviewing the dilemma regarding presidential power in 1975, then-Senator Walter Mondale said that we need a "working concept of the Presidency which is strong, yet legal; capable of leading, but without dictating. We have reaped the bitter harvest of fundamental failure in the accountability of our Presidency; now we must rebuild that accountability to ensure the success of our government."[20]

In retrospect, Mondale's observations imply that we have simply relearned Lord Acton's age-old maxim that "power corrupts and absolute power corrupts absolutely." To fully understand how we can keep the president accountable to the American people, however, requires an appreciation of the factors underlying presidential power and its use. What is needed, ultimately, is a theory of presidential power, and to this task the first chapter is directed.

NOTES

[1]Erwin C. Hargrove, *The Power of the Modern Presidency* (New York: Alfred A. Knopf, 1974), p. 21.

[2]See Thomas E. Cronin, *The State of the Presidency* (Boston: Little, Brown and Company, 1980), chapter 3. Cronin developed his thesis of "the textbook presidency" as early as 1970 in a paper delivered to the American Political Science Association.

[3]James MacGregor Burns, *Presidential Government: The Crucible of Leadership* (Boston: Houghton Mifflin, 1973), p. 308.

[4]Harold J. Laski, *The American Presidency* (New York: Harper and Brothers, 1940).

[5]See Arthur M. Schlesinger, "The U.S. Presidents," *Life* (November 1, 1948), pp. 65–74; Arthur M. Schlesinger, "Our Presidents: A Rating by 75 Historians," *The New York Times Magazine* (July 29, 1962), p. 12; Gary M. Maranell and Richard A. Dodder, "Political Orientation and the Evaluation of Presidential Prestige: A Study of American Historians," *Social Science Quarterly* (September 1970), pp. 415–421.

[6]Burns, *Presidential Government*, p. 83. According to one study, large majorities of the political scientists (71.8%) and the historians (68.7%) surveyed called themselves "left" or "liberal" politically. Also, 71.2 percent of the political scientists and 68.3 percent of the historians voted for Democrat Hubert Humphrey in the 1968 presidential election. See "Faculty Opinion Survey," *PS (Washington, D.C.: American Political Science Association, Summer 1970), pp. 383, 385.

[7]Willmoore Kendall, "The Two Majorities," *Midwest Journal of Political Science* (November 1960), p. 324.

[8]Congress' delegation of authority to the executive and its administrative agencies without explicit standards of implementation is a major criticism made by Theodore J. Lowi in *The End of Liberalism* (New York: W. W. Norton, 1969).

[9]See Arthur M. Schlesinger, Jr., *The Imperial Presidency* (Boston: Houghton Mifflin, 1973).

[10]Erwin C. Hargrove, "The Crisis of the Contemporary Presidency," in James David Barber, ed., *Choosing the President* (Englewood Cliffs, N.J.: Prentice-Hall, 1974), p. 17.

[11]Philippa Strum, *Presidential Power and American Democracy* (Pacific Palisades, Calif.: Goodyear Publishing Company, 1972), p. 29.

[12]David Halberstam, *The Best and the Brightest* (New York: Random House, 1972).

[13]See Martin Shapiro, ed., *The Pentagon Papers and the Courts* (San Francisco: Chandler, 1972).

[14]Carl Bernstein and Bob Woodward, *All the President's Men* (New York: Simon and Schuster, 1974).

[15]*U.S. v. Nixon* 418 U.S. 683, (1974).

[16]Louis W. Koenig, *The Chief Executive*, 3rd ed. (New York: Harcourt Brace Jovanovich, 1975), pp. 336–339.

[17]Edward Banfield, *The Unheavenly City Revisited* (Boston: Little, Brown and Company, 1974); Daniel P. Moynihan, *Maximum Feasible Misunderstanding: Community Action in the War on Poverty* (New York: Free Press, 1969); Daniel P. Moynihan, *The Negro Family: The Case for National Action* (Washington D.C.: U.S. Government Printing Office, 1965); James S. Coleman, *Equality of Educational Opportunity*, Office of Education, U.S. Department of Health, Education and Welfare (Washington, D.C.: U.S. Government Printing Office, 1966). See also Peter Steinfels, *The Neoconservatives* (New York: Simon and Schuster, 1979).

[18]Cited in Thomas Halper, *Power, Politics, and American Democracy* (Santa Monica, Calif.: Goodyear Publishing Company, 1981), p. 161.

[19]See Hargrove, *The Power of the Modern Presidency*, p. 28.

[20]Walter F. Mondale, *The Accountability of Power: Toward a Responsible Presidency* (New York: McKay, 1975), p. 278.

SUGGESTED READINGS

Binkley, Wilfred. *The Powers of the President.* New York: Doubleday and Doran, 1937.

Bryce, James. *The American Commonwealth.* London: The Macmillan Company, 1888.

Burns, James MacGregor. *Presidential Government: The Crucible of Leadership.* Boston: Houghton Mifflin, 1973.

Finer, Herman. *The Presidency: Crisis and Regeneration.* Chicago: University of Chicago Press, 1960.

Hargrove, Erwin C. *The Power of the Modern Presidency.* New York: Alfred A. Knopf, 1974.

Hargrove, Erwin C., and Hoopes, Roy. *The Presidency: A Question of Power.* Boston: Educational Association, 1975.

Herring, Pendleton. *Presidential Leadership.* New York: Farrar, Straus, 1940.

Hyman, Sidney. *The American Presidency.* New York: Harper and Row, 1954.

James, Dorothy B. *The Contemporary Presidency.* 2nd ed. New York: Pegasus, 1974.

Kallenbach, Joseph E. *The American Chief Executive.* New York: Harper and Row, 1966.

Laski, Harold. *The American Presidency.* New York: Harper, 1940.

McConnell, Grant. *The Modern Presidency.* 2nd ed. New York: St. Martin's Press, 1976.

Mondale, Walter F. *The Accountability of Power: Toward a Responsible Presidency.* New York: McKay, 1975.

Reedy, George. *The Twilight of the Presidency.* New York: World, 1970.

Schlesinger, Arthur M., Jr. *The Imperial Presidency.* Boston: Houghton Mifflin, 1973.

Strum, Philippa. *Presidential Power and American Democracy.* Pacific Palisades, Calif.: Goodyear Publishing Company, 1972.

Thach, Charles, Jr. *The Creation of the Presidency, 1775–1789.* Baltimore: Johns Hopkins Press, 1922.

Tugwell, Rexford. *The Enlargement of the Presidency.* New York: Doubleday, 1960.

CHAPTER ONE

Toward A Framework To Explain Presidential Power

Students of the presidency and citizens alike must understand the nature of presidential power so that its promise as well as its dangers can be appreciated. This balanced perspective requires a theoretical framework that analyzes the empirical foundations of presidential power; this volume is organized toward that end. Many books written about the presidency address only selected topics such as the electoral process, the advisory system, or legislative liaison, an approach perhaps dictated by the volume of research on those specific topics. Even textbooks that purport to survey the literature on the presidency often lack any overarching theoretical design and tend to focus on a narrow approach or normative perspective. In spite of the tremendous amount of research done on the presidency by political scientists, historians, journalists, and scholars in related fields, compared with the literature on other sociopolitical topics (such as voting behavior), much less attention to empirical theory has guided analyses of the presidency. For this reason, it may not be obvious how the varied and specialized studies of the presidency interrelate in a coherent framework for analysis.

Any analysis of presidential power must necessarily draw on the discussions by many scholars, journalists, and political leaders. In this book, their data is organized into a framework suggestive of a theory of presidential power. We will study the presidency in terms of role analysis, and this chapter outlines the components of our framework to be followed in chapters 3 through 7, which analyze five major presidential roles. An important requirement of empirical theory is that it incorporate the requisite knowledge about a political phenomenon so that explanation, and ideally prediction, is achieved. Included in our framework are five variables which seem paramount to determining the power available to a president in his various roles. This approach has utility when applied to any incumbent, during most historical periods, and regardless of the scope of government activity; it provides a balanced and comprehensive theory of presidential power.[1]

FIVE PRESIDENTIAL ROLES

Our discussion is based on these five presidential roles: *commander-in-chief, chief diplomat, chief executive, legislative leader,* and *opinion/party leader*. A role is defined by Andrew McFarland as "a regularly recurring pattern of social interaction that can be described by (1) who expects (2) whom (3) to do what (4) in which situation."[2] The use of role analysis is prevalent in the literature on the presidency. Roles are central to the texts written by Clinton Rossiter, Edward Corwin, and Louis Koenig, among others.[3] A study by Thomas Bailey cites no fewer than forty-three presidential roles as measures of presidential responsibility. The scholars in this analytic tradition view roles as jobs or functions; they also agree that certain roles are specifically mentioned in the Constitution (commander-in-chief) whereas others have evolved upon the president with the passage of time (legislative leader).

For our purposes, therefore, *a role is that set of expectations by other political elites and the citizenry which defines the scope of presidential responsibilities within a given sphere of action*. Each of the five presidential roles can be identified with a general sphere of action, and over time added responsibilities have accrued to the president in all these roles. Commander-in-chief is the nation's highest military leader, just as the title chief diplomat suggests that our relationship to other nations is largely defined by the president. Chief executive refers to the complex and ever-changing relationship of the president to his bureaucracy, the advisory system, and to the administration of public policy. A president's relationship to Congress is demarcated by the role legislative leader, and the role of opinion/party leader points to the linkage between a president and the public, whether organized into interest groups or viewed as an unorganized mass. In this work the five roles are organized along a *continuum*, from the most powerful to the least powerful. The continuum is shown below:

COMMANDER-IN-CHIEF	—	CHIEF DIPLOMAT	—	CHIEF EXECUTIVE	—	LEGISLATIVE LEADER	—	OPINION/PARTY LEADER
(most powerful)								(least powerful)

We maintain that any roles beyond these five are either subdivisions or amalgamations of these roles or misnomers for what essentially are *obligations*, not roles. For example, Clinton Rossiter defines the president as "World Leader," noting that he "has a much larger constituency than the American electorate; his words and deeds in behalf of our own survival as a free nation have a direct bearing upon the freedom and stability of at least several score other countries."[4] But the president as world leader is not a viable role in terms of theory building. At the outset, Rossiter admits that this role depends upon a president acting as commander-in-chief, chief of state, and chief diplomat, so clearly the resources available to the president as world leader must depend on the effective use of existing roles. Writing in the late 1950s Rossiter stated that the role of world leader was "not much more than a decade old," which implies that its definition is time-bound. Indeed, that particular role orientation reflected the tensions between the United States and the Soviet Union which became so exaggerated during the Cold War years following World War II. It is clear this role would have limited relevance to earlier historical periods. It appears in this instance what Rossiter calls a "role" is really an "obligation," for he is saying that the realities of international politics demand that the president be a leader of the "free" world. Thus, he is identifying a goal for the president to pursue.

As the previous example shows, authors who talk about a president's obligations are identifying an area of public policy requiring executive action, and they exhort the president to assume leadership in promoting those objectives.[5] Many writers on the presidency reflect the obligations approach by focusing on certain substantive policies that demand a president's attention, such as the economy or civil rights. Their implication is that the president has a special obligation to the country to discharge his authority and responsibilities in these policy areas.

Obviously, the ability to fulfill any objective depends on which roles are involved; most often a president will have to act in many roles in order to advance such goals as racial justice and economic well-being. Consider the matter of civil rights. As commander-in-chief, President Truman issued an executive order that integrated the armed forces. The extraordinary success of Lyndon Johnson as legislative leader resulted in the enactment of the Civil Rights Acts of 1964, 1965, and 1968. When John F. Kennedy put the civil rights question on the public agenda, he tried as opinion/party leader to educate the American people to understand the morality of equal rights in our society. And as chief diplomat, Kennedy's efforts to recognize the aspirations of African nations, an area of the world long ignored by the United States, may have earned him the added respect of black Americans.

A president advancing the cause of civil rights acts in a variety of roles, and the same applies to his efforts to direct the economy. All presidents have exhorted the public to hold down wage demands and businesses to limit price increases; such persuasion by the use of one's office is called "jawboning." As chief executive, a president, for example Ronald Reagan, may limit pay raises for federal employees to reduce expenditures. In his budget message to Congress, the president as legislative leader is expected to define a fiscal policy that coordinates the levels of spending, taxation, and indebtedness. The price of food and goods may be affected by a president's policy on importation. For instance, when President Carter eased restrictions on the amount of beef being imported from Argentina, this action slowed the rise in domestic beef prices. So a president's effective leadership in promoting any goal—be it social justice, economic growth, or world peace—may require action in many roles. The problem is that his success depends upon the political resources available to him, and these are mainly determined by the roles in which he is operating. The probability of success, therefore, decreases markedly if a president has to rely exclusively on his influence as legislative leader and opinion/party leader, the two least powerful roles on the continuum, to achieve some desired goal.

FIVE DETERMINANTS OF PRESIDENTIAL POWER

The interrelationships among five variables—authority, decision making, public input, expertise, and crisis—determine the political resources available to a president in each role. The fact that these variables have *differential* impact on each role explains why a president is more powerful in some roles than in others. The determinants of presidential power may be subdivided into their component parts, as follows:

Authority
1. constitutional mandate
2. statutory delegation
3. judicial precedent
4. customary practice

Decision Making
5. separation of powers
6. federalism
7. political institutions (for example, parties)

Public Inputs
8. political mobilization
9. public deference

Expertise
10. monopoly of information
11. technocratic knowledge

Crisis
12. likelihood of crisis
13. need for decision making

Authority

Perhaps the chief determinant of presidential power is the degree of authority available to the president. We can speak of authority to the extent that power has been "routinized" by constitutional mandate, statutory delegations, judicial precedent, and customary practice. Moreover, such authority can be passed on from president to president, and enlarged upon, unless, that is, Congress enacts new legislation or the Supreme Court reinterprets existing law. As will be documented, in its effort to regain a stronger voice in policymaking during the period after Watergate and Vietnam, the Congress in many instances has undermined the president's authority by legislation. Two examples are its use of the War Powers Act of 1973 to limit presidential war making and its enactment of the Budget and Impoundment

Control Act of 1974 to prevent the president from refusing to spend money appropriated by Congress. A substantial body of literature traces legislative/ executive relationships in terms of how the law defines the roles of Congress and the president.[6] Other scholars are concerned about how presidential power is expanded or limited by decisions of the federal judiciary, especially the Supreme Court.[7]

Under certain conditions a president can make legally binding decisions. We can estimate how much authority he enjoys in each role by studying the Constitution, judicial precedent, statutory delegations, and customs as they have evolved historically. Customs are authoritative to the extent that they are accepted as legitimate by the people, opinion leaders, and the other branches of government. For example, the cabinet is not established by any statute, the Constitution, or a Supreme Court decision; its use is based upon a custom begun by George Washington.

Decision making

The president's power is affected by the number of decision makers involved in formulating and implementing any policy. His power is strengthened when he shares decision making with few other political actors. This argument is predicated on E. E. Schattschneider's contention that, as the "scope of conflict" affecting an issue increases, the expansion in the number of participants in that dispute precludes its control by any small group of decision makers.[8] In terms of presidential power, the number of decision makers *formally* involved depends upon the role affected. One may conceptualize this variable as a series of concentric rings moving outward from the president, who is in the center (figure 1-1). As one moves along the continuum of roles, from commander-in-chief to opinion/party leader, the number of decision makers increases because of three factors: separation of powers, federalism, and political institutions.

The commander-in-chief often is portrayed by scholars as a "constitutional dictator," suggesting that during wartime the normal, external checks on his power all but disappear and decision making is lodged in the office of president and his key advisers. As chief diplomat, a president must contend with the constitutional role given to Congress in foreign affairs. As a chief executive, however, a very different picture emerges. In addition to the president, his advisors, and Congress, government administration also involves the Supreme Court, the bureaucracy, subnational political elites (for example, mayors, governors), and clientele groups. Why is this the case? First, the judiciary tends to defer less to the president in the realm of administration than with regard to his duties as commander-in-chief and as chief diplomat. Second, the implementation of federal laws often requires the assistance of federal, state, and local agencies as well as "private" groups, such as neighborhood organizations and professional associations.

As legislative leader, the president's major antagonist is Congress, which can exercise independent power over lawmaking. And there is always the

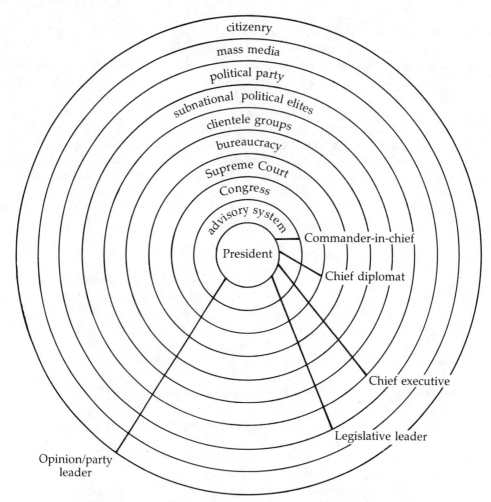

FIGURE 1-1. Decision makers affecting presidential power in five roles. (Source: Adapted from "Towards a Paradigm to Explain Presidential Power," by R. Tatalovich and B. W. Daynes. In *Presidential Studies Quarterly, 9(4),* Fall, 1979, p. 432. Copyright © 1979 by the Center for the Study of the Presidency.)

possibility that the Supreme Court may declare a president's programs to be unconstitutional, as happened to Franklin Roosevelt several times. Furthermore, in this role a president must contend with political party organizations, or the lack thereof; perhaps the major reason presidents are so ineffective as legislative leaders is the decentralized nature of our party system. The recruitment, nomination, and election of congressmen and senators are controlled by state and local political elites and by party activists who may have no loyalty to the president's program.

As opinion/party leader, finally, a president confronts the entire gamut of decision makers. At this role level the mass media and the citizenry take on great importance. Virtually any actor in the political system can affect a president's popularity and electoral success. The ordinary citizen participates in this role when casting a vote in elections, by recording his or her preferences with opinion pollsters, or demonstrating for or against policy decisions.

Public inputs

Besides studying the decision makers who formally share power with the president in each role, we must also consider those political actors who act as "veto groups," limiting the options available to a president. Proceeding along the continuum of roles, one may note that a president's policy options are restricted or opened up because (1) the level of political mobilization tends to fluctuate and (2) deference to the president's viewpoint by the people and various interest groups changes. Public opinion normally supports a president's policy initiatives when acting as commander-in-chief or as chief diplomat. In the role of chief executive, on the other hand, public opinion as such is less important than the intrigues of special interests and clientele groups who jockey to maintain their privileged access to government. There is a substantial increase in public inputs of all kinds when we consider the role of legislative leader. Interest groups, political parties, social movements, and voter blocs all try to influence the legislative process. Similarly, our analysis of public inputs in the least powerful role of opinion/ party leader suggests that the president's options are so limited that virtually no course of action can be implemented by him without incurring some political costs.

Expertise

A president's power is enhanced to the extent that decision making requires expertise. Of course, expertise is not equally available to everybody because it depends upon a monopoly of information sources and an understanding of technocratic knowledge. Here the expertise determinant refers to any use of information that prevents a president's critics from being able to evaluate his policies and actions, including secrecy, data manipulation, as well as expert testimony. Given its nature, expertise aids presidential power only insofar as other decision makers and citizens acknowledge its direct relevance to policy formation.

As commander-in-chief and chief diplomat, therefore, the expertise variable is very important; a president monopolizes information sources and is able to classify data or impose censorship to prevent their dissemination to the general public. As the facts about the Vietnam War became highly publicized in the media by journalists and commentators and in such documents as the Pentagon Papers, only then did we appreciate fully how often Presidents Johnson and Nixon had deceived the American people about the degree of our involvement there.

As chief executive and legislative leader, expertise is less beneficial. In the past, a president's reputed knowledge strengthened his position vis-à-vis

Congress when he submitted the budget for the federal government, and no doubt expertise aids his position when Congress must approve highly technical programs, such as the space program or medical research. But Congress gets much valuable and sophisticated information about proposed legislation from nongovernmental experts, from interest groups, and from its own committee staff.

In addition, the chief executive is very dependent upon public and private institutions beyond his immediate control for data the federal government needs to implement laws. A compelling argument can be made that a president's ability to manipulate our economy, to promote growth while reducing inflation, is severely limited by minimal knowledge about the multitude of social, political, and economic forces that shape our nation's economy. In trying to forge public opinion, similarly, a president's success is related less to expertise than to such factors as personality, historic events, patriotism, and partisan appeal. As was noted before, expertise aids presidential power only when others acknowledge its relevance, but in the role of opinion/party leader the citizenry rarely evaluates a president's performance or his policies in terms of his knowing what is best for us.

Crisis

As indicated before, crisis augments a president's power, especially in wartime and during periods of international turmoil. But the emergency variable should be viewed in its broadest sense: a crisis is a situation characterized by sudden, intense, and sometimes unexpected danger. It is manifested by wars, depressions, domestic violence, natural disasters, epidemics, and assassinations. In politics, crisis has the effect of undermining normal power relationships among the president, the Congress, and the Supreme Court because of the urgent need to mobilize a quick response to the danger. Couple the president's singular ability to act quickly with the urgency for action, and he gains leverage in whatever role is affected by crisis. In some nations constitutional provisions exist by which the chief executive may declare a state of national emergency and assume dictatorial powers. Such explicit authority is not given in our Constitution, but our political system does permit the extraordinary amplification of presidential power during crises.

Presidents are aware of the relationship between crisis and heightened executive power, and they try to use the crisis mentality for political advantage. William Mullen comments,

> In "doing what needs doing for the people," our chief executives have come to operate a crisis presidency as almost a routine way of doing business. Even relatively minor issues are now cased in terms of emergency.[9]

Thus, presidents refer to the oil crisis, the urban crisis, health care crisis, and the Middle East crisis in order to quickly mobilize resources but also to silence dissent. Lyndon Johnson declared "war" on poverty, and Jimmy Carter called the energy problem the moral equivalent of war. One might be tempted to perceive the crisis variable to be simply a facet of authority, since a president's powers often are based on statutory delegation. However, their use depends upon certain social, economic, and political conditions widely perceived to be crises. A president may routinely call any issue a crisis, but it is highly unlikely that the public will share that perception about all policy questions.

As commander-in-chief and chief diplomat, crises usually require a president to confront a threat to our national interest, if not our very survival. In these roles, therefore, a crisis quickly mobilizes a consensus behind the need for decisive action. As a chief executive, crisis augments presidential power during periods of domestic turmoil. Frequently the Congress delegates to the president the required authority to deal with threats to the nation's well-being when they can be anticipated. For example, the Taft-Hartley Act (1947) permits a president to delay strikes for 80 days should they imperil the nation.

The crisis variable is less effective in the roles of legislative leader or opinion/party leader. The major difficulty seems to be that congressmen and citizens often disagree with the president's definition of a problem as a crisis; moreover, there may be differences of opinion about the appropriate remedy. In evaluating this variable, therefore, it is not enough to find a relationship between a social problem and a legislative enactment, for in a sense all laws reflect societal demands. Rather, crisis suggests that a common feeling of urgency or danger exists, with Congress ready to rapidly answer a presidential initiative.

Similar problems impede the operation of the crisis variable in the role of opinion/party leader. Some events, such as a president's injury, heart attack, or assassination quickly generate a climate of opinion that a serious emergency has happened. Obviously, such real threats do not happen every day. For this reason, crises cannot be relied on for leverage by the opinion/party leader in any systematic way; they occur at random, the public may or may not react uniformly, and therefore a president's actions may not necessarily lead to his increased political popularity.

Summary

An inventory of the five variables indicates the power potential of the president at any period in our history. By our calculation (table 1-1), commander-in-chief and chief diplomat roles are very close in terms of the political resources available to the contemporary president; chief executive is a distant third in power potential, followed closely by the legislative leader role. Given the few resources available for opinion/party leadership, a president's power in this role would seem to be illusory, and essentially shaped by the incumbent's personality, political skills, and policy agenda, as well as the nature of the times. Although some very popular presidents have been elected to office, the acid test is that power as opinion/party leader cannot be routinized and passed on to a president's successor. The

TABLE 1-1   **Variables affecting presidential power***

Variable	Presidential Role				
	Commander-in-Chief	Chief Diplomat	Chief Executive	Legislative Leader	Opinion/Party Leader
Authority					
constitutional mandate	very strong	strong	moderate	moderate	none
statutory delegation	very strong	strong	strong	weak	none
judicial precedent	very strong	very strong	weak	very weak	none
customary practice	very strong	very strong	weak	moderate	moderate
Decision Making					
separation of powers	very weak	moderate	strong	very strong	strong
federalism	none	none	moderate	moderate	moderate
political institutions	weak	weak	moderate	very strong	very strong
Public Inputs					
political mobilization	very weak	weak	moderate	strong	very strong
public deference	very strong	strong	weak	weak	very weak
Expertise					
monopoly of information	very strong	strong	moderate	weak	weak
technocratic knowledge	very strong	strong	strong	moderate	weak
Crisis					
likelihood of crisis	very strong	strong	weak	weak	weak
need for decision making	very strong	very strong	moderate	moderate	moderate

*These values reflect our judgment about how each variable operates in the five presidential roles. For example, whereas public deference to the commander-in-chief is "very strong," it is "very weak" in terms of opinion/party leadership. Similarly, the commander-in-chief has a "very strong" constitutional mandate but the president as opinion/party leader has none from which to operate.

same drawback applies to the roles of legislative leader and chief executive. In relatively weaker roles, presidential power must be reestablished by each incumbent, for a president can rely on few antecedents established in these areas by his predecessors. In contrast, no president begins his term of office as commander-in-chief or chief diplomat with such a power vacuum.

Historic developments have affected the evolution of presidential roles; for example, the advent of mass media was essential to exploiting the full potential of opinion/party leadership. However, the relative position of each role on our continuum has changed very little over time. Any president acting as commander-in-chief and chief diplomat will be more powerful than when acting as chief executive, legislative leader, or opinion/party leader. Pointing out Thomas Jefferson as an extraordinary legislative leader supports this argument; in that role, Jefferson was one of few successful presidents. Moreover, was Jefferson any less effective as a commander-in-chief or chief diplomat? Presidential power depends upon political resources, and a president simply has more ammunition in some roles than in others.

Our analysis has implications for those reformers who seek to fundamentally alter the interrelationships between the presidency and the other branches of government, particularly Congress. It is doubtful that any single panacea will change the quality of executive/legislative relations. Enlarging Congress' formal authority over war making and foreign affairs may be inadequate if Congress lacks the information capability to evaluate presidential initiatives in these areas. It is unlikely that Congress can overcome the president's inherent advantages in conducting the day-to-day business of diplomacy, especially during an international crisis. On the other hand, presidential power has always been fragile, and vulnerable to assault by Congress, in the weaker roles in which the president lacks the requisite political resources: chief executive, legislative leader, and opinion/party leader. But in roles in which the president's power is firmly established, as commander-in-chief and chief diplomat, the composite of resources available to him is too great to be easily eclipsed by a few structural changes in executive/legislative relations. For the Congress to regain a meaningful say in foreign and military policy, what is required is a sustained congressional commitment to oversee executive initiatives in a variety of policy areas, during periods of "normalcy" *and* crisis, and *in spite of* the public's apparent complacent attitude towards foreign affairs.

We suspect any judgment about the decline of presidential power today is premature. Earlier periods of "congressional government" (for example, post–Civil War) did not last indefinitely, so one must determine whether the modern era has witnessed a change in variables underlying presidential power that indicates a fundamental realignment from the president to Congress. Recent literature alluding to a reassertion of Congress' role, even in foreign affairs, tends to emphasize the legal (War Powers Act) and institutional ("legislative veto") changes made by Congress to reassert its role in diplomacy and war making.[10] But these studies deemphasize the effect of such "political" variables as public opinion, expertise, and crisis in sustaining presidential power. The intellectual argument about the relative importance of "legal" versus "political" resources to a president's power is a long-standing one. A major advantage of the framework used here is that in addressing this question it poses a balanced alternative which seems more productive than either point of view alone. The following section briefly reviews the debate over the nature of presidential power.

PRESIDENTIAL POWER: AUTHORITY OR INFLUENCE?

Two diametrically opposing views of presidential power are offered by Richard Neustadt and Edward Corwin.[11] In the tradition of Machiavelli, Neustadt is concerned about understanding the realities of power. In the first edition of *Presidential Power,* based on the experiences of Harry Truman and

Dwight Eisenhower, Neustadt's original thesis was a straightforward one. Presidential power is not authority but rather *persuasion,* which derives from the effective use of (1) reputation, (2) prestige, and (3) bargaining. Neustadt begins his analysis with three case studies: Truman's seizure of the steel mills during the Korean War, Truman's dismissal of General Douglas MacArthur during the Korean War, and Eisenhower's decision to desegregate Little Rock, Arkansas High School by using federal troops. At first glance, all three decisions would seem to exemplify a president's use of "command" or formal authority to achieve results, but upon closer inspection Neustadt argues that all were "painful last resort" decisions suggestive more of failure than of success. Therefore, Neustadt doubts that any president acting within the confines of his formal powers can be any more than a "clerk;" to be a "leader" requires that the president use persuasion. Neustadt is clearly an advocate of the "heroic" or "textbook" president, for he prefers the active presidents such as Franklin D. Roosevelt and Harry Truman to the more passive ones, for example, Eisenhower. Neustadt implicitly recognizes the effect of a president's personality on his ability to exercise power. The cultivation of power requires an executive to be attuned to the needs of legislators, public opinion, civil servants, and other power brokers who can adversely affect a president's decision making.

Neustadt's research, while very influential, has been disputed by other political scientists on various grounds.[12] One criticism focuses on his neglect of formal authority as a source of presidential power. Peter Sperlich, for one, says Neustadt sees only two forms of presidential power, command or persuasion, and that "the former is underrated and the latter is overrated in Neustadt's schema."[13] One reason for this imbalance, according to Sperlich, is that the very controversial issues chosen by Neustadt as case studies may have depreciated the overall importance of command as a resource: "Less dramatic examples or influence attempts in matters of less importance might have produced a more positive picture of the use of command."[14] Certainly the day-to-day operations of government function according to legal authority, bureaucratic procedures, and routine, with little need for a president to use massive amounts of prestige, reputation, and bargaining to achieve results.

Neustadt's thesis exemplifies political "statecraft," argues David Paletz, who contrasts it with the "anti-aggrandizement" perspective found in Edward S. Corwin's seminal work, *The President: Office and Powers.*[15] Where Neustadt contends that an effective president has to augment his formal authority by exploiting political resources, Corwin is concerned that a president could assume too much power in our governmental system. Therefore Paletz argues that writers in the Corwin tradition tend to be constitutionalists who respect the separation of powers arrangement. While they may understand why presidential power has grown historically, they remain concerned that its growth has been at the expense of Congress. Corwin wrote the first edition of his text in 1940, but his argument is very compatible with the "revisionist" position articulated by liberal historians and political scientists two decades later.

Unlike Neustadt's approach, Corwin's analysis is highly legalistic; his understanding of presidential power (or authority) relates to the office, not the man himself. The powers of the president, he says, derive from the Constitution, Supreme Court rulings, statutes, and custom. Corwin feels more comfortable in designating Dwight Eisenhower as his model president rather than Franklin D. Roosevelt. Corwin approves of the collective responsibility fostered by Eisenhower's use of his cabinet rather than Roosevelt's "cult of personality" because, in FDR's case, the office became indistinguishable from the man. Since Corwin would like to deemphasize personality and the behavioral factors that underly presidential power, presumably he believes that a president can govern effectively solely by using the formal powers at his disposal.

A recent text in the Corwin tradition is Richard Pious's *The American Presidency.*[16] Pious's analysis touches on the Neustadt/Corwin dichotomy insofar as he differentiates between a president's "political" power and his "prerogative" power. Pious clearly discounts the importance of political statecraft in favor of prerogative or authority as the basis for presidential power. Pious claims that "the fundamental and irreducible core of presidential power rests not on influence, persuasion, public opinion, elections, or party, but rather on the successful assertion of constitutional authority to resolve crises and significant domestic issues."[17]

Pious's view of prerogative (or authority) as the mainstay of a president's power can be defended in some instances. Harry Bailey observes, "Vietnam and Watergate made it clear that some domestic and foreign policies could be accomplished without persuasion."[18] On the other hand, Pious's analysis would be troubling to scholars who study the historical events and political conditions affecting a president's use of power. Though it may be true that many presidents, even a majority, were unable to exploit "political" resources consistently for their advantage, this does not deny the importance of such resources to a handful of truly great presidents. The extraordinary success of FDR's New Deal was tied not to his formal authority but to political variables: the crisis of the Great Depression, the Democratic party control of Congress, his electoral landslide in 1932, a realignment in public opinion favoring governmental intervention in the economy, and his own cunning use of personal power.[19] Moreover, adverse political conditions, rather than any void in their authority, prompted Lyndon Johnson not to seek reelection in 1968 and forced Richard Nixon to resign in 1974.

Pious apparently fails to acknowledge the vital role that political variables play in his analysis. Pious refers to a "frontlash effect" and a "backlash effect." By the frontlash effect he means that Congress and the Supreme Court will often acquiesce to a president's claim of prerogative when his actions have been successful in meeting a domestic crisis. But the backlash effect has the opposite effect; sometimes even though a president successfully confronts a major issue, the Congress, the judiciary, and public opinion resist the president's claim of prerogative. Harry Bailey notes that this inconsistency contains "an element of Neustadt's persuasion model to which Pious gives very little attention. Clearly some persuasion of someone is necessary or how else does one account for frontlash over backlash or vice versa?"[20] Pious's account gives little credence to the notion of statecraft, as developed by Neustadt, and evinces less appreciation for the quality of "democratic statesmanship." Thomas Engeman, in assessing the inadequacy of a theory based solely on prerogative, states:

> The Office of the President . . . is the finest institution of democratic statesmanship currently known to us, and perhaps of all time. As a constitutional office, it is bound by custom, precedent, and statute; but, as the highest source of authority for a living people, it remains magnificently protean.
>
> The successful President will be one who combines an understanding of the democratic principles of the regime with a prudent assessment of his moment's possibilities.[21]

Our framework based on roles and variables resolves this intellectual dispute by synthesizing Neustadt's and Corwin's views of presidential power. Each writer is correct with regard to particular roles. As will be shown, the power of the commander-in-chief and the chief diplomat is best understood by applying Corwin's emphasis on formal, legal authority. Neustadt's insights are essential in explaining why certain presidents are more effective in the roles of chief executive, legislative leader, and opinion/party leader. As the formal authority available to a president is reduced, as is the case in these weaker roles, he must necessarily draw upon informal, personal resources in order to achieve his objectives. Thus, while any president *may* resort to bargaining, prestige, and reputation to bolster his position over military policy and foreign affairs, he *must* rely on these techniques of political "persuasion" to succeed in administration, legislative relations, and in cultivating a supportive public. In these areas the option of relying on authority is not open to presidents; the Constitution, statutes, judicial precedent, and customs have only marginally routinized power in these roles and each incumbent must in effect begin anew.

In summary, presidential power is a complex, elusive phenomenon, not amenable to simple explanations. Our approach is eclectic; our framework focuses on five key variables affecting presidential power in each role. What varies across roles is not the components of presidential power but how each operates within different roles. For example, whereas public opinion tends to unite behind a wartime president, it is extremely difficult to mobilize the American people behind a chief executive's program for reforming the bureaucracy. Similarly, though we worry that a commander-in-chief may take the nation into war without a "declaration" by Congress, we know that an opinion/party leader cannot command our obedience to his program or his party. *A president's power depends upon the roles in which he is operating*, and our great presidents have been successful in all five presidential roles.

NOTES

[1]For an interesting discussion of six approaches to studying the presidency, see David L. Paletz, "Perspectives on the Presidency," *Law and Contemporary Problems* (Summer 1970), pp. 429–445.

[2]Andrew S. McFarland, "Role and Role Conflict," in Aaron Wildavsky, ed., *The Presidency* (Boston: Little, Brown and Company, 1969), p. 3.

[3]Clinton Rossiter, *The American Presidency*, 2nd ed. (New York: Harcourt, Brace and World, 1960); Edward S. Corwin, *The President: Office and Powers*, 4th ed. (New York: New York University Press, 1957); Louis W. Koenig, *The Chief Executive*, 4th ed. (New York: Harcourt Brace Jovanovich, 1981). Also see Thomas A. Bailey, *Presidential Greatness: The Image and the Man from George Washington to the Present* (New York: Appleton-Century-Crofts, 1966).

[4]Clinton Rossiter, *The American Presidency*, pp. 39–40.

[5]A prominent example of the obligations approach is found in Richard Longaker, *The President and Individual Liberties* (Ithaca, N.Y.: Cornell University Press, 1963).

[6]A recent example of this legalistic approach is found in Louis Fisher, *The Politics of Shared Power: Congress and the Executive* (Washington, D.C.: Congressional Quarterly Press, 1981).

[7]Glendon A. Schubert, Jr., *The Presidency in the Courts* (Minneapolis: University of Minnesota Press, 1957); Arthur S. Miller, *Presidential Power in a Nutshell* (St. Paul: West Publishing Company, 1977).

[8]E. E. Schattschneider, *The Semi-Sovereign People* (New York: Holt, Rinehart and Winston, 1960), chapter 1.

[9]William F. Mullen, *Presidential Power and Politics* (New York: St. Martin's Press, 1976), p. 95.

[10]See Thomas M. Franck, ed., *The Tethered Presidency* (New York: Columbia University Press, 1981); Thomas M. Franck and Edward Weisband, *Foreign Policy by Congress* (New York: Oxford University Press, 1979).

[11]Richard E. Neustadt, *Presidential Power*, 3rd ed. (New York: Wiley, 1960); Edward S. Corwin, *The President: Office and Powers*, 4th ed. (New York: New York University Press, 1957).

[12]For a good overview of this literature see Harry A. Bailey, "Neustadt's Thesis Revisited: Toward the Two Faces of Presidential Power," paper delivered at annual meeting, Midwest Political Science Association, April 24–26, 1980.

[13]Peter W. Sperlich, "Bargaining and Overload: An Essay on Presidential Power," in Aaron Wildavsky, ed., *Perspectives on the Presidency* (Boston: Little, Brown and Company, 1975), p. 185.

[14]Ibid.

[15]Paletz suggests that Corwin's volume could be viewed within the "role" perspective, except that his conservative argument on presidential power is more indicative of what he calls the "anti-aggrandizement" perspective. See Paletz, "Perspectives on the Presidency," p. 440.

[16]Richard M. Pious, *The American Presidency* (New York: Basic Books, 1979).

[17]Ibid., p. 17.

[18]Bailey, "Neustadt's Thesis Revisited: Toward the Two Faces of Presidential Power," p. 14.

[19]The classic study of FDR during the New Deal is James MacGregor Burns, *Roosevelt: The Lion and the Fox* (New York: Harcourt, Brace, 1956).

[20]Bailey, "Neustadt's Thesis Revisited: Toward the Two Faces of Presidential Power," p. 10.

[21]Thomas Engeman, "Presidential Statesmanship and the Constitution: The Limits of Presidential Studies, *Review of Politics* (April 1982), p. 281.

SUGGESTED READINGS

Bailey, Harry A., Jr. *Classics of the American Presidency.* Oak Park, Ill.: Moore Publishing Company, 1980.

Bailey, Thomas A. *Presidential Greatness: The Image and the Man from George Washington to the Present.* New York: Appleton-Century-Crofts, 1966.

Corwin, Edward S. *The President: Office and Powers.* 4th ed. New York: New York University Press, 1957.

Goldsmith, William M. *The Growth of Presidential Power: A Documented History.* New York: Chelsea House, 1974.

Haight, David E., and Johnson, Larry D., eds. *The President: Roles and Powers.* Chicago: Rand McNally, 1965.

Koenig, Louis. *The Chief Executive,* 4th ed. New York: Harcourt Brace Jovanovich, 1981.

Longaker, Richard. *The President and Individual Liberties.* Ithaca, N.Y.: Cornell University Press, 1963.

Lowi, Theodore J. *The End of Liberalism.* New York: W. W. Norton, 1969.

Miller, Arthur S. *Presidential Power in a Nutshell.* St. Paul: West Publishing Company, 1977.

Mullen, William F. *Presidential Power and Politics.* New York: St. Martin's Press, 1976.

Neustadt, Richard E. *President Power: The Politics of Leadership from FDR to Carter,* 3rd ed. New York: Wiley, 1980.

Paletz, David L. "Perspectives on the Presidency." *Law and Contemporary Problems* (Summer 1970), pp. 429–445.

Pious, Richard M. *The American Presidency.* New York: Basic Books, 1979.

Rossiter, Clinton. *The American Presidency,* 2nd ed. New York: Harcourt, Brace and World, 1960.

Schubert, Glendon A., Jr. *The Presidency in the Courts.* Minneapolis: University of Minnesota Press, 1957.

Wildavsky, Aaron, ed. *The Presidency.* Boston: Little, Brown, 1969.

———. *Perspectives on the Presidency.* Boston: Little, Brown, 1975.

CHAPTER TWO

Recruiting A President: The Political Bases Of Opinion/Party Leadership

We have elected individuals to the presidency on a fairly routine basis for almost two hundred years. The election process has continued without interruption during peacetime as well as during wartime. And except for the first two presidential elections, all involved a choice between at least two candidates. Presidential campaigns, moreover, have been accompanied by the free exercise of civil liberties, open dissent, and at times by vigorous debate over controversial issues. The exact meaning of elections for presidential leadership, however, has prompted a continuing debate among political scientists.

Political scientists who subscribe to the "elitist" view of democracy argue that presidential elections are simply a means by which people choose between candidates for public office. According to this view, although elections permit us to select presidents who manage our government, elections do not allow popular control over the policies implemented by each president. Thus, as Richard Pious argues, "Elections are not true plebiscites and do not provide presidents with real mandates."[1] Pious contends that no close relationship exists between the margin of victory attained by a president in his election and the vigor with which he exercises leadership in the office. The viewpoint expressed by Pious is shared by many political scientists, who point out that campaign rhetoric often is general, vague, and ill-suited to guiding public policy after a candidate is elected to the presidency. Moreover, a president may have to reorder his domestic priorities in the face of unexpected world crises and changing economic conditions. In addition, no presidential campaign addresses every issue that will confront a president during his term of office. But most importantly, people vote for a presidential candidate for many differing reasons; therefore, a president's election "mandate" may represent public response to incompatible campaign promises.

For example, it appears that contradictory promises made by Ronald Reagan during the 1980 presidential campaign are a major reason for declining political support after his first year in office. As a candidate Reagan promised to increase defense spending, to enact a massive tax cut, and also to balance the budget. In 1981 President Reagan's budget proposals were supported by many congressmen and senators who sensed that, by defeating Jimmy Carter so handily, Reagan enjoyed widespread popular support for his economic programs. However, many legislators who backed Reagan's 1981 budget were opposed to his budgets for fiscal year 1982, and fiscal year 1983, which contained a deficit projected to exceed $120 billion. Many legislators, news commentators, and a growing segment of the electorate came to judge President Reagan harshly because he failed to fulfill a major campaign pledge, even though it is unlikely that any president could simultaneously increase defense spending, cut taxes, and balance the budget.

Thus, the very real constraints on policymaking suggest that any interpretation about an election "mandate" should be made cautiously. Still, the notion that elections have no meaning for the policymaking process does not appear justified. We will argue in this chapter that the recruitment-nomination-election process shapes public expectations about the direction of public policy and the use of presidential power. Formal election to office gives a president the degree of legitimacy needed to govern the nation so that his decisions will be accepted by the people as legal and morally binding. But the legitimacy of government also depends upon the "representative" quality of a president's substantive policies and symbolic acts. This relationship has special importance for the president's role as *opinion/party leader*, because his performance in office is judged partly in terms of the political agenda established during the election campaign.

Three specific linkages exist between the electoral process and the president's conduct of public policy. First, there are certain *watershed* elections in American history in which the direction of government policy is changed radically. The elections of 1800 (Jefferson), 1828 (Jackson), 1860 (Lincoln), and 1932 (Roosevelt) are examples. On these occasions, by choosing between the two parties' presidential candidates, the electorate also had the opportunity to select fundamentally different alternatives regarding the course of public policy in the United States. Second, in the wake of these "realigning" elections, the major political parties offer differing ideological orientations because they represent different political constituencies. Since 1932 the Democratic party has been more liberal than the Republican party on economic issues because its votes are drawn disproportionately from less affluent groups, minorities, and organized labor. Third, there are times during election campaigns when presidential candidates make explicit promises on issues of importance to certain voter and special interest groups. Research on the parties' platforms suggests that they are not just meaningless statements on current issues. Very often the presidential candidates are involved in drafting these platforms, which are taken seriously as guides to public policy. Within these three considerations, then, the recruitment-nomination-election process gains salience because it defines, in large measure, the democratic potential of presidential politics in the United States.

AVAILABILITY STANDARDS

The Constitution states only three formal requirements for president: "No person except a natural born citizen, or a citizen of the United States at the time of the adoption of this Constitution, shall be eligible to the office of President; neither shall any person be eligible to that office who shall not have attained to the age of thirty-five years, and been fourteen years a resident within the United States." By these criteria alone, millions of people would be eligible to run for president, but these formal requirements are augmented by equally important informal ones, which we call *availability standards*. One of the more vigorous analyses of these informal criteria for election to the presidency was provided by Clinton Rossiter in 1960. He argued that a candidate

> must be, according to unwritten law: a man, white, a Christian. . . . He almost certainly must be: a Northerner or Westerner, less than sixty-five years old, of Northern European stock, experienced in politics and public service, healthy. . . . He ought to be: from a state larger than Kentucky, more than forty-five years old, a family man, of British stock, a veteran, a Protestant, a lawyer, a state governor, a Mason, Legionnaire, or Rotarian—preferably all three, a small-town boy, a self-made man, especially if a Republican, experienced in international affairs, a cultural middle-brow who likes baseball, detective stories, fishing, pop concerts, picnics, and seascapes. . . .[2]

Some of Rossiter's insights may seem facetious, but others are very serious. In recruiting presidential candidates, both major political parties tend to adhere to the most important availability standards (see table 2-1). What our data suggest, therefore, is that presidents are sociologically representative of the demographic groups and social values that predominate in our culture. To the extent that these criteria become irrelevant to the recruitment of presidential candidates, this may be taken as one index of the democratization of the selection process.

Thus far, thirty-eight presidents have been white Anglo-Saxon Protestants, but after Rossiter composed his listing, John F. Kennedy became the first Catholic to be elected president. Herbert Hoover's defeat of Alfred E. Smith in 1928 had affirmed the conventional wisdom that no Catholic could win the presidency. When Kennedy was nominated his candidacy received even more support than usual from Catholic voters, but his Catholicism hurt him among fundamentalist Protestants. John F. Kennedy also lowered the age threshold by becoming the youngest (age 43) president-elect. On the other hand, age did not handicap Ronald Reagan, who was elected to the presidency at age 69. Moreover, since the Civil War no political party had dared to nominate a presidential candidate who resided in the Deep

TABLE 2-1   Demographic characteristics of presidents, 1789–1982 (N = 39)*

	n		n
Sex		**Office Held Before Presidency**	
Male	39	State Legislature	1
		Governor	8
Race		Federal Administration	8
Caucasian	39	House of Representatives	1
		Senate	4
Religion		Vice-President	13
Catholic	1	No Political Experience	4
Jewish	0		
Protestant	38	**Father's Occupation**	
Episcopalian	10	Statesman	4
Presbyterian	6	Businessman	16
Unitarian	4	Skilled Tradesman	6
Methodist	4	Military	3
Disc. of Christ	3	Learned Profession	7
Baptist	3	Farmer/Planter	3
Dutch Reformed	2		
Quaker	2	**State of Residence**	
Congregationalist	1	South (Confederacy)	11
Not Specified	1	Virginia	5
		Tennessee	3
Education Level		Louisiana	1
College Degree	26	Texas	1
Some College	5	Georgia	1
No College	8	Non-South	28
		Massachusetts	4
Age (When Inaugurated)		New York	8
35–45	2	Indiana	1
46–55	20	New Hampshire	1
56–65	15	Illinois	2
66+	2	Pennsylvania	1
		Ohio	6
Party Affiliation		New Jersey	1
Republican	16	California	2
Democrat	13	Missouri	1
Democratic-Republican	4	Michigan	1
Whig	3		
Federalist	2	**Mobility**	
Union/Republican	1	Resided in State of Birth	21
		Resided in State Not of Birth	18
Ethnic Origins			
English	17	**Occupation**	
Other Anglo-Saxon	16	Law	19
Dutch	3	Military	7
Swiss-German	2	Tailor	1
Irish	1	Educator/Teacher	2
		Engineer	1
Size of Birthplace		Farmer/Planter	3
Under 5,000	16	Actor	1
5,000–19,000	15	Haberdasher	1
20,000–99,000	5	Newspaper Editor	1
100,000–515,547	3	Writer	1
		Public Service	2

*Grover Cleveland is counted once in these distributions.

South, but in 1976 Jimmy Carter successfully overcame this obstacle when he was nominated by the Democratic party and elected to the presidency.

Studies of "elite" recruitment indicate that the degree of social homogeneity among political leaders increases as one proceeds from the local, to the state, and then to the federal levels of government. Given that the president is the highest ranking official in the country, it is not surprising to find that our thirty-nine presidents are more alike socially than, for example, the members of the House of Representatives or even the Senate. Except for John F. Kennedy, who was Irish, all presidents traced their ethnic origins to the United Kingdom or to another Northern European country. Most presidents attained higher levels of education and more prestigious occupations than the population in general, regardless of the historical period studied, and they probably came from more affluent class backgrounds. Apparently education, occupation, and class attributes are less relevant to political success because they are less "visible" to the public than are sex, race, or ancestry. Because both Democrats and Republicans usually follow availability standards, it is difficult to say whether any single criterion, if ignored, would affect the outcome of an election. Other "visible" attributes may influence voting as well; for example, it has been suggested that even a presidential candidate's height can affect voter perceptions of his leadership ability, noting that in every campaign between 1932 and 1968 except one (in 1940 when Willkie lost to Roosevelt) the taller candidate won the election.[3]

One background characteristic that clearly affects presidential recruitment is experience in public office. According to Donald Matthews, "The route to presidential prominence is overwhelmingly political—90 percent of the persons surfacing in the polls between 1936 and 1972 were public officeholders."[4] Holding a public office gives a candidate popular recognition and the necessary political connections with state and local leaders and his party organization. Our data show that thirty-five presidents held public office before their election. As might be expected, the largest number (one-third) succeeded to the highest office from the vice-presidency. In addition, sixteen presidents were elected after serving as governor or in the federal bureaucracy, usually as cabinet members. However, although both Jimmy Carter and Ronald Reagan were governors before their election to the presidency, most political scientists argue that this office has fewer advantages than other positions, such as senator, when seeking the presidency. Most governors do not receive much nationwide publicity, they are unable to travel as frequently in campaigning for president, and they are often identified with state and local issues rather than as experts on national policy. Governors who successfully enter the arena of presidential politics tend to come from more populous states—an important advantage given the workings of the electoral college system (discussed in detail later).

Although being a United States senator does not guarantee a successful candidacy, Matthews points out that a Senate seat "provides unique opportunities for those who wish to try."[5] He notes that since 1936, senators have had a better chance of becoming vice-president than have governors, cabinet members, or representatives. Therefore, most senators who succeed to the presidency do so by being nominated first to the vice-presidency, rather than moving directly from the Senate to the presidency. Our data show that only four presidents had been senators immediately before their election to the highest office.

Another political consideration is related to the electoral college method of electing our presidents; namely, the view that candidates ought to be recruited from states with large populations. By this strategy a candidate can begin his campaign for the presidency with a larger base of electoral votes. Overall, more than three-fifths of our presidents have been recruited from seven large states: Massachusetts, New York, Illinois, Pennsylvania, Ohio, California, and Michigan. However, this factor seems to have less importance today. With the advent of modern communications and the mass media, as well as the heavy emphasis on using television to reach the voting public, a presidential candidate can reside in a less-populated state and still mobilize the publicity needed to wage an effective campaign. For example, since 1960 the following presidential candidates were nominated by the major parties even though they lived in relatively small states: Goldwater in 1964 (Arizona), Humphrey in 1968 (Minnesota), McGovern in 1972 (South Dakota), and Carter in 1976 (Georgia). But although successful presidential candidates no longer need to reside in the largest states, it remains true that both parties' candidates must concentrate on winning the electoral votes in the larger states; this is why they focus campaign efforts on states such as California, New York, and Illinois.

Presidential succession without election

The large number of vice-presidents who became president is partly explained by the fact that eight presidents have died in office: William Henry Harrison, Zachary Taylor, Abraham Lincoln, James A. Garfield, William McKinley, Warren G. Harding, Franklin D. Roosevelt, and John F. Kennedy. Presidential succession also becomes an issue upon the impeachment or resignation of a president. Article II of the Constitution designates "treason, bribery, or other high crimes and misdemeanors," as grounds for impeachment. Only Andrew Johnson came close to being impeached. He was "impeached" by a majority vote in the House of Representatives, but the Senate fell one vote short of the needed two-thirds for conviction. Richard Nixon, who faced impeachment proceedings in the House, chose to resign from office. His removal afforded the first opportunity to use the provisions of the Twenty-fifth Amendment to the Constitution, which dictates vice-presidential succession after resignation or death. Ratified in 1967, the Twenty-fifth Amendment was the fourth attempt to resolve the question of presidential succession. (Previous attempts were the Succession Acts of 1792, 1886, and 1947, described later.)

Should the vice-presidency be vacant, the president can nominate a vice-president who assumes office after a majority vote in the House and Senate.

Thus, when Vice-President Spiro Agnew resigned in 1973, following allegations that as a Baltimore County official and as governor of Maryland he evaded income taxes and accepted bribes, President Nixon consulted with congressional leaders and chose House Minority Party Leader Gerald Ford (R.–Mich.) as his new vice-president. After Richard Nixon resigned in 1974, Ford assumed the presidency and proceeded to nominate New York Governor Nelson Rockefeller, who was confirmed as vice-president after some debate in Congress. By virtue of the Twenty-fifth Amendment, it is highly unlikely that the nation would suffer a double vacancy in both offices of president and vice-president. It also assures that the president and vice-president will represent the same political party and most probably be compatible personalities.

A more thorny issue pertains to presidential disability, and again the Twenty-fifth Amendment provides a satisfactory resolution to this matter, though questions persist concerning its exact implementation.[6] Long before the amendment's enactment, Presidents Garfield and Wilson had extended physical disabilities, and William McKinley lingered for about eight days after being shot by an assassin. Garfield was disabled for eighty days before he died, after an assassin's bullet lodged in his spinal column; Woodrow Wilson was disabled after suffering a paralyzing stroke from about September 25, 1919 until the end of his term in March 1921. During the disabilities of both Garfield and Wilson, however, the vice-presidents involved hesitated to assume presidential powers, and the cabinet in both instances did not force the issue. It was also unclear whether Garfield and Wilson would have legally resumed their official duties had they recovered, as this event was not addressed by the Constitution.

Under the Twenty-fifth Amendment a president now communicates in writing to the speaker of the House and the president pro tempore of the Senate that he is unable to discharge his duties. A president's disability also can be determined by the vice-president acting with a majority of the cabinet or "of such other body as Congress may by law provide"; again written communications are made to the speaker and president pro tempore. In either case, the powers and duties of the presidency are exercised by the vice-president as "Acting President." If the disability ends, the president indicates this by communicating to the speaker and president pro tempore in writing; thereupon he resumes the powers and duties of office, unless

> . . . the Vice President and a majority of either the principal officers of the executive department, or of such other body as Congress may by law provide, transmit within four days to the President pro tempore . . . and the Speaker . . . their written declaration that the President is unable to discharge the powers and duties of his office. Thereupon Congress shall decide the issue, assembling within 48 hours for that purpose if not in session. If the Congress, within 21 days after receipt of the latter written declaration, or, if . . . not in session, within 21 days after Congress is required to assemble, determines by two-thirds vote of both Houses that the President is unable to discharge the powers and duties of his office, the Vice President shall continue to discharge the same as Acting President; otherwise, the President shall resume the powers and duties of his office.

Before this amendment was enacted, Congress seemed little concerned about electoral accountability in matters of presidential succession. When a double vacancy in the presidency and vice-presidency occurred under the Succession Act of 1792, the president pro tempore became "Acting President." The Succession Act of 1886 provided that the presidency be assumed by members of the cabinet, beginning first with the secretary of state. The Succession Act of 1947, authored by Harry Truman, provided the least acceptable resolution of this problem; in the case of a double vacancy succession passed to the speaker, then to the president pro tempore, and then to the various cabinet members. Like the 1886 act, Truman's legislation allowed cabinet members, who were appointed to office, to become president; it also violated the separation of powers principle and made it possible for different political parties to control the presidency and vice-presidency. Most observers, therefore, were thankful when the Twenty-fifth Amendment was added in 1967. Its procedures are not perfect, however; when Gerald Ford and Nelson Rockefeller were president and vice-president, Senator Pastore (D.–R.I.) made this observation: "For the first time in the history of this great nation the President and Vice President will both be appointed—not elected by the people and not responsive to any mandate from the citizens."[7] But had the Succession Act of 1947 been in force, in this situation the president would have been the Democratic speaker of the House of Representatives, a far more serious blow to the notion of electoral accountability.

The electoral college

The framers of the Constitution were not especially concerned about making the president directly accountable to the people. The method of choosing a president through an electoral college is fairly complicated, and it puts the president's election on a *federal* rather than on a national basis (see table 2-2). The number of electoral college votes is equal to the total number of senators (100) and representatives (435), with three more allocated to the District of Columbia by the Twenty-third Amendment. A majority of electoral votes (270) is needed for a candidate to be elected president, but the electors in each state cast their electoral votes as a group. Should no candidate obtain the majority of electoral votes, the House of Representatives, where each state has only one vote to cast, chooses the president by majority vote from among the three candidates receiving the largest number of electoral college votes. The Constitution permitted each state, moreover, to appoint its electors "in such manner as the legislature thereof may direct."

When George Washington was elected in 1789 and 1792 and John Adams in 1796, the electors were chosen as intended, by the state legislatures. But after 1796, various states began to allow the electors to be chosen by popular vote. By 1832 all the states except South Carolina, which did not abandon the legislative method until 1864, authorized popular election of electors.

This development coincided with the rise of political parties in the country. To assure its electoral victory, the dominant political party in each state changed the law to allow the "general ticket" system. Under this plan, the presidential candidate who wins a *plurality* (not a majority) of the state's popular vote captures all the state's electoral votes.

The Founding Fathers intended that the electors use their independent judgment to choose the best man for president, which occurred when Washington was elected on two occasions. By 1796, however, the political rivalries that developed between the Federalists and the Anti-Federalists prompted the electors to cast their ballots according to partisan preference. Thus, the Federalist John Adams was selected over his opponent, Thomas Jefferson, who became the leader of the Anti-Federalists (known later as the Jeffersonian-Republicans). From this point on in our history, electors acted in the name of their political party. The possibility that electors may desert their party's candidate and support another presidential nominee rarely occurs (see table 2-2), so this problem of the "faithless elector" is relatively minor. In most instances, custom reinforced by state law and judicial decree assures that electors remain loyal to their party's presidential candidate.

A more serious threat to the political parties' monopoly over the electoral college is posed when the states modify their laws to allow the voters to choose, in addition to electors pledged to the Republican or Democratic candidates, "unpledged" electors. For example, in 1960 fourteen unpledged electors were chosen in Alabama and Mississippi. It is highly unlikely that unpledged electors could decide a presidential election, but usually that is not the intent. As when "minor" political parties nominate candidates for president, such as George Wallace's 1968 nomination by the American-Independent party, the purpose of selecting unpledged electors is to deny either major party candidate the majority of electoral votes, thus forcing the decision to be made by the House of Representatives. In this circumstance, the political balance of power shifts to the smaller (and usually more conservative) states, because in the House deliberations each state has only one vote to cast for president, regardless of its population.

The possibility that minor candidates or unpledged electors may distort the workings of the electoral college is one of many criticisms made against the existing system. Arguments against the electoral college are summarized as follows:

1. The electoral college exaggerates the margin of victory for the winning candidate because electoral votes are allocated on a winner-take-all basis in each state.
2. The electoral college system can permit the candidate with the most popular votes cast to lose the election, as occurred in 1824, 1876, and 1888.
3. On three occasions (1800, 1824, 1876) the electoral college has failed to elect the president.

TABLE 2-2   Distribution of electoral votes among presidential candidates according to state (1932–1980)*

	1932	1936	1940	1944	1948	1952	1956	1960	1964	1968	1972	1976	1980
Ala.	D	D	D	D	SR	D	D[2]	D[3]	R	AI	R	D	R
Alaska								R	D	R	R	R	R
Ariz.	D	D	D	D	D	R	R	R	R	R	R	R	R
Ark.	D	D	D	D	D	D	D	D	D	AI	R	D	R
Calif.	D	D	D	D	D	R	R	R	D	R	R	R	R
Colo.	D	D	R	R	D	R	R	R	D	R	R	R	R
Conn.	R	D	D	D	D	R	R	D	D	D	R	R	R
Del.	R	D	D	D	R	R	R	D	D	R	R	D	R
D.C.									D	D	D	D	D
Fla.	D	D	D	D	D	R	R	R	D	R	R	D	R
Ga.	D	D	D	D	D	D	D	D	R	AI	R	D	D
Hawaii								D	D	D	R	D	D
Idaho	D	D	D	D	D	R	R	R	D	R	R	R	R
Ill.	D	D	D	D	D	R	R	D	D	R	R	R	R
Ind.	D	D	R	R	R	R	R	R	D	R	R	R	R
Iowa	D	D	R	R	D	R	R	R	D	R	R	R	R
Kan.	D	D	R	R	R	R	R	R	D	R	R	R	R
Ky.	D	D	D	D	D	D	R	R	D	R	R	D	R
La.	D	D	D	D	SR	D	R	D	R	AI	R	D	R
Maine	R	R	R	R	R	R	R	R	D	D	R	R	R
Md.	D	D	D	D	R	R	R	D	D	D	R	D	D
Mass.	D	D	D	D	D	R	R	D	D	D	D	D	R
Mich.	D	D	D	D	R	R	R	D	D	D	R	R	R
Minn.	D	D	D	D	D	R	R	D	D	D	R	D	D
Miss.	D	D	D	D	SR	D	D	UE[3]	R	AI	R	D	R
Mo.	D	D	D	D	D	R	D	D	D	R	R	D	R
Mont.	D	D	D	D	D	R	R	R	D	R	R	R	R
Neb.	D	D	R	R	R	R	R	R	D	R	R	R	R
Nev.	D	D	D	D	D	R	R	D	D	R	R	R	R
N.H.	R	D	D	D	R	R	R	R	D	R	R	R	R

	1932	1936	1940	1944	1948	1952	1956	1960	1964	1968	1972	1976	1980
N.J.	D	D	D	D	R	R	D	D	D	R	R	R	R
N.M.	D	D	D	D	D	R	D	D	D	R	R	R	R
N.Y.	D	D	D	D	R	R	D	D	D	D	R	D	R
N.C.	D	D	D	D	D	D	R	D	D	R⁴	R	D	R
N.D.	D	D	R	R	R	R	R	R	D	R	R	R	D
Ohio	D	D	D	R	D	R	R	D	D	R	R	D	R
Okla.	D	D	D	D	D	R	R	R³	D	R	R	R	R
Ore.	D	D	D	D	R	R	R	R	D	R	R	D	R
Penn.	R	R	D	D	R	R	D	D	D	D	R	D	R
R.I.	D	D	D	D	D	R	D	D	D	R	R	D	D
S.C.	D	D	D	SR	D	R	D	D	R	R	R	R	R
S.D.	D	D	R	R	R	R	R	R	D	R	R	R	R
Tenn.	D	D	D	D¹	R	R	R	R	D	R	R	D	R
Texas	D	D	D	D	D	R	R	D	D	D	R	D	R
Utah	D	D	D	D	D	R	R	D	D	R	R	R	R
Vt.	R	R	R	R	R	R	R	R	D	R	R	R	R
Va.	D	D	D	D	D	R	R	R	D	R	R⁵	R	R
Wash.	D	D	D	D	D	R	D	D	D	D	R	R⁶	R
W.Va.	D	D	R	R	D	D	R	D	D	D	D	D	D
Wisc.	D	D	R	R	R	R	R	D	D	R	R	D	R
Wyo.	D	D	D	D	D	R	R	D	D	R	R	R	R

Legend: AI = American Independent Party; D = Democratic Party; R = Republican Party; SR = States Rights Party; UE = Unpledged Electors Slate. 1 = one Truman elector in Tennessee voted for States Rights Party; 2 = one Stevenson elector in Alabama voted for Walter Jones; 3 = electors in Alabama (6), Mississippi (8), and Oklahoma (1) voted for Senator Harry F. Byrd; 4 = Nixon elector in North Carolina voted for American Independent Party; 5 = Nixon elector in Virginia voted for Libertarian Party; 6 = Ford elector in Washington voted for Ronald Reagan.
*Source: Based upon information in: *Guide to U.S. Elections* (Washington, D.C.: Congressional Quarterly, Inc., 1975), pp. 289–298; *Congressional Quarterly Almanac* (Washington, D.C.: Congressional Quarterly, Inc.), 1976, p. 822; 1977, p. 4; 1980, p. 6B.

4. The electoral college benefits the smallest states and the largest states in the country.
5. The electoral college violates the democratic ideal of "one man, one vote" because it effectively disenfranchises the losing candidate's popular votes and because the value of each vote cast for president depends upon the state in which a voter resides.
6. The winner-take-all system of allocating electoral votes gives political leverage to pivotal groups located in the most populous, powerful states.
7. The electoral college discourages minor political parties and independent presidential candidates since it is so difficult for them to win the majority of electoral votes, which are allocated on a state-by-state basis.

The critics of the electoral college appear to be more concerned about the niceties of democratic theory than about the "political" implications of reforming the existing system. For example, they point out that fifteen times in our history the winning presidential candidate obtained less than a majority of the popular vote cast: John Quincy Adams in 1824, Polk in 1844, Taylor in 1848, Buchanan in 1856, Lincoln in 1860, Hayes in 1876, Garfield in 1880, Cleveland in 1884 and 1892, Benjamin Harrison in 1888, Wilson in 1912 and 1916, Truman in 1948, Kennedy in 1960, and Nixon in 1968. Implicit in this criticism is the view that somehow a president's actions are less legitimate when they are not mandated by a popular majority. But as Richard Pious has noted, the margin of victory attained by such presidents as Lincoln, Wilson, and Nixon did not prevent them from exercising the prerogatives of office in a decisive manner. More fundamental to the critics' arguments, however, are those elections in which the electoral college failed to work or when it is suspected of having distorted the popular will.

The experiences of 1800 led to the enactment of the Twelfth Amendment, which now requires the electors to cast two separate ballots, one for president and one for vice-president. Under the Constitution, each elector originally had two votes, and one had to be cast for a candidate who did not reside in the elector's home state. By this method the candidate with the highest number of votes was president and that candidate with the second-highest majority was vice-president. Obviously a problem would occur should two candidates tie in the electoral college voting. This happened in 1800, between Republicans Thomas Jefferson and Aaron Burr, and as a result this election was decided by the House of Representatives. The rival Federalist Party held the majority in Congress and, although Jefferson was his party's intended presidential candidate, many Federalists favored Burr's election. It took thirty-six ballots in the House before Jefferson, who was strongly backed by Federalist leader Alexander Hamilton, won.

In 1824 four candidates received electoral votes: Andrew Jackson (99), John Quincy Adams (84), William Crawford (41) and Henry Clay (37). In the eighteen states (of twenty-four in the Union) choosing electors by popular vote, Jackson captured the plurality of popular votes. Nevertheless,

Clay threw his support to Adams and the House of Representatives selected John Quincy Adams as president. In 1876 Democrat Samuel J. Tilden received 250,000 more popular votes than Republican Rutherford B. Hayes, but Hayes became president. That year fraud and violence affected voting throughout the nation, especially in the South. An electoral commission was established by Congress to determine which candidate won the disputed electoral votes in Florida, Louisiana, and South Carolina. By a strictly partisan vote the commission awarded all three states' electoral votes to Republican Hayes.

Perhaps the most blatant distortion of the popular will occurred in 1888, when incumbent Democrat Grover Cleveland won a plurality of the popular vote (48.6 percent) against Republican Benjamin Harrison (47.8 percent) but lost in the electoral college by a vote of 168 to 233. What happened in 1888 concerns political scientists anew every time a close election occurs. It is possible for a candidate to lose the popular vote in the large states (having many electoral votes) by small margins but to win the popular vote in smaller states by tremendous margins. As a result, a candidate could be the popular-vote winner but may lack the majority of electoral votes. During the elections of 1836, 1844, 1848, 1860, 1876, 1880, 1884, 1888, 1916, 1948, 1968, and 1976, a shift in the electoral outcome in one, two, or three states would have cost the winning candidate the election. Thus, had 25,000 votes in New York shifted from Abraham Lincoln to Stephen A. Douglas in 1860, the decision would have gone to the House of Representatives. Charles Evans Hughes in 1916 needed about 4,000 more votes in California to defeat Woodrow Wilson for president. And in 1976, Jimmy Carter would have lost to Gerald Ford had about 9,000 votes shifted in Hawaii and Ohio.

Apart from the nation's reluctance to reform governmental institutions and processes, the fact is that political considerations also affect the debate over the electoral college system. Defenders of the electoral college are generally more concerned about the long-term consequences of reform. They make the argument that the electoral college has a "liberalizing" impact on presidential politics because it gives disproportionate power to the larger states. In point of fact the existing system favors the smallest states as well as the larger ones, but for very different reasons. Because no state has fewer than three electoral votes, the least populated states hold a larger proportion of electoral votes than they do popular votes. More important politically, however, is the fact that a few large states hold a majority of electoral votes, and consequently the presidential candidates concentrate on winning these important states. In 1980 twelve states accounted for 284 electoral votes: Ohio, Texas, California, Pennsylvania, New York, Illinois, Massachusetts, New Jersey, Michigan, Indiana, Missouri, and Florida.

Furthermore, large numbers of racial, ethnic, and religious minorities, as well as unionized laborers, live in the highly populated states. These voter groups tend to be more liberal on economic issues, and presidential candidates are encouraged to address their concerns in an effort to win large states rich in electoral votes. For example, although the Jewish community has only about 3 percent of the total national vote, disproportionate numbers of Jews in New York, Illinois, and Florida, give them leverage in these important states. The bias of the electoral college violates the ideal of "one man, one vote" as well as that of "one weight" because all voters in the larger states, including pivotal minority groups, are more important polit- ically than voters in the smaller states. As Lawrence Longley explains, "A citizen voting in California in the present electoral college as apportioned in the 1970s, is found to have 2.5 times the potential for determining the outcome of the Presidential election as a citizen voting in the most disad- vantaged area—the District of Columbia."[8] Most political scientists agree with Longley's assessment of the political impact of the electoral college. Moreover, liberal organizations such as the NAACP and the Americans for Democratic Action (ADA) favor preserving the existing arrangements. In 1977 the ADA issued this statement in behalf of the electoral college:

> Perhaps the only way that significant American minorities can have an impact on the political process is as the deciding factor as to which major candidate can win a given state and a given set of electoral votes. In this way, urban interests and rural, blacks, Latinos, and other minorities, the handicapped and the elderly, the young, the poor, the rich, and the middle-aged can all compete for some attention and some share of public policy. If direct election were instituted, the need for taking into account the needs and desires of minorities would no longer exist. Candidates would campaign for the American middle as their particular pollster describes that middle and would be beholden to no group, no cause, and no interest. Those who constitute America's minorities, whether they are farmers or urban dwellers, would all suffer.[9]

Political scientist Richard Pious disagrees with the commonly held posi- tion that the electoral college permits political leverage by minorities. According to him, because these groups, such as blacks or Jews, are so pro- Democratic in their voting behavior, they do not constitute a "swing" voter bloc, whose allegiance shifts between the Republican and Democratic par- ties.[10] His argument does not seem consistent with political developments since the New Deal. As discussed previously, historians and political sci- entists admired "heroic" presidents because they are seen as promoting social legislation and the rights of minorities. But since these presidents mainly were Democrats, such as Franklin Roosevelt, Truman, Kennedy, and Johnson, one could suggest that the "liberal" bias of the electoral college has singular impact on the Democratic party. Voting studies since the 1930s affirm that Jews, blacks, union labor, and Catholics are heavily Democratic in their partisan identification, and these groups are generally found in the large urbanized states of the Northeast and Midwest. Thus, it may be more accurate to say that the presence of such minorities in the pivotal states *constrains* the leadership of the Democratic party in a liberal direction. How- ever, it may be that the liberal bias of the large states has similar effects, though to a lesser degree, on Republican presidential candidates as well.

Empirical research shows that both parties concentrate on the larger states in waging their presidential campaigns. When a candidate declares his intention to visit every state in the Union, as Richard Nixon did in 1960, it is considered a serious political mistake because that strategy undermines the candidate's ability to concentrate on the key states. A study that followed both parties' candidates on the campaign trail during the period between 1932 and 1976 found that in every election but one Republican and Democratic candidates devoted substantially more than 50 percent of their campaign appearances to those states having eleven or more electoral votes.[11] In the twelve elections studied, in fact, Republicans allocated more than three-fifths of their campaign stops to the larger states, and more than 70 percent in four cases. Democrats were even more committed to a large-state strategy, which provides added verification for the hypothesis that the electoral college has special importance for Democratic candidates. Democratic presidential candidates devoted more than 60 percent of their campaign appearances to the larger states, and in nine elections that proportion rose to more than 70 percent. Furthermore, both parties tended to focus on these larger states regardless of the states' political "competitiveness" during the election. That analysis, therefore, suggests that *size* rather than marginality is the salient reason why the parties' candidates allocate precious time and energy to the larger states.

Reform proposals. The major alternative to the electoral college is *direct popular election* of the president. This proposal was opposed by the ADA for the same reasons that they defended the electoral college. While there are variations to this scheme, the proposal advocated by former Senator Birch Bayh (D.–Ind.) provided for the president's election by a nationwide popular vote. A plurality would be enough for election so long as the winner achieved at least 40 percent of the vote cast. If he did not, then a run-off election would be held between the top two candidates. Jimmy Carter was the first Democratic president to favor this change, and at one time Senator Bayh was able to recruit about forty-five cosponsors for his amendment. Gallup Polls and Harris Surveys since 1966 indicate increased support by Americans for changes in the electoral college. And in 1969 the House of Representatives actually approved an amendment, but it died in the Senate. With Senator Bayh's reelection defeat in 1980, reformers lost their primary spokesman for direct election, and no other senator has emerged as the acknowledged leader favoring this alternative to the electoral college system.

Another proposal, the *proportional plan,* would allocate each state's electoral votes to the presidential candidates according to their share of the popular vote. A third alternative, the *single-member district system,* requires that each state be divided into districts equal to its number of representatives. The voters in each district would choose an elector, and two more electoral votes (for each state's senators) would go to that presidential candidate winning the plurality of popular votes statewide. Still a fourth option is called the *national bonus plan.* It would retain the electoral college but weigh it more heavily towards the candidate who wins the popular vote. Under this scheme, a "bonus" of 102 electoral votes would be given to that candidate who receives the most popular votes, but the existing number of electoral votes (538) would be allocated on a state-by-state basis as is traditionally done. This plan has been advocated by a task force of social scientists, including political scientist Thomas Cronin.[12]

By any standard, however, these reforms of the electoral college would have the effect of further insulating the president from strategically located minorities, thereby strengthening more conservative values and interests. In the final analysis, political bias of the electoral college depends on the role of the states in allocating the electoral votes among the presidential candidates, and our federal system has similar effects on how the parties nominate presidential candidates. The parties' nominating conventions are composed of delegates selected in the various states, and delegates from certain regions are more liberal than those coming from other areas.

PRESIDENTIAL NOMINATING CONVENTIONS

An index to the importance of political parties in any regime is the degree to which they monopolize the nominating process. When they dominate, aspirants for public office must establish their commitment to the party organization, and to its political principles, or they find it difficult or nearly impossible to secure elective office. In the beginning, nominees for president were chosen by legislative caucus, which consisted of each political party's members in Congress. This procedure was superseded by the nominating convention. The Anti-Masons held the first convention in 1830, but when the Democratic party nominated Andrew Jackson in 1832, it established the model by which our political parties have nominated presidential candidates ever since. The conventions do more than nominate candidates, however; they write the party platform, establish party rules, and launch the presidential campaign. A latent function of the convention, moreover, is to establish a working consensus among the various factions of a political party so that its candidate is supported by a unified party organization.

Delegates to the party conventions are selected according to party rules and state law. Historically the states have allowed differing methods for their selection: conventions, appointments, caucuses, primary elections, or some combination of these alternatives. The primary election has become the predominant method of choosing convention delegates. The majority of delegates to both parties' conventions in 1972, 1976, and 1980 were chosen this way. In contrast, during 1912 to 1968 delegates chosen by primary election were a majority in only one Democratic convention (1916) and in two Republic conventions (1916, 1920).[13] Delegate selection by primary election would seem to be more democratic than other methods, but this reform has weakened party organization in the United States. In addition, it often prevents a party from achieving internal unity needed to wage a presidential campaign effectively. A major reason for weakened party unity is that the use of primaries permits delegates to be selected by voters who may differ widely in their loyalty to the political party, ideological orientation and issue positions, and socioeconomic background.

The critics of primaries argue, therefore, that people who vote in the primaries are not always representative of the party's membership, and are certainly not representative of the entire electorate. A candidate selected by delegates chosen in primaries and a platform written by such delegates may handicap the party's ability to compete in the general election. On the other hand, those who defend the primary system of delegate selection argue that when the conventions were dominated by delegates chosen in state conventions, by appointment, or through local party caucuses, the parties too often abandoned their commitment to principles and favored nominees who simply maximized voter appeal. In the past, large numbers of delegates included elected officials, such as mayors, governors, and members of Congress, whose main interest was finding a strong candidate to wage an effective campaign against the opposition party. This tension between the need to win elections and the desire to promote certain policies and ideological commitments cannot be easily reconciled. In fact, this dichotomy is so important that many political scientists use it to differentiate between "professional" politicians who wish to win elections and "amateur" party activists who are ideologically motivated.

Most relevant to our analysis is the fact that nominating conventions can act as political constraints affecting the presidential candidates. Without suggesting that the convention actually manages the presidential campaign, within limits it can define the ideological tone of the campaign and commit the party's candidate to very specific programs. Frank Munger and James Blackhurst have shown that factionalism at the parties' national conventions reflects ideological differences that persist over time.[14] During 1940 to 1964, for example, two identifiable factions dominated Republican politics at the national conventions; namely, the "Taft wing" and the "Eastern wing." The moderate-to-liberal Eastern wing prevailed when the Republican party nominated Willkie in 1940, Dewey in 1948, and Eisenhower in 1952, but the Taft wing captured the party's nomination when Barry Goldwater was chosen in 1964. Six factions coexisted in the Democratic party during the same period, and Munger and Blackhurst determined that control over the nominations for president and vice-president shifted over time from a left-center coalition in 1940 (Roosevelt-Wallace), to a center-right coalition in 1944 (Roosevelt-Truman), back to a left-center coalition in 1948 (Truman-Barkley), to a center coalition in 1952 (Stevenson-Sparkman) and in 1956 (Stevenson-Kefauver), and back again to a left-center coalition in 1960 (Kennedy-Johnson). Thus, political coalitions in the nominating conventions are not forged only for the purpose of maximizing the power of each candidate; rather, they reflect different orientations toward public policy as well.

Gerald Pomper updated the Munger and Blackhurst analysis for the 1968 election and discovered that the traditional factional alignments in both parties had changed.[15] The nominations of both Richard Nixon and Hubert

Humphrey in 1968 suggested a greater influence in both parties by their conservative wings. Pomper concludes:

> A shift of power within the parties is clearly evident. The earlier control of the Republican party by the "Eastern establishment," seen in Eisenhower's reliance on the most liberal faction, was reversed by Goldwater's nomination. Nixon's nomination maintains the party's new leaning toward its more conservative wing. Even more startling is the shift within the Democratic party. . . . Humphrey's victory implies a realignment of the power structure within the party, and the potential primacy of the conservative delegations that have been subordinate within the party since John W. Davis was nominated in 1924.[16]

One explanation for these new political alignments, especially in the Democratic party, may be the changing policy agenda of the 1960s and 1970s. Many demands expressed in the 1960s and 1970s by antiwar protesters, civil rights activists, and advocates of women's rights involved social issues rather than the Democratic party's more traditional concern for bread-and-butter economic issues.

A study by Howard Reiter affirms that new cleavages within the parties' nominating conventions have developed since the early 1960s.[17] In the Democratic party he found a division between the liberal North and the conservative South, and another split between the "professional" politicians and the "amateur" reformers. The latter gap, however, affected only the most recent Democratic conventions. Reiter suggests that the differences between professionals and amateurs is related to the widely differing political cultures found in the various states: "so many recent conventions have involved clashes over reforms in party rules and 'style' issues such as foreign policy, feminism, abortion, homosexual rights, and affirmative action."[18]

Conservative influence in the Republican party is strongest in the Southeast and Far West, whereas liberalism is strongest in the Northeast and parts of the Midwest. Reiter's analysis seems to confirm Pomper's suspicion that a new kind of conservatism is dominating the Republican party today. He speculates that the conservatism is particularly evident in such issues as race relations and military spending, which have special relevance to, respectively, the Southeast and the Far West.

The problem of factional conflict is more serious for the out-party, because the president symbolizes for his political party its programmatic goals, ideology, and relationship to key voter groups. For this reason it is also difficult for a party to repudiate its president. Only a few incumbents, therefore, have been denied renomination: Tyler, Andrew Johnson, Pierce, Fillmore, Buchanan, and Arthur. This has not happened in the twentieth century, though a number of presidents have declined to seek renomination, including Theodore Roosevelt, Calvin Coolidge, Harry Truman, and Lyndon Johnson. Truman and Johnson clearly were prompted by a keen understanding that their performance in office had led to a steep decline in public approval. Once a president is renominated, it is not easy to defeat him. A president seeking reelection has been defeated only three times in this

century: Taft in 1912, Ford in 1976, and Carter in 1980. It may be significant
that the two most recent incumbents were defeated for reelection; some
observers suggest we may be witnessing the beginning of a period of "one-
term" presidents. Given today's myriad social and economic issues coupled
with the proliferation of single-issue groups, they argue that it may be too
difficult for a president to keep his majority coalition intact for a second
term.

On the other hand, in the party not controlling the presidency various
factions and presidential candidates jockey for power, exploiting issues,
voter groups, and ideology in an effort to capture the nomination. As a
result, since 1936 only two nominations by the out-party have been consensual: Landon's in 1936 and Dewey's in 1944. Since the Republican party
has been out of power most often since 1936 most of the serious battles over
the presidential nomination have affected its conventions: those nominating
Willkie in 1940, Dewey in 1948, Eisenhower in 1952, Goldwater in 1964,
Nixon in 1968, and Ford in 1976. Serious factional strife affected the Democrats in 1952 (Stevenson), in 1968 (Humphrey), when they were the in-
party, as well as in 1972 (McGovern).[19] In general, it appears that the conventions have provided a unified party organization behind nominees on
most occasions, although it is clear that candidates seeking election in a
party torn by serious dissidence, as suffered by the Democrats in 1968 and
1972, face insurmountable obstacles to running an effective campaign.

Conventions usually can establish a degree of unity behind the presidential candidates because the convention choice typically is the party
membership's choice as well. In a penetrating essay, W. G. Carleton argues
it is highly unlikely that political parties today can nominate an unknown
person for president.[20] Such "dark horse" presidential candidates were not
infrequently nominated before the 1920s; usually they appeared as nominees after the front-runners for the nomination were deadlocked. The last
times our conventions turned to a dark horse were in 1920 for the Republicans (Harding) and in 1924 for the Democrats (John W. Davis). Nowadays
the parties are compelled to turn to "celebrities" as their candidates. Among
the reasons cited by Carleton for this new strategy are the greater importance of mass media in campaigning, the impact of public opinion polling,
and the increased reliance on presidential primaries. Therefore, Carleton
argues that the recruitment of presidential nominees has been further
democratized, although he is concerned that these developments have less
impact on the process by which we select candidates for Congress.

Convention politics and public opinion

The relationship between public opinion, presidential primaries, and the
convention process has been analyzed by William Lucy.[21] In the elections
of 1936 to 1972 he found that in nineteen times out of twenty the final
preconvention leader in the opinion polls who actively wanted the nomination was nominated by his party. The lone exception to this trend was
Estes Kefauver's defeat by Adlai Stevenson in 1952. Moreover, only once

during 1936 to 1972 was the preprimary leader in the opinion polls defeated in presidential primaries and thereby lost his leadership position in the polls. Here the exception was in 1972, when Democrat Edmund Muskie faltered in the primaries and Sen. George McGovern was eventually nominated.

McGovern was the first candidate in modern times to overcome his weak support among party leaders as well as his low standing in the opinion polls to capture the nomination. This maneuver would have been impossible before the widespread use of presidential primaries. In 1972, 60.5 percent of the Democratic convention delegates were chosen through primaries; in 1976, thirty states used primaries to elect 72.5 percent of the party's delegates. Thus, Jimmy Carter, a one-term governor of Georgia who in 1973 could not be identified on the television show *What's My Line*, exploited media coverage to move from political obscurity to capture his party's nomination in 1976. He did this by using the primaries. Jimmy Carter ran in twenty-six primaries, won seventeen, and placed second in the rest. Many political commentators see a relationship between Carter's method of securing the nomination and his subsequent difficulties as president. Because he could win delegates in primaries without having to court the favor of the party leadership, President Carter lacked the ties to the party organization which might have assisted in cultivating support for his programs. In the past, a contender for the presidential nomination had to choose between being an "insider" working through party organization and cultivating leadership to support his candidacy or entering presidential primaries as an "outsider" to prove his superior vote-getting ability. This option has changed fundamentally today. Given the widespread use of the primaries, no serious contender for the presidency can ignore them and hope to be "drafted" by the convention for the nation's highest office.

The research by Lucy, therefore, shows a close relationship between the parties' rank-and-file preferences, as reflected in opinion polls, and the formal nominations made by the conventions. Since this linkage was firmly established throughout this century, even before primaries became widespread, one might wonder why the parties reformed their delegate selection process in the 1970s. To the extent that the views of a party's rank and file are reflected in its choice of a presidential candidate, one can argue that the convention is generally "representative" of the party membership. This, however, does not mean that all groups within the political party have an equal opportunity to participate in the convention's decision-making processes.

Democratic party reforms

The year 1968 was not a good one for the Democrats. The party was seriously divided after primary challenges against Lyndon Johnson were mounted by Eugene McCarthy and Robert Kennedy, who was assassinated after his victory in the California primary. When the Democratic convention was held in Chicago to nominate Vice-President Hubert Humphrey, the American people were exposed to a powerful media event. Inside the convention dissidents were charging "boss rule," and outside anti–Vietnam War demonstrators and student radicals were confronting the Chicago police in what one report terms a "police riot." Because Hubert Humphrey was nominated without having entered any presidential primaries, the dissidents charged that the decision-making processes of the convention were insensitive to the views of rank-and-file Democrats and were controlled by party "professionals," such as Chicago Mayor Richard J. Daley. To address this grievance, the delegates to the 1968 convention adopted a resolution requiring the state party organizations to give "all Democrats a full, meaningful, and timely opportunity to participate" in the selection of delegates to future Democratic conventions. As a result, Democratic National Committee Chairman Fred Harris appointed a Commission on Party Structure and Delegate Selection to be cochaired by Sen. George McGovern (D.–S.D.) and Rep. Donald Fraser (D.–Minn.). The McGovern-Fraser Commission recommended a series of party reforms aimed at making the 1972 convention more representative of the party's membership, increasing grass-roots participation in decision making, and assuring more open and democratic procedures. But the recommendations of the McGovern-Fraser Commission were short-lived insofar as its reforms were re-evaluated by other Democratic party commissions established during the 1970s and 1980s.

The changes made by the Democratic party in its selection of delegates to attend national conventions is the major reason why presidential primaries have become so important today. Moreover, since delegate selection is regulated by state law, various states had to incorporate these reforms into their statutes, which means that the Republican party could be affected by these changes as well. Included in the McGovern-Fraser reforms was the requirement that delegates be chosen only in the calendar year of the convention. Fees for entering the primaries were lowered or abolished; the old system of proxy voting—in which a state party leader could cast many votes for delegates—was ended; and now state party central committees could no longer appoint more than 10 percent of the delegates. In addition, three-fourths of the delegates had to be elected at levels no higher than congressional districts. But the most controversial proposal by the McGovern-Fraser Commission was a so-called quota system, which required the representation of "minorities, women, and young people in reasonable relationship to their presence in the population of the state."

Due to the complexity of these reforms, it was very difficult for state party organizations to implement them at every stage of the nominating process should they want to use caucuses and state conventions. As a result, many states turned to the primary election as the easiest method of reforming the delegate selection process. Primaries give the party's membership real power because, under "binding" primaries, those delegates elected in behalf of a candidate for the nomination must vote for him in the convention for a specified number of ballots, unless released by the candidate. However, disputes over whether the McGovern-Fraser Commission's rules had been properly implemented resulted in eighty-two challenges affecting thirty states and more than 40 percent of the delegates who attended the 1972 Democratic convention.[22] One dispute not easily resolved by the convention's Credentials Committee involved the makeup of the Illinois delegation under the leadership of Chicago's Mayor Daley. Eventually this question was taken to the convention floor, where the delegates voted not to seat the "regular" Democrats under Daley but approved a rival group led by "independent" Democratic alderman William Singer and civil rights leader Jesse Jackson. This action led to extensive litigation, until the Supreme Court in 1975 decided that the rules of the national political parties take precedence over state laws regarding the qualifications and eligibility of delegates to the conventions.[23]

These reforms had an impact on the 1972 Democratic convention. Between 1968 and 1972, the number of women delegates increased from 13 to 40 percent, blacks increased from 5.5 to 15 percent, and delegates aged 30 or under increased from 4 to 21 percent.[24] More important was the substantial increase in the number of "amateur" political activists who participated in the 1972 convention. As mentioned previously, research suggests that amateurs are motivated to engage in politics because of commitment to a certain candidate or single-minded devotion to an ideology or cause. In contrast, it is argued that professional politicians are more willing to compromise on candidates and on issues in order to achieve electoral victory. According to one study, the number of amateurs at Democratic conventions rose from 23 percent in 1968 to a majority of 51 percent in 1972. Most of these activists supported the candidacy of George McGovern.[25] Conversely, there was a sharp decline in the number of elected party officials attending the 1972 convention. For example, 90 percent of the Democratic senators, 33 percent of the Democratic representatives, and all Democratic governors attended the party's 1956 convention. The respective percentages for the 1968 convention were 68, 39, and 83; however, by 1972 all three groups had lost representation (18%, 15%, and 47%).[26] In 1972 eighty-three percent of the Democrats were attending their very *first* party convention.

The real impact of the reforms, however, was the fact that the Democratic convention in 1972 nominated George McGovern, who ultimately carried only Massachusetts and the District of Columbia against Richard Nixon. After reviewing survey data showing that the 1972 Democratic delegates were far more liberal than Democratic voters on such issues as busing, welfare, and crime, Everett Ladd concludes: "The convention that formally nominated McGovern was strikingly unrepresentative of the policy preferences of the mass of Democrats."[27] This observation is confirmed by an analysis done by Jeanne Kirkpatrick, who found in 1972 that Democratic voters were closer ideologically to the Republican convention delegates than to the Democratic delegates.[28] This situation was the reverse of what was found in 1956; at that time the Democratic delegates were closer ideologically to both Republican and Democratic voters than were the Republican delegates.[29] Thus, although delegates to the national conventions can be expected to be more issue-oriented than most voters, too great a disparity between the views of the delegates and the party's membership can undermine a presidential candidate's ability to win the necessary votes from his partisans, from independents, and from the opposition party to win the election.

By 1976 the ideological tone of the Democratic convention had been moderated. A study comparing the 1972 and 1976 conventions found that the number of "moderates" had increased whereas the proportion of delegates categorized as "very liberal" or "liberal" had declined.[30] Among the delegates to the 1976 Republican convention, ideology differentiated those delegates supporting Gerald Ford from those committed to Ronald Reagan. Whereas 76 percent of Reagan's supporters called themselves "conservative," the majority of Ford's supporters (67%) were called "moderate."[31] Reagan also relied more heavily on delegates committed to policy issues while Ford got more support from the party professionals.[32]

A relationship exists, therefore, between the delegate makeup of the national conventions and the ideological thrust of their presidential campaigns. Democratic candidates for president are nominated by more liberal conventions than are Republican presidential candidates, and these tendencies are pronounced whenever ideological purists dominate the convention deliberations. This happened to the Republicans in 1964 and in 1980 and to the Democrats in 1972. One cannot know for certain whether a Goldwater presidency would have been much different than Lyndon Johnson's or whether McGovern would have followed the same policies outlined by Richard Nixon. We doubt that they would have. In this regard the record of the Reagan administration may prove instructive; we can evaluate the degree to which a presidential candidate who is nominated by ideological purists, and who holds strong views on political issues, abides by those commitments after he is elected to office.

McGovern's massive defeat in 1972 caused the Democratic Party to reevaluate its party rules; ways had to be found to reduce the internal factionalism resulting from more democratic decision-making processes, as well as to guarantee that party professionals have a voice in the conventions. Since the party's elected officials ultimately must seek reelection with the president and vice-president, the entire ticket would be strengthened by allowing state and local political leaders to have influence in the national conventions. In 1972 George McGovern lost in part because many Democratic mayors, governors, congressmen, senators, and local officials refused to support his candidacy. A new commission was appointed to reduce factionalism in the 1976 election. Under the guidelines of this Mikulski Commission the quota rules were replaced with affirmative action programs and the candidates were allowed more control over the delegates selected to represent them. Another important change involved the "winner-take-all" system of voting for convention delegates. To assure the representation of minority viewpoints, the McGovern-Fraser Commission had recommended that delegates be allocated among the various candidates on the basis of "proportional representation" rather than the traditional "winner-take-all" system. That guideline was not required in 1972, but by 1976 the "winner-take-all" system was prohibited. However, in 1976 that prohibition was avoided by using the so-called loophole primary. What happened was that a loophole in the party rules permitting the election of delegates according to congressional districts resulted in winner-take-all systems being applied at that level. And because a candidate with a plurality of the vote in each congressional district could win all that district's delegates to the national convention, this method obviously helped the front-runners and disadvantaged minor candidates.

As a consequence, the new Winograd Commission received a charge from the 1976 Democratic convention to find an alternative for the "loophole" primary by the 1980 election. Its recommendations were also controversial. The Winograd Commission recommended that (1) the primary period be reduced to three months, (2) the "equal division" rule for equalizing the number of male and female delegates from each state be reinstated, (3) proportional representation be used in all states and the winner-take-all system be entirely eliminated, and (4) a 10 percent "add-on" policy be adopted to increase the number of officeholders and party professionals able to attend the convention. In 1980 many Democrats felt that the Winograd Commission had gone too far, with the result that yet another commission was convened to study the delegate selection process for 1984. The Hunt Commission on Presidential Nominations promised to make its recommendations based on the need to strengthen the party's control over its own internal procedures. Its goal is to avoid the convention battles of 1972 and of 1980, when Ted Kennedy opposed Jimmy Carter, by assuring that the party's presidential candidate is supported by all factions of the Democratic party.

About one-fourth of the seventy-member Hunt Commission are elected officials and party leaders, while the others represent various interests within the Democratic party. North Carolina Governor James B. Hunt, Jr., the chairman, is a Southern Democrat, and the cochairmen represent organized labor (Douglas Fraser, United Auto Workers president) and Democratic women (Dorothy Zug, vice-chairman of Pennsylvania). The Hunt Commission does not plan to alter the affirmative action programs or the "equal division" policy assuring equal numbers of men and women delegates. A major proposal is the recommendation that about 550 "superdelegates"— who would be unpledged and uncommitted party professionals and elected officials—be added to the convention. That group would represent about 14 percent of the convention's 3,850 members, and the hope is that they will play a key role in shaping the convention's choice of a presidential candidate. Another recommendation is the reinstatement of the "winner-take-all" rule as well as the "winner-take-more" principles. The first rule would allow a winning candidate to control all the delegates chosen within a congressional district, and the second would give the winning candidate a "bonus" delegate. Therefore, the Hunt Commission is following a very different philosophy from what motivated the McGovern-Fraser Commission. It wants to ensure party unity and candidate support, and there is also the desire to make the nominating convention a meaningful decision-making arena rather than simply a forum for ratifying decisions made in presidential primaries and state party caucuses.

Party platforms

Besides nominating candidates, national conventions also write party platforms, which are statements of past accomplishments and of future goals. Rather than taking platforms seriously, voters usually look toward the candidates' statements during the campaign to indicate the probable direction of public policy. But on occasion the party platforms do make explicit commitments to special interest and voter groups, which is one reason why presidential candidates try to make these documents compatible with their own personal views. As Judith Parris argues, many delegates and party leaders take the platform seriously as a guide to action.[33] For this reason also, platforms have been the cause for serious factional conflict within both parties from time to time.

Gerald Pomper studied both parties' platforms during 1944 to 1968. He found that one-third of the pledges were the same for both parties, that about one-half were made by only one of the two parties, and that on the remaining planks the Republican and Democratic parties had opposing positions.[34] More important, there is a relationship between the party platforms and public policymaking. Paul David analyzed Pomper's data and determined that a high percentage of the most specific planks have been enacted into law.[35] During 1944 to 1966 the Democratic party made 517 specific pledges in its platform, and 68 percent were fulfilled. The Republican party made 418 pledges and 62 percent were enacted. As one might expect, the success rate increases for any pledges made by both parties, and the party holding the presidency is able to fulfill more pledges than the out-party. For the in-party, David says that "platform drafting has come increasingly under the influence of the President, usually with active participation by White House staff at all stages."[36] In addition, the most specific planks were found in policy areas affecting clientele groups, such as labor, resources, welfare, and agriculture, whereas the pledges were most general in areas affecting foreign and defense policy and in economic affairs. Finally, the success rate on pledges by the in-party has increased since 1944. David found that about 60 percent were achieved during the period from 1944 to 1952, but at least 80 percent of the pledges were fulfilled during 1952 to 1966. Overall, these findings led David to conclude that platforms are not meaningless statements: "In the contemporary situation, the major party platforms have become important as alternative and partly overlapping national plans on which a substantial degree of execution can reasonably be expected. It is time that they were recognized as such."[37]

Conflict over party platforms is more evident in the period since 1964. One exception to this generalization, however, was the 1948 Democratic convention. Southern delegates tried to incorporate a states' rights plank onto the platform, but instead the convention adopted a very strong civil rights plank. This caused the Southerners to walk out and form the Dixiecrat party, which backed Strom Thurmond for president in 1948. In 1964, Republican moderates led by New York Governor Nelson Rockefeller urged the convention to condemn political extremism and to support civil rights, but Barry Goldwater succeeded in getting his anticivil rights plank adopted. The 1968 Democratic convention experienced a four-hour debate over Vietnam, but eventually Lyndon Johnson was able to gain convention approval for a plank supporting his war policies, even though it hurt the presidential candidacy of Hubert Humphrey. In 1972, the Democratic platform reflected the views of activists who supported George McGovern. It included very liberal planks on amnesty for Vietnam War resisters and on school busing; in addition, the convention debated planks on such controversial topics as abortion and homosexuality.

In 1980 the Democratic platform was the subject of conflict between the Carter and Kennedy forces, but the Republican party's platform was adopted with considerable unity. Though Jimmy Carter regained the presidential nomination, the convention adopted three minority planks in its platform which he opposed: a pro-choice stand on abortion, a $12 billion jobs program, and sanctions against Democratic candidates who did not support the Equal Rights Amendment. In contrast, the 1980 Republican platform conformed to Ronald Reagan's views on these issues, and it was approved by a convention heavily dominated by conservatives. The Republican platform favored a constitutional amendment banning abortions as well as the proposal that federal judges be screened according to their views on abortion. It also opposed ratification of the Equal Rights Amendment. Thus, the Republican and Democratic platforms of 1964, 1972, and 1980 reflected the fundamental differences in ideology that characterized the delegates to the two parties' conventions, as well as the differing views of their presidential candidates. In the assessment of Paul David, "Those who continue to believe that party platforms are meaningless and without consequence might well respond with some form of evidence that is more than fragmentary and anecdotal in support of their position."[38]

REALIGNING ELECTIONS, COALITION BUILDING, AND POLICY CHOICE

Angus Campbell has classified presidential elections as maintaining, deviating, and realigning.[39] A *maintaining* election occurs whenever the political party with the largest number of identifiers wins the election. Since most voters today are Democrats, seven recent contests are maintaining elections: 1936, 1940, 1944, 1948, 1960, 1964, and 1976. A *deviating* election takes place when the minority party is able to exploit short-term forces, such as issues, events, or a candidate's personality, to win the presidency. Such an outcome is a temporary deviation from what is expected, however, because the success of the minority party is not related to any shift in the partisan identification of voters. Examples of deviating elections have included Eisenhower's victories in 1952 and 1956, Nixon's victories in 1968 and 1972, and Reagan's election in 1980.

Realigning elections are extraordinary events and as mentioned earlier, few have occurred in our history: 1800 (Jefferson), 1828 (Jackson), 1860 (Lincoln), 1896 (McKinley), and 1932 (Roosevelt). In these instances the electoral outcome is shaped by massive shifts in the partisan identification of voter groups. V. O. Key referred to such contests as "critical" elections because they are important watersheds in American politics.[40] During realigning elections the relationship between the public's electoral choice and the direction of public policy is strengthened. Historically, these elections have occurred during crises, when issues of tremendous magnitude shook the nation to its foundations. The shifting of partisan loyalties by voter groups increases party conflict in the short term and affects the parties' ideological makeup over the longer run. Wayne Shannon observes that the degree of "party voting" in Congress, where a majority of Republicans oppose a majority of Democrats, dramatically increases after a realigning election.[41] Because each party's political constituency has been redefined and sharpened, due to the impact of issues, this conflict over public policy affects Congress when legislation is debated. Thus, the Republican party's domination of national politics from 1860 to 1932 followed the debate over slavery and the issue of secession.

The realignment associated with the Great Depression of the 1930s established a New Deal Coalition which sustained the Democratic party's hegemony ever since. Unlike the regional shifting that followed the Civil War, the Depression and Roosevelt's New Deal precipitated a reshuffling along class lines; many working-class people and minorities became Democrats whereas middle-class groups moved toward the Republican party. Therefore, as Angus Campbell argues, realigning elections are related more to ideology and issues and less to the candidates' personalities.

> . . . the realigning elections have not been dominated by presidential candidates who came into office on a wave of great personal popularity. . . . The quality which did distinguish the elections in which they came to power was the presence of a great national crisis, leading to a conflict regarding governmental policies and the association of the two major parties with relatively clearly contrasting programs for its solution. In some degree national politics during these realigning periods took on an ideological character.[42]

Franklin D. Roosevelt won the 1932 election by holding onto the solid Democratic South and adding voters who traditionally had voted Republican or had not voted at all. While these groups do not always vote Democratic to the same extent and though their loyalty to the Democratic party varies over time, disproportionate numbers of the following groups vote Democratic more often than Republican: blue-collar workers, immigrant groups who are largely Catholic, Jews and blacks, and residents of large central cities. Since we are living in the wake of this New Deal Coalition, it is important that we understand its impact on both the Democratic and Republican parties and their presidential candidates. The survey data in table 2-3 for the years 1952 to 1980 indicate that voter groups are generally consistent in their partisan loyalties in presidential elections. In the seven elections between 1952 and 1976 (excluding 1980 for the moment), the Democratic candidate always received more support than the Republicans from nonwhites; the same tendency applies to manual workers, Catholics, and members of labor union families in six cases, and to the grade-school educated in five elections. Republicans did better than Democrats among whites, the college-educated, Protestants, and people engaged in professional/business occupations in six of the seven elections. The greatest deviations in the expected vote by these groups occurred in 1964 and in 1972; many Republican-leaning groups supported Johnson in 1964, whereas in 1972 Democratic voters shifted to Richard Nixon.

To more precisely define each party's electoral coalition, Robert Axelrod studied the voting behavior of these groups not only in terms of their partisan loyalty but also in terms of their group size and their voting turnout. By this strategy he calculated the relative importance of each voter group to the Republican and Democratic electoral coalitions (table 2-4). Originally Axelrod applied his analysis to the elections during 1952 to 1968, but updated the study to include the 1972 and 1976 elections as well.[43] Axelrod's research is of paramount importance. Rather than simply confirming existing knowledge about the parties' electoral coalitions, he was able to show the shifts in the composition of those coalitions over time. For each election, Axelrod studied the Republican vote in terms of these groups: the nonpoor, whites, nonunion families, Protestants, Northerners, and residents outside the central cities. The reverse holds true for the Democrats, whose coalition relies disproportionately on the poor, blacks, union members, Catholics, Southerners, and central city residents.

In terms of Axelrod's formulation, the Republican coalition consists of overlapping "majorities" which are the precise complements of the "minorities" that compose the Democratic coalition. The problem for the Republican party, however, is that its huge voter blocs are much less loyal to Republican candidates than traditional Democratic voters are to their party's standard-bearers. Overall, the trends in Republican voting may be summarized as follows:

1. The nonpoor are barely more Republican than the nation as a whole.
2. Whites are 1 to 3 percent more pro-Republican in their voting than the nation as a whole.
3. Nonunion family members vote 5 to 6 percent more Republican than the nation as a whole.
4. Protestants vote about 5 percent more Republican than the nation as a whole, except in 1960 when their Republican vote increased markedly.

TABLE 2-3 Percentage vote by selected groups for Republican and Democratic presidential candidates (1952–1980)

	1952 (D) AS	1952 (R) DE	1956 (D) AS	1956 (R) DE	1960 (D) JFK	1960 (R) RN	1964 (D) LBJ	1964 (R) BG	1968 (D) HHH	1968 (R) RN	1968 (AI) GW	1972 (D) GM	1972 (R) RN	1976 (D) JC	1976 (R) GF	1980 (D) JC	1980 (R) RR	1980 (I) JA
Race																		
White	43	57	41	59	49	51	59	41	38	47	15	32	68	46	52	36	56	7
Nonwhite	79	21	61	39	68	32	94	6	85	12	3	87	13	85	15	86	10	2
Education																		
College	34	66	31	69	39	61	52	48	37	54	9	37	63	42	55	35	53	10
High School	45	55	42	58	52	48	62	38	42	43	15	34	66	54	46	43	51	5
Grade School	52	48	50	50	55	45	66	34	52	33	15	49	51	58	41	54	42	3
Occupation																		
Prof./Business	36	64	32	68	42	58	54	46	34	56	10	31	69	42	56	33	55	10
White Collar	40	60	37	63	48	52	57	43	41	47	12	36	64	50	48	40	51	9
Manual Labor	55	45	50	50	60	40	71	29	50	35	15	43	57	58	41	48	46	5
Religion																		
Protestant	37	63	37	63	38	62	55	45	35	49	16	30	70	46	53	39	54	6
Catholic	56	44	51	49	78	22	76	24	59	33	8	48	52	57	42	46	47	6
Region																		
East	45	55	40	60	53	47	68	32	50	43	7	42	58	51	47	43	47	9
Midwest	42	58	41	59	48	52	61	39	44	47	9	40	60	48	50	41	51	7
South	51	49	49	51	51	49	52	48	31	36	33	29	71	54	45	44	52	3
West	42	58	43	57	49	51	60	40	44	49	7	41	59	46	51	35	54	9
Age																		
Under 30	51	49	43	57	54	46	64	36	47	38	15	48	52	53	45	47	41	11
30–49	47	53	45	55	54	46	63	37	44	41	15	33	67	48	49	38	52	8
50 and Older	39	61	39	61	46	54	59	41	41	47	12	36	64	52	48	41	54	4
Politics																		
Republican	8	92	4	96	5	95	20	80	9	86	5	5	95	9	91	8	86	5
Democrat	77	23	85	15	84	16	87	13	74	12	14	67	33	82	18	69	26	4
Independent	35	65	30	70	43	57	56	44	31	44	25	31	69	39	57	29	55	14
Sex																		
Male	47	53	45	55	52	48	60	40	41	43	16	37	63	53	45	38	53	7
Female	42	58	39	61	49	51	62	38	45	43	12	38	62	48	51	44	49	6
Labor Union Family	61	39	57	43	65	35	73	27	56	29	15	46	54	63	36	50	43	5

Source: *The Gallup Opinion Index* (December 1980), report no. 183, pp. 6–7. Reprinted by permission.

Legend: D = Democratic; R = Republican; AI = American Independent; I = Independent. AS = Stevenson; DE = Eisenhower; JFK = Kennedy; RN = Nixon; LBJ = Johnson; BG = Goldwater; HHH = Humphrey; GW = Wallace; GM = McGovern; JC = Carter; GF = Ford; RR = Reagan; JA = Anderson

TABLE 2-4   Percentage contribution of demographic groups to Democratic and Republican electoral coalitions* (1952–1976)

Demographic Groups**	Year						
	1952	*1956*	*1960*	*1964*	*1968*	*1972*	*1976*
Democratic Party							
Poor	28%	19%	16%	15%	12%	10%	7%
Black	7	5	7	12	19	22	16
Union Member/Family	38	36	31	32	28	32	33
Catholic	41	38	47	36	40	43	35
South	20	23	27	21	24	25	36
Central Cities	21	19	19	15	14	14	11
Republican Party							
Nonpoor	75%	84%	83%	89%	90%	93%	97%
White	99	98	97	100	99	98	99
Nonunion Member/Family	79	78	84	87	81	77	80
Protestant	75	75	90	80	80	70	76
Northern	87	84	75	76	80	73	67
Outside Central City	84	89	90	91	92	95	98

*Source: Robert Axelrod, Letter to the Editor, *American Political Science Review* (June 1978), pp. 622–624; *Communications* (September 1978), p. 1011. Reprinted by permission. Table shows the percentage of each party's electoral coalition drawn from each demographic group. For example, in 1952 99 percent of the Republican party's vote was cast by whites.
**Poor refers to income under $3000 per year and nonpoor to income over $3000 per year; black includes other nonwhites; Catholic includes other non-Protestants; South includes border states; central city refers to residents of twelve largest metropolitan areas; and union member/family refers to union member or family with union member.

5. Northerners usually are not more than 3 percent more Republican than the nation as a whole, and their share of the Republican vote has decreased as Southerners have begun to vote Republican with more frequency.
6. Residents outside central cities are barely more Republican in their voting than the nation as a whole.

In his landslide defeat of George McGovern in 1972, Richard Nixon carried all six Republican-leaning voter groups by at least 60 percent of the vote cast and, in addition, majorities in four Democratic voter groups: the poor, members of union families, Catholics, and Southerners.

The experience of Democratic candidates is more revealing since they have dominated our politics for the past fifty years. Axelrod found that the poor are really not part of the Democratic coalition because only in 1964, and to a lesser degree in 1976, did they cast disproportionate votes for the Democratic presidential candidate. The contribution of union members and their families has dropped from 38 percent in 1952 to 28 percent in 1968, but it increased to one-third by 1976. Voters in central cities are another group whose contribution to the Democratic party has steadily declined over the past two decades, falling from 21 percent in 1952 to 11 percent in 1976. On the other hand, the importance of black voters to the Democratic party has grown during this time, and Catholics remain a generally reliable constituency for the party's presidential candidates. Perhaps the most significant trend documented by Axelrod pertains to the changing voting behavior by Southerners. As a group they were 10 percent more pro-Democratic than the nation in 1952 and 1956, only 2 percent more in 1960; but in 1964 (-3 percent), in 1968 (-4 percent), and in 1972 (-2 percent) they were less Democratic than the electorate as a whole. In 1976 Southerners rallied behind the candidacy of Jimmy Carter and voted more Democratic than the country, but only by 3 percentage points.

According to Axelrod's analysis, in 1976, for the first time since Lyndon Johnson's 1964 landslide, the Democratic party won a majority of votes in all categories of traditional Democratic voters. Yet Jimmy Carter almost lost to Gerald Ford, a circumstance that prompted Axelrod to suggest that the New Deal Coalition rests on a shaky foundation:

> One lesson from the 1976 election is that even when the Democrats put together all of the elements of their traditional coalition, the election can be very close. The experience of the Democrats after running a Catholic candidate in 1960 shows that the gains in Catholic deviation in loyalty may not be lasting. . . . The same may apply in the South after Carter. If the Democrats lose the South again, or if they lose the enthusiasm of the blacks or the loyalty of any of their other traditional groups, they will be in trouble. This could easily happen despite their large and steady lead in party identification.[44]

A new realignment?

Axelrod's analysis indicates that the New Deal Coalition has been weakened in recent decades, but as yet no single presidential election has prompted a new realignment among the major voter groups. After Richard Nixon's 1968 victory, Kevin Phillips wrote *The Emerging Republican Majority* suggesting that such an electoral realignment was underway.[45] Phillips saw contemporary demographic shifts reestablishing a conservative coalition in American politics. Fundamental to his thesis is the growth of the South and the Southwest, which Phillips argues is populated by members of

> . . . the rootless, socially mobile group known as the American middle class. Most of them have risen to such status only in the last generation, and their elected officials predictably embody a popular political impulse which deplores further social upheaval and favors a consolidation of the last thirty years' gains. Increasingly important throughout the nation, this new middle-class group is most powerful in the Sun Belt.[46]

Support for this argument is found in the research by Kirkpatrick Sale, who says that "the Southern Rim," which runs across the South and Southwest to California, has gained electoral votes in every census in this century.[47] According to Sale, 68 percent of the 270 electoral votes needed for election to the presidency are now controlled by "the Southern Rim." Moreover, this area has supplied eight of the last ten presidential candidates for both political parties: Johnson, Goldwater, Carter, Nixon, and Reagan.

Phillips also contends that the Democratic party is losing support from key voter groups, such as blue-collar labor and Southern whites; he suggests that an emerging minority Democratic party will represent primarily central city residents, blacks, and liberals. Much of Phillips's argument assumes that, had George Wallace not entered the presidential election as a minor candidate, Nixon's 1968 victory would have been a landslide equivalent to Franklin D. Roosevelt's in 1936. Research on the 1968 election shows that voters drawn to the American-Independent party shared Wallace's extreme conservatism on such issues as Vietnam, civil rights, and crime. In particular, Wallace's vote in large cities throughout the North has been traced to the hostile white, working-class, "ethnic" voter reactions to black encroachment into their neighborhoods.[48] Compared with both Nixon and Humphrey, Wallace's campaign was more issue-oriented, but this does not mean that Nixon and Humphrey offered the electorate no real alternative. An analysis by Benjamin Page shows that major differences separated Nixon and Humphrey on such issues as civil rights, law and order, and social welfare, but Page suggests that these party cleavages have been largely the same "since the New Deal and thus long antedated the campaign of 1968."[49]

It appears that Jimmy Carter's fragile victory over Gerald Ford in 1976 coupled with his defeat to Ronald Reagan in 1980 gives support to the argument that the New Deal Coalition is in the process of disintegrating. The 1980 election offers the opportunity for political scientists to evaluate many hypotheses regarding voting behavior, issue salience, and coalition building. Long before that election, Richard Scammon and Ben Wattenberg argued that Carter's 1976 electoral coalition was tenuous and would cause him serious problems in 1980.[50] Their data supported the view that Carter defeated Gerald Ford mainly because Southern white Protestants deviated from their historic movement away from the Democratic party to vote for Jimmy Carter. Scammon and Wattenberg plotted the percent deviation of this voter group from the nationwide vote for the Democratic presidential candidate during 1936 to 1976. Southern white Protestant voters were 19 percent more Democratic in 1936 and 1944 and 26 percent more so in 1940; their support for the Democrats then narrowed during 1948 (+5%), 1952 (+6%), and 1956 (+9%). After 1956 their index shows that Southern white Protestants became Republican-tending in their voting behavior: −4 percent in 1960, −14 percent in 1964, −18 percent in 1968, −19 percent in 1972, and −5 percent in 1976. Thus, Southern white Protestants still voted Republican in 1976, but many more supported the Democratic presidential candidate than in the previous three elections.

Scammon and Wattenberg argue that Carter's gain among these voters cannot be attributed to his political ideology because opinion polls showed that the electorate viewed Gerald Ford as more "conservative" than Carter. Moreover, since the South is generally more conservative than other regions, they ask why Carter did better than other Democratic candidates in this region. Scammon and Wattenberg conclude that Carter's Southern origin was the primary reason for this electoral deviation by Southern white Protestants, but they doubted that Southerners would continue to support Jimmy Carter for this reason indefinitely: "looking to the future, we can say that if a relatively few Southern conservatives perceive Carter as a liberal in 1980 and vote conservative instead of Southern, Carter could be in serious trouble." As president, therefore, Jimmy Carter's "problem" was that he would have a difficult time pursuing policies favored by Democratic, liberal activists outside the South while at the same time projecting a conservative image to Southern white Protestants. Scammon and Wattenberg's analysis seems to have been confirmed by the 1980 election.

THE 1980 PRESIDENTIAL ELECTION

Where Jimmy Carter narrowly defeated Gerald Ford in 1976, his defeat to Ronald Reagan in 1980 was massive (figure 2-1). Reagan carried forty-four states with 489 electoral votes; Carter won only six states and the District of Columbia, with forty-nine electoral votes. Reagan got a majority of the popular vote (51 percent) compared to 41 percent for Carter and 7 percent for Independent candidate John Anderson. In every state Carter's vote margin dropped below his 1976 level. The last time an incumbent Democrat lost reelection was in 1888, when Cleveland was defeated by Benjamin Harrison.

Data on how demographic groups voted in 1980 show that, except for blacks, Reagan made substantial inroads with all categories of Democratic-leaning voters. Gallup Poll analyses (see table 2-3 on page 59) and CBS News-*New York Times* surveys show that Reagan obtained a majority vote from these groups: men, whites, middle-aged and older, middle- and upper-income, college-educated, Southerners, Midwesterners, Westerners, Catholics and Protestants, Republicans and Independents, and people engaged in professional/managerial occupations.[51] In addition, Reagan won a plurality of the votes cast by Easterners, women, white-collar and blue-collar workers, and the grade-school educated. President Carter carried a majority vote only among Democrats, liberals, blacks and Hispanics, Jews, and voters in the youngest age grouping and the lowest income category.

Because Reagan won so handily, and in spite of the pollsters' predictions of a very close election in 1980, the matter of determining whether the electorate had expressed an ideological preference is more difficult to ascertain. According to George Gallup, ". . . the Reagan landslide was the result not so much of an ideological shift to the right among the electorate as of dissatisfaction with the leadership of the nation and a desire for change."[52] On the other hand, the voters also were aware that a rejection of President Carter would mean the election of a very conservative Republican. In Gallup's view, during the 1980 campaign "Reagan was perceived by voters to be not only to the right of President Carter but also to the right of where voters place themselves on the left-right scale."[53] On both points, it appears that Gallup's judgment is confirmed by scholarly analyses of the 1980 election.

Kathleen Frankovic studied public opinion during 1980 and concludes that "disapproval and dislike of the incumbent outweighed any other single explanation for supporting Ronald Reagan on Election Day."[54] She further

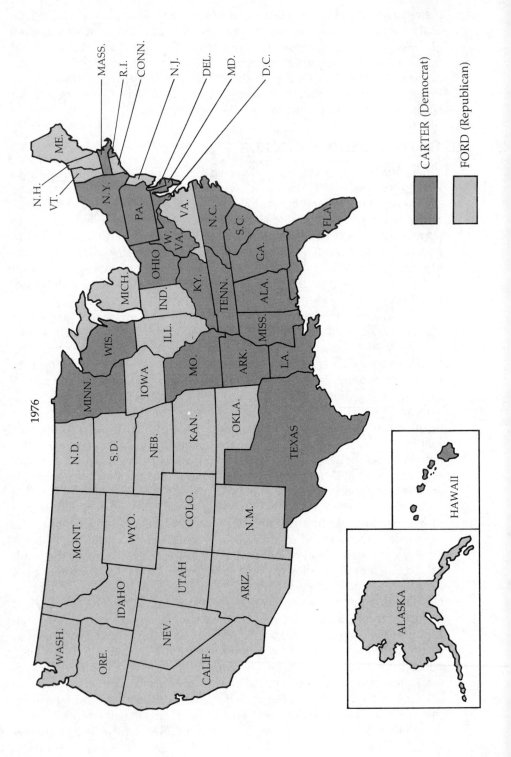

1976

CARTER (Democrat)

FORD (Republican)

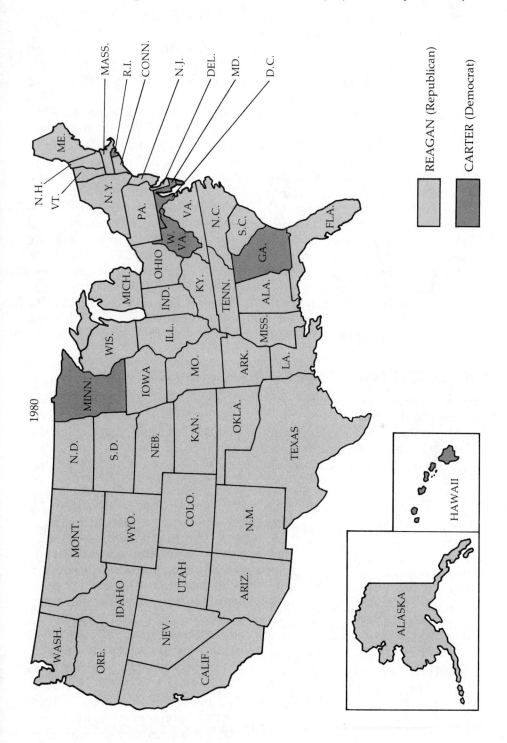

1980

REAGAN (Republican)

CARTER (Democrat)

notes that the public held a consistently negative image of Jimmy Carter throughout his term of office. With regard to the view that Reagan's election was a "mandate" for conservatism, she states, "Reagan was not elected because of increasing conservatism of the country."[55] This conclusion is based on survey data showing that public opinion did not shift much to the right between 1976 and 1980. Frankovic notes that "while some of the issues were related to candidate preference in 1980, these issues have historically separated Democratic and Republican voters."[56] Thus, such issues as balancing the budget, the relative importance of inflation and unemployment, the Equal Rights Amendment, tax cuts, and military preparedness separated Carter and Reagan supporters just as they have differentiated Democratic and Republican voters in the past. Throughout the campaign the electorate was more aware of Reagan's policy views than Jimmy Carter's, and the majority tended to agree with Reagan that the United States should be more forceful when dealing with the Soviet Union and that inflation, not unemployment, was the major economic problem facing the country. However, surveys indicate that the electorate did not share Reagan's views on killing the Equal Rights Amendment or on reducing income taxes by 30 percent. Based on extensive analysis, therefore, Frankovic concludes, "The new President does not have a mandate for conservative policies; instead, he has a mandate to be different from Jimmy Carter."[57]

REALIGNMENT AND THE CHANGING AMERICAN ELECTORATE

In the past, major political realignments have been caused by singularly important presidential elections, but it seems doubtful that this pattern will be repeated in the near future. We suspect that any fundamental reordering of American politics, such as that anticipated with the population shift to the Sun Belt, will be gradual. The American electorate as well as the character of presidential politics has been transformed during the past three decades. Although these developments are conducive to a political realignment, they do not signal any immediate *partisan* realignment. Foremost is the fact that both Republican and Democratic parties have been weakened, not only by the rise of the presidential primaries, reliance on the mass media, and use of public funds for elections but, most importantly, by a lessened partisan identification among large numbers of voters. Independents, who today constitute about 40 percent of the electorate, are double the number of Republicans. Moreover, there has been a decline in the number of "strong" Republican and "strong" Democratic voters, which indicates that even partisans are less committed to their party organizations than before.[58] For these reasons, it seems highly unlikely that any one election will prompt a plurality of voters to shift their allegiance from the Democratic party to the Republican party. On the other hand, Republicans have done fairly well in recent presidential elections. Republican candidates won only five (of thirteen) contests during 1932 to 1980 but five of the eight elections since 1952. The ability of the "minority" party to capture the presidency this often is explained partly by the rise in split-ticket voting, a trend which now seems to be an established fact about American politics.[59] But Republican successes may also relate to other considerations indicative of changes in the American electorate.

The 1980 election was affected by voter turnout which, at 52 percent, was the sixth consecutive decline since 1960. Since a higher proportion of nonvoters tend to identify with the Democratic party, any shrinkage in the size of the electorate tends to favor the Republican candidates. This hypothesis was confirmed for the 1980 election by a CBS News-*New York Times* survey which found that a higher percentage of Reagan supporters actually voted.[60] This trend in voting turnout, should it continue, may be yet another factor militating against the Democratic hegemony in American politics.

The seminal research on voting behavior during the 1950s was reported in *The American Voter*,[61] and its major conclusions have been affirmed by more recent studies, including that by Nie, Verba, and Petrocik.[62] Important changes in voting behavior have occurred since the 1950s. Most voters in the 1950s were ideologically moderate, but by the 1970s they seem to have become more conservative. For example, in 1956 41 percent were "middle of the road" but this number fell to 27 percent in 1973. In addition, whereas those on the left of the political spectrum increased only modestly in number (31% in 1956 and 33% in 1973), the voters called "rightist" or "moderate rightist" increased from 28 percent to 40 percent during this period.[63] Apparently the ideological shift since the early 1970s has been less impressive. This shift is indicated by Gallup Polls and CBS News-*New York Times* surveys shown in table 2-5.[64]

According to these data, both the right and the left have lost voters compared with the moderate position. These trends in public opinion during 1976 to 1980 suggest, as noted by Frankovic, that Reagan's landslide victory over Carter cannot be related to any massive rightward shift in public opinion during this period. However, when the public is questioned about specific policies, a more obvious conservative position emerges. CBS News-*New York Times* surveys taken during this period, for example, show that a majority of people feel that government should not fund abortions, that

TABLE 2-5   Gallup Poll and CBS News-*New York Times* survey results measuring ideological shift, 1976 and 1980

	1976	1980
Gallup		
right of center	31%	32%
middle of the road	45	49
left of center	24	19
CBS-New York Times		
liberal	20%	18%
moderate	48	51
conservative	32	31

most people do not need welfare payments, and that business is over-regulated by the government. Moreover, 45 percent in 1976 and 49 percent in 1980 agreed that domestic spending should be reduced.[65]

A most important change in voting behavior is the fact that public opinion on issues is now more closely related to how people choose between the Republican and Democratic presidential candidates. Gerald Pomper studied this relationship during 1956 to 1972.[66] Pomper found a stronger linkage between voters' attitudes and party preference beginning with the Goldwater-Johnson campaign in 1964. Therefore, he argues that the electorate today is more aware that Democrats are generally "liberal" and that Republicans are generally "conservative" as well as how the two parties differ on public policies. Related to this finding are studies indicating that voters today are more apt to evaluate issues from a broader, more ideological, framework, which supersedes the earlier research by Converse showing that the majority of voters were not ideological.[67] According to Nie and Andersen, however, analysis of the 1964, 1968, and 1972 presidential elections indicates that the voters' positions on domestic and foreign policy issues have become more consistent with one another.[68] Similarly, in the 1976 election voters' choice between Gerald Ford and Jimmy Carter was also affected by the linkage between party preference and issue attitudes.[69] Unlike 1972, however, voters in 1976 were less concerned about social issues and focused more on economic problems, such as unemployment. In general, the Democratic party is perceived by the voters to be more able and willing to address the problem of unemployment than the Republicans. By 1980, as noted already, voters felt inflation rather than unemployment was the most pressing economic problem, which helped Ronald Reagan because it symbolized Jimmy Carter's ineffectual leadership as president. Emerging literature on voting behavior adds credibility to V. O. Key's argument, which in 1966 was a dissenting viewpoint, that the electorate is rational insofar as voters do choose among the candidates for issue reasons.[70]

In evaluating the body of research on voting behavior, Richard Watson argues that increased issue salience is not caused by changes in the American electorate, such as increases in educational levels, but rather is related to changes in the political environment affecting presidential elections.

> . . . Political events such as the war in Vietnam and the developments in race relations in the United States were more dramatic and salient to voters than the issues of the 1950s. . . . Moreover, presidential candidates such as Barry Goldwater and George McGovern took more definite stands on controversial issues than candidates in the Eisenhower years did; they also tended to tie issues to the electorate on where the respective parties and candidates stood on the vital issues of the 1960s and 1970s.[71]

Voters will respond, therefore, to issue cues when the presidential candidates offer real policy differences. Traditional political wisdom argued that presidential candidates should occupy the "center" ideologically to attract votes from all segments of the electorate. This strategy would blur any differences between the Democratic and Republican candidates and prevent the voters from making a policy choice when casting their ballots. But Ronald Reagan's 1980 campaign, like Goldwater's in 1964 and McGovern's in 1972, is an exception to that rule, because Reagan made few concessions ideologically during the course of his campaign. From the beginning of his presidential campaign, according to Frankovic, "the electorate characterized Reagan as a conservative and as a strong leader, knew his advanced age, and expressed concern about his potentially aggressive character."[72] Political scientists are interested to see the degree to which Reagan, as president, remains committed to conservative principles. Will he abandon them in the face of social problems, or to bolster his political base? Ideologically committed Goldwater and McGovern were defeated in their bids to be president, so Reagan's election gives a real opportunity to study the correlation between the recruitment-nomination-election process and a president's conduct of public policy.

THE MEDIA CAMPAIGN

The mass media—print, radio, and television—have become an essential part of the presidential campaign. As early as 1880 advertisements and campaign literature distributed by mail were commonplace, and by 1928 political candidates began to use that new invention, radio. Television was first used during the 1952 campaign between Dwight Eisenhower and Adlai Stevenson. However, today presidential campaigns are conducted to maximize impact on the media. Doris Graber observes that "campaigns are arranged for the best media exposure before the largest suitable audience. To attract media coverage, candidates concentrate on press conferences, talk show appearances, or trips to interesting locations."[73] Though a media campaign is very expensive, the presidential candidates have no choice but to exploit the media, particularly television. In 1980 Jimmy Carter and Ronald Reagan devoted more than 50 percent of their campaign budgets to television advertising, which was about $31 million between them.[74] A Carter aide estimated that Jimmy Carter spent about $4 million for television ads in the last week of the election campaign, though Reagan spent twice that much.[75]

In 1968 Richard Nixon spent $12.1 million on radio advertisements and $6.1 million on television announcements.[76] The importance of the mass media, especially television, was dramatized by the 1968 election, when Nixon defeated Vice-President Hubert Humphrey. Nixon's feat was more impressive because he had suffered a series of political beatings; in 1960 he lost the presidency to John F. Kennedy and in 1962 he was defeated in the gubernatorial election in California. Humphrey's loss can be attributed to many factors, including widespread disaffection with the Vietnam War, but Nixon's victory was helped substantially by his effective use of television, described by Joe McGinnis in his book *The Selling of the President 1968.*[77] McGinnis comments, "Politics, in a sense, has always been a con game."

Unlike the printed media, where columnists focus on the candidates' issue positions, ideology, and rhetoric, the successful television campaigner needs the right image. McGinnis elaborates on this point:

> On television it matters less that he [candidate] does not have ideas. His personality is what the viewers want to share. He need be neither statesman nor crusader; he must only show up on time. Success and failure are easily measured: how often is he invited back? Often enough and he reaches his goal—to advance from "politician" to "celebrity," a status jump bestowed by grateful viewers who feel that finally they have been given the basis for making a choice.
>
> The TV candidate, then, is measured not against his predecessors—not against a standard of performance established by two centuries of democracy—but against [talk show host] Mike Douglas. How well does he handle himself? Does he mumble, does he twitch, does he make me laugh? Do I feel warm inside?
>
> Style becomes substance. The medium is the message and the masseur gets the votes.[78]

Thus, rather than the cold and grumpy Richard Nixon of the past, in 1968 television showed a "new" Nixon, who offered reassurance to the American people, projected warmth and sincerity, and promised the stability and maturity needed during that period of social turmoil. A key to Nixon's much improved image was the efforts of his media consultants and advertising experts to assure that he was portrayed to the voters in a "controlled" setting: loyal supporters filled his audiences, friendly and noncontroversial questions were asked of him, and the use of stage lighting and camera exposure presented him in the most appealing way. These conditions are not so easily manipulated when presidential candidates meet in a televised debate, which is a major reason why Vice-President Richard Nixon lost the election for president in 1960.

Television debates between the major presidential candidates were an important factor in three elections: 1960, 1976, and 1980. For many reasons the 1960 debates were the most influential; they provided the most spontaneous and lively exchanges between the candidates and apparently had an impact in changing some voters' opinions about the two contenders for president. About 100 million people saw Kennedy and Nixon debate on television, and 60 percent of the voters claimed that they had been influenced by the debates.[79] This election was very close, with John Kennedy winning by 112,000 votes. Kennedy had presented a more pleasing appearance—healthy, vigorous, and nicely tanned—compared to the sickly, gaunt figure of Richard Nixon. Opinion polls showed that relatively few voters actually shifted their allegiance from one candidate to the other because of the debates, but even a small change in voter preferences can matter in such a closely contested election.

In 1976 President Gerald Ford was encouraged to debate challenger Jimmy Carter. They had three debates while the candidates for vice-president had one debate. Two-thirds of the registered voters watched these debates, but apparently they made little difference in the election outcome. One aspect that may have damaged President Ford's credibility was his mistaken statement that Eastern Europe was not within the Soviet Union's sphere of influence. He was immediately challenged by Jimmy Carter on that score. A telephone survey taken just after this particular debate showed that Ford, nevertheless, had won; however, twenty-four hours after that debate, followup polls indicated that Carter's lead over Ford had increased.[80] One reason Ford's gaffe about Eastern Europe eventually did hurt him, says Graber, is that afterwards the reporters and journalists severely criticized the president for that remark.[81] The publicity given Ford's comment by the mass media also points out the great influence columnists, journalists, and broadcasters have in defining the policy agenda and the issues on which a presidential election is contested.

In 1980 a minor candidate for president posed problems for President Jimmy Carter. Carter refused to debate John Anderson, and reluctantly agreed to debate Ronald Reagan. Meanwhile Reagan agreed to debate both Carter and John Anderson. Anderson quickly accepted Reagan's offer, and the League of Women Voters, the group sponsoring the debates, invited President Carter to also participate. He refused, preferring to debate only Reagan. Eventually there was a Reagan-Anderson debate on September 22, 1980 and a Reagan-Carter debate one week before the November election. Reagan emerged the winner in his meeting with President Carter. Carter tried to emphasize his policy differences with Reagan, whom he tried to picture as an extremist, but the debate showed Reagan to be moderate and reasonable, personable and witty, and quite knowledgeable about the issues. About 60 percent of eligible voters watched the Reagan-Carter debate, and surveys taken afterwards indicated that Ronald Reagan had won. A CBS News poll taken October 28 showed Reagan winning by 44 percent to Carter's 36 percent. Another poll taken at the end of October by CBS News-*New York Times* indicated that the Reagan win was even greater (41 to 26%).[82]

Overall, the television debates made little difference in how the vast majority of people cast their ballots in 1960, 1976, or 1980. David Sears argues that most voters' views were more often reinforced, rather than changed, by the debates in 1976.[83] Because the candidates fear making any mistake, they prepare for the debates well in advance, are given practice questions by their staff, and have time to formulate the best answers. Given the format of the debates, the candidates have only a limited amount of time in which to reply to the panelists who ask the questions, and the panelists are given few opportunities to pursue the candidate's answers with more detailed questions. Thus, only a superficial discussion of complex policy issues is provided by the candidates in public debates. What is important is that the debates afford another opportunity to project the right image. For example, Ford agreed to debate Carter because he believed that his "presidential" image would be an advantage, but Carter saw the debate as a chance to enhance his credibility and competence to be president.

FLEA-MARKET POLITICS AND PRESIDENTIAL GOVERNMENT

We have argued in this chapter that the recruitment-nomination-election process imposes political constraints on a president in terms of the *direction* of public policy, though not always about the content of specific legislation. However, the recent tendency for presidential campaigns to be waged without the active support of the political party organizations deeply troubles many political scientists. Ladd describes this aspect of presidential campaigning as "flea-market" politics, pointing out that "in contrast to the situation that prevailed as recently as two decades ago, candidates for President now set up their own electoral organizations and go their own way with little regard for, or contact with, other sections of the party—including, surely, the congressional wing."[84] This pattern was illustrated by the Committee for the Reelection of the President (CREEP), an organization that managed the 1972 presidential campaign for Richard Nixon outside the regular Republican party machinery. The major concern is that the kinds of campaign techniques and political strategies needed to gain the nomination and election to the presidency may be ill-suited to, and in fact antithetical to, governing the nation.

Political scientists see two serious dysfunctions resulting from the democratization of the recruitment-nomination-election process in the United States. First, as implied throughout this chapter, a presidential candidate can be nominated by activists who are unrepresentative of the party's rank and file, let alone the general electorate. It is now possible for presidential candidates to establish a political base by appealing to narrow voter groups, addressing the concerns of special interest and single-issue groups, and win primary elections which are dominated by a relatively small segment of the voter population. As a consequence, an increased number of candidates are running for president. Moreover, during the past two decades contenders for the presidency have been able to mount serious challenges without summoning the support of their party's leadership: Democrats McCarthy in 1968, McGovern in 1972, and Carter in 1976, and Republicans Goldwater in 1964 and Reagan in 1976.

The second problem with democratization of the election process is that a president today can be nominated and elected in a way that alienates partisan supporters in states and localities and, most importantly, in Congress. In criticizing "free-lance" presidential politics, Robert McClure is especially worried about how political party "reforms" have weakened those institutions. Political parties, he argues, are among the few institutions in American society that ameliorate the effects of special interests and single-issue groups, and help forge political consensus. According to McClure,

> The ultimate folly associated with free-lance politics is that the forces in America that have advocated increased activity from the central government have been most often the forces favoring the reforms that together with technology and common attitudes are destroying American political parties. The irony is that without party as a meaningful organization this country's complicated govern-

ment grinds to a halt, cannot deliver necessary national policies, and cannot be a positive force for change. Party is the common organization that holds the disparate parts of the society together.[85]

McClure attributes the weakened state of political parties in the United States to three general causes. The first fundamental reason is the fact that the American people always have been skeptical, and often-times hostile, toward party politics, "bosses," and big city "machines." Second, as a consequence of that skepticism the primary election was instituted during the Progressive Era as a method to return power over party nominations to the ordinary citizen. This democratic sentiment continues to shape public policies aimed at reforming our political parties, for example, the extension of the primary for the selection of delegates to the nominating conventions. Similar motivations also influenced the recent legislation to provide government funding for presidential elections. The move was a serious mistake, McClure explains: "Although many other countries publicly finance their national elections, the government money in these instances is channeled through political parties. In this country the party is by-passed; the money is given directly to individuals. Once again, the policy frees the candidate from the necessity to work with the party."[86]

In 1971 Congress enacted, and amended in 1974 and 1976, the Federal Elections Campaign Act. Its purpose was to curb the escalating costs of campaigning, due primarily to media expenses; to reduce candidates' reliance on large contributors; and to prevent secret donations to the candidates. Campaign finances were to be monitored by a Federal Election Commission, though a 1976 Supreme Court ruling necessitated its reorganization by Congress.[87] This legislation provided for public funding of presidential elections (but not congressional elections); no candidate is required to accept federal money but those who do are limited to spending no more than $10 million in the primaries and another $20 million in the general election (adjusted for cost-of-living rises), plus 20 percent for fund-raising costs and an unlimited amount for legal and accounting expenses. Federal funds are allocated among the candidates as "matching" grants; the Revenue Act of 1971 allows taxpayers to "check-off" one dollar on their federal income tax for this purpose.

In one way the Federal Elections Campaign Act discourages "minor" political parties because, to receive public funds, a minor party must have received at least 5 percent of the total vote in the last presidential election. In 1980, when John Anderson ran for president as an Independent candidate, the Federal Election Commission (FEC) ruled that he could be reimbursed for his campaign expenses on the condition that he get at least 5 percent of the total vote cast. Anderson eventually received $4.2 million from the FEC. On the other hand, this legislation encourages many candidates to seek the Republican or Democratic nomination for president. In 1976, for example, the FEC distributed more than $24 million to *fifteen* presidential candidates during the primaries.[88] Not only does the promise of federal funds encourage lesser-known candidates to enter the race but, as Richard Watson argues, the "subsidy probably allowed some of them to remain in the race longer than would have been the case if they had had to depend on private donations alone."[89] This argument is illustrated by Stephen Wayne when he compares Edmund Muskie's (D.,Me.) plight in 1972 with Rep. Morris Udall's (D., Ariz.) performance in 1976.

> . . . As the front runner, Senator Edmund Muskie had raised over $2 million by January 31, 1972, before the primaries even began and eventually spent over $7 million in his campaign.Nonetheless, he was forced to abandon his quest for the nomination for lack of funds after only five primaries (two months). Representative Morris Udall, on the other hand, was not nationally known and had not demonstrated substantial fund-raising capacity. Yet, he was able to raise over $4.5 million, including almost $2 million from the Treasury, and to compete actively in more than one-third of the states without winning one primary or controlling one state delegation other than his own.[90]

McClure's third reason for "free-lance" presidential politics overshadowing party politics is modern technology; namely, the advent of opinion polling, computerized mailing systems, and the mass media. The presidential campaign today is not directed by party professionals but by public relations experts, media consultants, direct-mail fund raisers, pollsters, speech writers, and a cadre of loyal activists. Using these specialists in an ad hoc organization, a presidential candidate can now carry a political message directly to the people. However, the problem is that these communications specialists and the candidate's cadre of loyalists are less concerned about, and less able to guarantee the effectiveness of their candidate once elected to the presidency. A concern for actual government, in addition to the conduct of an effective election campaign, is more the domain of party professionals. Richard Watson points out

> Party professionals are generally more responsive and accountable as far as presidential nominations are concerned. Since they are in public life on a more permanent basis and want to remain in office if they can, professionals are likely to be sensitive and concerned about public sentiments. They also have a stake in ensuring that the person nominated and elected as president will reflect well on their party. Moreover, if their presidential candidate is elected, they continue to take an interest in what that person is doing.[91]

The fact that Jimmy Carter gained the Democratic party nomination without having to court the support of the party's leadership seems to be related to his inability to exert leadership over Congress. According to Ladd, "Few members of the Democratic majority of the U.S. House and Senate, for example, had anything to do with the nomination of Jimmy Carter. Most congressional Democrats [took] some satisfaction in the fact that one bearing their label [was] ensconced at the other end of Pennsylvania Avenue—but not all that much."[92]

To summarize, the democratization of presidential politics has been a mixed blessing. On one hand, the opportunity to seek the nation's highest office has been expanded markedly through primary elections, public financing, and the use of opinion polls to detect public preferences. And perhaps the increased reliance on mass media has made the electoral process more rational in recent years.The presidential candidates and the parties, argues Watson, "give clearer signals to the electorate than they formerly did on their stands on the major issues. As a result, voters are better able to distinguish between the general public policy approaches used by the contending groups."[93]

On the other hand, the skills needed to wage a media campaign are not necessarily the traits needed to manage the United States government. When our system is compared with the way Great Britain recruits its prime ministers, American presidents appear woefully ill-prepared to assume their awesome responsibilities. Robert Sickels contrasts the English and American systems of leadership recruitment as follows:

> . . . Their [British] system of selecting leaders has been characterized as one of apprenticeship, ours as entrepreneurial. The way to the top is more carefully defined in Great Britain, and when time comes for a choice the field is smaller. Those put under consideration are politicians, invariably, and beyond that have enjoyed a special combination of legislative and executive experience. . . . There is none of the American practice of sending strangers to the management of national executive or legislative affairs. And, too, there is a difference in the kind of personality felt to be suited to the chief executive in the two countries: An American must in some sense be popular in order to become president, but need not be adept at dealing with other politicians at close hand. A British prime minister must have proven his or her collegiality as a requisite of office.[94]

The lack of political experience can be a major deficiency for any president, and especially when acting as opinion/party leader. The successful use of power to mobilize the citizenry behind a president's election "mandate" cannot depend upon the formal resources of the office. Rather, the cultivation of a supportive public opinion requires a degree of political sophistication, collaboration with other decision makers including the mass media, and some managerial talent. Many Presidents have not excelled at these qualities, which suggests why so few strong opinion/party leaders have emerged in American politics.

Summary

The presidency is a more democratic office today than was intended by the framers of the Constitution. The advent of political parties as well as the enactment of state laws allowing the voters to select the presidential electors have changed the nature of the office. However, very few elections in American history have had singular impact on the presidency or the direction of public policy. The 1932 election, which ushered in Roosevelt's New Deal, was the last "realigning" election, and since then we have chosen between more "liberal" Democrats and more "conservative" Republicans when assessing social-welfare and economic programs. We have suggested that the ideological thrust of a presidential campaign is influenced by the makeup of the national conventions which formally choose the candidates and write the party platforms. With the widespread use of primary elections to choose delegates today, however, the party conventions merely ratify the decisions made within party primaries and caucuses.

The democratization of the delegate selection process has been accompanied by a weakening of the political party organizations, which suggests that the entire process by which we nominate and elect Presidents is more susceptible to pressures from single-issue groups, special interests, and voter blocs. In addition, surveys indicate that the electorate nowadays is somewhat more issue oriented, less loyal to party affiliation, and more likely to perceive partisan differences between presidential candidates. This is especially true when candidates, such as Goldwater, McGovern, and Reagan, hold extreme positions on controversial issues. Such trends, should they continue, may strengthen the linkage between the electorate's choice in a presidential election and the policy agenda established by the president. But they also may portend a weakening of opinion/party leadership in the future, because a president may face insurmountable problems to maintaining political popularity.

NOTES

[1]Richard Pious, *The American Presidency* (New York: Basic Books, 1979), p. 86.

[2]Clinton Rossiter, *The American Presidency* (New York: Harcourt, Brace and World, 1960), p. 201.

[3]*Jackson Clarion-Ledger* (October 8, 1972), Parade Sec., p. 6.

[4]Donald R. Matthews, "Presidential Nominations: Process and Outcomes," in James David Barber, ed., *Choosing the President* (Englewood Cliffs, N.J.: Prentice-Hall, 1974), pp. 43–44.

[5]Ibid., p. 45.

[6]For a discussion of these issues see Louis W. Koenig, *The Chief Executive*, 3rd ed. (New York: Harcourt Brace Jovanovich, 1975), pp. 81–84.

[7]Quoted in Arthur Schlesinger, Jr., "On the Presidential Succession," *Political Science Quarterly* (September 1974), p. 476.

[8]Lawrence Longley, "The Case Against the Electoral College," paper delivered at annual meeting, American Political Science Association, 1977. Quote also found in Thomas E. Cronin, "Choosing a President," *The Center Magazine* (September/ October 1978), pp. 5–15.

[9]Cited in Cronin, "Choosing a President," 1978, p. 9.

[10]Pious, *The American Presidency*, p. 112.

[11]Raymond Tatalovich, "Electoral Votes and Presidential Campaign Trails, 1932–1976," *American Politics Quarterly* (October 1979), pp. 489–498.

[12]The advantages of the national bonus plan in terms of both the electoral college and direct popular election are discussed in Thomas E. Cronin, "Choosing a President."

[13]F. Christopher Arterton, "Campaign Organizations Face the Mass Media in the 1976 Presidential Nomination Process," paper delivered at annual meeting, Amer-

ican Political Science Association, 1977. Cited in Stephen J. Wayne, *The Road to the White House* (New York: St. Martin's Press, 1981), p. 84.

[14]Frank Munger and James Blackhurst, "Factionalism in the National Conventions, 1940–1964: An Analysis of Ideological Consistency in State Delegation Voting," *Journal of Politics* (May 1965), pp. 375–394.

[15]Gerald Pomper, "Factionalism in the 1968 National Conventions: An Extension of Research Findings," *Journal of Politics* (August 1971), pp. 826–830.

[16]Ibid., pp. 829–830.

[17]Howard L. Reiter, "Party Factionalism: National Conventions in the New Era," *American Politics Quarterly* (July 1980), pp. 303–318.

[18]Ibid., p. 312.

[19]See William Keech and Donald R. Matthews, *The Party's Choice* (Washington, D.C.: Brookings Institution, 1976), pp. 157–213. The authors differentiate among consensual, semiconsensual, and nonconsensual conventions.

[20]W. G. Carleton, "The Revolution in the Presidential Nominating Convention," *Political Science Quarterly* (June 1957), pp. 224–240.

[21]William H. Lucy, "Polls, Primaries, and Presidential Nominations," *Journal of Politics* (November 1973), pp. 830–848.

[22]Richard A. Watson, *The Presidential Contest* (New York: John Wiley and Sons, 1980), p. 33.

[23]*Cousins v. Wigoda*, 419 U.S. 477 (1975).

[24]*Congressional Quarterly Weekly Report* (July 10, 1976), p. 1803.

[25]John W. Soule and Wilma E. McGrath, "A Comparative Study of Presidential Nominating Conventions: The Democrats 1968 and 1972," *American Journal of Political Science* (August 1975), pp. 501–517.

[26]Commission on Presidential Nomination and Party Structure, Openness, Participation and Party Building: Reforms for a Stronger Democratic Party (Washington, D.C.: Democratic National Committee, 1978), p. 18.

[27]Everett Carll Ladd, Jr., "Reform Is Wrecking the U.S. Party System," *Fortune* (November 1977), pp. 177–181, 184, 188.

[28]Jeanne Kirkpatrick, "Representation in the American National Conventions: The Case of 1972," *British Journal of Political Science* (July 1975), pp. 313–322.

[29]Herbert McClosky; Paul J. Hoffman; and Rosemary O'Hara, "Issue Conflict and Consensus Among Party Leaders and Followers," *American Political Science Review* (June 1960), pp. 406–427.

[30]John S. Jackson III; Jesse C. Brown; and Barbara L. Brown, "Recruitment, Representation and Political Values," *American Politics Quarterly* (April 1978), p. 197.

[31]Cited in Stephen J. Wayne, *The Road to the White House* (New York: St. Martin's Press, 1981), p. 95.

[32]Dennis Sullivan, "Party Unity: Appearance and Reality," *Political Science Quarterly* (Winter 1977–1978), p. 641.

[33]Judith Parris, *The Convention Problem: Issues in Reform of Presidential Nominating Procedures* (Washington, D.C.: Brookings Institution, 1972), p. 110.

[34]Gerald Pomper, *Elections in America: Control and Influence in Democratic Politics* (New York: Dodd, Mead and Company, 1970), chapters 7 and 8.

[35]Paul T. David, "Party Platforms as National Plans," *Public Administration Review* (May/June 1971), pp. 303–315.

[36]Ibid., p. 305.

[37]Ibid., p. 312.

[38]Ibid., p. 311.

[39]Angus Campbell, "A Classification of the Presidential Elections," in James I. Lengle and Byron Shafer, eds., *Presidential Politics: Readings on Nominations and Elections* (New York: St. Martins Press, 1980), pp. 502–513.

[40]V. O. Key, "A Theory of Critical Elections," *Journal of Politics* (1955), pp. 3–18.

[41]Wayne Shannon, *Party, Constituency, and Congressional Voting* (Baton Rouge: Louisiana State University Press, 1968), pp. 42–43.

[42]Angus Campbell, "A Classification of the Presidential Elections," p. 513.

[43]Robert Axelrod, "Where the Votes Come From: An Analysis of Electoral Coalitions, 1952–1968," *American Political Science Review* (March 1972), pp. 11–20; Letter to the Editor, *American Political Science Review* (June 1974), pp. 717–720; Letter to the Editor, "1976 Update," *American Political Science Review* (June 1978), pp. 622–624.

[44]Axelrod, Letter to the Editor, "1976 Update," p. 624.

[45]Kevin Phillips, *The Emerging Republican Majority* (New Rochelle, N.Y.: Arlington House, 1969).

[46]Ibid., p. 437.

[47]Kirkpatrick Sale, *Power Shift: The Rise of the Southern Rim and Its Challenge to the Eastern Establishment* (New York: Random House, 1975), pp. 89–90.

[48]See Samuel Lubell, *The Hidden Crisis in American Politics* (New York: W. W. Norton, 1970), p. 90.

[49]Benjamin I. Page, *Choices and Echoes in Presidential Elections* (Chicago: University of Chicago Press, 1978), pp. 76–90. Page also concludes that "voters fairly accurately perceived this contrast between candidate differences on foreign and domestic issues," p. 88.

[50]Richard M. Scammon and Ben J. Wattenberg, "Jimmy Carter's Problem," *Public Opinion* (March/April 1978), pp. 3–8.

[51]Cited in Stephen J. Wayne, *The Road to the White House*, pp. 286–287. Also see Gallup Opinion Index, report no. 183 (December 1980), p. 2.

[52]Gallup Opinion Index, report no. 183 (December 1980), p. 2.

[53]Ibid.

[54]Kathleen A. Frankovic, "Public Opinion Trends," in Gerald M. Pomper, ed., *The Election of 1980* (Chatham, N.J.: Chatham House Publishers, 1981), p. 97.

[55]Ibid., p. 113.

[56]Ibid., p. 115.

[57]Ibid., p. 117.

[58]See Philip Converse, *The Dynamics of Party Support: Cohort-Analyzing Party Identification* (Beverly Hills, Calif.: Sage Publications, 1976).

[59]Walter DeVries and Lance Tarrance, *The Ticket-Splitter: A New Force in American Politics* (Grand Rapids, Mich.: William B. Eerdmans, 1972). The research on split-ticket voting, however, has been complicated by methodological problems. See Alan R. Gitelson, "An Analysis of Split-Ticket Voting Patterns at the Micro-Analytic Level," *Political Methodology* (1978), 445–459.

[60]Cited in Stephen J. Wayne, *The Road to the White House*, pp. 285–286.

[61]Angus Campbell; Philip E. Converse; Warren E. Miller; and Donald E. Stokes, *The American Voter: An Abridgement* (New York: John Wiley and Sons, 1964).

[62]Norman H. Nie; Sidney Verba; and John R. Petrocik, *The Changing American Voter* (Cambridge: Harvard University Press, 1976).

[63]Ibid., p. 199.

[64]Drawn from Gallup Opinion Index, report no. 183 (December 1980), p. 2; Frankovic, "Public Opinion Trends," p. 114.

[65]Frankovic, "Public Opinion Trends," p. 114.

[66]Gerald Pomper, *Voters' Choice: Varieties of American Electoral Behavior* (New York: Dodd Mead, 1975).

[67]Philip Converse, "The Nature of Belief Systems in Mass Publics," in David Apter, ed., *Ideology and Discontent* (New York: Free Press, 1964), pp. 206–261.

[68]Norman Nie and Kristi Andersen, "Mass Belief Systems Revisited: Political Change and Attitude Structure," *Journal of Politics* (August 1974), p. 558.

[69]However, Carter and Ford stood much closer on the issues as compared with, for

example, the differences between Nixon and McGovern. See Page, *Choices and Echoes in Presidential Elections*, pp. 91–97. Also see Arthur Miller and Warren Miller, "Partisanship and Performance: Rational Choice in the 1976 Presidential Election," paper delivered at annual meeting, American Political Science Association, Wash., D.C., Sept. 1977.

[70] V. O. Key, with the assistance of Milton Cummings, *The Responsible Electorate: Rationality in Presidential Voting, 1936–1960* (Cambridge: Harvard University Press, 1966).

[71] Watson, *The Presidential Contest*, pp. 86–87.

[72] Frankovic, "Public Opinion Trends," p. 104.

[73] Doris A. Graber, *Mass Media and American Politics* (Washington, D.C.: Congressional Quarterly Press, 1980), p. 162.

[74] John W. Mashek, "$800 Million Price Tag on '80 election," *U.S. News and World Report* (September 22, 1980), p. 23.

[75] "Election Tab: A Billion Dollars, and Rising," *U.S. News and World Report* (December 15, 1980), p. 32.

[76] Robert S. Getz and Frank B. Feigert, *The Politics and Process of American Government* (Boston: Allyn and Bacon, 1982), p. 285.

[77] Joe McGinnis, *The Selling of the President 1968* (New York: Trident Press, 1969).

[78] Ibid., pp. 29–30.

[79] Richard E. Morgan; John C. Donovan; and Christian P. Potholm, *American Politics: Directions of Change, Dynamics of Choice* (Reading, Mass.: Addison-Wesley, 1982), p. 226.

[80] George F. Bishop; Robert G. Meadow; and Marilyn Jackson-Beecks, eds., *The Presidential Debates: Media, Electoral and Policy Perspectives* (New York: Praeger, 1978), pp. 81–101.

[81] Graber, *Mass Media and American Politics*, p. 124.

[82] Cited in Wayne, *The Road to the White House*, p. 282.

[83] David O. Sears, "The Debate in the Light of Research: An Overview of the Effects," paper delivered at annual meeting, American Political Science Association, Wash. D.C., Sept. 1977. Cited in Samuel C. Patterson; Roger H. Davidson; and Randall B. Ripley, *A More Perfect Union: Introduction to American Government* (Homewood, Ill.: The Dorsey Press, 1982), p. 278.

[84] Ladd, " 'Reform' Is Wrecking the U.S. Party System," 1977, p. 188.

[85] Robert D. McClure, "Misguided Democracy: The Policy of Free-Lance Politics," *Discourses* (Chicago: Institute for Political Philosophy and Policy Analysis, Department of Political Science, Loyola University, 1979), p. 29.

[86] Ibid., p. 9.

[87] *Buckley v. Valeo* 424 U.S. 1 (1976). The Supreme Court nullified two parts of this legislation, the limits on spending by congressional candidates and Congress' power to appoint four of the six members of the Federal Election Commission. Under 1976 amendments, Congress reconstituted the FEC as an executive agency; all six members are now nominated by the president subject to confirmation by the Senate.

[88] Charles Funderburk, *Presidents and Politics: The Limits of Power* (Monterey, Calif.: Brooks/Cole, 1982), p. 50.

[89] Watson, *The Presidential Contest*, p. 68.

[90] Wayne, *The Road to the White House*, p. 45.

[91] Watson, *The Presidential Contest*, p. 99.

[92] Ladd, " 'Reform Is Wrecking the U.S. Party System," 1977, p. 188.

[93] Watson, *The Presidential Contest*, p. 100.

[94] Robert J. Sickels, *The Presidency: An Introduction* (Englewood Cliffs: Prentice-Hall, 1980), p. 64.

SUGGESTED READINGS

Abramson, Paul R.; Aldrich, John H.; and Rohde, David W. *Change and Continuity in the 1980 Elections*. Washington, D.C.: Congressional Quarterly Press, 1982.

Barber, James David. *The Pulse of Politics: Electing Presidents in the Media Age*. New York: W. W. Norton, 1980.

Barber, James David, ed. *Choosing the President*. Englewood Cliffs: Prentice-Hall, 1974.

Barber, James David, ed. *Race for the Presidency*. Englewood Cliffs: Prentice-Hall, 1978.

Ceaser, James W. *Presidential Selection: Theory and Development*. Princeton, N.J.: Princeton University Press, 1979.

David, Paul T.; Goldman, Ralph M.; and Bain, Richard C. *The Politics of National Party Conventions*. Washington, D.C.: Brookings Institution, 1960.

Hess, Stephen. *The Presidential Campaign: The Leadership Selection Process After Watergate*. Washington, D.C.: Brookings Institution, 1978.

Keech, William, and Matthews, Donald. *The Party's Choice*. Washington, D.C.: Brookings Institution, 1976.

Ladd, Everett Carll, Jr., and Hadley, Charles D. *Transformation of the American Party System: Political Coalitions from the New Deal to the 1970's*. 2nd ed. New York: W. W. Norton, 1978.

Matthews, Donald. *Perspectives on Presidential Selection*. Washington, D.C.: Brookings Institution, 1973.

Nie, Norman; Verba, Sidney; and Petrocik, John R. *The Changing American Voter*. Cambridge: Harvard University Press, 1976.

Page, Benjamin I. *Choices and Echoes in Presidential Elections*. Chicago: University of Chicago Press, 1978.

Parris, Judith. *The Convention Problem: Issues in Reform of Presidential Nomination Procedures*. Washington, D.C.: Brookings Institution, 1972.

Pomper, Gerald. *Elections in America: Control and Influence in Democratic Politics*. New York: Dodd, Mead, 1970.

Pomper, Gerald. *The Election of 1980: Reports and Interpretation*. Chatham, N.J.: Chatham House, 1981.

Watson, Richard A. *The Presidential Contest*. New York: Wiley, 1980.

Wayne, Stephen J. *The Road to the White House: The Politics of Presidential Elections*. New York: St. Martin's Press, 1981.

Wildavsky, Aaron B., and Polsby, Nelson W. *Presidential Elections: Strategies of American Electoral Politics*. 5th ed. New York: Scribner, 1980.

CHAPTER THREE

Opinion/Party Leader: The Limits of Presidential Persuasion

The formulation of the president as opinion/party leader often is subdivided into more distinct roles by other political scientists. For example, Clinton Rossiter would include his "Chief of State," "Chief of Party," and "Voice of the People" roles as the primary manifestations of what we are calling the opinion/party leader.[1] We contend, however, that more is gained analytically by aggregating these elements into one role rather than by trying to study them separately. First of all, there is so little research on the president as "chief of state" that it is doubtful this generally ceremonial role is viable in terms of theory building. On the other hand, fundamental to all three orientations, chief of state, chief of party, and voice of the people, is their direct linkage to the people. Opinion/party leadership, therefore, has as its objective generating public support for the president's office, for his incumbency, for his public policies, and for his political party.

In terms of the resources available to a president, however, this role is the weakest of the five considered in this volume. This relative weakness is explained by the fact that opinion/party leadership evolved much later in our history. Indeed, effective use of presidential power in this role had to await the development of political parties and mass media. Few presidents have been master of public opinion throughout their terms of office; clearly, success in this role depends a great deal on the incumbent's personal skills— influence rather than authority. The importance of personal prowess is not surprising, since the authoritative bases for opinion/party leadership are not well established.

AUTHORITY

Consistent with the "heroic" image of presidents after the Franklin D. Roosevelt era, scholars argue that the power of this office can be magnified greatly when public opinion is mobilized by the executive. As Louis Koenig states, "The hours when the American Presidency has enjoyed its most brilliant effectiveness, when democracy and the strong executive seem in finest congruence, are those when the Chief Executive rallies public sentiment behind policies addressed to the common good."[2] In this context Koenig, like other political scientists, points to Teddy Roosevelt's campaign against the trusts, Woodrow Wilson's commitment to Progressivism, and Franklin Roosevelt's New Deal. That a relationship between presidential leadership and public opinion exists cannot be denied, but this linkage cannot be traced to the Founding Fathers. The Framers of our Constitution were wary of "direct" democracy and political parties, which is why the role of opinion/party leader is not alluded to in the Constitution.

The president's election by the electoral college resulted after the Framers debated and discarded other options. For instance, they disapproved his selection by the legislature on the grounds that the president's independence would be jeopardized. The electoral college was adopted because the Framers also feared choosing the executive by popular election. Their apprehensions about direct democracy have been aptly summarized by Corwin and Koenig:

> The people were liable to deceptions; the people in large areas were too ignorant of the characters of men; elective monarchies were turbulent and unhappy; the people would vote for their state candidates; the people would be led by a few active and designing men and would not be better able to judge than the legislature; "it were as unnatural to refer the choice of a proper character for chief magistrate to the people, as it would be to refer a trial of colours to a blind man"— so it was argued. . . .[3]

In contrast, it was believed that when the electors deliberated on the choice of an executive they would seek out "virtuous" men who would understand the needs of the entire community.

At the Constitutional Convention the main advocate of popular election was James Wilson of Pennsylvania. His views did not prevail because, according to Thach, "the force of anti-democratic sentiment was too strong."[4] Coinciding with this predisposition was the Framers' view that Congress, not the executive, was designed to be the primary mechanism for representative government. Moreover, by tying the election process to larger constituencies, the Framers expected this system would encourage more distinguished men to seek public office. Jean Yarbrough explains their intentions this way:

> Recognizing that the people would never accept a constitution which deprived them of the right to vote, the framers had to devise some means of promoting the candidacy of the best men which was consistent with the republican principle of popular election. Their solution was the extended electoral district, a necessary concomitant of the extended republic. By increasing the ratio of constituents to representatives, they were able to secure the best men and yet allow for widespread suffrage.[5]

Willmoore Kendall further argues that the notion of a presidential "majority" as opposed to a congressional "majority" was never even considered by the Founding Fathers. He states:

> One of the two majorities, the presidential, has . . . been *engrafted* on our political system: it was not intended by the Framers, not even present to their minds as something to be "frustrated" and have "barriers" put in its way. It is, in other words, insofar as we can satisfy ourselves that it exists *qua* majority and eventuates in "mandates," something new in our politics.[6]

Although Kendall is distressed about this change in our politics, other political scientists defend the rise of the plebiscitary president. Their counterargument, as noted earlier, is part of the widespread support for the strong, activist, and liberal-tending president. And by asserting that only the president and vice-president are elected from a national constituency, the impression is conveyed that the executive's popular mandate is more "legitimate" than Congress' because senators and representatives are beholden to local interests. Grant McConnell, for example, admits that both Congress and the president represent the people, though in differing ways. He clearly prefers representation through the executive branch, since "On the whole, the President tends to emphasize national considerations and the interests of a great diversity of people more often than Congress."[7] These sentiments are echoed, but with more certainty, by James MacGregor Burns. Burns agrees that legislative representation was the original, constitutional prescription, but he argues that any assessment of this issue requires a consideration of one's values. Burns stands in favor of "positive" government and of presidential government.

> We must, under modern conditions, reassess the old idea that the *main* governmental protection of civil liberty, social and economic rights, and due process of law lies in the legislature or the courts or state and local government. The main protection lies today in the national executive branch. As a general proposition the Presidency has become the chief protector of our procedural and substantive liberties; as a general proposition, the stronger we make the Presidency, the more we strengthen democratic procedures and can hope to realize modern liberal democratic goals.[8]

Thus, the evolution of the president as opinion/party leader has been accompanied by a new philosophical defense of presidential power. Proponents of this viewpoint argue that the executive is more "representative" than Congress insofar as democratic values, civil rights, and egalitarianism are concerned. A strong president, therefore, is needed to counterbalance the innate conservatism of the legislative branch. This position was steeped in the tradition of the "textbook" president discussed in the Introduction; this statement by James MacGregor Burns reflects those sentiments.

The development of opinion/party leadership required the abandonment of another intellectual underpinning of the Constitution. In this instance, public acceptance of political parties followed in the wake of their establishment during the earliest years of the Republic. The word "party" in the eighteenth century derived its meaning from partisanship, and the Framers saw factionalism as being disruptive to the stability of the regime. The primary cause of faction, argued James Madison in *The Federalist #10*, was human nature: "A zeal for different opinions concerning religion, concerning government, and many other points, as well of speculation as of practice . . . have . . . divided mankind into parties, inflamed them with mutual animosity, and rendered them much more disposed to vex and oppress each other than to cooperate for their common good." In Madison's opinion, the political cause of divisiveness was "liberty," but insofar as he did not want to destroy personal liberties, his solution was to design governmental arrangements that suppressed the ill-effects of factions. However, when political parties evolved in America, they did so outside the formal, legal structure of government; the very first party organization was the Jeffersonian-Republican party. According to Harry Jaffa, the party "was an outgrowth of democratic societies that had sprung up here during Washington's administration. These . . . in the main were the result of a conviction that Federalist policies would undo the work of the American Revolution, and lead us back into the fold of Britain and of monarchy."[9]

Our strongest party leaders have been Thomas Jefferson, Andrew Jackson, Woodrow Wilson, and Franklin D. Roosevelt. George Washington expressed his personal distaste for factionalism, but he became identified with those policies fashioned by the Secretary of the Treasury, Alexander Hamilton, who was an ardent Federalist. As a result, Secretary of State Thomas Jefferson resigned from Washington's cabinet in 1793 to join James Madison in rallying the opposition forces. The election of 1800 effectively ended Federalist rule, and it ushered in America's first real experience with party government. As will be shown (chapter 4), Thomas Jefferson was able to achieve major legislative successes because he could marshall the necessary votes in Congress from the Jeffersonian-Republican party. With Jefferson, therefore, we began to view the president as the "titular" head of his political party.

By custom, the political parties defer to the president's choice of a vice-presidential nominee when he seeks reelection, and even the out-party allows its presidential candidate to choose his own running mate. It is rare for an incumbent president to be denied renomination by his party, and today the president handpicks the chairman of his party's national committee to manage the party apparatus at the national level. The Jeffersonian-Republican party was the first "modern" political party insofar as it developed a grass-roots party organization to mobilize the voters and to recruit political leaders for elected offices at the local, state, and federal levels of government. Eventually the Jeffersonian-Republicans became known as the Democrats under President Andrew Jackson. Jackson was instrumental in strengthening the role of opinion/party leader in important ways.

Jacksonian democracy

The era of President Andrew Jackson was a time when presidential politics was brought closer to the average citizen and when political parties were strengthened. Jackson was the first Democrat by name (his party was also known as The Democracy) and, as already noted, in 1832 was the first president to be nominated by the prototype of the modern nominating convention. This change in procedure occurred because of widespread indignation following the outcome of the 1824 presidential election in which, although Jackson was the popular vote winner, the congressional "caucus" elected John Quincy Adams president instead. Also resulting from that contested presidential election of 1824 was a split in the Jeffersonian-Republican party: the National Republicans were headed by John Quincy Adams and Henry Clay whereas the Democratic Republicans were under the leadership of Andrew Jackson and John C. Calhoun, among others. By President Jackson's retirement, these respective factions became organized into two separate political parties, the Whigs and the Democrats. Thus, Jackson's reelection victory in 1832 had a major impact on the course of party politics in the United States; as William MacDonald argues, Jackson "made possible a new drawing of party lines," allowing a "reconstitution of parties on broad national lines, and a reformulation of political opinions such as had not been since the close of the War of 1812."[10] This development also marked the beginning of a "loyal opposition" in American politics. Though the Whigs and the Democrats disagreed over policies such as the Bank of the United States, and reflected differing constituencies, they shared an agreement on the fundamental, constitutional arrangements of the government.

Following in Jefferson's tradition, Andrew Jackson was a president who acted as "tribune" for public opinion, as both the people's educator and defender. Jackson's influence in this role is captured by Leonard D. White when he suggests that the Jackson years were "a huge experiment in the education of citizens in democracy by direct participation in officeholding, local, state and federal."[11] Andrew Jackson's democratic credo prompted him to urge many reforms allowing greater political participation by the ordinary citizen. He even favored abolishing the electoral college in favor of direct popular election of the president. Jackson once stated:

> To the people belongs the right of electing their Chief Magistrate; it was never designed that their choice should in any case be defeated, either by the intervention of electoral colleges or by the agency confided, under certain contingencies, to the House of Representatives. Experience proves that in proportion as agents to execute the will of the people are multiplied there is danger of their wishes being frustrated. Some may be unfaithful; all are liable to err. So far, therefore, as the people can with convenience speak, it is safer for them to express their own will.[12]

Jackson also favored limiting a president's tenure to one term of four-to-six years. Neither proposal was considered, though he believed both would contribute to the "prosperity and harmony of the country."

Jackson's desire to limit a president's term of office reflected his commitment to rotation of public offices as a major cornerstone of his "republican creed." Government ought to be returned to the people through mass participation in government. Toward this end Jackson defended and used the "spoils" system because "the duties of all public officers are . . . so plain and simple that men of intelligence may readily qualify themselves for their performances." Though Jackson did not invent the concept, he did nationalize the patronage system. He brought a host of new-style democratic politicians with him to Washington and, during his eight years in office, replaced about 2,000 of the 11,000 government employees. This number exceeded the removals by all his predecessors except Jefferson, whose equaled Jackson's. Beyond strengthening Andrew Jackson's political base, according to Arthur M. Schlesinger, Jr., the spoils system helped ". . . restore faith in the government."[13]

Related to his belief in rotation and the spoils system was Jackson's enthusiastic support for universal manhood suffrage. Of the six states which entered the union during Jackson's tenure, five rescinded the property requirement for voting and adopted universal manhood suffrage. As a presidential candidate Jackson encouraged the enfranchisement of adult males throughout the country. In the election of 1828, for example, only 1,155,340 adult males voted in a total population of nearly 13 million. However, this represented an increase of about 800,000 voters since the 1824 election, which can be attributed to the fact that only two candidates contested the 1828 election in addition to the role of the Democratic party. The Democratic party's grass-roots organization was improved in various states, and a concerted effort was made to increase voter turnout, a trend that continued until the Lincoln administration.

Andrew Jackson's egalitarianism and his belief in the common sense of ordinary citizens led him as president to articulate the grievances of workingmen, small farmers and merchants, and debtors and to encourage their participation in party politics through such devices as the nominating convention, officeholder rotation, political patronage or spoils, and universal manhood suffrage.

Modern party leaders

Another Democrat who relied heavily on his political party and public opinion was Woodrow Wilson. As a political scientist and as president, Woodrow Wilson fully understood the importance of political parties for a democracy. He favored reforms aimed at strengthening the party organizations, and he believed that a president's power was greatest when he exerted leadership over both his party and public opinion. This exalted statement by Wilson shows the perfect synthesis embodied in opinion/party leadership:

[The President] cannot escape being the leader of his party except by incapacity and lack of personal force, because he is at once the choice of the party and the nation. He is the party nominee, and the only party nominee for whom the whole nation votes. . . . There is no national party choice except that of President. No one else represents the people as a whole exercising a national choice . . . the President represents not so much the party's governing efficiency as its ideals and principles. He is not so much a part of its organization as its vital link of connection with the thinking nation. He can dominate his party by being spokesman for the real sentiment and purpose of the country, by giving direction to opinion, by giving the country at once the information and the statements of policy which will enable it to form judgments alike of parties and of men.[14]

Wilson tried to apply this concept to government. He used the Democratic party caucus in the House of Representatives to formulate legislative strategy, and urged "progressive" Democrats to seek leadership positions in the Congress. Woodrow Wilson was the second Democrat (besides Grover Cleveland) to occupy the White House between 1861 and 1933; the Democratic majorities which gained control of the House and Senate in 1913 were essential to his legislative successes. Wilson also began the practice, now commonly accepted, of a president campaigning for his party during the midterm congressional elections. Wilson, however, was not effective in this regard—the Republicans regained control of both houses of Congress in 1918.

Franklin D. Roosevelt's attempt to "purge" conservative Democrats from Congress in the 1938 midterm elections was extraordinary in that FDR tried to influence the primaries, not just the general elections. Roosevelt's famous purge was precipitated by Congress' defeat of his Supreme Court "packing plan" in 1937, a defeat caused by several Democrats who had consistently opposed Roosevelt. In a "fireside chat" President Roosevelt declared his intention to become involved in Democratic primary contests:

> As the head of the Democratic party . . . charged with the responsibility of the definitely liberal declaration of principles set forth in the 1936 Democratic platform, I feel that I have every right to speak in those few instances where there may be a clear issue between candidates for a Democratic nomination involving these principles, or involving a clear misuse of my own name.[15]

Despite his many campaign trips across the nation in behalf of his political allies and in opposition to his enemies, Roosevelt's strategy was a failure. While some of the candidates he supported did win, every senator and congressman he marked for defeat (except one) won reelection. As a result of what Louis Koenig called "Franklin Roosevelt's grisly and unforgettable failure, no President has ventured onto the purge trail since his day."[16]

The practice of presidents campaigning for their parties' candidates for Congress suggests that the role of opinion/party leadership has become routinized in recent years, but this does not mean that all presidents exert equal influence over their party organizations. In spite of his tremendous popularity ("I Like Ike"), Dwight Eisenhower—following the example set by George Washington—desired to stay above partisan politics and refrained from actively supporting Republican candidates. Thus, Ike's personal appeal was not translated into voter support for the Republican party; the Republicans controlled Congress only during two years (1953–1954) of Eisenhower's eight-year tenure and failed to win any seats in the House or Senate despite the president's landslide reelection in 1956.

Ambiguity impinges on the public's perception of the executive acting as opinion/party leader, however, because a president's efforts in behalf of his party seem so obviously political. Unlike the situation in nations like Great Britain, where a constitutional monarchy exists, tradition in the United States has not clearly defined our expectations regarding the proper division of a president's official duties as "head of state" and his activities as a political leader. As a result, serious political infractions as witnessed during Watergate can adversely affect the institution of the presidency and not simply the reputation of the incumbent. On the other hand, when a president welcomes visiting foreign dignitaries or proclaims a national holiday, he reaps political gain from these "symbolic" acts, particularly during an election campaign. For this reason the president may adopt a "Rose Garden" strategy during the reelection campaign. By staying close to the White House and acting "presidential," a president tries to convey the impression that, while his opponents are allowed the luxury of campaigning full-time, he is busily engaged in the pressing business of state. This tactic is reflected in data on presidential campaign trails during 1932–1976. From the records it can be determined that incumbents actively campaigned much less than their challengers.[17]

Apparently a fusion of a president's "civic" and "political" responsibilities into one role helps the executive cultivate a supportive public opinion, one inclined to accept the primacy of a president's leadership position in our system of government. However much the fusion of civic and political roles in one person may bolster the institution of the presidency in public opinion, it is also true that the popularity of presidents can vary greatly during their terms of office. This circumstance is related to the fact that presidents are limited in their ability to influence the news media; they cannot monopolize all the decision-making processes in the workings of the communications industry. Opinion leaders in the mass media often play an independent role in projecting a president's image to the people, and this, in turn, is affected by the structure, composition, and ideological makeup of that profession.

DECISION MAKING

In our society, public opinion is shaped to a large extent by the daily newspapers, magazines, radio and television stations that constitute the mass media. This industry is huge in terms of the number of decision makers involved. Today there are about 6,700 commercial radio stations, 7,000 commercial television stations, and 1,750 daily newspapers in the United States. Every day more than 30 million Americans watch the news on the three major networks, ABC, NBC, and CBS. An estimated 100 million persons watched the Reagan–Carter debate televised one week before the 1980 election. Newspapers rival television as the source of news information for the average citizen, and about 62 million newspapers are purchased each day in this country. It is true that monopolistic pressures affect the mass media and that the ownership of media outlets has concentrated in recent decades; nevertheless it is also the case that the opportunity exists for the public to have a view of politics from media elites very different from, and often at odds with, the version supplied by the government. And media elites can be very persuasive for large numbers of people; various polls, for example, indicated that in the 1970s Walter Cronkite, the former CBS evening news anchorman, was "the most trusted person in America."[18]

Many media outlets, particularly newspapers and magazines, are directed to specialized clientele groups. Most newspapers, including such big city dailies as the *Chicago Tribune*, are oriented to local markets, while many magazines and newspapers are aimed at ethnic or racial groups (for example, *Ebony*), at women (for example, *Ms*), at special interests, and at economic constituencies (such as *Fortune*). In addition, a tremendous amount of literature is disseminated by interest groups to their memberships as well as to the general public. The size, diversity, and range of the mass media in the United States make it impossible for a president to monopolize the processes by which the citizenry receives information about the government and upon which it makes political judgments.

Nevertheless, the government is a major source of news stories for the media, and this fact gives the president special access to this extensive communications network. The president's actions are an ongoing "media event," and a shrewd politician can exploit the media's need for "news" to his political advantage. George Reedy, one of Johnson's press secretaries, characterized the relationship between the president and the news media in this way:

> The principal source of the leverage is the unusual position of the President as one of the very few figures in public life who has in his exclusive possession a type of news virtually indispensable to the social and economic security of any reporter assigned to cover the White House full time. This category of newsworthy material consists of the President himself—his thoughts, his relationship with his friends and employees, his routine habits, his personal likes and dislikes, his intimate moments with his family and his associates.[19]

Thus, a president can monopolize publicity because reporters always want a story. This is a major way the president becomes transformed into a celebrity. But merely the fact that a president is "visible" to the public does not mean that his point of view is communicated to the citizenry. Most news reporting is not an objective process. Scholars use the concept "gatekeeping" to describe the many ways the press influences the content of "news." Our perception of any political leader is colored by the views of journalists, the slant given to reporting a president's activities, and the use of certain code words to describe his position on issues. In the same way, the meaning of current events depends on how the media interpret them for the public. For example, when George McGovern tried to make Watergate a campaign issue in the 1972 presidential election, the established media elites generally downplayed the entire episode. The serious implications of Watergate for democratic government were later revealed by two lesser-known reporters for the *Washington Post*, but by this time the 1972 election was over.

Press biases toward the president

Franklin D. Roosevelt exploited the radio by use of his fireside chats to reach the American people directly. He feared that the majority of newspaper editors, who were heavily Republican in sympathies, would not report accurately his New Deal policies. The pro-Republican disposition of certain periodicals, such as *Time* when it was managed by Henry Luce, is well-known. The political bias among newspaper owners has persisted over the past five decades.[20] One study found that, during 1932–1980, the vast majority of daily newspapers surveyed endorsed Republican presidential candidates in every election except two: in 1964 and in 1980.[21] In 1964 the plurality of newspapers endorsed Lyndon Johnson (42.4%) rather than Barry Goldwater (34.7%), and in 1980 an equal number endorsed Ronald Reagan as remained neutral or independent. But only 12 percent of the newspapers endorsed Jimmy Carter for reelection in 1980. These two exceptions to the rule may suggest that, although solidly Republican in orientation, newspaper editors stop short of endorsing avowed conservatives in their party.

Of course, newspaper reporters may not agree politically with their editors. Polsby and Wildavsky observe, "Democratic candidates probably have to work . . . at cultivating good relations in order to help counteract the editorial slant of most papers. But Republicans have to work a little harder to win the sympathies of reporters of liberal tendency who dominate the national press corps."[22] The traditional political sympathies of the working press were documented as early as the 1930s, when various observers determined that the majority of reporters favored the New Deal and were committed personally to Franklin D. Roosevelt.[23]

It is also significant that most newspapers rely on the Washington press corps for their news about the national government, because few media outlets assign their own reporters to the capital. A study by Ralph Nader showed that 72 percent of all daily newspapers, 96 percent of all television stations, and 99 percent of all radio stations did not have their own Washington correspondents.[24] Most reporters in the Washington press corps represent the print media, and some of these journalists are extremely influential with political decision makers as well as with the ordinary citizen. Among these "heavies," as Timothy Crouse calls them, are writers David S. Broder, James Reston, Mary McGrory, Jack Nelson, Joseph Kraft, and Robert Novak.[25] The Washington press corps tends to be liberal and Democratic, which suggests that they are in an important position to evaluate critically the policies of any president with whom they disagree, particularly a conservative Republican.

A recent study by Lichter and Rothman, based on interviews with 240 members of the "media elite," found that these prestigious journalists were overwhelmingly white, male, college-educated, and had incomes well in excess of $30,000 a year.[26] In addition, two-thirds came from the region extending from New England to Chicago. This study also showed that the journalists' political biases were the opposite of those held by newspaper editors. These reporters overwhelmingly favored the Democratic presidential candidate in 1964, 1968, 1972, and 1976; even in 1972, they preferred McGovern over Nixon by a margin of 81 percent to 19 percent even though Richard Nixon defeated George McGovern in a landslide victory that year. In terms of policy preferences, this sample of reporters favored such policies as redistribution of income, affirmative action, and government-guaranteed job programs.

It was his perception of this political bias in the working press corps that led Vice-President Spiro Agnew to make a speech in 1969 attacking news commentators, charging that a handful of journalists were imposing their views on millions of citizens. Agnew argued that the media elites reflected the social values of their limited geographical surroundings, namely the East Coast between New York City and Washington, D.C. Agnew's outburst simply underlined the intense feelings in the Nixon administration that the news media were its enemy. Several years later, Richard Nixon defended Agnew's charges. "As far as Spiro Agnew is concerned," Nixon said, "because he was conservative, because he was one who took on the press, he got a lot rougher treatment than would have been the case had he been one of the liberals' favorite pin-up boys."[27] There is some truth to the argument, for empirical research indicates that the press *was* more critical of Nixon's presidency, and Lyndon Johnson's administration, than of their predecessors and successors in the presidency.

Grossman and Kumar undertook a content analysis of the news stories reported in the *New York Times* and in *Time* during 1953–1978 and on CBS News during 1968–1978.[28] Their data contradict the commonly held view of presidents that they are involved "in an ongoing war with the news media, a war in which they believe they lose most important battles." The content analysis showed an opposite pattern:

> A striking feature . . . is the consistent pattern of favorable coverage of the President. The number of negative articles has grown, but the favorable still outnumber the unfavorable. Johnson's successors have not received the same level of favorable coverage that he did early in his term, but in the post-Vietnam and Watergate period, the balance of press coverage of the White House has been favorable. Yet Presidents Ford and Carter, like their predecessors, complained about media treatment of their administrations.[29]

Given below are the percentages of "favorable" stories about the president in the *New York Times* and *Time* during three periods.

	1953–1963	*1966–1976*	*1974–1978*
New York Times	50.0%	28.5%	37.5%
Time	58.9	28.7	43.3

The data indicate that these publications were more sympathetic to Dwight Eisenhower, John F. Kennedy, and Lyndon Johnson (at least during his early years) than their successors in the presidency. If this pattern is representative of the news media across the nation, it suggests one reason why the general level of public approval for Presidents Nixon, Ford, and Carter was lower than the degree of popularity achieved by their predecessors.

The useful work done by Grossman and Kumar points to other potent dynamics affecting the media's coverage of the presidency. First, the media concentrates on the president; he is the most important continuing story in Washington and virtually every edition of the *New York Times*, *Time*, and the CBS evening news had a story on the president in the years studied. This finding is confirmed by Charles Hamilton, who determined that during 1958–1977 the coverage of the president in two newspapers (*New York Times* and *Buffalo Evening News*) had increased from 61.9 percent to 73.1 percent, whereas coverage of the Congress dropped from 33 percent to 17.8 percent.[30] Second, more stories about the president are published during his first year in office; indeed, the number of favorable stories is greatest during this period. This phenomenon means a president can look forward to a "honeymoon" period at the beginning of his term, because the media, for various reasons, avoids antagonizing the new administration. Finally, the tone of the news stories about the president in all three media outlets was remarkably similar. For example, any story about the president's "personal" life or about his day-to-day "activity" invariably was favorable in tone. On the other hand, articles about his programs and policies or relationship with Congress tended to be more negative.

We would add, however, that the various kinds of news stories on a president's power may not have the same impact. Richard Neustadt differentiates between a president's "prestige" with the American public and his "reputation" with the Washington establishment, including congressmen, bureaucrats, and advisers as well as the media elites.[31] The fact that most stories about a president's personal life may be favorable, and therefore supportive of his popular image, may have little effect in counteracting the adverse publicity resulting from executive/legislative conflicts or from stories about infighting among his key advisers. Such negative information, although it may not be typical of all news about a president, nonetheless can do substantial damage to his leadership position vis-à-vis other decision makers in Washington. Thus, throughout his presidency Jimmy Carter was perceived by the American people to be a good and honorable man, but he also was judged by many citizens, including members of the Washington establishment, to be ineffectual in his dealings with Congress. On the other hand, because the news coverage of certain topics, such as a president's personal qualities, is so predictable and favorable, presidents may try to develop public relations strategies to focus the media's attention on subjects that bolster his image.

THE ART OF NEWS MANAGEMENT

Many observers have pointed out the symbiotic relationship between the president and the news media. The press needs stories and the president needs a way to sell his programs. But James Thomson, Jr. argues this relationship is doomed because, "to each, the other is a convenient means; but their ends are usually quite different."[32] Though the media and the executive attempt to seduce one another by developing mutual friendships, more often they become adversaries.[33] Lyndon Johnson once told Richard Nixon that he never understood why, after he wined and dined reporters at the White House, the press remained his enemy. But Nixon understood; he believed that all reporters were after a "story" and a negative story makes better copy than a positive one.[34]

The relationship between the media and the White House, however, is never static; it changes over time. When a president is elected to office, he promises an "open" administration and wants to be accessible to the press.[35] In turn, the reporters try to cooperate with the new president, and oftentimes the media simply acts as a conduit for whatever information the president wants to disseminate to the public. The major reason for this so-called honeymoon period is that both the media and the executive have common interests in getting exposure for the new administration. The press focuses on "human interest" stories about the president, his family, and close advisers, or discusses the president's policy agenda or style of decision making. For his part, the president tries to promote cordial relations with the press and to establish a rapport with key journalists. Thus, there are usually more press conferences and informal meetings with reporters held during the first year of a president's term.

This cooperative phase between the media and the president yields to a new phase involving competition. Reporters now begin to probe more deeply into policy issues and disputes among decision makers, problems that typically confront any president intent on serious change. As a result, the White House becomes upset about press coverage and the slant given to the news stories; it is troubled by rumors and news "leaks" by insiders. Soon the ideal of an open presidency is replaced by a desire to manipulate the press.

The art of news management is utilized most aggressively by the president during this period to regain the political advantage. Grossman and Kumar define news management as the "manipulation by the President and his advisers of the kinds of information that will be made available to reporters and of the forums in which information is given to them."[36] In general, news management involves (1) controlling access to the president, (2) manipulating the timing, content, and setting of information provided,

(3) courting the favor of reporters and media elites, and (4) attacking the credibility of the press.

Since the president is the focus of media attention, the White House tries to shape the content of news by controlling access to the president and his advisers. The president also may try to overshadow opponents' activities with his own news. For example, in 1967 President Johnson took various steps to undercut the news coverage given to a Senate speech by Robert Kennedy (D.–N.Y.) which criticized his Vietnam War policies. Prior to the time of the speech, Johnson called some newspapermen to announce that he had just received a letter from the Soviet Union indicating that talks were progressing toward an arms control agreement. That same day he went to Howard University and affirmed his commitment to racial justice; Johnson then appeared before the Office of Education and pledged to continue programs to educate the nation's children. Finally, President Johnson told the press that his daughter Luci was pregnant.[37]

A similar maneuver was used by Jimmy Carter when he was campaigning in the Wisconsin primary in 1980. He called a press conference at 7:00 A.M. to announce a new development in the Iranian hostage crisis; this assured him exposure in the mass media the same day Wisconsin voters were going to the polls. After Carter had won the Wisconsin primary, however, it was announced that his earlier declaration about a pending breakthrough in hostage negotiations was in error. By that time it had had its intended effect.[38]

A president can influence news content by requiring the press to agree to certain conditions before giving them access to the White House. Friendly reporters are welcomed whereas members of the press who are hostile are simply ignored or punished. For example, in 1964 when an Associated Press photographer snapped a picture of President Johnson picking up his beagles by their ears, a storm of protests from dog lovers assailed the White House. In reaction, Johnson banned that reporter from the White House for a week. It is more difficult for a president to monitor the contacts between his advisers and the press, though both Lyndon Johnson and Richard Nixon tried to do this as well. Unauthorized leaks of information to the media can seriously damage a president's reputation, although very often such disclosures to the press by the president are deliberate. Columnist Joseph Kraft observes, "In the typical Washington situation, news is not nosed out by keen reporters and then purveyed to the public. It is manufactured inside the government, by various interested parties for purposes of their own, and then put out to the press in ways and at times that suit the source."[39] Still, leaks may hurt a president's credibility. Richard Nixon's decision allowing the formation of the "Plumbers" unit in the White House was related to his desire to plug leaks in his own administration.

More effective than trying to prevent the leaks of information to the press are the president's efforts to win the support of the working press. Serving the legitimate needs of the reporters for news, giving friendly reporters restricted information, allowing a political ally an exclusive interview, and ingratiating oneself with the more prestigious journalists or newspaper editors are various methods used. President Kennedy excelled at the use of "social flattery" to win media support. For example, during one period Kennedy had invited to White House luncheons groups of editors and publishers from Florida, New Jersey, and the State of Washington. Similarly, columnists Stewart Alsop and Charles Bartlett, close friends of President Kennedy, apparently received privileged access to National Security Council proceedings for a magazine article they coauthored on the Cuban missile crisis.[40] It seems to be easier for Democrats—such as Roosevelt, Kennedy, and Johnson—to use these tactics of news management than Republicans, because the working press generally considers itself to be part of the Democratic party constituency.

When all efforts at news management fail, a president may resort to an attack on the integrity of the news media. By this strategy a president tries to discredit reporters with their own news organizations or a particular media outlet with the public. All presidents challenge certain reporters at one time or another, but no president impugned the integrity of the news media in quite the same fashion as Richard Nixon. According to Grossman and Kumar, "Attacks on the media during the Nixon administration were different in scale from those of previous administrations; they constituted a massive and unprecedented assault on the legitimacy of news organizations' activities."[41] As a result, in the short term the media did soften its strident criticism of the Nixon administration, but the Nixon–Agnew attack on the press did not save the Nixon presidency. The media's attention to the Watergate scandal continued, and its persistence was one factor that undermined public support for President Nixon, resulting in his forced resignation from office.

PUBLIC INPUTS

Columnist Russell Baker once wrote that "Americans tend to like the President and dislike the people who oppose him. The President is one of those universally revered modern American institutions like Mother, Friday night, the flag, burgers, progress, and plenty of free parking which everybody assumes that all decent, right-thinking citizens approve of and support."[42] There is some truth to this statement. The president is the best-known political leader in the United States, and citizens support him more often than not. Even though Watergate severely damaged Richard Nixon's credibility with the American people, it had less effect on public attitudes toward his successors. Gerald Ford, Jimmy Carter, and Ronald Reagan all began their terms of office with majority "approval" in public opinion. To what can we attribute the respect given to the president by the public? The research indicates that various social, economic, and political conditions can influence how public opinion evaluates the performance of specific presidents, but it appears that our attitudes toward the presidency as an institution of government are grounded in deep-seated emotional underpinnings.

Apparently our attachment to the presidency begins very early—during childhood. Studies show that children at an early age know who is president and they develop a positive attitude about his role in our system of government.

How children view the president

Research on political socialization has interested political scientists only in recent decades. Beginning in the 1960s, several studies were published detailing how children perceived the political system.[43] In retrospect, we have learned that those early studies were somewhat biased because they focused on suburban, middle-class, white children rather than on minorities or the poor. Their findings are not irrelevant, however, insofar as the largest numbers of Americans do belong to those racial, income, and geographic groupings. To the extent that such children are socialized effectively, it would seem that the future stability of our government is being enhanced. The early research on political socialization, by Greenstein, Hess and Torney, and Easton and Dennis, moreover, drew the same broad conclusions.

White, middle-class, suburban children hold highly idealized and positive views of our political system. Their primary orientation toward government is through "authority figures," mainly the president. Children are aware of the president at an early age, but this fact cannot be attributed to their level of political knowledge. Greenstein summarizes this research finding:

> By the age of nine (and, evidently earlier) virtually every child is aware of the Presidential role and the name of the incumbent President. Children of this age resemble the least informed members of the adult population in that they have almost no further political information. For example, most of them have not heard of Congress and cannot provide even a vague specification of what the President's duties are.[44]

In addition, children perceive the president as being more important than any other public official, as someone to be trusted, and as a benevolent leader. Based on their studies on children in metropolitan Chicago, and other cities across the nation, Hess and Torney characterize the attitudes of children this way:

> Young children relate to the president as they do to figures they know personally, expressing strong emotional attachment to him and expecting protection from him. They believe that the president is intimately involved not only in momentous decisions concerning the fate of the country but also in more mundane decisions that affect them and their neighborhood. . . . A strong sense of trust is evident in their responses; they think that the president is personally responsive to children's wishes and believe that they could even go to the White House and talk to him.[45]

The researchers who conducted the early studies on political socialization advanced several reasons why children react so positively towards the president. Children may idealize authority because they are so dependent on it and therefore feel vulnerable. It is also suspected that parents teach their children about the idealized, formal aspects of government rather than about the more corrupt and seedy realities of politics. As children grow older, they do acquire a more realistic viewpoint about government, and at higher grade levels their extent of political knowledge increases. Nonetheless, it appears that a child's favorable disposition to the president carries over into adulthood. Survey data indicate that Americans apparently have a reservoir of good will toward the president.

Later studies of political socialization added caveats to the original research on this question. One qualification pertains to the finding that children from minority or poverty groups do not hold such idealistic perceptions of government. Children in less affluent circumstances are aware of racial and class barriers, and they relate their immediate life experiences to the larger political system. Robert Coles remarks that "a black child of eight, in rural Mississippi or in a northern ghetto, an Indian or Chicano or Appalachian child, can sound like a disillusioned old radical: down with the system, because it's a thoroughly unjust one."[46] This observation is substantiated by a study of poor, rural Kentucky schoolchildren in 1967 by Jaros, Hirsch, and Fleron. These scholars replicated many survey questions used earlier by Hess and Easton, but poor Kentucky children were found to be less positive about the president. Instead of regarding him as a superior person, the authors found that

> for all five President-evaluation items, the distribution of responses of the Knox County youngsters is significantly less favorable than that of the Hess and Easton sample. In fact, when compared against "most men," the President does not do particularly well. In aggregate, he is not a paramount figure, and there are a fair number of youngsters (about a fourth) that express overtly unfavorable reactions to him.[47]

Jaros, Hirsch, and Fleron acknowledge that Appalachia constitutes a distinct subculture, one that exhibits more political cynicism than elsewhere in the country, but they further suggest that the political values expressed by these children may be transmitted by their families. The data point to a correspondence between the family's political orientation and their children's attitudes. Thus, Jaros, Hirsch, and Fleron caution that the original studies of political socialization may not be applicable to every segment of our society.

Compounding the fact that the early research was culture-bound is the problem that it may have been time-bound as well. We know that adult opinions about politics, and especially those concerning presidential performance, are colored heavily by current events. It is very probable that the children studied during the 1950s and 1960s were affected by historical circumstances. The early studies were done during the terms of Eisenhower and Kennedy, generally popular presidents; those research findings have not been sustained by research undertaken during Richard Nixon's tenure. In 1974, for example, Dennis and Webster revisited Tacoma, Washington, a city studied in 1962, and found that levels of support for the president had dropped substantially.[48] Another study by Jaros and Shoemaker in 1974 evaluated the attitudes of Appalachian schoolchildren toward Richard Nixon (who had resigned), Gerald Ford, and "the president."[49] Overall the children's view of Nixon was less favorable, but they exhibited more support for Gerald Ford as well as the unspecified "president." This finding suggests that the children's negative attitudes toward Nixon did not transfer to his successor or to the institution of the presidency.

Surveys of more affluent suburban children in Massachusetts also indicate attitude changes between 1973 and 1975.[50] During 1973, in Arterton's first study, children's attitudes toward Richard Nixon were very negative at the time the president was being severely criticized by the press and Congress. By 1975, however, Arterton determined that the children's hostility toward the president had lessened markedly.

With so few studies of political socialization, it is difficult to pinpoint all the variables that influence children's attitudes toward the president, or toward politics in general. Apparently such attitudes can vary according to subculture as well as time period. However, there has been little research undertaken on the relationship between childhood attitudes and adult opinions, a question most relevant to understanding the impact of political socialization on maintaining loyalty to the regime. Public opinion surveys find that adults generally have a positive attitude towards the president, which is consistent with the findings on middle-class, white, and suburban children.

How adults view the president

Compared with other public officials, the president clearly is the best-known political figure in the country. Data gathered by Greenstein shows that virtually all adult Americans (98%) know who the president is.[51] On the other hand, a majority of respondents did not know the name of the secretary of state or the secretary of defense, the speaker of the House of Representatives or the Senate majority party leader, their state's senators or their own congressman. Only the vice-president elicited name recognition (87%) near the level achieved by the president.

The American people also have deep respect for the office of the president; they rank it above the other branches of government in importance. Moreover, we tend to admire activist presidents, and most of the time more people approve of the incumbent president's performance than disapprove. It is true that, in recent years, public trust in the major institutions of society has been weakened. This distrust extends to the presidency also. For example, the average approval rating for Richard Nixon (49%), for Gerald Ford (46%), and for Jimmy Carter (47%) was much lower than the averages achieved by earlier presidents: Franklin D. Roosevelt (75%), Dwight Eisenhower (64%), John Kennedy (70%), and even Lyndon Johnson (55%). Part of the reason for this downward tendency, we suspect, is that the onslaught of so many pressing social, economic, and political issues faced by the contemporary president makes it more difficult to govern, and to satisfy the demands of the variety of voter groups in America. Yet, the increased skepticism of the American people has had an even more adverse impact on how they evaluate the Congress, as will be shown later.

To a remarkable degree, the public's view of "great" presidents closely parallels the judgment held by historians and political scientists. This suggests that the mythology surrounding such men as Washington and Lincoln makes them larger than life heroes, but the public lacks a historical perspective for making this kind of evaluation, with the result that incumbent presidents tend to be ranked higher relative to even the "great" presidents. A 1946 Gallup Poll, for example, asked Americans which president, among four named, was the greatest. These presidents were ranked as follows: Franklin D. Roosevelt (39%), Lincoln (37%), Washington (15%), and Wilson (5%).[52] A more objective measure of public opinion on this matter was taken in 1956 when Gallup asked this open-ended question: "What three United States presidents do you regard as the greatest?" Again Lincoln, Washington, and Franklin Roosevelt topped this listing, but the incumbent, Dwight Eisenhower, scored higher than Wilson, Theodore Roosevelt, or Thomas Jefferson.[53] The number of people choosing each president in this Gallup Poll follow: Franklin D. Roosevelt (891), Lincoln (864), Washington (648), Eisenhower (468), Truman (180), Wilson (177), Theodore Roosevelt (136), Jefferson (93), Hoover (83), Coolidge (42), McKinley (13), Other (44), No Answer/Don't Know (106).

When Gallup asked a nationwide sample in 1975 to name the three greatest presidents, the findings showed continued admiration for Lincoln, Franklin Roosevelt, and Washington. However, more contemporary presidents were named more often than prominent leaders of the eighteenth or nineteenth centuries. The percentages citing each president in the 1975 survey are given below:[54]

Kennedy (52%)	Theodore Roosevelt (9%)
Lincoln (49%)	Lyndon Johnson (9%)
Franklin Roosevelt (45%)	Nixon (9%)
Truman (37%)	Jefferson (8%)
Washington (25%)	Wilson (5%)
Eisenhower (24%)	

Thus, seven of the eleven presidents ranked by historians as "great" or "near-great" in the 1962 Schlesinger poll (see box in Introduction) are included in this group named by the public. (Those omitted were Jackson, Polk, John Adams, and Cleveland.) Moreover, it appears that the American people are more impressed by the accomplishments of contemporary presidents than are historians and political scientists. Kennedy, Eisenhower, Lyndon Johnson, and Richard Nixon were not ranked as high by the historians polled by the U.S. Historical Society in 1977 or by the *Chicago Tribune* in 1982.[55]

To what extent, therefore, does the public's respect for "activist" presidents translate into a more generalized support for presidential leadership? Further, will the public tolerate executive action even at the expense of Congress' prerogatives? Little research addresses these salient issues, but those few studies that do suggest the American people are inclined to support presidential leadership, particularly when exercised to solve pressing national problems.

An analysis by Sigel and Butler indicates that a degree of ambivalence affects the public's perception of presidential power. They conclude, "We have managed to *admire* strong men who know how to use power well and have suspected them of wanting to become autocrats, tyrants, and dictators."[56] This observation was prompted by the finding that their sample favored enactment of the Twenty-second Amendment, which limits the president to two terms, even though the respondents also admired dynamic leadership by the president. Elsewhere, Roberta Sigel tests this "ambivalence theory" and finds support for it.[57] Particularly in foreign affairs (though her question actually pertained to sending troops), Sigel found the public to be very dependent on the president. She argues, "it must be pointed out that the willingness to delegate decision making to the president stems not only from the public's view of his better knowledge . . . but also from the public's trust that as a rule presidents are not wont to abuse their decision-making power." With regard to domestic policy, Sigel found that, though public support for the president decreased somewhat, the majority of respondents still relied more on the president than on Congress. Based upon these findings, Sigel concludes that "the public's preference for the presidential *office* is one of broad scope and wide powers but that excess of power should be guarded against by the imposition of limited tenure."

Longitudinal data of another kind shows the primacy of the executive relative to the Congress. Long before Watergate and the end of the Vietnam War, commentators pointed to an increased cynicism, political malaise, or even alienation affecting public opinion.[58] In 1964 for example, 76 percent of Americans surveyed indicated that one could trust the national government to do what is right "just about always" or "most of the time."[59] By 1972 this proportion had already dropped to 53 percent. Moreover, Louis Harris has documented the decline in public confidence which affected the major institutions of our government between 1966 and 1971. In every case, fewer Americans in 1971 had a "great deal" of confidence in these institutions:[60]

	1966	1971
Executive branch	41%	23%
Supreme Court	51	23
Congress	42	19
Military	62	27

Note that the decline in confidence affecting the executive branch (not specifically the presidency) was less than the erosion recorded for the Supreme Court, the Congress, or the Military.

The fact that Lyndon Johnson and Richard Nixon carried on the Vietnam War during this period apparently had no effect in strengthening the public's respect for the Congress. Nor did the Watergate scandals do much, over the long-term, to improve Congress' overall image. Although some polls taken during the Watergate era showed that public opinion favored a reassertion of legislative authority over the executive, nonetheless the public's view of Congress has remained basically negative over these years.[61] Louis Harris studied public attitudes toward the Congress in a series of eight polls taken during 1965–1978. Only once (in 1965 during the Great Society era) did a majority of Americans hold "positive" rather than "negative" evaluations of the Congress. In 1965, 64 percent rated Congress positively but by 1978 63 percent held negative views of the legislative branch.[62]

One legacy of the Watergate and Vietnam eras is the fact that public support for the presidency—as well as for incumbent presidents—has been weakened. Daniel Yankelovich argues that the "crisis of confidence" affecting public opinion toward government is the primary reason why the American people no longer believe that the president "knows best," even in foreign affairs.[63] Yankelovich found that "automatic support" for the president traditionally reached 50 percent whenever he made a decision in foreign affairs—and regardless of the policy made. Since the end of the Vietnam War, however, the level of "automatic support" has diminished substantially. Yankelovich predicts, "Increasingly, the President may find himself having to justify his initiatives to a critical, reluctant public, with few citizens going along just because the president is presumed to know best."[64] This research by Yankelovich is consistent with the trends uncovered by Jack Dennis as well as by Kernell, Sperlich, and Wildavsky.

Using statewide samples of Wisconsin adults taken once in 1972 and twice in 1974, Dennis wanted to determine the impact of Watergate on the public's "diffuse" support for the presidency.[65] His findings affirm that Watergate did undermine public esteem for the presidency, as is shown in the responses to these questions:[66]

	Nov./Dec. 1972 (agree)	Nov./Dec. 1974 (agree)
"Office of the president has done some good"	52%	38%
"People have a say in what the president does"	19	10
"Office of the president should be reformed"	18	45

During this two-year period, moreover, the losses in "diffuse" support for the presidency were greater than what was recorded for the Supreme Court, Congress, or federal administrative agencies. The more important question raised by Dennis had to do with the relationship between "specific" support for the incumbent president and "diffuse" support for the presidency. When Gerald Ford succeeded to the presidency, Ford's initial popularity did not immediately reverse the loss of public respect for the institution. This led Dennis to conclude "the actions of an incumbent can be significant for public support for the presidential institution. Thus the performance of presidents and the resulting public image have determinate effects on the authority they leave their successors."[67]

On the other hand, Dennis acknowledged that "diffuse" support is not entirely dependent on the public's attitude toward specific presidents. He determined that public support is also influenced by our socioeconomic backgrounds and ideological orientations. For example, older citizens, people with less education, and political conservatives Dennis found to be more supportive of presidential authority than younger people, those with more education, and political liberals. Similar relationships affect public opinion toward the president, according to the research by Kernell, Sperlich, and Wildavsky. They further suggest that demographic changes in our population may yield a greater skepticism by the public regarding the president.[68] These political scientists measured public attitudes in terms of three indices: "I like presidents," "Our presidents right or wrong," and "rally round presidents in a crisis." They found that presidential support is "disproportionately located among citizens who are older, of fundamental religious persuasion, have fewer years of formal schooling, and may be described as psychologically inflexible." They conclude that because ". . . the population is becoming younger, less likely to belong to fundamentalist sects, possessing additional years of formal education, and is more likely to be psychologically flexible," such "long-term, secular changes in the population would lead to a drop in support for Presidents."[69]

Thus, Watergate and Vietnam eroded the public's respect for the presidency, in addition to crippling Richard Nixon's incumbency. The research by Kernell and colleagues, moreover, predicts that presidents in the future may have a more difficult time in cultivating a supportive public opinion. Apart from these social trends, however, is the fact that public attitudes toward the president on a day-to-day basis are influenced by myriad other forces. A substantial body of research indicates that presidential popularity is quite volatile, shaped by historic events, sudden crises, economic conditions, and policy decisions. But even more significant, in addition to these social, economic, and political conditions, public attitudes toward the president may be conditioned by our psychological needs and fears.

Psychological factors

The leading advocate of the view that psychology has a great deal to do with presidential perceptions by the public is Fred Greenstein. Though Greenstein admits that the empirical verification for his hypothesis is tenuous, he argues that the president serves at least five important psychological functions for the people.[70] First, the president is a cognitive aid: "The existence of this highly publicized national figure who combines the roles of political leader and head of state *simplifies perception* of government and politics."[71] The public, in other words, focuses on public affairs by following the actions of the president. Second, the president provides an emotional outlet, meaning that we become involved emotionally with his life. "The detailed preoccupation of the media with the president's hobbies and social activities has become an American equivalent of the more cere-monial displays of symbolic activity associated elsewhere with monarchs."[72]

Next, as a means of "vicarious participation," Greenstein maintains that citizens can identify with the president when he acts effectively, thus enhancing our desire for "a world in which one is not completely dependent upon external circumstances and events." A fourth psychological function of the president involves his position as a symbol of national unity; when a president dies or suffers serious illness, as a society we are overwhelmed. For example, when Dwight Eisenhower suffered a heart attack in 1955, the stock market dropped to its lowest point since the Great Crash of 1929. Finally, the president is a symbol of stability and predictability. In this rela-tionship he signifies social stability and continuity; according to Greenstein, one aspect of a president's assassination that particularly disturbs people is its implications for domestic and international order.

In his analysis of these psychological variables, Greenstein sees obvious parallels between the needs satisfied by our president and those provided by a king or queen in other countries. His argument, therefore, bolsters the view that the fusion of "civic" and "political" functions in one authority figure—the president—probably has the effect of strengthening his position as opinion/party leader.

Social, economic, and political factors

Scholars also analyze the trends in public approval of the presidents' performance in office to determine their underlying causes. Listed below are the scores achieved by our past eight presidents. These are based upon the Gallup Poll question asked regularly since the 1930s: "Do you approve or disapprove of the way _____ is handling his job as president?"[73]

	Percent Approval		
	High	*Low*	*Average*
Franklin Roosevelt	84	54	75
Harry Truman	87	23	41
Dwight Eisenhower	79	48	64
John Kennedy	83	56	70
Lyndon Johnson	80	35	55
Richard Nixon	67	24	49
Gerald Ford	71	37	46
Jimmy Carter	75	21	47

The seminal research on this topic was done by John Mueller, whose major conclusion was that, during their terms of office, the popularity of presidents declines.[74] This Mueller attributed to the hypothesis that a pres-ident's election is based upon a "coalition of minorities" rather than a "majority" coalition in any meaningful sense. As a president is forced to address a wide variety of controversial issues during his tenure, he eventually will alienate the various components of his electoral coalition. The accumulation of disaffected minorities, therefore, causes a downturn in the president's popularity. Mueller's research focused on presidents from Truman to Johnson, but a cursory review of the approval ratings for their successors (figure 3-1) also shows a decrease in popularity for Nixon, Ford, and Carter. With regard to Ronald Reagan, things looked particularly bleak. Fourteen months after taking office, in March 1982, a Gallup Poll showed that about as many Americans approved (46%) as disapproved (45%) of his performance. At this point in his term, therefore, Reagan had the lowest approval rating of any contemporary president. Thus, it appears that the downward trend in Reagan's approval ratings has proceeded at a faster rate than that experienced by his immediate predecessors. To this extent, Mueller's hypothesis is confirmed for Ronald Reagan as well. During March through August of 1981 Reagan's performance was approved by at least 60 percent of the respondents; this approval rating dropped to 52 percent in September of 1981, rose slightly to 56 percent in October 1981, and then fell to 54 percent in November 1981; from December 1981 through March 1982, less than a majority of respondents approved of Reagan's performance in office.

The downward trend affecting the presidents' approval ratings, however, occurs after an initial "honeymoon" period, which begins the term of a newly elected president. All presidents seem able to build upon their electoral victory by sustaining a degree of public enthusiasm for their incumbency. Based on Mueller's analysis, Dwight Eisenhower was able to sustain the most consistent, and high, levels of public approval for his performance. Eisenhower clearly was our most popular president since World War II, and Mueller suggests that Ike's singular performance in this regard may be related to his ending the Korean War as well as to the fact that he did little as president, thus offending relatively few people.

This inevitable downward trend in public approval can be reversed temporarily by the so-called rally-round-the-flag effect (see chapter 6). International crises prompt a short-term, sharp increase in the president's popularity, regardless of the wisdom of his foreign policies, because public opinion unites behind the nation's leader. But domestic crises do not necessarily generate widespread support for the president. Theodore Lowi observes that such incidents as urban riots or racial disturbances, though they may involve violence, hurt the presidents' approval ratings.[75] Unlike the deference paid by the public to a president's conduct of foreign affairs, people tend to have very different views about how best to handle lawlessness or social unrest. This argument is related to Mueller's finding that domestic events, such as scandals, inflation rates, or levels of unemployment, generally harm rather than help a president's standing in the opinion polls. However, these variables are much less important in explaining the trends in presidential popularity. For example, Mueller determined that economic downturns tend to depress presidential popularity somewhat,

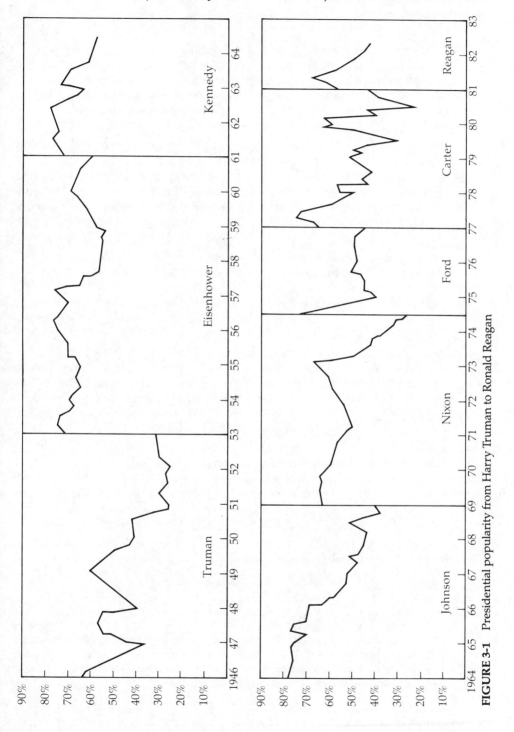

FIGURE 3-1 Presidential popularity from Harry Truman to Ronald Reagan

but periods of economic growth do not appreciably improve his approval ratings.

Other scholars have documented the negative relationship between presidential popularity and the passage of time, though serious methodological questions have been raised about this formulation of the problem.[76] A study that essentially confirms Mueller's argument was conducted by James Stimson.[77] However, Stimson contends that a president can do little to reverse this decline in popularity because, fundamentally, it relates more to public misperceptions regarding his capabilities rather than to the specific actions taken. According to Stimson, presidential popularity increases as an incumbent begins his term, because the president has support from some citizens who did not vote for him. In time the president's popularity will "bottom out" to reflect the plurality that elected him. In order to rebuild his support, a president becomes more active toward the end of his term, with the result that his popularity begins to rise slightly. Stimson, unlike Mueller, views the long-term trend in presidential popularity as being cyclical but, like Mueller, relies on the time variable as the major determinant of any president's popularity.

Domestic economic conditions seem to have less impact on a president's popularity than one may think. Any relationship appears to be stronger between the rate of inflation and presidential popularity rather than between the rate of unemployment and his standing in the polls. Presumably this means many more people are adversely affected by rising prices, whereas incremental jumps in the unemployment rate have a disproportionate impact on smaller numbers of people. Research on this question by Henry Kenski[78] was inconclusive, and a study by Samuel Kernell found that unemployment rates were not an important determinant of presidential popularity and, moreover, that price levels had some effect in only two of the five administrations studied (Kennedy's and Nixon's).[79]

A more productive research strategy was used by Kristen Monroe, who argued that people do not respond immediately to fluctuations in prices but rather react to the accumulation of price changes over time.[80] She says that presidential popularity responds to inflation "in a gradual, cumulative and lagged fashion." Therefore, prolonged inflation will hurt a president's standings in the polls, as Monroe explains:

> While there is some immediate response to inflation, the major response is a cumulative one. This suggests that the public does not blame the president for brief periods of inflation but will hold him responsible for sustained inflation. The lagged impact suggests the public has a long memory. The public is not easily distracted by sudden declines in inflation which immediately precede an election. Rather, it sees beyond tinkering with the economy for immediate political gain and bases its political response to the economy primarily on more stable periods of economic improvement or decline.[81]

Thus, the general state of the economy can affect the president's approval ratings, but day-to-day economic fluctuations probably have little immediate impact.

Finally, presidential popularity may be influenced by current events in addition to the presence of war or crises and economic trends. Richard Brody and Benjamin Page tried to explain the president's approval ratings according to their "news discrepancy" theory.[82] The theory maintains that public support will rise or fall depending upon the balance between good and bad news reported in the mass media. Brody and Page tested this theory during the Johnson and Nixon years. Poll-to-poll changes in the presidents' approval ratings were predicted based upon the discrepancy between the level of presidential support in the previous month and the "goodness or badness" of news content in the current period. Their results were more conclusive for Lyndon Johnson than for Richard Nixon.

The body of literature, therefore, implies that the amalgam of forces which affect presidential popularity are, to a large degree, beyond the scope of any president's control. One possible exception to this generalization is the "rally-round-the-flag" syndrome, which may be exploited by the president for political gain. During his first term, for example, President Nixon made eleven major trips abroad, including his historic visits to the People's Republic of China and the Soviet Union.

One research question thus far ignored by political scientists concerns the relationship between a president's electoral coalition and his long-term approval ratings. Data on Ronald Reagan, for example, suggest the hypothesis that a president may depend upon the same voter groups which had voted for him to continually support his policies during his term of office. On the other hand, voter groups which opposed his election may constitute the groups that most consistently disapprove of his performance as president. The March 1982 Gallup Poll showing that only 46 percent of Americans "approved" of Reagan's performance also indicated the level of support by various demographic groups. The "approval" ratings by some of these voter groups are given below:

Group	% Approval	Group	% Approval
men	52	women	41
Republicans	84	Democrats	26
whites	51	blacks	12
college-educated	54	grade-school educated	30
family income $15,000+	54	family income under $15,000	35

Notable in these data is the fact that all the voter groups with a majority approving of Reagan's performance as president gave a majority of their votes to him in the 1980 election. In contrast, women, Democrats, blacks, and people whose family income was under $15,000 tended to favor Jimmy Carter in 1980, and these voter groups are now very disapproving of Reagan's performance as president. This relationship is only suggestive, but one suspects that it may indicate that a president's declining approval ratings depend specifically on the greater disapproval of members of "minorities" who had opposed his election in the first place.

Midterm elections

Another relationship that has been verified empirically is that a president's popularity affects his political party's fortunes in the midterm congressional elections. The failure of Roosevelt's 1938 "purge" underscores the difficulty presidents face in trying to persuade the voters to support their chosen candidates. Indeed, the historic record suggests that a president more often is a political liability rather than an asset to his party's candidates for Congress. It is well known that the president's party usually loses seats in the House of Representatives in the midterm election following the presidential election. This has occurred every midterm election since the Civil War except for 1934.

Research conducted in the 1950s argued that midterm House losses were a function of voter turnout.[83] The size of the electorate does shrink in the midterm election following the presidential election. But more importantly, according to this study the increased turnout during presidential elections is caused by "weak" partisans and independents whose voting is stimulated by short-term variables, such as candidate personality or issues. Because these short-term variables tend to favor the winning presidential candidate (who at the time of the study was Eisenhower), the "surge" in voting turnout also benefited his party's candidates for Congress. During the midterm election, however, voting turnout declines because those short-term factors are less important; more voters act according to their "normal" party preference, thus causing the president's party to lose seats in the House of Representatives.

The foregoing thesis has been reevaluated by scholars who suggest that voting in midterm elections may be viewed as a referendum on the incumbent president's popularity. According to Austin Ranney, moreover, Democrats are generally less successful in midterm elections than Republicans, even though most voters call themselves Democrats.[84] On the average, Ranney calculated that Democrats lost thirty-eight House seats in midterm elections to the Republican party's thirty-one. He subscribes to the view that in midterm elections the voters are reacting to the president's performance in office; therefore "congressional candidates eagerly seek close association with popular Presidents, as in 1934, 1954, and 1962, but put all the distance they can between themselves and an unpopular administration as in 1946, 1966, and 1974."[85]

Some empirical support for Ranney's argument is provided by Samuel Kernell and Edward Tufte. Kernell argues that midterm elections are dominated by "negative voting," which means that voters are motivated more by their opposition to policies and candidates than by their support. He contends that the voters who participate in midterm elections are probably more inclined to disapprove of the president's programs, as well as his party, when casting their ballots.[86] Edward Tufte supplies a mathematical formula indicating that, for every 10 percent loss in the president's approval rating between the presidential election and the following midterm election, the president's party will lose 1.3 percent of its share of the House vote in the midterm election. And this translates into a 2.6 percent loss in its share of seats in the House of Representatives.[87] Austin Ranney applied Tufte's model to the 1978 midterm elections, and predicted that the Democrats would lose fifteen to twenty-five seats in the House; as it turned out, they lost fifteen seats. In the 1982 midterm elections Republican moderates tried to dissociate themselves from President Reagan's economic policies, apparently without much success. That year the Republicans lost 26 seats in the House of Representatives. From this perspective, clearly the president's record in office has an effect on his political party's electoral fortunes, but apparently a president's ability to influence the midterm elections is limited by his overall success in cultivating a favorable public opinion.

EXPERTISE

The function of opinion/party leader, as noted before, was the latest role to evolve, mainly because media technology was limited until this century. "Until the twentieth century," Corwin and Koenig observe, "the limitations of scientific developments in communications enabled even the most effective Presidents to shape public opinion only at a moderate pace and on few issues in the course of a four-year term."[88] In a sense, however, this new role is a mixed blessing for the president. The tremendous opportunity today for a president to influence mass opinion is limited by the president's inability to completely control the media and by the structure of the communications industry itself.

Furthermore, the success of an opinion/party leader may depend upon his objectives. Koenig identifies three general themes a president may articulate to his political constituencies: (1) conservator, (2) protector, and (3) innovator.[89] As a "conservator," the president affirms established values and safeguards the economic, social, and political status quo. Presidents who cultivate this style work to minimize controversy, thus they may become extremely popular figures. Dwight Eisenhower no doubt was a president who acted very effectively as a conservator, but he did not exploit his personal popularity for political gain. Therefore, the popular slogan "I Like Ike" was not extended by voters to his Republican party.

By being "protective," a president "provides security against external danger to society's survival and well-being and protects its members from bodily harm and physical destruction."[90] Obviously, this theme arises during international crises, wartime, and domestic turmoil, such as after an assassination. In putting forth both of these roles, conservator and protector, a president's ability to communicate with the American people is enhanced because, in a sense, he is saying what they want to hear. A far more difficult task faces the president who is "innovative," for Koenig argues that the advocacy of social change undercuts a president's popularity:

A President who responds to the forces of change undertakes novel action and revises the existing economic, political, or social order by enacting new laws and establishing new accords and arrangements among nations. To make innovations he must sustain controversy and even risk political defeat.[91]

During his first year in office, Ronald Reagan's dealings with the mass media suggested that he, in addition to Kennedy and Franklin Roosevelt, would be one of the more effective opinion/party leaders in recent decades. After his first year, however, his popularity dropped and support for domestic programs decreased markedly. Reagan's difficulties stemmed partly from the themes he emphasized as opinion/party leader. Even in calling for a "new beginning," Reagan's rhetoric was indicative of the "conservator," because he embraced fiscal restraint, reliance on capitalism and the free market, and the delegation of more power to the states and localities. Such arguments have been made in American politics for many years, especially by Republicans. But Reagan was also "innovative" to the extent that he wanted to reverse the New Deal and Great Society liberal agenda. Thus he needed to convince the electorate that a reassessment of social priorities was in order to allow reduced governmental benefits. Any president who advocates innovation, therefore, must be combative to some degree, because he is challenging long-standing assumptions about politics. His objective is to "educate" the people about the necessity and desirability of change. For example, Harry Truman waged his 1948 reelection campaign by conducting a whistle-stop tour in which he blasted the "bloodsuckers of Wall Street" and the Republican-dominated "Idiot 80th," "Do-Nothing Congress."

The role of opinion/party leader has been institutionalized in many ways; namely, the use of press conferences and reliance on press secretaries. The president is expected to carry on a dialogue with the American people: to avoid this obligation damages his credibility. However, given the adversary nature of the press, it is not easy for all presidents to cultivate the kind of media coverage they want, with the result that even activist presidents cannot exploit this role consistently for political advantage. As Lyndon Johnson once told a reporter, "Our most tragic error may have been our inability to establish a rapport and a confidence with the press and television . . . I don't think the press has understood me."[92] Johnson attributed the lack of rapport to the bias against his Texas origins held by Eastern reporters, particularly in light of Kennedy's assassination.

Theodore Roosevelt's legacy

In developing the role of opinion/party leader, major precedents were established by Theodore Roosevelt, who pioneered many of the public relations techniques used today. His lasting contribution was the viewpoint that a president should articulate popular reforms. As one observer summarized TR's impact: "To a superactive, but squeaky-voiced Roosevelt, the presidential podium was a 'bully pulpit,' and his pontifical moral judgments echoed throughout the land. From his office, the President preached righteousness, national honor, prestige, patriotism, 'square deal,' world peace, and progressivism. So articulate and vehement was the Rough Rider, that he virtually drenched Congress with words."[93]

Theodore Roosevelt was the first president to use the presidential junket as a calculated publicity stunt. In 1907, for example, he made a trip down the Mississippi River with members of the Inland Waterways Commission. This trip attracted "wide public attention" and gave the commission "standing in the public esteem."[94] Twice during his term TR made extended nationwide speaking tours to prepare the citizenry for his new programs and to familiarize the people with ideas he felt would not be read in the newspapers. Theodore Roosevelt was the first president, in addition, to create press offices in the White House. He held off-the-record news conferences with reporters, in which he would provide background information or release "trial balloons" on issues to test their political acceptance. Roosevelt also was known to reveal information confidentially to newsmen in the hope that it would undermine his opponents in the Congress.

Theodore Roosevelt never permitted news to be distributed from the White House without his approval. Not only did he have ready access to the editorial pages and news columns of hundreds of newspapers across the country that supported him—he also knew how to exploit them for best effect. Since a Sunday news release would make the front page of Monday's otherwise routine news coverage, he delayed the distribution of information to the press until Sundays. Such tactics were extremely effective, and Roosevelt's antics made tremendous news copy. Moreover, he made sure to know who the leading journalists were to assure positive reactions to his announcements in the mass circulation newspapers and magazines. Many of Theodore Roosevelt's informal techniques to manipulate the media have been used by more aggressive successors in the presidency. One aspect, however, has become formalized in the role of opinion/party leader; that is, the use of the press conference.

The press conference

The press conference is a forum whereby a president states his views on policy questions asked by reporters. During Woodrow Wilson's term, reporters gathered by general invitation in his office for a question-and-answer session.[95] This procedure replaced the traditional pattern in which presidents would grant interviews to only selected reporters. Although Wilson formalized the press conference, he was not entirely effective in these meetings, given his reserved nature and because he came to view the reporters' persistence as an insult to his integrity.

Since press conferences are now usually televised events, these occasions allow the president to communicate directly to the people. The advent of radio and television was a major technological advance for the opinion/party leader, for now a president's political statements are not as easily distorted by reporters, partisan newspapers, and journalists. Franklin D. Roosevelt quickly grasped the great potential of radio in this regard. Faced with heavy opposition from Republican-dominated newspaper editors, he turned to his fireside chats on the radio to bring messages about the New Deal directly to the American people.

Since its formal establishment under Woodrow Wilson, the press conference has had varied uses by our presidents. Some incumbents, such as Franklin D. Roosevelt and John F. Kennedy, were especially adept in using this forum for political advantage whereas others, such as Richard Nixon, were ineffective because the process revealed too much about themselves. As shown in table 3-1 Roosevelt and Truman held many more press conferences than their successors, a circumstance probably related to the absence of television and to the urgency of the Great Depression, World War II, and the Korean War which prompted them to keep the public informed about current events and their programs.

The modern press conference as we know it began with Franklin D. Roosevelt. He arranged two meetings with the press a week, and abandoned Herbert Hoover's requirement that written questions be provided. Roosevelt did establish his own ground rules for these conferences, for example, he often provided "background" information not to be attributed to the White House or "off the record" materials for reporters' information only. At his first press conference, FDR established the rule that nothing he said could be "quoted" without his express permission. Research indicates that FDR was, without doubt, the most effective opinion/party leader. Apparently his press conferences were lively sessions dominated by his charm. Consider this firsthand impression of Roosevelt's press conference style by journalist John Gunther:

> In twenty minutes Mr. Roosevelt's features had expressed amazement, curiosity, mock alarm, genuine interest, worry, rhetorical playing for suspense, decision, playfulness, dignity, and surpassing charm. Yet he *said* almost nothing. Questions were deflected, diverted, diluted. Answers—when they did come—were concise and clear.[96]

Franklin D. Roosevelt was a hard act to follow but, of more consequence, his use of the press conference set a major precedent. As Cornwell comments, the institution "was rescued from the doldrums and disrepute into which it had fallen, and used with unsurpassed skill and subtlety."[97] Cornwell affirms that as the press conference forged a link between the president

TABLE 3-1   Presidential press conferences, 1932–1980*

President	Number	Average per year in office
Roosevelt	998	83
Truman	322	40
Eisenhower	193	24
Kennedy	64	21
Johnson	126	25
Nixon	37	7
Ford	39	16
Carter	59	15

*Milton C. Cummings, Jr. and David Wise, *Democracy Under Pressure* (New York: Harcourt Brace Jovanovich, 1981), p. 380.

and the people, it was destined to gain vital importance in the modern era of big government and world crises.

Harry Truman began his tenure by following the procedures set by his predecessor. Though the number of press conferences was much less than the number held by Roosevelt, Truman came to win the affection of the press corps. But Truman's use of the press conference was probably less effective than Roosevelt's because he was less manipulative and apparently had no strategy in mind. Moreover, Truman's impetuous and quarrelsome nature was revealed to the reporters at times.

Under Dwight Eisenhower the press conference became a televised event, presented to the people with only minor editing. Ike's relationship with the press was distant, and when he began his term as president there were concerns among reporters that Eisenhower and certain staff aides might not favor continuing the tradition of the press conference. Eisenhower's popularity with the American people, coupled with his nonpartisan stance, suggested that a strong relationship with the press was less important to him. Knowing this, the reporters in turn were not inclined to incur Eisenhower's disfavor. Thus, the Eisenhower press conference was an infrequent, formal affair, with less personal interaction between the president and reporters. Whereas Roosevelt held press conferences on the average of almost seven per month, the frequency was reduced to less than four under Truman and cut further to two under Eisenhower. It is relevant to note that the advent of television allowed more opportunity for the public to follow Eisenhower's daily activities, so the president's reduced use of the formalized press conference did him little harm. In fact, Cornwell suggests that the infrequency may have helped Eisenhower by reaffirming his noncontroversial image. Eisenhower's modifications in the timing of press conferences encouraged his successors to schedule press conferences for best political impact, rather than solely as a medium for keeping the press informed. Even Kennedy, a master at public relations, held fewer press conferences than did Eisenhower.

John F. Kennedy's press conferences were televised to the American people without any editing; Kennedy was extremely effective in these encounters with the press. For some, JFK's skill at exploiting public relations, matched only by Franklin D. Roosevelt, brought to mind Hollywood epics. Elmer Cornwell remarks that

> The reporters grew to feel that they were extras in the recurring drama. . . . So efficient had the transcript system become that the first five or six pages were ready for use by the time "Thank you, Mr. President" was uttered, and stories could be written from the conference by newsmen who had not even bothered to attend. The point had almost been reached, in short, at which the only real excuse for holding the conference was the vast unseen audience.[98]

Like FDR, therefore, Kennedy saw the press conference primarily as a means of communicating directly with the public. In 1961 Richard Rovere observed that Kennedy felt "he must attempt direct communication with the people because, in the first place, he wishes to awaken and arouse them, and because, in the second place, he fears that a predominantly Republican press will not deal objectively with him and his views."[99]

Presidents Johnson, Nixon, and Ford tried to avoid the formal, televised press conference, perhaps because they feared being compared with Kennedy. Lyndon Johnson preferred highly informal meetings with small groups of reporters. His style of holding impromptu news conferences at almost any time and anywhere came to annoy the press since not all reporters could be on hand, and television coverage also was precluded. In 1966, for example, one-half of Johnson's news conferences were impromptu. This arrangement allowed him the opportunity to badger reporters in his familiar, one-on-one manner. In terms of content, Johnson's approach to the press conference was cautious, and more typical of Eisenhower; he rarely shocked his audience, seldom showed anger (at least not until Vietnam dominated the discussions), and tended to give lengthy responses to questions to consume time.

Richard Nixon had the fewest press conferences of any contemporary president, and rarely made himself available to the press through impromptu meetings. As already noted, Nixon and his vice-president, Spiro Agnew, viewed the press as suspect, and an enemy. But his efforts to avoid reporters only prompted them to ask highly critical questions whenever the opportunity arose. When first elected president, Nixon's press conferences were more successful than later in his term, when such political controversies as Watergate surfaced. In contrast to Nixon, Gerald Ford promised an "open presidency," and courted a favorable press. Ford preferred a structured meeting with reporters rather than the televised news conference, but also held meetings with non-Washington reporters as well as the regular White House press corps.

Jimmy Carter generally had good relations with the press; obviously he understood the importance of maintaining effective public relations. His movement from political obscurity to the White House was in part engineered by exploiting the mass media. Besides holding formal press conferences, Carter also met with non-Washington reporters. Carter tried to hold press conferences regularly twice a month.

Ronald Reagan held very few formal press conferences during his first year in office, apparently preferring to appear on television to appeal to people directly, for example when he discussed his budget cuts or the imposition of martial law in Poland in 1981. In spite of his conservative ideology, Reagan had good relations with the press, but this can be expected of any president during his so-called honeymoon period. The fact that presidents begin their term of office with high levels of public approval is related to the way they are treated by the mass media. Greenstein observes that media coverage of a new president in the first few months

tends to emphasize the endearing personal touches—Ford's preparation of his own English muffins, Carter's fireside chat in informal garb. No wonder both of these Presidents enjoyed high poll ratings during their initial months in office. But the trend can only go downward . . . after idealizing Presidents, the media quickly search out their warts.[100]

Press secretary

The task of protecting the president from the media as well as promoting his positive achievements in the press falls to the president's press secretary. Like the press conference, this position has been routinized since its establishment in the 1930s. Prior to Franklin D. Roosevelt no one presidential adviser served as press secretary. Such aides as James P. Tumulty, who served Woodrow Wilson, had other duties besides press relations, but Franklin Roosevelt's extensive reliance on the mass media necessitated that these disparate responsibilities be delegated to a separate assistant. Most press secretaries have had experience in the mass media, but their effectiveness depends largely upon how they are utilized by the president.

Perhaps the most effective functionary in this capacity was James C. Hagerty, who was Eisenhower's press secretary. According to William Spragens, Hagerty could be considered the model for a modern press secretary: ". . . he gave the media as much news as he could . . . but he also was loyal and painstaking in his work performed for Eisenhower. He was also consulted by Eisenhower as a trusted aide during his eight-year term."[101] During John F. Kennedy's thousand days in office, his only press secretary was Pierre Salinger. In general, few presidents have had only one person serve them as press secretary during their entire term of office. Lyndon Johnson had three press secretaries, including Bill Moyers, George Reedy, and George Christian; Franklin Roosevelt and Harry Truman also had three persons serve in this position. The turnover among press secretaries sometimes is related to their lack of credibility with the press. Since their importance depends upon their position as the president's key spokesman, any sign that a president lacks confidence in his press secretary can reduce that adviser's impact with the media. Turnover in the position of press secretary under Lyndon Johnson was related to the president's credibility gap regarding the Vietnam War, and apparently two of his press secretaries, Bill Moyers and George Reedy, disagreed with Johnson over matters of policy. Ron Ziegler was press secretary for Richard Nixon during most of Nixon's tenure, but his credibility was destroyed by Watergate, in addition to the fact that the press knew that he was not privy to high-level decision making in the Nixon administration. After saying that Watergate was nothing more than a "third-rate" burglary, as the facts surfaced Ziegler later was obliged to declare previous White House denials to be "inoperative." Gerald Ford was served by Jerald TerHorst and later by Ron Nessen. TerHorst resigned as press secretary one month after his appointment, because he could not support the Nixon pardon. Jimmy Carter's only press secretary was Jody Powell, who was also a close adviser to the president. For this reason Powell was highly respected by the working press. During 1971–1975, Jody Powell had acted as press secretary to Carter when he was governor of Georgia.

The press secretary's duties include the management of the press office, the conduct of presidential press conferences, and the handling of daily press briefings. His position is central to opinion/party leadership. As Grossman and Kumar observe, the relationship of the press secretary to the media "is second only to that of the President in its importance in framing the public's perception of the Chief Executive."[102] But as noted above, the press secretary's effectiveness depends on how he is utilized by the president. Presidents Carter, Eisenhower, Roosevelt, and Kennedy delegated much responsibility to this person, whereas Nixon, Johnson, and Ford restricted their press secretaries to more routine tasks. Moreover, the position of the press secretary today has been complicated somewhat by the increased reliance on White House aides. At times these senior advisers try to manipulate the press to protect their own image. Clearly, no president can tolerate an adviser who cultivates media coverage at his expense. During the Nixon and Ford administrations Secretary of State Henry Kissinger allegedly used his contacts with the press to protect his reputation as the Watergate scandal began to unfold. As a result, the press did not scrutinize Henry Kissinger's role in that affair.

An effective press secretary enhances the president's image by being able to represent the president's viewpoints accurately and fully. "Press secretaries need to know how to convey the President's messages in a manner that increases the likelihood that the media will portray them the way the White House intended."[103] When this position was established in the Roosevelt administration, it involved many diverse functions. Roosevelt's first press secretary, Stephen T. Early, prepared correspondence and public statements for the president, held daily press briefings, answered reporters' requests for information, scheduled appointments with Roosevelt, edited the president's speeches, advised the first lady on public relations matters, acted as liaison between the White House and the Democratic National Committee, and coordinated the public relations activities of the departments. Today these differing functions are assigned to more specialized agencies, such as the Press Office which handles regular contacts with the press; the Media Liaison (established by Nixon as the Office of Communications) to make contacts with non–Washington-based media outlets; the public information officers who serve the departments and major bureaus; Office of the Appointments Secretary to the President; the White House Photo Office; and the Office of Public Liaison, which provides linkages to special interest groups.

The press secretary plays four general roles for the president—conduit, staff, policymaker, and agent.[104] His most important function is that of a conduit to routinely transmit information from the president to the mass media. The daily press briefings by the press secretary are extremely valuable, particularly when a president such as Richard Nixon holds few formal press conferences. A press secretary who has the confidence of the president can speak for him on a wide variety of topics, and the daily press briefing sets the tone for the administration's policies and priorities. By this means the press secretary is able to control the "agenda" pertaining to the media's coverage of the White House and, therefore, can influence the public's expectations about what events and issues are important. The daily press briefing can be very effective in defining news content because the reporters, constrained to meet deadlines for that evening's broadcast or newspaper publication, cannot do much more than simply report the president's activities.

In his staff role the press secretary is supposed to coordinate the contacts made by the president's senior advisers with the media so that one coherent and consistent message is conveyed to the press. Most press secretaries are not involved in policymaking per se, but they do participate in decision making about the overall strategy to be employed in any communications policy. As already noted, Eisenhower, Kennedy, and Carter relied heavily on their press secretaries to formulate policy in this area, but Lyndon Johnson and Richard Nixon kept direct control over these kinds of operations.

Finally, a press secretary is an agent for three constituencies: the president, the White House staff, and the media. He must educate the president and his senior advisers about the legitimate needs of the working press, not an easy task since most presidents sooner or later come to be annoyed with the news media. The secretary tries to provide reporters with access to the administration as well as the information they need. The press secretary who fails to perform these elementary services for the news media cannot adequately promote the president's agenda. For example, Charles G. Ross, one of Truman's press aides, knew President Truman's views on most issues but was unable to meet the information requests of the press, with the result that complaints about his handling of the job mounted.

The press secretary stands at the apex of a huge public relations apparatus in the executive branch, which devotes an extraordinary amount of staff, resources, and time to generating a positive image of the president. One cannot estimate with precision the extent of these public relations activities in the White House, but one high-ranking official in the Ford administration suggested that more than 60 percent of the political staff was employed in publicizing the president.[105] As another index to these public relations activities, it was determined that, of the forty-nine White House assistants making more than $40,000 in 1977, slightly more than 30 percent were assigned to positions involving media relations.[106] Thus, the president's role as an opinion/party leader is buttressed by a large professional staff, whose establishment has evolved mainly in the period since Franklin D. Roosevelt.

CRISIS

The extraordinary degree of public commitment to the presidency is highlighted by the political crisis caused when a president is stricken by illness or by an assassin. There have been assassination attempts on nine presidents and four (Lincoln, Garfield, McKinley, and Kennedy) were killed. It seems the number of assassination attempts on presidents or on presidential candidates has increased in recent years. Senator Robert Kennedy was killed in Los Angeles on the day he won the 1968 California presidential primary, and Alabama's Governor George Wallace was crippled by an assassin's bullet as he campaigned in the 1972 Maryland primary. There were two attempts on President Ford's life, and in 1981 a would-be assassin shot President Ronald Reagan.

There is some data to assess the public's reaction to the attempted assassination of Reagan. His approval rating increased 8 percentage points in less than a month.[107] In early March 60 percent of Americans approved his performance as president; by April 3–6 (days after the March 30 assassination attempt) Reagan's popularity rose to 67 percent; by May it reached 68 percent approval. By June, with Reagan no longer hospitalized and recovering from his wounds, his approval rating fell to 59 percent. Moreover, in light of this attempt on Reagan's life, a Gallup Poll found that the majority of Americans now believed that a president's safety was more important than his mingling with crowds. In 1975, following an assassination attempt on President Ford, a plurality of respondents (49%) still believed that the president should mingle with the people. The attack on Reagan, however, caused an 11 percent shift in public opinion, with 55 percent agreeing that such gestures are too risky today.

The popular mood following the murder of John F. Kennedy has been studied in more detail, and that research points up the great emotional attachment we, as a society, have for the president.

Kennedy's assassination

Based on a nationwide survey conducted by the National Opinion Research Center (NORC) within days of President Kennedy's assassination, Sheatsley and Feldman documented the ways people were affected by that tragedy. The public's reactions were coded as follows:[108]

"Felt sorry that a strong young man had been killed at the height of his powers"	88%
"Felt ashamed that this could happen in our country"	83%
"Felt the loss of someone very close and dear"	79%
"Felt angry that anyone should do such a terrible deed"	73%
"Worried about how his death would affect the political situation in this country"	47%
"Worried about how his death would affect our relations with other countries"	44%
"Felt worried about how the United States would carry on without its leader"	31%

As Greenstein observes, although the vast majority of Americans do not regularly engage in political conversations, the distress at President Kennedy's death was almost universal.[109] In many cases the reaction to his assassination was so profound and personalized that it resulted in physical symptoms. The NORC survey found that 43 percent of its sample experienced a loss of appetite during the four days following Kennedy's death, 48 percent reported insomnia, 25 percent had headaches, 68 percent reported feeling nervous and tense, and many Americans said they experienced "rapid heart beats" (26%) and perspiring (17%).[110]

Throughout the weekend following Kennedy's assassination, people seemed unable to carry on their normal activities. According to Sheatsley and Feldman, "The average adult spent eight hours on Friday, ten hours on Saturday, eight hours on Sunday and another eight hours on Monday listening to television and radio reports of the assassination and its aftermath."[111] This reaction to Kennedy's murder may be related to its violent nature as well as to his youthfulness, but Fred Greenstein argues that such considerations were less important than the fact that our president had been killed. Such mass outpourings of emotion do not generally accompany the deaths of other public figures, or even ex-presidents. However, the historical record suggests that comparable public reactions occurred after the deaths of President Garfield, McKinley, Harding, and Franklin D. Roosevelt. Research on how people reacted to Roosevelt's death, though he died of natural causes, showed a pattern similar to that exhibited after Kennedy's assassination.[112]

Consider this report of the popular mood after the unexpected death due to illness of Warren Harding, a president now considered to be one of our "failures":

> People in the streets around Times Square could hardly believe the news. A man in evening dress said, "It can't be true." There was a steady stream of telephone calls to newspaper offices by persons seeking to verify the news.
>
> Taxicab drivers, waiters, conductors, and people in all walks of life . . . echoed the same comment. "Why did not the doctors prepare the people for this sad announcement?"
>
> Meyer London, Socialist Congressman: "Oh, what a calamity. This is a tremendous shock. . . Politics are now forgotten in the love all factions had for him as a man."
>
> August 10, 1923, was the official day of mourning. All public activity was suspended for that day; banks, stores, theaters, and movie houses were closed. At noon, the entire nation observed two minutes' silence in honor of the dead President.[113]

The assassination of a president obviously has profound consequence for our society, and the public clearly shares this perception of such an event. Greenstein argues that the degree of psychological stress witnessed after Kennedy's death was greater than during the Cuban missile crisis, when a naked confrontation between the United States and the Soviet Union was taking place.

Watergate

Another crisis that deeply affected the nation, though it was of a very different nature, was Watergate. Although Richard Nixon's behavior was scandalous, surveys of public opinion indicated the degree to which Americans wanted to believe in their president and in the presidency as an institution of government. The impact of Watergate on public opinion was documented in numerous Gallup Polls taken during 1973 and 1974. Three general conclusions can be drawn from these data.[114] First, the Watergate scandal was chiefly responsible for undermining President Nixon's public support. Nixon's approval rating reached a high of 67 percent in January 1973, which reflected his Vietnam peace settlement. But over the next six months it fell 44 points to a record low of 24 percent in mid-July. Before this decline began, in all but a few Gallup Polls taken during 1969–1972 and through April 1973, Richard Nixon's performance as president was "approved" by a majority of the respondents. However, beginning in April 1973 less than a majority approved of his performance. After John Dean implicated President Nixon in the Watergate cover-up in his testimony before Congress, Nixon's popularity fell below 40 percent. When, in October 1973, Richard Nixon fired Archibald Cox, the first special prosecutor appointed to investigate the charges, the president's approval rating dropped below 30 percent and never rose above that level. From October 1973 through August 1974 Nixon's approval ratings fluctuated between 24 and 28 percent.

The survey data also indicate the public came to perceive Watergate as a serious matter, and one that directly involved President Nixon. During the 1972 presidential election, George McGovern was unable to convince the electorate that the burglary and illegal wiretapping of the Democratic National Committee in the Watergate complex in June 1972 disclosed corruption in the government. Three months after the break-in, in September 1972, a bare majority (52 percent) had heard or read about this incident. Moreover, Gallup Polls showed that eight of ten voters did not think that Watergate was important enough to convince them to vote for McGovern. As more details about Watergate and related illegalities began to surface, the scandal dominated the news. In April 1973, eighty-three percent of the respondents had heard or read about Watergate, and by June 1973 virtually everybody (98 percent) had heard or read about it. At first the public viewed Watergate as "just politics"; this was the judgment held by 67 percent of the people surveyed by Gallup in April 1973. But this assessment changed radically. By June 1973 a plurality (47 percent) thought that Watergate revealed corruption in the Nixon administration, and in August 1973 a majority (53 percent) held this view of the matter. Moreover, public opinion implicated Richard Nixon in the Watergate affair.

During the period from June 1973 through August 1974 several Gallup Polls asked respondents to assess the degree of Nixon's involvement in this scandal. Four options were provided:

1. Nixon planned the Watergate 'bugging' from the beginning.
2. Nixon did not plan the 'bugging' but knew about it before it took place.
3. Nixon found out about the 'bugging' after it occurred, but tried to cover it up.

4. Nixon had no knowledge of the 'bugging,' and spoke up as soon as he learned about it.

On this series of Gallup Polls, 8–11 percent believed that Nixon "planned" Watergate, whereas those respondents feeling that he had "no knowledge" of it ranged from 15–23 percent. Therefore, a consensus emerged in public opinion, beginning at least by June 1973, that Nixon either had known about Watergate in advance (24–32 percent) or had tried to cover it up (31–40 percent). The final Gallup Poll taken in August 1974 showed that 64 percent of Americans surveyed held one or the other of these views regarding Nixon's involvement in Watergate.

In the public's mind, Watergate was not simply political mischief but a serious matter of corruption at the highest level of government. A plurality of Americans believed that Nixon tried to cover up the bugging, and the second largest number of respondents thought that he knew about Watergate in advance. As a result, Nixon suffered in his approval ratings and, beginning in January 1974, a plurality of respondents said that they wanted Vice-President Gerald Ford, rather than Nixon, to be president. And yet despite Richard Nixon's culpability, the American people resisted his removal from office.

Public sentiment to actually remove Richard Nixon from the presidency developed more slowly. Not until August 1974, just days before his resignation and amidst rumors of Nixon's pending departure from office, did a majority (57 percent) favor his removal from the presidency. In analyzing the impeachment proceedings against President Nixon, Robert Sherrill argues that Congress

> moved with extreme reluctance and only after many felonies and subversions of statutory law had been traced to the White House. If a Democratic Congress was that hesitant to move against a Republican President so plainly guilty of having violated the law . . . then it is clear that the impeachment process has little appeal to Congress.[115]

Apparently the public had a similar view of the matter.

From June 1973 through February 1974, this question was asked by Gallup Polls on eight occasions: "Do you think President Nixon should be impeached and compelled to leave the presidency, or not?"[116] While there was a trend in public opinion favoring Nixon's removal from office during this nine-month period, in every survey a majority was opposed to that action. Thus, in June 1973 19 percent had answered "yes" to that question while 69 percent said "no"; by February 1974 these statistics were, respectively, 38 percent and 51 percent. Thereafter, the Gallup Polls asked respondents these two related questions:

> Now let me ask you first of all, if you think there is enough evidence of possible wrongdoing in the case of President Nixon to bring him to trial before the Senate, or not?

Just from the way you feel now, do you think his actions are serious enough to warrant his being removed from the presidency, or not?

The percentage of responses to each question in the *affirmative* for five Gallup Polls is given below.[117]

	"Yes" Response	
	Trial	*Removal*
April 1974	52%	46%
May 1974	51	48
June 1974	50	44
July 1974	51	46
August 1974	65	57

In spite of the fact that the majority of Americans consistently believed that the seriousness of Nixon's crimes warranted a trial for impeachment in the Senate, less than a majority was willing to see him forced from office. The marked increase in the percent favoring Nixon's removal between July and August probably was influenced by the general expectation that he would be leaving his office soon. That final Gallup Poll was taken during August 2–5, and Richard Nixon announced his resignation on August 8. Once Richard Nixon became a private citizen, however, public opinion favored his prosecution to the extent allowed by the law. No doubt this sentiment was affected by the very act of his resignation (which implied guilt) coupled with Nixon's pardon by President Ford "for all offenses against the United States which he . . . has committed or may have committed." Ford took this action, he said, to avoid a "divisive debate" over Watergate, but it hurt him politically. After he announced the pardon, President Ford's popularity fell 22 percent.[118]

CONCLUSIONS

The president's weakness as opinion/party leader is tied to the fact that little authority is available in this role and to the decentralized nature of decision making that affects public opinion. Political activity in this role is very fluid and open to citizen influences. Parties, social movements and dissident protests, interest groups, the mass media, and opinion polls all influence the president's standing in public opinion; they shape the political agenda by which his performance in office is measured. Thus, as the "civic" embodiment of the nation, the people rally around the presidency as an institution of government. This consensus, however, deteriorates once a president begins to exert his "political" leadership. Fundamental to opinion/party leadership is the problem that a president's electoral majority is ephemeral, with the result that every president in modern times suffers a long-term decline in approval ratings. This pattern suggests, therefore, that virtually no course of action by the president can be undertaken without some measure of political liability.

The public response to President Kennedy's assassination shows, in a positive way, the tremendous affection Americans have for a president. Yet a similar lesson can be drawn from the public's reaction to Watergate, though for precisely the opposite reasons. In this case, the reluctance of citizens and Congress to remove Nixon from the presidency, in spite of his criminal conduct, shows that people hold a reservoir of good will for that institution of government. For this reason it is unlikely that Watergate will tarnish permanently our admiration for the office of the president. As Patterson, Davidson, and Ripley argue, "Average citizens apparently continue to *want* to believe in the presidency, even when incumbent presidents betray their trust."[119]

NOTES

[1]Clinton Rossiter, *The American Presidency*, 2nd ed. (New York: Harcourt, Brace and World, 1960), chapter 1.

[2]Louis W. Koenig, *The Chief Executive*, 3rd ed. (New York: Harcourt Brace Jovanovich, 1975), p. 92.

[3]Edward S. Corwin and Louis W. Koenig, *The Presidency Today* (New York: New York University Press, 1956), pp. 13–14.

[4]Charles C. Thach, *The Creation of the Presidency* (Baltimore: Johns Hopkins Press, 1922), p. 86.

[5]Jean Yarbrough, "Representation and Republicanism: Two Views," in Daniel J. Elazar, ed., *Republicanism, Representation, and Consent: Views of the Founding Era* (New Brunswick, N.J.: Transaction Books, 1979), p. 97.

[6]Willmoore Kendall, "The Two Majorities," *Midwest Journal of Political Science* (November 1960), p. 336.

[7]Grant McConnell, *The Modern Presidency* (New York: St. Martin's Press, 1967), p. 35.

[8]James MacGregor Burns, *Presidential Government* (Boston: Houghton Mifflin, 1973), p. 330.

[9]Harry V. Jaffa, "The Nature and Origin of the American Party System," in Robert A. Goldwin, ed., *Political Parties, U.S.A.* (Chicago: Rand McNally, 1964), pp. 71–72.

[10]William MacDonald, *Jacksonian Democracy: 1829–1837* (New York: Harper and Brothers, 1906), pp. 185–186.

[11]Leonard D. White, *The Jacksonians: A Study in Administrative History, 1829–1861* (New York: The Free Press, 1954), p. 17.

[12]Francis N. Thorpe, ed., *The Statesmanship of Andrew Jackson* (New York: Tandy-Thomas Company, 1909), p. 42.

[13]Arthur M. Schlesinger, Jr., *The Age of Jackson* (New York: Book Find Club-Little Brown, 1945), p. 46.

[14]Cited in Rowland Egger, *The President of the United States* (New York: McGraw-Hill, 1972), p. 172.

[15]Louis W. Koenig, *The Chief Executive*, p. 132.

[16]Ibid., p. 133.

[17]Raymond Tatalovich, "Electoral Votes and Presidential Campaign Trails, 1932–1976," *American Politics Quarterly* (October 1979), pp. 489–498.

[18]Cited in David V. Edwards, *The American Political Experience* (Englewood Cliffs: Prentice-Hall, 1979), p. 373.

[19]George Reedy, *The Twilight of the Presidency* (New York: World, 1970), pp. 100–101.

[20]For an excellent discussion of the establishment of four major news organizations—*Time*, the *Los Angeles Times*, CBS News, and the *Washington Post*—see David Halberstam, *The Powers That Be* (New York: Knopf, 1979).

[21]Cited in Milton C. Cummings, Jr. and David Wise, *Democracy Under Pressure* (New York: Harcourt Brace Jovanovich, 1981), p. 282.

[22]Nelson Polsby and Aaron Wildavsky, *Presidential Elections* (New York: Scribner's, 1968), p. 181.

[23]Elmer E. Cornwell, Jr., *Presidential Leadership of Public Opinion* (Bloomington: Indiana University Press, 1966), p. 145.

[24]Cited in Samuel C. Patterson; Roger H. Davidson; and Randall B. Ripley, *A More Perfect Union* (Homewood, Ill.: Dorsey, 1979), pp. 357–358.

[25]See Timothy Crouse, *The Boys on the Bus* (New York: Ballantine, 1972).

[26]S. Robert Lichter and Stanley Rothman, "Media and Business Elites," *Public Opinion* (October/November 1981), pp. 42–46, 59–60.

[27]Quoted in Edwards, *The American Political Experience*, p. 387.

[28]Michael Baruch Grossman and Martha Joynt Kumar, *Portraying the President: The White House and the News Media* (Baltimore: Johns Hopkins University Press, 1981), chapter 10.

[29]Ibid., p. 253.

[30]Charles V. Hamilton, *American Government* (Glenview, Ill.: Scott, Foresman and Company, 1982), p. 329.

[31]Richard Neustadt, *Presidential Power: The Politics of Leadership with Reflections on Johnson and Nixon* (New York: John Wiley & Sons, 1976), ch. 4–5.

[32]James C. Thomson, Jr., "Government and Press: Good News about a Bad Marriage," *New York Times Magazine* (November 25, 1973), p. 44.

[33]For an elaboration on the conflicts between the executive and the media see Byron W. Daynes, "Press Access to and Government Control Over Public Information: Criminal Justice Issues," *Occasional Paper*, Division of Governmental Studies and Services, Washington State University, Pullman, Wash., May 1980.

[34]From an interview between Richard Nixon and Howard K. Smith, "Every Four Years: A Study of the Presidency," part 2, PBS Television Documentary on the Presidency, 1980.

[35]Grossman and Kumar, *Portraying the President: The White House and the News Media*, chapter 11. Their analysis is followed in our discussion in this section.

[36]Ibid., p. 280.

[37]Robert MacNeil, *The People Machine* (New York: Harper and Row, 1968), p. 294.

[38]David S. Broder, "The 'Good News' School of Politics," *Boston Globe* (April 6, 1980), p. A7.

[39]Joseph Kraft, *Profiles in Power: A Washington Insight* (New York: New American Library, 1966), p. 93.

[40]These episodes are cited in Louis W. Koenig, 3rd ed., *The Chief Executive*, p. 108

[41]Grossman and Kumar, *Portraying the President: The White House and the News Media*, p. 290.

[42]Cited in David V. Edwards, *The American Political Experience* (Englewood Cliffs, N.J.: Prentice-Hall, 1979), p. 188.

[43]Fred I. Greenstein, *Children and Politics* (New Haven: Yale University Press, 1965); Robert D. Hess and Judith V. Torney, *The Development of Political Attitudes in Children* (New York: Anchor Books, 1968); David Easton and Jack Dennis, *Children in the Political System* (New York: McGraw-Hill, 1969).

[44]Fred I. Greenstein, "More on Children's Images of the President," in Aaron Wildavsky, ed., *The Presidency* (Boston: Little, Brown and Company, 1969), p. 290.

[45]Hess and Torney, *The Development of Political Attitudes in Children*, p. 45.

[46]Robert Coles, "The Politics of Middle-Class Children," *New York Review of Books* (March 6, 1975).

[47]Dean Jaros; Herbert Hirsch; and Frederic J. Fleron, Jr., "The Malevolent Leader: Political Socialization in an American Sub-Culture," *American Political Science Review* (June 1968), p. 569.

[48]Jack Dennis and Carol Webster, "Children's Images of the President and of Government in 1962 and 1974," *American Politics Quarterly* (October 1975), p. 394.

[49]Dean Jaros and John Shoemaker, "The Malevolent Unindicted Co-Conspirator: Watergate and Appalachian Youth," *American Politics Quarterly* (October 1975), pp. 483–506.

[50]F. Christopher Arterton, "The Impact of Watergate on Children's Attitudes Toward Political Authority," *Political Science Quarterly* (June 1974), pp. 269–288; F. Christopher Arterton, "Watergate and Children's Attitudes Toward Authority Revisited," *Political Science Quarterly* (Fall 1975), pp. 477–496.

[51]Fred I. Greenstein, "What the President Means to Americans," in James D. Barber, ed., *Choosing the President* (Englewood Cliffs, N.J.: Prentice-Hall, 1974), p. 125.

[52]Hadley Cantril, ed., *Public Opinion 1935–1946* (Princeton, N.J.: Princeton University Press, 1951), p. 590.

[53]American Institute of Public Opinion, survey no. 558 (January 4, 1956). Cited in Burns, *Presidential Government*, p. 100.

[54]American Institute of Public Opinion, *Public Opinion 1972–1977*, vol. I (Wilmington, Del.: Scholarly Resources Inc., 1978), pp. 641–643.

[55]A U.S. Historical Society Poll in 1977 ranked the top ten presidents as follows: Lincoln, Washington, Franklin Roosevelt, Jefferson, Theodore Roosevelt, Wilson, Jackson, Truman, Polk, and John Adams. Kennedy was ranked thirteenth, Eisenhower sixteenth, Lyndon Johnson eleventh, and Nixon shared the twenty-second ranking with six other presidents. Cited in John A. Moore, Jr. and Myron Roberts, *The Pursuit of Happiness* (New York: Macmillan, 1981), p. 110. In 1982 the *Chicago Tribune* asked its respondents to choose the ten best and the ten worst presidents. The best were Lincoln, Washington, Franklin Roosevelt, Theodore Roosevelt, Jefferson, Wilson, Jackson, Truman, Eisenhower, and Polk. The ten worst were Harding, Nixon, Buchanan, Pierce, Grant, Fillmore, Andrew Johnson, Coolidge, Tyler, and Jimmy Carter. See "Our Best and Worst Presidents," *Chicago Tribune*, magazine section (January 10, 1982), p. 9. Eisenhower's improved standing in these surveys indicates that many observers are reevaluating his presidential impact. As one example of this kind of analysis, see Fred I. Greenstein, "Eisenhower as an Activist President: A Look at New Evidence," *Political Science Quarterly* (Winter 1979–1980), pp. 575–599.

[56]Roberta S. Sigel and David J. Butler, "The Public and the No Third Term Tradition: Inquiry into Attitudes Toward Power," *Midwest Journal of Political Science* (February 1964), pp. 39–54.

[57]Roberta S. Sigel, "Image of the American Presidency: Part II of an Exploration into Popular Views of Presidential Power," in Aaron Wildavsky, ed., *The Presidency* (Boston: Little, Brown and Company, 1969), pp. 296–309.

[58]See James D. Wright, "The Real Danger in Alienation," *The Nation* (January 17, 1976).

[59]Cited in Erwin C. Hargrove, *The Power of the Modern Presidency* (New York: Alfred A. Knopf, 1974), p. 17.

[60]Ibid.

[61]A poll taken by the Michigan Survey Research Center in November 1973, for example, showed that 44 percent believed that the president should have less influence over policy whereas 45 percent said that Congress should have more influence. Cited in Hargrove, *The Power of the Modern Presidency*, pp. 17–18.

[62]Cited in Milton C. Cummings, Jr. and David Wise, *Democracy Under Pressure* (New York: Harcourt Brace Jovanovich, 1981), p. 440.

[63]Daniel Yankelovich, "Farewell to 'President Knows Best,' " *Foreign Affairs* (1979), pp. 670–693.

[64]Ibid., p. 670.

[65]Jack Dennis, "Who Supports the Presidency?," *Society* (July/August, 1976), pp. 48–53.

[66]Ibid., p. 51.

[67]Ibid., p. 53.

[68]Samuel Kernell; Peter W. Sperlich; and Aaron Wildavsky, "Public Support for Presidents," in Aaron Wildavsky, ed., *Perspectives on the Presidency* (Boston: Little, Brown, 1975), pp. 148–181.

[69]Ibid., p. 178.

[70]These five psychological functions were formulated by Fred I. Greenstein during the early 1960s; see his analysis in "The Psychological Functions of the Presidency for Citizens," in Elmer E.Cornwell, *The American Presidency: Vital Center* (Glenview, Ill.: Scott, Foresman and Company, 1966), pp. 30–36. Later he added a sixth function, the president as " 'lightning rod' or object of displacement." By this Greenstein means that the people also tend to blame the president personally when things go badly. This is implied in such phrases as "Hoover's Depression" or Nixon's "mess in Washington." See the discussion in Greenstein, "What the President Means to Americans," in James David Barber, ed., *Choosing the President* (Englewood Cliffs, N.J.: Prentice-Hall, 1974), pp. 146–147.

[71]Greenstein, "The Psychological Functions of the Presidency for Citizens," p. 35.

[72]Greenstein, "What the President Means to Americans," p. 144.

[73]*The Gallup Opinion Index*, report no. 183 (December 1980), p. 57.

[74]John E. Mueller, "Presidential Popularity from Truman to Johnson," *American Political Science Review* (March 1970), pp. 136–148.

[75]Theodore J. Lowi, *American Government: Incomplete Conquest* (Hinsdale, Ill.: Dryden Press, 1976), pp. 440–442.

[76]See Samuel Kernell, "Explaining Presidential Popularity: How Ad Hoc Theorizing, Misplaced Emphasis, and Insufficient Care in Measuring One's Variables Refuted Common Sense and Led Conventional Wisdom Down the Path of Anomalies," *American Political Science Review* (June 1978), pp. 506–522.

[77]James A. Stimson, "Public Support for American Presidents: A Cyclical Model," *Public Opinion Quarterly* (Spring 1976), pp. 1–21.

[78]Henry C. Kenski, "The Impact of Economic Conditions on Presidential Popularity," *Journal of Politics* (August 1977), pp. 764–773.

[79]Samuel Kernell, "Explaining Presidential Popularity," p. 518.

[80]Kristen R. Monroe, "Inflation and Presidential Popularity," *Presidential Studies Quarterly* (Summer 1979), pp. 334–340.

[81]Ibid., p. 339.

[82]Richard A. Brody and Benjamin I. Page, "The Impact of Events on Presidential Popularity: The Johnson and Nixon Administration," in Aaron Wildavsky, ed., *Perspectives on the Presidency* (Boston: Little, Brown and Company, 1975), pp. 136–148.

[83]See Angus Campbell, "Surge and Decline: A Study of Electoral Change," *Public Opinion Quarterly* (Fall 1960), pp. 397–418.

[84]Much of this discussion is based on Austin Ranney, "The 1978 Congressional Elections: A Renaissance for Republicans?" *Public Opinion* (March/April 1978), pp. 17–20.

[85]Ibid., p. 18.

[86]Samuel Kernell, "Presidential Popularity and Negative Voting: An Alternative Explanation of the Midterm Congressional Decline of the President's Party," *American Political Science Review* (March 1977), pp. 44–66.

[87]Edward R. Tufte, "Determinants of the Outcomes of Midterm Congressional Elections," *American Political Science Review* (September 1975), pp. 812–826.

[88]Edward S. Corwin and Louis W. Koenig, *The Presidency Today*, p. 66.

[89]Louis W. Koenig, *The Chief Executive*, 2nd ed. (New York: Harcourt Brace Jovanovich, 1968), p. 184.

[90]Ibid.

[91]Ibid., p. 185.

[92]Louis W. Koenig, *The Chief Executive*, 3rd ed. (New York: Harcourt Brace Jovanovich, 1975), p. 104.

[93]Thomas Bailey, *Presidential Greatness* (New York: Appleton Century, 1967), p. 201.

[94]Erwin Hargrove, *Presidential Leadership* (New York: Macmillan, 1966), p. 20.

[95]The discussion to follow is based on the analysis in Elmer E. Cornwell, Jr., *Presidential Leadership of Public Opinion* (Bloomington: Indiana University Press, 1966), especially chapters 7 and 8.

[96]John Gunther, *Roosevelt in Retrospect* (New York: Harper, 1950), p. 22.

[97]Cornwell, *Presidential Leadership of Public Opinion*, p. 160.

[98]Ibid., p. 192.

[99]Richard Rovere, "Letter from Washington," *New Yorker* (February 4, 1961), p. 112.

[100]Fred I. Greenstein, "Change and Continuity in the Modern Presidency," in Anthony King, ed., *The New American Political System* (Washington, D.C.: American Enterprise Institute for Public Policy Research, 1978), pp. 74–75.

[101]William C. Spragens, *The Presidency and the Mass Media in the Age of Television* (Washington, D.C.: University Press of America, 1979), p. 253.

[102]Grossman and Kumar, *Portraying the President: The White House and the News Media* (Baltimore: Johns Hopkins University Press, 1981), p. 130. This volume gives a very comprehensive analysis of media relationships in the executive branch, and we rely on its argument for much of the discussion to follow.

[103]Ibid., p. 149.

[104]These four roles are elaborated on ibid., pp. 136–147.

[105]Ibid., p. 83.

[106]Ibid., p. 84.

[107]The opinion data on Reagan's popularity and on the public's view regarding the president's safety are found in *The Gallup Report*, report no. 187 (April 1981), pp. 2–3 and report no. 189 (June 1981), pp. 11–13 (Princeton, N.J. The Gallup Poll, 1981).

[108]Paul B. Sheatsley and Jacob J. Feldman, "The Assassination of President Kennedy: A Preliminary Report on Public Reactions and Behavior," *Public Opinion Quarterly* (Summer 1964), pp. 189–215.

[109]Greenstein, "What the President Means to Americans," pp. 123–124.

[110]Sheatsley and Feldman, "The Assassination of President Kennedy: A Preliminary Report on Public Reactions and Behavior," pp. 189–215.

[111]Ibid., p. 197.

[112]See Harold Orlansky, "Reactions to the Death of President Roosevelt," *Journal of Social Psychology* (1947), pp. 235–266.

[113]Ibid., p. 264.

[114]The discussion to follow is based on selected Gallup Polls reported in American Institute of Public Opinion, Public Opinion 1972–1977, vol. 1 (Wilmington, Del.: Scholarly Resources Inc., 1978), pp. 128, 133, 139, 158, 167, 184, 208, 311–314.

[115]Robert Sherrill, *Governing America* (New York: Harcourt Brace Jovanovich, 1978), p. 318.

[116]American Institute of Public Opinion, *Public Opinion 1972–1977*, p. 334.

[117]Ibid.

[118]A special survey conducted immediately after Ford announced Nixon's pardon on September 9, 1974 showed that 62 percent disapproved of that action. Two years later, a Gallup Poll taken in June 1976 showed that 55 percent still believed that the pardon was the wrong thing for Ford to do. A Gallup Poll taken during August 1974 showed that 58 percent felt that Nixon should "be tried for possible

criminal charges arising from Watergate," and 53 percent stated that Ford should not give him a pardon "if Nixon is brought to trial and found guilty." See ibid., pp. 354–359, 799–801.

[119]Patterson; Davidson; and Ripley, *A More Perfect Union*, p. 396.

SUGGESTED READINGS

Bloom, Melvyn. *Public Relations and Presidential Campaigns.* New York: Thomas Y. Crowell, 1973.

Broder, David. *The Party's Over.* New York: Harper and Row, 1972.

Burnham, Walter Dean. *Critical Elections and the Mainsprings of American Politics.* New York: W. W. Norton, 1970.

Burns, James MacGregor. *Deadlock of Democracy: Four Party Politics in America.* Englewood Cliffs, N.J.:Prentice-Hall, 1963.

Chambers, William, and Burnham, Walter Dean, eds. *The American Party System: Stages of Political Development.* London: Oxford University Press, 1967.

Cornwell, Elmer E., Jr. *Presidential Leadership of Public Opinion.* Bloomington: Indiana University Press, 1965.

────── *The American Presidency: Vital Center.* Glenview, Ill.: Scott, Foresman, 1966.

Grossman, Michael B., and Kumar,Martha J. *Portraying the President: The White House and the News Media.* Baltimore: Johns Hopkins University Press, 1981.

Hardin, Charles. *Presidential Power and Accountability.* Chicago: University of Chicago Press, 1974.

Ladd, Everett Carl, Jr. *American Political Parties.* W. W. Norton, 1970.

McGinnis, Joseph. *The Selling of the President, 1968.* New York: Trident Press, 1969.

Mendlson, Harold, and Crespi, Irving. *Polls, Television and the New Politics.* Scranton, Penn.: Chandler Publishers, 1970.

Minow, Newton N., Martin, John Bartlow, and Mitchell, Lee M. *Presidential Television.* New York: Basic Books, 1973.

Nimmo, Dan, and Savage, Robert. *Candidates and Their Images: Concepts, Methods and Findings.* Pacific Palisades, Calif.: Goodyear Publishing Co., 1976.

Novak, Michael. *Choosing Our King: Powerful Symbol in Presidential Politics.* New York: Macmillan, 1974.

Patterson, Thomas, and McClure, Thomas. *The Unseeing Eye.* New York: Putnam's Sons, 1976.

Spragens, William C. *The Presidency and the Mass Media in the Age of Television.* Washington, D.C.: University Press of America, 1979.

Sundquist, James L. *Dynamics of the Party System: Alignment and Realignment of Political Parties in the United States.* Washington, D.C.: Brookings Institution, 1973.

CHAPTER FOUR

Legislative Leader: An Uncertain Mandate For Presidential Power

Over the years the president has become known variously as "legislative leader," "chief legislator," and even "initiator-in-chief."[1] These titles imply an active relationship between the president and Congress, with policy-making at its core. Without question this relationship is one of the most important in our political system, yet it is not well understood. Arthur Schlesinger, Jr. makes the analogy to guerrilla warfare, with Congress attacking in ambush against the commanding forces and firepower of the executive.[2] Other scholars have made similar allusions in describing this relationship. Joan MacLean called it one of "deadlock, intermittent warfare, even hostility."[3]

Conflict is a notable attribute of the relationship between the president and Congress. The causes of this contentious behavior are many: the president may veto important acts of Congress, refuse to appoint persons having legislative support to administrative offices, or neglect to consult with congressmen or senators on key policy issues. Conflict results also when the president tries to insulate his staff, and himself, from legislative inquiries. But more fundamentally, conflict results because the president and Congress represent different constituencies and must contend with differing electoral cycles. All members of the House of Representatives, in particular, must face the electorate every two years, and for this reason congressmen may be especially beholden to constituents when they vote on legislation. On the other hand, senators have six-year terms, meaning that one-third of the Senate never faces reelection during the tenure of a one-term president, such as Jimmy Carter. Moreover, ideological and partisan differences can affect executive/legislative relations. When John F. Kennedy launched his New Frontier in 1961, his clashes with Congress over social-welfare programs affirmed the suspicion of many political scientists that Congress was indeed the bastion of conservatism, localism, and special interests. This was not the case, however, when Richard Nixon confronted a more liberal Congress, one dominated by the Democratic party. Yet both Nixon's and Kennedy's experiences show that ideological differences between the president and Congress can be the underlying cause of much conflict between the branches of government.

Conflict does not characterize the entire relationship between the president and Congress, for cooperation does occur at times. During international crises as well as in matters affecting foreign policy, a large measure of cooperation displaces conflict as the salient pattern of executive/legislative interaction. Moreover, the separation of powers principle has been undermined by acts of Congress that delegate policymaking functions to the president. The Budget and Accounting Act of 1921, for example, enabled the president to prepare the federal budget for the Congress. On the other hand, in reaction to Nixon's excessive impoundment of funds appropriated by the Congress, the legislative branch regained a measure of control over the budgetary process by enacting the Congressional Budget and Impoundment Control Act of 1974.

The fact that both conflict and cooperation affect the legislative leader role has implications for the presidency, because a president's domestic leadership is judged largely in terms of his being able to enact major legislation. Edward Corwin and Louis Koenig suggest that "virtually all presidents who have made a major impact on American history have done so in great degree as legislative leaders."[4] They point to Andrew Jackson's crusade against the National Bank, Theodore Roosevelt's Square Deal, Woodrow Wilson's New Freedom, Franklin D. Roosevelt's New Deal, and Harry Truman's Fair Deal. As these examples show, Democrats rather than Republicans have had singular impact on developing the role of legislative leader. One is hard pressed to remember the legislative agendas set forth by Harding, Coolidge, Hoover, or Eisenhower, although Ronald Reagan's reordering of domestic priorities and his New Federalism may be an exception to this pattern.

The majority of American presidents have not been effective legislative leaders, and most presidents have been frustrated in this role at one time or another. Gerald R. Ford, who was a congressman before he became president, was especially sensitive to these frustrations. He articulated the hope of all presidents who want to be effective leaders when he said, "As president, within the limits of basic principles, my motto towards the Congress is communication, conciliation, compromise and cooperation . . . I do not want a honeymoon . . . I want a good marriage."[5] Unfortunately for Gerald Ford, he had neither a successful marriage with the Congress nor a very long honeymoon period. In the wake of Richard Nixon's confrontations with Congress, the legislative branch insisted on regaining a measure of control over policymaking after Ford assumed the presidency.

THREE CASES OF LEGISLATIVE LEADERSHIP

Success as legislative leader requires an appreciation of the subtle uses of political persuasion, for no president has enough authority in this role to meet his needs. Though most presidents have had only modest success in this role, certain presidents have achieved tremendous successes in shaping the lawmaking process for their own ends. By comparing the leadership style of two presidents who effectively wielded political power in this role with the leadership style of a president who was quite ineffectual as legislative leader, one can begin to understand which factors underlie presidential power as legislative leader. In this discussion, we will focus on Thomas Jefferson, the most effective legislative leader of the nineteenth century, and Lyndon Johnson, whose twentieth-century achievements may eclipse even those of Franklin D. Roosevelt. We will also analyze the serious problems faced by Jimmy Carter in trying to deal with the Congress.

Jefferson

Thomas Jefferson was the first president to exert recognized leadership in Congress. To do so he had to work to create a "party," assist in the election of its members to Congress, and maintain constant contacts with his supporters in Congress to assure acceptance of his proposals. The Jeffersonian-Republicans were a rather loosely knit group sharing a common dislike for the Federalist "aristocrats" and what they represented.[6] Moreover, the Jeffersonian-Republicans were a heterogeneous, often disunited group in Congress. They did not support Thomas Jefferson's programs in every instance. To the contrary, Jefferson's success with Congress, in part, was based on his personal involvement in the legislative process, his understanding of congressional politics, and his ability to bargain and persuade.

Congress itself was very different during that period. Committee chairmen were not as strong, nor were leadership positions routinized. There were no formalized party leaders, party whips, or party committees as we find today in Congress. James Young suggests that for these reasons legislative politics during Jefferson's day is not comparable to the situation in Congress during the twentieth century. In addition, there was high membership turnover, conflicting constituency interests, and internal procedures that encouraged party factionalism. Young concludes, "parties on the Hill were largely unorganized groups."[7]

Perhaps this is too harsh an appraisal. Party caucuses became organized as early as 1801, and discernible voting blocs were evident in Congress even before Thomas Jefferson was elected president.[8] There were designated, though informal, floor leaders for the Jeffersonian-Republicans in Congress. Among these party leaders was John Randolph, but according to Robert Johnstone, as many as twenty men functioned as "leaders" for the administration during the Jefferson years.[9] These party leaders worked closely with Thomas Jefferson to gain adoption of his programs. Since Thomas

Jefferson was swept into office in 1800 with party majorities in both houses of Congress, he had a potentially firm base of support from which to operate. Jefferson's major accomplishment was Congress' approval of the 1803 Louisiana Purchase and a bill establishing a government for that territory. President Jefferson called the Congress into session three weeks early to capitalize on the groundswell of public support for the treaty, and it took the Senate only four days to approve the document, with voting strictly following party lines. The legislation governing the Louisiana Territory also was approved in spite of Federalist opposition.

A key to Jefferson's success as legislative leader was his attitude toward Congress along with his personal involvement in the lawmaking process. His attitude has been described as "deferential."[10] He vetoed no legislation, and in an early presidential message Jefferson indicated that ". . . nothing shall be wanting on my part to inform as far as in my powers the legislative judgment, nor to carry that judgment into faithful execution."[11] Jefferson's approach was not overt but indirect: he constantly made suggestions to Congress though he did not let it be known that they were his ideas. He was always careful to keep his role in Congress from public view.[12] His pressures on the legislative branch, while ever-present, were never overbearing.

Jefferson seemed to enjoy active involvement in this role. He visited Congress frequently, personally interviewed the legislators, and helped to recruit and select party leaders. He even wrote many of his own bills and amendments for Congress' consideration. In addition, he would supply other relevant information to committees when needed, as Noble Cunningham indicates:

> Jefferson's annual and special messages presented numerous recommendations for action; and, while these messages contained only broad outlines, he privately communicated specific details to legislative leaders and members sympathetic to presidential proposals.[13]

Jefferson also utilized cabinet members and department secretaries to lobby in Congress and to testify before committees in behalf of his policies.

Jefferson encouraged his administrative secretaries to help write pieces of legislation. The relationship between Sen. Abraham Baldwin and Secretary of the Treasury Albert Gallatin shows that the contact between Congress and the administration was often close. Senators thought nothing of asking the administration for direct input into legislation before Congress. As Senator Baldwin wrote Secretary Gallatin in 1802, ". . . the enclosed Bill has just been referred to a Select committee in the Senate. . . . Will you have the goodness to note on the bill any amendments which you think proper to recommend to their consideration?"[14]

Thomas Jefferson also used social contacts as an opportunity to win support from congressmen. He entertained various legislators at his home, and his dinners became well-known settings for encouraging party unity among the Jeffersonians. By bringing his partisans together, these dinners allowed them to interact with each other and with the president in an informal setting.

As effective as Jefferson was in the role of legislative leader, however, his power had its limits. Not only did opposition to his policies grow in the Federalist ranks, but occasionally Republican congressmen grew tired of the president's interference in the legislative process. Jefferson was even accused of violating the principles of the Jeffersonian-Republican party. One such clash involved his legislation establishing a government for the newly acquired Louisiana Territory. Some Republicans argued that Jefferson's bill gave the residents of that territory little say in their own government insofar as the president was empowered to select the governor and judges, while the legislature was to be appointed by the governor rather than elected.[15] The most damaging threat to party unity that Jefferson faced during his tenure concerned John Randolph, who had acted in Congress as House Ways and Means Committee chairman and as floor leader for the Republicans. Randolph was retained by Jefferson as floor leader until he came out in open opposition to the president on two issues: the president's compromise settlement of the Yazoo land claim controversy in 1804–1805 and the intended impeachment of Federalist Supreme Court Justice Samuel Chase. Jefferson had offered a compromise solution to the Georgia state legislature over its questionable cession of the disputed lands, but Randolph fought the compromise from the beginning and threatened to create disunity within the party. Jefferson was also upset with Randolph's mishandling of the Chase impeachment trial, which resulted in Chase's final acquittal in the Senate.

The formal break between Jefferson and Randolph came in 1805. This rupture in party unity affected other Republicans in the House of Representatives who had supported Randolph. So many Republicans, in fact, joined Randolph that a serious schism within the party was threatened, which could have destroyed the cordial relationship Jefferson had enjoyed with Congress over the years.[16] By early 1806, however, this threat to party unity had subsided, with Jefferson the victor. Unfortunately, the party reconciliation came just before Jefferson was to retire.

Thomas Jefferson showed his greatest strength as legislative leader during the first five years in office. During these early years the United States came as close to having "party government" as it has ever come. Not only did the Jeffersonian-Republicans control the presidency, the Senate, and the House of Representatives, but in the House the party had authority to select the speaker, who then could appoint all the standing committees and designate their chairmen.[17] This situation had the effect of centralizing power within Congress in the hands of the party organization. Clearly, Jefferson benefited from the arrangement. At the end of his first year in office, Jefferson wrote that Congress had "carried into execution steadily almost all the propositions submitted to them in my message at the opening of the session."[18] By 1805, however, his control over Congress waned, and after he announced his retirement in 1805 (to take effect at the end of his second term) Jefferson's ability to lead Congress was never again so strong.

Thus, the crucial element to Jefferson's success was his leadership of a *new* political party, dedicated not only to opposing the Federalists but also to following another set of governing principles. By having a sizable majority of his party in control of the House and Senate, Jefferson could exert his influence over the lawmaking process in subtle and indirect ways. Historians view the presidential election of 1800 as a watershed era in American politics. In ending Federalist rule, it created a new political agenda which mobilized the executive and legislative branches into a unified governing force. The Jeffersonian-Republicans had criticized Alexander Hamilton's direct intervention into the lawmaking process, but Jefferson had done exactly the same through the informal machinery of the political party. As James MacGregor Burns argues, Jefferson ". . . blithely ignored his own constitutional principles of earlier days and established a powerful regime of party government."[19] Although the nation changed dramatically in the next century and a half, the successes of Lyndon B. Johnson in the legislative leader role were also based on the strength of political party organizations.

Johnson

Unlike the Congress of Jefferson's period, by the late twentieth century the legislative process had become highly institutionalized.[20] Formalized party leadership positions and a highly decentralized decision-making system developed, based on the standing committees, whose members and chairmen were chosen by "seniority." Even though only two political parties now control all the seats in Congress, the Republican and Democratic parties are not unified organizations. Often Republicans and Southern Democrats join forces in a "conservative coalition" against Northern Democrats to oppose, and often defeat, key social-welfare programs. The fact that Lyndon Johnson overcame these difficulties to fashion an impressive number of Great Society victories was chiefly due to his political instincts and sophisticated knowledge of how Congress works, coupled with the party composition of the legislature. Moreover, Johnson assumed office following Kennedy's death, the first assassination of a president in about sixty years. Thus Lyndon Johnson began his tenure with an unusual degree of political unity in the country. The early 1960s were also times of relative economic prosperity and stability, which established a positive setting for Johnson's Great Society proposals. Finally, LBJ exploited his honeymoon period at the beginning of his term to present to Congress a massive agenda for domestic reforms.

Congress was especially responsive to Johnson's overtures, for one of their own members was now president. Although John Kennedy had served in Congress for fourteen years, he had not been a party leader, nor had he an especially distinguished legislative career. Lyndon B. Johnson had been the Democratic majority party leader in the Senate throughout the 1950s;

many observers argue that he exerted disproportionate power over law-making then because President Eisenhower assumed such "quiet leadership" over Congress.[21] As party leader, Johnson was a member of the Senate's "club," and enjoyed the respect of many senior Southern Democrats both in the Senate and in the House of Representatives. George Edwards points out that during this time the party was strong and party leaders could command the support needed to enact a presidential program.[22] This meant that Lyndon Johnson, as president, could deal with relatively few leaders in Congress and receive assurances of support for his programs. Important leaders, such as Speaker John McCormack and House Majority Party Leader Carl Albert, were confidants of the president.

In the election of 1964, Lyndon Johnson's margin of victory over Barry Goldwater constituted a landslide, and many more Democrats were elected to Congress. Democrats had majorities in both House (295 to 140) and Senate (68 to 32), the largest majorities the Democrats had enjoyed since 1937. This fact alone led one scholar to conclude that such majority rule in Congress would have allowed any president to successfully pass his legislative program.[23] Of more significance was the fact that a great many liberal Democrats were elected to Congress in 1964.[24] This sent a large "freshman" class to Congress, many of whom were carried into office on Johnson's broad coattails. These freshmen Democrats were especially supportive of Great Society legislation. Coinciding with this shift in the political control of Congress was Lyndon Johnson's great popularity with the American people at the beginning of his term. Johnson's approval rating in 1965 reached 66 percent, although his five-year average was only 56 percent.

The political environment, therefore, was extremely amenable to Johnson's legislative proposals. His success in getting them enacted, however, was also due to Johnson's own legislative skills and his use of liaison staff. President Johnson had inherited from John Kennedy astute personnel to operate the Office of Congressional Relations (OCR). Lawrence O'Brien, who was Kennedy's chief liaison aide, remained in this capacity during the first years of the Johnson administration. O'Brien's tasks were many, but his primary objective, as John Manley explains, was

> not unlike that of many successful bargainers in politics: to establish and maintain a bargaining relationship in which the flow of mutual support continued without the need for specific accounting or explicit trading. Tacit exchanges between the administration and Congressmen were the best exchanges: they testified to a high quality working relationship.[25]

The liaison staff under O'Brien provided Congress with information on administration proposals and actively solicited support for them. Thus, the OCR tried to maintain regular contact with congressmen and congressional leadership in both the House and Senate. The OCR also served Johnson as an intelligence network to gather data similar to what is collected by the party whip system. It polled Congressmen about pending legislation and tried to determine the probable vote outcome on specific bills. In doing this, the OCR attempted to guarantee Johnson that sufficient support for his policies was available both in the committees as well as on the floor. The liaison staff also made regular contact with the press to encourage favorable coverage of the president's programs. Lyndon Johnson insisted that liaison work be of high quality; after the 1964 election, he told Cabinet members, "I want to be especially sure that each of you selects a top man to serve as your legislative liaison. Next to the Cabinet officer himself, I consider this the most important office in the department."[26]

Lyndon Johnson's use of the Office of Congressional Relations was only part of a broad-based lobbying effort during his tenure. The OCR coordinated the lobbying efforts of all the departments, agencies, and major interest groups that might support administration policies. Furthermore, contact was made with groups who were against Johnson's programs, in an effort to soften their opposition. The lobbying strategy used for Johnson's Aid to Education Bill of 1965 is summarized by Richard Pious.

> U.S. Commissioner of Education Francis Keppel won support from Catholic lay organizations, Jack Valenti at the White House maintained communication with the Vatican apostolic delegate, Lee White worked with Jewish groups, Henry Hall Wilson rounded up southern support, and Douglas Cater drummed up support from the National Education Association.[27]

Although the OCR and other administration lobbyists were important in winning legislative support for Johnson's Great Society, Eric Davis's research suggests that the OCR "had little impact on the processes of policy development."[28] The OCR performed its major function as Johnson's primary observer of the legislative process, and as such served to protect the administration's interests. In addition, Davis concludes that the OCR acted as a "two-way transmission belt between President and Congress, serving as a conduit for messages flowing both ways along Pennsylvania Avenue."[29]

A legislative staff has only limited impact, however, unless the president fully supports its efforts. Lyndon Johnson certainly did. Johnson knew Congress' machinery, its processes, and the people to approach to get things done. According to Lawrence O'Brien, "President Johnson's knowledge in depth of the Congress and his close relationship with so many members" added much to the administration's liaison efforts. O'Brien added, "No detail of the legislative program was too minute to involve him. . . . For Johnson, Congress was a twenty-four-hour-a-day obsession."[30] Johnson not only made demands on Congress; he also wanted to service its members. Ralph Huitt recalls that Johnson told one of his subordinates, "We are always asking Congress to help us. Let's offer to help them."[31] Each liaison officer, therefore, was assigned to several congressmen to determine what the administration could do for them. As Johnson viewed it there is "but one way for a President to deal with the Congress, and that is continuously, incessantly, and without interruption. If it's really going to work, the relationship between the president and the Congress has got to be almost incestuous."[32]

Clearly Lyndon Johnson's "personal touches" with congressmen and the congressional leaders of both parties made him effective as a legislative leader, and distinguished him from other presidents. For example, he reached out for bipartisan support immediately after the Kennedy assassination. He approached various state governors about his legislative proposals, and those who became Johnson supporters pressured the congressmen from their states to follow Johnson's leadership. He posed for color photographs at the White House to give to legislators and their wives who were invited to the White House for dinner, signed bills in public before cameras to publicize those legislators who supported him, and made personal telephone calls saying "thank you" to congressmen who delivered votes on crucial bills. Johnson missed no opportunity to win the support of individual legislators. For instance, he personally apologized to Rep. William Hungate (D.–Mo.) when Hungate had to stay in Washington on a Friday for a critical vote and nearly missed a breakfast appointment the next morning in Springfield, Missouri. Johnson wired him at that breakfast apologizing for delaying "his outstanding young Congressman" and then commending him for his "patriotic commitment to the great goals in the path-breaking education bill now on the floor."[33]

Johnson also sent letters of thanks to politicians across the nation who supported the administration. Mayor Richard J. Daley of Chicago received one of these letters, in recognition that three of the most loyal supporters of the president were Democratic congressmen from Chicago. The message also acknowledged Daley's role in encouraging the congressmen to support Johnson's program.[34] In 1965, Johnson invited every senator and congressman to the White House for buffets and briefings. Over five-hundred accepted these invitations to come with their spouses, in groups of fifty, during five weeks in February and March.

Johnson was an activist legislative leader, personally involved—even more directly than Jefferson—in courting the Congress. He delighted in shepherding a bill through Congress from beginning to end, confronting committee chairmen when necessary, and making appeals to individuals on committees and on the floor. Deliberations on the 1965 Foreign Aid Bill illustrate this pattern. When Otto Passman, then chairman of the House Appropriations Subcommittee responsible for this legislation, wished to reduce the total amount of aid in this bill, Johnson sent one of his liaison people, Agency for International Development Director David Bell, to brief the members of Congress who supported foreign aid. With the support of the Speaker and the majority party leader, LBJ then telephoned fifty-three Democratic House members who had a record of cutting foreign aid bills. His primary appeal to them was based upon party loyalty. President Johnson kept in constant contact with the floor leadership of the House as the bill was being debated. As a result, the president was the eventual victor because—even though Johnson's aid request was cut—the reduction in foreign aid was the smallest in seventeen years.[35]

Johnson's success as legislative leader was fundamentally due to the fact that during most of his tenure Congress was the president's major focus of attention. As Doris Kearns has suggested,

> He persuaded elected senators and representatives to serve on many of the task forces that generated ideas for Great Society legislation; he involved them in drafting the presidential messages that accompanied legislative requests; he briefed congressmen on messages before they were sent to the Hill; he selected and sought out the congressmen he wanted to introduce bills and he followed up all this by closely watching and frequently directing the process of enacting legislation.[36]

Specifically, Kearns argues that Johnson's intimate knowledge of the South, and its membership in the Congress, helped him understand what approach to use in mobilizing votes on such sensitive legislation as civil rights.

On the other hand, George Edwards feels Johnson's legislative skills have been exaggerated and that they had little effect on his relationship with Congress. Edwards claims that if Johnson's political skills were so important, he should have won even more legislative victories in 1965 and 1967. Edwards further suggests that Kennedy actually had more support from Northern Democrats than Johnson did, in spite of the increased number of liberals elected in 1964. Obviously, Edwards's analysis deemphasizes the importance of a president's personal skills as a factor underlying effectiveness in this role.[37]

Although success as legislative leader is grounded in more fundamental causes, such as the degree of political party organization in Congress, the record nevertheless shows that Johnson was more effective than either his immediate predecessors or those presidents who succeeded him in office (table 4-1). For the years 1953 to 1981, Johnson had the highest number of victories on roll call votes of any president: 93 percent during the first session of the 89th Congress in 1965. As impressive as this statistic seems, however, many Democratic presidents achieved success in at least three-fourths of their key votes in Congress. In 1963, for example, Kennedy's 87.1 percent was higher than what Johnson achieved in 1966, 1967, or 1968. (As table 4-1 shows, the records of Eisenhower, Johnson, Nixon, and Ford indicate more legislative success during the early years of their terms than in later years.)

A more revealing indication of presidential effectiveness in this role is the percentage of victories on legislation rather than on individual votes (table 4-1). Again, Johnson's 68.9 percent success rate in enacting legislation during 1965 is exceeded only by Eisenhower's 72.7 percent success rate in 1953. Yet this comparison also highlights Johnson's success as a legislative leader, since Eisenhower submitted only 44 proposals in 1953 whereas Johnson's 1965 rate was based upon 469 pieces of legislation. When Johnson is compared with Kennedy on these terms, moreover, LBJ's superiority in getting legislation enacted is obvious.

Compared with Kennedy, Johnson's greater effectiveness was related, in part, to his ability to mobilize more support from Southern Democrats, especially in the House of Representatives (see table 4-2). Table 4-2 shows

TABLE 4–1   Presidential success rates on key roll call votes and on legislation, 1953–1981

Year/ President	Success on Votes*	Success on Legislation**	
		N Submitted	Approved
Eisenhower			
1953	89.0%	44	72.7%
1954	82.8	232	64.7
1955	75.0	207	46.3
1956	70.0	225	45.7
1957	68.0	206	36.9
1958	76.0	234	47.0
1959	52.0	228	40.8
1960	65.0	183	30.6
Kennedy			
1961	81.0	355	48.4
1962	85.4	298	44.6
1963	87.1	404	27.2
Johnson			
1964	88.0	217	57.6
1965	93.0	469	68.9
1966	79.0	371	55.8
1967	79.0	431	47.6
1968	75.0	414	55.8
Nixon			
1969	74.0	171	32.2
1970	77.0	210	46.1
1971	75.0	202	19.8
1972	66.0	116	44.0
1973	50.6	183	31.1
1974	59.6	97	34.0
Ford			
1974	58.2	64	35.9
1975	61.0	—	—
1976	53.8	—	—
Carter			
1977	75.4	—	—
1978	78.3	—	—
1979	76.8	—	—
1980	75.1	—	—
Reagan			
1981	82.4	—	—

Congressional Quarterly Almanac, 1981 (Washington, D.C., Congressional Quarterly Press, 1982), p. 18C.

**Congressional Quarterly Almanac, 1968* (Washington, D.C., Congressional Quarterly Press, 1968), p. 97; the data for 1953 and for 1969–are found in the *Congressional Quarterly Almanac* for those years. *CQ* cautions the reader that the score for 1953 was not comparable to those for subsequent years insofar as legislation was grouped differently that year. After 1975 *CQ* discontinued publishing this statistic.

TABLE 4-2   Analysis of voting on key presidential roll calls in 1963, 1965, and 1978 in House and Senate

	1963 (Kennedy)	1965 (Johnson)	1978 (Carter)
House of Representatives			
Party (Support Score)*			
Democrats	72%	74%	60%
Republicans	32	41	36
Region (Support Score)*			
Democrats			
East	82	83	66
West	80	80	62
South	60	57	47
Midwest	79	82	68
Republicans			
East	41	54	45
West	30	37	29
South	25	29	28
Midwest	27	37	37
Senate			
Party (Support Score)*			
Democrats	63%	64%	66%
Republicans	44	48	41
Region (Support Score)*			
Democrats			
East	78	73	77
West	67	68	66
South	48	49	53
Midwest	70	71	70
Republicans			
East	59	60	64
West	34	44	29
South	39	44	28
Midwest	37	42	44
Conservative Coalition (House and Senate)**			
Percent of recorded votes when coalition appeared	17%	24%	21%
Percent of votes won by coalition	50%	33%	52%

**Congressional Quarterly Almanac, 1963,* pp. 712–713; *1965, pp.* 1099–1100; *1978,* pp. 24C–25C. The "support score" for political party and region is the average percentage of votes in which each category of congress members supported the president where he indicated his policy preference.

***Congressional Quarterly Almanac 1978,* p. 35C. Whereas the "support score" is given for key votes on the president's legislative agenda, voting by the conservative coalition pertains to all recorded votes in the session.

that the "conservative coalition" between Southern Democrats and Republicans prevailed on fewer votes during 1965, compared with both 1963, when Kennedy was president, and 1978, when Jimmy Carter was president. Unlike Kennedy, Johnson also obtained more support from Republican congressmen and senators for his program. This fact suggests that

Johnson's legislative skills may have had an effect on the Republican legislators, for he was successful in gaining Republican support for his programs even though the Republican party in 1964 had nominated a presidential candidate (Barry Goldwater) diametrically opposed to LBJ's Great
Society.

Despite all that can be said about Lyndon Johnson's strength as legislative
leader, even he could not sustain Congress' continued support throughout
his term. As Vietnam absorbed more and more of his time and energies,
he devoted less attention to Congress. Thus, as already noted, his number
of victories on key roll call votes fell during 1966, 1967, and 1968. Because
Johnson was less involved in the lawmaking process, the Office of Congressional Relations became less effective. Even some of Johnson's most loyal
supporters in Congress began to desert him, as John F. Manley relates.

> Late in 1967, when LBJ was fighting a losing battle on behalf of a 10 percent surtax
> and the war in Vietnam was going badly, a reporter asked a normally loyal big
> city Democrat what he thought of the President's recent attack on Congress. The
> reply was "f—— him" said with more indifference than rancor.[38]

This incident suggests that presidential power in the role of legislative leader
is quite fragile and that it requires full-time attention to Congress, its politics,
and to the needs of its members. A president's leverage is further weakened
when public opinion drifts away from the president's policy positions, as
occurred when Lyndon Johnson persisted in waging the war in Southeast
Asia. Nonetheless, in retrospect we have come to appreciate Johnson's effectiveness in dealing with Congress. No doubt his relatively high ranking by
historians reflects the immensity of his Great Society legislative victories.
Many have also come to respect Lyndon Johnson's achievements after witnessing the inept performance of another Democrat who succeeded to the
presidency, James Earl Carter.

Carter

The contrast between Lyndon B. Johnson and Jimmy Carter as legislative
leader is stark. As George Edwards remarks, on one hand is the "ultimate
professional, the 'insider' Lyndon Johnson," and on the other, the "amateur
outsider with no Washington experience at all, Jimmy Carter."[39] Table 4-1
shows that, in terms of victories on key roll call votes, Carter's best year
was only 3.3 percent better than Lyndon Johnson's worst year. An analysis
by Lee Sigelman suggests that Carter's performance in domestic legislation
was especially ineffective in contrast to Johnson's, though Carter fared better in foreign affairs.[40] Moreover, Sigelman notes that many of Carter's
legislative victories came as a result of extremely close votes in the Congress.
For example, Carter's five-part energy program passed the House by one
vote and his lifting of the Turkish arms embargo won by a three-vote margin. A similar margin killed the B-1 bomber bill. These narrow victories
mean that Jimmy Carter appears stronger in the presidential box scores
than he was in reality.

Unlike Lyndon Johnson, Carter's only previous experience with legislative assemblies was his four years in the Georgia state senate and his one term as Georgia's governor. As governor, his difficulties in dealing with the state legislature were characterized by the same kinds of problems he faced as president. Gary Fink, in an incisive study of Jimmy Carter, points out that Carter was very reluctant to "wheel and deal" as a politician with the legislators. It seemed alien to his personality. Carter also had problems in cementing party coalitions.[41] His experience in state government was not entirely without successes, however. Carter's ability to enact a government reorganization plan in Georgia, often cited in his campaign for president, was based on his willingness to compromise and aggressively lobby in the state legislature. Gary Fink suggests that, in this case, Carter effectively used a variety of political strategies:

> In retrospect, Carter's success resulted from a complex, interrelated combination of circumstances that included the long Public Awareness campaign preceding the General Assembly session, the administration's effective management of the bill in the legislature, the cooperative attitude of House leaders, Carter's timely compromises and personal lobbying among legislators, Republican support of the measure, and the arrogant pettiness of the Senate opposition.[42]

A persistent difficulty for Carter in Washington, D.C., is best summed up by a Georgia legislative leader: "Jimmy's his own worst enemy [in] getting something done. . . . He feels he's right . . . he's got a lot of integrity, but he doesn't communicate."[43] This same criticism of Carter was made by Sen. Dale Bumpers (D.–Ark.) in October 1977. Commenting on the faultering legislative tactics of the Carter administration, Bumpers observed that "the President has a tendency to think . . . this is right, 'this is what needs to be done'—and he expects Congress to see it the same way."[44] Bumpers added that Congress needed to be "sold" on the virtues of Carter's proposals. Failure to communicate troubled President Carter from the very beginning in trying to deal with Congress. His failure to alert Congress about his forthcoming energy program is viewed as one reason why he had great difficulty getting it enacted by Congress.

Carter was seen by Congress and the press as indecisive and irresolute in his dealings. He caused unnecessary opposition to be mobilized by legislators who would have liked to support him. One example occurred when Carter was promoting his $50 tax rebate plan to reduce the voters' tax burden. Once it appeared that the vote would be close in Congress, President Carter lost interest in this proposal and suggested that the improved economy no longer made the tax rebate plan a reasonable option. Little effort was expended by the Carter administration to soften the embarrassment suffered by his legislative supporters, who had vigorously backed this plan.[45] Carter also refused to campaign in 1979 for Democratic congressmen. To one Democratic congressman, who had voted against Carter on several occasions, the president was heard to say, "I'll be damned if I'll send my wife into your district for a fund-raiser."[46] Carter's White House staff added insult to the list of injuries when one of his aides publicly offered this observation: "Harry Truman ran against the 'do-nothing 80th Congress' . . . Carter ought to run against the gutless 96th."[47] The irony is that, whereas Truman campaigned against the Republican 80th Congress, Carter faced problems created by his own political party.

Carter failed to consult with Congress at all stages of the legislative process, and his failure to lobby the legislators vigorously for his programs resulted in some very close victories, some narrow defeats, and much unnecessary criticism. Majority Party Leader Jim Wright (D.–Tex.) said of Carter in 1978, "In dealing with Congress, he doesn't twist arms nor promise favors. Some in his Cabinet can be disdainful of Congressional advice. And that has cost him some support."[48] Carter's attitude may have been a by-product of his 1976 election campaign in which, as the once obscure Georgia governor, he campaigned against the inefficiency and incompetence of the Washington establishment. It may have been difficult for him to abandon that posture and approach the Congress in a more positive, traditional way.

Not all of Jimmy Carter's problems were of his own making, for Congress in 1977 was a very different institution than it had been during Johnson's term. In the aftermath of Vietnam and the Watergate scandals, Congress tried to reassert its authority in various policy areas. Since the early 1970s a greater gulf between the Congress and the president had developed. Unlike Lyndon Johnson's landslide defeat of Barry Goldwater in 1964—when Johnson carried into office many indebted freshmen Democrats—in 1976 Jimmy Carter ran well behind most of the Democratic legislators seeking reelection. For this reason, the veteran Democrats in Congress felt that they owed little of their election victory to the president.

The party leadership in Congress, moreover, had to contend with the various "reforms" adopted in the 1970s which were intended to democratize Congress' decision-making processes. Though the Speaker was given new powers during this period, at the same time decision-making authority was fragmented among the many subcommittees and the Democratic party membership ("caucus") took a more active role in policymaking. Greater factionalism began to emerge in Congress during the 1970s. Long-standing organizations, such as the Democratic Study Group (liberal Democrats), the House Wednesday Group (moderate Republicans), and the House Republican Study Committee, were joined by newer groups representing more specialized interests: the Black Caucus, the Congressional Travel and Tourism Caucus, the Hispanic Caucus, the Congressional Steel Caucus, the Congressional Caucus for Women's Issues, and the Blue Collar Caucus. Ever since the late 1930s, the "conservative coalition" (Southern Democrats and Republicans) has acted to block liberal programs; more recently, however, other voting blocs have developed: the Conservative Democratic Forum ("Boll Weevils") and the moderate Committee of Northeast-Midwest Republicans ("Gypsy Moths"). Such groups articulate specific demands in the Congress and prevent the party leadership from unifying the rank-and-file members. No longer can a president rely on the party leaders to "deliver" the votes. Furthermore, simple reforms, such as the introduction of electronic voting in the House of Representatives in 1973, added to these difficulties; in this case the voting by congressmen is more visible to their constituents and thus facilitates grass-roots pressure on the legislative process.

Besides weakening the party leadership, as Eric Davis points out, the reforms of the 1970s restricted the power of the standing committee chairmen and reduced the importance of the "seniority" rule when making appointments to the various committees.[49] An analysis of the House Ways and Means Committee, for example, suggests that its operations under Rep. Al Ullman (D.–Ore.) in the 1970s were less effective than when it was chaired by powerful Rep. Wilbur Mills (D.–Ark.) during the 1960s.[50] All these changes mean that no president can influence the legislative process simply by dealing with a few influential congressmen and senators who are the leaders of the committees and the party organizations. Now presidents must contend with a multiplicity of decision makers who share influence in the Congress today.

In trying to deal with this array of influences on the lawmaking process, President Carter's first efforts proved to be more combative than effective. For example, two Republicans from Massachusetts were given important positions in the administration without first checking with House Speaker "Tip" O'Neill. Next, President Carter removed Robert T. Griffin from his position in the General Services Administration without explanation, though Griffin had been O'Neill's handpicked man for the job. As might be expected, these incidents caused a serious breach between the Speaker and the Carter administration, which was healed only after Griffin was given a White House post.[51] The lack of political experience of Carter and his aides was reflected as early as the 1976 presidential primaries. Eric Davis maintains they felt that "since they did not have to engage in bargaining to get the nomination or to win the election, they would not have to engage in bargaining or exchange to get their programs passed on Capitol Hill." Davis continues:

> Because they did not recognize the importance of coalition-building through brokerage, they did not, at the very outset of the administration, make an effort to establish cooperative lobby relationships with the other participants in the legislative process.[52]

Thus, this political lesson had to be learned during Carter's early years in the White House, which took valuable time and tarnished the image of the Carter presidency. One Democratic congressman was heard to remark, "Every night is Amateur Night at the White House."[53]

Carter began to learn from his mistakes. White House liaison activities had decidedly changed by 1978. Carter was beginning to lobby congressmen effectively enough to win some narrow victories. For example, he was able to barely defeat a plan to build the B-1 bomber. To secure this legislative victory President Carter telephoned several House members, including Rep. Melvin Price (D.–Ill.)—chairman of the House Armed Services Committee—to convince them to support the administration's views. He sent similar letters to all the Democratic members of the House Appropriations Committee. To win approval in the Senate for his Panama Canal Treaties, Carter unleashed the entire administration to argue the president's case. Influential in this lobbying effort were Vice-President Mondale, Secretary of State Vance, Secretary of Defense Brown, National Security Adviser Brzezinski, Ambassador Bunker, Deputy Secretary of State Christopher, presidential aide Hamilton Jordan, and other legislative liaison officers.

To promote the Natural Gas Bill of September 1978, top industrial leaders, including bankers, automobile manufacturers, and construction and steel industry executives, were called together in a series of meetings at the White House. In these sessions the president tried to anticipate opposition to the bill and to win important support from the business community. Carter personally telephoned all the uncommitted senators, and Vice-President Mondale stayed on the Senate floor to contact other senators directly. Carter appealed to major interest groups to put pressure on the Senate and House membership. In addition, an appeal was made by the Carter strategists to the effect that support for the president on this legislation would allow him to "save face politically" and recapture the prestige needed by Carter to wage his diplomatic overtures.[54] Apparently all these tactics were effective, for this legislation was enacted in October of 1978.

One fundamental change made by the Carter administration in 1978 was to reduce the number of priority bills, from about sixty to thirty. This allowed Carter's liaison staff and the administration spokesmen to concentrate their limited resources on fewer bills. Greater reliance on task forces to lobby Congress was also in evidence in 1978. The hiring of new staff personnel strengthened Carter's position with Congress. Gerald Rafshoon, Assistant to the President for Communications, for example, established the Carter image for decisiveness, and Anne Wexler, Assistant to the President, helped win support from important interest groups for the president's proposals.[55] The administration also adopted some of Lawrence O'Brien's old techniques, including "dividing coverage of the House by his lobbyists on a geographic basis, servicing of lawmakers' needs, closely coordinating departmental lobbyists and having the president personally intervene when rounding up votes on crucial issues."[56] By 1978, Carter's liaison staff began to be effective in using political bargaining and patronage as well as contacts with the Democratic leadership in Congress. They also stopped focusing on issues that affected the internal operations of Congress, since these cause serious divisions among the membership. However, unlike Lyndon Johnson, who was able to obtain bipartisan support for many of his proposals, Carter concentrated mainly on the Democrats in Congress, appealing to Republicans only when their votes were absolutely crucial.

Compared with his first year in office, Carter in 1978 and 1979 (but not in 1980) increased his number of victories on key roll call votes (see table 4-1), which suggests that these changes in legislative liaison had an effect. An observer noted the improved Carter appeal: "What began as a comedy of errors has definitely matured. . . . Now people on the Hill are more willing to work with Frank Moore [Assistant to the President for Congressional Liaison]."[57]

Summary

The experiences of Thomas Jefferson, Lyndon Johnson, and Jimmy Carter highlight certain variables affecting legislative leadership which have long been documented by political scientists. A fundamental consideration affecting executive/legislative interactions is political party organization. Having the same party control the presidency and the Congress is helpful, but is not enough. To mobilize the party's membership in support of the executive's policy objectives requires pressure from the public or a "mandate" for substantive reforms. Jefferson's victories came in the wake of the watershed election of 1800 which eliminated the Federalists from serious political contention and established the Jeffersonian-Republicans as the new majority party. Johnson's effectiveness was essentially related to his electoral coattails, in which a disproportionate number of liberal, freshmen Democrats were elected to Congress. Lyndon Johnson also profited from the nation's unity resulting from John Kennedy's assassination. Thus, *new* legislative majorities are more creative than old majorities, which are composed of veteran congressmen and senators who may have opposed social change for many years. This factor is the essential underpinning for Jefferson's and Johnson's successes as legislative leaders. Whereas Thomas Jefferson fashioned a strong party apparatus in Congress under his personal leadership, Lyndon Johnson exploited the more unified and disciplined party organization which existed in Congress during the 1960s. By the time Jimmy Carter assumed the presidency, both political parties had been severely weakened as mechanisms for majority rule.

Another major lesson to be learned from these case studies is that effective legislative leadership requires aggressive, personal, and continued involvement by the president and his liaison staff. A working coalition in Congress is never the result of half-hearted or bungling attempts by amateurs, as the experience of Carter's first year in office shows. Just as this role implies, success with Congress demands *leadership:* presidents cannot enact legislation unilaterally. As we review the five determinants of presidential power in this role, it is obvious that a president's political resources are too few to routinize power firmly as a legislative leader.

AUTHORITY

A basic obstacle in legislative leadership is that the president has little real authority to exert over Congress. To begin with, the Framers—though establishing policymaking as a shared responsibility—lodged primary authority in the Congress. Article II, Section 3 of the Constitution allows the president to "give to the Congress Information on the State of the Union, and recommend to their consideration such measures as he shall judge necessary and expedient." He is also given authority to call the Congress into special session and to adjourn Congress in instances when the House and Senate disagree over adjournment. The clearest source of legal authority is his veto power, but the veto does not allow a president to initiate policy. In contrast, Congress was granted those specific legislative powers listed in Article I, Section 8 of the Constitution. Among these are the powers to: lay and collect taxes, duties, imposts, and excises; borrow money; regulate commerce; establish naturalization and bankruptcy laws; coin money and regulate its value; establish post offices and postal roads; declare war; raise and support armies; maintain a navy; and provide for a militia. Through the use of the "necessary and proper" clause of the Constitution, Congress also can make policy in areas beyond those enumerated. Thus, because Congress holds both enumerated and "implied" powers over lawmaking, the president must utilize resources beyond his meager grants of authority to shape the legislative process.

A president's effectiveness as legislative leader depends on his relationship with the Congress, which can be affected by his previous political experience, particularly in Congress, as well as by the president's attitude towards the legislative branch. We routinely talk about the legislative leader role today, but historically not all presidents were so involved in these matters. George Washington, for example, remained aloof in his dealings with Congress. Though Washington did give an annual State of the Union Message to a joint session of Congress, he made only three recommendations to Congress during his entire term of office. Moreover, he relied heavily on Secretary of the Treasury Alexander Hamilton to mobilize the votes behind Federalist policies. On the other hand, Woodrow Wilson was an activist legislative leader. He did not wait to be invited to advise Congress but, rather, surprised the legislators by personally addressing Congress on several different occasions during his term. Not since John Adams had any president delivered the State of the Union Message in person.

Dwight Eisenhower, upon his election to the presidency in 1952, acted much as George Washington had in this role. During his first two years in office, Eisenhower failed to establish his legislative agenda for Congress' consideration. He abandoned this aloof posture after the 1954 midterm elections, however, for his party—which lost its control over the Congress—now insisted that he supply proposals for Congress' consideration. All presidents since Eisenhower have submitted legislation to the Congress, suggesting that this role has become more institutionalized in this century than it was in earlier periods.

By statutory delegation the Congress has strengthened the president's powers as legislative leader. The Budget and Accounting Act of 1921 delegated to the president the power to formulate an "executive budget." Although this law was superseded by the 1974 Congressional Budget and Impoundment Control Act, which permits Congress to formulate a budget along with that one prepared by the executive, the president still controls much of the budget-making process. He also delivers an annual Budget Message to Congress. And under the Employment Act of 1946, the president is required to give Congress an Economic Report, in which he describes such economic problems as inflationary trends and unemployment rates along with his plans for sustaining the nation's economic health. These statutes are important because they permit the president to initiate the budgetary agenda that Congress will consider.

Whether the president submits a budget or legislation to Congress, it is very probable that Congress will take issue with his priorities and enact legislation of its own. When these first skirmishes of an executive/legislative battle occur, a president may use the veto, or may hope that the threatened use of the veto will prompt Congress to reconsider his policy objectives in whatever legislation is approved. The veto would appear to be a major power available to any president, but on further examination it is unclear whether the veto is an index of a president's strength or weakness as legislative leader.

The veto power

The presidential veto was not an original invention of the Framers of the Constitution. The governors of the royal colonies, as well as the English monarch, held an absolute veto power over legislation. In the Constitutional Convention there was general support for the presidential veto, though few delegates would allow it to be absolute. The Framers reasoned that the veto would be a way of preserving executive power from the excesses of legislative intervention. But early presidents rarely exercised the veto, and when they did, they used it against legislation they thought unconstitutional. George Washington vetoed two bills, but the veto was never used by John Adams or Thomas Jefferson (table 4-3). James Madison vetoed five bills, four because of constitutional reasons and the fifth because he believed it was ill-designed to achieve the intended purpose. It was President Andrew Jackson, however, who discovered the full potential of the veto. His twelve vetoes were the most used by any president until Andrew Johnson. More important, however, was Jackson's justification for using the veto rather than the absolute number of vetoes cast. Jackson established the precedent of using the veto to shape public policy, and his own dislike of legislation was sufficient justification for using the veto power. President Polk later defended Andrew Jackson's use of the veto as a necessary element in the checks and balances system.

Since Jackson's time, the veto has been used widely by most presidents, especially in the twentieth century. Recent presidents exercised the veto to publicize their stands on policy issues. Harry Truman, for example, directed his veto messages as much to the American people as to Congress. Since Congress in 1947–1948 was controlled by the Republican party, Truman believed that the public would support his programs once it understood the reasons underlying his veto of key legislation.

The veto is an extremely effective power. Overall, only about 7 percent of all presidential vetoes have been overridden by Congress. The mere

TABLE 4-3   The use of presidential vetoes, 1789–1981*

President	Regular vetoes	Pocket vetoes	Regular vetoes overriden
Washington	2	0	0
J. Adams	0	0	0
Jefferson	0	0	0
Madison	5	2	0
Monroe	1	0	0
J. Q. Adams	0	0	0
Jackson	5	7	0
Van Buren	0	1	0
W. H. Harrison	0	0	0
Tyler	6	4	1
Polk	2	1	0
Taylor	0	0	0
Fillmore	0	0	0
Pierce	9	0	5
Buchanan	4	3	0
Lincoln	2	4	0
A. Johnson	21	8	15
Grant	45	48	4
Hayes	12	1	1
Garfield	0	0	0
Arthur	4	8	1
Cleveland (1st term)	304	110	2
B. Harrison	19	25	1
Cleveland (2nd term)	42	128	5
McKinley	6	36	0
T. Roosevelt	42	40	1
Taft	30	9	1
Wilson	33	11	6
Harding	5	1	0
Coolidge	20	30	4
Hoover	21	16	3
F. D. Roosevelt	372	263	9
Truman	54	29	11
Eisenhower	36	45	2
Kennedy	4	5	0
Johnson	6	7	0
Nixon	24	16	5
Ford	35	11	8
Carter	13	16	2
Reagan (1981)	1	1	0
TOTALS:	1,185	886	87

*Congressional Quarterly, *Guide to Congress*, 2nd edition (Washington, D.C.: Congressional Quarterly Press, 1976), p. 628. Data on Carter is from *Congressional Quarterly Almanac 1980*, p. 7; Data on Reagan is from *Congressional Quarterly Almanac 1981*, p. 9.

threat of a veto, moreover, can be used by presidents as a way of influencing the legislative process. Thus, when Jimmy Carter announced his intention to veto any bill that granted tuition tax credits, Congress proceeded to remove this provision from the 1978 education bill even though the Senate had previously approved such tax credits. Similarly, Ronald Reagan effectively used the veto warning in 1981 against "budget-busting" legislation that threatened his economic program.

It is doubtful, however, that the veto power is an effective method of molding legislation in most instances. As shown in table 4-4, presidents labeled "near great" by historians used the veto power most frequently, followed by the "great" presidents. Democrats are more than two times more likely to use the veto as Republican presidents; moreover, the veto is used much more often during periods of "presidential dominance" rather than during eras of congressional domination. Franklin D. Roosevelt and Grover Cleveland account for nearly one-half of all the regular vetoes cast. After them, the top ten are: Harry Truman, Dwight Eisenhower, Gerald Ford, Ulysses S. Grant, Theodore Roosevelt, Benjamin Harrison, Woodrow Wilson, and Calvin Coolidge. Among these presidents one finds both active and passive types, though the overall listing suggests that the veto is used

TABLE 4-4   Classification of 2,071 presidential vetoes during 1789–1981 according to party affiliation, ranking by historians, and historical era*

Variable	Number	Percent	Number per president	Number per year
Party				
Republican	622	30.0	36.6	8.5
Democratic	1429	69.0	119.1	19.8
Other	20	.1	2.0	.4
Ranking				
Great	687	33.2	137.4	17.2
Near great	764	36.9	127.3	19.1
Average	306	14.8	25.5	5.1
Below average	76	3.7	12.7	3.8
Failure	99	4.8	49.5	8.3
Not ranked	139	6.7	23.2	6.6
Historical Era				
Presidential dominant	1105 }	53.4	69.1	10.6
Modified pres. dominant	1 }			
Congressional dominant	434 }	40.9	42.4	11.2
Modified cong. dominant	414 }			
Not classified	117	5.6	9.0	29.3

*The ranking of Presidents is based on the 1962 Schlesinger survey as found in: Arthur M. Schlesinger, "Our Presidents: A Rating by 75 Historians," *New York Times Magazine* (July 29, 1962), p. 12. The years included in the periods of presidential or congressional dominance can be found in Rowland Egger, *The President of the United States* (New York: McGraw-Hill, 1972), p. 162. This categorization of presidential vetoes is based on the data in Table 4.3.

more often by more activist presidents. The case of Grover Cleveland, however, lends support to the hypothesis that the veto is a power to be used as a last resort. Many of Cleveland's vetoes involved bills providing pensions for Civil War veterans. Congress persisted in approving such pensions, against Cleveland's expressed opposition, and this situation left him with no option except to continually veto those bills.

Excessive use of the veto can damage a president's relations with Congress. This seems to be the case during Gerald Ford's term, and it certainly was during Richard Nixon's. In one instance, Nixon used the "pocket veto" against a Family Practice of Medicine Act that had been overwhelmingly passed in 1970 by the Senate (64 to 1) and by the House of Representatives (412 to 3). A pocket veto occurs whenever a president fails either to sign or return a bill to Congress within ten days during which time the Congress has adjourned. Unlike a regular veto, a pocket veto cannot be overridden by the Congress; therefore, Congress has to reintroduce legislation. In the case of the Family Practice of Medicine Act, Sen. Edward Kennedy (D.– Mass.), its chief sponsor, and other senators sued President Nixon for misusing the pocket veto. In the case of *Edward M. Kennedy v. Arthur F. Sampson, Acting Administrator, General Services Administration*, the Court of Appeals in 1974 affirmed a district court decision that Richard Nixon had acted unconstitutionally in casting the pocket veto during the five-day Christmas recess.[58] This action by Nixon, clever but also provocative, did not help his relations with the Democratic-controlled Congress.

As mentioned previously, it is unclear whether the veto is an indication of presidential strength or weakness. While a threat to veto legislation can be used to influence Congress, the actual use of a veto shows that neither branch of government prevailed and that cooperation broke down. In any event, it is clear that the veto cannot be used repeatedly as a reliable source of power for the president as a legislative leader.

DECISION MAKING

Under the British parliamentary system, the fact that the prime minister is guaranteed the majority of seats by his political party in the House of Commons means that virtually the entire program of the government will be enacted. Should the prime minister fail to gain approval for his or her programs in the Parliament, this would signal a vote of "no confidence" by the prime minister's own political party. In Great Britain the legislative branch is, to a much greater degree, simply a means of ratifying or legitimizing public policy formulated by the executive branch. Parliamentary government in England, therefore, stands in marked contrast to the role of Congress in the United States. Although Congress expects the president to submit a legislative program for its consideration, Congress by no means simply approves the president's program. Congress has an independent impact on policymaking in this country. For example, during the first session of the 96th Congress (1979), only 20 of the 187 public bills enacted into law were key pieces of legislation in President Carter's program.

Lawrence Chamberlain was one of the first political scientists to document that Congress, not the president, was the primary initiator of legislation.[59] Chamberlain analyzed some ninety different statutes drawn from a cross section of public laws enacted between the 1880s and the 1940s, during the terms of such strong presidents as Theodore Roosevelt, Woodrow Wilson, and Franklin D. Roosevelt. The legislation studied covered ten major policy areas, including agriculture, labor, and national defense. Chamberlain determined whether the president, the Congress, or both branches of government had primary influence in shaping these bills. He concluded that, despite the number of strong presidents in office during this time period, only about 20 percent of the laws studied could be considered "Presidential Influence Preponderant." Nearly 40 percent of the bills were classified as "Congressional Influence Preponderant" and another 30 percent had "Joint Presidential–Congressional Influence." Moreover, Chamberlain found that seventy-seven of these ninety bills had their origins in the Congress, not in the executive branch. In light of these findings, Chamberlain, rather than depreciate the president's role in policymaking, simply declared: "Congress is more important."[60]

Chamberlain's research suggests a reassessment of assumptions about the extent of legislative leadership by the president. Ronald Moe and Steven Teel have done a followup study of Chamberlain's analysis for the period 1940–1967.[61] In their work, Moe and Teel paid more attention to the legislative activity that occurred before a bill was ready for final passage. They evaluated legislation in twelve policy areas: economics, tariff, labor, transportation, urban, technology, agriculture, conservation, immigration, civil rights, national defense, and foreign policy. Their conclusions were that Congress had substantial impact in virtually every policy area and that Congress continued to be an active initiator of legislation.

A different conclusion was reached by William Goldsmith, whose study covered the twenty-year period from 1945 to 1964.[62] Goldsmith focused on sixty-three statutes he deemed significant. Of this number, he found that only 11 percent could be attributed to Congress alone, whereas 41 percent originated within the executive branch. The other 44 percent of the bills had input from both Congress and the executive (the remaining 3% was attributed to interest group influence). Goldsmith argued that, whereas in Chamberlain's study 47 percent of the statutes became law without presidential influence, in the period he studied only 14 percent of the laws were enacted in that way. Thus, he concluded that the president's role in policymaking had become more important than ever before. The discrepancy between Goldsmith's findings and those of Moe and Teel, who surveyed the same general period, may be related to differing methodologies. Moe and Teel gave more attention to the process of lawmaking rather than simply the final enactment of a bill. Clearly, a more productive role by Congress in the legislative process would be revealed by an analysis that focused on the various stages affecting the content of a bill. Nonetheless, regardless of which study one prefers, all show a substantial impact by the Congress on a significant number of statutes.

Given these kinds of studies, one may wonder why political scientists and opinion leaders stress the policymaking role of the president instead of Congress. One explanation may be the greater public visibility of the president's actions. Gary Orfield contends that this enhanced visibility gives a president more credit than he deserves as an initiator of public policy.[63]

Congress' role in policymaking, moreover, is greater in domestic areas than in foreign affairs or military policy. In his article on "The Two Presidencies," Aaron Wildavsky's argument that the executive predominates in foreign affairs was substantiated by *Congressional Quarterly* data for 1948–1962.[64] During this period, Congress approved 73 percent of the presidents' legislation affecting defense policy and 59 percent in foreign policy, but only 40 percent in domestic policy. These figures are revealing since, during this fifteen-year period, there were about four times as many bills considered in domestic policy areas than in foreign and defense policy combined.

Analysis of this kind has been updated by LeLoup and Shull for the years 1965–1975.[65] Again, domestic legislation represented almost four times as many bills as foreign and defense policy. Although the executive/legislative relationship in 1965–1975 changed somewhat from the 1948–1962 period, the president still maintained his dominance in winning Congress' approval for his foreign and defense legislation. LeLoup and Shull found that Congress approved 61 percent of the defense bills, 50 percent of the foreign policy legislation, and 46 percent of the domestic legislation. These findings seem consistent with the public's expectations regarding the role of the Congress and the president in lawmaking. In 1979 Thomas Cronin determined that the public wants Congress to remain important in overall policymaking but prefers the executive to maintain a dominant position in foreign affairs.[66] However, it is also true that the president *loses* a substantial number of bills in both domestic policy and foreign/military policy.

Political parties

The separation of powers and the checks and balances system assures multiple decision makers in the legislative process. But as Thomas Jefferson soon learned, executive/legislative cooperation can be enhanced when a president's political party controls the Congress. Joan MacLean has suggested that

> Legislation is not a one-man affair. The synchronized efforts of many individuals requires some kind of propulsive energy to maintain momentum. Party harmony is an important generative force, but the wellsprings of party lie deep and are not always easily tapped.[67]

A president whose political party has a majority of seats in the House of Representatives and the Senate has a better chance of getting his program enacted than if either or both houses of Congress are controlled by the opposition party. In recent years, Democratic presidents have benefited more often than Republican presidents from party control of Congress. During 1933–1983, Democratic presidents worked with Democratic-controlled Congresses for thirty of thirty-two years; Republican presidents, on the other hand, had their party in control of Congress only two of eighteen years. During the 97th Congress (1981–1982), President Ronald Reagan confronted a situation in which his party controlled the Senate while the Democrats held a majority in the House. Given the fact that many presidents have been able to obtain legislative approval for their domestic programs less than 50 percent of the time, it would appear that the presidents' parties in Congress are not unified in their support of the executive. This problem notwithstanding, it is also true that the impact of presidential leadership on domestic policymaking would be even worse had "divided" government been the normal state of political affairs over the past five decades.

In general, presidents can rely on getting more support from their own political party, as table 4-5 shows. According to this study by Lee Sigelman, the six recent presidents obtained 88 percent support on key legislation from their own political party during the period 1957–1978. But the oppo-

TABLE 4-5   Patterns of presidential victories on key domestic legislation during 1957–1978*

President	Years	N	Percent victories
			(By all congressmen)
Eisenhower	1957–1960	51	.608 ⎫
Kennedy	1961–1963	47	.702 ⎪ .732
Johnson	1964–1968	95	.853 ⎬
Nixon	1969–1972	46	.652 ⎭
Nixon	1973–1974	20	.500 ⎫
Ford	1974–1976	27	.593 ⎬ .565
Carter	1977–1978	22	.591 ⎭
			(By congressmen of president's party only)
Eisenhower	1957–1960	51	.863 ⎫
Kennedy	1961–1963	47	.830 ⎪ .879
Johnson	1964–1968	95	.926 ⎬
Nixon	1969–1972	46	.848 ⎭
Nixon	1973–1974	20	.950 ⎫
Ford	1974–1976	27	.852 ⎬ .884
Carter	1977–1978	22	.864 ⎭
			(By congressmen of opposition party only)
Eisenhower	1957–1960	51	.412 ⎫
Kennedy	1961–1963	47	.128 ⎪ .293
Johnson	1964–1968	95	.337 ⎬
Nixon	1969–1972	46	.239 ⎭
Nixon	1973–1974	20	.300 ⎫
Ford	1974–1976	27	.185 ⎬ .217
Carter	1977–1978	22	.182 ⎭

*Drawn from Lee Sigelman, "A Reassessment of the Two Presidencies Thesis," *Journal of Politics* (1979), p. 1201.

sition party supported their legislation much less than one-third of the time. In particular, the study noted the heavy resistance by Democrats to Gerald Ford's proposals and that by Republicans to the legislation offered by Jimmy Carter.

Political party is important to the decision-making process in Congress because it serves as a vital communications link between Congress and the president. It is the party's floor leadership in Congress that maintains contact with the president and the White House liaison staff. Randall Ripley points out, for example, that the majority party leader and the speaker of the House of Representatives, when of the president's party, try to support the president's legislation whenever possible.[68] Such presidents as Thomas Jefferson, Theodore Roosevelt, Woodrow Wilson, and Ronald Reagan recognized the importance of working through their party's leadership to facilitate passage of legislation. Wilson took an active role in helping the Democratic rank and file in Congress to strengthen the party's organization, and was instrumental in encouraging his Progressive allies to seek leadership positions in Congress. Presidents whose party is the minority in Congress find it more difficult to be effective legislative leaders. Eisenhower, for example, had to contend with a Democratic Congress, with the result that only 37 percent of his priority legislation was approved in 1957.

The decision-making process in Congress is complicated by the decentralized nature of the legislative branch, with its numerous standing committees and subcommittees having jurisdiction over policy areas. We have come to recognize that "subgovernments" made up of legislative committees, administrative agencies, and clientele groups virtually create public policy in certain policy arenas, and their recommendations are usually ratified by the entire Congress. An early scholar to discuss the effects of subgovernments was Ernest Griffith, who wrote about these "whirlpools" where policy is made with little presidential influence.[69] His observation has been confirmed by many political scientists, including Theodore Lowi, whose case studies of public policymaking show how these "iron triangles," as he refers to them, limit the influence of any legislative leader.

Functional arenas

Theodore J. Lowi classifies public policy as being distributive, regulatory, or redistributive, while arguing that a different constellation of political structures, decision makers, and processes affect lawmaking in each of these "arenas of power."[70] More important for our consideration is his view that the president's influence over the legislative process depends on the type of policy being considered by Congress. Distributive policy, which may be likened to "pork-barrel" appropriations or subsidy, allows very little involvement by a president, and Congress' role as a collectivity is reduced. Distributive policymaking is dominated by a subgovernment in most instances. To illustrate this, Lowi described the alliance among the Soil Conservation Service (of the Department of Agriculture), the Agriculture

Subcommittee of the House of Representatives Committee on Appropriations, and the local committees of the National Association of Soil Conservation Districts (the associations through which farmers control this program).[71] President Eisenhower's secretary of agriculture, Ezra Taft Benson, tried to consolidate all federal farm programs and increase the president's control over them. But given the power of this subgovernment constellation, his objective was doomed to failure. Similarly, John Kennedy's farm program of 1961 was rejected largely because of the might of this alliance structure. It was Lowi's conclusion, therefore, that the existence of these so-called iron triangles "limited the capacity of the public government to govern responsibly and flexibly."[72] Similar political relationships predominate in other distributive policies, such as rivers and harbors projects, highway construction, research and development grants, agricultural price supports, the "protective" tariffs of the late nineteenth and early twentieth centuries, public works, and health research funds.

An entirely different cast of political actors makes regulatory policy, which involves an element of coercive control by government over the behavior of private individuals or businesses. Included among these policies are minimum wage and maximum hours legislation, antitrust regulation, pure food and drug laws, strip-mining controls, and air and water pollution standards. Because so much conflict among interest groups affects any move by government to impose added regulatory controls, policymaking in this arena is not limited to the standing committees but extends beyond them to the House and Senate floors. In issues affecting regulation, therefore, Lowi argues that the president has a "moderate" level of influence over the legislative process. But in this "arena of power," ultimately Congress is the most important decision maker in formulating public policy.

On the other hand, redistributive policy involves the deliberate attempt by government to reallocate resources—wealth, property, rights, or power— among broad classes or groups in our society. Such redistributive policies as public welfare, Social Security, Medicare, the income tax, model cities, federal aid to education, the Comprehensive Employment and Training Act (CETA), and Lyndon Johnson's War on Poverty generate an ideological debate between "liberals" and "conservatives" because such legislation is viewed as a threat to established privilege. The predominate influence over redistributive policy is not the standing committees or even Congress as a whole, according to Lowi. Most often the successful enactment of redistributive policy requires the determined legislative leadership of the president. Indeed, most of the above-mentioned programs were strongly supported by Democratic Presidents Franklin D. Roosevelt and Lyndon Johnson.

An important followup study by Robert Spitzer applied Lowi's conceptual scheme to analyzing the president's impact on the legislative process.[73] He studied 5,463 bills included in the *Congressional Quarterly* "Presidential Boxscore" during 1954–1974. Overall, the largest number of executive proposals were categorized as "redistributive" issues (30.2%), but Spitzer was impressed by the fact that more "distributive" (25.6%) than "regulatory"

(18.6%) policies were included in these presidents' legislative agendas. During this twenty-one-year period, the Kennedy administration proposed the highest percent of redistributive bills, surpassing even the Johnson administration. This finding gives added credence to the thesis that John F. Kennedy in large measure established the legislative agenda which, though resisted by Congress, was later adopted by Lyndon Johnson. Moreover, except for Eisenhower, the presidents' success rate in enacting legislation is highest in redistributive policy (though Spitzer notes that success in foreign policy is greater than in any domestic arena). The outstanding record of achievement in promoting redistributive policies is held by Lyndon Johnson; he achieved legislative victory in almost 68 percent of the cases. Eisenhower, on the other hand, was successful in only 42 percent of the cases, Kennedy in about 41 percent, and Richard Nixon in barely 36 percent. While Spitzer is careful in his conclusions, he agrees that these findings seem to confirm Lowi's argument regarding the pivotal role of the president in promoting redistributive policies.

Executive/congressional interaction in budgetary policy

Budgeting is one of the most important interactions between Congress and the president. Beyond simply providing funds to implement governmental programs, the budget is fundamentally an ordering of our national priorities. Aaron Wildavsky describes this process as a "series of goals with price tags attached."[74] Because government budgets set priorities in such areas as defense policy, social-welfare programs, and economic development, major confrontations between the president and Congress do occur. However, conflict over budgeting is a relatively contemporary development, for the federal budget was modest until recent decades. In 1929, for example, the budget was less than $3 billion, which means that the federal budget grew more than 23,000 percent by 1980, even though the nation's population grew less than 100 percent during that time. Political scientist David Edwards calculated that the entire budget for George Washington's eight-year term would finance less than two minutes of the government's operations today.[75] The very size of today's federal budget seems to signify that the president has an advantage over Congress in formulating and evaluating this document, but this was not always the case.

The Founding Fathers intended Congress to be the primary decision maker in budgeting. The legislature was given the power to "lay and collect Taxes, Duties, Imposts and Excises, to pay the Debts and provide for the common Defense and general Welfare of the United States." Legislation for raising taxes had to originate in the House of Representatives before proceeding to the Senate and then to the president. James Madison predicted, in *Federalist #58*, that this power over the "purse" would be "the most complete and effectual weapon with which any constitution can arm the immediate representatives of the people, for obtaining a redress of every grievance, and for carrying into effect every just and salutary measure."

In 1789, with the creation of the Department of the Treasury by Congress, the secretary of the treasury was given the dual responsibility of reporting both to the Congress and to the president. As the first secretary of the treasury, Alexander Hamilton worked closely with Congress. At times this relationship was collegial, but at other times it became strained. In 1790, for example, Congress asked Hamilton to formulate a plan to establish public credit. He proceeded to exercise the broad authority given to him by Congress by writing a series of extensive reports on fiscal policy. In his *Report on the Public Credit* (1790), Hamilton proposed that Congress should pay for the national debt at full value and should also assume the debts of the states, which amounted to more than $77 million. After much haggling, Congress agreed to these proposals, and accepted his recommendation for imposing excise taxes to supplement government revenues. Congress resisted the suggestion made in his *Report on Manufactures* to establish a tariff to protect infant American industries. Hamilton was convinced that fiscal policy could best be made, as he wrote in *Federalist #36*, by "single men or boards composed of a few individuals" who formulated the plan for taxation to be submitted to the legislature for approval. Hamilton came to regret his aggressive role over budgetary policy, however, because the Congress in 1793 moved to regain its control over these matters. In fact, that year a resolution by the House of Representatives charged Hamilton with violating the law, ignoring instructions from the president, and committing an "indecorum against the House."[76]

Tension between the president and Congress over budgetary issues has persisted since Hamilton's time. But prior to 1921, despite the pattern set by Hamilton, Congress predominated in budgetary matters. During these previous years the legislative budget was simply the product of differing committees and subcommittees in the Congress. Included in this decentralized process was the House Ways and Means Committee (which raised revenues), its counterpart in the Senate (Finance Committee), and the Appropriations Committees of the House and Senate. Yet this procedure was adequate only as long as government's responsibilities remained modest. As Congress eventually learned, its decentralized decision-making process did not produce a unified, coherent budget that interrelated levels of taxation, spending, and indebtedness. This inadequacy led to the enactment of the landmark Budget and Accounting Act of 1921. It authorized the president (beginning with Warren G. Harding), rather than Congress, to assume primary responsibility for developing an "executive budget." This statute, more than any other, firmly placed control over the budget process in the hands of the president.

The 1921 law established a Bureau of the Budget in the Department of the Treasury, its director appointed by the president to be accountable exclusively to him. Upon passage of this act, President Harding immediately issued Budget Circular No. 49 declaring that, henceforth, all bureaus and agencies would submit their budget requests to the Bureau of the Budget before being forwarded to the Congress. Before 1921 each administrative agency submitted its budgetary request directly to Congress. In 1939 the Budget Bureau was transferred from the Treasury Department to the newly created Executive Office of the President, giving the president more direct control over its operations. In 1970, the Bureau of the Budget was reorganized by President Nixon into the Office of Management and Budget (OMB).

The 1921 Budget and Accounting Act required the president to submit an annual budget to Congress. The role of Congress now would be to approve or disapprove its provisions as well as to audit its expenditures. However, as in the pre-1921 period, the decentralized budgetary process within Congress remained. The Senate Finance Committee, the House Ways and Means Committee, and both chambers' Appropriations Committees continued to be the major decision makers in this process. Moreover, during the period 1921–1974, Congress typically agreed to the president's budgetary requests. It was very difficult for the legislators, many of whom lacked training in financial management, to oversee the executive budget. Inadequate time to study the budget was also a problem; before 1974, the fiscal year for the federal government ran from July 1 to June 30. Since the president had to submit his budget to Congress on the first day of each session of Congress in January, this meant Congress had only about six months to scrutinize a budget document which easily ran over 1,000 pages. Accordingly, Congress tended to focus on those budget items having importance to powerful interest groups and voter blocs. Congress generally made only marginal changes in the levels of spending requested by the president.

Before budgetary reforms were enacted by Congress in 1974, budgetary policy was a classic example of "incrementalism," according to the seminal study by Aaron Wildavsky.[77] In other words, agencies would ask for substantial increases in their appropriations for the next fiscal year; Congress would then reduce those requests by smaller amounts, with a resulting increase in the level of expenditures for most agencies. This process of making incremental, though upward, adjustments in each year's budget is one explanation for the federal budget's multiplication almost every year over the past two centuries.

Some agencies fare better in appropriations than others, and in those cases Congress simply increases their appropriations beyond the level requested by the president. Francis Rourke studied the level of appropriations given to various agencies in the executive branch, and determined that during 1947–1962, agencies which received disproportionately more funding than most had substantial political support from both the Congress and interested clientele groups. During that period, the most successful agencies in this regard included the Soil Conservation Service, the Office of Education, the Forest Service, and the Food and Drug Administration.[78] Thus, having political allies in Congress and among constituency groups can provide a degree of autonomy to government agencies and insulate them from the president's budgetary control.

In most cases, however, the Congress accedes to the president's budgetary requests. An insightful analysis by Arnold Kanter, based on the fiscal years 1960–1970, indicates how minor the changes were that Congress made in the president's requests for defense spending. Concludes Kanter:

> From fiscal 1960 through fiscal 1970, five annual appropriations involved changes of less than 1 per cent, seven of less than 2 per cent, and nine appropriations out of eleven varied from the President's request by less than 4 per cent.[79]

Kanter's findings are supported by a more recent study by Ahrari and McNitt for the period covering 1954–1978.[80] They determined that except for one year (-7.5% in 1970) Congress never reduced the president's requests for defense spending by more than 7 percent. Most often the reductions were far less than this; ten of the seventeen times the defense budget reductions were under 4 percent. The greatest reductions in defense spending tended to occur when Presidents Nixon or Ford confronted a Democratic Congress, during the years 1969, 1970, 1973, 1974, 1975, and 1976. Ahrari and McNitt also reviewed the spending pattern for appropriations to the Departments of Labor and Health, Education and Welfare (HEW). Here Congress tended to increase the president's requests for appropriations. The largest increases came during 1959 and 1960 (Eisenhower), 1961, and in 1972, 1973, and 1974 (Nixon). One would expect that a Democratic-controlled Congress would add to the social-welfare spending proposed by Republican presidents, but again in fifteen of the twenty-five fiscal years studied, the increases or decreases in Labor–HEW appropriations by Congress were under 4 percent, and none during this twenty-five-year period exceeded 8.3 percent.

1974 budget reforms

By 1974 the relationship between the president and Congress had deteriorated, a situation resulting from Congress' battles with Richard Nixon. In 1973 President Nixon had refused to spend, that is, impounded, certain moneys which Congress had appropriated (impoundment is discussed further in chapter 5). In reaction, Congress enacted the Congressional Budget and Impoundment Control Act of 1974 (see page 161). The act was intended to focus Congress' energies on the budget and to centralize decision making over budgetary matters within Congress. As mentioned before, by allocating responsibility over finances to many subcommittees and committees, the legislative branch was unable to view the budget as an entity. According to Sen. Edmund Muskie (D.–Me.).

> Congress has seen its control over the federal pursestrings ebb away over the past fifty years because of its inability to get a grip on the overall budget, while the Office of Management and Budget in the executive branch has increased its power and influence.[81]

The 1974 act created two new standing committees—the House and Senate Budget Committees—a new staff agency, the Congressional Budget Office (CBO), and a new schedule and procedures for evaluating the budget. The House Budget Committee originally consisted of twenty-three members but

Congressional Budget and Impoundment Control Act of 1974
Public Law 93-344
July 12, 1974
(Excerpts)

Purposes

Sec. 2. The Congress declares that it is essential—

(1) to assure effective congressional control over the budgetary process;

(2) to provide for the congressional determination each year of the appropriate level of Federal revenues and expenditures;

(3) to provide a system of impoundment control;

(4) to establish national budget priorities; and

(5) to provide for the furnishing of information by the executive branch in a manner that will assist the Congress in discharging its duties . . .

House Budget Committee
(membership)

Sec. 101. "(e) Committee on the Budget, to consist of twenty-three members as follows:

"(1) five Members who are members of the Committee on Appropriations;

"(2) five Members who are members of the Committee on Ways and Means;

"(3) eleven Members who are members of other standing committees;

"(4) one Member from the leadership of the majority party; and

"(5) one Member from the leadership of the minority party. No Member shall serve as a member of the Committee on the Budget during more than two Congresses in any period of five successive Congresses beginning after 1974 (disregarding for this purpose any service performed as a member of such committee for less than a full session in any Congress). All selections of Members to serve on the committee shall be made without regard to seniority." . . .

Senate Budget Committee
(duties)

Sec. 102 "(2) Such committee shall have the duty—

"(A) to report the matters required to be reported by it under titles III and IV of the Congressional Budget Act of 1974;

"(B) to make continuing studies of the effect on budget outlays of relevant existing and proposed legislation and to report the results of such studies to the Senate on a recurring basis;

"(C) to request and evaluate continuing studies of tax expenditures, to devise methods of coordinating tax expenditures, policies, and programs with direct budget outlays, and to report the results of such studies to the Senate on a recurring basis; and

"(D) to review, on a continuing basis, the conduct by the Congressional Budget Office of its functions and duties." . . .

Congressional Budget Office

Sec. 201. (a) In General—

(1) There is established an office of the Congress to be known as the Congressional Budget Office (hereinafter in this title referred to as the "Office"). The

Office shall be headed by a Director; and there shall be a Deputy Director who shall perform such duties as may be assigned to him by the Director and, during the absence or incapacity of the Director or during a vacancy in that office, shall act as Director.

(2) The Director shall be appointed by the Speaker of the House of Representatives and the President pro tempore of the Senate after considering recommendations received from the Committees on the Budget of the House and the Senate, without regard to political affiliation and solely on the basis of his fitness to perform his duties. The Deputy Director shall be appointed by the Director . . .

Data, Availability

Sec. 201. (d) Relationship to executive branch—The Director is authorized to secure information, data, estimates, and statistics directly from the various departments, agencies, and establishments of the executive branch of Government and the regulatory agencies and commissions of the Government. All such departments, agencies, establishments, and regulatory agencies and commissions shall furnish the Director any available material which he determines to be necessary in the performance of his duties and functions (other than material the disclosure of which would be a violation of law). The Director is also authorized, upon agreement with the head of any such department, agency, establishment, or regulatory agency or commission, to utilize its services, facilities, and personnel with or without reimbursement; and the head of each such department, agency, establishment, or regulatory agency or commission is authorized to provide the Office such services, facilities and personnel . . .

Rescision of Budget Authority

Sec. 1012. (a) Transmittal of Special Message.—Whenever the President determines that all or part of any budget authority will not be required to carry out the full objectives or scope of programs for which it is provided or that such budget authority should be rescinded for fiscal policy or other reasons (including the termination of authorized projects or activities for which budget authority has been provided), or whenever all or part of budget authority provided for only one fiscal year is to be reserved from obligation for such fiscal year, the President shall transmit to both Houses of Congress a special message specifying—

(1) the amount of budget authority which he proposes to be rescinded or which is to be so reserved;

(2) any account, department, or establishment of the Government to which such budget authority is available for obligation, and the specific project or governmental functions involved;

(3) the reasons why the budget authority should be rescinded or is to be so reserved;

(4) to the maximum extent practicable, the estimated fiscal, economic, and budgetary effect of the proposed rescission or of the reservation; and

(5) all facts, circumstances, and considerations relating to or bearing upon the proposed rescission or the reservation and the decision to effect the proposed rescission or the reservation, and to the maximum extent practicable, the estimated effect of the proposed rescission or the reservation upon the objects, purposes, and programs for which the budget authority is provided.

(b) Requirement to Make Available for Obligation.—Any amount of budget authority proposed to be rescinded or that is to be reserved as set forth in such special message shall be made available for obligation unless, within the prescribed 45-day period, the Congress has completed action on a rescission bill rescinding all or part of the amount proposed to be rescinded or that is to be reserved . . .

was increased to thirty by the 97th Congress. Its membership includes Congressmembers from the Appropriations Committee and the Ways and Means Committee. Its membership was to rotate so that nobody would serve more than four years in any ten-year period. The 22-member Senate Budget Committee was intended to be more permanently staffed, with its membership selected by the parties' steering committees and committees on committees. Neither the House nor the Senate Budget Committees was to have subcommittees, thus permitting their entire memberships to monitor budgetary issues. The budget committees were supposed to assess the overall budget and to prepare the joint budgetary resolutions to guide both House and Senate consideration of legislation affecting taxing, spending, and deficits.

The Congressional Budget Office was designed, according to some legislators, to be Congress' "think tank" on fiscal policy. It was intended to develop for Congress the kind of expertise and sophisticated data the executive branch had generated over the years. Its use of budget experts and computer services would provide Congress with current estimates of expenditures and costs to be used for fiscal policymaking. The CBO also would make budgeting assessments based on data sources independent of the White House's OMB; for the first time in history Congress would gain access to alternative data bases on fiscal matters. By using CBO data, moreover, the Congress would assess the "executive budget" in terms of its own fiscal priorities. As Sen. Lee Metcalf (D.–Mont.) once said, "Information is the name of the game in budget control."[82] Since its establishment, the CBO has provided research to Congress of a very high quality. Joel Havemann comments,

> Not only did the Congressional Budget Office perform much of the mathematics that was vital to the new congressional budget process, but it also developed into one of the most capable shops in town for analyzing the pros and cons of alternative federal policies.[83]

The director of the CBO by law is authorized to obtain information and data estimates from agencies within the executive branch if needed, and the departments must provide it. The CBO director can gather information from the General Accounting Office, the Office of Technology Assessment, and the Library of Congress. The CBO is not limited to responding to requests from the budget committees of Congress but rather can supply data to any member of Congress, House or Senate committee, or even to interested citizens. Congress hopes that the CBO will become its research arm for bridging the "information gap" between Congress and the executive. This gap had been a serious problem limiting Congress' oversight capacity. Sen. Frank Church (D.–Id.) argued in 1973 that the president "commands full and immediate access to information and can tell as little or as much as he likes, while the individual member of Congress must largely rely on the uninhibited, informed reporting of a free press."[84]

In the 1974 budgetary reforms, Congress allowed itself more time to evaluate the federal budget, by moving the beginning of the fiscal year from July 1 to October 1 (table 4-6). As Davis and Ringquist remind us, from 1964 to 1974 ". . . only six money bills were passed before the July 1 deadline. Consequently, Congress often had to pass temporary funding measures to keep programs going."[85] Under the new timetable (table 4-6), Congress has about nine months to approve a budget after receiving the president's "executive budget" on January 18—fifteen days after Congress convenes. Actually the budgetary process begins during the previous calendar year; by November 10 the 1974 law requires the OMB to submit to Congress a "current services budget." This budget lists all activities and programs funded during the past fiscal year along with estimates of how much it will cost to maintain these same programs *unchanged* in the new fiscal year.

Congress' role in the budgetary process begins when the standing committees which deal with taxation or other fiscal matters submit formal recommendations concerning program priorities to the House and Senate bud-

TABLE 4-6   Schedule and timetable for congressional budget*

On or before:	Action to be completed
November 10	President submits current services budget
15th day after Congress meets	President submits his budget
March 15	Committees and joint committees submit reports to budget committees
April 1	Congressional Budget Office submits report to budget committees
April 15	Budget committees report first concurrent resolution on the budget to their Houses
May 15	Committees report bills and resolutions authorizing new budget authority
May 15	Congress completes action on first concurrent resolution on the budget
7th day after Labor Day . .	Congress completes action on bills and resolutions providing new budget authority and new spending authority
September 15	Congress completes action on second concurrent resolution on the budget
September 25	Congress completes action on reconciliation bill or resolution, or both, implementing second required concurrent resolution.
October 1	Fiscal year begins

*Public Law 93-344, July 12, 1974, 88 Stat. 306.

get committees. After receiving the "executive budget," the CBO submits a data report on it to the budget committees, which study those budget figures and assess fiscal options available to the Congress. The budget committees then prepare for hearings on the budget based upon their studies, the "current services budget," the president's final "executive budget," and a report by the Joint Economic Committee which evaluates the economic impact of the president's budgetary priorities. Using the information in these reports, and that from the hearings, a "concurrent" resolution is formulated by the House and Senate budget committees. The final version of this concurrent resolution, which will become the budgetary agenda for both House and Senate, usually is not written until a conference is held to settle any differences between the House and the Senate. This concurrent resolution, and its accompanying report, must be approved by Congress by May 15; it includes budget outlays, any new budgetary authority for proposed programs, projections for future budgetary expenditures, estimated revenues with any surpluses or deficits, and the level of taxation for the next five fiscal years. Any proposed changes in the levels of federal support to state and local government are also noted.

Other standing committees of the Congress must report any other legislation designed as appropriations measures by the May 15th deadline, the same day Congress must decide whether to accept the first concurrent resolution drawn up by the budget committees. Once Congress approves this resolution establishing general budgetary goals, Congress begins debating the individual taxing and appropriations bills. Unlike the practice before 1974, now *all* spending bills must be appropriated. Before the 1974 reforms, agencies could borrow funds directly from the Treasury without first getting approval of the appropriations committees. These "back-door" expenditures precluded the Congress from coordinating spending and taxing priorities.

After adopting the first concurrent budget resolution (on May 15), Congress must conclude action on all taxing and appropriations legislation seven days after Labor Day. By September 15, a second concurrent budget resolution is adopted by the House and Senate to modify or reaffirm the first concurrent resolution in light of the actions Congress had taken on the various taxing and revenue bills. Acceptance of this second budget resolution prevents Congress from enacting any spending bill beyond its guidelines or from passing any tax measures which undercut its revenue estimates. Should there be a need to reconcile any legislation in conflict with the second concurrent resolution, such action must be completed by September 25. Once this is completed, the concurrent budget resolution becomes law without the president's signature. Thus, the entire process involving the executive and Congress takes about two years prior to the fiscal year in question. For example, for fiscal year 1982 (beginning October 1, 1981), the president submitted his budget January 18, 1981 based on fiscal data which the executive agencies collected beginning in February and March of 1980 (see chapter 5).

Effects of budgetary reforms

Several policy objectives were intended by the 1974 budget reforms, but to date not all of them have been fully realized. As intimated earlier, the CBO established for Congress the independent sources of expertise needed to evaluate or challenge the budgetary decisions of the president and the OMB staff. The changes in the timing of the fiscal year, along with the requirement that spending, taxing, and borrowing be interrelated in con-current resolutions, have permitted congressmen to view the budget as a unified document. Moreover, the budget committees have vigorously mon-itored legislative actions taken pursuant to the first concurrent resolution in order to assure the integrity of Congress' overall ceilings on revenues and expenditures.

In 1976, the first year in which all provisions of the 1974 act were imple-mented, Congress passed all its regular appropriations bills before October 1, the start of the new fiscal year. However, in 1977 three appropriations measures were not enacted until nearly three months into the next fiscal year; one of these bills, Labor-HEW appropriations, had been stalled by a debate over funding abortions.

Besides delays, a more serious problem with the budgetary reforms is that Congress has yet to consolidate its ability to evaluate differing priori-ties. Voting for or against plans to build the B-1 bomber is a relatively simple matter compared with trying to review the broad range of choices involved in budgetary allocations. Given the serious economic problems facing the nation during this time, Congress was too preoccupied with fiscal issues to modify domestic priorities. As a result, Congress' changes in the executive budget did not indicate any obvious shifts in domestic priorities. Indeed, as Joel Havemann has suggested, one "can prove either that Congress became more liberal or that it became more conservative with the onset of budget reform."[86]

Another consideration occupying the budget committees during those early years was their very survival. Because they were trying to impose a new arrangement on powerful existing subcommittees and committees whose chairmen could be adversely affected, the budget committees tended to assume a more passive role when formulating the concurrent resolutions. They merely incorporated the anticipated spending requests to be author-ized by the various standing committees. Havemann concludes, "The sur-vival instinct greatly reduced the opportunities for the Budget Committees to influence budget policy in the short term. The committees only rarely tried to use the budget process to force Congress to do that which it would not otherwise have done."[87]

A major test for Congress' budgetary reforms came with the election of Carter to the presidency in 1976. Heretofore, the reforms had strengthened a Democratic Congress' ability to oversee Gerald Ford's fiscal policies. But when one political party controls the White House and Congress, can these budget reforms still maintain Congress' policymaking independence vis-à-vis the president? From the experience of 1977, it would appear that Congress had more difficulty in asserting its prerogatives over budgetary policy. There was less than a 1 percent difference between Carter's budget for fiscal 1979 and the amount authorized in Congress' second concurrent resolution. James Thurber affirms that Congress' role in budgetary policy has remained independent of the executive, but that Congress was more sympathetic to Carter's policy goals than to Ford's objectives. He argues, "Although President Carter and his advisers . . . lost several major policy battles to Congress, the budget committees seem to be taking their major cues from the President."[88] Thus Thurber concludes that the most important factor explaining the difference in how Congress viewed those budgets formulated by Ford and Carter was the fact that the majority party in Congress was the same party that held the presidency in 1978. From this perspective, then, even the new budget reforms can be undermined by the informal influences of political party organization.

Reagan's budget battles

Ronald Reagan came into office believing that he had a mandate to reduce the scope of government activity and to cut federal expenditures. This was Reagan's avowed top priority in 1981: "There is nothing more important than putting America's economic house in order."[89] His first public appearance after the assassination attempt was a prime-time television speech to a joint session of the Congress. He pleaded for Congress to accept his budget proposals and not to make any major changes. The president then sent cabinet members into the districts of undecided House Democrats, and made numerous telephone calls to win support from representatives and senators. He even telephoned Rep. Eugene Atkinson (D.–Penn.) while he appeared on a talk show in Beaver Falls, Pennsylvania.[90] At the same time, opposition by the Democratic party was in disarray. As House Speaker "Tip" O'Neill said after the Easter recess, "I've been in politics an awful long time and I know when you fight and when you don't fight."[91] Thus, on July 29, 1981, Ronald Reagan won a major budget victory when Congress approved a 30 percent reduction in personal income taxes.

Reagan's success can be attributed to many factors. There was heavy lobbying of Congress by the White House. Rep. Claude Pepper (D.–Fla.) remarked he had seen nothing to compare with it in his thirty-three years in office.[92] The president was very persuasive in communicating directly with the American people; in response to his appeals, people contacted their legislators by mailgrams, telephone calls, and letters. The day after Reagan's televised speech, Rep. Dan Glickman (D.–Kan.) received some fifteen thousand telephone calls—many more than usual. Congressmen who remained undecided were flown to Camp David for discussions with the president on July 26. Fifteen congressmen met with the president, twelve of whom eventually voted for Reagan's tax cut. Moreover, Reagan was not above trading favors for votes; he made promises to various legislators to oppose certain bills, such as imposing a windfall profits tax on natural gas, keeping military installations open, and allowing the unrestricted production of peanuts.

Critical to Reagan's victory on the budget for fiscal year 1982 was an important parliamentary maneuver. The president's supporters in Congress were able to incorporate all appropriations for federal programs and Reagan's budget cuts into one bill. By this tactic, lengthy hearings were avoided and the various standing committees and subcommittees were prevented from rearranging Reagan's budget priorities by selectively funding each particular program. At issue was the Reconciliation Bill, Public Law 97-35 (but following the *first* concurrent resolution) that required the Congress to adjust expenditures for programs in terms of overall budgetary ceilings. President Reagan essentially forced the Congress to accept his budgetary priorities when the majority of representatives and senators voted to debate the budget as one bill, rather than as separate programs. This ploy subverted a budget process newly established in 1974, since as Alan Schick observes, Congress was constrained to accept the budget on Reagan's terms.[93] Aside from reducing Congress' role in formulating a 1982 fiscal budget, this legislative tactic heightened the public's understanding of the budget battle. Elizabeth Wehr observes that this factor helped Ronald Reagan because "it simplified public perceptions of what was an extraordinarily complex issue, enabling the White House to ask Americans—who then asked their Congressmen—whether they were 'for' or 'against' an immensely popular president's budget."[94]

Another budget victory for Reagan came in 1981, as the deadlock between Congress and Reagan over the fiscal 1982 budget continued. In November 1981, Reagan cast his first veto of legislation (HJ Res 368) that would have continued funding for all federal agencies through mid-December 1981 at existing levels. Although this stopgap measure was needed because final action on the fiscal 1982 budget had not been completed, Reagan vetoed that bill because it funded various social programs at higher levels than he wanted. As a result, offices were ordered to begin closing their doors; Congress' hand was forced and eventually new legislation, which Reagan could support, was enacted. Some members of Congress complained that Reagan was grandstanding by his use of the veto in this instance, and Sen. Walter D. Huddleston (D.–Ky.) echoed the sentiments of other legislators when he said that ". . . Ronald Reagan is now running against the Congress, like every president."[95]

President Reagan had more problems in dealing with the Congress his second year in office, mainly because it appeared to many congressmen, the press, and the public that his economic policies were not working. Congressmen were just recovering from the budget battles of 1981 when the new battles of 1982 began. Massive deficits exceeding $100 billion were proposed in Reagan's fiscal year 1983 budget; this deficit was the highest in history, an extraordinary problem given that Reagan had campaigned in 1980 on the need to curb government spending. When the Reagan budget for fiscal year 1983 was submitted to Congress, immediately there was talk of an alternative budget being formulated by a bipartisan coalition in Congress. In the Senate, Senators Domenici (R.–N.M.), Baker (R.–Tenn.), Dole (R.–Kan.), Hatfield (R.–Ore.) and Laxalt (R.–Nev.) had a major role in developing alternatives to Reagan's budget; in the House, Democratic Representatives Gephardt (D.–Mo.), Panetta (D.–Calif.), Mineta (D.–Calif.), Wirth (D.–Colo.), and Aspin (D.–Wis.) were heavily involved in this effort. By April 1982, key members of the House and Senate began meeting with the Reagan administration; included in these negotiations were the chairmen of the two budget committees, the chairman of the Senate Finance Committee, and the chairman of the House Ways and Means Committee.

Heightened conflict attended the preparation of the 1983 budget, and partisan antagonisms grew more intense. As Representative Tauke (R.–Iowa) put it: "The partisan juices are flowing because leaders in both parties are trying to prove their control of the process."[96] However, in the House of Representatives the Republican floor leader, Robert H. Michel (R.–Ill.), failed to endorse the Reagan budget because the Republican party was divided between Reagan loyalists and moderates (known as the Gypsy Moths). A major point of contention involved Reagan's proposal that Social Security benefits be cut. By May 1982, after some twenty-seven days of negotiations, the congressional leaders and administration spokesmen still could not reach agreement. On April 29, President Reagan made a televised address to the American people, asking their support for his budget, and indicating that he was willing to work with "responsible" Democrats in Congress. In the Democrats' response to Reagan's speech, Rep. Richard Bolling (D.–Mo.) told the television audience that bipartisan agreement was essential if any budget was to be passed that year. Bolling was correct, and executive/congressional negotiations began in earnest again. During this time, about seventeen negotiators held some twenty secret meetings in an effort to minimize the differences between Congress and the president. Eventually, the deadlock was broken; on May 6 the Senate Budget Committee accepted a budget that Reagan would support. By June 1982—after five frustrating months for both sides—President Reagan won a narrow victory when the Conference Bill (S Con. Res. 92) was adopted in the House of Representatives by a vote of 210 to 208, and in the Senate, 54 to 45.

Another major victory on the budget came when Congress approved President Reagan's request for $98.3 billion in new taxes over the next three fiscal years. On August 19, 1982, this request barely passed in the House by a vote of 226 to 207 and in the Senate, 52 to 47. But whereas Reagan's partisan strategy was the basis for his success in enacting the 1982 budget, this tax increase and the 1983 budget required bipartisan support. Without the support of Democratic Speaker O'Neill and 51 percent of the Democratic members, both liberal and conservative, Reagan would not have won this issue. Only 54 percent of the House Republicans voted for this measure; moreover, nine House Republicans joined nine House Democrats to sue President Reagan in a federal district court, challenging the 1982 tax bill on the grounds that revenue-raising bills should originate in the House of

Representatives and not in the executive branch.[97] Some of the most vocal in their opposition to new taxes had been Reagan's staunchest allies in 1981: Rep. Jack Kemp (R.–N.Y.), a conservative proponent of "supply-side" economics, and such conservative interest groups as the National Association of Manufacturers and Business Roundtable. To win this battle, President Reagan again appeared on television in a nationwide appeal for support. He favored the taxes to reduce the huge budget deficit and also as a way of taking money from "those who are not now paying their fair share."[98]

Thus, no sooner had the new budget process become an established routine when the entire procedure collapsed over spending priorities: namely, Reagan's intention to increase defense spending while cutting social services and the desire of Democrats in Congress to do the opposite. In preparing the 1982 and 1983 budgets, moreover, the fragile timetable requiring agreement between the House and Senate by May 15 broke down, especially during the proceedings of 1981. In making the 1982 budget, President Reagan held the dominant position, mainly because his party was strongly united in the Senate and the House Democrats could not define a satisfactory alternative. In 1982, however, as work on the fiscal 1983 budget began, it was obvious both Congress and the president shared the responsibility and frustrations in trying to develop a compromise document. Ultimately, the Reagan budget battles of 1981 and 1982 reveal the gravity of "political" factors underlying presidential power. The executive/legislative relationship in the budgetary process cannot be codified by statutes. Rather, Reagan's ability to influence the budgetary process in Congress was related to his 1980 electoral landslide, his initial political popularity, the fact that Republicans held the Senate for the first time in twenty-eight years, his skill in mobilizing public opinion and persuasiveness in personally lobbying the congressional leadership and rank-and-file members, and his clever use of parliamentary procedure to force the Congress to vote on his budget as one package. Political scientists who have studied Reagan's early budget victories agree that his performance as legislative leader was unmatched in recent decades.[99]

PUBLIC INPUTS

A serious obstacle to any president's effectiveness in the role of legislative leader is that the lawmaking process allows innumerable opportunities for public opinion, social movements, and interest groups to shape the outcome of pending legislation. Insofar as political conflict accompanies the legislative process, the probability that the president will achieve his policy objectives is markedly reduced. In 1980 there were over 13,500 private associations in the United States, the largest of which have full-time, professional staff located in Washington D.C. to monitor legislative developments continually. While it is true not all special interests in the nation are organized and not all pressure groups are equally effective, nonetheless an extraordinary number of special interests lobby Congress on a daily basis. The degree of interest group activities is so pervasive in the United States that some political scientists view this "pluralism" as the functional equivalent to democracy. As E. E. Schattschneider has argued, people as individuals do not have much political influence, but in groups they can exert disproportionate leverage over the lawmaking process.[100] Thus, compared to the relatively minor role public inputs play in determining a president's power as commander-in-chief, as chief diplomat, or even as chief executive, presidential power as legislative leader is undeniably shaped by the type and vigor of public pressures influencing Congress.

Gaining access to Congress

The very organization of our Congress facilitates the communication of demands from constituency groups. The heterogeneity of Congress' membership, especially in the House of Representatives, is one method by which ethnic, religious, racial, and other minorities can bring their grievances before the legislative assembly. For example the Harlem congressman, Rep. Adam Clayton Powell (D.–N.Y.), developed a personal style of leadership that dramatized the social grievances of blacks in America.[101] As chairman of the House Committee on Education and Labor during the 1950s and early 1960s, he was famous for his persistent sponsorship of the Powell Amendment banning federal aid to schools that segregate. When Bella Abzug (D.–N.Y.) was elected to the House of Representatives in the 1970s, the cause of women's rights gained a well-known and energetic supporter in Congress. Congress' deliberations on legislation in the late 1970s and early 1980s banning public funds for abortions were greatly affected by the legislators' religious backgrounds. One study of legislative voting on abortion found that religion was second only to political ideology as a determinant of voting by congressmen on these bills.[102] Catholic representatives, whose religion equates abortion with murder, are overwhelmingly opposed to public funding of abortions whereas Jewish and Protestant congressmen tend to favor such programs.

Public inputs also are channeled into Congress by the electoral system. Legislators are recruited, nominated, and elected to public office by local and state party organizations which are more attuned to constituency opinions than to the needs of the president. On certain kinds of bills, the relationship between constituency opinion and legislative voting is very close. Seminal research by Miller and Stokes, for example, shows that congressmen are guided mainly by their perceptions of constituency opinions when voting on civil rights legislation.[103] On social-welfare programs, however, Miller and Stokes found that constituency attitudes were filtered through the congressmen's political party affiliation. Democratic congressmen voted for social-welfare programs because they assumed that the voters, by voting Democratic, preferred such programs; Republican congressmen make the opposite assessment. This linkage between constituency opinions and partisan preference is confirmed by other important studies of roll call voting.

Research on legislative voting by political scientists in the 1950s and 1960s[104] has been updated by using more elaborate methodologies and simulation theory.[105] Regardless of approach used, however, most researchers agree that political party affiliation is the single most important determinant of voting in the Congress. On most bills Democrats vote with Democrats and Republicans vote with Republicans. This tendency, moreover, is reinforced by political ideology as well as by constituency variables. Thus, "liberal" Democrats are more loyal to the Democratic party whereas "conservative" Republicans are more loyal to the Republican party, leading some scholars to argue that political ideology is the underlying, and paramount, reason for "party voting" in Congress.[106] Yet another consideration is the fact that certain types of constituencies elect Democrats and other types elect Republicans to Congress. Lewis Froman, for example, demonstrated that Northern Democrats are elected from districts heavily populated by blacks and urban dwellers, with higher population densities, and with lower percentages of single-family dwellings.[107] Congressional districts with the opposite demographic characteristics tend to elect Republicans. The literature on legislative behavior concludes that Republicans and Democrats vote differently in Congress because their opposing ideologies reflect different socioeconomic constituencies. As a consequence, interlinkage between constituency, party, and policymaking has strong implications for executive/legislative relations.

Because Republicans are more conservative than Democrats, some political scientists argue that the president, in general, will be ideologically more "liberal" than the Congress in three of four situations: (1) when the president is a Democrat and Congress is controlled by the Democratic party, (2) when the president is a Democrat and Congress is controlled by the Republican party, (3) when the president is a Republican and the Congress is controlled by the Republican party. Only when Congress is controlled by the Democrats and a Republican is president is it hypothesized that Congress will be more liberal than the president.[108] This situation existed during the years 1969–1977, when Richard Nixon and Gerald Ford confronted a Democratic-controlled Congress. The theory partly explains why Nixon and Ford had less success as legislative leaders than their Democratic predecessors who worked with a Democratic party majority in both House and Senate. Hence, the problems of legislative leadership under conditions of "divided" government are aggravated because partisan differences are reinforced by the parties' opposing ideological positions.

On the other hand, the Republican and Democratic parties are not unified and disciplined organizations, such as are found in the House of Commons among the English political parties. On any particular bill, a minority of congressmen in both our parties can be expected to withdraw support from their party's leadership. The literature on voting behavior indicates that the primary reason why legislators vote against their party is counterpressure from their districts. Among Republicans, those congressmen who deviate more often from "party voting" tend to be "liberals," whereas "conservative" (and Southern) Democrats tend to be less loyal to the Democratic party leadership.

The split between Northern and Southern Democrats originated in the Civil War era. Because the Republican party dominated the nation's politics between 1860 and 1932, the Democratic party retained the loyalty of the conservative Old South. This historic legacy helps explain the reason why it is Southern Democrats who opposed civil rights legislation during the 1930s, 1940s, 1950s, and 1960s. It is a common occurrence for Southern Democrats to join Republicans in a "conservative coalition" to defeat liberal programs. Indeed, this coalition defeated much of John F. Kennedy's New Frontier legislation (see table 4-2). Moreover, Ronald Reagan's budget victories during 1981 can be attributed, in part, to the support given him by Southern Democratic congressmen who belong to the Conservative Democratic Forum, also known as the Boll Weevils. Many of these Southern Democrats abandoned their party's leadership to give Reagan the margin needed for victory.

Constituency groups enjoy their greatest access to Congress through the standing committee system. The committees of the House and Senate are organized according to subject matter; farm bills go the agriculture committees, bills affecting the military go to the committees on armed services, and tax legislation to the House Ways and Means Committee and the Senate Finance Committee. Because the same type of legislation usually is referred to the same committees of the House and Senate, this procedure allows special interests with a stake in those programs to develop close, working relationships with the congressmen and senators who are members of those committees. One can understand, then, how "subgovernments" can become established in the Congress; they result simply because interest groups, standing committees, and government agencies deal with programs in which all these parties have a strong vested interest.

Access to standing committees by special interests is facilitated because representatives, in particular, and senators prefer to be members on committees that control programs of direct benefit to their constituents. In the House of Representatives, for example, congressmen from farm areas desire membership on the Agriculture Committee; those from coastal states, the Merchant Marine and Fisheries Committee; and representatives from industrial states who want to promote labor-oriented legislation, the Committee on Education and Labor. By this method of "functional" representation, certain strategically located interests in the country enjoy more access to decision making in Congress than their numbers warrant. A well-known example is the "farm bloc"; though farmers are only a fraction of the labor force, they have disproportionate influence in Congress because congressmen and senators from farm states dominate the House and Senate committees on agriculture.

Special interests versus political parties

To establish a working majority behind his legislative program, a president must cooperate with the party leadership in Congress. During the 1950s, for example, Senate Majority Party Leader Lyndon Johnson did not exploit his position for partisan advantage, because he believed that he had a responsibility to help Dwight Eisenhower govern the country. Similarly, President Lyndon Johnson called upon Everett McKinley Dirksen (R.–Ill.), the Senate minority party leader, to rally Republican senators behind Johnson's civil rights program. Many political scientists argue, therefore, that our political parties ameliorate the worst effects of pluralism in America, because the parties' leadership, which is mainly concerned with creating a majority coalition for effective government, tends to moderate political conflict and emphasize compromise rather than exaggerate policy differences. To the extent that party organization in Congress is weakened, the influence of special interests will be strengthened. Apparently this happened during the 1970s.

A *Time* essay in 1978 focused on "the startling increase in the influence of special interest lobbies" in Congress, and suggested that this development was the primary reason why so many of President Carter's legislative proposals had been defeated or stalled.[109] The power of special interests, moreover, was further strengthened by the various reforms in the 1970s, which promised to democratize decision making in the Congress. The power of party leaders and committee chairmen was reduced and authority over legislation was diffused among the various subcommittees, but these changes also had the effect of giving special interests more access to decision makers in Congress. In addition, membership turnover increased during the 1970s and, in general, newcomers to the Congress are more susceptible to grassroots pressures than veteran congressmen; those representatives having more seniority in Congress enjoy a degree of political independence vis-à-vis organized interests. At the same time the "seniority rule" was weakened, allowing the appointment of freshmen congressmen to such powerful standing committees as Ways and Means. The increased work load of Congress compounds these problems. Though congressmen and senators traditionally consult interest groups for information about pending bills, and despite the fact that more staff assistance is available to legislators today, the tremendous increase in Congress' work load forces the rank and file to rely even more heavily on special interests when evaluating and voting on legislation. On the other hand, legislators may defer to special interests because these groups also provide the resources needed to wage a campaign for reelection.

Important interests in the United States, such as labor unions, trade associations, and professional groups, always had the capability to generate huge amounts of manpower and financial resources to protect their legislative interests. A classic example involved the multimillion-dollar public relations campaign waged by the American Medical Association (AMA) against President Truman's program for national health insurance. By labeling the plan "socialized medicine," the AMA made certain the legislation was never enacted, and Congress did not seriously consider government-funded medical care for almost two decades. In 1965 Medicare was enacted, but only after another major battle with organized medicine.[110] Money can buy influence. This problem is a persistent one for any democracy, but apparently has grown to new proportions in recent years, with the increase in Political Action Committees coupled with escalation in costs of running a reelection campaign.

By law corporations and labor unions are prohibited from directly contributing to election campaigns. Such groups circumvent the law by forming Political Action Committees (PACs), which collect voluntary contributions. The Federal Election Campaign Act of 1974 did not extend public financing of campaigns to congressional elections (only to presidential primaries and elections). The ceilings imposed on total spending by senators and congressmen in that legislation were nullified by a 1976 Supreme Court decision, which deemed them a violation of the First Amendment.[111] This ruling opened the door to extensive fund-raising activities on behalf of legislative candidates by special interests. Thus, in 1974 there were 457 PACs registered in Washington, D.C., whose contributions totaled $12.5 million; by the 1978 congressional elections, there were 1,938 PACs, whose efforts raised $35.1 million.[112] Funds raised through PACs are fast becoming the second most important source of revenue for congressmen and senators, and obviously most of this money is channeled to incumbents. Moreover, the funds are distributed to members on the standing committees with jurisdiction over programs affecting special interests. For example, in 1976 Common Cause, the public interest lobby, determined that maritime unions distributed $104,338 among thirty of the forty members of the House Committee on Merchant Marine and Fisheries; dairy interests gave $205,986 to twenty-three of forty-six members on the House Agriculture Committee; the AMA channeled $74,503 to twenty-nine of thirty-seven members on the House Committee on Ways and Means; and the National Education Association provided $54,080 to twenty-five members on the thirty-seven-person House Education and Labor Committee.[113] Thus, at a time when public financing of presidential elections serves to minimize the reliance of presidential candidates on special interests for their campaign financing, members of Congress have become much more dependent on those sources for revenue.

The role of legislative leader is weakened because the lawmaking process is heavily influenced by public inputs. When groups lobby the Congress, they want to protect their self-interest, therefore political conflict often results. Conflict over public policy prevents legislators from following a president's leadership, because their actions in Congress become too visible to special interests and public opinion. Research on party leadership in Congress indicates that a key variable underlying the leaders' effectiveness in persuading the party's rank and file is the degree of visibility surrounding legislative actions.[114] When votes taken or amendments proposed are hidden from public view, the rank-and-file party members follow their leadership's position. But when these actions are visible to outside interests and to voter groups, then legislators tend to yield to public pressures and abandon their party's position. Thus, in the role of legislative leader, two predictors of presidential power—public inputs coupled with the nature of decision-making—work to the distinct disadvantage of the president. The legislative leader finds that these handicaps are not easily overcome, even when he attempts to exploit his expertise or a crisis situation.

EXPERTISE

Compared with the roles of commander-in-chief and chief diplomat, the president cannot monopolize information and expert opinion in the role of legislative leader. Nonetheless, a president does gain leverage over Congress whenever the expertise variable is operative. Prior to 1974, for example, the budgetary process was dominated by the president because Congress lacked the capability to make independent policy evaluations and economic projections. That imbalance was to be rectified, as we noted, by establishing the Congressional Budget Office. In the case of highly technical and complex legislation, expertise aids presidential power. When Congress appropriates funds to land a man on the moon, it can only assume that the National Aeronautics and Space Administration (NASA) has the capability to actually achieve that feat. In general the executive branch enjoys an advantage in being able to mobilize the data base, statistical analysis, and historical documentation pertaining to establishing an agenda for legislative action on any particular problem. David Price studied fourteen major bills to determine the role of various decision makers in the Congress, the executive branch, and among special interests in the various stages of program development.[115] The one function in which the executive had primary responsibility in most legislation was what Price referred to as "information gathering." This does not mean that Congress will necessarily accept the president's definition of a problem, and his choice of remedial legislation, but it is well known that the person who controls the legislative agenda enjoys an advantage in getting his point of view accepted. However, Congress does not lack alternative sources of information with which to counter the executive's arguments. When many outside experts, academics, and interest groups can intelligently discuss and supply information relating to such questions as medical costs, crime rates, or abortion, Congress has no need to rely on the president's judgment alone. Moreover, the tradition that congressmen and senators are appointed to standing committees important to the members' constituency groups, and the "norm" that legislators—especially members of the House—specialize in narrow policy areas, permit the standing committees to accumulate substantial expertise in specific policy areas. An illustration is Rep. Wilbur Mills (D.–Ark.), whose sixteen-year chairmanship of the House Ways and Means Committee gave him a reputation for knowing the complexities of our tax code.

To strengthen his ability to communicate effectively with members of Congress, the president has come to rely on the Office of Congressional Relations. The establishment of the OCR in 1953 signaled the further routinization of the role of legislative leader and indicated that effective leadership by a president requires continuing liaison by a staff armed with the requisite knowledge about the legislative process and the substance of legislation.

Office of Congressional Relations

Before 1953, liaison between the president and Congress was informal and quite unstructured. Thomas Jefferson, as noted, made contacts with congressmen through his dinner invitations and visits to Capitol Hill. Teddy Roosevelt met frequently with House Speaker Joe Cannon; Woodrow Wilson maintained contact with his party's leadership and committee chairmen. Even Calvin Coolidge invited congressmen to breakfasts, though for the most part these gatherings were more social than political. As late as Harry Truman's administration, presidents still relied on their own means to lobby the Congress about legislation. In Truman's case, aides were sent to the Hill only when the president's legislative proposals were in serious trouble.

President Dwight Eisenhower established the OCR. This action reflected his emphasis on formalized staffing procedures. It was a good beginning, for Eisenhower made use of professionals in the OCR who were very familiar with the lawmaking process. Bryce Harlow (later to become a White House assistant to President Nixon) and Jerry Parsons assumed direction over legislative liaison for Eisenhower. Because in its early years the Eisenhower administration produced few major legislative proposals, the OCR focused its energies on preventing the enactment of legislation opposed by the president and on protecting Eisenhower from demanding congressmen.[116] Harlow and Parsons took a bipartisan approach to their work. As Parsons stated, the OCR's original goal was to ". . . create a mutual understanding between downtown and uptown so that [president and Congress] would not have . . . misunderstandings through the news media."[117] The OCR also encouraged other departmental liaison personnel to lobby congressmen to support Eisenhower's policies. In this manner, Eisenhower's OCR succeeded in, according to Stephen Wayne, "formalizing institutional relationships with Congress and thereby establishing a presidential presence on Capitol Hill."[118]

Under John F. Kennedy, the work of OCR was crucial to the president's few legislative successes. Lawrence O'Brien, Kennedy's aide in the OCR, proved to be its most valuable member. His close relationship with President Kennedy gave him the necessary authority and fully identified him with Kennedy's policy aims. For Kennedy, and later for Lyndon Johnson, the OCR became more active in promoting legislation. It became a primary function of OCR to help determine the administration program, and then to decide on the necessary strategy to obtain its approval in Congress.

During the Nixon years, OCR divided its personnel into a Senate and House staff with Bryce Harlow, and later William Timmons, in charge of its operations. Timmons did not have the close relationship that Harlow had with President Nixon. Therefore, he had to rely more heavily on Nixon's White House aides, especially H. R. Haldeman. This did not win Timmons and the OCR much support from congressmen, since Nixon's senior aides were not well respected by the Congress.

Congressional affairs under Jimmy Carter in 1978 were handled by Frank B. Moore, assistant to the president for congressional liaison. Although Moore enjoyed a close relationship with Carter, having served him in Georgia, Moore was a novice to Washington politics. For the first eighteen months Carter suffered frequent legislative defeats, and offended such important Democrats as Speaker O'Neill because of his lack of consultation. By late 1978 the Carter liaison office recovered some lost ground by increasing their lobbying staff from four to seven and by limiting their legislative objectives. The OCR under Ronald Reagan was first directed by Max Friedersdorf, a former liaison head for Gerald Ford. Reagan's early legislative successes can be attributed partly to Friedersdorf's effectiveness as well as to the President's personal involvement in the legislative process. In January 1982, Friedersdorf was succeeded by Kenneth M. Duberstein, a White House liaison aide during 1981.

Since OCR's establishment, it has performed the same functions under both Republican and Democratic presidents. Regular contact with congressmen at all levels is central to its operations, for most presidents want liaison input into the subcommittees, committees, and floor operations of Congress. The OCR tries to assure legislative support for the executive's program, and provides information about the president's program to members of Congress. Over the years, OCR staff members have attempted to coordinate the liaison activities of department and agency personnel, which includes making regular contacts with state and local party leaders and the pertinent interest groups. When the OCR staff has close rapport with the president, they are able to speak with greater authority in Congress, and are listened to more often. During Lyndon Johnson's tenure, the OCR staff had a close relationship with the president. The staff was able to exchange patronage appointments for legislative support or offer project grants to individual congressmen. They utilized other means of social contact, such as sending birthday wishes or pens used by the president in bill-signing ceremonies, and inviting legislators to social events at the White House. In general, OCR's effectiveness depends on the scope of the president's legislative proposals. The more limited were his objectives, the more successful was OCR. During the Eisenhower years, when fewer proposals were submitted to Congress than during Kennedy's or Johnson's terms, OCR was more successful in promoting the Eisenhower legislative agenda. Of course, the success of OCR fundamentally hinges on the president's view of legislative leadership, for OCR has never been effective without the commitment of a president willing to fight for his goals in the Congress.

CRISIS

Crisis seems to be an unreliable variable in the role of legislative leader. The strongest presidents, such as Franklin D. Roosevelt, have profited greatly from the existence of domestic turmoil, but weaker executives have not taken full advantage of crisis conditions. For example, the pending Civil War crisis did little to strengthen Buchanan's leadership, and the debate over Reconstruction after the Civil War only undermined Andrew Johnson's already faltering leadership in Congress. In spite of the Great Depression, Herbert Hoover did not exploit the potentials of this disaster to strengthen his legislative leadership, because he disapproved of government intervention in the economy. Sometimes domestic crisis can strengthen a president's power, if he wishes to use it for those purposes. Koenig reminds us, ". . . in the gravity of the peril, national opinion demands action and the population looks to the President for initiative and brooks no denial. . . ."[119] The economic crisis of the 1930s gave Franklin D. Roosevelt, during his first one-hundred days, the leverage he needed to enact major New Deal proposals. For example, the seriousness of the Great Depression prompted the Congress to approve the Emergency Banking Act literally before copies could be duplicated for all congressmen to read. Even Republican leaders supported this measure, saying, "The House is burning down and the President of the United States says this is the way to put out the fire."[120] Certainly the crisis of assassination helped Lyndon Johnson's success with social-welfare programs which, when John Kennedy was alive, were stalled in the Congress.

During our history Congress has responded quickly to shocking events which demanded remedial action. The Pendleton Act of 1883, for example, which established the federal civil service system, was passed after President Garfield's assassination by a disgruntled job-seeker. The enactment of federal antikidnapping legislation in 1932 was a response to the sensational outcry following the abduction and murder of the infant son of Charles Lindbergh, the hero of early aviation. In 1958 a concerned Congress speedily passed the National Defense Education Act to increase educational opportunities for graduate students; this law was directly related to the Soviet launch of the first Sputnik satellite in 1957. Dr. Martin Luther King's murder in 1968 prompted Congress to consider seriously, and approve, an Open Housing Act.

The Congress answered President Reagan's request for emergency legislation to stop a nationwide railroad strike in September 1982. On September 19, 1982 a walkout by railroad engineers threatened the jobs of over one-million people, promised to cost nearly $1 billion a day, and inconvenienced nearly 250,000 commuters across the nation. Negotiations between the Brotherhood of Locomotive Engineers and the railroad industry had begun in 1981—prior to that time twelve other railroad unions reached an agreement with the industry. In June 1982, however, the engineers indicated to the National Mediation Board that the union planned to strike in July.

Thereupon President Reagan used the 1926 Railway Labor Act to establish an Emergency Board to negotiate a settlement during a sixty-day mandatory cooling-off period. When the engineers rejected that settlement and again threatened to go on strike on September 19, Reagan asked Congress to enact emergency legislation ordering the 26,000 striking engineers back to work. The president also asked the union to accept the contract negotiated by the Emergency Board, which provided a 28.8-percent wage increase over thirty-nine months, and requested a moratorium on any strikes until at least June 1984.

The last time Congress intervened in a railroad strike was in 1971, at the request of President Nixon. When they were faced with this situation again in 1982, Congress acted quickly. The Senate's Labor and Human Resources Committee reported a resolution (SJ Res. 250) on September 21, the third day of the strike. That evening the Senate passed this "joint" resolution by voice vote. The next day the House of Representatives approved the legislation by a lopsided vote of 383 to 17; President Reagan signed the legislation on September 22, forcing the engineers back to work.

Congress acted in the face of another, very different, crisis in 1976. The following case study discusses Congress' response to President Ford's legislative requests during an impending swine flu epidemic.

The swine flu case

In January 1976 the Center for Disease Control in Atlanta identified an illness that afflicted a number of recruits at New Jersey's Fort Dix as swine flu.[121] The concern was raised that, should the disease reach epidemic proportions, few people would have immunity to this infection. By February a nationwide search for other cases had begun. Cases of swine flu were diagnosed in Virginia, Mississippi, and Pennsylvania. Based on fragmentary evidence, the Army estimated that at least five hundred men probably had been exposed to the virus, and by March the Center for Disease Control had informed HEW Secretary David Matthews of its findings. Matthews then notified James Lynn of the OMB of this possible threat to the public health, and Lynn informed President Gerald Ford.

By March 22, various officials at HEW and OMB as well as several White House aides had recommended to Ford that the federal government begin a mass vaccination program for all Americans. Little thought was given at the time to the problems of implementing such a massive undertaking. By March 24, 1976, Ford was convinced, and announced his recommendation on nationwide television. He urged the Congress to appropriate $135 million for this purpose. Following the broadcast, Ford sent a memorandum to all federal departments urging their support for his program.

Although the threat of an epidemic was unproven and still relatively controversial among health experts, Congress nevertheless responded to Ford's request. On March 31 a hearing was held before the House of Representatives Interstate and Foreign Commerce Committee's Subcommittee on Health and Environment on the need for authorizing the funds for a mass inoculation program. By April 9, the House of Representatives had approved both an authorization bill and the necessary appropriations. The Senate approved its version of the appropriations bill, but failed to act on an authorization measure. Both houses of Congress passed an amended appropriations bill by April 12; authorization was found under Title III of the Public Health Act.

On April 15, just one month after Gerald Ford had first heard about the swine flu problem, the president signed the special appropriations bill into law. In December 1976, after some forty million Americans had been inoculated, the swine flu program was suspended to assess the potential side effects from the inoculations. The program was never revived, having lasted less than three months.

We have seen that executive/legislative cooperation does not result in every instance of an alleged "crisis," for often the president and Congress disagree on the appropriate remedy. For example, Congress armed Nixon with wage and price controls to combat inflation, but President Nixon remained opposed to using this legislation. In 1973, after the Arab oil embargo, Congress passed sweeping emergency legislation in the Omnibus Emergency Energy Bill (S 2589). This legislation empowered the president to ration oil and oil products and to take other conservation measures to save energy. The bill levied a windfall profits tax on oil, and modified certain clean air standards to allow the burning of coal. Nixon vetoed this legislation, arguing that certain provisions threatened to infringe upon the executive's autonomy. Even in the midst of the Great Depression, and after Franklin D. Roosevelt's landslide reelection victory in 1936, the political crisis triggered by the Supreme Court's invalidation of key New Deal law did not persuade the Congress to approve the president's "court-packing" plan. Democrats held large majorities in the House and Senate, but they were concerned that Roosevelt's action threatened the separation of powers system. The impact of crisis on legislative leadership depends on a common feeling of urgency, and a Congress ready to answer the president's initiatives. It is obvious that this consensus between the two branches of government does not always occur.

CONCLUSION

For many reasons a president's power as legislative leader is problematic. He lacks the authority to force Congress to enact his programs. Instead he must rely upon informal, political resources to shape the legislative arena for his advantage. The president can exert leadership by establishing Congress' agenda through such devices as the State of the Union Message, the executive budget, and his legislative program. He can expect to get more support from members of his party in Congress than from the opposition, which is why legislative leadership suffers during an era of "divided" government. But no president is able to rely upon a disciplined party organization in the Congress. The lawmaking process is continually buffeted by voter groups, constituency pressures, and special interests. It can be argued that these forces became more powerful in the 1970s. A modern president can rely on his liaison staff to lobby the Congress, but he cannot monopolize all the information relevant to assessing the desirability of each legislative proposal. It is rare for Congress to evaluate a bill simply on its merits; political calculations as well as normative considerations influence how legislation is judged. Crises do strengthen the president's leadership over Congress, as was shown, but this variable cannot be relied upon in terms of his day-to-day priorities. Thus, to understand the role of legislative leader, we must appreciate how myriad "political" conditions increase or reduce the executive's ability to influence the majority of congressmen and senators to support his programs. The dynamic quality of legislative leadership is *not* equivalent to those legal relationships affecting the president and Congress.

NOTES

[1] It was Howard Lee McBain who allegedly used the term "Chief legislator" for the first time in his 1927 book, *The Living Constitution* (New York: Macmillan Company, 1948), pp. 115–118.

[2] Arthur Schlesinger, Jr. and Alfred deGrazia, *Congress and the Presidency: Their Role in Modern Times* (Washington, D.C.: American Enterprise Institute for Public Policy Research, 1967), pp. 4–5.

[3] Joan C. MacLean, *President and Congress: The Conflict of Powers* (New York: H. W. Wilson Company, 1955), p. 15.

[4] Edward C. Corwin and Louis W. Koenig, *The Presidency Today* (New York: New York University Press, 1956), p. 83.

[5] Quoted in Stephen J. Wayne, *The Legislative Presidency* (New York: Harper and Row, 1978), p. 1.

[6] William M. Goldsmith, *The Growth of Presidential Power: A Documented History* (New York: Chelsea House Publishers, 1974), vol. 1, p. 347.

[7] James Sterling Young, *The Washington Community, 1800–1828* (New York: Columbia University Press, 1966), p. 147.

[8] Mary P. Ryan, "Party Formation in the U.S. Congress, 1789–1796: A Quantitative Analysis," *William and Mary Quarterly* (October 1971), pp. 523–542.

[9] Robert M. Johnstone, Jr., *Jefferson and the Presidency: Leadership in the Young Republic* (Ithaca, N.Y.: Cornell University Press, 1978), p. 133.

[10] James W. Davis and Delbert Ringquist, *The President and Congress: Toward a New Power Balance* (Woodbury, N.Y.: Barron's Educational Series, 1975), p. 21.

[11] James D. Richardson, *Messages and Papers of the Presidents*, vol. 1 (Washington, D.C.: Government Printing Office, 1897), pp. 331–332.

[12] Noble E. Cunningham, Jr., *The Process of Government under Jefferson* (Princeton, N.J.: Princeton University Press, 1978), p. 192.

[13] Ibid., p. 188.

[14] Ibid., p. 200.

[15] Johnstone, *Jefferson and the Presidency*, p. 151.

[16] Ibid., pp. 158–159.

[17] "Rules and Orders for Conducting Business in the House of Representatives," U.S. Congress, *House Journal* (December 17, 1805), vol. 5, p. 200.

[18] Noble E. Cunningham, *The Jeffersonian Republicans in Power, 1801–1809* (Chapel Hill: University of North Carolina Press, 1963), p. 74.

[19]James MacGregor Burns, *Presidential Government* (New York: Houghton Mifflin, 1973), p. 32.

[20]See the seminal work by Nelson W. Polsby on this topic, "The Institutionalization of the U.S. House of Representatives," *The American Political Science Review* (March 1968), 144–168.

[21]See Howard J. Silver, *Presidential Performance With Congress: 1954–1973*, Ph.D. diss. Ohio State University, 1975, p. 34.

[22]George C. Edwards III, "Presidential Legislative Skills as a Source of Influence in Congress," *Presidential Studies Quarterly* (Spring 1980), p. 216.

[23]"Congress 1965—The Year in Review: Johnson Leadership, Large Majority Win Legislative Grand Slam for Democrats," *Congressional Quarterly Almanac*, 1965, p. 65. Also see Erwin Hargrove, *Presidential Leadership: Personality and Political Style* (New York: Macmillan Company, 1966), p. 151.

[24]Milton Cummings, ed., *The National Election of 1964* (Washington, D.C.: Brookings Institution, 1966), pp. 247–248.

[25]John F. Manley, "Presidential Power and White House Lobbying," *Political Science Quarterly* (Summer 1978), p. 261.

[26]Quoted in Abraham Holtzman, *Legislative Liaison* (Indianapolis: Bobbs-Merrill, 1970), p. xii.

[27]Richard M. Pious, *The American Presidency* (New York: Basic Books, 1979), p. 188.

[28]Eric L. Davis, *Building Presidential Coalitions in Congress: Legislative Liaison in the Johnson White House*, Ph.D. diss., Stanford University, 1977, p. 53.

[29]Ibid., p. 284.

[30]Lawrence F. O'Brien, *No Final Victories: A Life in Politics—From John F. Kennedy to Watergate* (Garden City, N.Y.: Doubleday, 1974), p. 170.

[31]Ralph K. Huitt, "White House Channels to the Hill," in Harvey G. Mansfield, Sr., ed., *Congress Against the President* (New York: Praeger, 1975), p. 74.

[32]Quoted in Doris Kearns, *Lyndon Johnson and the American Dream* (New York: Harper and Row, 1976), p. 226.

[33]Alan L. Otten, "By Courting Congress Assiduously, Johnson Furthers His Program," *Wall Street Journal* (April 9, 1965), p. 1.

[34]Manley, "Presidential Power and White House Lobbying," p. 263.

[35]Reo M. Christenson, "Presidential Leadership of Congress: Ten Commandants Point the Way," *Presidential Studies Quarterly* (Summer 1978), p. 263.

[36]Kearns, *Lyndon Johnson and the American Dream*, p. 185.

[37]Edwards, "Presidential Legislative Skills as a Source of Influence in Congress," pp. 220–222.

[38]Manley, "Presidential Power and White House Lobbying," p. 269.

[39]Edwards, "Presidential Legislative Skills as a Source of Influence in Congress," p. 214.

[40]Lee Sigelman, "A Reassessment of the Two Presidencies Thesis," *Journal of Politics* (1979), p. 1201.

[41]Gary M. Fink, *Prelude to the Presidency: The Political Character and Legislative Leadership Style of Governor Jimmy Carter* (Westport, Conn.: Greenwood Press, 1980), p. 108.

[42]Ibid., p. 143.

[43]Ibid., p. 169.

[44]Quoted in Bob Rankin, "Senate Rejection of Carter Energy Proposals Attributed to Belief They Were Unwise," *Congressional Quarterly Weekly Report* (October 22, 1977), p. 2236.

[45]*Presidency 1977* (Washington, D.C.: Congressional Quarterly, Inc., 1978), p. 1.

[46]Tom Morganthau et al., "Carter Can't Get Up the Hill," *Newsweek* (October 1, 1979), p. 18.

[47]Ibid.

[48]Quoted in Richard E. Cohen, "The Carter-Congress Rift—Who's Really to Blame," *National Journal* (April 22, 1978), p. 630.

[49]Eric L. Davis, "Legislative Reform and the Decline of Presidential Influence on Capitol Hill," *British Journal of Political Science* (1979), p. 468.

[50]Ibid., 469.

[51]*President Carter 1978* (Washington, D.C., Congressional Quarterly, Inc., 1979), p. 12.

[52]Eric L. Davis, "Legislative Liaison in the Carter Administration," *Political Science Quarterly* (Summer 1979), p. 301.

[53]Charles Mohr, "Carter's First Nine Months: Charges of Ineptitude Rise," *New York Times* (October 23, 1977), p. 36.

[54]"White House Lobbyists Employ the Hard Sell . . . to Win Senate Support for Natural Gas Bill," *Congressional Quarterly Weekly Report* (September 16, 1978), p. 2453.

[55]Larry Light, "White House Lobby Gets Its Act Together," *Congressional Quarterly Weekly Report* (February 3, 1979), p. 196.

[56]Ibid.

[57]Ibid., p. 200.

[58]*Kennedy v. Sampson* (73-2121-22) (1974).

[59]Lawrence H. Chamberlain, *The President, Congress and Legislation* (New York: Columbia University Press, 1946).

[60]Ibid., p. 454. Another ten percent of the bills were classified by Chamberlain as "Pressure Group Influence Preponderant."

[61]Ronald C. Moe and Steven C. Teal, "Congress as Policy-Maker: A Necessary Reappraisal," *Political Science Quarterly* (September 1970), pp. 443–470.

[62]William M. Goldsmith, *The Growth of Presidential Power: A Documented History*, vol. III, p. 1400.

[63]Gary Orfield, *Congressional Power: Congress and Social Change* (New York: Harcourt Brace Jovanovich, 1975), p. 54.

[64]Aaron Wildavsky, "The Two Presidencies," *Trans-Action* (December 1966), pp. 7–14.

[65]Lance T. LeLoup and Steven A. Shull, "Congress Versus the Executive: The 'Two Presidencies' Reconsidered," *Social Science Quarterly* (March 1979), p. 707.

[66]See the Gallup Poll for Fall 1979 cited in Thomas E. Cronin, "A Resurgent Congress and the Imperial Presidency," *Political Science Quarterly* (Summer 1980), p. 211.

[67]MacLean, *President and Congress*, p. 61.

[68]Randall Ripley, *Party Leaders in the House of Representatives* (Washington, D.C.: Brookings Institution, 1967), p. 17.

[69]Ernest S. Griffith, *The Impasse of Democracy.* (New York: Harrison-Hilton Books, 1939).

[70]See Theodore J. Lowi, "American Business, Public Policy, Case Studies, and Political Theory," *World Politics* (July 1964), pp. 677–715.

[71]Theodore J. Lowi, "How the Farmers Get What They Want," in Lowi, ed., *Legislative Politics, U.S.A.* (Boston: Little, Brown and Company, 1965), pp. 132–139.

[72]Ibid., p. 139.

[73]Robert J. Spitzer, "The Presidency and Public Policy: A Preliminary Inquiry," *Presidential Studies Quarterly* (Fall 1979), pp. 441–457.

[74]Aaron Wildavsky, *The Politics of the Budgetary Process*, 3rd ed. (Boston: Little, Brown and Company, 1979), p. 1.

[75]David V. Edwards, *The American Political Experience* (Englewood Cliffs, N.J.: Prentice-Hall, 1979), p. 207.

[76]Louis Fisher, *President and Congress: Power and Policy* (New York: The Free Press, 1972), p. 87.

[77]See Aaron Wildavsky, *The Politics of the Budgetary Process*, 1979. The first edition of this volume was issued in 1964.

[78]Francis E. Rourke, *Bureaucracy, Politics and Public Policy* (Boston: Little, Brown and Company, 1969), p. 27.

[79]Arnold Kanter, "Congress and the Defense Budget: 1960–1970," *American Political Science Review* (March 1972), p. 131.

[80]Mohammed Ahrari and Andrew D. McNitt, "The Two Presidencies Reconsidered: Is There a Post-Imperial Presidency?," paper delivered at annual meeting, Midwest Political Science Association, Chicago, April 19, 1979. Cited in Charles Funderburk, *Presidents and Politics: The Limits of Power* (Monterey, Calif. Brooks/Cole, 1982), p. 272.

[81]"Budget: 'Congress Shall . . . Pay the Debts,' " *National Journal* (May 29, 1976), p. 742.

[82]"Budgetary Information," *Congressional Record* (March 19, 1974), 93rd Congress, 2nd Session, vol. 120, part 6, p. 7151.

[83]Joel Havemann, *Congress and the Budget* (Bloomington: Indiana University Press, 1978), pp. 100–101.

[84]"Congress: Servant or Equals? A Constitutional Question," *Congressional Record* (January 18, 1973), 93rd Congress, 1st Session, vol. 119, part 2, p. 1496.

[85]James W. Davis and Delbert Ringquist, *The President and Congress: Toward a New Power Balance*, p. 111.

[86]Joel Havemann, *Congress and the Budget*, p. 199.

[87]Ibid., p. 202.

[88]James A. Thurber, "New Powers of the Purse: An Assessment of Congressional Budget Reform," in Leroy N. Rieselbach, ed., *Legislative Reform* (Lexington, Mass.: Lexington Books, 1978), p. 168.

[89]Gail Gregg, "Swift Action: Reagan Proposes Dramatic Reduction in Federal Role," *Congressional Quarterly Weekly Report* (March 14, 1981), p. 443.

[90]Gail Gregg, "New Round of Budget Bargaining Begins," *Congressional Quarterly Weekly Report* (April 25, 1981), p. 705.

[91]Quoted in Dale Tate and Gail Gregg, "Targeting Savings: Congress Set for Showdown on First Budget Resolution," *Congressional Quarterly Weekly Report* (May 2, 1981), p. 743.

[92]Elizabeth Wehr, "White House's Lobbying Apparatus . . . Produces Impressive Tax Vote Victory," *Congressional Quarterly Weekly Report* (August 1, 1981), p. 1372.

[93]Allen Schick, "How the Budget Was Won and Lost," in Norman J. Ornstein, ed., *President and Congress: Assessing Reagan's First Year* (Washington, D.C.: American Enterprise Institute for Public Policy Research, 1982), pp. 25–26.

[94]Wehr, "White House's Lobbying Apparatus . . . Produces Impressive Tax Vote Victory," p. 1373.

[95]Elizabeth Wehr and Irwin B. Arieff, "Reagan's Veto Tactic Unsettling to Congress," *Congressional Quarterly Weekly Report* (November 28, 1981), p. 2328.

[96]Richard E. Cohen, "The Fiscal 1983 Budget Equation: Election and Recession = Frustration," *National Journal* (May 29, 1982), p. 944.

[97]"Congressmen Go to Court to Block Tax-Increase Bill," *Christian Science Monitor,* Midwest Edition (August 19, 1982), p. 2.

[98]Dale Tate, "Spending Stalemate Broken: President Hawks Tax Increase as Conferees Haggle Over Bill," *Congressional Quarterly Weekly Report* (August 14, 1982), p. 1947.

[99]See the excellent essays by Norman J. Ornstein; Allen Schick; Stephen J. Wayne; and I. M. Destler in Norman J. Ornstein, ed., *President and Congress: Assessing Reagan's First Year,* 1982.

[100]E. E. Schattschneider, *The Semi-Sovereign People: A Realist's View of Democracy in America* (New York: Holt, Rinehart and Winston, 1960).

[101]James Q. Wilson, "Two Negro Politicians: An Interpretation," *Midwest Journal of Political Science* (1960), pp. 346–369.

[102]Maris A. Vinovskis, "The Politics of Abortion in the House of Representatives in 1976," *Michigan Law Review* (1979), p. 1806.

[103]Warren Miller and Donald E. Stokes, "Constituency Influence in Congress," *American Political Science Review* (March 1963), pp. 45–56.

[104]Julius Turner, *Party and Constituency: Pressures on Congress* (Baltimore: Johns Hopkins Press, 1951); Duncan MacRae, Jr., *Dimensions of Congressional Voting* (Berkeley: University of California Press, 1958); David Truman, *The Congressional Party* (New York: John Wiley and Sons, 1959); Lewis A. Froman, Jr., *Congressmen and Their Constituencies* (Skokie, Ill.: Rand McNally, 1963).

[105]See John W. Kingdon, *Congressmen's Voting Decisions* (New York: Harper and Row, 1973); Donald R. Matthews and James A. Stimson, *Yeas and Nays: Normal Decision-Making in the U.S. House of Representatives* (New York: John Wiley and Sons, 1975); Aage R. Clausen, *How Congressmen Decide* (New York: St. Martin's Press, 1975); Cleo H. Cherryholmes and Michael J. Shapiro, *Representatives and Roll Calls* (Indianapolis: Bobbs-Merrill Company, 1969).

[106]See Jerrold E. Schneider, *Ideological Coalitions in Congress* (Westport, Conn.: Greenwood Press, 1979).

[107]Froman, *Congressmen and Their Constituencies*, pp.

[108]For an extensive analysis of the relationship between the president and the majority party in Congress see Randall B. Ripley, *Majority Party Leadership in Congress* (Boston: Little, Brown and Company, 1969).

[109]See "The Swarming Lobbyists," *Time* (August 7, 1978).

[110]The best account of the AMA's campaign against Truman's proposals is in Stanley Kelley, Jr., *Professional Public Relations and Political Power* (Baltimore: Johns Hopkins Press, 1956). On AMA's battle against Medicare see Theodore R. Marnor, *The Politics of Medicare* (London: Routledge and Kegan Paul, 1970).

[111]*Buckley v. Valeo*, 424 U.S. 1936 (1976).

[112]Robert S. Getz and Frank B. Feigert, *The Politics and Process of American Government* (Boston: Allyn and Bacon, 1982), p. 291.

[113]Robert Sherrill, *Governing America* (New York: Harcourt Brace Jovanovich, 1978), p. 133.

[114]See Lewis A. Froman, Jr. and Randall B. Ripley, "Conditions for Party Leadership: The Case of the House Democrats," *American Political Science Review* (March 1965), pp. 52–63.

[115]David Price, *Who Makes the Laws?* (Cambridge, Mass.: Schenkman, 1972), table 7, pp. 290–291.

[116]Eric L. Davis, *Building Presidential Coalitions in Congress: Legislative Liaison in the Johnson White House*, p. 33.

[117]Stephen J. Wayne, *The Legislative Presidency*, p. 142.

[118]Ibid., p. 145.

[119]Louis W. Koenig, *The Chief Executive*, 2nd ed. (New York: Harcourt, Brace, World, 1968), pp. 125–126.

[120]Robert Sherrill, *Why They Call It Politics* (New York: Harcourt Brace Jovanovich, 1972), p. 67.

[121]For this discussion we have relied on the excellent case study by Richard E. Neustadt and Harvey V. Fineberg, *The Swine Flu Affair: Decision-Making on a Slippery Disease* (Washington, D.C.: United States Department of Health, Education and Welfare, 1978).

SUGGESTED READINGS

Chamberlain, Laurence H. *The President, Congress and Legislation.* New York: Columbia University Press, 1946.

Davis, James W., and Ringquist, Delbert. *The President and Congress: Toward a New Power Balance.* Woodbury, N.Y.: Barron's Educational Series, 1975.

deGrazia, A. *Congress and the Presidency: Their Role in Modern Times.* Washington, D.C.: American Enterprise Institute, 1967.

Edwards, George C. III. *Presidential Influence in Congress.* San Francisco: W. H. Freeman, 1980.

Fisher, Louis. *President and Congress: Power and Policy.* New York: Free Press, 1972.

────── *The Constitution Between Friends: Congress, the President and the Law.* New York: St. Martin's Press, 1978.

────── *The Politics of Shared Power: Congress and the Executive.* Washington, D.C.: Congressional Quarterly Press, 1981.

Holtzman, Abraham. *Legislative Liaison: Executive Leadership in Congress.* Chicago: Rand McNally, 1970.

Johannes, John. *Congress and Policy Innovation.* Morristown, N.J.: General Learning Press, 1972.

Kessel, John. *The Domestic President.* Belmont, Calif.: Wadsworth, 1975.

Livingston, William S.; Dodd, Lawrence C.; and Schott, Richard L. *The Presidency and the Congress: A Shifting Balance of Power.* Austin, Tex.: LBJ School of Public Affairs, 1979.

Mansfield, Harvey, Sr., ed. *Congress Against the President.* New York: Praeger, 1976.

Moe, Ronald, ed. *Congress and the President.* Pacific Palisades, Calif.: Goodyear Publishing Co., 1976.

Orfield, Gary. *Congressional Power.* New York: Harcourt Brace Jovanovich, 1975.

Ornstein, Norman J., ed., *President and Congress: Assessing Reagan's First Year.* Washington, D.C.: American Enterprise Institute for Public Policy Research, 1982.

Schlesinger, Arthur M., Jr., and deGrazia, Alfred. *Congress and the Presidency: Their Role in Modern Times.* Washington, D.C.: American Enterprise Institute for Public Policy Research, 1967.

Wayne, Stephen J. *The Legislative Presidency.* New York: Harper and Row, 1978.

Wildavsky, Aaron. *The Politics of the Budgetary Process.* 3rd ed. Boston: Little, Brown and Company, 1979.

CHAPTER FIVE

Chief Executive: The Struggle Against Congressional Government

At first glance, the president as chief executive appears quite powerful because he shares this power with no other elected official or board. Yet the chief executive is often frustrated by opposition in this role because the Constitution fragments control over the bureaucracy, making it difficult for any president to dominate the executive branch of government. Not only does the president share jurisdiction over the bureaucracy with Congress but, as James MacGregor Burns indicates, "one finds lines of authority running horizontally from committee or Congressman to department or bureau chief." This means "authority is shifted from the President and dispersed throughout the bureaucracy."[1] Moreover, a president's management function does not command high priority, for his other political concerns usually take precedence. The role of chief executive is complicated further by the very size of the federal government, and by the thousands of statutes, regulations, executive orders, and agency rules that are promulgated each year. In addition to the 3 million civilian employees now working for the federal government (table 5-1), a president occasionally interacts with some of the 13 million employees of state and local governments as well as another 6 to 7 million employees in the private sector who are hired for government projects.

The complexity of the federal government is also evident in the multitude of administrative units and subunits into which the executive branch is organized (figure 5-1). Grant McConnell has estimated that there are at least 1,800 administrative units in the executive branch.[2] For example, the Department of Health and Human Services alone has more than forty major

TABLE 5-1   Civilian employment in the federal government, 1816–1980

Year	Total employees	President
1816	4,837	Madison
1851	26,274	Fillmore
1881	100,020	Arthur
1901	239,476	T. Roosevelt
1921	561,142	Harding
1930	601,319	Hoover
1940	1,042,420	F. Roosevelt
1945	3,816,310	Truman
1950	1,960,708	Truman
1955	2,397,309	Eisenhower
1960	2,430,000	Eisenhower
1965	2,539,000	Johnson
1970	2,928,000	Nixon
1975	2,882,000	Ford
1980	2,987,000	Carter

Source: U.S. Bureau of the Census, *Historical Statistics of the United States: Colonial Times to 1957* (Washington, D.C.: U.S. Government Printing Office, 1957), p. 710; *Statistical Abstract of the United States, 1981*, p. 266.

subdivisions. The bureaus and agencies owe some loyalty to Congress—since it established them and funds their activities each year—and to certain clientele groups that give them political support, so there is a constant pull away from allegiance to the chief executive. In addition, an entire group of agencies, boards, commissions, and corporations is independent of the president's direct control (table 5-2). These independent units of government cover a variety of policy areas, with the ability to resist both the president and Congress. For example, when Congress approved a tax increase in 1968 to reduce inflationary pressures caused by the Vietnam War, the Federal Reserve Board offset that action by increasing the money supply. Such divergent policies, argues Rep. Henry S. Reuss (D.–Wis.), raise the question: "with fiscal and monetary policy pulling in opposite directions, how is one to pinpoint responsibility for the nation's economic performance?"[3]

Obviously, this huge bureaucracy is so complex, chaotic, confused, and dispersed, that the system is too cumbersome for one president to manage alone. Alexander Hamilton had warned about this danger when he argued in *Federalist #70* for unity in the executive branch. He further suggested in *Federalist #72* that to preserve this unity, administrators should be appointed and remain accountable to the executive. Harry Truman was equally sensitive to this problem; from time to time he would show visitors a wall chart depicting more than one-hundred offices which directly reported to him. And each time Truman would complain, "I cannot even see all these men, let alone actually study what they are doing."[4] The task facing a chief executive looks almost insuperable, but each president has tried to cope with these responsibilities by using his constitutional mandate and whatever power accrues to him by statute, custom, and judicial precedent.

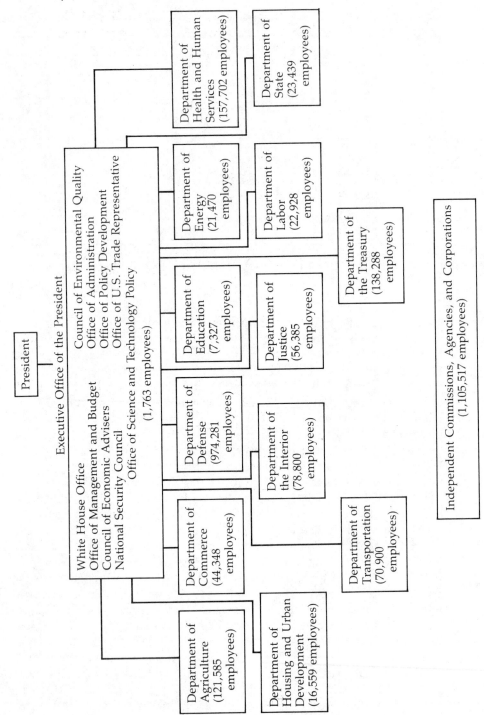

FIGURE 5-1 Executive branch of government (1981). *Source: Statistical Abstract of the United States, 1981,* p. 268.

TABLE 5-2 Independent agencies, commissions, and corporations (1980)

Action (1971)[1]	International Communication Agency (1978)[1]
Administrative Conference of the United States (1964)[1]	Interstate Commerce Commission (1887)[2]
American Battle Monuments Commission (1923)[2]	Merit Systems Production Board (1978)[1]
Appalachian Regional Commission (1965)[2]	National Aeronautics and Space Administration (1958)[1]
Board for International Broadcasting (1973)[1]	National Capital Planning Commission (1952)[2]
Central Intelligence Agency (1947)[1]	National Credit Union Administration (1970)[1]
Civil Aeronautics Board (1938)[1]	National Foundation on the Arts and Humanities (1965)[1]
Commission on Civil Rights (1957)[2]	National Labor Relations Board (1935)[1]
Commission on Fine Arts (1910)[2]	National Mediation Board (1934)[1]
Commodity Futures Trading Commission (1974)[2]	National Science Foundation (1950)[1]
Community Services Administration (1974)[1]	National Transportation Safety Board (1975)[1]
Consumer Product Safety Commission (1972)[2]	Nuclear Regulatory Commission (1974)[2]
Environmental Protection Agency (1970)[1]	Occupational Safety and Health Review Commission (1970)[2]
Equal Employment Opportunity Commission (1964)[2]	Office of Personnel Management (1978)[1]
Export-Import Bank of the United States (1934)[3]	Panama Canal Commission (1979)[2]
Farm Credit Administration (1971)[1]	Pension Benefit Guaranty Corporation (1974)[3]
Federal Communications Commission (1934)[2]	Postal Rate Commission (1970)[2]
Federal Deposit Insurance Corporation (1933)[3]	Railroad Retirement Board (1935)[1]
	Securities and Exchange Commission (1934)[2]
Federal Election Commission (1974)[2]	Selective Service System (1948)[1]
Federal Emergency Management Agency (1978)[1]	Small Business Administration (1953)[1]
Federal Home Loan Bank Board (1932)[1]	Tennessee Valley Authority (1933)[3]
Federal Labor Relations Authority (1978)[1]	United States Arms Control and Disarmament Agency (1961)[1]
Federal Maritime Commission (1961)[2]	United States International Development Cooperation Agency (1979)[1]
Federal Mediation and Conciliation Service (1947)[1]	United States International Trade Commission (1974)[2*]
Federal Reserve System (1913)[1]	United States Metric Board (1975)[1]
Federal Trade Commission (1914)[2]	United States Postal Service (1970)[1]
General Services Administration (1949)[1]	Veterans Administration (1930)[1]
Inter-American Foundation (1969)[3]	

Source: *U.S. Government Manual 1981/1982* (Washington, D.C.: U.S. Government Printing Office, 1981), pp. VI–VII.
Legend: [1]Independent agencies
[2]Independent commissions
[3]Independent corporations
*Formerly known as U.S. Tariff Commission (1916).
Year of establishment is shown in parentheses.

AUTHORITY

The president is expected to manage a bureaucracy, supervise subordinates, and implement public policies, yet has little authority to carry out such responsibilities. Louis Koenig contrasts this dilemma of the president with the authority of a business executive.

Unlike the typical business chief, the President finds no designation in his fundamental charter, the Constitution, as administrative chief. Neither do its collective provisions confer any equivalent authority. The Constitution does grant him the "executive power," language the Supreme Court has sometimes interpreted to include certain powers normally associated with an administrative chief. He is charged to see that the laws are "faithfully executed," which suggests a general administrative responsibility, but duty is not power. He also enjoys express powers such as the power to make appointments. Still other authority is conferred by act of Congress and by weight of custom.[5]

As is the case in other roles, authority based on statute and custom can be fragile, especially when executive/legislative tensions heighten. In the Constitution, the president's authority as chief executive is established in Article II in two clauses. One specifies that "the executive power shall be vested in a President of the United States of America," and the other indicates that the president has the responsibility to "take care that the laws be faithfully executed." This provision is very different from the way legislative power is granted to the Congress. The Framers chose to give Congress specific grants of power in very precise terms but the vague manner in which the president was granted administrative powers makes it unclear exactly what a president was supposed to do. For example, the president was to receive "opinions in writing" from the principal advisers he appoints to the executive departments, but the relationship of these officers to each other and to the president, as well as their duties and functions, was unspecified. Even in the usually explicit language of the Constitution, therefore, it was left unclear how far presidential power could extend in the role of chief executive.

Appointment

A primary means by which the president directs the executive branch is the appointive power. However, though a president may delay nominations to appointive positions, he cannot refuse to fill them, as Richard Nixon discovered when he refused to make appointments to the National Advisory Council on Indian Education. Nixon was taken to court when he failed to fill vacancies on the council. A district court said that, while a president has discretion to decide who would sit on this agency, he had no right to determine whether the council would be constituted or not.[6]

Nevertheless, it is not easy for a modern president to make the number of appointments available to him during a term. In 1796 George Washington submitted only eighty-five names to the Senate for civil and military positions in his administration. In fact, Robert Sickels reminds us, "George Washington supervised more people on his plantation in Virginia than in any of the executive department's central offices."[7] Yet by 1834, under Andrew Jackson, the president could appoint 785 positions. In 1914 this number had grown to 3,418 appointees; in 1935, to 14,998 positions; and by 1945 this figure increased to 40,557.[8]

Today a president appoints 100,000 positions throughout the federal government, including military commissions and advisory committees, but he is able to fill less than 3,000 top-level policymaking positions. This small number in a 3 million-person bureaucracy shows that no chief executive can assume direct control over any agency. In 1977, for example, there were eleven appointive positions in the 15,650-person Department of Housing and Urban Development, twenty in the 129,525-person Department of Health, Education and Welfare, and ten in the 14,910-Department of Labor.[9] This circumstance can frustrate a newly elected president. When Jimmy Carter became president he wanted to remake the General Services Administration (GSA) but quickly learned that the president could appoint only twenty-one positions in that 37,000-person agency. Consequently the GSA lacked Carter's stamp of "newness."

The same story applies to any modern president. Dwight Eisenhower found this problem especially troublesome, because it had been so many years since a Republican occupied the White House. Civil servants who had been "blanketed-in" during the Roosevelt and Truman administrations, he believed, did not share his political philosophy. Roosevelt staffed newly created New Deal agencies with his loyal appointees, and then put these employees under the protection of civil service. Truman followed a similar policy to insure support for his Fair Deal. Eisenhower had to find ways of releasing some of these positions from civil service protection. He implemented a Schedule "C" allowing such "supergrade" positions as GS16–GS18 to be removed from civil service and made available for political appointments. As a result, today there are approximately 1,100 such positions open to presidential appointment.[10]

Once positions are available for appointment by the president, it is necessary to find appointees who are loyal, have managerial experience, and represent important political constituencies. Richard Nixon began his personnel search by using a mass mailing system to solicit names, and a large number of prominent citizens were contacted in 1969 for suggestions for prospective appointees. Most presidents automatically limit their search to their political party; whenever a president appoints somebody from the other party to high office, such as the cabinet, part of the intent is to convey the impression that his administration has broad-based, bipartisan support. For example, President Nixon appointed Peter J. Brennan the secretary of labor and Daniel P. Moynihan his urban affairs adviser, though both men were Democrats. Jimmy Carter chose James Schlesinger, a Republican, to be his secretary of energy. President Reagan included Democrats in his administration: United Nations Ambassador Jeane Kirkpatrick and John O. Marsh, Jr., secretary of the army. But such appointments are the exception, not the rule.

Additional political constraints on the appointment power are imposed on the president by special interests and voter blocs. When filling the position of secretary of agriculture, for example, a Democratic president will try to satisfy the National Farmers Union, whereas a Republican president looks to the American Farm Bureau Federation for advice. In recent administrations, a black has been chosen as secretary of the Department of Housing and Urban Development (HUD) to suggest that the president is committed to solving the problems of big cities where minority groups reside. As secretary of HUD, President Carter appointed Patricia Harris and Ronald Reagan named Samuel R. Pierce, Jr. According to William Lammers, moreover, certain departments are given appointees from identical professions regardless of which president makes the appointments. Most secretaries of defense and of treasury have business experience in large corporations; treasury secretaries often have banking experience in their backgrounds.[11] Secretaries of agriculture typically have farming backgrounds and often are recruited from the Midwest; President Reagan's Secretary of Agriculture, John Block, was an Illinois farmer. Finally, political appointments can be payments for campaign debts, and large contributors historically have been rewarded with important positions in the administration, such as ambassadorships. Though there has been improvement in the quality of appointments to the foreign service since 1975, patronage appointments are still made.[12]

The Constitution requires that certain presidential appointees be confirmed in the Senate by majority vote, but generally the president is allowed to make his executive appointments without much Senate interference. This pattern may be changing, however. Calvin MacKenzie determined that only eleven major presidential nominations were rejected by the Senate during 1961–1973, whereas almost three times as many rejections occurred in 1974 (six), 1975 (seven), 1976 (ten), and 1977 (six).[13] These data imply that the Senate may be scrutinizing the president's nominees more carefully in the post-Watergate era. Rejection usually follows charges that the appointee is controversial, represents an extremist position, or is involved in a conflict of interest. In 1973, for example, the Senate refused to confirm Robert H. Morris for a position on the Federal Power Commission because he had an especially close relationship with the industries he would be regulating. One of Reagan's first defeats in Congress in 1981 involved his nomination of Ernest W. Lefever to be assistant secretary of state for human rights and humanitarian affairs. Since this position was created at Congress' urging, it had symbolic importance for U.S. commitment to human rights. Lefever was supported by right-wing Republicans in the Senate and he was not sympathetic to promoting human rights overseas. After the Senate Foreign Relations Committee voted against his nomination, Lefever's name was withdrawn from consideration.

Although not all appointments by a president require Senate confirmation, Congress has discretion to designate which positions need Senate approval. At first the director of the Office of Management and Budget (formerly Bureau of the Budget) was not subject to Senate approval, but during the Nixon administration the Senate recognized the importance of this position. With the passage of the Budget and Impoundment Control Act of 1974, both the director and deputy director of OMB became subject to Senate confirmation.

Removal power

There is no mention of a removal power in the Constitution, except concerning impeachment, and for this reason the president's power to remove administrators is even more tenuous than his power to appoint them in the first place. In fact, interpretations of a president's removal power have varied since the Constitutional Convention. Alexander Hamilton in *Federalist #77* suggested that the removal power could be presumed from the power to appoint, but he also favored a Senate role over removals insofar as it had to approve appointments. In the first Congress James Madison argued in favor of a removal power, saying that it was implied in the president's authority to "take care that the laws be faithfully executed." Other members of the first Congress supported the idea of allowing Congress to delegate removal authority to the president, if necessary, or giving such power to the judiciary or to Congress. However, a majority of congressmen adhered more closely to Madison's view, which granted removal power to the president.

Today removals from office are often subject to administrative rules and regulations and to decisions issued by the courts and by Congress. As a result, certain appointments made by a president have greater immunity from his removal power than do others. In 1935 the Supreme Court protected members of the "independent" regulatory commissions from being arbitrarily removed by a president, but a member of the cabinet is not so protected. In general, a chief executive has more control over removal when applied to presidential advisers, such as the cabinet or White House staff. Few people today would question a president's absolute right to control his own cabinet and staff, but this was not always the case.

Prior to President Jackson's removal of Treasury Secretary Duane, there was more sympathy for Senate participation in this kind of decision. Although Jackson had removed 252 officers within the executive branch (more removals than all his predecessors combined), his firing of Duane for refusing to follow Jackson's order to remove deposits from the United States Bank and to distribute them to state banks prompted Senate opposition to President Jackson in 1833. In reaction, the Senate censured Andrew Jackson for assuming powers not granted to him. Its resolution stated *"Resolved,* That the President, in the late Executive proceedings in relation to the public revenue, has assumed upon himself authority and power not conferred by the Constitution and laws, but in derogation of both."[14]

Eventually President Jackson was able to have that censure resolution expunged from the official record, and his ultimate victory helped to secure a president's removal power over his own cabinet members. In 1867, however, this authority was again challenged by Congress. The 1867 Tenure of Office Act specified that all officers appointed under one president were to serve for the duration of that president's term. Furthermore, it stated that such officers could not be removed by the president without Senate concurrence. Andrew Johnson felt that this law was unconstitutional, and he proceeded to remove Secretary of War Stanton from his cabinet. The reaction to Stanton's removal was, of course, the near-impeachment of President Johnson by the Congress.

Although firing members of the cabinet is not as tenuous today as it was under the Tenure of Office Act, removing a cabinet member may incur political costs. According to David Truman, even department secretaries who have a strong and independent power base with supportive clientele groups can be removed from office, but in doing so the president may jeopardize his relationship with those interest groups. For this reason Franklin D. Roosevelt refused to remove Jesse Jones, his secretary of commerce and liaison with the business community. However, after Washington gossip labeled Jones unsupportive of the Democratic party's national ticket, it became safe for Roosevelt to replace him.[15] As distasteful as it may be to him, sometimes a president has no choice but to remove an executive officer when an impropriety is alleged amid much publicity. Though he was eventually vindicated, Richard Allen—Reagan's first national security adviser—was encouraged to resign amidst charges that he received expensive gifts from Japanese businessmen.

Resignation is also the preferred way to eliminate an adviser who is a constant source of conflict within the administration. This is how Ronald Reagan handled the case of Alexander Haig, his first secretary of state; Haig resigned after a series of highly publicized disputes with other presidential advisers over the conduct of foreign policy. Less political fallout will accompany a resignation, compared with a removal, because fewer people are implicated. In addition, the president does not have to admit that he made a mistake in appointing that person to the office in the first place.

In summary, it is clear that much less authority has evolved upon the chief executive through customary practice, judicial precedent, or statutory delegation. Unlike their strong support of the commander-in-chief and the chief diplomat, the Supreme Court and Congress defer less to a president acting as chief executive. Accordingly, whenever the legislative and judicial branches become involved in the administration of government, it is more likely that they will share authority with the president in ways that limit his supervisory powers over the bureaucracy. The role of Congress and the Supreme Court in the administrative arena, consequently, should be viewed in terms of their participation in decision making rather than in terms of partners supportive of a greater constitutional role by the president in this sphere.

In addition, decision making in the chief executive role involves the bureaucracy, subnational political elites, and even clientele groups. It obviously includes the president and his advisory system, for the degree of control a chief executive wields over the bureaucracy depends in large measure on how he utilizes his advisers, cabinet, and staff. Although the scope of governmental activities has increased greatly since Franklin D. Roosevelt's New

Deal, the existence of so many decision makers in the bureaucratic arena hints that perhaps the chief executive was stronger during earlier periods of smaller government.

DECISION MAKING

Supreme Court

An issue that illustrates the degree of judicial intervention in governmental administration is the president's removal power.[16] As early as 1803, in the well-known case of *Marbury* v. *Madison*, the Supreme Court decided that a president had removal authority only until an appointment was actually made, at which point it ended. The Court said, "[t]he right to the office is *then* in the person appointed, and he has the absolute, unconditional, power of accepting or rejecting it." In subsequent cases the Court's support of the chief executive in firing subordinates was quite uneven. In *U.S.* v. *Perkins* (1886), the Supreme Court said that the secretary of the Navy had no authority to relieve a cadet naval officer of his duty since he had not been charged with violating the law or misconduct. And though Presidents Grover Cleveland, William McKinley, and Woodrow Wilson were supported by the rulings in *Parsons* v. *U.S.* (1897), *Shurtleff* v. *U.S.* (1903), and *Wallace* v. *U.S.* (1922) when they terminated various administrative officials, the Supreme Court hinted in these decisions that the Senate had a role in approving removals. That is, the Court reasoned that Senate approval for a removal was indicated whenever it confirmed the successor for that person's position. Moreover, it stated that a president's removal authority could be limited by the statute that established the position affected by the removal power.

These limits to the president's power to fire subordinates were put aside, though only temporarily, by the Court's landmark decision in *Myers, Administratrix* v. *U.S.* in 1926. Woodrow Wilson had appointed Frank S. Myers in 1917 to the position of first-class postmaster in Portland, Oregon, for a four-year term. Before the term expired, however, Wilson removed him from office. An Act of Congress of 1876 stated that the appointment or removal of postmasters of the first, second, or third class required the advice and consent of the Senate. The Senate had played no role in dismissing Myers, who sued for eighteen months of back pay. The Supreme Court's lengthy majority decision in the *Myers* case was delivered by Chief Justice Taft, whose prior experience as president no doubt led him to fully support Wilson's action. Taft argued that, since no limit on the removal power existed in the Constitution and since it is as important as the appointment power, a president should have an unchecked power to remove subordinates from office. That the Senate had a role in the appointment process is no reason, he argued, for extending its role to removals as well. Taft saw no difference between removing inferior or superior offices, and therefore concluded that the 1876 law limiting a president's removal power was unconstitutional.

This 1926 decision, justifying a president's unrestricted power to terminate subordinates, was amended just nine years later in the equally famous case of *Humphrey's Executor (Rathbun)* v. *U.S.* (1935). In this instance, Roosevelt had asked Hoover-appointee William E. Humphrey to resign from the Federal Trade Commission (FTC), though his term did not end until 1938. His resignation was requested because Roosevelt believed that FTC policies should be implemented by people loyal to the New Deal. Humphrey refused to resign and Roosevelt removed him from office in 1933; Humphrey said he deserved his salary and, after he died in 1934, his executor sued. The question eventually came before the Supreme Court. The fundamental issue considered by Justice Sutherland was whether a president could remove an FTC commissioner even though the act creating the FTC stipulated that a commissioner could be removed by the president only for inefficiency, neglect of duty, and malfeasance of office. Sutherland concluded for the Court that Congress' intent was written clearly in the FTC statute; its intent was to establish an independent body of experts outside the control of the executive. Sutherland drew the distinction between the position of postmaster, the focus of attention in *Myers,* and that of FTC commissioner and concluded that there was no similarity. Whereas the postmaster was an "executive officer," the independent regulatory commissions such as the FTC possess quasi-judicial and quasi-legislative functions. By this decision, therefore, the Supreme Court set a precedent for judicial intervention in questions affecting a president's removal power, for the Court indicated that the degree of presidential removal authority depends on the character of the office in question.

In the years since *Humphrey's Executor,* various appeals of the president's use of removal power have been taken to the federal judiciary.[17] One of these cases, *Wiener* v. *U.S.* (1958), affirmed *Humphrey's Executor,* and thus prevented President Eisenhower from removing a member of the temporary War Claims Commission. Eisenhower wanted his own nominee on that commission and removed Wiener, who was appointed by Truman; Eisenhower's argument was similar to Roosevelt's in *Humphrey's Executor.* But the Court rejected his plea, saying that the president was not given this removal power by the Constitution or by any statute.

During the Nixon administration, a widely publicized case involved Nixon's firing of the special Watergate prosecutor, Archibald Cox, in the so-called 1973 Saturday Night Massacre. Nixon's action prompted much opposition and was immediately challenged in Court in the case of *U.S.* v. *Nixon* (1974). Here the Supreme Court said that the president could not remove the special prosecutor because he was appointed with the concurrence of congressional leaders. Removal of the special prosecutor was possible only for "extraordinary improprieties" and only after the president conferred with the majority and minority party leaders in Congress and the chairmen and ranking minority members of the Senate and House judiciary committees. This had not been done, and Nixon was denied authority to remove the special prosecutor.

In a recent case, the Supreme Court protected the president from civil law suits resulting from his use of removal power, but did not extend this immunity to presidential aides. The Supreme Court in *Nixon* v. *Fitzgerald* (1982) did not question Nixon's dismissal in 1970 of A. Ernest Fitzgerald, an Air Force management analyst who had in 1968 called Congress' attention to the cost overruns in constructing C5A cargo planes for the Air Force. The Court did rule 5 to 4 that current and former presidents had "absolute immunity" from law suits that sought money damages for misconduct in office. Justice Lewis F. Powell stated, "[w]e consider this immunity a functionally mandated incident of the President's unique office, rooted in the constitutional tradition of the separation of powers and supported by our history." The Court said that the president's actions must be within the "outer perimeter" of his official duties to receive this protection and, in this case, the removal of Fitzgerald was so considered. In his dissent, Justice White charged that giving a president absolute immunity from suit allows the president to ". . . injure Federal employees or any other person within or without the Government." Nonetheless, as a result of this decision, it would appear that the president has a freer hand in removing subordinates without fear of civil suit.

Another aspect of the chief executive role that has received some attention by the courts is the degree of latitude a president has when implementing the law. All presidents enjoy some discretion in administering government policies, but occasionally Congress tries to limit his range of options. In the famous case of *Mississippi* v. *Johnson* (1867), the Supreme Court argued that a president is legally immune from being forced to carry out his duties or prevented from going beyond his powers, though the Justices acknowledged that no president is immune from political reprisals.[18] Richard Nixon's impoundment of funds appropriated by Congress, however, complicated this precedent, and Arthur Miller contends that impoundments will not be upheld by the courts when congressional appropriations are mandatory, not discretionary.[19] However, the question of impoundment is more clearly legislative in nature insofar as such authority is delegated by statute.

Congress' role

From the discussion so far, it is clear that Congress affects decision making in the chief executive role in a wide variety of ways. Virtually the entire bureaucracy is established by law, and statutes detail the organization of the federal civil service regarding examination, selection, and promotion; classification of positions and pay scales; collective bargaining rights; "bonus" points in hiring veterans; and medical, life insurance, and retirement benefits. Funding for the agencies depends on their annual appropriations by Congress. As noted, the Senate has a voice in confirming executive appointees, but Congress can stipulate the qualifications, powers, and duration of whatever executive position is created, in addition to indicating what reasons justify the official's removal. In a few cases, congressmen or senators are included in the membership of executive agencies. For example, the Trade Act of 1974 included ten members of Congress as advisers to the United States trade delegation when involved in international trade negotiations. The Federal Election Commission's membership also included the president's appointees as well as members of the Senate and the House of Representatives (before being nullified by the Supreme Court).

Moreover, Congress can require the agencies of government to give "due process" in their decision making and implementation of policies. The Administrative Procedure Act of 1946 requires public notification and testimony regarding administrative rule making, and provides that boards or committees—representing private interests—be constituted to advise the federal agencies on the implementation of legislation. The Freedom of Information Act (1966) and the Sunshine Act (1976) are intended to assure citizens and private groups more access to administrative decision-making processes, along with access to public documents.

The federal civil service system was established when Congress passed the Pendleton Act in 1883. This law originally applied to only 10 percent of government employees, and was administered by a three-member Civil Service Commission apart from the president's direct control. Today over 90 percent of federal civilian employees are under the civil service system. Though civil service was intended to assure that federal employees are recruited according to "merit" rather than patronage considerations and to guarantee them a degree of job security, the system also can handicap a president who tries to exercise managerial controls over the federal bureaucracy. It is difficult for the president to reassign key personnel where needed, to institute cost-effective methods, and to reward superior performance by individuals. In an effort to redress these deficiencies in the civil service system, President Jimmy Carter proposed a series of reforms (the Civil Service Reform Act) which Congress enacted in 1978.

The Civil Service Commission was replaced with three separate agencies. The Office of Personnel Management (OPM) assumed most of the personnel management tasks previously handled by the Civil Service Commission; it is headed by a director who is appointed by the president upon Senate approval. The Merit Systems Protection Board (MSPD) is charged with protecting the integrity of the merit system by reviewing OPM rules and hearing appeals about employee grievances. The MSPD is a three-member, bipartisan board appointed by the president for one seven-year term; the members also are confirmed by the Senate. The Federal Labor Relations Authority (FLRA) hears complaints about unfair labor practices within the federal government, particularly regarding the government's relationship with employee bargaining agents. It is also a bipartisan, three-member board, whose members serve five-year terms after being appointed by the president and confirmed by the Senate. Thus, by enacting the Civil Service Reform Act of 1978, Congress tried to strengthen the president's managerial capability while, at the same time, adhering to the traditional view that civil service should be protected from partisan, political influences.

The major change accomplished by this legislation, however, was Congress' acceptance of the Carter administration proposal for a Senior Executive Service (SES). Agencies would now designate positions, mainly within the supergrades, to be included in the SES. The objective was to increase productivity by offering merit pay raises and bonuses for superior performance. On the other hand, these senior executives could be assigned throughout the federal government, and individuals who fail to meet its performance standards could be removed from the SES without long delays or red tape. The concept of an elite managerial corps in the federal bureaucracy was slow to develop in the Congress, though various students of public administration have pointed to the advantages of the senior civil service system used in Great Britain. A fundamental problem facing any president is the fact that our traditional civil service system assures that federal employees, particularly the careerists at high levels, will be more loyal to their agencies and programs than to the goals of the chief executive. The 1978 reforms were intended to rectify this situation, as a Carter aide who authored this legislation stated, "The underlying theory of the SES is that the top layer of bureaucracy will be more responsive to the President."[20]

In terms of the day-to-day operations of the federal government, the president enjoys substantial discretion based on statutory delegations to implement the law. But, as noted throughout this volume, powers given to the chief executive can be taken back by Congress. This fact was illustrated many times during the Nixon administration. The uneasy relationship between the president and Congress was apparent in the 1970s in three aspects of administration: impoundment, government reorganization, and legislative oversight.

Impoundment.   A president "impounds" funds when he refuses to spend moneys appropriated by the Congress. Most court cases involving impoundments have been decided against the president, precisely because that authority is derived from statutes. To this extent, therefore, legislative or judicial controls on a president's impoundment authority can prevent him from using that power to shape the nation's fiscal policy, at least insofar as the rate of government spending is concerned. Serious intervention by Congress in this area really began in 1974. Prior to 1974 Congress was willing to support the president's control over funding. The Anti-Deficiency Act of 1905 has been used by presidents to justify their impoundments; it allowed the chief executive to parcel out appropriations to the bureaus and agencies to assure that their expenditures did not exceed the sums appropriated. Franklin D. Roosevelt was the first contemporary president to make significant use of his impoundment authority. He did so during the Depression and World War II to gain a degree of flexibility over government spending in coping with those emergencies. Though Congress set limits on the total amounts Roosevelt could spend, he would impound funds he did not use. Presidents Truman, Eisenhower, Kennedy, and Johnson also impounded funds during their terms.[21] Although their impoundments primarily involved defense spending, the sums involved were substantial; Eisenhower, for example, impounded nearly $7 billion yearly, while Kennedy's total reached more than $6 billion.

Lyndon Johnson resorted to impoundments as a way of imposing his will on Congress in both domestic and foreign policy as well as a way of keeping control over inflation. Richard Nixon impounded funds most extensively—more than $30 billion during his first term and $12.2 billion in 1972 alone.[22] Nixon impounded one-half of the $18 billion earmarked by Congress for sewer programs, and reduced the funding allotted to four housing programs, seven community development projects, five agricultural projects, and several health and educational programs.[23] Nixon ended all funding for the Rural Electrification Act of 1936, and refused to spend all moneys appropriated for water pollution control. In the latter case, Nixon's impoundment of funds allocated under the Federal Water Pollution Control Act Amendments of 1972 prompted many states and localities, which were to receive those federal funds, to challenge those impoundments in court.[24] Eventually the Supreme Court reviewed two cases involving funds for water pollution control, and ruled against President Nixon.[25] The Court did not address the question of whether the president had "executive" authority to impound funds but rather said that, in this instance, the impoundments infringed on Congress' control over appropriations. Those funds had already been obligated according to statutory guidelines, and thus Nixon could not refuse to spend that money. In using his impoundment authority, therefore, President Nixon, unlike his predecessors, utilized this power as an "item veto" to undermine certain programs he opposed. As Sen. Hubert Humphrey (D.–Minn.) observed:

> Under policy impoundment, funds are withheld not to effect savings, nor as directed by Congress, nor as Commander-in-Chief, but because the President has unilaterally decided to impound money for programs that are not his priorities. It is a method for substituting executive will for congressional purpose.[26]

As a consequence, Congress in 1974 proceeded to enact the Congressional Budget and Impoundment Control Act, which dramatically reduced the president's ability to impound funds (see page 161). Title X of the law specifies that a president can impound funds only to provide for "contingencies" or "savings" when "greater efficiency of operations" is demanded. No longer can presidents control the flow of funds to agencies the way they could before 1974. Now they can delay funding ("deferral") for a period not to exceed one fiscal year, and either House or Senate can disallow that action at any time. Rescissions (or permanently cutting funds) are more difficult; to cut funds from the budget that have already been appropriated, the president must get majority approval in the House and the Senate within forty-five days, otherwise the funds must be released. In the president's request for such authority, Congress must be assured that the original budget intent will not be altered by such an action.

Immediately after the 1974 law was enacted, however, the Ford administration impounded $28.9 billion—more than any other president had reported for one year. Two large projects accounted for most of this total, a highway construction project amounting to $10.7 billion and a sewer project of $9 billion. Congress now had its first opportunity to apply the 1974 budget law to Ford's impoundments; it refused to rescind $102.5 million from the handicapped education bill and overturned the president's deferral of $50 million in planning grants.[27] Allen Schick analyzed Congress' response to Ford's efforts to impound funds.

> Congress appears to have drawn a fairly clear distinction between routine and policy impoundments . . . The President was repeatedly rebuffed in his efforts to convert impoundment controls into reordering the budget priorities established by Congress.[28]

Thus, during fiscal years 1975–1977 the Congressional Budget and Impoundment Control Act had an impact; the number of rescissions by the president fell dramatically from what they had been in the years immediately prior to 1974.[29] In addition, Congress seems to be more likely to approve the president's requests for deferrals rather than rescissions. In 1978, 1979, and 1980 Congress approved the vast majority of President Carter's requests for deferrals. The tension between Congress and the Executive over impoundments, therefore, has eased considerably in the period since the Nixon Administration.

Reorganization plans. Congress, through the "necessary and proper" clause of Article I in the Constitution, has the authority to oversee a president's reorganization plans. Before the 1930s, reorganizations of the federal government as well as decisions to abolish or transfer various functions were implemented by Congress through legislation. During the Hoover administration, Congress enacted legislation allowing the president to propose reorganization by "executive order" unless either the House or the Senate disapproved that action within sixty days. President Hoover issued eleven executive orders, all of which were disapproved by the House of Representatives. Since Hoover had lost the 1932 presidential election to Franklin D. Roosevelt, the Democratic-controlled House preferred to wait until Roosevelt assumed the presidency before considering plans for government reorganization. In 1933 Congress delegated to Roosevelt the power to reorganize the government for two years without having to worry about the legislative branch. When the Reorganization Act of 1939 was enacted, however, Congress established the procedure of governing reorganizations which has continued to the present day. The president now proposes a reorganization "plan" subject to its disapproval by either the House or the Senate (before 1949 disapproval by both House and Senate was required).

Where successful, reorganization of the federal government can strengthen the chief executive's management capabilities. In the past reorganization has been used to reduce personnel on various commissions, to limit the autonomy of certain agencies, to reduce funding for some bureaus, and to reduce the number of supergrade positions in the civil service. During the period 1939–1977, Congress rejected only 23 of the 115 reorganization plans submitted by the president.[30] Included in these 23 defeats were some major reorganization proposals. For example, 4 of Kennedy's 10 reorganization plans were rejected, including one that would have created the Department of Urban Affairs. In 1977 Jimmy Carter wanted to establish a new Department of Energy to consolidate authority over energy policy which was dispersed among various agencies, including the Federal Energy Administration, the Federal Power Commission, and the Energy Research and Development Administration. Although Congress did create a Department of Energy, it refused to give that department authority to control prices; that power was lodged in an independent Federal Energy Regulatory Commission.

Congress also can limit the effects of governmental reorganization by exempting certain agencies from these plans besides circumscribing the latitude a president has in this area. The Reorganization Act of 1939 exempted the Federal Communications Commission, the Federal Power Commission, the National Labor Relations Board, the Interstate Commerce Commission, the Federal Trade Commission, and the Securities and Exchange Commission. These last three agencies were also exempted from the 1945 Reorganization Act. The Reorganization Act of 1977 prohibited Jimmy Carter from submitting any reorganization plan to Congress that would ". . . abolish, merge or create either departments or independent regulatory agencies, abolish any function mandated by statute or extend or expand agency functions."[31] However restricted this authority seems to be, it was better than nothing at all. The president's power to initiate reorganization plans had lapsed in 1973, as the Watergate scandal broke, and thus had to be authorized again in 1977, at President Carter's request.

Perhaps the most ambitious reorganization plan was proposed by Richard Nixon. Louis Koenig observes, "no other President has unloosed a heavier barrage of department reorganizations. Through them, Nixon moved to reduce or abolish agencies that were ill-suited to his administration's philosophy."[32] In Nixon's 1971 State of the Union Message, he promised, "I shall ask not simply for more new programs in the old framework, but to change the framework itself—to reform the entire structure of American government so we can make it again fully responsive to the needs and wishes of the American people." His reforms of the federal government reflected the philosophy of the Advisory Council on Executive Organization (Ash Council) which Nixon created in 1969. A major purpose was to weaken the clientele-related Departments of Agriculture, Commerce, Labor, and Transportation and allocate their functions to four "super" departments: Community Development, Economic Affairs, Human Resources, and Natural Resources. Under Nixon's scheme, the Departments of State, Defense, Treasury, and Justice would remain—making a total of eight departments rather than the existing eleven. But, as Harold Seidman observes, in preparing this reorganization plan Nixon's "solicitude shown for pork barrel programs did not extend to the social and economic programs identified with the New and Fair Deals and President Johnson's 'Great Society.' "[33] President Nixon planned to minimize changes in the operations of the U.S. Army Corps of Engineers and the Soil Conservation Service, whereas the Office of Economic Opportunity (OEO)—which administered antipoverty programs—would be retained without much program jurisdiction, and the Farmers Home Administration and Small Business Administration would be abolished, with their programs also transferred to other agencies. Nixon's major reorganization proposal was not approved. Though Congress was sympathetic to the need for overall government reorganization, it was not convinced that Nixon's bold strategy was the best one. Obviously, the threatened agencies and clientele groups opposed any changes, and in some cases members of the Nixon administration did not show any real enthusiasm for specific recommendations.

"It is no accident," Robert J. Sickels observes, "that the executive branch after years of reorganization, still does not resemble the ideal of the Hoover Commission as expressed in the 1949 act. Hundreds of functions are carefully tucked away in the care of regulatory commissions, independent agencies, governing corporations, institutes, boards, councils and committees."[34] By one count, for example, in 1977 there were 228 separate health programs, 156 separate programs for income security and social services, and 83 different housing programs.[35]

What the first Hoover Commission (Commission on Organization of the Executive Branch of the Government) in 1949 had proposed was a model based on its view of sound business management. Related functions were supposed to be grouped together, the "independent" agencies and commissions would be consolidated under the departments, and authority ran up the hierarchy to the president, who is held responsible for the management of government. Apart from the fact that many public administration practitioners and scholars have become disenchanted with those "principles" of sound management, is the more relevant consideration that every reorganization plan expresses a political bias. These decisions are not made in a vacuum, as Seidman argues: "Organization is one way of expressing national commitment, influencing program direction, and ordering priorities. Organizational arrangements tend to give some interests and perspectives more effective access to those with decision making authority, whether they be in the Congress or in the executive branch."[36]

When Jimmy Carter campaigned for president in 1976, he pledged to reduce 1,900 federal agencies to 200; as president he did the opposite. According to Ronald C. Moe, "On balance, [Carter's] reorganization effort has resulted in more, not fewer, agencies and in more agencies and programs being placed outside direct accountability to the President."[37] For many reasons, therefore—sheer size of government, continued opposition of interest groups and agencies, Congress' resistance, and ill-conceived notions of reorganization by the executive—the organization of the federal government remains a primary factor why the chief executive cannot oversee the implementation of policy effectively.

Congressional oversight. Because legislation must necessarily be formulated in broad language, Congress relies on the chief executive and the bureaucracy to provide the specific rules and regulations to implement those policies. Nevertheless, Congress does not abdicate its responsibility to monitor program implementation. This responsibility is known as its "oversight" function. Various statutes affirm Congress' intention to closely watch the executive branch. For example, the Legislative Reorganization Act of 1946 authorized each standing committee to exercise "continuous watchfulness" over those agencies of government within its program jurisdiction. The Reorganization Act of 1970 made this charge even more specific: "Each standing committee shall review and study, on a continuing basis, the application, administration, and execution of those laws, or parts of laws, the subject matter of which is within the jurisdiction of that committee."

Related to its oversight function is Congress' legitimate need to obtain information in order to enact legislation. From time to time highly publicized investigations by the Congress occur. Some investigations are effective in uncovering executive wrongdoing (Watergate), whereas others are more infamous, for example, the "Red Scare" promoted by Sen. Joseph McCarthy (R.–Wis.) during the early 1950s. Sen. William Proxmire (D.–Wis.) is well known for his "Golden Fleece Awards," which he gives to government projects he considers wasteful of public moneys.[38]

During the 1970s, it would seem that Congress has intervened in government administration in more direct ways than simply by its powers to investigate. By using a "legislative veto" Congress can amend regulations promulgated by the agencies without approval by the president. A legislative veto means that a program or regulation can be disapproved by the House and Senate ("two-house veto"), by either House or Senate ("one-house veto"), or by a committee or subcommittee of either/both House and Senate ("committee veto"). In most cases, therefore, a program or rule can be disapproved before it is implemented by the agency; in some instances a program or rule must be approved before it can take effect.

The legislative veto was first adopted in 1932; as noted, during the Hoover administration it was applied to "reorganization" plans submitted to Congress by the president. By one count, there are now 186 laws that have 264 provisions for some kind of legislative veto. The various techniques used in these laws are listed below:[39]

Methods	No. Provisions
Disapproval by House or Senate	93
Disapproval by House and Senate	55
Disapproval by standing committee of either/both House and Senate	12
Approval by House and Senate	40
Approval by committee/subcommittee of House and Senate	55
Other methods	9

For the period 1976–1978 alone, Congress enacted twenty-two statutes with legislative vetoes, and during the Carter administration Congress imposed a "one-house veto" on all regulations issued by the FTC.[40] President Carter was forced to accept this wide application of the legislative veto in order to get funding for the FTC; it came amidst calls for deregulation and complaints that the FTC was overregulating business in behalf of consumer interests. Either the House or the Senate can veto FTC regulations by a majority vote, the first such use of the legislative veto against an agency of government. Similarly, a one-house legislative veto was added to the Trade Act of 1974. Although this law empowered the president to negotiate the lowering of tariff barriers with other nations, either the House or the Senate could disallow a president's decision within ninety days.

In 1978 Congress enacted legislation requiring HUD to submit proposed regulations to the House and Senate banking committees. Either committee can review a regulation before it is published in the *Federal Register;* moreover, once published in the *Federal Register,* either committee can delay its implementation for ninety days by reporting a "joint" resolution intended to nullify or to modify that regulation.[41] No doubt the provision for a "legislative veto" may influence administrative decision making; however, one analysis found that since 1932 Congress vetoed only eighty-one actions by the executive branch.[42]

An even more ambitious oversight technique is the so-called sunset legislation which Congress nearly approved. In 1978, the Senate by a 88 to 1 vote approved a bill requiring a regular review of all governmental programs every ten years; because it was late in the session the House never acted on that bill. The 96th Congress (1979–1980) considered a modified version of this legislation, authorizing a selective review of government programs by the standing committees. In the end, however, key congressmen and committee chairmen became concerned about the added work load that would result from such a law, and the House has yet to bring this measure to the floor for a vote. On the other hand, the House of Representatives does integrate or "build in" limits for specific programs. In the 1979 Civil Service Authorization Bill (HR 5138), the House stopped its "open-ended" authorization and permitted only a two-year authorization. That same year the House amended the Child Health Assurance Program (HR 4962) so that, after four years, the program would terminate unless Congress voted to extend it.

Finally, Congress can use its "power of the purse" to stipulate how laws are administered. In 1977 a proposed regulation by HUD caused an outcry in Congress. Intended to define which family groups are eligible for public housing, this HUD regulation included in the definition of "stable family relationships" the category of unmarried couples. Such a definition could extend to homosexual couples. In reaction, on July 15, 1977, the House of Representatives added a "rider" to an appropriations bill nullifying that HUD regulation, and this amendment was shortly thereafter enacted into law.[43] Another issue that prompts a concerted effort by Congress to intervene in policy implementation is abortion. Since 1976 every Congress has approved a version of the so-called Hyde Amendment to appropriations bills for the Department of HEW/Department of Labor. Such "riders" prohibit the use of Medicaid funds to pay for abortions for indigent women except in specific cases, such as when the woman's life is endangered. Moreover, Congress enacted "conscience clauses" permitting hospitals (or physicians) receiving federal funds to refuse to terminate a pregnancy. The House of Representatives sponsored legislation that prohibited antipoverty lawyers employed by the Legal Services Corporation from representing clients in abortion cases; another bill forbids the U.S. Commission on Civil Rights from collecting any data about the abortion policies of various government agencies.[44]

The bureaucracy

Decision makers throughout the federal government also share authority with the chief executive. Agencies and bureaus survive much longer than any president. In 1976, the citizen's lobby group Common Cause reported that, during the past fifteen years, whereas 236 new federal agencies were created only 21 had been abolished.[45] Herbert Kaufman found that 148 of the 175 agencies operating in 1923 existed in 1973, fifty years later.[46] Not only do agencies have time to develop relationships with clientele groups and to cultivate political support in the Congress, but they also establish methods of operation and reflect certain ideological and professional biases. For this reason, a president wanting fundamental changes in domestic priorities will probably face resistance from the civil servants who have implemented policies in certain ways for many years. One study found that bureaucrats recruited during the Kennedy and Johnson administrations, a period of much expansion in social-welfare programs, were unsympathetic to President Nixon's efforts to consolidate or to end those various programs.[47] In another example, the Saint Lawrence Seaway is an atypical "inland waterway" insofar as it imposes user fees although it was built by the Army Corps of Engineers. According to Harold Seidman,

> Devotion to these "historic" policies endures in the face of changing circumstances and challenges by presidents and prestigious study commissions. The U.S. Army Corps of Engineers adheres rigidly to the policy first enunciated in 1787 that inland waterways should be regarded "as public highways open to use of the public generally without restriction," although every president since Franklin Roosevelt has recommended the imposition of user charges.[48]

The heads of agencies and bureaus prepare budgetary increases each year, request new program authority, and pressure the chief executive to fill high-level appointments with people from their agencies. The Foreign Service, for example, lobbies the president to appoint careerists to ambassadorships. Civil servants interpret the meaning of statutes and lay down regulations, and senior administrators make substantive policy decisions.

In 1982, HUD threatened to withhold federal moneys for public housing in Chicago until the executive director of the Chicago Housing Authority stepped down. In this manner, the bureaucracy makes law as much as any Congress. As Sen. James G. Abourezk (D.–S.D.) observed in 1975:

> Last year the Congress enacted 647 public laws while approximately 6,000 administrative rules were adopted by 67 Federal agencies, departments, and bureaus. More law, in the sense of rules governing our society, is produced by the executive branch and independent agencies than is produced by the national legislature.[49]

In certain instances, agency heads have so much influence that they are virtually immune from presidential control. This situation was exemplified by J. Edgar Hoover, the late director of the Federal Bureau of Investigation. Hoover turned the FBI into a personal fiefdom during his half-century as its director, and used information gathered in secret to intimidate his allies and to frighten his enemies. Critics of the FBI during Hoover's era argue that, although organized crime was becoming established in America, Hoover spent disproportionate energy monitoring left-wing groups, Communists, and civil rights leaders, including Dr. Martin Luther King. One source determined that 40 percent of the FBI's time was used for political surveillance, largely because Hoover had a personal dislike of leftist causes.[50] But no attorney general directly confronted J. Edgar Hoover, and Presidents Kennedy, Johnson, and Nixon all reappointed him to office. In fact, Hoover was allowed to remain as FBI director despite the fact that he was past the legal retirement age for federal employees. Only after Hoover's death did the scope of his operations become known. Robert Sherrill notes that ". . . the Director had been downright quirky about some other things, too. He liked to put together files that could have been—even if they weren't—used for blackmail: files full of data about the private lives of important people." Hoover's files on presidents and members of Congress included "their sexual and drinking habits."[51]

Though an extreme case, Hoover's control of the FBI shows that a president's managerial authority is limited to the extent that an agency is beyond his administrative reach and enjoys political support independent of the executive branch. The "independent" regulatory commissions, therefore, pose a special problem in this regard, for they were established by the Congress to be isolated from the president's direct supervision. Though their memberships are appointed by the president with Senate approval, the fact that they serve long, staggered terms means that no chief executive can easily replace the majority who serve on such agencies as the Interstate Commerce Commission and the Federal Trade Commission. In addition, the membership of these independent regulatory commissions must be bipartisan in makeup. And as noted earlier, usually a president cannot remove the members of these commissions except for reasons authorized by Congress.

However, a president can exert some influence over these independent agencies, commissions, and corporations through subtle, political means.

William Brigman maintains in fact, that the president has more influence over such commissions than is commonly believed.[52] The president controls their budgets, makes legislative recommendations, appoints the commissioners and designates the chairmen, and the solicitor general gains access for these agencies before the courts. In reviewing the Nixon, Ford, and Carter administrations, Brigman concluded that the politics of the independent regulatory commissions were generally acceptable to those presidents.

Subnational elites and clientele groups

The chief executive's responsibility for supervising government administration is not limited to the federal bureaucracy. Federal programs also are implemented by state and local political elites as well as clientele groups. By 1980, 30 percent of state and local government revenue came from the federal government.[53] As Grodzins and Elazar observe, "there is hardly any activity that does not involve the federal, state, and some local government in important responsibilities. Functions of the American governments are shared."[54] As early as the 1880s the federal government provided "grants-in-aid" to the states, but such programs were markedly expanded since the Depression. By the mid-1970s there were at least 442 different "categoric" grant programs, as they are also known, which in 1977 allocated $55 billion to states and localities. Grant-in-aid moneys are earmarked for specific purposes, and the federal government monitors their use by the states and imposes standards for planning and operations.

When Congress enacted "revenue-sharing" under the Nixon administration (State and Local Fiscal Assistance Act of 1972) and "block" grants under such legislation as the Comprehensive Employment and Training Act of 1973 (CETA), such programs allowed the states and localities more discretion to use federal funds in general policy areas, such as criminal justice, job training, community development, and health care. The use of revenue-sharing and block grants was advocated by local officials and state governors precisely because they had fewer federal constraints. Thus, decision makers at the state and local levels of government enjoy more latitude in utilizing federal moneys, which in some instances caused problems. Block grants were provided in the Omnibus Crime Control and Safe Streets Act of 1968, which established the Law Enforcement Assistance Administration (since abolished). Federal moneys were channeled by the LEAA through state planning agencies (for example, Illinois Law Enforcement Commission) which in turn would allocate grants to the various municipal, county, and state agencies as well as nonprofit organizations. This arrangement was criticized because it led to excessive spending by local police departments for "hardware" and antiriot equipment, with the result that Congress' 1970 amendments required that 60 percent of those funds be used for corrections institutions, programs for probation and bail, and court systems upgrading.

To deal with the 50 states, 3,042 counties, 18,862 municipalities, 16,822 townships, 25,962 special districts, and 15,174 school districts in the nation (as of 1977), the federal government operates through "regional" offices. Beginning in 1969 the nation was subdivided into ten standard regions, and federal agencies were supposed to organize the administration of programs according to those regions. This policy acknowledged a greater need to delegate program authority to the regions, rather than to centralize it in Washington, D.C., and affirmed the fact that many federal programs necessarily require substantial federal–state–local cooperation to be effective. Federalism remains a powerful influence in American politics. Its profound effect, Peter Woll observes,

> has necessitated various devices to aid the administrative branch in carrying out its programs in areas involving federal–state cooperation. Frequently, for example, federal and state agencies must cooperate in program implementation if national policy is to be effective . . . such cooperation has fostered a decentralized federal bureaucracy, and an emphasis upon field organizations. In turn, this development has caused various problems of control in the federal bureaucracy, for a field agency always has a certain amount of autonomy resulting not only from such factors as distance, but also from local political support for program implementation that may or may not accord with central directives and policy.[55]

The delegation of administrative responsibility extends into the private and nonprofit sectors, involving clientele groups as well. At the outset, the federal government relies heavily on "contract" employees to do specialized tasks. In 1977 the Subcommittee on Reports, Accounting and Management of the Senate's Governmental Affairs Committee estimated that 1.3 million employees worked under contract for the federal government—about 40 percent of the federal civilian work force.[56] The Army Corps of Engineers is entirely dependent upon private contractors in its construction projects, and the same applies to the Atomic Energy Commission. According to Seidman, "The Atomic Energy Commission was practically incapable of operating anything except by contract, and went so far as to contract out administration of the city of Oak Ridge."[57] The excessive use of employees under contract further complicates a chief executive's managerial task. Robert Sherrill notes that "this contractual, quasi arm of the government exists in virtual anonymity, and it is only remotely responsible to the general public."[58] Moreover, it provides a setting for collusion between federal agencies and private businesses. In the Department of Defense, 80,000 employees are used to make contracts with private companies at an annual cost of $48 billion.[59] In 1970, A. Ernest Fitzgerald, who was a financial analyst for the Department of Defense, testified before Congress about a $2 billion cost overrun in Lockheed's production of the C-5A cargo plane, and alleged that the Pentagon and Lockheed cooperated in concealing this expenditure. Rather than having been commended for his vigilance, however, Fitzgerald was dismissed in January 1970 when his job was eliminated in a government reorganization approved by President Nixon.

Federal agencies implement programs through various clientele groups. The Department of Agriculture carries out its various programs through the state land grant colleges, soil conservation districts, and elected farmer committees. Another example of such subdelegation, and one that was politically controversial, involved President Johnson's War on Poverty. Central to the Economic Opportunity Act of 1964 was the Community Action Program, which was to be implemented at the local level using federal funds. That legislation stipulated that such community action programs were to be "developed, conducted, and administered with the maximum feasible participation of the residents of the areas and members of the groups served." The ambiguity of this language was interpreted by administrators in the Office of Economic Opportunity (OEO) to mean that the poor and minorities should be organized not only to improve their economic condition but also to capture political power. Congress did not have this in mind, and obviously local officials became hostile to federal programs that encouraged community groups to develop political power. The 1964 act permitted local community participation through a "public or private nonprofit agency," but obviously the optimal choice—from the standpoint of antipoverty activists—would be an organization separate from city government. Thus, by June 1968, only 34 of the 1,012 "community action agencies" established across the nation were public agencies.[60] Moreover, in the local elections held to select community representatives to those community action agencies, it was not uncommon to find that only 1 percent of the population participated, meaning that authority was lodged in the hands of very few community activists.

In the end, though mismanagement plagued the Community Action Program and appropriated federal funds made little impact in improving the lives of the poor residents, it was the political backlash resulting from its administration that made the War on Poverty so unpopular. Opposition in Congress to the OEO began even before Johnson left the presidency; this ill will allowed President Nixon to cut funding for those programs and to transfer OEO's remaining functions to other agencies.

Advisory system

There are many actors who affect decision making in the role of chief executive, a scenario very different from that in the stronger roles of chief diplomat and commander-in-chief. To overcome such countervailing forces in the administrative arena a president must rely on his advisory system. No one person can control a government of such magnitude—the so-called institutionalized presidency was intended to help the president govern the nation. However, scholars have recognized that a president's advisers may further complicate the decision-making process and frankly undermine his effectiveness in this role.

Included in the advisory system are such groups as the cabinet, informal "kitchen cabinets," the Executive Office of the President, and whatever ad hoc or permanent commissions and advisory committees a president chooses to utilize. These advisers are supposed to give the chief executive the information and expertise needed to manage the government, but their importance depends ultimately on how the president uses them. Each president arranges his advisory system according to his own personality and style.

The growth of the institutionalized presidency cannot be traced to the Constitution. Rather, since the 1930s it has evolved as the chief executive tries to make routine certain functions previously accomplished in an ad hoc or impromptu manner. Louis Koenig describes this development.

> Much of the staffing . . . [begun] as personal staffs—for national security, press relations, Congressional affairs, for example—becomes institutionalized. Jurisdictions, once blurred and overlapping, become clarified and delineated. Tasks once handled by generalists are committed to specialists. . . . Formalization, routinization, records, files, meetings—the standard paraphernalia of bureaucracy—have overtaken the presidency and implanted a presidential bureaucracy.[61]

The cabinet. The oldest institution to advise the president is the cabinet. The first cabinet created in George Washington's administration had four officials: secretary of state, secretary of the treasury, secretary of war, and attorney general. Although the number of departments in the cabinet has increased to thirteen (table 5-3), there has been no corresponding increase in the power of the cabinet. While individual members of a president's cabinet may be very influential, unlike in Great Britain the cabinet has no tradition of "collective" responsibility to the chief executive. Members of the cabinet are not recruited from the same political constituency; they vary in their loyalty to the president, and often act to safeguard the interests of their own departments. Since the 1930s, moreover, presidents have come to rely more heavily on the White House staff, who are rivals to the department secretaries. This problem affected the Kennedy administration when McGeorge Bundy, who was Kennedy's national security adviser, undermined the Department of State by having all important communications transmitted directly to him at the White House rather than through the State Department. Thus, Bundy always knew what State was doing. This kind of intervention by the president's senior aides, argues Thomas Cronin, can ". . . diminish self-confidence, morale, and initiative within departments."[62]

Richard Pious contends that the cabinet no longer is an important source of policy or advice for the president and that it has little use except to function "for public relations symbolism."[63] His assessment is shared by many political scientists insofar as the cabinet's role in policymaking is concerned, but one should not underestimate the importance of its "representative" function. Each cabinet member can represent important interests within the president's political party. As Richard Fenno, Jr. says,

> He is a man with a particular departmental viewpoint, responsive to particular clientele interests and pursuing a particular program. His political behavior is shaped to a large degree by the kinds of extra-presidential relationships he estab-

lishes as he seeks solutions to his particular problems—the support of his policies, the survival of his organization, the control of his environment.[64]

From a different perspective, Herman Finer adds that, "the Cabinet is an instrument of information . . . the cabinet aids the President in gauging public opinion and in evaluating the opinions of special groups."[65] Moreover, when a cabinet appointment satisfies an important interest group or a major geographical area, it can mean the difference between whether the president's party wins or loses at the polls.

By custom, all presidents since Washington have had a cabinet of separate departments. Overall, the importance of cabinet members, like all advisory groups, depends on how the president uses them; presidents have granted the cabinet varying amounts of authority and responsibility. Woodrow Wilson allowed departments with domestic responsibilities much independence, and Calvin Coolidge permitted wide discretion to his entire cabinet. Harry Truman's modus operandi emphasized his cabinet's independence

TABLE 5-3   The cabinet, 1981

Department	Year Created	President	1981 Budget rank*	1981 Personnel rank*	Political "power" rank**
State	1789	Washington	13	9	2
Treasury	1789	Washington	3	3	3
Interior	1849	Polk	10	5	5
Agriculture	1862	Lincoln	6	4	8
Justice	1870	Grant	12	7	4
Commerce (formerly Department of Commerce and Labor, 1903)	1913	Wilson	11	8	9
Labor (formerly Department of Commerce and Labor, 1903)	1913	Wilson	4	10	7
Defense (consolidated Department of War, 1789, and Department of Navy, 1798)	1947	Truman	2	1	1
Housing and Urban Development	1965	Johnson	8	12	10
Transportation	1966	Johnson	5	6	11
Energy	1977	Carter	9	11	—
Health and Human Services (formerly Department of Health, Education and Welfare, 1953)	1980	Carter	1	2	6(HEW)**
Education (separated from Department of Health, Education and Welfare, 1953)	1980	Carter	7	13	—

*Source: *Statistical Abstract of the United States, 1981*, p. 250.
**This is the ranking made by Stewart Alsop in *The Center: People and Power in Political Washington* (New York: Harper and Row, 1968), p. 254. Alsop judged the Department of Health, Education and Welfare to be the sixth most powerful.

and dependence: "The President stays out of the secretary's way in departmental matters, and the secretary defers to the president on questions of policy."[66] Eisenhower placed more confidence in his cabinet than did any recent president. He held regular cabinet meetings, had minutes taken, and based discussions on a formal agenda. In 1954 he created a cabinet secretariat. Next to Sherman Adams, Eisenhower's chief of staff, the cabinet secretaries were the most important advisers to the president. Like field generals in the military, Ike's cabinet members were given "broad initiative and responsibility for their allotted sectors of operation."[67] John Kennedy believed that regularly held cabinet meetings wasted his time, and doubted that secretaries had the kind of far-ranging perspective helpful to a chief executive. As a consequence, Kennedy held only six full cabinet meetings during his three-year tenure.

When campaigning for president in 1976, Jimmy Carter criticized the power of presidential aides who were unaccountable to the Congress and the people, and suggested that he would rely more heavily on the cabinet. Carter intended to use his cabinet to coordinate policy matters and to advise him; he appointed a cabinet secretary with duties equivalent to a "domestic" ambassador. But the cabinet secretary became little more than a "public relations man for the administration rather than a coordinator of programs."[68] After one year in office, seeing that his objectives were not being achieved, Jimmy Carter began to meet less frequently with the cabinet. As a result, cabinet members began to define their own priorities and conflicts between Carter's senior advisers and various secretaries began to surface. By 1979 President Carter needed to reorganize his administration. His approval rating now at its lowest point, Carter sought advice through a series of Camp David meetings with individuals within and outside the government. As one aide described this process, Carter wanted to know "the whole stance and style of this Administration, the question of how we pull it back together."[69] After meeting with about one-hundred and thirty religious, political, economic, social, business, and labor leaders, President Carter proceeded to reorganize his advisory system. During this period, five cabinet members departed from the administration—Energy Secretary James Schlesinger, HEW Secretary Joseph Califano, Treasury Secretary W. Michael Blumenthal, Transportation Secretary Brock Adams, and Attorney General Griffin Bell (though both Adams and Bell resigned mainly for personal reasons).

The problem of "departmentalism" among cabinet members apparently frustrated Ronald Reagan's desire to dismantle the Departments of Education and of Energy. Reagan made this a campaign pledge in the 1980 election, and chose secretaries for these two departments who shared his viewpoint. But the Department of Education maintains old ties with such traditional and powerful clientele groups as the National Education Association, which opposes its termination. The Department of Energy, established much more recently, lacks support from as many clientele groups.

Although the cabinet does not act as an advisory body to the president, individual secretaries can be very influential. Quite often these key cabinet members come from the so-called inner cabinet: Justice, State, Defense, and Treasury. Unlike the "clientele" departments (Agriculture, Interior), these four departments monopolize the president's attention because they handle policy areas that are important to the entire nation. Moreover, they are somewhat less concerned about representing the demands of special interests, though in some cases they are supported by powerful constituency groups (for example the Department of Defense and the military-industrial complex). The first secretary of the treasury, Alexander Hamilton, was the primary adviser to George Washington. More recently, those cabinet members who have shared power with the president's inner circle of advisers have included four secretaries of state—Dean Acheson under Truman, John Foster Dulles under Eisenhower, Henry Kissinger under Nixon, and Cyrus Vance under Carter—as well as Ronald Reagan's Secretary of Defense Caspar Weinberger. In addition, in a pattern that concerns some commentators, contemporary presidents have appointed a close "political" confidant as attorney general. Kennedy chose his brother Robert, Nixon appointed John Mitchell, Carter appointed Griffin Bell, and Reagan selected his long-time legal adviser, William French Smith. The ideal cabinet member should be loyal to the president but not blindly uncritical of his mistakes. Norman Thomas asserts that "what is called for is a Cabinet-presidential relationship that is at once highly autonomous and deeply responsive."[70]

Kitchen cabinet and inner circle. A president's "kitchen cabinet" is an informal advisory group. The tradition has a long history. These advisers are as close to being "alter egos" of the president as anyone can be. They do the president's bidding, bolster his confidence when necessary, act as counsel, relieve his loneliness, and give advice on the most serious issues. And they do even more. Lester Seligman identifies seven roles now played by a president's kitchen cabinet, also known as his "inner circle":

> At times they are buffers to absorb pressures which the President must avoid or divert. Some serve as catalysts to expedite administrative or political action when it is in danger of being bogged down. . . . They are liaison men and fixers with the press, Congressmen, administrators, party leaders. . . . They are "needlers" who, acting for the President, may expedite action at key points where bureaucratic resistance threatens. Others serve as communications experts with the mass media. They are policy-advisers and experts supplying data, advice, criticism, and suggestion for overall policy-thinking. They are sometimes ideologists, whose task it is to intellectualize the policies of the President.[71]

Whether a president's kitchen cabinet is recruited from inside or outside the government, these individuals have held a pivotal role ever since George Washington's administration. One of Andrew Jackson's confidants was Amos Kendall, whose extraordinary duties have been described in this way:

> He [Kendall] was the President's *thinking* machine, and his *writing* machine, ay, and his *lying* machine . . . the chief overseer, chief reporter, amanuensis, scribe,

accountant general, man of all work—nothing was well done without the aid of his diabolical genius.[72]

Members of a president's inner circle are close friends or privileged aquaintances, and quite often they are members of the president's family. Mrs. Woodrow Wilson's relationship to her husband was crucial after President Wilson was incapacitated from a stroke. She selected the important issues to bring to his attention and, in effect, made the important decisions. As noted, President Kennedy appointed his brother attorney general, and Jimmy Carter's wife, Rosalynn, attended cabinet meetings on a regular basis and participated in other official gatherings.

The advisers who constitute the president's inner circle share common attributes. One study found that 96 percent were young or middle-aged, 86 percent were college-educated, 60 percent came from the private sector, and 77 percent were recruited from the East Coast.[73] Most importantly, members of a president's inner circle are appointed because they are loyal to him. But their effectiveness—and survival—depends on how useful they are in addition to the accuracy and importance of the information and advice they provide to the president. At times an adviser grows so close to the president that he becomes a literal reflection of his boss. William Loab, Jr., an aide to Theodore Roosevelt, wore a pince-nez and a hair style and mustache identical to the president's. Nebraska-born Theodore Sorenson associated so closely with John Kennedy that he began to speak with an Eastern accent and to imitate Kennedy's gestures and behavior.[74]

When loyalty is overemphasized by a chief executive, however, the conformity and deference that characterizes the inner staff can cause problems for the president. Pederson and Williams contend that

> the most dangerous problem of the modern presidency concerns the excessive mutual dependence that develops between Presidents and their aides. The personalities of the "inner circle" and the President become crucial in determining the degree of isolation of the Oval Office from outsiders.[75]

The intimate relationship between a president and his kitchen cabinet has been institutionalized to the extent that a modern president can include his closest confidants within the Executive Office of the President, particularly in the White House Office.

Executive office of the president

In contrast to the "line" departments responsible for implementing public policies, the president's "staff" agencies, which have advisory functions, are located in the Executive Office of the President. In 1939 the President's Committee on Administrative Management said, "The President needs help. His immediate staff assistance is entirely inadequate. He should be given a small number of executive assistants who would be his direct aides in dealing with the managerial agencies and administrative departments." That year President Roosevelt created the Executive Office of the President, which today contains ten units (table 5-4). It is rare for a "line" agency to be

TABLE 5-4   **Executive office of the president, 1981**

Office	Year created	President
White House Office	1939	Roosevelt
Intelligence Oversight Board	1947	Truman
Office of Management and Budget (formerly Bureau of the Budget, established in 1921)	1970	Nixon
Council of Economic Advisers	1946	Truman
National Security Council	1947	Truman
Office of Science and Technology Policy (formerly Office of Science and Technology, established 1962–73)	1975	Ford
Council on Environmental Quality	1969	Nixon
Office of Policy Development (formerly Domestic Council, 1970–76, and Domestic Policy Staff, 1977–80)	1981	Reagan
Office of Administration	1977	Carter
Office of United States Trade Representative (formerly Office of Special Representative for Trade Negotiations, 1963–78)	1979	Carter

Source: *U.S. Government Manual 1981/1982* (Washington, D.C.: U.S. Government Printing Office, 1982), pp. 87–99, 815.

housed in the Executive Office, but during the 1960s the Office of Economic Opportunity was located there. President Johnson wanted to maximize his control over its administration of the War on Poverty and to assure that other governmental agencies did not sabotage OEO's operations.

As will be shown, the OMB is the most important agency in the Executive Office of the President. First established in 1921 as the Bureau of the Budget, it was transferred by Roosevelt from the Treasury Department to the Executive Office. Its major responsibility is to formulate the "executive" budget to be submitted to the Congress. Moreover, OMB performs "central clearance" by screening the agencies' legislative requests before they are sent to Congress by the president. In 1970 Richard Nixon added its management function and renamed the Bureau of the Budget the Office of Management and Budget. In this capacity it gathers information and data on programs in an effort to promote efficiency and greater coordination.

The Council of Economic Advisers (CEA) was created by the Employment Act of 1946. Intended to advise the president on economic trends so that policies can be devised to promote economic growth, stable prices, and high employment levels; its three members, who are academic economists, are appointed by the president with the approval of the Senate. Very often a president will appoint CEA members to various task forces to study economic problems, such as trade relations or energy policy. The National Security Council was established in 1947 to coordinate domestic, foreign, and military policies affecting national security, but its role in decision making varies according to which president is in office (see chapter 6).

A more recent addition to the Executive Office was the Domestic Council, begun by President Nixon in 1970. Its membership included the president, vice-president, an executive director, the OMB director, and cabinet members and agency heads responsible for "domestic" policy areas. Its role in formulating domestic policy was intended to be analogous to the National Security Council's deliberations over foreign and military affairs. However, President Carter downgraded the Domestic Council to the Domestic Policy Staff in 1977, and President Reagan changed its name again to the Office of Policy Development in 1981. President Nixon viewed the Domestic Council as yet another unit for increasing his control over domestic policy—rather than for strengthening his policymaking capabilities—and given its changing status under Ford, Carter, and Reagan, this particular unit in the Executive Office has yet to attain the organizational standing or policy focus achieved by the National Security Council or the OMB.[76]

The White House Office has grown from a small number of ad hoc personal advisers into a highly specialized staff (table 5-5). Before 1939 the president's staff had no formal positions and, in fact, Franklin Roosevelt's aides had been borrowed from the regular departments. The "institutionalization" of the presidency is manifested in the expansion of the White House Office; most chief executives since FDR have added members to this advisory body. The number of senior advisers peaked during the Nixon administration; since then there has been a reduction in the number—if not the power—of these senior aides. Some advisers are mere reflections of the president's power. As Lee C. White, special counsel to John Kennedy, described this role, he said such an adviser is a "user of another man's power, another man's authority, another man's responsibility."[77] Other senior aides are more than just reflections of the president; they exercise power in their own right. This was the case with Sherman Adams, Eisenhower's chief of staff, and with John Ehrlichman and H. R. Haldeman, who served Richard Nixon. In 1974 experts from the National Academy of Public Administration testified before Congress about the power of key White House assistants in the Nixon administration:

> Centralization of power in the Presidency has increased over the years to the present extreme situation in which the prevailing view is that the whole government should be run from the White House. The role of the principal assistants to the President has been virtually transformed to one of "assistant Presidents."[78]

In recent years the workings of the White House staff have been criticized by congressmen, political scientists, and journalists. Critics charge that accountability is an urgent problem because of the magnitude of the staff. Whereas presidents such as Truman could meet regularly with their senior advisers, more contemporary presidents such as Kennedy saw their aides recruiting their own staffs. Moreover, few of these top advisers are confirmed by the Senate, thus giving the president an unchecked power of appointment. Although the White House staff was intended to increase the chief executive's control over the bureaucracy, a large staff may actually cripple the president by isolating him from the public, the Congress, and even the cabinet. One reason this is likely to happen is the tendency for a

TABLE 5-5   White House Office under Reagan, 1982

Counsellor to the President	Deputy Assistant to the President for National Security Affairs
Chief of Staff and Assistant to the President	Deputy Assistant to the President for Political Affairs
Deputy Chief of Staff and Assistant to the President	Deputy Assistant to the President and Deputy Press Secretary
Assistant to the President for National Security Affairs	Deputy Assistant to the President for Communications and Director of the Office of Communications
Assistant to the President for Policy Development	Assistant Counsellor to the President
Assistant to the President and Press Secretary	Deputy Counsel to the President
Assistant to the President for Public Liaison	Deputy Press Secretary to the President
Counsel to the President	Special Assistant to the President for Public Liaison
Assistant to the President for Legislative Affairs	Special Assistant to the President
Assistant to the President and Staff Director	Special Assistant to the President for Public Liaison
Assistant to the President	Special Assistant to the President for Public Liaison
Assistant to the President for Presidential Personnel	Special Assistant to the President for Public Liaison
Assistant to the President for Political Affairs	Special Assistant to the President
Assistant to the President for Intergovernmental Affairs	Special Assistant to the President for Policy Development
Deputy Counsellor to the President	Special Assistant to the President for Public Liaison
Deputy Assistant to the President for Public Liaison	Special Assistant to the President and Deputy Director of Special Support Services
Deputy Assistant to the President and Deputy to the Chief of Staff	Special Assistant to the President for Public Liaison
Deputy Assistant to the President and Director of the Office of Cabinet Administration	Special Assistant to the President for Intergovernmental Affairs
Deputy Assistant to the President and Director of the Office of Policy Development	Special Assistant to the President for Intergovernmental Affairs
Deputy Assistant to the President and Director of Special Support Services	Special Assistant to the President for Administration
Deputy Assistant to the President and Deputy to the Chief of Staff	Special Assistant to the President and Director of the Advance Office
Deputy Assistant to the President for Intergovernmental Affairs	Special Assistant to the President for Public Liaison
Deputy Assistant to the President and Director of Staff for the First Lady	Special Assistant to the President
Deputy Assistant to the President for Legislative Affairs	Special Assistant for Scheduling
	Curator
	Physician to the President
	Chief Usher

Source: *The U.S. Government Manual, 1981/1982* (Washington, D.C.: U.S. Government Printing Office, 1982), pp. 88–89.

president to encircle himself with like-minded persons he trusts. Thus, the so-called Irish Mafia of the Kennedy administration was replaced by the "Texas Mafia" of the Johnson administration. Richard Nixon came to depend on a group of "public relations" experts from California. Many of President Ford's confidants, for example Press Secretary Jerry TerHorst, knew Ford when he was a congressman from Michigan.

Presidential isolation caused by the growth of the White House Office is a consequence unintended by the 1939 President's Committee on Administrative Management. It had recommended a small number of presidential assistants (not to exceed six), who were to make no decisions by themselves but rather were to strengthen the president's managerial capabilities. They were supposed to

> . . . assist him in obtaining quickly and without delay all pertinent information possessed by any of the executive departments so as to guide him in making his responsible decisions; and then when decisions have been made, to assist him in seeing to it that every administrative department and agency affected is properly informed.[79]

That scenario is very different from the way these advisers affect the chief executive today. As Christopher Lasch warns, they can render the President ". . . deaf and dumb, dangerously oblivious to ordinary facts." Lasch continues, "Paranoia, far from being an unfortunate aberration and a special trait of the current incumbent of the office [Nixon], is built into the Presidency at every level."[80]

Nevertheless, the White House staff shares a unique perspective with the president, as Cronin and Greenberg observe, "These few assistants are the only other men in Washington whose responsibilities both enable and require them to look, as he does, at the government as a whole."[81] This "presidential" perspective brings the senior advisers into conflict with the "departmentalism" of secretaries and career civil servants.[82] For example, presidential aides complain about bureaucratic red tape and the parochialism of many agencies, because they want to achieve results during a president's four-year term. The careerists say that presidential aides are abrasive and intrude into agency operations and, since their tenure is more permanent, civil servants view problems over the long term. Fundamentally, whether these advisers strengthen or weaken the chief executive depends on how a president uses them. The use of advisers reflects the president's personality and style, and each chief executive since Franklin D. Roosevelt has structured his advisory system to meet his own needs. The following sections review these systems of management, with special attention to the changing relationships between the cabinet and the White House staff.

Roosevelt's system. Franklin D. Roosevelt adopted an unusual method of administration, for he wanted his organization to be flexible and informal. Two of FDR's underlying principles were "competition" and "tension." To maximize his access to information, Roosevelt would pit a liberal against a conservative, for example when he solicited advice from conservative Secretary of the Treasury Will Woodin and from liberal presidential assistant Harry Hopkins. Conflict also was fostered when the Office of Production Management was established. President Roosevelt staffed this agency with William Knudsen of General Motors and Sidney Hillman from the Congress of Industrial Organizations (CIO); they had co-equal authority. Roosevelt also would encourage overlapping jurisdictions by creating an ad hoc agency rather than assigning a function to an existing bureau. Thus, instead of allowing the Treasury Department to supervise the stock exchanges, that authority was given to the newly created Securities and Exchange Commission. And though the project to generate energy and control flooding in the Tennessee River Valley would normally have been housed in the Department of Interior, Roosevelt established a new Tennessee Valley Authority.

FDR's White House assistants—known as Roosevelt's "brain trust"—were often used to undermine department jurisdictions in order to obtain information for the president. Roosevelt's aides would be assigned to investigate an issue or problem even though the matter was also being studied by a cabinet secretary. Roosevelt did not abide by clear lines of authority if they did not suit his purposes, and often elicited information by directly contacting individuals throughout his bureaucracy. There were as many as one-hundred people in top, middle, and low-level positions in the bureaucracy who had Roosevelt's permission to call him directly if necessary.[83] Though these practices irritated the department heads, they strengthened Roosevelt's control over his administration. Louis Koenig summarizes the impact of Roosevelt's advisory network this way:

> The Roosevelt method is the surest yet invented for maximizing the President's personal influence and for asserting his sway over the executive branch. It spurred the flow of information and ideas into his possession and magnified his impact on policy.[84]

Truman's system.   Harry Truman dismantled much of the Roosevelt system of management. He explained, "I wanted to establish governmental lines so clearly that I would be able to put my finger on the people directly responsible in every situation."[85] He did away with "competition" as a principle of staffing and did not encourage staff conflict. Truman relied more heavily on his personal staff and the Bureau of the Budget to provide information and data. Truman increased his staff from 60 to 200, giving each person a specialized task to perform; designated a division of his staff to handle congressional liaison; and added the National Security Council to the Executive Office of the President. Truman's management system was more ordered and formalistic than Roosevelt's, and the cabinet members and the president's staff had primary influence over decision making. The cabinet, in essence, became a "board of directors," with the president as chairman of the board ". . . hearing sundry expert opinions on each aspect of the problem, then making a synthesis of them and announcing the decision."[86] Truman met twice a week with the full cabinet and also individually with cabinet members; during these meetings with each secretary he would deal with departmental problems.

In Truman's opinion, the president made the final decision after getting advice from his staff, and he expected his advisers not to criticize that decision. Truman's performance as chief executive was not notable in terms of the quality of his top-level staff, however. He selected many aides who were past political associates, except for Clark Clifford and Averell Harriman, who were exceptions to this pattern. Truman's staff was "long on loyalty and short on ability and ethics."[87] President Truman's management style was, in differing ways, similar to both Franklin Roosevelt's and Dwight Eisenhower's. His methods, observes Richard Neustadt,

> followed forms somewhat like Eisenhower's to results somewhat like Roosevelt's. In theory Truman was as much committed as was Eisenhower to straight lines and tidy boxes on the organization chart, and to "completed staff work." But in practice Truman had more feel for personalities than jurisdictions, and his instinct was to improvise arrangements around problems rather than to work through fixed procedures.[88]

Eisenhower's system.   Quite naturally, Dwight Eisenhower developed a hierarchical model with lines of authority pyramiding down through his staff to the subordinates, a pattern that resembled the military staffing with which he was familiar. President Eisenhower's was an orderly system very different from what Roosevelt had devised. Ike once claimed

> organization makes more efficient the gathering and analysis of facts, and the arranging of the findings of experts in logical fashion. Therefore organization helps the responsible individual make the necessary decision, and helps assure that it is satisfactorily carried out.[89]

Unlike Roosevelt, Eisenhower did not relish conflict or dissent among his staff; he tried to keep his advisers working in a congenial relationship.

After Eisenhower appointed Sherman Adams as his chief of staff, Adams controlled the flow of information to the president and Eisenhower's contact with the cabinet secretaries. Appointments and policy decisions from subordinates all passed through Adams first, and all cabinet members, except for Secretary of State John Foster Dulles, reported to Sherman Adams too. Thus, Eisenhower's management system allowed subordinates much say in decision making, for he saw his role as one of giving direction and establishing goals for his administration. The motto of the Eisenhower staff said in essence: "Nothing should go to the President's desk if it could be handled elsewhere, and, if it had to go to the President, it should be condensed to a one page memo."[90] Sherman Adams was told that Eisenhower wished him to ". . . simplify and expedite the urgent business that had to be brought to [the president's] personal attention and keep as much work of secondary importance as possible off his desk."[91]

Through this style of operations, according to Stephen Hess, "Eisenhower gave himself considerable freedom of action by giving his subordinates considerable latitude to act."[92] Eisenhower's decision making in the White House differed little from his experiences as a general, when his military chief of staff had played the role now exercised by Sherman Adams, that of sifting out the decisions important enough to go to Eisenhower.

Eisenhower's experience in the military also affirmed his commitment to the "team approach" in decision making. Many commentators see this aspect as Eisenhower's real genius: his ability to get the staff and the cabinet to work together. Decisions reached in cabinet meetings were implemented with the help of cabinet assistants, assistant secretaries, and department executive assistants who were assigned to a given task. Cabinet secretaries were expected to make formal reports outlining how they planned to implement the president's decisions.

Kennedy's system.   In contrast to Dwight Eisenhower, John F. Kennedy wanted a less formal decision-making apparatus. In April 1961 he dismantled forty-one committees in the executive branch to achieve greater simplicity and to place more responsibility on key individuals.[93] Theodore Sorensen, a principal aide during this period, offered this "football game" analogy between the Kennedy and Eisenhower styles: "The Eisenhower football method relied on regular huddles and rigid assignments. In the Kennedy administration all team members were constantly on the move."[94]

As an institution, the cabinet played a much less important role under Kennedy. The secretaries and their departments were not immune from intrusion by the "best and the brightest" staff, and members of the cabinet, though they could gain access to the president, often would work through important aides such as Robert Kennedy. Cabinet meetings were held infrequently, and the few that were called were designed to reassure the public that the administration was working to solve some problem. Kennedy's feelings about cabinet meetings are well known: "Cabinet meetings . . . are simply useless. Why should the Postmaster General sit there and listen to a discussion of the problems of Laos? . . . I don't know how Presidents functioned with them or relied on them in the past."[95]

Unlike Eisenhower, Kennedy wanted to be at the center of all decision making affecting both major and minor issues, and wanted to receive maximum information and contact from multiple sources of input. The role of Kennedy's staff was to structure options, encourage debate and analysis, and help to implement decisions once they were announced. Therefore Kennedy relied extensively on individual advisers who became quite influential. These aides were assigned to specialized areas, such as legislative relations and national security. Kennedy also used his aides as "generalists" to investigate problems in many areas. All advisers had access to the president. Moreover, there was no "chief of staff," an arrangement that permitted Kennedy to rely less on an "inner circle" of advisers than any other contemporary president. In addition, John Kennedy—like Roosevelt—would circumvent the established lines of authority, and encouraged his aides to do the same.

An advantage of Kennedy's "fluid" system of management was that he could direct his staff's attention to whichever problem had top priority. Such flexibility gave Kennedy more information sources when he made a decision. However, at times the advice of his senior advisers was of limited value because the generalists around Kennedy lacked the expertise in some areas they were asked to study. The Bay of Pigs invasion, for example, was formulated even though Kennedy failed to ask the opinion of a single Cuban expert in the Department of State.[96] The Bay of Pigs fiasco profoundly influenced John Kennedy, for thereafter he began to scrutinize more carefully those entrusted to positions of responsibility. He became suspicious of the Central Intelligence Agency, which had engineered the Bay of Pigs operation, and the military establishment. Eventually, Kennedy replaced Lyman Lemnitzer with Maxwell Taylor as chairman of the Joint Chiefs of Staff. He also checked on the CIA through the Foreign Intelligence Advisory Board and instructed the National Security Council to watch over the State Department.

A disadvantage of Kennedy's system, in which the president stands at the hub of the wheel of decision making, is that it exhausts a president's time and resources, allowing little time for long-term reflection. A chief executive can become buried in details. Using the Bay of Pigs operation as an example, Irving Janis further argues that the desire among Kennedy's aides to achieve a consensus on that issue subjected the advisory system to intragroup pressures. Janis's central thesis suggests that "the more amiability and esprit de corps among the members of a policy-making in-group, the greater is the danger that independent critical thinking will be replaced by groupthink, which is likely to result in irrational and dehumanizing actions against out-groups."[97] When Kennedy became aware of this problem, Janis notes, he strived to correct it by taking measures designed to make each adviser a skeptic and critic. Robert Kennedy and Theodore Sorensen were instructed to assure that intellectual mistakes did not occur; Kennedy subdivided the National Security Council Executive Committee into groups which met separately on important decisions and then met together for discussions. To ensure uninhibited discussions among his aides, Kennedy frequently would not attend these meetings. Unfortunately, this style of decision making is rare among chief executives, for too often presidents strive to generate consensus behind their policies and demand loyalty from their staff rather than criticism and healthy debate.

Johnson's system. Just as Eisenhower brought his experience as a military commander to the presidency, Lyndon Johnson's management of the White House reflected his experience in the Senate. As majority party leader in the Senate, Johnson excelled at the art of compromise and bargaining, and was central to the decision-making process. As president, Johnson wanted to remain at the center of decision making, with the cabinet and the staff supplying information to him. Johnson did not have a chief of staff, nor did his aides have definite assignments. To the outsider, staff activities in the Johnson administration seemed chaotic and confused while inside, everyone knew who was in charge. Johnson's attitude toward his staff was "essentially feudal," one critic commented.

He was the head of the duchy with all rights thereto pertaining. When he did not like the length of a Special Assistant's hair, he told him to go to a barbershop; he ordered a secretary to enroll in a charm school. He expected aides to be available at any time for any function. They were as likely to be asked to phone the tailor . . . as to confer with an ambassador.[98]

Not surprisingly, the decisions that were most important to Lyndon Johnson were legislative in nature. Certainly one reason for his success as legislative leader was the staff Johnson recruited, which, in the words of one observer, was "capable of mass producing legislative initiatives."[99]

President Johnson made more use of the cabinet and the National Security Council than had Kennedy, and he appointed a cabinet secretary. George Reedy observes, "Cabinet meetings were held with considerable regularity, with fully predetermined agendas and fully prewritten statements."[100] Actual decision making tended to focus on the White House staff, which became the primary body for establishing policy and policy goals. In this process Johnson received input from a very cohesive staff. Joseph Califano was a key aide to formulating policy recommendations. At the beginning of his term, Johnson consulted with many advisers before making decisions, but his circle of confidants grew increasingly small as the Vietnam War began to eclipse other issues. As Johnson's energies were absorbed by the conflict in Southeast Asia, Marvin Watson, his appointments secretary, began limiting access to the president, even protecting Johnson from his major advisers, such as McGeorge Bundy. Lyndon Johnson also became increasingly difficult to work for. If he detected that any aide was becoming especially popular, Johnson would take immediate action. For example, when Johnson read in a newspaper that Jack Valenti was the president's "primary" aide, Johnson had Valenti's office moved further from the Oval Office and demanded that Valenti also make appointments through Watson, as others did, to see the president.

Nixon's system. When Richard Nixon came into office he decided to concentrate on international relations and to delegate much responsibility over domestic policy to others. Delegating too much responsibility, however, can jeopardize a president's control, so Nixon wanted all business transacted in written form. In Erwin Hargrove's view, Nixon preferred "working with documents rather than people and . . . dealing with others through a key intermediary."[101] President Nixon's system of decision making by "memo" allowed him to minimize personal interactions, a method that, as Stephen Wayne observes, "provided Nixon with time to think and things to think about." Wayne explains that this control "allowed the presentation of alternatives in a way that did not challenge the president. Together, style and structure created an ordered, harmonious environment for Nixon, one that seemed to enhance and thereby encourage his capacity to control events."[102]

As a manager, Richard Nixon wanted to control the situation at hand. In choosing his cabinet, Nixon began with independent and strong figures, like Interior Secretary Walter Hickel, Agriculture Secretary Clifford Hardin, and Secretary of HUD George Romney. At first Nixon tried to balance his cabinet philosophically; liberal Daniel Patrick Moynihan and conservative Arthur Burns were both aides, while Romney became a spokesman for liberal Republicans. But Nixon also believed that an efficient White House staff was essential to a smoothly operating presidency, and for a time it appeared that he was following Eisenhower's model rather than Kennedy's or Roosevelt's. The staff saw its role as being supportive of the departments. H. R. Haldeman stated "Our job is not to do the work of government, but to get the work out to where it belongs—out to the Departments."[103] Initially Nixon planned on using a limited number of aides, including John Ehrlichman, Bryce Harlow, and H. R. Haldeman. He wanted a staff free from the conflict that had characterized previous administrations.

Before Nixon's first term ended, however, this original scheme was abandoned; Nixon decided to centralize and strengthen the White House staff and drastically reorganize the departments. Department secretaries encountered greater difficulty gaining access to the Oval Office, a major reason Interior Secretary Walter Hickel resigned in 1972. Other cabinet members followed Hickel during Nixon's second term, forcing the president to appoint some thirty cabinet members—more than any other president.[104]

Under the new structure there were five senior assistants to the president: H. R. Haldeman was chief of staff, John Ehrlichman headed domestic affairs, Henry Kissinger (national security adviser) managed foreign policy, Roy Ash (OMB director) handled executive management, and Treasury Secretary George Schultz was responsible for economic affairs. These persons constituted Nixon's "inner circle" of advisers, while outsiders, including the cabinet secretaries, communicated with the president through the senior assistants. In particular, Haldeman's job as chief of staff was to block access to Richard Nixon. In Haldeman's words, "Every President needs a son of a bitch, and I'm Nixon's. I'm his buffer and I'm his bastard. I get done what he wants done and I take the heat instead of him."[105]

The reorganization plan (Reorganization Plan No. 2) Nixon submitted to Congress in 1970 changed the Bureau of the Budget to the Office of Management and Budget and also established a Domestic Council in the Executive Office of the President. The prime movers behind these changes were the Ash Council, Ehrlichman, and Haldeman. John Ehrlichman wanted the Domestic Council to be his power base in a manner comparable to Kissinger's use of the National Security Council. In fact, Ehrlichman's desire that the Domestic Council staff not be included under civil service and his insistence that its executive director not be answerable to Congress almost defeated that proposal in the House of Representatives.

Harold Seidman maintains that Reorganization Plan No. 2 is important "because it marks the beginning of the trend toward formalizing the transfer of power to the president's personal staff."[106] Emerging during the Nixon administration, therefore, was "a three-tiered structure with the assistants to the president at the top and department and agency heads (other than those designated as counsellors) at the bottom," whose "clear intent was to transfer to the president's immediate staff effective control over executive branch policies and programs and to reduce Cabinet officers to an essentially ministerial role."[107]

By 1973 President Nixon had appointed more than one-hundred loyal staff members to key positions in the various departments and agencies to increase his control over their operations. These appointees were drawn from the White House, OMB, and the Committee to Re-elect the President (CREEP). Furthermore, Nixon created undersecretaries in Health, Education and Welfare, in Interior, and in Transportation, the deputy director of OMB, the Federal Aviation administrator, and the director of the National Parks Service.[108] In addition, Richard Nixon continued to appoint personnel to the White House staff until it had grown larger than ever before. Estimates of its size in 1973 vary from 3,562 to 5,395 persons; even based upon the most conservative estimate, this means that its size doubled from the 1,798 persons employed under Lyndon Johnson. Organizational lines stiffened, and subordinates operated in highly specialized assignments. The White House staff expansion meant that President Nixon could no longer personally direct its decision-making processes; thus, Nixon had to rely that much more on his senior advisers. Alexander Butterfield, a Nixon aide, estimated that in 1972 Nixon spent more than ". . . 70 percent of his staff time with Haldeman alone."[109] Haldeman, Ehrlichman, and Kissinger were the advisers who monopolized Richard Nixon's time during this period.

After the Watergate scandals were publicized, Nixon's plans for wholesale government reorganization were scrapped, especially when Haldeman and Ehrlichman resigned in the spring of 1973. Although Richard Nixon's "counter bureaucracy," as it has been called, did not achieve its objective of bringing the federal government under the president's control, he probably came closer than any other chief executive in devising a scheme to achieve that goal.[110]

Post-Nixon chief executives. No president since Richard Nixon has developed a unique style of decision making; rather, they borrowed various techniques already used by Nixon, Kennedy, or Eisenhower. Gerald Ford selected many senior advisers to manage the White House Office, and they all had access to the president—Ford had no chief of staff. He tried to hold the reigns of power loosely instead of with a tight grip, as had Nixon. President Ford fostered an openness in decision making because he wanted information from diverse sources before making a decision. He would gather his principal advisers around him, listen to them debate the issues, and then make his decision. One Ford adviser described the process this way:

> In all the meetings I've had with him, he insists on having written analyses of the issues before he meets and he likes to have a night to read them over. He likes to have the issue presented to him in cogent terms and described analytically and objectively. He likes to have alternatives and know who is for and against each alternative.[111]

Apparently Ford enjoyed making the hard decisions, such as his pardon of Richard Nixon, and once made he insisted on adhering to them. President Ford wanted "competence, loyalty, hard work" from his staff; he frowned on conflict among his advisers.[112] Ford wanted policy debate, not personal conflict. When Gerald Ford assumed the presidency on Nixon's resignation, he had every intention of moderating the presence of the White House staff, one visible sign of Nixon's "imperial" presidency. Ford was more accessible to cabinet members, meeting with them whenever possible. No secretary or senior aide seemed to dominate Ford's attention as was the case with Richard Nixon. Despite Ford's need to guard his time schedule more carefully later in his term, cabinet meetings remained in vogue and once a month the secretaries, senior aides, and Ford would meet to handle problems and discuss issues. But Gerald Ford could not turn the clock back. Stephen Wayne writes that Ford "soon found that there was no turning back. In terms of size, structure, and administrative procedures, his White House was much more like Nixon's than Truman's."[113]

Jimmy Carter's election represented a change in political party as well as in management style. Although he related to his advisers in ways similar to Ford by being open to consultations, the analogy ends there. Unlike Fo.d, Jimmy Carter was ignorant about Washington politics, particularly about Congress, and this lack of experience was not overcome by his choice of senior advisers. Six of Carter's top seven aides (except Stuart Eizenstat who had experience in Washington) came to the White House from Georgia, knowing only about Georgia politics. Carter wanted to be involved in all the decisions, much like Kennedy, but he also used the written memo to convey information as Nixon had done. Like Kennedy, President Carter also directed his staff to consider a wide range of problems, though this approach sometimes led to disagreements among his staff.

When Jimmy Carter became president, he intended to rely on the cabinet to administer the government. During 1977 he convened weekly cabinet meetings, more often than under any president since Eisenhower. The department secretaries could name their own deputies and had great discretion within their jurisdictions; Carter also relied on members of his cabinet for advice. President Carter retained final decision making authority: "The major decisions will be made ultimately by me as president, which is my constitutional prerogative and responsibility."[114] Carter's arrangement had its disadvantages. Louis Koenig argues that it placed demands on Jimmy Carter to allow people to be appointed to subsecretarial positions who represented interest groups, causes, and voter blocs.[115] As a consequence, the departments appeared to be sending conflicting messages to the public, resulting in the general perception that the Carter administration lacked unity and purpose. One particular conflict that troubled the Carter administration, though similar rivalries surfaced in other presidencies, involved the Secretary of State (Cyrus Vance) and Carter's National Security Adviser (Zbigniew Brzezinski). Priorities in foreign affairs were constantly subject to debate and open jockeying by these advisers for the president's support.

These kinds of problems eventually forced Jimmy Carter to restructure his advisory system, reducing the autonomy of the department secretaries. In effect Hamilton Jordan became Carter's "chief of staff," and the cabinet and senior advisers had to report to Jordan. Gerald Rafshoon, a Carter loyalist, was given the responsibility over communications to insure that the Carter administration spoke with one official voice. In addition, Carter tightened his control over domestic policymaking; he alerted the cabinet that White House policy would prevail over the departments. His staff adopted a system for making domestic policy that had been used by the National Security Council. This "Presidential Review Memorandum" allowed Carter greater control over both the hiring of administrative personnel and the drafting of policy recommendations within the departments. Under this reorganization, the cabinet members had to report on all their activities to President Carter's top aides, and were then briefed on what the White House policy was. The secretaries were expected to support the president's programs and priorities over their departments' in the event the two should be in conflict. Few notable domestic programs emerged from the Carter administration, but some innovative proposals were tried. As previously mentioned, one was the establishment of a Senior Executive Service for about 9,000 top-grade careerists. Carter also decreased the number of White House staff personnel, abolished the Council on International Economic Policy (within the Executive Office of the President), and replaced the Domestic Council with a Domestic Policy Staff.

When Ronald Reagan assumed the presidency, it became clear that he was not going to make the same mistakes that plagued Jimmy Carter. All of Reagan's nine senior aides had previous political experience of some kind; five had experience in Washington and three had worked in Reagan's California political campaigns. Max Friedersdorf, a veteran of the Nixon and Ford years, was responsible for congressional liaison, and was a key strategist in Reagan's remarkable first-year successes with the Congress. When Friedersdorf resigned, he was replaced in January 1982 with Kenneth M. Duberstein, who had been an effective administration lobbyist in Congress the previous year. With this experienced team Reagan could "hit the ground running" when he began his term, unlike Jimmy Carter who had to waste valuable time learning about Washington politics.

President Reagan also wanted a cabinet-directed government similar to the system he operated as governor of California. Not all cabinet members had equal influence, however. Initially an inner-three cabinet advisory system, which included Secretary of State Alexander Haig (succeeded by George Schultz), Secretary of the Treasury Donald Regan, and Defense Secretary Caspar Weinberger, was established. Later a triumvirate of key advisers emerged in the Reagan administration: Edwin Meese, presidential counselor; James A. Baker, chief of staff; and Michael Deaver, deputy chief of staff. These men were to oversee the White House staff and have direct access to the president.

President Reagan expected his cabinet and senior aides to work as a team to implement his policy goals. Since budget cutting was the top economic priority of his new administration, Reagan's advisers were expected to find ways of reducing government expenditures rather than to initiate new domestic programs. In an effort to assure that policymakers were loyal to the Reagan administration, David Edwards notes that "it fired virtually all former Carter appointees in an unusually thorough housecleaning."[116] Final decisions bore the Reagan stamp, therefore, although apparently the president allowed advisers considerable discretion to make secondary decisions, even in foreign affairs. For example, Edwin Meese, in consultation with other aides, made the decision in August 1981 to let U.S. fighter planes shoot down attacking Libyan aircraft sixty miles from Libya in disputed coastal waters. The U.S. F-14 jets were engaged in naval exercises in the area.

Changing role of OMB

The most important unit in the Executive Office of the President is the Office of Management and Budget, though its functions have changed somewhat since its establishment as the Bureau of the Budget in 1921. Foremost among OMB activities is the preparation of the "executive" budget, which is submitted to Congress by the president in January, whereupon the new "congressional" budget process begins (see figure 5-2). In addition, OMB exercises "central clearance" over program development by the executive agencies. In both these areas, however, OMB has lost some power in recent years.

Budget formation. Beginning about March of the year preceding the new fiscal year, the bureaus and agencies in the executive branch begin to evaluate ongoing programs and future changes in terms of projecting their budgetary estimates for the coming fiscal year. During this period the president confers with the Council of Economic Advisers about economic trends and with the OMB regarding overall budget estimates. Through May and June the president and the OMB make tentative decisions on the anticipated spending levels, which are communicated to the departments. Within each department, a budget unit reviews the budgetary requests by various agencies in terms of the president's guidelines. The information supplied by the bureaus, agencies, and departments offers the first indication of the scope of the budget for the new fiscal year. By September, the bureaus and agencies will have submitted their formal budget requests to OMB, and during the period August to October the Office of Management and Budget holds hearings with the various administrative units. Since the OMB has the reputation of reducing agency requests, these units typically include a higher funding level in anticipation of OMB cuts. As OMB begins its review of agency requests, interest groups and officials from states and localities can be expected to lobby the OMB to protect programs endangered by serious budget cuts.

During September and October the director of OMB confers with the president pursuant to his review of agency requests. At this time the president again consults with the Council of Economic Advisers and the Treasury Department regarding any changes in fiscal policy or economic conditions that may require modifications in the budget. The president makes his final budgetary decisions in November and December, which are transmitted to the agency heads, who must revise their budgetary estimates to conform with the president's. The month of December is devoted by the OMB to preparing the budget for submission to Congress in January as well as to drafting the president's Budget Message. Once the "executive" budget goes to Congress, the OMB director becomes its chief advocate. As OMB director, David Stockman was a strong proponent of Ronald Reagan's 1981 budget cuts and was extremely effective in his testimony before the Congress. However, Stockman's credibility was badly damaged later that year when, in a published interview, he questioned the wisdom of "supply-side" economic theory, which had thus far guided President Reagan's budgetary decisions.[117] (See figure 5-2.)

The president can exert control over executive agencies through the OMB's role in the budgetary process. When the Bureau of the Budget (BOB) was created in 1921, Presidents Harding, Coolidge, and Hoover did not exploit its full potential.[118] Under Charles Dawes, BOB's first director, it focused mainly on "economy" in government by guarding against excessive agency spending. This approach was too narrow for Franklin D. Roosevelt, who at first tended to ignore the BOB and rely on his "brain trust" to develop program and budget strategies. The (Brownlow) Committee on Administrative Management advocated using the BOB as the president's instrument for fiscal management; FDR's Executive Order 8248 broadened its scope and transferred BOB from the Treasury Department to the Executive Office of the President. By Truman's administration, BOB was a changed agency. According to Allen Schick

> it still reviewed agency estimates, but it had become the general staff for the president. The institutional presidency was in place, and the bureau's resources, skills, memory, and loyalty to the president could be passed on from one chief executive to the next.[119]

The Bureau of the Budget was most effective during the Truman and Eisenhower presidencies because its procedures had become routinized. Since Kennedy, however, the budgetary process has become much less "routine"; domestic and foreign crises happen unexpectedly, economic conditions are volatile and not entirely predictable, and a larger share of the budget consists of "uncontrollable" expenditures. The preparation of the budget today entails substantial guesswork, and estimates of spending and revenues are modified until a few days before the published document is released. Schick relates that the calm, stable budget process managed by Eisenhower gave way to frenetic budgeting by later presidents who were forced to frequently adjust their spending and revenue targets in order to accommodate last-minute policy decisions and changing economic conditions. Since Kennedy, the president's "mark" or initial spending target . . . has been nothing more than a starting point and the levels actually recommended in the published budget have often diverged sharply from it.[120]

The most fundamental change in budgeting relates to the growth in so-called uncontrollable or entitlement spending; these are funds that must be appropriated by law. One example is Social Security. So long as the number of recipients increases and they live longer, Congress liberalizes their benefits, and their pensions receive "cost-of-living" increases, more funds must automatically go to Social Security. Uncontrollable spending increased from 59 percent in fiscal year 1967 to 76 percent of the budget in fiscal year 1981—meaning that about $500 billion was spent for those programs in 1981.[121] These social-welfare programs are particularly susceptible to economic fluctuations, moreover; unemployment benefits depend on the unemployment rolls and cost-of-living allowances are affected by inflation rates. More than 40 percent of the budget is now indexed to inflation rates, leading Schick to observe, "It does not take the president long to realize that his budget is largely shaped by outside forces, not by White House decisions."[122]

Given these trends, therefore, the OMB has become primarily an "accounting" agency to provide technical support to the agencies in preparing the federal budget, rather than a decision maker. Whereas the BOB acted as a watchdog of the Treasury during its early days—when budgets were relatively small—the federal budget today is more obviously a political document because decision makers focus mainly on that share of federal spending that is "controllable." However, in evaluating this shrinking proportion of the budget, a president relies on cabinet members, the White House staff, as well as the OMB director in assessing his policy alternatives. For much the same reason, OMB's dominant role in reviewing legislative proposals has also been reduced.

Central clearance.   Until the New Deal, the Bureau of the Budget used central clearance—or "legislative clearance"—to prevent agencies from going to Congress for new program authority. It began with President Harding and was routinized during the Coolidge administration. This function was naturally delegated to the BOB, argues Richard Neustadt, due to its pivotal role in budget making: "The making of the budget is still the prime general-purpose, decision-and-action-forcing process yet institutionalized in the executive."[123] Nonetheless, the clearance procedure under Franklin D. Roosevelt retained its "negative" orientation; the major New Deal proposals were not submitted to the BOB, since that approach would have slowed their consideration in Congress.

Under President Truman, the central clearance procedure was transformed into a mechanism for preparing the president's legislative program,

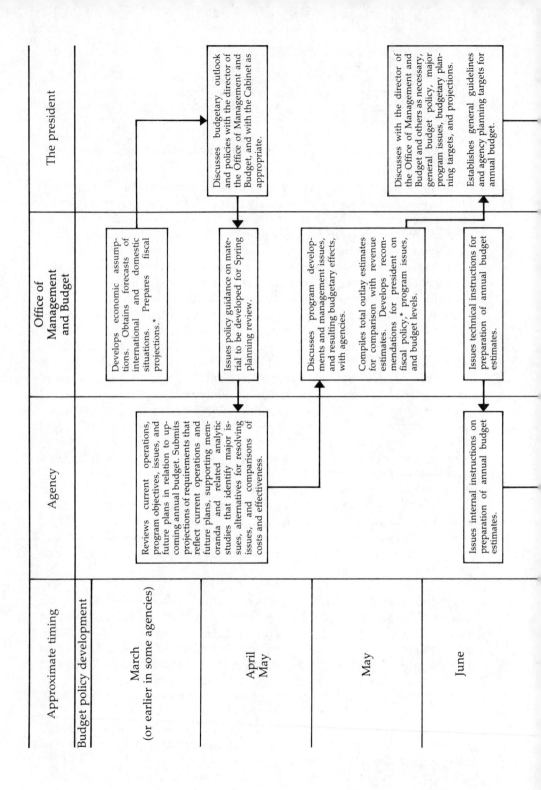

Approximate timing	Agency	Office of Management and Budget	The president
Budget policy development			
March (or earlier in some agencies)		Develops economic assumptions. Obtains forecasts of international and domestic situations. Prepares fiscal projections.*	
April May	Reviews current operations, program objectives, issues, and future plans in relation to upcoming annual budget. Submits projections of requirements that reflect current operations and future plans, supporting memoranda and related analytic studies that identify major issues, alternatives for resolving issues, and comparisons of costs and effectiveness.	Issues policy guidance on material to be developed for Spring planning review.	Discusses budgetary outlook and policies with the director of the Office of Management and Budget, and with the Cabinet as appropriate.
May		Discusses program developments and management issues, and resulting budgetary effects, with agencies. Compiles total outlay estimates for comparison with revenue estimates. Develops recommendations for president on fiscal policy,* program issues, and budget levels.	
June	Issues internal instructions on preparation of annual budget estimates.	Issues technical instructions for preparation of annual budget estimates.	Discusses with the director of the Office of Management and Budget and others as necessary, general budget policy, major program issues, budgetary planning targets, and projections. Establishes general guidelines and agency planning targets for annual budget.

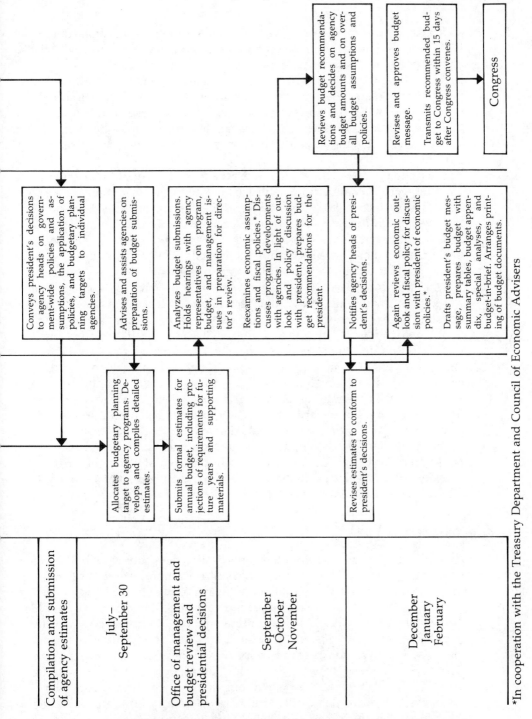

FIGURE 5-2 Preparation of the executive budget. *Source:* Office of Management and Budget, Executive Office of the President, *Major Steps in Budget Process*, Washington, D.C.: Government Printing Office, 1977.

and this enlarged mission survived during the Eisenhower administration. With the elections of John Kennedy and Lyndon Johnson, however, the greater use of legislative liaison personnel by these presidents—who personally advocated a far-reaching domestic policy agenda—meant that the initiative for policy development shifted from BOB to the White House. As a result, the BOB's role in central clearance was reduced to handling the "thousands of legislative items not commanding presidential attention, with the White House handling the major items and articulating the president's priorities."[124]

When the Bureau of the Budget was renamed the Office of Management and Budget, it became a more politicized organization—and there are signs that it has lost its professional standing. There has been increased personnel turnover in OMB; OMB officials have become involved in political issues and in controversial actions (such as Nixon's impoundments); and more political appointees have been added to its staff. In 1960 the BOB had only five appointed officers, but the 1970 reorganization added a new layer of "PADs" (program associate directors), who were White House political appointees. In addition, the OMB directors under Richard Nixon—George Schultz, Caspar Weinberger, and Roy Ash—saw themselves as the president's senior advisers rather than as impartial agency heads, with the result that OMB was identified "more as a member of the President's own political family and less as a broker supplying an independent analytic service to every President."[125] These trends concern Hugh Heclo, who decries the assault on OMB's "neutral competence"; he admits that OMB may be stronger than ever before, but toward what end? "Has OMB balanced the demands placed on it for policy advocacy outside and for quiet diplomacy within government? Has it succeeded in being a close member of the President's political family yet maintaining itself as a detached staff for the ongoing Presidency?"[126] Heclo argues that only a return to an objective, professional role will safeguard OMB's credibility and political power in the future.

PUBLIC INPUTS

A president acting as chief executive cannot effectively mobilize public inputs to strengthen his control over government operations. Political scientists differentiate between public opinion, or the majority's opinion, and publics' opinions. What public opinion says about government may not be reflected in the lobbying activities of interest groups that represent segments of the population. However, just as the term "bureaucrat" has a negative connotation, so it is that the American people have a disapproving image of the 2.8 million employees who constitute the federal government. For example, a 1977 Gallup Poll found that, when compared to nongovernmental workers, most Americans feel that federal employees are paid more (64%), get more fringe benefits (77%), but do not work as hard (67%); in addition, 67 percent of the respondents feel that there are too many federal employees.[127] When asked "Which of the following will be the biggest threat to the country in the future—big business, big labor, or big government?" a plurality of the respondents in 1967 (49%), in 1968 (46%), in 1977 (39%), and in 1979 (43%) said "big government."[128] No doubt flowing from this perception is the widespread view among Americans that government spending must be limited by a constitutional amendment. The Gallup Poll question asked in 1976, 1978, and 1979 with responses is given below.[129]

"Would you favor or oppose a constitutional amendment that would require Congress to balance the federal budget each year— that is, keep taxes and expenditures in balance?"

	Favor	*Oppose*
February 1979	78%	12%
July 1978	81	11
March 1976	78	13

Since presidents are aware of this undercurrent of antibureaucracy sentiment they often make the bureaucracy a scapegoat for the nation's problems, and their own failures. This strategy is used by both political parties. Ronald Reagan in 1980 campaigned against the growth in federal expenditures, yet as president his $100-plus billion deficit was the largest in the nation's history. When Reagan in 1982 publicly called for a constitutional amendment requiring a balanced budget, many Democrats in Congress said he was grandstanding and saying one thing while doing the opposite. In 1976 both Gerald Ford and Jimmy Carter made government reorganization a campaign issue. Carter boasted about the government reforms he achieved as governor of Georgia and promised to reduce the number of federal agencies from 1,900 to 200. In his 1971 State of the Union Message to Congress, President Nixon departed from his prepared speech to say, "Let's face it. Most Americans today are simply fed up with government at all levels."[130] Even Franklin Roosevelt in 1932 advocated a balanced budget alongside his promise for a New Deal.

The fundamental problem in trying to mobilize the public behind government reorganization is that individuals, though they want smaller government, do not want cuts in programs that benefit them. Reagan has been criticized for slashing social programs while increasing defense spending, but he has minimized the outcry from middle-class groups by reducing expenditures disproportionately for those programs designed for the poor. Even with regard to welfare, not a popular notion with Americans, the public seems to be more hostile to welfarism rather than to specific welfare programs. For example, a *New York Times*-CBS News Poll in 1977 questioned people on various aspects of this issue.[131] Most people disapproved of "most government-sponsored welfare programs" (58%) and "a guaranteed minimum income" (50%). Some 54 percent said they believed that most people "could get along" when asked "Do you think that most people who receive money from welfare could get along without it if they tried, or do you think they really need this help?" On the other hand, larger majorities favored "a national health care program" (60%), "food stamps for the poor" (81%), "aid to poor families with dependent children" (81%), and "health care for the poor" (82%). Similar findings by Free and Cantril led them to conclude that most Americans are ideological conservatives but operational liberals; that is, the public is conservative on fiscal matters but unwilling to end programs which provide them with benefits.[132] Such ambivalence in public attitudes toward the government prevents a chief executive from taking decisive action to eliminate federal programs or to implement major government reorganization plans.

Moreover, such questions as government reorganization lack political "sex appeal." In spite of his tremendous success in getting Congress to approve landmark social-welfare programs, Franklin Roosevelt was less successful in getting all his reorganization plans enacted. In reviewing Roosevelt's failures in this area, Richard Polenberg asserts that such administrative changes lacked public support. He says,

> People failed to get excited about administrative reform because it promised no immediate, tangible, or direct benefits. In this respect it differed fundamentally from other New Deal measures—such as river valley development, agricultural price supports, wages and hours legislation, relief programs—all of which enjoyed the support of certain geographic regions or social classes. There was no constituency for reorganization and, in its absence, no countervailing power to offset the opposition of special-interest groups.[133]

On the other hand, the clientele groups that influence the executive branch are not so opposed to big government. They want those programs benefiting them protected and expanded. As Irish, Prothro, and Richardson observe, "Every bureaucratic agency was created in response to pressures from outside the government itself, from good citizens who hate bureaucracy in general but want something done for themselves."[134] In this arena of bureaucratic intrigue, say Prewitt and Verba, small, well-organized interests have more access than they would have in trying to influence the more publicized legislative process in the Congress.[135] Access to government need not depend entirely on a group's size—access is also facilitated by its expertise, wealth, and degree of political organization. When the AMA, for example, calls a physician unfit to serve as surgeon general, its professional credibility is greater than counterarguments made by lay organizations.

In the sphere of "economic" regulatory policy, one finds the influence of business groups to be especially strong. After studying business regulation, Roger Noll concluded that "rarely does the President appoint, and the Senate confirm, a commissioner if the regulated industry is politically aligned against him."[136] Economic interests, as well as professional groups, gain access to government through a multitude of advisory committees. When Jimmy Carter took office he was amazed to find about 1,300 such advisory groups employing more than 22,000 people in the federal government. Nonetheless, like his predecessors President Carter allowed this number to grow. During his first year in office he added four more advisory groups:

the Commission on Mental Health, the U.S. Circuit Judiciary Nomination Commission, the Committee on Selection of the Director of the Federal Bureau of Investigation, and the Advisory Board on Ambassadorial Appointments.

In his study of private associations in the United States, Grant McConnell makes a compelling argument that government's intervention in the economy is limited by the executive's reliance on such advisory groups, for example the Aluminum Industry Advisory Committee, the Industry Advisory Committee on Bacon, and the Industry Advisory Committee on Peanut Butter.[137] According to Seidman, moreover, the executive is less concerned about what these groups know than who they know:

> What the government basically wants from advisory committees is not "expert" advice, although occasionally this is a factor, but support. Advisory boards may be utilized to lend respectability to new or controversial programs. . . . It is hoped that board members will act as program missionaries and assist in mobilizing support for the program both in their home communities and in the Congress.[138]

At times the relationship between government and such advisory groups becomes so intimate that the opinions of these private organizations are equivalent to being government policy. An extreme case of this collaboration occurred during the Eisenhower administration. The Anti-Trust Subcommittee of the House Judiciary Committee found that the advisory system established by Secretary of Commerce Sinclair Weeks had

> effected a virtual abdication of administrative responsibility on the part of Government officials in that their actions in many instances are but the automatic approval of decisions already made outside the Government in business and industry. The Secretary of Commerce. . . . has created an organization which in the name of the Government has been used to advance throughout the Government the cause of private interests. Failing to control its activities, he has allowed an agency of the Government to become an instrument for inside influence and advancement of special interests.[139]

To a lesser degree, similar cases are found in any administration, Democratic as well as Republican. A classic study of the Tennessee Valley Authority, for example, documented how the efforts of the TVA to co-opt local farmers and landowners into supporting the agency had unintended effects on its policies. Despite President Roosevelt's New Deal and his commitment to progressive social changes, the TVA's impact was more "conservative" than was intended; for example, its programs did not infringe upon the patterns of racial segregation which existed during that time.[140] On the other hand, advisory groups can be mobilized to defend a program placed in jeopardy by a president's reorganization plans. In 1960 the Advisory Council to the National Institute of Mental Health (NIMH) and the director of NIMH cooperated in opposing a scheme to reorganize the Public Health Service; it would have transferred certain NIMH programs to a new Division of Mental Health. In the face of the Advisory Council's resistance, the proposal was dropped.[141]

Finally, close collusion between government and business interests is especially evident during wartime. The president needs the support of the business community to mobilize the nation's resources for combat. Typically the chief executive will appoint corporate leaders to those agencies responsible for wartime production. For example, Franklin D. Roosevelt appointed William Knudsen, president of General Motors, to head the Office of Production Management in 1940 and Donald M. Nelson, a vice-president of Sears, Roebuck and Company, to direct the Office of Price Administration and Civilian Supply in 1941.

Graham Wilson suggests that "clientele" agencies are especially sensitive to constituency influences because they know that legislation, program authority, personnel, and funding are all provided by congressmen who view those interest groups as being "reasonably numerous, politically significant and sufficiently concentrated geographically to be of outstanding importance."[142] Whereas the departments are less susceptible to clientele pressures, given their large size and many functions, clientele groups are able to exert more influence over those agencies charged with specific responsibilities. And where clientele politics is especially strong, bureaus and agencies can be insulated from the president's control. According to Seidman, the Federal Housing Administration, the Office of Education, the Federal Highway Administration, and the Federal Aviation Administration are agencies with substantial political autonomy.[143] Regarding the Federal Housing Administration, Seidman notes that its operations reflect the values of the real estate men and mortgage bankers who founded it. The FHA cooperated with lending institutions to "red line" areas of our central cities populated by the poor and minority groups. Housing loans to these groups were denied because these people were viewed as bad credit risks. In the words of one study made in the 1960s, "the main weakness of FHA from a social point of view has not been what it has done but in what it has failed to do—in its relative neglect of the inner cities and of the poor, and especially black poor."[144]

The Army Corps of Engineers, which maintains and constructs dock facilities, dams, and harbors, is perhaps the most famous example of an agency whose close relationship with Congress and private interests has protected it from presidential controls. Formally the Corps is under the Department of the Army and indirectly under the Defense Department, but these lines of authority do not explain how the Corps actually operates. In fact, Peter Woll observes,

> the Corps has developed exceptionally strong *political* support from outside groups, many of which have a local orientation that is reflected in Congress. Thus, Congress is intensely interested in preserving the Corps on an independent basis in order to enable it to act in congressional interests. The dominant forces in its constituency are private and congressional, and hence the decisions of the Corps are oriented in this direction.[145]

The Army Corps of Engineers gets political clout from its association with the National Rivers and Harbors Congress. Established in 1901, this group has more than 7,000 voluntary members. Its affiliates are found in all fifty states and include private contractors, water and land development associations, businesses, members of Congress, and government agencies at the state, county, and local levels. Clientele agencies by definition have the support of powerful interest groups; for example, the Rural Electrification Administration—a Depression-era agency—could rely upon the National Rural Electric Cooperative Association; the Bureau of Reclamation looks to the National Reclamation Association for help; and the Soil Conservation Service gets assistance from the National Association of Soil and Water Conservation Districts. In his indictment of "interest group liberalism," Theodore Lowi is especially disturbed because these private groups have special access to governmental authority.

> The American Farm Bureau Federation is no "voluntary association" if it is a legitimate functionary within the extension system. Such tightly knit corporate groups as the National Association of Home Builders . . ., National Association of Real Estate Boards . . ., or American Federation of Labor-Congress of Industrial Organizations . . . are no ordinary lobbies after they become part of the "interior processes" of policy formation.[146]

Certain professions dominate the memberships of government agencies. Members of the Council of Economic Advisers are academic economists, recruited from prestigious universities, such as Harvard and the University of Chicago, rather than from the ranks of big business. According to statute, whenever a president nominates anyone to the National Science Board he must give consideration to the recommendations submitted by the National Association of State Universities and Land Grant Colleges, the National Academy of Sciences, the Association of American Universities, the Association of State Colleges and Universities and "other scientific or educational organizations." When making five of the fifteen appointments to the board of directors of the Federal National Mortgage Association, the president must find at least one member from the home-building industry, one from the mortgage lending industry, and one from the real estate industry. An obvious example of this cozy relationship affects appointments to the federal judiciary. The American Bar Association (ABA) usually is asked by the Congress to submit a report on the qualifications of the president's nominee; the ABA has a permanent committee responsible for such investigations. If the candidate for a judicial post is unqualified or is not an attorney or a lower court judge, the ABA probably will not approve the nominee. Moreover, if the candidate was a lower court judge whose decisions were frequently overridden, it is unlikely that his candidacy will be supported by the ABA. As President Nixon learned, ABA opposition to Judges Clement Haynesworth and G. Harrold Carswell, his nominees for the Supreme Court, provided additional support for the Senate's rejection of their nominations. Finally, some agencies have organized their own professional associations to safeguard their interests. The Foreign Service Association and the Navy League are composed of past and present members of the Foreign Service and the U.S. Navy.

In the role of chief executive, therefore, public opinion is not easily mobilized behind a president's management objectives. Instead, private groups are strongly organized to protect those programs in which they have a vested interest. This is especially true when a governmental agency serves a discrete constituency, a "clientele" group, which also has political support in Congress.

EXPERTISE

The president's expertise as chief executive does give him some leverage vis-à-vis the Congress. The legislative branch must delegate to the president authority to implement public policy because it lacks the capability to detail administrative regulations in highly technical areas. This rationale was fundamental to Congress' allowing the "independent" regulatory commissions to exercise quasi-legislative and quasi-judicial as well as executive powers in monitoring specialized aspects of the economy, such as transportation, business competition, and communications. Volumes of the *Federal Register,* which embody agency rules and regulations, accompany the laws enacted by Congress in the *Statutes at Large;* each year as many as 60,000 pages are added to the *Federal Register.* Certainly the growing complexity of modern government is a variable that frustrates Congress in its attempt to oversee the operations of the federal bureaucracy. Morris Ogul explains the dilemma.

> The more technical and complex the subject matter is perceived to be, the less the likelihood of oversight. Only a few members of the Congress are experts in *any* area of bureaucratic operations. Those who are, master very few. Fulfilling the obligations of a congressman requires more time than a member has available. Ease of immersion into a subject will then be one factor governing his activity.[147]

On the other hand, expertise does not operate completely in favor of the chief executive. Just as Congress must depend on the president for information, the president's subordinates very often must rely on data monopolized by public and private institutions beyond their control. Examples of this kind of dependency are numerous. For many years the FBI crime index was subject to serious biases, because traditionally the reporting of violent crimes to the FBI was done by state and local law enforcement agencies voluntarily, and not uniformly. In a larger context, much government regulation depends upon the expertise, know-how, and information held by industries that are being regulated. This problem was documented by the Ralph Nader Study Group when it examined such regulatory agencies as the Interstate Commerce Commission (ICC), the Federal Trade Commission (FTC), and the Food and Drug Administration (FDA).[148] It seems apparent that often the "independent" regulatory commissions (ICC and FTC) are "captive" of the industries they regulate. The Ralph Nader Study Group's conclusions about the FDA were quite similar. In spite of the fact that the FDA is under the direct authority of the Department of Health and Human Services (formerly HEW) and the president, it experienced the same problems as the FTC and the ICC. FDA staff resources were inadequate, meaning that it often relied on test results supplied by the pharmaceutical or food industry. Moreover, the FDA even lacked the subpoena authority to summon witnesses or to require firms to divulge pertinent records. In a statement by the Department of HEW's Task Force on Environmental Health and Related Problems, it was asserted that "the [FDA] must have, as it does not now, adequate authority to inspect and evaluate the processing of foods to make certain that their safety is not impaired through the effect of a process which may or may not involve the use of additives."[149]

The lack of manpower and resources seriously limits the ability of these agencies to protect public safety and welfare. For example, the Federal Railroad Administration has only 376 safety inspectors to monitor 330,000 miles of track, 1.8 million freight cars, and 30,000 locomotives. The Securities and Exchange Commission had only 119 employees in the mid-1970s to oversee a huge stock exchange industry:

> It means supervising the activities of about 5,000 broker-dealers and 3,500 investment advisers, regulating 1,300 investment companies, bringing enforcement actions to assure financial responsibility and fair dealing, studying 1,000 corporate reorganizations each year, obtaining full and accurate information from 10,000 corporations and watching the trading in another 10,000.[150]

The cozy relationship between the regulators and the affected industry can subvert government's best intentions. This problem was dramatized by the crash of a DC-10 at Chicago's O'Hare Airport on Memorial Day 1979. This air disaster, the nation's worst, killed 275 people. The tragedy implicated the Federal Aviation Administration (FAA), which is responsible for issuing rules on aircraft design, testing, and maintenance. As one congressman observed, "It appears almost certain that the FAA's certification of the DC-10 components directly involved in . . . the tragedy may have been faulty."[151] Not only had the FAA not discovered the defects in the aircraft which caused the engine of the ill-fated Chicago DC-10 to fall off during takeoff, but critics argued that the FAA consistently has been slow in pressuring the industry to correct design problems. They point to the FAA's handling of the DC-10's long-standing cargo-door problem. As early as 1970 FAA inspectors were aware that a cargo hatch had been blown off a DC-10 during certification tests, but the agency did little more than order the manufacturer, McDonnell-Douglas, to correct the problem. When another cargo door burst open in 1972, the FAA reached a "gentleman's agreement" with McDonnell-Douglas allowing it to make the necessary repairs at its own convenience. But the company failed to do this until a Turkish Airlines DC-10 crashed near Paris in 1974, killing 346 people.[152]

In many ways private industry stays one step ahead of the government regulators. In the first place, many employees of the regulatory agencies are recruited by these industries. Common Cause, the public interest lobby, determined that 52 percent of the forty-two regulatory commissioners appointed during 1971–1975 came from companies regulated by their agencies or from the law firms retained by those companies. Similarly, 48 percent of the thirty-six commissioners who left government service during this period became employed by those industries or their law firms.[153] Furthermore, nobody is appointed to the independent regulatory commissions unless they are informally approved by the affected industries. "CAB [Civil Aeronautics Board] appointees are cleared with airline executives, FPC [Federal Power Commission] appointees with gas and electric companies, ICC [Interstate Commerce Commission] appointees with railroad officials and usually truckers, too," reports one observer. Furthermore, "Every president in recent history has run some sort of check with industry before appointing or reappointing a regulator."[154]

The fact that government decision makers come to rely upon the experience of businessmen who sit on various advisory committees works to the distinct advantage of private enterprise. As Sen. Lee Metcalf (D.–Mont.) once argued,

> Industry committees perform the dual function of stopping the government from finding out about corporations while at the same time helping corporations get insider information about what the government is doing. Sometimes, the same company that sits on an advisory council that obstructs or turns down a government questionnaire is precisely the company that is withholding information the government needs in order to enforce a law.[155]

These difficulties arise mainly at the implementation stage of policymaking, but they also can limit the chief executive in formulating policy guidelines and in preparing legislative recommendations. Therefore, presidents often turn to outside advisers to study major public policy issues in order to generate more information and to broaden their options. The experience with these presidential commissions, however, has been uneven; at times they assist the chief executive but on other occasions they simply embarrass him politically.

Presidential advisory commissions

A presidential advisory commission is an ad hoc advisory group appointed directly by the president and whose report is public. In his extensive analysis of presidential advisory commissions from Truman to Nixon, Thomas Wolanin describes their five general functions.[156] Most presidential advisory commissions are constituted to study a specific problem, to assess existing efforts to solve it, and to recommend an appropriate course of action. For example, the findings of the President's Commission on Law Enforcement and Administration of Justice (1965–1967) led to Congress' enactment of the Omnibus Crime Control and Safe Streets Act of 1968. Other presidential advisory commissions serve the purpose of "window dressing," in order to persuade decision makers, such as Congress or the bureaucracy, and the general public, to support a proposal to which the president is already committed. Thus, the reasoning behind John Kennedy's creation of the President's Advisery Panel on Federal Salary Systems (1961–1963) was described as follows: "The President intends to submit a proposal on Federal pay to the Congress in January. He feels the need, however, for your advice and the advice of others on the panel before firming up his proposal."[157] Similarly, a president may use this kind of group for long-range educational purposes; here the intent is to help create a milieu receptive to changes in the future.

A few presidential advisory commissions are established in response to crisis, although this is not generally how they are used. Several have had this objective as a secondary purpose. A well-known example of this maneuver was Lyndon Johnson's appointment of the National Advisory Commission on Civil Disorders (Kerner Commission, 1967–1968). A White House aide pointed out, "The Kerner Commission was created in the wake of the riots. You can be damn sure that the President was not going to let the people think that he was not doing anything about the riots."[158] Other examples of commissions created in response to crisis include: the President's Commission on the Assassination of President Kennedy (1963–1964), the National Commission on the Causes and Prevention of Violence (1968–1969), and the President's Commission on Campus Unrest (1970).

Presidential advisory commissions, finally, can be used by a president to avoid an issue or to "take the heat off" the administration by delaying any meaningful remedial action. Skeptics would argue that this is the major reason for creating presidential commissions; such groups are created simply to make their recommendations after months of deliberations and public fanfare, only to have their advice ignored by the president. According to Wolanin's research on ninety-nine presidential commissions during a twenty-five year period, this characterization is not true. The recommendations of most presidential advisory commissions have had substantive impact on policymaking. Nonetheless, the general perception that presidential commissions are largely ignored is related to the fact that the recommendations of those "crisis" commissions have not been supported entirely by our presidents. One problem is that our governmental system only allows modest or incremental policy changes to be made whereas these "crisis" commissions tend to recommend widespread socioeconomic changes. Wolanin explains these drawbacks in feasibility.

A President may indeed want to enlarge civil rights, end poverty, banish racism from America, instill in the nation a new sense of purpose, and do all of the other things recommended by these commissions. Their broad and sweeping recommendations, however, tend to lack both concreteness and political feasibility. The commissions call for basic changes in national direction and for large-scale new legislative programs and executive actions . . . but by the time of their reports the sense of crisis which spawned them has abated, if indeed it ever existed with sufficient intensity to support the implementation of their recommendations.[159]

In addition, the president simply may reject the commission's major conclusions. Lyndon Johnson was embarrassed by, and flatly disagreed with, the assertion of the Kerner Commission that America was racist. Similarly, Richard Nixon refused to endorse the permissive views of the President's Commission on Obscenity and Pornography in 1970. In this case, however, that group had been appointed by President Johnson; Nixon was able to exploit the antipornography sentiment in the country during the 1970 midterm elections.

In summary, in many ways a president as chief executive lacks the requisite expertise because a tremendous amount of technological information, scientific data, and knowledge about private decision making and societal trends is unavailable to him, or is inaccurate. Simply consider the possibility that the 1980 Census may have undercounted hundreds of thousands of minorities and Spanish-speaking populations in our central cities. The census data on population and demographic composition is absolutely essential for a multitude of government programs which distribute public works and social welfare funds among the various states and cities. Moreover, the information given to a president may be incompatible with his ideological preferences, or it can damage him politically with Congress, the bureaucracy, and the people. Yet, should advisers agree too readily on policy issues, the president may be hindered in fully understanding the complexities of policy questions.

Above all these considerations is the simple fact that no president is able to cope with the mountains of information and advice that he receives daily. Aaron Wildavsky sums up the problem of diminishing returns this way:

> There is a limit to the amount of information or advice that is useful for the President to have or on which he has time to act. After a while, the addition of new staff just multiplies his managerial problems without giving him valuable service in return.[160]

CRISIS

A domestic crisis augments the president's power to implement public policies because those clauses in the Constitution giving him "executive power" and authorizing him to "take care that the laws be faithfully executed" imply that initiatives may be taken to enforce the laws. The use of force by a president, moreover, is supported by Article IV of the Constitution directing the national government to protect every state "against Invasion . . . and against domestic Violence." In various statutes the Congress explicitly directs the president, as chief executive and commander-in-chief, to enforce these "obligations" to the states. Such use of federal power may be requested by a state's governor or legislature, although a president can refuse to send assistance. On the other hand, a president may intervene in local disturbances when he believes that the state and local authorities are not enforcing federal laws. Federal troops, the ("federalized") National Guard, or U.S.

marshals were used without state consent when Dwight Eisenhower desegregated Little Rock High School in 1957 and when John F. Kennedy desegregated the University of Mississippi (1962) and the University of Alabama (1963). Lyndon Johnson used the National Guard to restore order in the 1967 Detroit riots, even though he and Michigan Governor George Romney had disagreed about when and whether to deploy federal troops there.

Congress may delegate extraordinary authority to the chief executive to deal with crises whenever they can be anticipated. Using statutory authority, Richard Nixon in 1970 declared a national emergency and used troops to deliver the mail during a postal strike. And in 1968 Lyndon Johnson invoked another law allowing the president to restrict the investment of American capital abroad in order to improve our unfavorable balance of payments. To curb labor strikes that threaten the national interest, the Taft-Hartley Act of 1947 permits the president to impose an eighty-day "cooling-off" period, thus preventing a walkout from taking place. Federal aid to counties suffering natural disasters, such as floods and hurricanes, requires a presidential declaration that such areas qualify for assistance. In 1933 Franklin Roosevelt resurrected a 1917 law (Trading with the Enemy Act) to justify his declaring a bank "holiday" to stem massive withdrawals of funds from financial institutions until public confidence in them was restored.

Perhaps the most extensive delegation of authority to a president during peacetime occurred when Congress enacted the landmark National Industrial Recovery Act. A cornerstone of Roosevelt's plans for combating the Great Depression, it attempted to reduce competition, increase prices, and control production through a series of codes adopted by industrial and trade associations. Acceptable codes for each industry had to be approved by the president, or the chief executive was empowered to prescribe his own codes and enforce them. This extraordinary delegation of power to the president, however, was declared to be unconstitutional by the Supreme Court in the equally famous case of *Schechter Corp. v. United States* (1935).[161] Therefore, as Theodore Lowi argues, "the area of 'emergency power' does not involve any presidential prerogative on the domestic side, even though a cooperative Congress helps make it unnecessary for the president to make a claim to prerogative."[162]

There is a long history of presidents using federal force to resolve labor/management disputes that disrupt the national economy. In the famous Pullman Strike, President Grover Cleveland, over the objections of Illinois' governor, dispatched federal troops to Chicago to protect U.S. property and "to remove obstructions to the United States mails." Cleveland's action was upheld by the Supreme Court in a ruling that suggested the president enjoyed wide discretion in determining whether a crisis situation necessitated the use of force.[163] When the nation was threatened by an anthracite coal strike as winter approached in 1902, Theodore Roosevelt actively intervened in this dispute. After an investigation he forced the union and management to submit their disagreement to an arbitration commission; had this plan failed Roosevelt was ready to use the army to "dispossess the operators and run the mines as a receiver."[164] Ronald Reagan's handling of the air traffic controllers' strike in 1981 illustrates how a perceived crisis can strengthen the chief executive's role. By reviewing this labor dispute, which directly involved the federal government, we can understand how President Reagan overcame the relative weaknesses of this role to essentially destroy the union representing the nation's air traffic controllers.

The PATCO strike

The Professional Air Traffic Controllers Organization (PATCO) represented 85 percent of the 17,500 federal employees who direct the country's air traffic. After two and one-half months of bargaining with the government, PATCO's president stated in May 1981 that his members would strike one month later unless an acceptable offer was made by their employer, the Federal Aviation Administration (FAA). After frenzied last-minute negotiations, the PATCO leadership reached a tentative settlement with the government, the strike was called off, and the benefit package was submitted to the union members for approval. When the settlement was rejected by 95 percent of the PATCO membership, talks were resumed at the end of July. Negotiations reached a stalemate over the terms of the FAA's final offer, the strike action began, and the Reagan administration reacted with a hard-line position.

After Reagan threatened that the striking employees would be terminated, only about 1,200 PATCO workers returned to their jobs. Within a few weeks, therefore, dismissal notices were sent to the more than 11,000 striking air controllers. Then the government went to court. Federal judges ordered U.S. marshals to jail five union leaders who refused to obey a back-to-work injunction. Judges also began levying fines against the union and its leadership totaling $1 million a day. PATCO's $3.5 million strike fund was also frozen, essentially bankrupting the union.

Even after the strike had been broken, President Reagan refused to hire back PATCO members as air traffic controllers, though in December 1981 he announced that the dismissed controllers could seek employment elsewhere in the federal government. Reagan described this decision as an act of "compassion"; however, given his cutbacks in federal employment, it remained to be seen how many PATCO members would get other federal jobs.

In a matter of five months the Reagan administration had broken the union of air traffic controllers. The legal basis for the government's action against PATCO lay in the antistrike oath that every federal employee must sign. It reads in part:

> I am not participating in any strike against the government of the United States or any agency thereof, and I will not so participate while an employee of the government of the United States or any agency thereof.

The fate of PATCO was sealed when, at the end of October, the Federal Labor Relations Authority, which grants unions the right to represent certain groups of workers, revoked that authority from the Professional Air Traffic Controllers Organization. This action was the first time that a union representing federal employees had been literally abolished.

Ronald Reagan's tough position against PATCO was related, in part, to his desire to send a message to other government unions whose contracts would be expiring soon. Presumably his victory over the air controllers would prompt other unions to moderate their wage demands. In spite of the political difficulties that could arise when a Republican President tries to destroy a collective bargaining organization, Reagan was able to minimize this problem by defining the controversy on his own terms. Before he began the dismissals, President Reagan summoned reporters to the White House Rose Garden and read a prepared statement. He said he respected the right of employees in the private sector to strike and recalled that, as president of the Screen Actors Guild in 1959, Reagan had called the first strike ever by that union. In this instance, however, he said that government "has to provide without interruption the protective services which are Government's reason for being," noting that in 1947 Congress passed a law forbidding strikes by federal employees. He read aloud the antistrike oath signed by all PATCO members and said: "They are in violation of the law, and if they do not report for work within 48 hours, they have forfeited their jobs and will be terminated."[165] The chief executive charged that PATCO was breaking the law, and the public sided with the president rather than the union.

Even though the American people support collective bargaining and unions in the private sector, Gallup Polls show that most people do not favor allowing public employees the right to strike.[166] The PATCO strike, similarly, was opposed by the majority of Americans; moreover, its effectiveness was undermined by other unions which refused to support it. Had the other unions serving the nation's airports honored the picket lines, these facilities would have been shut down. But such powerful unions as the International Association of Machinists, the International Brotherhood of Teamsters, the Air Line Pilots Association, and the Association of Flight Attendants did not support PATCO's walkout. A few leaders of other unions, such as Auto Workers President Douglas Fraser and AFL-CIO President Lane Kirkland, simply voiced their support for collective bargaining and the right to strike.

The argument that Reagan was "union-busting" did not seem credible to many people because the other unions did not honor PATCO's picket lines. PATCO's grievances stemmed from their argument that air controllers are responsible for more lives than commercial pilots but are paid much less than pilots and that the stresses faced on the job threatened to "burn out" these workers much earlier than people in other occupations. On the other hand, the PATCO strike caused a slowdown in air traffic and auxiliary personnel had been laid off; to shut down the airline industry completely could have damaged the companies' profit margin to the extent that many thousands of jobs would have been jeopardized. Thus, lesser-paid machinists, baggage handlers, and flight attendants felt little sympathy with air controllers who earned relatively high salaries. A prolonged PATCO strike could have cost them their jobs.

President Reagan's success in defeating the air controllers union also was related to his ability to replace the striking personnel with others trained to do their jobs. At the outset, about 3,000 supervisors and 2,000 nonstriking or nonunion controllers stayed on the job. To this number was added about 500 military controllers from an available pool of 10,000. To allow the government time to properly man the towers and radar centers across the nation, the FAA ordered airlines to cut their scheduled flights 50 percent for at least one month. The FAA proceeded to increase the number of air controllers being certified and announced plans to triple the number of new air controllers it trains, which was about 1,800 a year. Thus, ultimately the PATCO strike failed because air traffic, though affected by delays and a reduced schedule, continued throughout the duration of the walkout. As the Secretary of Transportation Drew Lewis commented, "To all intents and purposes, the strike is over. Our concern is to rebuild the system."[167]

Three lessons can be learned from the PATCO strike. First, the chief executive was able to use his formal authority against the strikers. Reagan did not have to share decision making with the Congress. Moreover, Reagan acted pursuant to a statute that prohibited strikes by federal employees, and the judiciary backed the president in this confrontation. Second, public opinion and those interests directly affected by the strike—the airline industry and unions of other airline personnel—either supported the president's action or avoided taking a stand that would undermine its effectiveness. Third, the president in this situation could rely upon substitute personnel with the requisite experience and knowledge to man the airport control towers during the strike. The various agencies of government involved, such as the FAA and the Department of Transportation, worked cooperatively under White House supervision, and without internal bickering, to accomplish Reagan's objectives.

CONCLUSION

According to our framework of analysis, the location of the chief executive role at the midpoint of the continuum suggests that both authority and influence are central to presidential power in this role. The chief executive is neither the strongest role, nor is it the weakest role. Congress understands that the president must be responsible for the day-to-day management of government, but it is unwilling to abdicate its power to intervene in public administration on behalf of constituency groups and special interests. Public opinion, moreover, is mostly benign in this role because the American people—though they hold an antibureaucracy viewpoint and are disturbed about the rising costs of government—are unable to translate those concerns into direct political action. On the other hand, agencies which have the support of clientele groups and the Congress are able to resist the president's direct control. Each president tries to arrange his own advisory system to supervise the government bureaucracy, though most employees are protected by civil service. Eisenhower's and Reagan's advisory systems were formalistic; Kennedy's flexible method of operations was akin to Franklin D. Roosevelt's; and Richard Nixon used his senior aides as assistant presidents. No president has mastered the bureaucracy entirely for his own purposes; Nixon tried to do so but was unsuccessful with the advent of Watergate.

When crises affect the domestic economy or our society, Congress seems quite willing to delegate to the president the authority to act, but obviously presidential power in this instance depends on the continuation of whatever emergencies exist. Thus, the evidence supports Louis Koenig's observation, quoted at the start of this chapter, that a president might well be envious of how much authority is allowed a typical business executive in the United States.

NOTES

[1] James MacGregor Burns, "Our Super-Government—Can We Control It?" *New York Times* (April 24, 1949), p. 32.

[2] Grant McConnell, *The Modern Presidency* (New York: St. Martin's Press, 1976), p. 65.

[3] Henry S. Reuss, "A Private Club for Public Policy," *The Nation* (October 16, 1976), p. 372.

[4] Quoted in Burns, "Our Super-Government—Can We Control It?" p. 30.

[5] Louis W. Koenig, *The Chief Executive*, 2nd ed. (New York: Harcourt, Brace and World, 1968), p. 155.

[6] See *Minnesota Chippewa Tribe v. Carlucci*, 358 F. Supp. 973, 975–976 (D.D.C. 1973).

[7] Robert J. Sickels, *The Presidency: An Introduction* (Englewood Cliffs, N.J.: Prentice-Hall, 1980), p. 206.

[8] Herman Finer, *The Presidency: Crisis and Regeneration* (Chicago: University of Chicago, 1968), p. 45. Raymond Chambers estimates that the president today can appoint no more than 103,500 positions in the federal service, most of which are in the armed services. See Edward N. Kearny, ed., *Dimensions of the Modern Presidency* (St. Louis: Forum Press, 1981), p. 123.

[9] Samuel C. Patterson; Robert H. Davidson; and Randall B. Ripley, *A More Perfect Union* (Homewood, Ill.: The Dorsey Press, 1982), p. 426.

[10] Richard M. Pious, *The American Presidency* (New York: Basic Books, 1979), p. 218.

[11] William W. Lammers, *Presidential Politics: Patterns and Prospects* (New York: Harper and Row, 1976), p. 100.

[12] In 1975 Congress passed the Foreign Relations Authorization Act, which demanded that the position of ambassador should be filled by those possessing "clearly demonstrated competence" and that financial contributions to a president's campaign should not be the primary qualification for the position. See P.L. 94–141, 89 Stat. 757, sec. 104 1975. For an essay critical of Jimmy Carter's diplomatic appointments see Roger Morris, "Diplomatic Spoils," *Harper's Magazine*, (November, 1978), pp. 69–75.

[13] Calvin MacKenzie, *The Politics of Presidential Appointments* (New York: The Free Press, 1981), p. 177.

[14] James D. Richardson, *A Compilation of the Messages and Papers of the Presidents, 1789–1887* (Washington, D.C.: U.S. Government Printing Office, 1896), vol. 3, p. 69.

[15]David B. Truman, "Presidential Executives or Congressional Executives," in Aaron Wildavsky, ed., *The Presidency* (Boston: Little, Brown, 1969), p. 489.

[16]These cases involving the president's removal power are cited in the discussion to follow: *Marbury v. Madison*, 5 US (1 Cr.) 137, 162 (1803); *U.S. v. Perkins*, US 483, 485 (1886); *Parsons v. U.S.*, 167 US 324, 343 (1897); *Shurtleff v. U.S.*, 189 US 311, 317 (1903); *Wallace v. U.S.*, 257 US 541, 545–46 (1922); *Myers, Administratrix v. U.S.*, 272 US 52 (1926); *Humphrey's Executor (Rathbun) v. U.S.*, 295 US 602 (1935).

[17]These cases are discussed in this section: *Wiener v. U.S.*, 357 US 349 (1958); *U.S. v. Nixon*, 418 US 683 (1974); *Nixon v. Fitzgerald* (No. 79–1738), June 25, 1982. Regarding the last case, also see Justice Powell, "Excerpts From Ruling by High Court," *New York Times* (June 25, 1982), p. 9.

[18]*Mississippi v. Johnson*, 4 Wall. 475 (1867).

[19]Arthur S. Miller, *Presidential Power in a Nut Shell* (St. Paul: West Publishing Company, 1977), p. 258.

[20]Quoted in G. Calvin MacKenzie, "The Paradox of Presidential Personnel Management," in Hugh Heclo and Lester M. Salamon, eds., *The Illusion of Presidential Government* (Boulder, Colo.: Westview Press, 1981), p. 130.

[21]Lammers, *Presidential Politics: Patterns and Prospects*, p. 214.

[22]William F. Mullen, *Presidential Power and Politics* (New York: St. Martin's Press, 1976), p. 67.

[23]Joel Havemann, *Congress and the Budget* (Bloomington: Indiana University Press, 1978), pp. 176–177.

[24]See James P. Pfiffner, *The President, the Budget, and Congress: Impoundment and the 1974 Budget Act* (Boulder, Colo.: Westview Press, 1979), chapter 5.

[25]*Train v. City of New York*, 420 U.S. 35 (1975).

[26]Quoted in Pious, *The American Presidency*, p. 282.

[27]Havemann, *Congress and the Budget*, p. 181.

[28]Ibid.

[29]Ibid.

[30]Harvey C. Mansfield, "Federal Executive Reorganization: Thirty Years of Experience," *Public Administration Review* (July/August 1969), p. 339.

[31]"Carter Given Reorganization Authority," *Congressional Quarterly Weekly Report* (April 12, 1977), p. 616.

[32]Koenig, *The Chief Executive*, 3rd ed. p. 206.

[33]Harold Seidman, *Politics, Position, and Power: The Dynamics of Federal Organization*, 3rd ed. (New York: Oxford University Press, 1980), p. 118.

[34]Sickels, *The Presidency: An Introduction*, p. 218.

[35]Rochelle Jones and Peter Woll, "The Interest Vested in Chaos," *The Nation* (April 2, 1977), p. 402.

[36]Seidman, *Politics, Position, and Power*, p. 15.

[37]Ronald C. Moe, "The Reorganization Efforts at Mid-Term," *Congressional Research Service Report* no. 79–56 (January 20, 1979), p. 10. Cited in Seidman, *Politics, Position, and Power*, p. 131.

[38]Louis Fisher, *The Politics of Shared Power* (Washington, D.C.: Congressional Quarterly Press, 1981), pp. 84–85.

[39]Patterson; Davidson; and Ripley, *A More Perfect Union*, p. 394.

[40]Clark F. Norton, "Congressional Review, Deferral and Disapproval of Executive Actions: A Summary and Inventory of Statutory Authority," *Congressional Research Service Report* no. 76–88G (April 30, 1976) and "Congressional Acts Authorizing Prior Review Approval or Disapproval of Proposed Executive Actions 1976–1977," *Congressional Research Service Report* no. 78–117 (May 25, 1978). Cited in Joseph M. Bessette and Jeffrey Tulis, *The Presidency in the Constitutional Order* (Baton Rouge: Louisiana State University Press, 1981), pp. 195–233.

[41]Fisher, *The Politics of Shared Power*, p. 99.

[42]"Using Its Legislative Veto Power," *National Journal* (January 13, 1979), p. 48.

[43]Fisher, *The Politics of Shared Power,* p. 99.

[44]See Raymond Tatalovich and Byron W. Daynes, *The Politics of Abortion: A Study of Community Conflict in Public Policy-Making* (New York: Praeger, 1981), pp. 186–188.

[45]*Sunset: A Common Cause Proposal for Accountable Government* (Washington, D.C.: Common Cause, 1976).

[46]Herbert Kaufman, *Are Government Organizations Immortal?* (Washington, D.C.: Brookings Institution, 1976).

[47]Joel D. Aberbach and Bert A. Rockman, "Clashing Beliefs within the Executive Branch," *American Political Science Review* (June 1976), pp. 456–468.

[48]Seidman, *Politics, Position, and Power,* p. 168.

[49]Quoted in Robert Sherrill, *Governing America* (New York: Harcourt Brace Jovanovich, 1978), p. 424.

[50]Thomas Emerson, "The FBI as Political Police," in Pat Watters and Stephan Gillers, eds., *Investigating the FBI* (New York: Doubleday, 1973), pp. 239–254.

[51]Sherrill, *Governing America,* p. 435.

[52]William E. Brigman, "The Executive Branch and the Independent Regulatory Agencies," *Presidential Studies Quarterly* (Spring 1981), pp. 244–246.

[53]Advisory Commission on Intergovernmental Relations, *Intergovernmental Perspective* (Summer 1980).

[54]Morton Grodzins and Daniel Elazar, "Centralization and Decentralization in the American Federal System," in Robert A. Goldwin, ed., *A Nation of States: Essays on the American Federal System* (Chicago: Rand McNally, 1974), pp. 1–2.

[55]Peter Woll, *American Bureaucracy* (New York: W. W. Norton, 1977), p. 64.

[56]Sherrill, *Governing America,* p. 418. One study which is critical of the federal government's use of contract employees is: D. Guttman and B. Willner, *The Shadow Government: The Government's Multi-Billion-Dollar Giveaway of Its Decision-Making Powers to Private Management Consultants, "Experts," and Think Tanks* (New York: Pantheon, 1976).

[57]Seidman, *Politics, Position, and Power,* p. 166.

[58]Sherrill, *Governing America,* p. 418.

[59]Ibid.

[60]Seidman, *Politics, Position, and Power,* p. 185. Also see the critical analysis of this program in Daniel P. Moynihan, *Maximum Feasible Misunderstanding: Community Action in the War on Poverty* (New York: The Free Press, 1969).

[61]Koenig, *The Chief Executive,* 4th ed., p. 205.

[62]Thomas Cronin, "The Swelling of the Presidency," in Harry A. Bailey, Jr., *Classics of the American Presidency* (Oak Park, Ill.: Moore Publishing Company, 1980), p. 154.

[63]Pious, *The American Presidency,* p. 240.

[64]Richard F. Fenno, Jr., "President-Cabinet Relations," in David E. Haight and Larry D. Johnson, eds., *The President: Roles and Powers* (Chicago: Rand McNally, 1965), p. 214.

[65]Finer, *The Presidency: Crisis and Regeneration,* p. 232.

[66]Quoted in Sickels, *The Presidency: An Introduction,* p. 156.

[67]Koenig, *The Chief Executive,* 3rd ed., p. 198.

[68]Pious, *The American Presidency,* p. 241.

[69]Terence Smith, "President Summons Aides to Camp David for a Broad Review," *New York Times* (July 7, 1979), p. 1.

[70]Norman C. Thomas, ed., *The Presidency in Contemporary Context* (New York: Dodd, Mead, 1975), p. 168.

[71]See Lester G. Seligman, "Presidential Leadership: The Inner Circle and Institutionalization," *Journal of Politics* (1956), pp. 412–413.

[72]Quoted in Finer, *The Presidency: Crisis and Regeneration,* pp. 186–187.

[73]Cited in Kearny, *Dimensions of the Modern Presidency,* p. 141.

[74]Ibid., p. 143.

[75]William D. Pederson and Stephen N. Williams, "The President and the White House Staff," in Kearny, *Dimensions of the Modern Presidency*, p. 141.

[76]See Lester M. Salamon, "The Presidency and Domestic Policy Formulation," in Heclo and Salamon, eds., *The Illusion of Presidential Government*, p. 183.

[77]Quoted in R. Gordon Hoxie, ed., *The White House: Organization and Operations* (New York: Center for the Study of the Presidency, 1971), p.71.

[78]Dom Bonafede, "White House Staffing: The Nixon-Ford Era," in Thomas E. Cronin and Rexford G. Tugwell, eds., *The Presidency Reappraised*, 2nd ed. (New York: Praeger, 1977), p. 154.

[79]The President's Committee on Administrative Management, *Report of the Committee with Studies of Administrative Management in the Federal Government* (Washington, D.C.: U.S. Government Printing Office, 1937), p. 5.

[80]Christopher Lasch, "Paranoid Presidency," *The Center Magazine* (March/April 1974), p. 26.

[81]Thomas E. Cronin and Sanford D. Greenberg, *The Presidential Advisory System* (New York: Harper and Row, 1969), p. 8.

[82]See the excellent analysis of these conflicts by Thomas E. Cronin in "Everybody Believes in Democracy until He Gets to the White House—An Analysis of White House–Departmental Relations," in Norman C. Thomas and Hans W. Baade, eds., "The Institutionalized Presidency," *Law and Contemporary Problems* (Summer 1970), pp. 573–626.

[83]Mullen, *Presidential Power and Politics*, p. 196.

[84]Koenig, *The Chief Executive*, 3d ed. p. 192.

[85]Harry S. Truman, *Memoirs*, vol. 1 (Garden City, N.Y.: Doubleday, 1955), p. 226.

[86]Stephen Hess, *Organizing the Presidency* (Washington, D.C.: Brookings Institution, 1976), p. 46.

[87]Sickels, *The Presidency: An Introduction*, p. 176.

[88]Richard Neustadt, *Presidential Power: The Politics of Leadership* (New York: John Wiley, 1960), pp. 171–172.

[89]Dwight D. Eisenhower, *Mandate for Change, 1953–1956* (Garden City, N.Y.: Doubleday, 1963), p. 114.

[90]Alex B. Lacy, Jr., "The Development of the White House Office: 1939–1967," paper delivered to annual meeting, American Political Science Association, 1967. Cited in Dorothy B. James, *The Contemporary Presidency*, 2nd ed. (Indianapolis: Pegasus, 1973), p. 155.

[91]Sherman Adams, *Firsthand Report: Eisenhower Administration* (New York: Harper and Brothers, 1961), p. 50.

[92]Hess, *Organizing the Presidency*, p. 65.

[93]"President Ends 41 Committees," *New York Times* (April 9, 1961), p. 32.

[94]Theodore C. Sorensen, *Kennedy* (New York: Harper and Row, 1965), p. 282.

[95]Arthur M. Schlesinger, Jr., *A Thousand Days* (Boston: Houghton Mifflin, 1965), p. 688.

[96]Irving L. Janis, *Victims of Groupthink* (Boston: Houghton Mifflin, 1972), p. 25.

[97]Ibid., p. 13.

[98]Eric F. Goldman, *The Tragedy of Lyndon Johnson* (New York: Knopf, 1969), p. 102.

[99]Hess, *Organizing the Presidency*, p. 101.

[100]George E. Reedy, *The Twilight of the Presidency* (New York: New American Library, 1970), p. 78.

[101]Erwin C. Hargrove, *The Power of the Modern Presidency* (New York: Knopf, 1974), p. 243.

[102]Stephen J. Wayne, *The Legislative Presidency* (New York: Harper and Row, 1978), p. 51.

[103]Hess, *Organizing the Presidency*, p. 113.

[104]Mullen, *Presidential Power and Politics*, p. 206.

[105]Quoted in Pious, *The American Presidency,* p. 244.

[106]Seidman, *Politics, Position, and Power,* p. 115.

[107]Ibid., p. 121.

[108]Ibid., p. 122.

[109]Wayne, *The Legislative Presidency,* p. 47.

[110]See Richard P. Nathan, *The Plot That Failed: Nixon and the Administrative Presidency* (New York: John Wiley and Sons, 1975).

[111]Wayne, *The Legislative Presidency,* p. 51.

[112]John Hersey, "The President," *New York Times Magazine* (April 20, 1975), p. 76.

[113]Wayne, *The Legislative Presidency,* p. 58.

[114]Joel Havemann, "The Cabinet Band—Trying to Follow Carter's Baton," *National Journal* (July 16, 1977), pp. 1104–1112. Cited in David V. Edwards, *The American Political Experience* (Englewood Cliffs, N.J.: Prentice-Hall, 1982), p. 255.

[115]Koenig, *The Chief Executive,* 4th ed., p. 202.

[116]Edwards, *The American Political Experience,* p. 255.

[117]William Greider, "The Education of David Stockman," *The Atlantic Monthly* (December 1981), pp. 27–54.

[118]This discussion is based on Allen Schick, "The Problem of Presidential Budgeting," in Heclo and Salamon, eds., *The Illusion of Presidential Government,* pp. 85–111.

[119]Ibid., p. 89.

[120]Ibid., p. 92.

[121]Ibid., p. 97.

[122]Ibid., p. 98.

[123]Richard E. Neustadt, "Presidency and Legislation: The Growth of Central Clearance," in Aaron Wildavsky, ed., *The Presidency* (Boston: Little, Brown, 1969), p. 630.

[124]Allen Schick, "The Budget Bureau That Was: Thoughts on the Rise, Decline, and Future of a Presidential Agency," *Law and Contemporary Problems* (1970), p. 527.

[125]Hugh Heclo, "OMB and the Presidency—The Problem of 'Neutral Competence,' " *The Public Interest* (Winter 1975), p. 87.

[126]Ibid., p. 89.

[127]American Institute of Public Opinion, *Public Opinion 1972–1977,* vol. 2 (Wilmington, Del.: Scholarly Resources Inc., 1978), pp. 1111–1114.

[128]*The Gallup Opinion Index,* report no. 167 (June 1979), pp. 18–19.

[129]*The Gallup Opinion Index,* report no. 164 (March 1979), pp. 21–22.

[130]Quoted in Sherrill, *Governing America,* p. 421.

[131]Cited in ibid., p. 163.

[132]See Lloyd A. Free and Hadley Cantril, *The Political Beliefs of Americans* (New York: Simon and Schuster, 1968), chapter 3.

[133]Richard Polenberg, "Roosevelt, Carter, and Executive Reorganization: Lessons of the 1930s," *Presidential Studies Quarterly* (Winter 1979), p. 45.

[134]Marian D. Irish; James W. Prothro; and Richard J. Richardson, *The Politics of American Democracy* (Englewood Cliffs, N.J.: Prentice-Hall, 1977), p. 337.

[135]Kenneth Prewitt and Sidney Verba, *An Introduction to American Government* (New York: Harper and Row, 1974), pp. 221–222.

[136]Roger G. Noll, *Reforming Regulation* (Washington, D.C.: Brookings Institution, 1971), p. 43.

[137]Grant McConnell, *Private Power and American Democracy* (New York: Knopf, 1966), chapter 8.

[138]Seidman, *Politics, Position, and Power,* p. 280.

[139]Ibid., p. 282.

[140]See the classic study in Philip Selznick, *TVA and the Grass Roots* (Berkeley: University of California Press, 1949).

[141]Seidman, *Politics, Position, and Power,* pp. 280–281.

[142]Graham K. Wilson "Are Department Secretaries Really a President's Natural Enemies?" in Bailey, ed., *Classics of the American Presidency,* p. 137.

[143]Seidman, *Politics, Position, and Power,* p. 153.

[144]Cited in ibid., p. 155.

[145]Woll, *American Bureaucracy,* p. 67.

[146]Theodore J. Lowi, *The End of Liberalism,* 2nd ed. (New York: W. W. Norton, 1979), p. 60.

[147]Morris S. Ogul, *Congress Oversees the Bureaucracy* (Pittsburgh: University of Pittsburgh Press, 1976), p. 14.

[148]These studies by the Ralph Nader Study Group are authored by different individuals and include the following: James S. Turner, *The Chemical Feast* (New York: Grossman Publishers, 1970) and Robert Fellmeth, *The Interstate Commerce Omission* (New York: Grossman Publishers, 1970).

[149]Turner, *The Chemical Feast,* p. 45.

[150]Sherrill, *Governing America,* p. 438.

[151]"Why FAA Draws Fire after DC-10 Crash," *U.S. News and World Report* (June 11, 1979), p. 8.

[152]See "Debacle of the DC-10," *Time* (June 18, 1979), pp. 14–16.

[153]Cited in Patterson, Davidson, and Ripley, *A More Perfect Union,* p. 585.

[154]Louis M. Kohlmeier, Jr., *The Regulators: Watchdog Agencies and the Public Interest* (New York: Harper and Row, 1969), p. 48.

[155]Lee Metcalf, "The Vested Oracles: How Industry Regulates Government," *Washington Monthly* (July 1971), p. 231.

[156]Thomas R. Wolanin, *Presidential Advisory Commissions* (Madison: University of Wisconsin Press, 1975), chapter 2.

[157]Cited in ibid., p. 17.

[158]Cited in ibid., p. 21.

[159]Ibid., p. 194.

[160]Aaron Wildavsky, "Salvation by Staff: Reform of the Presidential Office," in Wildavsky, ed., *The Presidency* (Boston: Little, Brown, 1969), p. 697.

[161]*Schechter Poultry Company v. United States,* 295 U.S. 495 (1935).

[162]Theodore J. Lowi, *American Government: Incomplete Conquest* (Hinsdale, Ill.: The Dryden Press, 1976), p. 404.

[163]*In re Debs,* 158 U.S. 564 (1895).

[164]Louis W. Koenig, *The Chief Executive,* 2nd ed. (New York: Harcourt Brace and World, 1968), p. 288.

[165]"Turbulence in the Tower," *Time* (August 17, 1981), p. 16.

[166]For example, a June 1979 Gallup Poll found that, although most Americans approve of labor unions, majorities of the respondents did not approve allowing such public employees as policemen, firemen, or teachers the right to strike. See *The Gallup Opinion Index,* report no. 167 (June 1979), pp. 14–17. In August 1981 68 percent of the respondents said that air traffic controllers should not be permitted to strike. See *The Gallup Report* no. 191 (August 1981), p. 35.

[167]"Turbulence in the Tower," *Time,* p. 15.

SUGGESTED READINGS

Anderson, Patrick. *The President's Men.* Garden City, N.Y.: Doubleday, 1968.

Cronin, Thomas E. *The State of the Presidency.* Boston: Little, Brown, 1975.

Cronin, Thomas E., and Greenberg, Sanford D., eds. *The Presidential Advisory System.* New York: Harper and Row, 1969.

Fenno, Richard F. *The President's Cabinet.* New York: Vintage Books, 1959.

Hess, Stephen. *Organizing the Presidency.* Washington, D.C.: Brookings Institution, 1976.

Hobbes, Edward. *Behind the President.* Washington, D.C.: Public Affairs Press, 1954.

Hoxie, R. Gordon, ed. *The White House: Organization and Operations.* New York: Center for the Study of the Presidency, 1971.

Janis, Irving L. *Groupthink.* 2nd ed. Boston: Houghton Mifflin, 1982.

Johnson, Richard T. *Managing the White House.* New York: Harper and Row, 1974.

Koenig, Louis. *The Invisible Presidency.* New York: Holt, Rinehart and Winston, 1960.

MacKenzie, Calvin. *The Politics of Presidential Appointments.* New York: The Free Press, 1981.

Nash, Bradley D. *Staffing the Presidency.* Washington, D.C.: National Planning Association, 1952.

Nathan, Richard P. *The Plot that Failed: Nixon and the Administrative Presidency.* New York: John Wiley and Sons, 1975.

Rose, Richard. *Managing Presidential Objectives.* New York: The Free Press, 1976.

Seidman, Harold. *Politics, Position, and Power: The Dynamics of Federal Organization.* 3rd ed. New York: Oxford University Press, 1980.

Thomas, Norman C. and Baade, Hans W., eds. *The Institutionalized Presidency.* Dodds Ferry, N.Y.: Oceana, 1972.

Wolanin, Thomas R. *Presidential Advisory Commissions.* Madison: University of Wisconsin Press, 1975.

Woll, Peter. *American Bureaucracy.* New York: W. W. Norton, 1977.

CHAPTER SIX

Chief Diplomat: The Primacy of Executive Authority

Most presidents consider foreign affairs to be more important than their management of domestic policy. Foreign policy defines our nation's relationship to other countries, whether ally or enemy. Major trends in U.S. diplomacy can be identified with specific presidents. George Washington's Neutrality Proclamation of 1793 and his Farewell Address in 1796 articulated a commitment to isolationism. This sentiment was affirmed by James Monroe's Monroe Doctrine, which warned European powers not to meddle in the western hemisphere. President James K. Polk's belief in Manifest Destiny was reflected in his involvement in the Mexican War to acquire new territories in the Southwest. Similar motivations affected our conduct of foreign policy in 1898, with the Spanish-American War and President William McKinley's annexation of the Philippines.

Theodore Roosevelt built the Panama Canal and used a "Big Stick" in dealing with Latin America; that heavy-handed approach was moderated by Franklin D. Roosevelt's promise of a Good Neighbor Policy toward the countries in Central and South America. Although Woodrow Wilson, after World War I, failed to achieve his League of Nations, Franklin D. Roosevelt's plans for a United Nations came to fulfillment under Harry Truman. Since World War II, our foreign policy has been shaped by "Cold War" tensions between the United States and the Soviet Union. The Cold War began when President Truman declared a "containment" policy directed toward the Soviet Union and its allies: during his tenure, Truman instituted the Marshall Plan to aid European economic recovery after World War II, gave assistance to Greece and Turkey when they were threatened by communist takeovers, and entered the Korean War to prevent the communist government in North Korea from occupying South Korea.

President Dwight Eisenhower held a Geneva Summit Conference in 1955. Although that particular meeting had little effect on U.S. relations with the Soviet Union, it marked the beginnings of "summitry," whereby high-level meetings with foreign leaders, including the Russians, are staged in an effort to promote world peace and cooperation. In 1962 President John F. Kennedy confronted the Soviet military presence in the Caribbean during the Cuban missile crisis. Perceptions of a communist threat to Southeast Asia led Presidents Johnson and Nixon to become deeply involved in the Vietnam War. The Nixon administration was known for its efforts to ease East–West tensions through détente. President Nixon visited the Soviet Union and made a historic trip to the People's Republic of China. Nixon's visit to Communist China paved the way for President Carter's formal "recognition" of the People's Republic of China; however, when the Soviet Union invaded Afghanistan in December 1979, Jimmy Carter felt obliged to resist this aggression by organizing an international boycott of the 1980 Olympics. When Ronald Reagan became president, he faced the imposition of martial law in Poland by its Soviet-backed government. Reagan promulgated various sanctions against the Russians, including a ban on the sale of U.S.-made equipment for construction of a Soviet gas pipeline to Western Europe.

As this cursory review suggests, the direction of our foreign policy has not always had enlightened, or entirely successful, leadership. Nonetheless individual presidents have left their imprint on the chief diplomat role. In contrast, it is difficult to recall any momentous decision in foreign affairs during historical periods when Congress dominated our government, for example, after the Civil War. As Alexander Hamilton and John Jay argued in the Federalist period, the president enjoys certain advantages in making foreign policy that Congress lacks. Since the president is always in office, unlike Congress which adjourns from time to time, he can act quickly and can maintain secrecy in his communications. Even beyond these "inherent" advantages, the chief diplomat is a powerful role in view of the political resources available to the president.

The conduct of foreign affairs is both a "plenary" and "exclusive" power of the national government. It is plenary (or complete) because the United States is a sovereign nation within the international community. This means our conduct of foreign policy is not "limited" in the same way government's power over domestic society is restricted. Moreover, jurisdiction over foreign affairs is exclusively a federal matter, notwithstanding the fact that the Constitution makes references to a potential role for the states in this area. Article I, Section 10 includes the following statement: "No State shall enter into any Treaty, Alliance, or Confederation; grant Letters of Marque and Reprisal"; nor "without the Consent of Congress . . . enter into any Agreement or Compact with another State, or with a foreign Power. . . ." Congressional consent has never been given for individual states to make compacts with other countries. Moreover, the few Supreme Court cases involving the federal government's exclusive rights in foreign affairs usually find the judiciary upholding the national government's prerogative in this arena.

The fact that foreign policy is a concern of the national government, however, does not show where among the branches of government that authority ultimately lies. The president's constitutional mandate in the chief diplomat role is not as well entrenched as is the case in the commander-in-chief role. Corwin summarizes the intent of the Constitution this way:

> What the Constitution does, *and all that it does*, is to confer on the President certain powers capable of affecting our foreign relations, and certain other powers of the same general kind on the Senate, and still other such powers on Congress; but which of these organs shall have the decisive and final voice in determining the course of the American nation is left for events to resolve.[1]

AUTHORITY

The president's authority over foreign affairs, therefore, needed to be routinized by custom, judicial precedent, and statutory delegation. This development began early in the nation's history. In at least five ways George Washington established customs that were inherited by his successors, thereby paving the way for the executive's predominance in foreign affairs. First, he received envoys from foreign countries and thus "recognized" their governments. Second, he refused to give the House of Representatives documents relating to the Jay Treaty, an unpopular agreement that made trade concessions to the English without safeguarding American shipping interests, thereby asserting executive privilege. Third, he issued a Proclamation of Neutrality and so invoked "executive" power over foreign policymaking. Fourth, he refused to allow the Senate to participate in negotiating treaties and, therefore, denied its constitutional right to give "advice" as well as "consent" to treaty making. Fifth, implicit in these actions was Washington's role as the "sole organ" in the conduct of foreign affairs.

Sole organ of diplomacy

In 1790 Sec. of State Thomas Jefferson said, "The transaction of business with foreign nations is executive altogether. It belongs, then, to the head of that department, except as to such portions of it as are specially submitted to the Senate. Exceptions are to be strictly construed." In 1800, Congressman John Marshall argued that the president "is the sole organ of the nation in its external relations, and its sole representative with foreign nations." But a certain ambiguity is evident in these sentiments because it was unclear whether the president simply received and transmitted communications on behalf of the country or actually made policy. The issue prompted a debate between Alexander Hamilton and James Madison, precipitated by Washington's Proclamation of Neutrality of 1793. Washington took that action during the outbreak of war between France and Great Britain; it was not entirely popular because many citizens wanted to ally the United States with France.

Alexander Hamilton, writing under the pseudonym "Pacificus," wrote a series of articles in *The Gazette of the United States*, in which he essentially argued that the conduct of foreign affairs was inherently an executive function. In his defense of George Washington's action, Hamilton claimed that since the power to declare neutrality does not belong to the legislature or the judiciary, it ". . . of course must belong to the executive." He insisted that the executive was to act as the

> . . . *organ* of intercourse between the nation and foreign nations; as the *interpreter* of the national treaties, in those cases in which the judiciary is not competent . . . as the *power* which is charged with the execution of the laws, of which treaties form a part; as that which is charged with the command and disposition of the public force.

Hamilton also argued that, since the president is empowered to be commander-in-chief, to make treaties, to receive ambassadors, and to "take care that the laws be faithfully executed," he has the authority to execute "all laws, the law of nations, as well as the municipal law." Finally, Hamilton concluded his defense by suggesting that "the President is the Constitutional *EXECUTOR* of the laws. Our treaties, and the laws of nations, form a part of the law of the land. He, who is to execute the laws, must first judge for himself of their meaning."

James Madison, at the urging of Thomas Jefferson, joined the debate by responding as "Helvidius" in the same newspaper. Charging that Alexander Hamilton was trying to give the president the "royal" prerogative of the English monarch, Madison argued that Congress, by virtue of its power to declare war, should make foreign policy. The president's role, he said, was merely instrumental to the ends set by Congress. History suggests that Madison won the political battle, but that Hamilton won the war.[2]

Congress in 1794 proceeded to enact our first Neutrality Act. Yet Alexander Hamilton's view that foreign policy is an executive power to be used independently of the Congress has prevailed. In the landmark case, *United States v. Curtiss-Wright Export Corporation* (1936), the Supreme Court legitimized a broad interpretation of the president's "executive" power over foreign affairs as sole organ of diplomacy. It said in part:

> It is important to bear in mind that we are here dealing not alone with an authority vested in the President by an exertion of legislative power, but with such an authority plus the very delicate, plenary and exclusive power of the President as the sole organ of the federal government in the field of international relations— a power which does not require as a basis for its exercise an act of Congress, but which, of course, like every other governmental power, must be exercised in subordination to the applicable provisions of the Constitution.[3]

Treaty making

Presidents can also negotiate international agreements. The Constitution reads, "He shall have power, by and with the advice and consent of the Senate, to make treaties, provided two-thirds of the Senators present concur." The Constitutional Convention had considered a plan to allow the Senate the power to negotiate treaties, but it finally decided to allow both the president and the Senate a role in this process. Apparently George Washington had this in mind, for as president in 1789 he personally asked the Senate for its advice and consent regarding some proposed Indian treaties. The Senate refused to talk to him; since that time no president has tried to consult with the Senate as a collectivity. Presidents do consult with the party leadership or with key senators to ease the passage of treaties, however. Even George Washington consulted with Senate leaders when he negotiated the Jay Treaty. Harry Truman, when negotiating the Japanese Peace Treaty at the end of World War II, chose Republican John Foster Dulles (later secretary of state under Eisenhower) to help convince the Senate Foreign Relations Committee to give bipartisan support to that treaty. Since Washington established the precedent, presidents now involve the Senate in the treaty-making process only at the point of final ratification. On the other hand, a president may modify a proposed treaty to accommodate the prevailing sentiment in the Senate to assure its passage. Thus, most treaties negotiated by the president are given approval by the Senate.

Throughout our history the Senate has refused to approve only about 1 percent of all treaties; another 15 percent have been accepted by the Senate after it added amendments, or "reservations." For example, in his 1978 effort to renegotiate the Panama Canal Treaties governing United States access to the canal until 1999, President Carter was forced under pressure from conservatives to accept a Senate amendment, the DeConcini Reservation, that gives the United States the right to use force to keep the canal open after 1999, when its operations are transferred to the Republic of Panama. With this important proviso, the Panama Canal Treaties passed the Senate with bipartisan support. By negotiating "executive agreements" rather than treaties, a president can avoid the need to obtain a two-thirds vote in the Senate for approval.

In the well-known case of *U.S. v. Belmont* (1937) the Supreme Court recognized the legal authority of executive agreements.[4] This case involved the Communist government of the Soviet Union in 1918, which had nationalized the Petrograd Metal Works and confiscated its assets, including those held in the New York bank of August Belmont and Company. When the United States in 1933 recognized the Soviet Union's Communist government, President Franklin D. Roosevelt negotiated a series of "executive agreements" with the Russian government, which ensured that the title to all nationalized properties of the Soviet Union in this country would be turned over to the U.S. government. The U.S. government would then determine whether those assets would be returned to the Soviet Union. The Belmont Bank objected to this procedure, charging that it violated New York State law. Upon hearing this case, Justice Sutherland for the Supreme Court said that "executive agreements" had the same force in law as treaties, and they superseded state law even though such agreements had not been ratified by the Senate. The Supreme Court also argued that the president's authority as "sole organ" allowed him to recognize foreign governments and to negotiate executive agreements. Thus, the State of New York had no authority to interfere with the president's making of international policies.

The historic trend (table 6-1) shows that presidents increasingly have relied on executive agreements to establish various military, political, and economic relationships with other nations. This trend also signals a degree of congressional acquiescence to executive policymaking in foreign affairs because the majority of these executive agreements are made pursuant to some kind of legislative action. Overall, presidents have negotiated over seven times as many executive agreements as treaties. Since World War II that ratio has grown to perhaps twenty times as many. About four hundred of these executive agreements are classified and thus are kept secret from the Congress.[5] Franklin D. Roosevelt negotiated fewer executive agreements relative to the number of treaties than any of his successors. Executive agreements have been used for such purposes as defining fishing rights between nations, settling boundary disputes involving the United States, and providing for annexation of territory.

President Franklin Roosevelt made several important agreements with our World War II allies by this method. For example, in September 1940, he negotiated the famous Fifty Destroyer Deal, in which the United States exchanged ships in return for leases on British territory in the North Atlantic for our naval bases. FDR took this action in an effort to assist Great Britain, which had suffered heavy losses from German submarine warfare,

TABLE 6-1 Treaties versus Executive Agreements, 1789–1978

Years	President	Agreements	Treaties	Ratio agreements:treaties
1789–1839	—	27	60	1 : 2.2
1839–1889	—	238	215	1.1 : 1
1889–1929	—	763	382	2 : 1
1930–1932	Hoover	41	49	1 : 1.2
1933–1944	Roosevelt	369	131	2.8 : 1
1945–1952	Truman	1,324	132	10 : 1
1953–1960	Eisenhower	1,834	89	20.6 : 1
1961–1962	Kennedy	579	19	30.5 : 1
1963–1968	Johnson	1,317	84	15.7 : 1
1969–1973	Nixon	1,087	80	13.6 : 1
1974	Nixon/Ford	230	13	17.7 : 1
1975–1976	Ford	666	26	25.6 : 1
1977–1978	Carter	841	32	26.3 : 1
TOTAL	—	9,316	1,312	7.1 : 1

Sources: *Congressional Quarterly Weekly Report* (August 2, 1975), p. 1714; John H. Ferguson and Dean E. McHenry, *The American System of Government* (New York: McGraw-Hill, 1981), p. 488.

and he did so with the knowledge that Congress probably would not have approved this policy in legislation. Roosevelt also made executive agreements with Britain's Winston Churchill and the Soviet Union's Joseph Stalin at conferences (such as Yalta) near the end of World War II. In these agreements, without Senate input, FDR made major decisions with world leaders affecting territories and their populations.

In September 1951, the first Bricker Amendment was considered in Congress. It was, according to Sidney Warren, "an expression of intense disapprobation of Roosevelt's and Truman's personal diplomacy, of the conviction that agreements made at the various wartime conferences were responsible for the cold war."[6] By 1953 this legislation by Ohio's Republican senator, John W. Bricker, had been endorsed by sixty-two senators of both political parties. It provided that a treaty conflicting with the Constitution would be invalid, that a treaty could become law only after passage of federal or state enabling legislation, and that Congress could "regulate" executive agreements. Dwight Eisenhower was convinced that this measure posed a serious threat to executive leadership and to the nation's leadership in the world community. Ultimately the Senate backed down from enacting the Bricker Amendment, but this issue surfaced again during the Vietnam War. In 1969 the Senate Foreign Relations Committee sponsored a "National Commitments Resolution" which proposed that

> (1) a national commitment for the purpose of this resolution means the use of the armed forces of the United States on foreign territory, or a promise to assist a foreign country, government, or people by the use of the armed forces or financial resources of the United States, either immediately or upon the happening of certain events, and (2) it is the sense of the Senate that a national commitment by the United States results only from affirmative action taken by the executive and legislative branches of the United States Government by means of a treaty, statute, or concurrent resolution of both Houses of Congress specifically providing for such commitments.[7]

President Nixon ignored this resolution, and in 1970 negotiated a military base agreement with Spain, which included security guarantees. Nixon's action prompted the Senate to pass a resolution stating that his agreement with Spain did not constitute a United States commitment.[8] In 1972, moreover, Congress passed legislation providing that

> the Secretary of State shall transmit to the Congress the text of any international agreement, other than a treaty, to which the United States is a party as soon as possible after such agreement has entered into force with respect to the United States, but in no event later than sixty days thereafter.[9]

But Congress refused to pass any stronger measures: in 1974, for example, the House failed to enact a Senate-approved bill to provide that executive agreements could be disapproved by a concurrent resolution. It appears that Congress is unwilling to disallow the use of executive agreements, although it has tried to monitor their use by presidents.

Ending treaties

In addition to the negotiations process, there is a related issue of how treaties may be terminated. The question of whether this can be done by the president unilaterally arose when Jimmy Carter announced that he was ending a defense treaty with Taiwan. He did this pursuant to his establishing full diplomatic relations with the People's Republic of China. As justification he cited a provision of that treaty allowing its termination upon one year's notice. The defense treaty with Taiwan did not specifically require Senate approval for its termination, and the Constitution makes no mention of a Senate role in ending treaties. Sen. Barry Goldwater (R.–Ariz.) and others argued that Senate consent was required for Carter's action, but in *Goldwater* v. *Carter* the Supreme Court sided with the president.[10] The Court judged the controversy premature and decided to withhold judgment and to dismiss the complaint. Nevertheless, where treaties or executive agreements require legislative action for their implementation, such as appropriations, Congress may refuse to support the president's initiatives.

Executive privilege

Another precedent set by George Washington in regard to treaty making is "executive privilege" (discussed in detail later in the chapter). In 1796, Washington became the first president to refuse to comply with the House of Representatives when it called for documents pertaining to the negotiations of the Jay Treaty. James Madison authored this request, which reflected his view that the president's role in foreign affairs was only instrumental. Washington refused because the House was not a partner to the treaty-making process and because the papers were "of a nature that did not permit of disclosure at this time." Through his action, therefore, Washington established executive privilege in matters affecting diplomacy, although it was not so labeled for another 150 years. The use of executive privilege has been extended by presidents to justify their refusal to supply information to both the House and Senate on a variety of matters.

Recognition

The Constitution empowers the president to receive ambassadors, an action tantamount to our "recognizing" foreign governments. This power is fully executive in nature, as Corwin observes: "Throughout the entire course of our national history the President has performed dozens of acts of recognition of new *governments* without consulting, or being expected to consult, Congress."[11] It is a potent authority since the president can use it to affect international events or to set the tone of our foreign policy. For example, when President Carter extended recognition to the People's Republic of China, and at the same time withdrew it from Taiwan, his act signaled an end to our refusal to acknowledge the legitimacy of the Communist regime that, during 1947–1949, defeated the Nationalist forces under Chiang Kai-shek. The Communist victory in China, observes Sidney Warren, "precipitated one of the lengthiest and most divisive political controversies the United States had ever experienced."[12] Truman's administration, in power when the fall of China came, was under attack from conservative Republicans, including then-Congressman Richard Nixon.

The experience with Communist China is not atypical, for the United States quite often refuses to grant legitimacy to communist regimes. Not until 1933, sixteen years after the Russian Revolution, did Franklin D. Roosevelt finally recognize the Soviet Union. And in 1982, for example, we still had not legally recognized the governments of Cuba, Vietnam, North Korea, or Albania. The power to recognize governments may be traced to George Washington, who granted recognition to the new French Republic.

Ambassadors and special agents

The Constitution states that the president "shall nominate, and by and with the Advice and Consent of the Senate, shall appoint Ambassadors, other public Ministers and Consuls." This power is somewhat limited by the fact that the entire diplomatic and consular establishment is organized in detail by statute in terms of grades, salaries, appointments, promotions, and duties. On the other hand, this power has been superseded by the president's ability to use "personal agents" to conduct diplomacy. These officials are appointed by the president without Senate confirmation, and their use, though not explicitly provided for in the Constitution, is yet another manifestation of Alexander Hamilton's view of "executive" power. Special agents are often used to assure the president's direct control over diplomatic missions. They typically enjoy the full confidence of the executive. The use of these secret, private, or personal agents can be traced back to the Washington administration, when George Washington sent John Jay to England to negotiate the Jay Treaty. Later, President Jefferson asked James Monroe to assist him in completing the Louisiana Purchase with France. More recently, in 1982 after Israeli troops had trapped Palestine Liberation Organization (PLO) forces in Beirut, Lebanon, along with thousands of civilians, President Ronald Reagan dispatched Philip Habib to the Middle East to resolve the stalemate. His delicate negotiations with all parties, including the PLO, Israel, and Lebanon, led to the eventual (peaceful) evacuation of the PLO troops from Beirut.

To summarize, the chief diplomat has an impressive array of formal powers affecting foreign policy. Included in these are his dominant position in treaty making, the authority to negotiate executive agreements, and the ability to act as "sole organ" in foreign affairs through the use of special agents. Though his "executive" authority is not dependent on Congress, the legislature has the political resources to potentially limit a president's control over foreign policy. The decision-making process affecting foreign policy suggests that historically Congress has been unwilling or unable to oppose the chief diplomat, although in recent years the legislative branch has tried to assert its constitutional role over the content of U.S. foreign policy.

DECISION MAKING

In managing the conduct of diplomacy the president can rely on his secretary of state—an office that dates back to George Washington's cabinet—and the Department of State. But the advisory system has been further institutionalized. The 1947 National Security Act established the National Security Council (NSC) and the Department of Defense. Located in the Executive Office of the President, the NSC is chaired by the president and its members include the vice-president, the secretary of state, and the secretary of defense. By statute the chairman of the Joint Chiefs of Staff is its military adviser, and intelligence information is supplied by the director of the Central Intelligence Agency. In addition, the president may include other agency heads, for example the director of the Office of Management and Budget and the treasury secretary.

The Special Assistant for National Security Affairs (also known as the National Security Adviser), who is a member of the president's White House staff, is another key element of this decision-making apparatus. In recent years this position has grown in importance with the appointment of such men as McGeorge Bundy under President Kennedy and Henry Kissinger under President Nixon. The purpose of the National Security Council involves "advising the President with respect to the integration of domestic, foreign and military policies relating to the national security,"[13] but one can readily appreciate that the makeup of a president's advisory system can result in tension and the clash of interests among the participants.

Not only is there the fundamental problem of maintaining civilian control over the military, but the armed services themselves may disagree over tactics as well as the proper balance of land, sea, and air power. The Departments of State and Defense tend to compete on questions of emphasis on diplomatic or military strategies. Moreover, the secretary of state often contends with the special assistant for national security affairs for primacy in this area. Jimmy Carter appointed Columbia University professor Zbigniew Brzezinski his national security adviser, whose views clashed with those of Secretary of State Cyrus Vance. President Carter's decision to follow Brzezinski's advice to stage the aborted rescue of American hostages in Iran, against Vance's arguments, led to Vance's resignation.

A highly publicized example of this bureaucratic infighting occurred in the Reagan administration. From the day of his inauguration as president, Reagan's choice for secretary of state—Alexander Haig, Jr.—moved to consolidate his dominance over foreign policymaking. In the process Haig confronted other decision makers who shared authority over foreign affairs: National Security Adviser Richard Allen, and his successor William Clark; Defense Secretary Caspar Weinberger, and UN Ambassador Jeane Kirkpatrick. In particular, Haig found his position being undercut by the Pentagon and its spokesman, Weinberger. Haig and Weinberger disagreed about U.S. policy in the Middle East, with the result that no clear policy was articulated by the Reagan administration. After the imposition of martial law in Poland, Weinberger also encouraged Reagan, much to Haig's dismay, to impose sanctions on the Soviet Union to delay construction of the Siberian pipeline to Western Europe. Haig argued that this action would unnecessarily alienate our European allies without stopping the pipeline construction. Moreover, on many occasions Weinberger made statements on various foreign policy issues, such as Latin America and rearmament in Japan. Defenders of the defense secretary suggested that:

> the line between defense and foreign policy is so thin and blurred that it is unrealistic to expect an activist secretary of defense to deny himself the right of speaking out on problems concerning the activities of his department.[14]

Haig had differences of opinion with UN Ambassador Jeane Kirkpatrick over the Falkland Islands War between Argentina and Britain. Haig was given no role in Reagan's selection of Philip C. Habib as the Middle East emissary to persuade Israel to withdraw from Beirut. The most serious intrusion into Haig's role as secretary of state came from Reagan's White House advisers. When he appointed Haig secretary of state, Reagan had led Haig to believe that he would be the principal adviser in foreign affairs. But Haig proved to be an outsider, rather than one of Reagan's inner circle of advisers; thus, Haig found that his advice was ignored. For example, when a special study on national security problems was conducted for President Reagan by William Clark in 1982, Clark involved the NSC staff, the Joint Chiefs of Staff, Caspar Weinberger, the secretary of treasury, the commerce secretary, UN Ambassador Kirkpatrick, senior officials from the Defense and State Departments, and the CIA. Alexander Haig's name was never mentioned, suggesting that his days in the Reagan administration were numbered.

Control over foreign policy was taken from the secretary of state and given to the Department of Defense, the NSC, and White House advisers James Baker, Edwin Meese, and Michael Deaver—a group Haig referred to as "the three-headed monster."[15] Meese became especially important in this area. Richard Allen, as national security adviser, had to report directly to Meese rather than to the president. It was Meese who, in August 1981, alerted Secretaries Weinberger and Haig—but failed to awaken President Reagan—when two U.S. Navy F-14 fighters shot down two Libyan SU-22 aircraft sixty miles from the Libyan coastline. This incident occurred after one of the American planes had been fired upon. However, Meese did not think the incident was important enough to disturb the president's sleep until 7:24 AM, about six hours later.

Eventually, with power over foreign policy delegated to so many others and with such a limited role in decision making, Alexander Haig resigned on June 25, 1982. Haig's troubles in dealing with other foreign policy advisers in the Reagan administration, like those disagreements involving Cyrus Vance under President Carter, seem to suggest that the importance of the secretary of state and his department has been reduced somewhat in the president's advisory network, especially after the position of national security adviser was added in the 1950s.

Secretary of State

A serious difficulty facing any secretary of state is the tendency for activist presidents to assume direct responsibility for foreign policymaking, as did Theodore Roosevelt, Woodrow Wilson, Franklin D. Roosevelt, and John Kennedy. Such presidents are personally involved in the details of diplomacy, even negotiations, with the result that much less delegation of authority is given to the secretary of state. In contrast, Dwight Eisenhower relied heavily on his secretary of state, John Foster Dulles, so much so that Sen. William Fulbright once observed that Dulles "seemed at times to be exercising those 'delicate, plenary, and exclusive powers' which are supposed to be vested in the President."[16] Henry Kissinger, who became secretary of state under Richard Nixon, traveled to the countries of the Middle East, India, and the Soviet Union, and personally negotiated an end to the 1973 Middle East War.

A drawback associated with this cabinet position is that relatively few secretaries of state have been chosen for their diplomatic experience. The exceptions are Kissinger, Dulles, Cyrus Vance,[17] and Truman's George Marshall. Most other secretaries of state have lacked a distinguished career in foreign affairs, an indication that their role would be secondary to either the president or his special assistant for national security affairs. For example, when Kissinger was Nixon's special assistant, the Secretary of State was William Rogers, a lawyer with little diplomatic experience.

Department of State

A factor that complicates the role of the secretary of state is the reputation of the Department of State as an ineffectual guardian of our foreign policy. It is argued that the State Department is too cautious in problem solving, too rigid in bureaucratic procedures, and too biased in its perception of world affairs. These problems are partly related to the fact that the State Department, unlike the "clientele" departments such as Labor or Agriculture, lacks a domestic political constituency that can be aroused to defend it when necessary. The State Department must rely on fewer groups, such as the Council on Foreign Relations, organizations that are not as powerful or as broadly based as the interest groups that support the other departments. Moreover, the State Department is especially vulnerable to criticism because the American public does not always appreciate the department's function in representing the attitudes of foreign peoples to our leadership.

The State Department's cautious approach to diplomacy may be related to the vicious attacks launched against it by right-wing congressmen and

Sen. Joseph McCarthy during the late 1940s and early 1950s. Career diplomats were labeled Communists and "fellow travelers," and the loyalty-security investigations conducted by Congress during this time ruined the good reputations of many civil servants. President Truman resisted those legislative investigations, with the result that the "red-baiting" criticisms leveled at Secretary of State Dean Acheson and the State Department helped to undermine his own popularity. President Eisenhower did not act decisively to end the Red Scare; instead he appeased the right wing by allowing Secretary of State Dulles to appoint a McCarthy ally to direct the State Department's personnel and security operations. In time, when Senator McCarthy shifted his attack from the State Department to the Army, the Defense Department, and to Dwight Eisenhower himself, his tactics became thoroughly discredited. The notion that Eisenhower, a World War II hero, and other officials in the Defense Department were left-wing sympathizers was too incredible to be taken seriously; in the end McCarthy was censured by the Senate for bringing such discredit to that institution.

However, a result of the confrontation with McCarthyism, argues Dorothy James, is that the State Department "learned that policy identification could be dangerous in some later post mortem."[18] No doubt this would pose special difficulties for diplomats sensitive to the problems of leftist regimes or political movements. During the 1980 presidential election, U.S. policy toward El Salvador was severely criticized by Ronald Reagan, as was the role of our ambassador there. El Salvador is governed by one of the most elite and authoritarian regimes anywhere in Latin America, and has been the target of guerilla warfare from rightist as well as leftist factions. President Carter, driven by his commitment to human rights, tried to moderate that regime by pressuring it to accept land reforms, and Ambassador Robert White fully identified with this policy. But Ronald Reagan favored supplying military aid to the government of El Salvador, arguing that it was under siege by communists who were getting aid from Cuba.

U.S. experience in El Salvador highlights another reason for the Department of State's ineffectiveness. Ambassador White was criticized by conservatives because he was "too sympathetic" to the needs of El Salvador's masses. Yet too often such sympathy is the exception, because the information the State Department gathers is colored by its reliance on "elites" for that input and may be influenced by preconceived expectations. Its contacts with foreign countries are mainly conducted through existing governmental agencies, whose officials are drawn from the upper socioeconomic strata. Therefore the State Department may lack an understanding of popular grass-roots movements and may antagonize leftist factions trying to reform authoritarian regimes, by either peaceful or violent means.

A fundamental reason why the State Department is limited in its ability to make foreign policy is that most contemporary presidents assume full responsibility in this area. Moreover, foreign policymaking is not dominated by career diplomats in the State Department but by the president's political advisers as well. This, in turn, causes the civil servants in State to feel that domestic "politics" unduly influences judgments about U.S. diplomacy. It is true that there is high turnover among the assistant secretaries of state and that important ambassadorships are often filled by loyalists who worked in the president's campaign.[19] On the other hand, presidents do violate the command structure by communicating directly, and secretly, with certain ambassadors, as did President Kennedy in his dealings with John K. Galbraith, the ambassador to India. Kennedy's approach, in this instance, may have reflected his and Galbraith's skeptical view of State. As John K. Galbraith once remarked, "You'll find that it's the kind of organization [State Department] which, though it does big things badly, does small things badly too."[20]

Apart from all these difficulties is the fact that the State Department must compete with military intelligence and the Central Intelligence Agency for the president's attention. The military advisers tend to predominate during crises, and when gathering intelligence in foreign countries the CIA typically is exempted from control by the ambassadors and the embassy staffs. Although President Carter gave his ambassadors the authority to supervise all diplomatic personnel in their countries, nonetheless the CIA issued guidelines limiting the information that ambassadors could obtain from CIA sources.[21]

NSC and the National Security Adviser

To mold these disparate personalities and institutions in such a way that decision making is facilitated is, ultimately, the president's task. Obviously, the chief diplomat brings to his office a style and view of foreign affairs that influences his use of the advisory system. The role of the National Security Council is pivotal to foreign policymaking, but not all presidents utilize the NSC in the same way. Before the outbreak of the Korean War, President Truman participated in only eleven of the fifty-six meetings of the newly established National Security Council; rather, he relied more heavily on his secretary of state, George Marshall, to formulate policy.[22] When the Korean War began, Truman made greater use of the NSC as a sounding board for policy recommendations, and participated in its meetings more frequently. Nonetheless, the NSC was not the predominant policymaker in foreign affairs during this time either, as one observer notes:

> NSC no doubt considered the staff papers, debated policy and arrived at recommendations, but every glimpse we have been given of the actual policy-making process in this period shows Defense, State, the Budget Bureau, the White House, making the independent determinations—usually on a hasty if not extemporaneous basis—which really counted.[23]

President Eisenhower expanded the use of the NSC; its membership was increased and it began to meet on a regular basis. Eisenhower also formalized its internal procedures and used the NSC to formulate policy that could be implemented by the line agencies. During Eisenhower's first three years in office, consequently, NSC met 145 times and took 829 policy actions, compared with the 128 meetings and 699 policy actions during its five years under Truman.[24]

The role of NSC changed again under President John Kennedy; he proceeded to dismantle the elaborate and formal machinery established by Eisenhower in favor of a loose, flexible, and pragmatic arrangement more amenable to his personal style. NSC's size was limited to its statutory membership, though other high-level advisers were consulted on an ad hoc basis. Under Kennedy the NSC was only one of the several forums that JFK used for debate on foreign policy and to review policy alternatives; he did not want the NSC to undermine the role of his secretary of state (Dean Rusk) or his secretary of defense (Robert McNamara) as principal advisers in these areas. The position of special assistant for national security affairs, though first established by Eisenhower, was given new importance by Kennedy's appointment of McGeorge Bundy. Bundy monitored proposals coming from the departments and strengthened the president's control over the implementation of foreign policy. During the Cuban missile crisis, however, Kennedy met almost daily with the Executive Committee of the NSC; this group included the secretaries of state, defense, and treasury, the attorney general (Robert Kennedy), the CIA director, the chairman of the Joint Chiefs of Staff, McGeorge Bundy, and Special Counsel Theodore Sorenson. Occasionally, JFK also invited others to attend, such as vice-president Johnson.

President Lyndon Johnson made little use of the National Security Council; instead he convened the "Tuesday lunch" with the secretaries of state and defense, the special assistant (Walt Rostow), the CIA director, and the chairman of the Joint Chiefs of Staff. This ad hoc arrangement, says Richard Pious, served to limit dissent and "to shield the president and reinforce his conviction that he was pursuing the right policies."[25] As public opinion shifted against LBJ's war policies and our military position in Vietnam remained stalemated, Johnson tolerated no dissent among his advisers and sought counsel only from those individuals who backed his objectives in Vietnam. Many observers, therefore, agree that Johnson's decision-making style rendered it almost impossible to reevaluate our goals in Southeast Asia. As Robert L. Galluci concludes, "the way we make and carry out foreign policy appears to have a lot to do with the quality of the policy that is produced and the chances of it succeeding. Of the many lessons that might be learned from Vietnam, this ought to be among the least debatable."[26]

When Richard Nixon became president, he wanted to combine the Eisenhower system with Kennedy's personalized style to maximize White House control over foreign policy. Nixon achieved this objective through Henry Kissinger, who chaired the various committees of the NSC. Kissinger used the NSC staff to articulate various foreign policy options, which reflected the differing perspectives of the departments and advisers, but ultimately the NSC served to ratify the decisions made by the White House. The position of national security adviser had its greatest influence over foreign policy during this time, mainly because Kissinger's views so closely paralleled Nixon's. As Sen. Stuart Symington (D.–Mo.) once declared, Kissinger had become "Secretary of State in everything but title."[27] In 1973 Henry Kissinger further consolidated his position by becoming the secretary of state, while also retaining his position as special assistant.

During his tenure, Henry Kissinger enjoyed much discretion to conduct "personal" diplomacy on a variety of delicate questions, such as the Vietnam peace, SALT talks, and opening relations with Communist China. When President Nixon became embroiled in his Watergate defense, the management of foreign affairs was firmly entrusted to Kissinger and to Secretary of Defense James Schlesinger; they referred important matters to President Nixon only for his final approval. The Nixon style of decision making in foreign affairs, therefore, reflected his personality as well as his view of international politics. According to Sam Sarkesian,

> The Nixon–Kissinger team was under no illusions. The world was viewed as a dangerous place and the real solutions for the United States were in dealing with the world from a central decision-making point. Thus, the Nixon–Kissinger national security policy process operated on the basis of a one man show, linked directly to the president . . . [it] under Nixon evolved into a structure dominated by one man and functioned like a "fiefdom."[28]

When Gerald Ford succeeded to the presidency after Nixon's forced resignation, he also relied on Kissinger's advice at first. Eventually President Ford became convinced that a more balanced approach to policymaking was needed. Ford appointed General Alexander Haig as his special assistant; moreover, he sought advice from Secretary of Defense Donald Rumsfeld and Secretary of the Treasury William Simon as well as from Kissinger when evaluating foreign policy. A similar philosophy influenced Jimmy Carter, who was very opposed to Kissinger's pivotal role in policymaking.

Jimmy Carter believed that the president is responsible for making foreign policy, and tried to deal directly with those senior officials charged with given responsibilities. In this way, his approach was similar to Kennedy's. President Carter also tried to separate the National Security Council from the Department of State. He appointed Zbigniew Brzezinski as his national security adviser, thinking that he would be subordinate to the secretary of state. Moreover, the Carter–Brzezinski team reduced the number of NSC committees chaired by the national security adviser, though no fundamental changes in the overall national security establishment were made. According to Donald Neuchterlein,

> As for the NSC papers prepared in the Carter NSC system, only the names have changed. . . . The process of preparing and reviewing these [presidential review memorandums] is similar to the process under Kissinger, except that the secretary of state now has a larger role in bringing the studies to final form for the president's decision.[29]

In contrast to Richard Nixon, Carter wanted to be personally involved in the policymaking process. He met with various staff informally, tried to master the substantive issues of national security, and operated a managerial type office, which "was attuned to a logical, neat, purposeful structure and a world viewed in 'engineering' terms, with each problem in its own, neat and separate little box."[30]

A very different decision-making style characterized the Reagan administration. "The philosophy, the policy and the major decisions are Reagan's," said White House Chief of Staff James Baker, "the details he delegates to others."[31] Like Dwight Eisenhower, President Reagan delegated substantial authority to his cabinet officials, did not immerse himself in operational details, and respected his organizational structure. As Sarkesian notes, Reagan "clearly prefers a pyramid plan of organization. Policy options move to the top of the pyramid through an orderly chain of command. Reagan decides among the options, then delegates authority to follow through."[32]

When Reagan became president, he expressed a view of foreign affairs that stressed American military preparedness and the need to confront the Soviet Union wherever that nation posed a threat to U.S. interests. The importance of the national security adviser was reduced insofar as Reagan's first appointment, Richard Allen, did not have the prominence of a Kissinger or a Brzezinski. Nonetheless, various foreign policy advisers, including Allen, had difficulties in dealing with Reagan's secretary of state, Alexander Haig, and apparently Haig's inability to be a team player led President Reagan to accept his resignation. Haig was succeeded by George Schultz (secretary of the treasury under Ford). Later President Reagan appointed William Clark as national security adviser, following Allen's resignation in the midst of allegations that he was involved in "influence peddling." The fact that Defense Secretary Caspar Weinberger, Secretary of State George Schultz, and National Security Adviser William Clark generally shared Reagan's outlook, therefore, indicated that the president would enjoy more harmonious relationships among his key advisers.

Summary. The confused and competitive relationship between the National Security Council and the Department of State has led many observers to suggest that the lines of responsibility between these agencies should be more clearly spelled out. The Murphy Commission on the Organization of the Government for the Conduct of Foreign Policy in 1975 recommended that the president make foreign policy and then delegate to the State Department the primary responsibility for carrying it out.[33] It would also strengthen the advisory role of NSC. Political scientist Alexander George has argued in favor of a "multiple advocacy" approach to foreign policymaking.[34] As it now stands George argues that policymaking can be seriously distorted in any one of nine ways:

1. The president and his advisers agree too readily on the nature of the problem and on a response to it.
2. The president's advisers do not consider the full range of policy options.
3. There is no advocate for an unpopular policy position.
4. The advisers thrash out their own disagreements and provide the president with a unanimous recommendation.

5. A president's advisers are unwilling to alert him to the need to make a difficult decision.
6. The president depends on a single channel of information.
7. The key assumptions and premises of a policy option are evaluated only by its advocates.
8. The president does not examine more carefully the negative opinions offered by any of his advisers.
9. A president fails to determine how firm a consensus among his advisers is, how it was achieved, and whether it was justified.

According to Alexander George, in order to properly cultivate advice on an issue, the president "must define his own role as that of a magistrate who evaluates, judges, and chooses among the various policy options articulated by advocates."[35]

This style of decision making occurred during the Cuban missile crisis, and Alexander George would like to see this system institutionalized. During the Cuban missile crisis, President Kennedy allowed his staff and advisers to openly debate the issues, unrestrained by position or rank, and various policy options were fully aired in the discussion. On occasion Kennedy permitted these discussions to proceed in his absence so that he would not unduly influence the arguments being made; moreover, there was no need to compromise differing positions or to reach some artificial consensus. Unfortunately, this manner of policymaking was atypical even for Kennedy, for most of his decisions were not handled in this manner. The fundamental problem is that presidents want to believe that their policies are supported by a consensus, and most executives—though Franklin D. Roosevelt may have been an exception—do not fully appreciate dissent among their key advisers and staff.

Congress' role

To provide an overview of executive/legislative relationships in foreign policy, let us consider the role of Congress in foreign affairs during the past five decades. James Robinson studied the decision-making process affecting twenty-two foreign policy decisions during 1930–1961. His analysis includes such events as the establishment of NATO, the Marshall Plan, Lend-Lease Act, the Truman Doctrine, building the atomic bomb, the Korean War, the Berlin Airlift, and the Bay of Pigs invasion.[36] In table 6-2 we extend Robinson's analysis by focusing on another twenty-four decisions made between 1962 and 1980. Robinson evaluates each decision according to certain variables, such as whether Congress or the executive initiated the decision, and proceeds to analyze the interrelationships among these variables in the decision-making process. These interrelationships are summarized in table 6-3, where Robinson's data are contrasted with our own analysis. Clearly, this sample of 46 cases is not indicative of all foreign policy decisions made during the past five decades. This listing is also biased in some respects, for example by the fact that most decisions analyzed are "successful" ones.

TABLE 6-2 Congressional/executive interaction on major foreign/military policy decisions, 1962–1980

Decision	Congressional involvement	Initiator	Predominate influence	Resolution/ legislation	Threat of violence	Decision time
Cuban Missile Crisis, 1962	low	Exec.	Exec.	yes	yes	short
Limited Test-Ban Treaty, 1963	high	Exec.	Exec.	yes	no	long
Gulf of Tonkin Res. 1964	high	Exec.	Exec.	yes	yes	short
Dominican Intervention, 1965	none	Exec.	Exec.	no	yes	short
First Hanoi Bombing, 1966	none	Exec.	Exec.	no	yes	long
Foreign Aid Auth. (To Israel) 1968	high	Exec.	Exec.	yes	no	long
Vietnam Peace Talks Begin, 1968	high	Exec.	Exec.	no	yes	long
First U.S. Veto in UN, 1970	low	Exec.	Exec.	no	no	long
U.S. Troops into Cambodia, 1970	none	Exec.	Exec.	no	yes	long
Okinawa Returned to Japan, 1971	high	Exec.	Exec.	yes	no	long
Devaluation of Dollar, 1971	low	Exec.	Exec.	no	no	long
SALT I, 1972	high	Exec.	Exec.	yes	no	long
U.S.–USSR Wheat Sale, 1972	low	Exec.	Exec.	no	no	long
Vietnam Involvement Ended, 1973	high	Cong.	Cong.	yes	yes	long
U.S.–East Ger. Est. Relations, 1974	none	Exec.	Exec.	no	no	long
Military Aid Cutoff to Turkey, 1974	high	Cong.	Cong.	yes	no	long
Vladivostok Accord, 1974	none	Exec.	Exec.	no	no	short
Mayaguez Incident, 1975	none	Exec.	Exec.	no	yes	short
Panama Canal Treaty, 1978	high	Exec.	Exec.	yes	no	long
Camp David Accord, 1978	none	Exec.	Exec.	no	no	long
People's Rep. China–U.S. Est. Relations, 1978	none	Exec.	Exec.	no	no	long
Shah enters U.S., 1979	none	Exec.	Exec.	no	no	short
SALT II, 1980	high	Exec.	Cong.	no	no	long
Iran Hostage Rescue, 1980	none	Exec.	Exec.	no	yes	long

TABLE 6-3 Legislative/executive relationships in major foreign policy decisions, 1930–1980

		1930–1961*	1962–1980**
Degree of congressional involvement			
	High	16(2)†	10(3)†
	Low	4(3)	5(1)
	None	2(2)	9(5)
Initiator of decision			
	Executive	19(7)	22(8)
	Congress	3(0)	2(1)
Predominate influence in decision			
	Executive	16(6)	21(8)
	Congress	6(1)	3(1)
Formal legislation or resolution			
	Yes	17(3)	9(3)
	No	5(4)	15(6)
Decision-making time available			
	Long	20(5)	18(5)
	Short	2(2)	6(4)

*This analysis is based on documentation supplied by James A. Robinson in *Congress and Foreign Policy-Making* (Homewood, Ill.: Dorsey Press, 1962), pp. 64–69.

**This analysis is based on our classification of policy decisions found in table 6-2.

†The cases in parentheses involved the threat of violence. In Robinson's sample they included the following seven: Building the A-Bomb (1944–1945), Lend-Lease (1941), Berlin Airlift (1948), Korean War Decision (1950), Indochina (1954), Formosan Resolution (1955), and the Bay of Pigs Invasion (1961). In our sample these had violence potential: Cuban Missile Crisis (1962), Gulf of Tonkin Resolution (1964), Dominican Intervention (1965), First Hanoi Bombing (1966), Vietnam Peace Talks Begin (1968), Sending Troops into Cambodia (1970), Ending the Vietnam War (1973), Seizure of the *Mayaguez* (1975), and the Iran Hostage Rescue Attempt (1980).

One is further cautioned when interpreting data based on subjective judgments. Given these caveats, however, our findings with regard to the years 1962–1980 parallel Robinson's conclusions, and the interrelationships affecting Congress and the executive persist across the largest number of cases.

These data verify the overwhelming advantage that the president has, relative to Congress, in managing foreign affairs. Overall, the executive held the predominant influence in 77 percent of the cases during 1930–1961 and in 88 percent during 1962–1980. This finding is even more impressive because most foreign policy decisions allow the opportunity for Congress to assert its prerogatives. The time involved in making these decisions was relatively "long" in over two-thirds of the cases during both historical periods. In addition, Congress had enacted resolutions or statutes to express its policy preferences in two-thirds of the cases during 1930–1961 and in two-fifths of the decisions since then. Therefore, although Congress passed legislation and had enough time to evaluate the executive's foreign policy initiatives, the president still held predominant influence in the vast majority of decisions during both time periods.

On the other hand, where Congress did *not* enact a statute or resolution, the proportion of cases in which the president predominated increased during 1930–1961 (80%) and during 1962–1980 (93%). This suggests that Congress' leverage over foreign policymaking depends mainly on its use of formal authority. Robinson's analysis showed that Congress held the predominant influence on the questions of repealing Chinese exclusion (1943), the Fulbright Resolution (1943), and the Monroney Resolution (1953). We have added three more decisions in which Congress held the upper hand: ending the Vietnam War (1973), the military aid cutoff to Turkey (1974), and SALT II (1980). All these policy decisions in which Congress predominated over the executive involved Congress' use of legislation, whether through treaty ratification, budget appropriation, or resolutions by the Senate or the House of Representatives.

Robinson argues that the ability to *initiate* foreign policy largely determines which branch of government will ultimately prevail in the decision-making process. Clearly, the executive is better equipped to initiate foreign policies than the Congress. Robinson concludes his study with the observation that Congress is severely handicapped in its ability to formulate foreign policy, and the situation seemed to have deteriorated during the years he studied. He stated in 1962:

> Foreign policy-making today is characterized by the need for large amounts of technical *information*, short decision *time*, and by great financial *cost*. Only the fact that Congress controls the purse makes it relevant to these three policy needs, but even its power to appropriate (or not to appropriate) can hardly be employed for positive or initiating purposes. In short, the nature of foreign policy-making requirements stands as an obstacle to Congressional initiative.[37]

Power of the purse.   In its control over appropriations, Congress has a potentially important power over foreign policy. But given Congress' nature, this control only enables Congress to resist a president after the fact rather than to initiate foreign policy. For example, in 1974 Congress cut off military aid to Turkey after its invasion of Cyprus, in spite of President Ford's objections, and in 1976 the Congress took similar action with regard to Angola. Congress amended the $112.3 billion defense budget to forbid any covert CIA activities or military assistance on behalf of pro-Western factions fighting Cuban and Soviet-backed leftist groups in Angola.

However, a president generally can expect to have most of his foreign policy approved by Congress. After the Yom Kippur War of 1973, for example, Congress affirmed President Nixon's commitments to Israel by providing over $2.2 billion in aid. In addition, Congress allowed and funded Nixon's use of American observers in the Middle East to monitor the Sinai

Accords between Egypt and Israel. For the period 1948–1964, an analysis of voting behavior in Congress found that 58.2 percent of the 1,929 bills proposed by the president in foreign affairs had been approved by the Congress.[38] Another study by LeLoup and Shull found that every president during 1965–1975 had more legislative successes in foreign and defense policy than in domestic policy.[39] However, in one particular area of foreign affairs, this generalization does not hold: Congress can be expected to oppose most presidents' foreign aid requests.

One study found that Congress reduced the president's requests for foreign assistance every year during 1958–1967. In 1958, Eisenhower requested $3.86 billion for foreign aid but only $2.77 billion was appropriated; in 1962, John F. Kennedy requested $4.77 billion but only $3.91 billion was approved; and in 1967, President Johnson requested $3.35 billion but only $2.94 billion was granted.[40] Taking into account inflationary trends over that decade, the amounts of money allocated to foreign assistance suggests that Congress, in real terms, actually made even greater reductions in its commitment to other nations in terms of economic aid. Another study of foreign aid appropriations during the period 1957–1978 shows that Congress cut the president's requests every year; in nineteen years (of the twenty-three years studied) the foreign aid reductions exceeded 13 percent.[41] Foreign aid programs are not popular with the citizenry; they seem analogous to domestic "welfare" spending. This means that congressmen who support our foreign aid commitments are acting more in terms of their perception of the national interest rather than according to grass-roots opinions. One study of legislative voting on foreign aid determined that no relationship existed between how congressmen vote and constituency attitudes.[42]

In certain policy areas, therefore, Congress' power over the purse can be used to shape the direction of our foreign policy. One of the best illustrations of this was Congress' ability to force an end to the Vietnam War.

How Congress ended the Vietnam War.   Although President Nixon on January 23, 1973, announced the signing of the Paris Peace Accord ending the Vietnam War, he proceeded to bomb Cambodia because the communist forces there wanted an outright victory against the Americans.[43] Since the Gulf of Tonkin Resolution had been repealed by Congress in 1970, his action appeared to be war making without any legislative authorization. Nixon argued that he could bomb Cambodia based on his authority as commander-in-chief. The funds for this purpose had been transferred from other uses. During fiscal year 1973, the Department of Defense had shifted about $750 million for Cambodia bombing missions, but failed to so inform the House and Senate appropriations committees. Therefore, when the Nixon administration went to Congress for additional "back-door" funding in 1973, there was open hostility by rank-and-file legislators.

The House of Representatives in 1973 passed an amendment banning all such transfers and another amendment, sponsored by Clarence D. Long (D.–Mo.), forbidding the use of any Defense Department moneys for combat activities in Cambodia. In the Senate, Thomas Eagleton (D.–Mo.) sponsored an even more restrictive cutoff amendment: "None of the funds herein appropriated under this act or heretofore appropriated under any other act may be expended to support directly or indirectly combat activities in, over or from off the shores of Cambodia or in or over Laos by United States forces."[44] Eventually a conference committee reconciled the House and Senate versions of this cutoff legislation, but Nixon vetoed that bill. In reaction, Congress proceeded to attach the Eagleton Amendment to various kinds of legislation, for example, an authorization bill for the Department of State, a pay bill for the federal bureaucracy, and a bill extending the debt limit. Eventually a cutoff amendment was enacted, which, since it permitted President Nixon forty-five additional days to continue the bombing, Nixon signed into law. Nixon later blamed the Congress for prematurely ending the conflict in Southeast Asia, remarking in his memoirs: ". . . [the] war and the peace in Indochina that America had won at such cost over 12 years of sacrifice and fighting were lost within a matter of months once Congress refused to fulfill our obligation. And it is Congress that must bear the responsibility for the tragic results."[45] Congress proceeded to impose similar funding cutoffs to other bills, and during 1974 and 1975 it systematically reduced the level of appropriations requested by the Nixon and Ford administrations for military and economic aid to the governments of Laos, Vietnam, and Cambodia.

However, the fundamental problems in trying to legislate a foreign policy were manifested during the final days of the Vietnam War, after the Saigon regime had collapsed. Because the Eagleton Amendment remained in force, President Ford was technically in violation of that law when he used U.S. helicopters to rescue the Vietnamese from our embassy there. During this evacuation process, Congress was debating the merits of allowing the president to undertake that action, a circumstance that prompted this commentary by Sen. Barry Goldwater:

> When the North Vietnamese [get] within rocket range of Tonsonhut Air Base, there is not going to be any more evacuation unless we want to go to war. I think we are spinning our wheels. The President, and I am proud of him for having done this, has taken into his own hands the protection of Americans and American property and American freedoms, wherever they might be, around this world, regardless of the legislation that we, in my opinion, foolishly passed last year. . . . I suggest that we're being a little foolish, a little redundant. We're not accomplishing anything. We may not pass this bill until the day after tomorrow, at which time, I think the whole action will be over and we will have again engaged ourselves in ridiculous debate. . . .[46]

In the end, Congress never did agree on legislation to permit the president's evacuation of Saigon.

Congressional oversight.   Using its power over the purse, Congress can oversee the conduct of foreign affairs in other ways. Congress can require the president to issue periodic reports on various programs, notify the

Congress about actions taken pursuant to legislation, or simply provide additional information or supporting data to the Congress. In a variety of ways, therefore, the implementation of foreign policy can be subjected to statutory provisions. For example, when voting funds for the Agency for International Development or other foreign aid programs, Congress often adds "buy American" provisos to how foreign countries may use those funds, or it may require that American ships transport the purchased goods.

Before Jimmy Carter became president, the Congress tried to apply a "human rights" standard to our provision of military and foreign aid to other countries. In 1974, for example, Congress reduced U.S. economic aid to Chile and ended all military assistance to that nation. It also made a token reduction in the military assistance flowing to South Korea. These actions by Congress reflected the nonbinding "sense of Congress" resolution, which had been passed that year. It stated that "the President shall substantially reduce or terminate security assistance to any government which engages in a consistent pattern of gross violations of internationally recognized human rights, including torture or cruel, inhuman or degrading treatment or punishment; prolonged detention without charges; or other flagrant denials of the right to life, liberty and the security of the person."[47]

In 1975 Congress passed legislation requiring "human rights reports" for all nations that receive U.S. assistance, and provided for the cutoff of aid by concurrent resolution of Congress. When the Department of State reported gross violations by these nations, President Carter moved to reduce or to end aid to Uruguay, Ethiopia, and Argentina. Both liberals and conservatives in Congress have used "human rights" to justify cuts in military and economic assistance to other nations, though they have focused on very different regimes. Whereas conservatives disliked the governments in Angola, Mozambique, and North Vietnam, liberals wanted to reduce assistance to the regimes in South Korea, Indonesia, Iran, Uruguay, Argentina, Chile, and the Philippines.[48] Nobody in Congress spoke up for Uganda when it was ruled by dictator Idi Amin, and in 1978 Congress ignored President Carter's opposition and enacted a total trade embargo against that country.

Another area with major implications for foreign policy is the sale of arms to other nations. Since Vietnam, Congress has tried to exercise oversight over arms shipments. Until 1974 the law simply required the secretary of state to report semiannually to Congress any significant arms sales, but this procedure was changed in 1974 by the Nelson-Bingham Amendment. Sponsored by Sen. Gaylord Nelson (D.–Wis.) and Rep. Jonathan Bingham (D.– N.Y.), though opposed by President Ford, Congress enacted this legislation requiring the president to give Congress a detailed description of any weapons sale involving $25 million or more. An arms sale can be vetoed by a concurrent veto of Congress within thirty days unless the president stipulates that an emergency exists.

During the first five years under this 1974 legislation, no arms sale was vetoed by Congress, but there have been instances when the president had to modify his proposals to obtain legislative approval. In 1975, the Ford administration wanted to sell fourteen Hawk missile batteries to Jordan; the deal had been arranged secretly to minimize the time available for Israeli lobbyists to oppose the sale. When Congress was informed, a controversy erupted. Jordan's King Hussein journeyed to the United States to persuade key congressmen. In the end the Ford administration modified the Hawk system to comply with legislative recommendations aimed at assuring its defensive rather than offensive use. After these modifications were made, President Ford was allowed to proceed with the sale.

In 1977 a proposed arms sale by the Carter administration to Iran, involving the very sophisticated AWACS (Airborne Warning and Control System) planes, aroused stiff opposition in Congress. It was feared that this equipment might fall into the hands of the Soviet Union, and again, after precautions were included in the terms of that sale, Congress withdrew its threat to veto the entire package. In retrospect, Congress' foresight was superior to the president's; when the Iranian revolution began in 1978 and the Shah's regime began to collapse, the agreement was cancelled. In 1981 the same concerns plagued Congress when President Reagan proposed to sell AWACS planes to Saudi Arabia. The issue then was complicated by the assassination of Egypt's President Sadat. However, when the Senate refused to join the House of Representatives in approving the concurrent resolution to veto that arms package, the AWACS sale to Saudi Arabia was approved.

Summary. No doubt Congress' heightened role in foreign policymaking since the Vietnam War is a reaction to the excesses of Lyndon Johnson and Richard Nixon. Yet the situation in the 1970s and 1980s is not unique in American history. Franck and Weisband argue that the post-Vietnam era is the fourth period in U.S. history when Congress tried to reassert its power in foreign affairs. The earlier periods were: (1) the era beginning with President Martin Van Buren and ending with the election of Abraham Lincoln (1837–1861), (2) the period covering the administrations of Presidents Grant, Hayes, Garfield, Arthur, Cleveland, and Harrison (1869–1893), and (3) the administrations of Presidents Harding, Coolidge, and Hoover (1921–1933). In each case, they argue, war facilitated a swing toward the power of the president whereas peace triggered a shift toward Congress.[49] One problem with their formulation is that those historic eras typified by Congress' dominance are also associated with weak presidents. On the other hand, those periods when strong presidents dominated the national government were eras characterized by domestic reform legislation as well as by important foreign policy achievements. Obviously, it is difficult to unravel these parallel trends to pinpoint any causal relationship over time.

As evidence for their position, Franck and Weisband point to Congress' part in nearly defeating the Panama Canal Treaties, its role in ending the Vietnam War, and its cutoff of military aid to Turkey in 1974 and to Angola in 1976. Analysis of legislative enactments by LeLoup and Shull also indicates that Presidents Nixon and Ford had less success in getting legislative approval for their foreign and military policies than Presidents Eisenhower, Kennedy, or Johnson.[50] Apparently there has been a reaction in Congress in the wake of Vietnam. The more important question, however, is whether Congress' renewed interest in foreign affairs suggests any fundamental realignment in the balance of power between the executive and the legislature in foreign policy. Although Franck and Weisband argue that Congress' increased role in foreign policymaking will be relatively permanent, that prognosis seems doubtful.

In the first place, Congress lacks the capability to make foreign policy decisions during "crises," when advantages still accrue to the executive. (This aspect is discussed later in the chapter.) Second, although Congress' ability to review the actions of presidents may have been strengthened by legislation enacted during the 1970s, collectively Congress cannot *initiate* policy, let alone *react* when a speedy response is necessary. This problem was illustrated by Congress' inability to pass legislation allowing the rescue of Vietnamese during the final days before the total collapse of Saigon's government. Third, legislative decision making may not be the optimal method of handling foreign policy issues. Even Franck and Weisband are concerned that laws denying to the president discretion in foreign affairs may be inappropriate to the ever-changing needs of diplomacy in the modern world. In evaluating the conflict between the president and Congress on the issue of cutting military aid to pro-Western factions in Angola, Franck and Weisband make this observation:

> If Angola, as a special circumstance enveloped in special circumstances, teaches few generally applicable lessons, it does pose crucial questions about power-sharing, about the ability of the United States to play a coherent, effective role as a superpower in the new era of Congressional activism.[51]

PUBLIC INPUTS

A perplexing question haunting democratic theorists is how to assure that public policy represents the opinions and demands of the citizenry. Presidents often legitimize their policies by referring to their "mandate" from the people, but generally elections are very imprecise barometers of public opinion on specific issues. To forge a linkage between public opinion and governmental decision making, we have come to rely on interest groups and single-issue movements to articulate the views of certain "publics" in our society on policy questions. This mode of representation, however, can severely distort an understanding of the "public interest." Moreover, scholars tend to agree that the relationship between public opinion and policy-making is more direct in domestic affairs than it is in foreign policy, because citizens rarely understand how foreign policy affects their lives. For this very reason, a president normally enjoys great discretion in conducting diplomacy without much interference by public opinion.

Public opinion

The impact of public opinion on foreign policy is a very complicated issue to unravel. Political scientists have offered various hypotheses to explain how citizens react to the chief diplomat's initiatives. One argument is based on the finding that different clusters of public attitudes, or "moods," toward foreign affairs characterize certain historical periods. In observing public opinion before and after World War I, for example, Walter Lippmann was concerned about its seemingly "volatile and irrational" nature.[52] Before World War I the country was in an "isolationist" mood and public opinion was unsympathetic to our becoming involved in the European conflict. Once America entered the war, the people became zealots who wanted to crush the enemy and win a total victory. The war crisis obviously aroused popular emotions, but Lippmann viewed this aspect as a threat to rational decision making in foreign affairs. Thus, he preferred to let the president make foreign policy.

The public's vacillating attachment to both isolationism and internationalism was studied by Gabriel Almond, who linked this schizophrenic attitude to the fact that the public's views of foreign affairs are influenced to a great extent by events.[53] Prior to World War II Americans were suspicious of international politics and wanted to withdraw from world affairs. But after Pearl Harbor our attitudes shifted toward a commitment to internationalism, whereby we established alliances (NATO) and hoped for world peace. The optimistic view yielded again to cynicism during the Cold War, and the rise of McCarthyism in the early 1950s probably reflected the public's feeling that the United States was somehow being betrayed by our leadership. In this context, Theodore Lowi suggests that political intolerance usually follows in the aftermath of war, mainly because the citizenry is not easily calmed after being emotionally aroused and seeks scapegoats.[54]

The view that public attitudes toward foreign affairs are "volatile and irrational" suggests that democracy is basically incompatible with the requirements of international relations. The scholars who subscribe to this interpretation argue that stable opinions about foreign policy are related to a person's educational level. Accordingly, they argue that "elites" have a role in educating the masses about foreign affairs so that the potential for major fluctuations in United States foreign policy is reduced. Compared with the general public, which has little knowledge about foreign affairs and whose opinions lack stability and consistency, these writers claim the "elites" and so-called attentive publics are much better informed and more concerned about foreign policy.

For example, Robert Dahl argued that congressmen, by their public statements and voting on legislation, transmit foreign policy positions to the mass population.[55] A later study by James Rosenau formulated a linkage showing that attitudes about foreign affairs were communicated from policymakers to opinion leaders and "attentive" publics, who in turn influenced the general public.[56] Rosenau's argument was that the elites and the attentive public—about 10 percent of the citizenry—shape the public's attitudes to foreign policy initiatives and thereby create a degree of consensus behind the president. Many studies do suggest that a kind of political consensus supporting internationalism did develop after World War II. The research by Martin Patchen found "involvement" to be a primary dimension in public attitudes toward foreign affairs,[57] while Modigliani reported that "international intervention" was the salient attitude dimension for most people.[58] On the other hand, evidence suggests that the post-World War II consensus in foreign affairs was undermined by the Vietnam War. In the view of Mandelbaum and Schneider, the "cold war consensus" has been eroded, with the result that public opinions now can be categorized as liberal internationalist, conservative internationalist, and noninternationalist (a lack of interest in foreign affairs).[59] Moreover, these divisions are linked to certain domestic ideological positions. Mandelbaum and Schneider are concerned that this "cleavage in public opinion will hobble the conduct of foreign policy" in the future.

A study by Bardes and Oldendick is one of very few to contrast elite and mass attitudes on a variety of foreign policy issues during 1974–1978. After reviewing their data, the authors conclude that there are indeed definite distinctions between elite and mass opinion in foreign affairs. In their words,

> Elites are much more supportive of an activist role for the U.S. in world affairs than is the general public, and also demonstrate far greater understanding of the interdependence of nations. The leadership group is also much more favorable towards detente, advocates advancing human rights positions, and believes that the U.S. should be a leader in solving world problems. The electorate, on the other hand, tends to be much more chauvinistic, to believe that the U.S. is strong enough to go it alone, and that its primary concerns should be at home. Paradoxically, the general public also wants the U.S. to continue to play a strong international role in world affairs.[60]

The research by Bardes and Oldendick also reveals the ambivalence Americans exhibit toward foreign affairs; the public seems to vacillate between the desire to withdraw from the world and the desire to overwhelm and dominate it. Another interesting finding pertains to the president's ability to educate public opinion regarding foreign affairs. Even though Jimmy Carter made "human rights" a campaign issue in 1976 and gave it high priority during his term, data show that "public support for U.S. actions to secure human rights in other nations did not increase during the Carter presidency."[61] From this perspective, therefore, one can only speculate about the degree to which public opinion restrains the president in foreign policymaking.

Erwin Hargrove argues that public opinion defines the permissible boundaries within which presidents must conduct foreign policy.[62] As one example, he asks whether John F. Kennedy could have allowed the Russians to establish a missile base in Cuba, just ninety miles from Florida. In this instance, given that the country was involved in midterm congressional elections and the Republicans were charging that the Soviets were building missiles in Cuba, no doubt Kennedy sensed that serious political damage could result by his failure to take decisive action. The American people expect a president to meet a Soviet challenge, and apparently this is a stronger constraint on Democrats than on Republicans. As Hargrove explains it,

> This has been a particular problem for Democratic Presidents, who have been saddled by Republican rhetoric [blaming them for] loss of China and softness on communism. Republican Presidents have ironically been much freer to be moderate in the Cold War than Democrats because Republican political rhetoric has had more of a claim on patriotism and anticommunism and because the vocal Republican right wing is more neutralized when the Republicans are in the White House.[63]

Opinion surveys generally indicate that voters perceive the Republicans as being more effective in addressing foreign policy issues, whereas Democrats are seen as being more skillful in handling domestic policy. During the 1952 and 1956 presidential campaigns, for example, Dwight Eisenhower was judged by the electorate to be more capable than Adlai Stevenson to deal with foreign affairs.[64] Similarly, whereas President John F. Kennedy had to take a hard-line position against the Soviets in the Cuban missile crisis, President Richard Nixon—who had a strong anti-communist reputation—could begin an era of detente with the Soviet Union without damaging his political position.

To the degree that Hargrove's argument is valid, this interpretation suggests that the president must "educate" the public before making any fundamental shifts in U.S. foreign policy. For example, Hargrove cited President Roosevelt's 1937 speech about the need to "quarantine" European dictators in order to test public opinion on this sensitive issue.[65] Since the reaction to Roosevelt's address was negative, he had to postpone any changes in foreign policy until the Lend-Lease program, when Great Britain's wartime difficulties became more obvious to Americans. However, Hargrove's viewpoint remains an open question, because presidents often initiate foreign policies *despite* public opinion.

Consider public opinion during 1954–1963 on the matter of stopping atomic weapons tests in the earth's atmosphere.[66] Before 1958, the majority of Americans favored a multilateral agreement to stop these tests but opposed a unilateral cessation by the United States. In April 1958, a majority remained opposed to American suspension of atmospheric tests; that summer the Eisenhower administration announced cessation of all such weapons tests; and one year later (November 1959) 77 percent of Americans favored that moratorium. However, by June 1961, the majority wanted to resume American testing of atomic weapons, though the Kennedy administration was trying to negotiate a test-ban treaty with the Soviet Union. By January 1962, public opinion was deadlocked on this question, but in March 1962, shortly after President Kennedy announced his decision to resume weapons testing, 67 percent of Americans supported that policy. The final reversal in public opinion in the years studied came seventeen months later when, in August 1963, 61 percent expressed approval for the Senate's ratification of a partial test-ban treaty with the Russians. In evaluating the erratic nature of public opinion on that issue, the author of this research concluded that public attitudes did not enfeeble the president's decision making on this matter; moreover, "mass opinion did not compel the government to be 'too pacifist in peace' at the 'critical junctures' examined here."[67] Rather, public opinion regarding the desirability of banning weapons tests in the atmosphere was shaped by the views expressed and the actions taken by our political leadership as well as by the attentive "elites" in the mass media who supported President Kennedy's initiatives.

In a different example, President Ronald Reagan's intervention in the Falklands War between Great Britain and Argentina illustrates that a lukewarm public opinion may not deter a president from exercising leadership in foreign affairs. During 1982, public support for Reagan's foreign policy had been decreasing, a trend consistent with the decline in his overall popularity. In Spring of 1982 Argentina landed troops on the Falkland Islands, located off its coast, though that territory was under British rule. Great Britain demanded their withdrawal and Prime Minister Margaret Thatcher ordered a naval task force to sail to the Falklands. Secretary of State Alexander Haig tried unsuccessfully to resolve the dispute peacefully, but President Reagan aligned the United States with Great Britain. He offered the British war supplies, repair facilities for its fleet, and intelligence information about Argentine troop movements and the location of Soviet naval vessels in the vicinity. Congress stood firmly behind Reagan's position in backing Great Britain. On April 29, 1982, the Senate by a 79 to 1 vote approved a resolution stating that the United States could not remain neutral but rather supported Britain's efforts to "achieve full withdrawal of Argentine forces" from the Falklands. The House of Representatives, on May 4, 1982, by a two-thirds vote adopted a nonbinding resolution that stated:

> *Resolved*, That it is the sense of the House of Representatives that—
> (1) in compliance with United Nations Security Council Resolution 502, Argentina should withdraw its forces from the Falkland Islands; and
> (2) if the efforts to resolve the conflict through peaceful means fail, the United States should provide full diplomatic support to Great Britain in its efforts to uphold the rule of law.[68]

Public opinion in the United States, however, showed only a modest increase in approval for Reagan's leadership during this period. One survey by ABC News-*Washington Post* taken during April 21–25, 1982 found that 53 percent of the respondents approved Reagan's leadership in foreign affairs, a 10 percent increase in his approval rating since March 1982.[69] But a Harris Survey found that, during April 16–22, 1982, only 39 percent of Americans approved of Reagan's handling of foreign policy; this percentage was slightly higher than the president's rating on foreign policy in March (36%).[70] The fact that Reagan's popularity in March 1982 was at its lowest point since he assumed office, therefore, did not deter him from entering the Falklands dispute as Britain's ally. Apart from the diplomatic calculations that affected Reagan's decision in this matter, however, is the additional consideration that, as president, he probably believed that decisive leadership during the Falklands War would strengthen his popularity with the American people. The historical record shows, in fact, that international crises do help a president's approval ratings because the public tends to "rally round the flag," an aspect of public opinion in foreign affairs to be discussed in the following section.

Rallying round the flag

It may seem that international crises are a permanent condition of the world community, especially given Cold War tensions, but this perception is not exactly true. A nation can tire of almost any pressure when it becomes too routine. As the Iran hostage "crisis" dragged on for more than a year, it became difficult for Jimmy Carter to rally the nation around his leadership. And in the end, that incident undermined his credibility. Similar observations can be made about the Korean and Vietnam wars (see chapter 7). As those conflicts persisted, our willingness to make sacrifices and to accept inconveniences for the sake of the war efforts diminished. When body counts and reports from the battlefield become daily occurrences, eventually the public becomes disillusioned with the war effort and with political leadership. Thus, although a war may be an acute international crisis when it begins, prolonged involvement in war hurts a president's popularity.

The impact of an international crisis on the president's popularity is limited to the short term, when such incidents are immediately grasped by the public as posing a threat to national security. One must seriously question whether public opinion can limit a president's authority in foreign affairs. For survey respondents to express an opinion on a variety of questions affecting foreign policy during times of international stability is one matter, but those attitudes may have little meaning if public opinion is radically transformed under conditions of stress.

Research by John Mueller shows that public opinion can be expected to coalesce around a president's leadership during international crises, when political issues are sensational and a need for decisive action is recognized.[71] On these occasions the president truly is the symbol of our nation. Nelson Polsby observes, "Invariably, the popular response to a President during international crisis is favorable regardless of the wisdom of the policies he pursues."[72] Consider these four examples. After Pearl Harbor, Franklin D. Roosevelt's popularity rose from 72 to 84 percent approval. When President Truman decided to resist the communist invasion of South Korea, his popularity rose 9 points within one month. In the 1950s, the Suez Canal crisis, which involved Egypt and Great Britain, caused Dwight Eisenhower's approval rating to increase from 67 to 75 percent, also during one month. In spite of the Bay of Pigs fiasco, President Kennedy's popularity rallied by

10 percentage points. Regardless of whether international events are judged to be "good" or "bad" by the American people, Mueller's analysis found that the president's popularity increases in the short term.

This relationship has persisted since Mueller completed his study. In 1978 Jimmy Carter gained 11 points in his approval rating as a result of his successfully negotiating the Camp David Accords between Egypt's President Sadat and Israel's Prime Minister Begin. Even more impressive is the fact that President Carter's popularity rallied from a low of 29 percent approval before the Iran hostage crisis to 61 percent approval within one month after the embassy takeover. This was the single largest jump in popularity experienced by any president during the four decades that such approval ratings have been recorded.

This tendency to "rally round the flag" during an international crisis is based upon our psychological needs, argues Fred Greenstein. He explains:

> To the degree that the President's actions are effective, citizens who identify themselves with him may experience heightened feelings of strength—of being in a world which is not completely dependent upon external circumstances and events.[73]

An inherent danger in this "rally-round-the-flag" syndrome is the fact that it may encourage presidents to favor aggressive actions in the face of an international challenge rather than judiciousness and restraint. This prospect concerns Erwin Hargrove, for example, who notes that many foreign crises during the 1940s, 1950s, and 1960s reflected the Cold War. To this extent, therefore, Hargrove argues that our presidents are given yet another reason for maintaining a firm posture vis-à-vis the Soviet Union.[74] Thus, the "rally-round-the-flag" phenomenon suggests that when public opinion becomes activated around foreign policy goals, it generally supports, rather than limits, those initiatives undertaken by a president.

Election campaigns

Not only is public opinion permissive in terms of following the president's lead in foreign affairs, but the presidential election campaign gives the president few cues regarding the conduct of diplomacy. While there are occasions when partisanship influences the content of our foreign policy debate, more often partisan conflicts focus on domestic issues. This was not always the case in American history. During the era between World War I and World War II political parties mirrored different attitudes toward foreign affairs. In general, the Republican party, reflecting its "isolationist" constituency in the Midwest, resisted the efforts by the Democratic party under Franklin D. Roosevelt to involve the country in the impending European conflict. After World War II, however, the negative effects of party competition have been neutralized by a spirit of "bipartisanship" in foreign affairs. For example, in Congress the major legislation affecting foreign policy is often enacted by majorities of Republicans and Democrats.

The zenith of bipartisanship in foreign policy occurred immediately after World War II. President Harry Truman perceived a serious communist threat to Eastern Europe, and solicited the assistance of Sen. Arthur Vandenberg (R.–Mich.), the distinguished Republican chairman of the Senate Foreign Reiations Committee. Vandenberg, who had been an avid isolationist during the 1930s, was persuaded by Truman, and proceeded to rally Republican support for the president's initiatives in foreign affairs. This alliance between Truman and Vandenberg was very important at that time, because the Republicans gained control of both the House and the Senate during the 80th Congress (1947–1948). As a result, Truman's major proposals—the Marshall Plan to aid European economic recovery; the Truman Doctrine, which enunciated a "containment" policy toward the Soviet Union; NATO; and aid to Greece and Turkey, which were threatened by communist take-over—were enacted with bipartisan support.

This era of bipartisanship faded by the end of Truman's term, especially when conservative Sen. Robert Taft replaced Vandenberg as chairman of the Foreign Relations Committee. Not only did Taft harbor isolationist sentiments, but the Republicans harassed Truman and the Democrats about events in Korea, the fall of China to the Communists, and the role of Secretary of State Dean Acheson. During the 1952 presidential campaign the Korean stalemate worked to the disadvantage of Democrat Adlai Stevenson. Eisenhower, a World War II hero, promised to "save" Korea. After soundly defeating Stevenson in the election, Eisenhower went to Korea, and eventually he did end that war.

In the 1960 presidential election between Vice-President Richard Nixon and John F. Kennedy the tables were turned. The Russians launched their Sputnik satellite in 1957, which came as a shock to Americans who had been told throughout the decade that our technology and military power were supreme. Soviet prestige soared, and it now appeared that the United States was falling behind in the technological race. This development set the stage for Kennedy's charge that a "missile gap" existed between the United States and the Soviet Union. This one issue alone cannot account for Kennedy's narrow victory over Nixon, however, since other events served to discredit the Republicans during the years before the election: Castro established his communist regime in Cuba, and the Russians shot down an American U-2 spy plane, though Eisenhower denied for a time that the aircraft was ours.

In 1964, as the Vietnam War was commencing, incumbent Lyndon Johnson used heavy-handed public relations techniques against Barry Goldwater on the issue of tactical nuclear weapons. Goldwater favored giving control over these devices to military commanders, whereas Johnson, who had cultivated a more pacifist image, argued that the president should never relinquish authority over such awesome weapons. For the most part, the war in Vietnam was not the subject of partisan debate. Indeed, more Republicans were "hawkish" on Vietnam than many Democrats. Clearly, the leading "doves" on the question were Democratic senators, such as Foreign Relations Committee Chairman William Fulbright and Oregon's Sen. Wayne Morse. The Vietnam War generated factional infighting within the Democratic party in 1968. That year, faced with serious challenges from Sen. Eugene McCarthy (D.–Minn.) and later Robert Kennedy (D.–Mass.), Lyndon Johnson chose not to run for reelection.

In the 1968 presidential election, Nixon was helped to the extent that liberal Democrats refused to rally around the Humphrey candidacy. But, among the voting public, the majority could not readily differentiate between Humphrey's and Nixon's views on the Vietnam War.[75] Both men favored ending the conflict—though Humphrey's position was somewhat constrained by his being Johnson's vice-president. Although he won the election, Richard Nixon continued the Vietnam War up to the time of the 1972 campaign, when it did become a partisan issue differentiating President Nixon and Democrat George McGovern. Compared with its impact in 1968, withdrawal from Vietnam was now even more salient for Democratic activists than for Republicans. McGovern was nominated in 1972 by a Democratic convention controlled by liberal activists who wanted the United States to get out of Southeast Asia and to grant amnesty to draft evaders. Nixon won 61 percent of the vote in 1972, but this electoral outcome cannot be entirely explained by public perceptions about foreign affairs. McGovern alienated large segments of the electorate with his liberal views on welfarism, racial justice, abortion, and marijuana use, as well as on Vietnam.

Foreign policy had less impact on the Carter–Ford election in 1976. Gerald Ford, however, made a grave political error when he suggested during a debate that Poland was not within the Soviet sphere of influence. Although he later clarified his statement, Ford's blunder allowed Jimmy Carter to question Ford's comprehension of world affairs. Overall, that year's important campaign issues focused on the record of Nixon's presidency: the Watergate scandals, Nixon's near-impeachment, and Ford's decision to pardon the former president. In 1980, foreign policy was highly politicized by Ronald Reagan, who forcefully challenged the policies of the Carter administration. Reagan, the most conservative Republican to be nominated since Barry Goldwater, argued that America's prestige in the world was deteriorating and that our military power was second to that of the Soviet Union. He ridiculed Carter's response to the Soviet invasion of Afghanistan and to the Iranian crisis, exploited conservative opposition to the Panama Canal Treaties, and suggested that he would reaffirm U.S. commitment to Taiwan. Carter was judged to be vulnerable on his foreign policy record; his domestic policies also hurt him. During Carter's term, the nation had experienced an economic slowdown along with double-digit inflation rates.

This cursory review of presidential politics suggests that foreign affairs rarely dominates an election campaign. With the possible exception of the Nixon–McGovern debate over Vietnam, presidential candidates usually do not offer the voters a fundamental choice between foreign policy options. Rather, we experience partisan debate over which candidate can best perform in this arena; criticism of executive leadership typically is related to Cold War issues. Usually Republicans, but sometimes Democrats, claim that the incumbent has failed to meet the Soviet challenge effectively. Finally, whereas errors in the conduct of our foreign affairs may cost a president votes in a forthcoming election, elections provide few cues about how diplomacy should be conducted. Only in rare instances do campaign promises constrain candidates; for example, Eisenhower probably felt an obligation to end the Korean War. It appears that President Ronald Reagan strove to honor his campaign commitment to strengthen the U.S. military stance. Although he made substantial reductions in expenditures for social-welfare programs, Reagan also provided increases in defense spending. Our bipartisan posture vis-à-vis the Soviet Union in the three decades since World War II has prevented the development of fundamentally different viewpoints on foreign affairs in the United States, in contrast to the situation that typified the 1930s.

Interest groups

There are two major policy areas that elicit concerted efforts by interest groups to shape the direction of American diplomacy. One area is international trade and finance, a subject of interest to domestic industries and their work forces. The other area involves the activities of "ethnic" groups in behalf of their "homelands." Serious lobbying by both interest groups occurred during the 1970s.

Trade relations is a policy issue in which Congress has exerted much influence in behalf of domestic industries desiring protection against foreign competition. In the nineteenth and twentieth centuries trade legislation erected barriers to imports by use of tariffs and quotas. Trade policy is a classic example of pork-barrel politics, in which members of Congress support colleagues who want trade protection for goods produced in their regions of the country in return for similar favors.

This horse trading of votes was exemplified by the Smoot–Hawley Tariff Act of 1930. Indiscriminate reciprocal concessions gave rise to legislation imposing high tariffs on hundreds of imported goods and commodities. Under the Reciprocal Trade Agreements Act of 1934, Congress articulated a "free-trade" policy by delegating to the president (beginning with Roosevelt) authority to negotiate the lowering of trade barriers between the United States and other nations. As a result, less control over trade policy is now retained by Congress. Occasionally, various industries appeal to Congress to exempt their businesses from having to compete with foreign goods.

Those businesses favoring trade liberalization speak through the Emergency Committee for American Trade (ECAT). In 1974, when the Trade Reform Act was an issue, ECAT helped to organize about 1,200 corporate executives to lobby for its passage. The American Iron and Steel Institute, which represents an industry facing serious competition from German and Japanese firms, tends to pressure Congress for trade protection; its arguments are often supported by the United Steelworkers of America. In the early 1970s, the matter of ocean fishing rights prompted such groups as the Atlantic States Marine Fisheries Commission, the National Coalition for

Marine Conservation, and the Maine Sardine Packers Association to lobby (successfully) Congress to enact a 200-mile fishing zone around the U.S. coast. In 1978 the U.S. sugar beet industry was able to prevent U.S. ratification of the International Sugar Agreement (assuring sugar price stability) until President Carter agreed to increase domestic subsidies for that commodity. The latter negotiations were characterized by Vincent Mahler in this way:

> Senate ratification of the International Sugar Agreement [ISA] thus became for the sugar lobby a vehicle to force the Carter administration to support an acceptable *domestic* sugar program to supplement the ISA mechanisms. The administration found itself caught between conflicting desires. On the one hand it strongly favored Senate ratification of the ISA. . . . On the other hand, though, the administration was firm in its conviction that large supplementary domestic sugar price supports would be inflationary. . . . Throughout 1978 sugar policy was the object of a truly byzantine series of maneuvers within Congress and by the administration. Central to the maneuvering was the stubborn refusal of generally liberal and internationalist Senator Frank Church of Idaho (a major beet sugar state) to move the ISA through the Senate Foreign Relations committee, of which he was chairman, unless acceptable supplementary sugar price supports were forthcoming.[76]

President Carter faced similar conflicts with the farming community and exporters when he imposed an embargo on grain sales to the Soviet Union in 1980.

The grain embargo. President Carter's embargo of January 4, 1980 blocked the shipment of about 17 million tons of grain to the Soviet Union. Though this embargo was the fifth one in the past ten years, its purpose was unique.[77] By denying it grain shipments for its invasion of Afghanistan the president intended to punish the Soviet Union. The grain embargo was only part of the Carter administration sanctions against the Soviets; included were prohibitions on Soviet–U.S. cultural exchanges, limits on Soviet licenses for high technology and oil-drilling equipment, and restrictions on fishing rights in U.S waters. At first, the grain embargo appeared successful. The Soviets regularly imported grain for two-thirds of their domestic needs and in 1979 unfavorable weather conditions had reduced the Soviet Union's grain harvest by about 21 percent.

To protect American farmers, several costly programs were undertaken by the Carter administration. The government agreed to purchase and store some of the grain, while new markets would be sought for the rest of it. Other programs, at a cost of $2.8 billion, would ease the burdens resulting from the embargo. The Commodity Credit Corporation assumed contracts from the exporters now unable to deliver grain to the Soviets, which meant that the U.S. government took ownership of 4.2 million tons of wheat and another 9 million tons of other grains. On the other hand, the Carter administration rejected a proposal supported by many farmers to establish a crop diversion program; the farmers viewed this alternative as a hedge against falling prices in the event of a record harvest. Instead, the government allowed farmers to withhold grain from the markets and to use it as collateral for federal loans. When farm prices rose, that grain could then be sold on the open market.

In the end, the grain embargo failed in its purpose. Moreover, it undermined President Carter's popularity with the farm community. Not only did the United States grossly underestimate the Soviet Union's ability to buy grain elsewhere, but the Carter administration supplied the Soviets with 8 million tons of grain that had been promised under a five-year U.S.–Soviet agreement negotiated during the Ford administration in 1975. Carter was unable to justify his support for that five-year-old policy while, at the same time, he was imposing a new embargo. Nor could he persuade other nations (Argentina, Australia, and Canada) to join the embargo. Eventually the Soviet Union imported a total of 31 million tons of grain, only 2.5 million tons less than what it had planned to buy from the United States.

The Carter administration also miscalculated the degree of opposition from the American farmers. Many factors worked against the president. U.S. crop production was extremely productive and the USSR had already promised to purchase an exceedingly large amount of American grain surplus that year. These two facts alone caused great antagonism between the farm community and the Carter administration. The farmers resented the intervention of the federal government in agriculture policy, which was necessitated by the embargo. In the words of one Iowa farmer, the embargo "hurt the farmers and hurt our balance of trade and hurt our economy." He added that it was done for no reason other than to "make us feel moral."[78] The American Farm Bureau Federation opposed the embargo and later accused the Carter administration of breaking its word to protect the farmers from the ill effects of that policy. By the time of the 1980 elections, congressional and presidential candidates in both political parties criticized Carter's embargo—Ronald Reagan, Sen. Edward Kennedy (D.–Mass.), Sen. George McGovern (D.–S.D.), Sen. Birch Bayh (D.–Ind.), Sen. Thomas Eagleton (D.–Mo.), Sen. Robert Dole (R.–Kan.), and Sen. John C. Culver (D.–Iowa). In Congress there was talk of adding a legislative veto to the Export Administration Act of 1979, which was used to authorize the embargo, and by July 1980 four antiembargo measures had been introduced in the House and Senate. No legislation was enacted by the 96th Congress, but Ronald Reagan attacked Carter's grain embargo throughout the 1980 presidential campaign. Ultimately, the embargo caused Jimmy Carter more political harm than its impact on foreign policy warranted. According to one observer's assessment of the embargo, "No future President should wish to find himself uncomfortably positioned, as was President Carter earlier this year, with his most visible trade and security policies toward the Soviet Union moving in opposite directions."[79]

Various trends have so increased the American economy's vulnerability to worldwide economic forces that the traditional distinction between domestic and foreign policy is blurred. The United States exports about 20 percent of its industrial production and more than one-third of its agricultural output. One-third of the profits earned by American companies derive from their foreign-based operations. Related to these developments is the fact that, although our domestic economy is more dependent on the international economy, the importance of the U.S. economy has dropped relative to its position at the end of World War II. In the future, therefore, we may anticipate even more lobbying by special interests trying to influence U.S. policy on trade relations and international finance. The rise of multinational corporations with financial interests across the globe poses special problems for the president.

Since 1945, U.S. corporations have developed about 8,000 overseas subsidiaries. Because mergers, licensing requirements, and equipment sales must take place across national boundaries, any one government is unequal to the task of monitoring those transactions. To facilitate their business transactions in foreign countries, moreover, many American firms resort to "bribes" and questionable payments to officials in the host countries. In 1976, for example, Exxon Corporation admitted to the Senate Subcommittee on Multinational Corporations that it had paid some $46 million to several government ministers and political parties in Italy during the 1970s for the privilege of operating there.[80] Lockheed Corporation, involved in numerous cases of "kickbacks" to foreign governments, acknowledged that it had hired a Japanese agent, who was a member of a right-wing political faction, to intercede for the company in Japan. Since the United States had opposed the same right-wing faction for many years, the irony of these conflicting policies led Sen. Frank Church (D.–Idaho) to conclude that

> in effect, we have had a foreign policy of the U.S. Government which has vigorously opposed this political line in Japan and a Lockheed foreign policy which has helped to keep it alive through large financial subsidies in support of the company's sales efforts in that country.[81]

Among the other American companies making illicit payments to foreign officials and agents was Gulf Oil, which paid $4.8 million to persons within the United States and another $4.3 million to overseas political leaders. About $4 million of that sum went to government officials in Korea.[82] Mobile Oil Italiana, a subsidiary of Mobil Oil, paid an average of $534,000 a year to political parties in Italy during 1970–1975. The Northrop Corporation admitted to spending $450,000 in 1975 to bribe the Minister of Aviation in Saudi Arabia in hopes of selling its products there.[83] The full extent of Northrop's involvement in these activities was carefully hidden from the Senate investigation. Senator Church pointed out:

> The documents show payments made by Northrop to agents and business partners in a way that would permit the company to disclaim knowledge or responsibility for the uses to which it was put. . . . We are shown military officers of the highest rank and members of parliament of foreign governments on the Northrop payroll as "consultants" under arrangements which permitted them to keep their Northrop connection concealed.[84]

ITT and Chile. The record of unsavory business practices by certain companies operating in foreign countries is extensive, yet none compares to the involvement by International Telephone and Telegraph (ITT) in 1970–1971 in Chile. Even before Salvador Allende, an avowed Marxist, was elected president of Chile ITT was concerned that if the conservative party lost the election, foreign capital would be seized and ITT profits would be threatened. In putting their case to Henry Kissinger, national security adviser to President Nixon, however, ITT officials stressed other concerns: ". . . a communist-dominated Chile in the Southern cone of the hemisphere in tandem with Communist Cuba in the north at our doorstep represents a new critical challenge to the national security and interest of the United States."[85] ITT had a plan to undermine Allende's government through the concerted efforts of various businesses, banks, and the U.S. government; among its plans were the following objectives:[86]

1. Restrict loans to Chile by such international banks as the Export-Import Bank; have private banks in the United States do the same. Confer with foreign banking institutions toward the same objective.
2. Delay buying commodities from Chile during the next six months, bringing about a scarcity of U.S. dollars there.
3. Delay shipments of fuel to Chile's navy and gasoline to its air force; U.S. manufacturers stop or delay any shipments of small arms and ammunition to Chile.
4. Terminate U.S. aid to Chile now in "pipeline," amounting to about $1 million per month; rescind Inter-American Development Bank aid in "pipeline" for Chile's earthquake emergency fund.
5. Close U.S. markets to Chile's exports, annually valued at $154 million.
6. Consult with other foreign governments adversely affected by the Allende regime, including those to which Chile is indebted.

In an attempt to gain support for these measures from other American businesses and banks, ITT organized an ad hoc committee on Chile. Companies invited to participate in these deliberations included Anaconda, W. R. Grace, Ralston Purina, Kennecott Copper, Bank of America, and Pfizer Chemicals. Several meetings were held during 1971, and ITT believed that if all the companies would agree on a strategy they could pressure the State Department and the CIA to support their objectives. Ultimately, however, no other corporation or bank agreed to join ITT in this venture, so that the full impact of those plans was never felt in Chile. Nonetheless, ITT's efforts proceeded without support from other American businesses.

Prior to Allende's election, ITT agreed to make a substantial election contribution to conservative presidential candidate Jorge Alessandri Rodriquez. This proposal was made to William V. Broe, CIA's head of clandestine activities in the western hemisphere in July 1970, but the CIA rejected the idea. In September 1970, a substantial grant of $1 million was offered to the State Department, National Security Adviser Kissinger, and to the CIA if any of them would develop a plan to protect American private investment in Chile. That money could be used, ITT reasoned, to unify opposition to Allende and help prevent his election, to bring about economic turmoil in the country, or, as Senator Church surmised, to "... promote a military coup d'etat in a foreign land to thwart the results of an election."[87]

Although the CIA disapproved the ITT proposal, it did provide an alternative strategy to interfere with Allende's election by creating economic disruption in Chile, influencing Chile's congressional elections, and urging Christian Democratic representatives to withdraw support from Allende. ITT disagreed with this CIA plan, thinking it unworkable.

Although U.S. foreign policy was not changed because of the ITT–CIA collaborations, nor was there a conspiracy of American multinational corporations to undermine Allende's position, one cannot ignore the serious implications of ITT's proposals. In the first place, the entire ITT–CIA scheme proceeded without the knowledge of the State Department, the president, or other major policymakers responsible for foreign policy. Moreover, ITT's clandestine planning shows how difficult it would be for the president to control such intrigues by American companies doing business in foreign countries.

If ITT had accepted the CIA proposal and the other companies had joined the ITT–CIA partnership to create economic havoc in Chile, the consequences for United States foreign policy would have been disastrous. A wave of anti-Americanism throughout Latin America would have resulted and the president's diplomatic options in the western hemisphere would have been severely limited. Indeed, ITT officials were warned by a political journalist from Chile that, should they try to support the Alessandri faction and the Christian Democrats in the Chilean elections, that action could result in a civil war or at the very least in serious bloodshed. Another consequence of such intervention could have been Allende's conversion to a hard-line communist position.[88]

The ITT case shows that the president cannot easily apply sanctions on multinational corporations without violating the sovereignty of other nations. Meanwhile, borders do not prevent the multinational corporations from using a country's economic resources for political purposes. As one White House aide observed, "The multinationals can orchestrate pressure on foreign governments because of this network of relationships. . . . It certainly is extensive."[89]

Ethnic groups. When the United States undertakes foreign policies that threaten the interests of countries from which some Americans have emigrated, certain ethnic groups can be expected to lobby the president and Congress. For example, in his study of legislative voting on foreign aid bills throughout the 1950s, Rieselbach found that Catholics generally were more supportive of foreign aid than were Protestants.[90] He speculated that this behavior was related to the fact that many U.S. Catholics had emigrated from Eastern Europe, which had faced economic hardship in the postwar period. By voting for foreign aid the Catholic congressmen intended to help those nations with which they held an ethnic identification. In recent years, however, the most active ethnic lobbies have been the Jewish and the Greek communities in the United States.

The efforts of the American Jewish community in behalf of Israel are long standing, but they have received greater media attention in the 1970s given concerns about Middle East peace and the problem of maintaining a supply of oil from the Arab states in that region. In terms of the Jewish–Arab conflict in the Middle East, however, the strength of the Arab lobby in the United States is simply no match for the resources available to the Jewish community.[91] Consequently, the Arab countries of the Middle East typically lobby Congress directly for military sales, whereas Israel refrains from such activities and relies on the American Jewish community to promote its interests indirectly. Founded in 1951, the American Israel Public Affairs Committee (AIPAC) has been called "the most effective citizen-ethnic lobby" in America.[92] Supported by only 11,000 dues-paying members and operating on a modest budget of about one million dollars a year, AIPAC speaks for all major Jewish organizations in this country. Its role is to represent the Jewish community on issues directly affecting Israel. AIPAC is effective because its professional staff provides well-documented, expert opinion on issues of Israeli concern; it is also able to mobilize grass-roots opinion behind its objectives. A majority of Americans have tremendous sympathy for Israel in its dealings with the Arab states. During the 1970s AIPAC was extremely active, although it was not successful in every lobbying effort.

In 1973–1974 the National Conference on Soviet Jewry, an umbrella organization of Jewish groups, organized a grass-roots lobbying effort supporting the Jackson-Vanik Amendment. The amendment tied U.S. trade concessions for the Soviet Union to its allowing more Jewish emigration from Russia. President Gerald Ford opposed this approach, and eventually the Soviets—who originally had promised to ease their restrictions on emigration—reneged because of Congress' overt pressure tactics. Another important issue involved the matter of trying to prohibit American firms from cooperating with the Arab League's boycott of Israel. In establishing its boycott, the Arab League required firms doing business with them not to subcontract with companies that refused to honor the Arab boycott. In 1976 the American Jewish Congress and the Anti-Defamation League of B'nai B'rith lobbied both the House of Representatives and the Senate to enact legislation making it a crime to participate in such secondary and tertiary boycotts. The Ford administration opposed this bill, and it failed to pass in the final hours of the 94th Congress. This question was renewed in 1977, during the Carter administration. Although President Carter denounced the Arab boycott during the 1976 presidential campaign, his administration could not draft an acceptable policy on this problem. Therefore, both the Congress and the president were content to allow the Jewish groups and the business interests negotiate the matter. Eventually the Jewish and business groups' compromise agreement was incorporated into legislation, which was approved by Congress.

The influence of Jewish lobbyists also frustrated President Reagan when he proposed to sell five AWACS radar planes to Saudi Arabia in 1981. These aircraft were designed to strengthen the force of sixty F-15 fighters that President Carter had sold to Saudi Arabia in 1978. Opposition in Congress was strong even before Reagan announced the proposed sale. The 1974 Arms Export Control Act allowed a majority of the House and Senate (by concurrent resolution) to disapprove any arms sale within thirty days of the notice of that agreement. Thus far, no arms sale by the president had been stopped, but Reagan's AWACS deal came close to being vetoed by Congress. AIPAC actively lobbied against the sale. The AIPAC director was instrumental in getting 54 senators and 224 representatives to sign a petition opposing the arms sale, and that letter was sent to President Reagan on June 24, 1981.[93] The opposition raised two arguments against Reagan's proposal: they feared that Israel's position in the Middle East would be jeopardized and that this military technology would not be secure given the political instability of nations such as Saudi Arabia.

The House of Representatives passed a resolution disapproving the sale (H. Con. Res. 194), which was cosponsored by fifty senators. President Reagan countered the resolution by arguing that disapproving the sale would jeopardize U.S. relations with Saudi Arabia and, furthermore, would weaken the president's leadership position. Reagan's appeal to party loyalty was especially effective in the Senate, where eight first-term senators (seven of them Republicans) changed their position to support the president. The *Wall Street Journal* indicated that political favors were swapped by the administration for support for Reagan's position; for example, Senator DeConcini (D.–Ariz.) was told by White House aides that President Reagan would not campaign against him in 1982 if he supported the AWACS deal.[94] In the end, the Senate rejected the House resolution 48 to 52, but this vote was not decided on the strength of the Arab lobby in Washington. Rather, the victory required a massive commitment by President Reagan; the AWACS vote was judged to be a "major test of his authority in foreign policy."[95] The victory was not without a price. I. M. Destler, director of the Carnegie Endowment Project on Executive–Congressional Relations in the Middle East, commented that "because of the failure to be sensitive to the politics of this issue, [Reagan] dug himself an enormous hole, and was only able to dig out of it with great effort and at a considerable cost."[96]

The Greek-American lobby was most articulate in 1974, after Turkey invaded the island of Cyprus. That aggression prompted Greek-American organizations to urge Congress to end U.S. arms shipments to Turkey. An embargo was imposed by Congress against the advice of President Ford and the leadership of both parties in Congress. This action resulted from the lobbying campaign orchestrated by Father Evagorus Constantinides and a very small number of congressmen of Greek nationality. Added leverage was gained because Constantinides resided in the district of Rep. Ray Madden (D.–Ind.), then chairman of the House Rules Committee. The American Hellenic Institute was established three days after the second Turkish offensive in Cyprus; its lobbying arm—the American Hellenic Institute Public Affairs Committee—mobilizes grass-roots pressure on Congress every time a president suggests lifting that embargo. Eventually, in August 1978, Congress did repeal the arms embargo to Turkey.

To summarize, foreign policy generally is less affected by interest group lobbying except in cases in which trade relations, international finance, and ethnic homeland interests are affected. One would expect, however, to see an increase in lobbying by special interests in foreign affairs in the future, should Congress take a more active role in these issues. The Jewish–Arab confrontation, in particular, allows Congress to exert more influence over U.S. foreign policy in the Middle East, precisely because organized interests are so actively involved in that issue.

EXPERTISE

One of the chief diplomat's major advantages when dealing with outsiders, whether Congress or the public, is his control over information affecting foreign policy. The president's authority to maintain the confidentiality of such data is related partly to statute; the Federal Register Act of 1935 and the Administrative Procedures Act of 1946 have provisions for withholding information from public scrutiny. Until 1958, the executive relied on various laws enacted between 1789 and 1872 (known collectively as the "housekeeping statutes"), intended to regulate the use of government documents. Even the Freedom of Information Act (1966) exempted documents "specifically required by executive order to be kept secret in the interest of national defense or foreign policy"; this loophole has been upheld by the Supreme Court.[97] In addition, presidents use executive orders to implement classification systems. The modern system began with President Roosevelt, who classified War and Navy Department information as "secret," "confidential," and "restricted." After World War II Truman extended the system to all agencies, nonmilitary and military alike. By 1953, when Eisenhower created the Interagency Committee on Internal Security to monitor the system he limited the number of agencies with classifying authority to forty-seven and the number of officials involved to about 1.5 million.

Beyond this, classification systems are used by the president's staff to prevent information from being obtained by other agencies of government as well as Congress and media. These procedures have evolved so that even Congress does not know which materials are being classified or at what level. During a 1964 Senate Foreign Relations Committee hearing, Secretary of Defense Robert McNamara refused to testify on certain matters because not all the committee's staff had been given the necessary clearance. He further admitted that perhaps twenty-five different clearances existed above the "top-secret" classification.[98]

The president sometimes institutes classification plans in order to prevent his own departments from knowing about his foreign policy initiatives. For example, John F. Kennedy in 1963 used such methods to communicate directly with Averill Harriman who was negotiating a test-ban treaty with the Soviet Union. Only six persons in the Kennedy administration had access to that information so that those delicate negotiations would not be revealed to the Department of Defense or to the Joint Chiefs of Staff.[99]

Executive privilege

The president's monopoly over information sources can be safeguarded by the doctrine of "executive privilege." When that doctrine is invoked, the president can deny to Congress either information or testimony by his subordinates. During the Vietnam War years (1964–1973) the Senate Committee on the Judiciary documented numerous occasions when this doctrine was used by the executive to withhold materials from the legislative branch. Precedent for this doctrine, as was noted, can be traced to George Washington's refusal to give the House of Representatives papers on the Jay Treaty negotiations; similar actions were taken by Presidents John Adams, Jefferson, Monroe, Jackson, and James Buchanan. Executive privilege usually was applied to information affecting military or foreign policy, but nowadays it has been extended to all kinds of interagency communications, records, files, reports, and to the advice given a president by his staff.

The practice of executive privilege was institutionalized by President Taft's Executive Order 1062, but only rarely did the president deny information to the Congress during the period before World War II. The claim of executive privilege in its broadest scope is credited to Dwight Eisenhower, who refused to give personnel records of military officers to Sen. Joseph McCarthy. President Eisenhower defended his prerogative in this area, and the Congress as well as the judiciary—sympathetic to his efforts to resist McCarthy— never challenged his broad interpretation of executive privilege. Presidents Kennedy and Johnson did not exploit this doctrine for political advantage, and it did not become an issue dividing the Congress and the president during their terms. But Richard Nixon, who claimed an absolute right to deny information to Congress, brought this matter to a political climax during the revelations about Watergate.

In the case of *United States v. Nixon* (1973), although the Supreme Court required President Nixon to release the Watergate tapes, it also upheld the legality of executive privilege. Professor Arthur Miller explains: "the Court unanimously recognized a 'presumptive privilege' for presidential communications, asserting that such a privilege 'is fundamental to the operation of government and inextricably rooted in the separation of powers under the Constitution.' "[100] In this case, Chief Justice Warren Burger suggested that Nixon's defense of executive privilege had been weakened because he did not make a justification based on national security needs. Burger said, "When the privilege depends solely on the broad, undifferentiated claim of public interest in the confidentiality of such conversations, a confrontation with other values arises. Absent a claim of need to protect military, diplomatic or sensitive national security secrets, we find it difficult to accept the argument."[101]

Problems of legislative oversight

Congress' ability to monitor foreign affairs is frustrated by its lack of information and expertise in such matters. Moreover, many legislators are not very interested in such issues, as the 1975 Murphy Commission on the Organization of the Government for the Conduct of Foreign Policy observed.

> Congress does not have the information, and some congressmen do not have the understanding, sophistication, and interest to support independent judgment. Inevitably, then, Congress is compelled to accept the grand design, the general direction, the mood of presidential foreign policy.[102]

On the other hand, the Department of State wants to protect its autonomy and resists Congress' overtures in foreign policymaking. According to Rep. Patsy T. Mink (D.–Hawaii), foreign service officers view Congress' interest in foreign policy as being tainted by public opinion: "Thus, Congress is believed to reflect an amateurish, uninterested, unschooled, and mildly xenophobic middle America, to hold in the lowest possible regard anything 'foreign' and to believe that State regularly plots to give away what rightfully belongs to the American people."[103] While the generalization is not entirely accurate, Mink suggests that the main effect of such stereotypes is to persuade the State Department that "Congress should have no active role in foreign policy and that Congress cannot be trusted with highly sensitive information."[104]

In most cases, the executive can obstruct Congress' oversight functions without having to invoke the doctrine of executive privilege. There are many strategies agencies can use to avoid or minimize the need to supply privileged information to Congress.[105] For example, agencies can delay responding to Congress' information requests for several months, and sometimes for an entire year. Moreover, no agency will provide comprehensive information for a congressional inquiry unless a "memorandum of understanding" (MOU) is agreed on; it establishes a procedure under which classified data will be supplied to the congressional committees and outlines the extent of any public disclosure. In addition, the "third agency rule"—a National Security Council directive affecting the disclosure of intelligence information—prohibits one agency from providing materials that originated in another agency without obtaining the consent of that agency first. But however much these tactics frustrate Congress' oversight function, the major obstacle is a political consideration. According to Michael Glennon, public opinion may not support a serious investigation of the executive by the legislature for fear that important government activities, such as intelligence operations, may be impaired. He states:

> The sensitivity, or vulnerability, of Congress to every change in the political climate poses the principal obstacle to effective legislative oversight. To a large extent, legislative action and inaction should reflect the popular will. But this is likely to mean that legislative committees responsible for various intelligence oversight functions normally will be only as vigorous as the popular will allows.

. . . in periods of relative public indifference, a subpoena will simply not be issued by the committee when the executive refuses to reveal a significant document.[106]

The fact of the matter is that very few conflicts between the president and Congress involve access to privileged or secret information. Most requests by committees of Congress are routine and are answered by the agencies. This tradition of executive/legislative cooperation, however, should not obscure the importance of the president's ability to use "executive privilege" to guard his information sources. According to George Calhoun's assessment, based on the reasoning by a circuit court of appeals in *Senate Select Committee* v. *Nixon* (1974), "congressional requests for information, in the face of an assertion of executive privilege, are not as 'strong' as those of the judiciary in a criminal proceeding or of a grand jury. In the former, the privilege can prevail; in the latter, it will usually fail."[107] For this reason, Calhoun doubts that Congress will be eager to challenge the doctrine of executive privilege in the courts.

Apart from Congress' difficulties in exercising oversight in foreign affairs is its more serious problem of trying to monitor the president's diplomatic initiatives as they occur. For example, after Egypt and Israel signed the second Sinai disengagement agreement, Congress learned that Secretary of State Henry Kissinger had made commitments to both parties which, though secret, involved the United States. Section 10 of Secret Agreement E stated that, should Israel be faced with a security threat, the United States would "consult promptly with the Government of Israel with respect to what support, diplomatic or otherwise, or assistance it can lend to Israel in accordance with its constitutional practices."[108] In like fashion, although the Panama Canal Treaties took thirteen years to negotiate, Congress was never informed about the negotiations so that it could not interfere in that delicate process. When the U.S. negotiators finally briefed the Senate Foreign Relations Committee in 1977, the Panama Canal Treaties had been finalized.

Congress does not have an easy task trying to penetrate the secrecy that surrounds high-level diplomatic negotiations, a primary reason why legislators can exercise oversight only after the fact. In recent years, however, Congress has tried to improve its capacity for legislative oversight. These attempts are manifested in the growth of its professional staff, a development suggesting that Congress itself has become a minibureaucracy as extensive as the executive branch. There are now more than 17,000 staff members assigned to Congress; the number is more than 23,000 if one includes the General Accounting Office, Congressional Research Service, Office of Technology Assessment, and the Congressional Budget Office. Today the number of staff available to Congress exceeds the number of employees in the Department of State.

An organizational problem that reduces Congress' ability to oversee foreign affairs is its fragmented committee system. Neither the House of Representatives Committee on Foreign Affairs nor the Senate Committee on Foreign Relations have comprehensive jurisdiction in this area. In the House of Representatives, for example, foreign trade is under the jurisdiction of the Ways and Means Committee; valuation of the dollar is given to the Committee on Banking, Currency, and Housing; matters affecting shipping, fisheries, and the Panama Canal are under the Committee on Merchant Marine and Fisheries; and U.S. membership in international organizations is controlled by the Committee on Government Operations. Even more complicated is the financial responsibility for such programs. Foreign aid appropriations must be considered by the House and Senate budget committees, the House Foreign Affairs and the Senate Foreign Relations committees, and the relevant subcommittees of the House and Senate appropriations committees.

Problems of assuring coordination in foreign policymaking are further compounded by the fact that all standing committees may not have the same viewpoint on foreign affairs. Committees may be dominated by "hawks" or "doves," liberals or conservatives, and internationalists or isolationists. Moreover, foreign policy areas that affect domestic interests, such as trade relations, may prompt congressmen to be more attuned to the needs of special interests rather than to the national interest. Although Franck and Weisband welcome Congress' attempt to regain influence over foreign affairs, they express great concern about these problems:

> It is at least paradoxical, and also probably dangerous to the national interest, that at the very time Congress has taken to itself so large a share of responsibility for the conduct of foreign affairs, it should be scattering substantial, even crucial, bits and pieces of that responsibility among committees established for quite different purposes and holding other perspectives.[109]

This fragmented responsibility is precisely the reason so many scholars, before Vietnam, were concerned about Congress' involvement in foreign affairs. The fact that Congress has strengthened its staff capability and has achieved greater expertise in foreign policy does not in itself ameliorate the effects of politics on the legislative process. Politics simply receives more impact in that area because of the way in which Congress is organized.

CRISIS

During international crises, interest groups enjoy little, if any, influence in the decision-making process. As already observed, crises tend to rally public opinion behind the president's leadership in foreign affairs. More significant is the qualitative change in executive/legislative relations during foreign crises, which greatly reduces Congress' influence in foreign policymaking. In our framework of analysis (see figure 1-1), we argued that foreign policy is normally controlled by the president, his advisers, and Congress—given its constitutional role. When the president confronts a crisis in foreign affairs the pattern of decision making is analogous to that exhibited by the commander-in-chief: only the president and his key advisers are privy to those decisions. Evidence for this interpretation is provided by scholars who analyze case studies of decision making in different policy areas.

Drawing on Lowi's functional approach to policymaking, various political scientists differentiate three types of foreign policy issues.[110] As an example of pork-barrel foreign policy, Ripley and Franklin cite the Food for Peace Program which, since its enactment in 1954, mainly has been used to reduce surpluses of our farm commodities. In this case, the important decision makers are the Foreign Agricultural Service (Department of Agriculture), the relevant subcommittees of the House and Senate agriculture committees, and the farmer and merchant shipping interests. In "regulatory" foreign policy the objective is to influence the strategic relationships between the United States and other countries. Examples include U.S. trade relations with the Soviet Union and the matter of ending foreign aid to Turkey in 1974 because it invaded Cyprus. Such regulatory foreign policies generate serious debate in Congress, and the legislative branch may be expected to modify the president's proposals.

On the other hand, Ripley and Franklin argue that "crisis" decisions in foreign affairs are a third category because the decision-making process is greatly simplified. Crises are handled by

> the President and whomever he chooses to consult. Mostly he will choose to consult only a few of his top advisors; sometimes he will bring in leading individual members of Congress or occasionally "peak association" leaders. The issues are defined quickly, debated in private by the executive actors, and responded to quickly in a highly centralized fashion through executive (presidential) action. Of course, the decisions may provoke considerable public debate after they are announced.[111]

This pattern is illustrated by a subcategory of foreign policy decisions analyzed during the periods 1930–1961 and 1962–1980 (see table 6-3). In his study, James Robinson differentiated between seven foreign or military policy decisions that involved the potential for *violence* and those that did not. Violence was a factor in building the A-bomb, Lend-Lease, Berlin Airlift, Korean War decision, Indochina in 1954, Formosan resolution (1955), and the Bay of Pigs invasion. His data show, moreover, that the executive both initiated and had predominant influence in all of these cases except one; this proportion is *higher* than what Robinson found for his entire sample of twenty-two cases. In the one exception, when Congress held the predominant influence rather than the president, President Eisenhower had consulted with congressional leaders when the French requested U.S. military assistance to relieve their embattled garrison at Dienbienphu in Indochina in 1954. Eisenhower decided against sending aid.

During 1962–1980 we determined that nine decisions had a potential for violence: Cuban missile crisis (1962); Gulf of Tonkin Resolution (1964); Dominican intervention (1965); first Hanoi bombing (1966); Vietnam Peace Talks begin (1968); sending troops into Cambodia (1970); ending the Vietnam War (1973); seizure of the *Mayaguez* (1975); and the Iran hostage rescue attempt (1980). Again, in every case but one (ending the Vietnam War) the executive initiated the decision and had the predominant influence. This percentage is also higher than that found for our entire sample of twenty-four cases. Thus, crisis decisions tend to further consolidate power in the hands of the president. As shown in these examples, a major reason for this concentration of power is that international crises very often involve the potential for violence.

Panama Canal treaties

The nature of executive/legislative relations in the Panama Canal Treaties is shown in table 6-2. (See page 311 for excerpts from the treaties.) The executive initiated the process of renegotiating the treaties, and he predominated in this decision mainly because the Senate did eventually ratify those agreements. Legislative involvement was high; President Carter was forced to accept Senate amendments to the treaties. In this instance, Congress' leverage was based on its formal role in the decision-making process. Thirteen years passed between the time that negotiations with the Republic of Panama opened and the time that the treaties were signed, and no real threat of violence surrounded the deliberations, despite President Carter's urgent appeals that Congress quickly approve those agreements. The renegotiation of the Panama Canal Treaties was controversial and attracted both opposition and public dispute.[112]

Relations between the Republic of Panama and the United States have been strained ever since 1903, when the first treaty giving control over the Panama Canal to the United States was signed. By the Hay–Buneau-Varilla Treaty of November 18, 1903, the United States secured possession of a ten-mile-wide strip of land (the Canal Zone) to construct, operate, and maintain a canal through Panama. The canal's operation was to conform to an earlier treaty between the United States and Great Britain—the Hay-Pauncefote Treaty of 1901—which guaranteed that the canal would be "free and open to the vessels of commerce and of war of all nations observing these Rules, on terms of entire equality, so that there shall be no discrimination against any such nation, or its citizens or subjects, in respect of the conditions or charges of traffic, or otherwise. Such conditions or charges of traffic shall be just and equitable." In return for the land acquired from Panama, the United States agreed to pay Panama $10 million in addition to $250,000 annually, to begin in 1913; this annual fee has been increased on several occasions until it reached $1.93 million yearly after 1955.

Talks aimed at renegotiating this agreement between the United States and Panama began as early as 1964, after rioting erupted in the Canal Zone. In 1967 President Johnson indicated that three different treaties had been negotiated and written, one of which established a binational commission to control the Canal Zone. Strong opposition in Congress prevented approval of these measures. Negotiations were reopened in 1970, 1973, and 1974. Substantive progress developed in these talks after Secretary of State Henry Kissinger in 1974 agreed to "Eight Principles" with Panama. One of these principles declared that the United States intended to transfer control over the canal and the Canal Zone to the Republic of Panama. When Jimmy Carter became president, he named Sol Linowitz and Ellsworth Bunker as treaty negotiators. No senators were on the negotiating team, despite the fact that in 1975, thirty-one senators had voted for Senate Resolution 97 opposing any transfer of sovereignty over the canal to Panama. The treaty negotiations followed customary practice insofar as the Senate was not consulted prior to ratification, at which time President Carter tried to rally the necessary two-thirds votes for approval. Given the controversial nature of these treaties, this strategy was no minor error by the Carter administration. Moreover, the tactic led to differences of interpretation among members of the Senate, Panama, and the Carter administration regarding the treaty language.

Two new treaties finally were signed on September 7, 1977, a major achievement of the Carter administration. Both were controversial, but the one that attracted most opposition was the Treaty Concerning the Permanent Neutrality and Operation of the Panama Canal; it provided that the canal would be permanently neutral and would remain open to all vessels on an equal basis both in times of peace and war. The United States would have priority in times of an emergency insofar as its ships would go through the canal ahead of other nations' vessels. The treaty also gave the United States and Panama the right to maintain its neutrality until 1999, after which Panama would have the primary responsibility for operating and protecting the canal. In defending this provision, President Carter argued that, should the United Sates have to intervene in Panama after the year 2000 to protect the canal, such action would occur with the endorsement of Panama as well as the forty or fifty nations that agreed to uphold the neutrality of the canal. This method of intervention, according to President Carter, would give "legitimacy and an endorsement of the rest of the world to do what we want in the first place to keep the Canal open, well managed, and to meet the security needs, the trade needs of our own country."[113]

The other treaty—the Panama Canal Treaty—guaranteed the right of the United States to operate and manage as well as defend the canal until December 31, 1999, when Panama would assume complete control over it. Until that date canal operations are to be managed by a Panama Canal Commission, having five U.S. and four Panamanian members; the administrator must be a U.S. citizen. The treaty also prohibited either nation from constructing a new waterway without the consent of both countries. Finally, it guaranteed that Panama would be paid some $10 million annually from canal revenues, plus additional amounts not to exceed $10 million should operating revenues exceed yearly expenses.

President Carter had a difficult task trying to convince the Senate to ratify these agreements. He also had to persuade the House of Representatives to support them. Though the House usually is not involved in the treaty-making process, conservative congressmen quoted Article IV, Section 3, Clause 2 of the Constitution regarding the House's responsibility in dis-

posing of U.S. property. Other congressmen favored the House's partici-
pation based on Article I, Section 9, Clause 7, which gives the House of
Representatives control over funding and appropriations. The Panama Canal
Commission required funding each year from the Congress.

The Panama Canal Treaties prompted an outcry from certain segments
of the population. Opposition to the canal "give-away" mobilized a coalition
of conservative groups, known as the Emergency Coalition to Save the
Panama Canal. It included such organizations as the American Conservative Union, the American Legion, the Conservative Caucus, Young Republicans, the National Conservative Political Action Committee, Citizens for
the Republic, the American Security Council, Young Americans for Freedom, Veterans of Foreign Wars, and the Committee for the Survival of a
Free Congress. The treaty opponents used a direct mail campaign, television advertisements and documentaries, and radio announcements to
mobilize public opinion. Richard Viguerie—the well-known direct mailer
for conservative causes—estimated that between five and ten million letters
were mailed by his organization by the Spring of 1978.[114] Senators and
representatives opposed to the treaties were organized by Sen. Paul Laxalt
(R.–Nev.) and Rep. Philip Crane (R.–Ill.). About twenty legislators formed
"truth squads" to educate the public and to encourage them to pressure
uncommitted Congressmen to vote against these treaties.

On the pro-treaty side were the U.S. Chamber of Commerce, the AFL-
CIO's Committee on Political Education, and the American Institute of Mer-
chant Shipping, as well as actor John Wayne, who was a personal friend of
Panamanian General Omar Torrijos. The Committee for Ratification of the
Panama Canal Treaties included various liberal groups, such as the Americans for Democratic Action, the United Auto Workers, and the Democratic
National Committee. In addition, a leading ad hoc organization supporting
the treaties had as members such prominent persons as George Meany,
Lady Bird Johnson, former President Gerald Ford, Averill Harriman, and
former Senate Minority Party Leader Hugh Scott (R.–Penn.). The Carter
administration sent spokesmen throughout the country to encourage approval
of the treaties. Officials from the State Department made about eight hundred
speaking engagements, appearing on television talk shows and giving
interviews. President Carter gave a "fireside chat" in support of the treaties,
and Secretary of State Vance, Vice-President Walter Mondale, and Secretary
of Defense Harold Brown all made formal speeches on this issue. To persuade opinion leaders across the nation, a White House Conference was
called in January 1978: writers, educators, and public officials from twenty-
five states came to hear briefings on the Panama Canal Treaties by President
Carter, National Security Adviser Brzezinski, and General George S. Brown
of the Joint Chiefs of Staff.

Given the ideological nature of the debate over these treaties, those senators who eventually supported the president probably did so based upon
their perception of the national interest. Not only were the treaties strongly
opposed by conservatives, but they were unpopular with the general pub-

lic. In the Senate, conflict focused on the ambiguous language of the treaties, which was interpreted in different ways by the Carter administration,
the Senate, and Panama. With regard to Article VI of the "neutrality" treaty,
the secretary of state told the Senate Foreign Relations Committee that its
language allowed the United States to guarantee the canal's neutrality after
the year 2000, but Panamanian negotiators said that, under this provision,
the United States had no right to intervene militarily there. To resolve this
dispute, President Carter and General Torrijos met on October 14, 1977,
and issued a Joint Statement of Understanding to clarify U.S. rights pertaining to the defense of the canal. The Foreign Relations Committee recommended that this Carter–Torrijos statement be included in the treaty
document. It was added as the so-called leadership amendments sponsored
by Majority Party Leader Robert Byrd (D.–W.Va.) and Minority Party Leader
Howard Baker (R.–Tenn.).

In addition to those changes, the Senate added other conditions, reservations, and understandings to the Panama Canal Treaties. The most serious challenge to President Carter's leadership came from Arizona's freshman Democratic senator, Dennis DeConcini. Should the canal be closed or
its operations interfered with, the "DeConcini Reservation" allowed the
United States to take whatever action it deemed necessary, including the
use of military force, to reopen the canal or to restore its operations. In the
face of this threat, President Carter became personally involved in the treaty
battle, because he viewed this issue as affecting his prestige. Eventually the
president had to accept the DeConcini Reservation to save the treaty, even
though Torrijos threatened to reject the entire agreement if it were added.
The impact of this proviso was moderated by other language incorporated
in the treaty document. Nonetheless, the problem caused by Senator
DeConcini resulted from a major tactical error by the Carter administration.[115] At first, President Carter had relied on White House aides to win
Senate approval for the treaties, bypassing his party leadership. But, before
concluding the second treaty, which governed the canal until the year 2000,
President Carter allowed the Senate's party leadership to handle DeConcini's
objections. As a result, the treaty was passed without any damaging
amendments.

To get Senate approval of the Panama Canal Treaties required some old
fashioned "log-rolling" on the part of Jimmy Carter. For Georgia's Democratic Senator Herman F. Talmadge, President Carter ended his opposition
to a subsidy program for cotton and grain farmers. To appease DeConcini,
the president announced the purchase of $250 million of surplus copper
for the nation's strategic stockpile. These kinds of political payoffs became
a laughing matter on Capitol Hill; it is said that Republican Senator Robert
Dole joked about holding out his vote for the treaties in exchange for a naval
base in Kansas. In the end Carter prevailed; both Panama Canal Treaties
were approved by one vote more than necessary, 68 to 32. The victory came
at a high price. In Pious's view, President Carter had "bungled his dealings
with the Senate, antagonized Panama and other Latin American nations,

and suffered political damage at home."[116] Conflict over these treaties continued, as opponents worked to undermine those agreements by obstructing the legislation necessary to implement them. Congress failed to authorize funding for the Panama Canal Commission in fiscal years 1980, 1981, and 1982. Finally, Congress included the funding in the budget for fiscal 1983.

Several limits on presidential power were manifested in this case. In considering the Panama Canal Treaties in terms of our framework of analysis, it is clear that President Carter had the "authority" to negotiate those agreements unilaterally. But, in view of the constitutional role of the Senate in the ratification process, Carter should have considered ways to facilitate its passage in Congress. Carter's difficulties were compounded because interest groups, usually unaffected by such matters, became politicized along ideological lines. The strong opposition to the treaties underscored the fact that public opinion was unsympathetic to Carter's proposals. He was unable to exploit presidential expertise and knowledge for political advantage. Not only did the senators, Panama's negotiators, and administration spokesmen disagree about the language of the treaties, but the president's liaison with Congress was handled by his legislative staff, not by specialists in foreign affairs or the party leadership in the Senate. Finally, there was no crisis atmosphere surrounding the treaty deliberations. Though President Carter urged the Senate to act expeditiously to avoid jeopardizing U.S. relations with Panama, the senators delayed. Their delays allowed many opportunities for grandstanding by individual members of Congress.

CONCLUSION

The chief diplomat role is second only to the commander-in-chief in power potential. The constitutional basis for the president's role in foreign diplomacy has been greatly strengthened by precedent and customary practice, as well as by Congress' historic abdication of much responsibility over foreign affairs. Yet no president can ignore the legislature entirely, given its power over the purse. Congress moved to reassert its role in foreign policymaking during the 1970s. Whether Congress' heightened interest in foreign affairs was a temporary reaction to the Vietnam War, encouraged by the relatively passive leadership styles of Presidents Ford and Carter, or a more permanent change in executive/legislative relations cannot yet be determined. Diplomacy was not President Reagan's major focus, and the 97th Congress did not move into that leadership vacuum. In his confrontations with Congress over foreign policy (for example, the AWACS sale to Saudi Arabia), Reagan predominated.

In general, the president tends to dominate in foreign affairs because Congress lacks the capability to limit his foreign policy *initiatives*. Indeed, that is the fundamental source of a president's power; Congress can only react to the chief diplomat's activities and is therefore reduced to making modifications after the fact. In addition, public opinion usually defers to the president's leadership in foreign affairs, especially during an international crisis. It is extremely rare for a presidential election campaign to commit a president to any specific course of action in foreign policy. Compared with domestic policymaking, fewer interest groups lobby in foreign affairs. (One exception to this generalization involves U.S. policy in the Middle East; here real political constraints are imposed on all presidents by lobbyists and their allies in the Congress.)

It is highly improbable that the chief diplomat's preeminence in foreign affairs would be challenged under the following conditions: (1) when the president has explicit legal authority to act; (2) when he monopolizes decision making as well as the requisite information and expertise; (3) when he is unconstrained by interest groups or public opinion; and (4) when he faces a crisis situation. Not every decision in foreign affairs allows a president to exploit all these political resources; thus, foreign policy can become politicized and can lead to the president's defeat on major issues. The sometimes-fragile quality of presidential power in foreign affairs was illustrated by President Carter's mishandling of the Panama Canal Treaties.

PANAMA CANAL TREATIES
(excerpts)

1978 Panama Canal Treaty

The United States of America and the Republic of Panama,

Acting in the spirit of the Joint Declaration of April 3, 1964, by the Representatives of the Governments of the United States of America and the Republic of Panama, and of the Joint Statement of Principles of February 7, 1974, initialed by the Secretary of State of the United States of America and the Foreign Minister of the Republic of Panama, and

Acknowledging the Republic of Panama's sovereignty over its territory,

Have decided to terminate the prior Treaties pertaining to the Panama Canal and to conclude a new Treaty to serve as the basis for a new relationship between them and, accordingly, have agreed upon the following:

Article II
Ratification, entry into force, and termination

1. This Treaty shall be subject to ratification in accordance with the constitutional procedures of the two Parties. The instruments of ratification of this Treaty shall be exchanged at Panama at the same time as the instruments of ratification of the Treaty Concerning the Permanent Neutrality and Operation of the Panama Canal, signed this date, are exchanged. This Treaty shall enter into force, simultaneously with the Treaty Concerning the Permanent Neutrality and Operation of the Panama Canal, six calendar months from the date of the exchange of the instruments of ratification.

2. This Treaty shall terminate at noon, Panama time, December 31, 1999.

Article III
Canal operation and management

3(a) The Panama Canal Commission shall be supervised by a Board composed of nine members, five of whom shall be nationals of the United States of America, and four of whom shall be Panamanian nationals proposed by the Republic of Panama for appointment to such positions by the United States of America in a timely manner . . .

Article IV
Protection and defense

1. The United States of America and the Republic of Panama commit themselves to protect and defend the Panama Canal. Each Party shall act, in accordance with its constitutional processes, to meet the danger resulting from an armed attack or other actions which threaten the security of the Panama Canal or of ships transiting it.

2. For the duration of this Treaty, the United States of America shall have primary responsibility to protect and defend the Canal. The rights of the United States of America to station, train, and move military forces within the Republic of Panama are described in the Agreement in Implementation of this Article, signed this date. The use of areas and installations and the legal status of the armed forces of the United States of America in the Republic of Panama shall be governed by the aforesaid Agreement . . .

Treaty Concerning the Permanent Neutrality and Operation of the Panama Canal

Article IV

The United States of America and the Republic of Panama agree to maintain the regime of neutrality established in this Treaty, which shall be maintained in order that the Canal shall remain permanently neutral, notwithstanding the termination of any other treaties entered into by the two Contracting Parties.

Article V

After the termination of the Panama Canal Treaty, only the Republic of Panama shall operate the Canal and maintain military forces, defense sites and military installations within its national territory.

". . . [I]f the canal is closed, or its operations are interfered with, the United States of America and the Republic of Panama shall each independently have the right to take such steps as it deems necessary, in accordance with its constitutional processes, including the use of military force in Panama, to reopen the Canal or restore the operations of the Canal, as the case may be."
Note: DeConcini Reservation approved by Senate, March 16, 1978

Statement of Understanding signed by President Carter and General Omar Torrijos Herrera on October 14, 1977 (Incorporated into Neutrality Treaty as "Leadership Amendments")

Under the Treaty Concerning the Permanent Neutrality and Operation of the Panama Canal (the Neutrality Treaty), Panama and the United States have the responsibility to assure that the Panama Canal will remain open and secure to ships of all nations. The correct interpretation of this principle is that each of the two countries shall, in accordance with their respective constitutional processes, defend the Canal against any threat to the regime of neutrality, and consequently shall have the right to act against any aggression or threat directed against the Canal or against the peaceful transit of vessels through the Canal.

This does not mean, nor shall it be interpreted as a right of intervention of the United States in the internal affairs of Panama. Any United States action will be directed at insuring that the Canal will remain open, secure and accessible, and it shall never be directed against the territorial integrity or political independence of Panama.

The Neutrality Treaty provides that the vessels of war and auxiliary vessels of the United States and Panama will be entitled to transit the Canal expeditiously. This is intended, and it shall so be interpreted, to assure the transit of such vessels through the Canal as quickly as possible, without any impediment, with expedited treatment, and in case of need or emergency, to go to the head of the line of vessels in order to transit the Canal rapidly.

NOTES

[1] Edward S. Corwin, *The President: Office and Powers*, 4th ed. (New York: New York University Press, 1957), p. 171.

[2] See "Pacificus" Essay no. 1, June 29, 1793, in John. C. Hamilton, ed., *The Works of Alexander Hamilton*, vol. 7 (New York: John F. Trow, 1851), p. 79. Madison's argument as "Helvidius" is discussed in Edward S. Corwin, *The President: Office and Powers*, 4th ed. (New York: New York University Press, 1957), pp. 180–181. The quote by Thomas Jefferson is found in Andrew A. Lipscomb and Albert Ellery Bergh, eds., *The Writings of Thomas Jefferson* (Washington, D.C: Thomas Jefferson Memorial Association, 1905), vol. V, pp. 161–162. John Marshall's quote is cited in Corwin, *The President: Office and Powers*, p. 177.

[3] *United States* v. *Curtiss-Wright Export Corporation*, 299 U.S. 304 (1936).

[4] *U.S.* v. *Belmont*, 57 S.Ct. 758–764, (1937).

[5] Richard M. Pious, *The American Presidency* (New York: Basic Books, 1979), p. 341.

[6] Sidney Warren, *The President as World Leader* (New York: McGraw-Hill, 1964), p. 379.

[7] Senate Resolution 85, *Congressional Record*, 91st Congress, 1st Session, June 25, 1969, p. 17245.

[8] Senate Resolution 469, *Congressional Record*, 91st Congress, 2nd Session, December 11, 1970, p. 41167.

[9] Public Law 92–404.

[10] *Goldwater* v. *Carter*, 444 U.S. 996 (1979).

[11] Corwin, *The President: Office and Powers*, p. 189.

[12] Warren, *The President as World Leader*, p. 333.

[13] Public Law 80–253, Section 101(a).

[14] Tad Szulc, "Dateline Washington: The Vicar Vanquished," *Foreign Policy* (Summer 1981), p. 181.

[15] Quoted in David M. Alpern et al., "The Resignation That Took," *Newsweek* (July 5, 1982), p. 18.

[16] Quoted in Louis W. Koenig, *The Chief Executive*, 3rd ed. (New York: Harcourt Brace Jovanovich, 1975), p. 223.

[17] For an interesting discussion of Vance's personality and diplomatic style see Bernard Gwertzman, "Cyrus Vance Plays It Cool," *New York Times Magazine* (March 18, 1979), p. 32.

[18]Dorothy Buckton James, *The Contemporary Presidency* (New York: Pegasus, 1969), p. 149.

[19]For a critical assessment of Jimmy Carter's choice of top-level diplomats see Roger Morris, "Diplomatic Spoils: The Washington Bureaucracy Abroad," *Harper's Magazine* (November 1978), pp. 69–75.

[20]Quoted in Pious, *The American Presidency*, p. 359.

[21]Ibid., p. 361.

[22]Stanley L. Falk, "The National Security Council under Truman, Eisenhower, and Kennedy," in Aaron Wildavsky, ed., *The Presidency* (Boston: Little, Brown and Company, 1969), p. 673. We rely on Falk's discussion of the NSC in the sections to follow.

[23]Ibid., p. 677.

[24]Ibid., p. 685.

[25]Pious, *The American Presidency*, p. 366.

[26]Robert L. Galluci, *Neither Peace Nor Honor: The Politics of American Military Policy in Vietnam* (Baltimore: Johns Hopkins University Press, 1975), p. 156.

[27]Quoted in Koenig, *The Chief Executive*, 3rd ed., p. 225.

[28]Sam C. Sarkesian, "The President and the National Security Policy Process," unpublished manuscript, Loyola University of Chicago 1982, pp. 12–13. To appear in the forthcoming publication *Defense Policy and the Presidency: The View from the Oval Office*, edited by Sam C. Sarkesian.

[29]Donald E. Neuchterlein, *National Interests and Presidential Leadership: The Setting of Priorities* (Boulder, Colo.: Westview Press, 1978), pp. 130–131.

[30]Sarkesian, "The President and the National Security Policy Process," pp. 14–15.

[31]Quoted in "The 9-to-5 Presidency, Is It Working?" *U.S. News and World Report* (March 23, 1981), p. 30.

[32]Sarkesian, "The President and the National Security Policy Process," p. 19.

[33]Commission on the Organization of the Government for the Conduct of Foreign Policy, *Final Report* (Washington, D.C.: Government Printing Office, 1975), pp. 5–39.

[34]Alexander George, "The Case for Multiple Advocacy in Making Foreign Policy," *American Political Science Review* (September 1972), pp. 751–785.

[35]Ibid., p. 761.

[36]James A. Robinson, *Congress and Foreign Policy-Making* (Homewood, Ill.: The Dorsey Press, 1962), pp. 64–69.

[37]Ibid., p. 192.

[38]Aaron Wildavsky, "The Two Presidencies," *Trans-Action* (December 1966), p. 8. This percentage is calculated from Wildavsky's data on three categories of foreign policy issues.

[39]Lance LeLoup and Steven Shull, "Congress Versus the Executive: The 'Two Presidencies' Reconsidered," *Social Science Quarterly* (March 1979), pp. 707, 710.

[40]James, *The Contemporary Presidency*, p. 147.

[41]Mohammed Ahrari and Andrew D. McNitt, "The Two Presidencies Reconsidered: Is There a Post-Imperial Presidency?" paper delivered at annual meeting, Midwest Political Science Association, 1979. Cited in Charles Funderburk, *Presidents and Politics: The Limits of Power* (Monterey, Calif.: Brooks/Cole, 1982), p. 272.

[42]Warren E. Miller and Donald E. Stokes, "Constituency Influence in Congress," *American Political Science Review* (March 1963), pp. 45–56.

[43]This discussion is based upon the analysis in Thomas M. Franck and Edward Weisband, *Foreign Policy by Congress* (New York: Oxford University Press, 1979), pp. 13–33. This volume details Congress' role in foreign affairs during the 1970s and we rely on its argument throughout the remainder of this chapter.

[44]Ibid., p. 18.

[45]Richard M. Nixon, "RN: The Memoirs of Richard Nixon," *New York Times* (May 3, 1978), p. 10.

[46]U.S. Senate, *Congressional Record* (April 23, 1975), S. 6611.

[47]Cited in Franck and Weisband, *Foreign Policy by Congress*, p. 86.

[48]Ibid., p. 91.

[49]Ibid., p. 6.

[50]LeLoup and Shull, "Congress Versus the Executive: The 'Two Presidencies' Reconsidered," p. 710.

[51]Franck and Weisband, *Foreign Policy by Congress*, p. 57.

[52]See Walter Lippmann, *The Public Philosophy* (Boston: Little, Brown and Company, 1950).

[53]Gabriel Almond, *The American People and Foreign Policy* (New York: Praeger, 1960). Also see William Caspary, "The 'Mood Theory:' A Study of Public Opinion and Foreign Policy," *American Political Science Review* (June 1970) pp. 536–547.

[54]See "Postwar Panic and the Chilling of Dissent," in Theodore J. Lowi, *The Politics of Disorder* (New York: Basic Books, 1971), pp. 102–119.

[55]Robert A. Dahl, *Congress and Foreign Policy* (New York: Harcourt Brace, 1950).

[56]James Rosenau, *Public Opinion and Foreign Policy: An Operational Formulation* (New York: Random House, 1961).

[57]Martin Patchen, "Social Class and Dimensions of Foreign Policy Attitudes," *Social Science Quarterly* (December 1970), pp. 649–667.

[58]Andre Modigliani, "Hawks and Doves, Isolationism and Political Distrust: An Analysis of Public Opinion on Military Policy," *American Political Science Review* (September 1972), pp. 960–978.

[59]Michael Mandelbaum and William Schneider, "The New Internationalism: Public Opinion and American Foreign Policy," in Kenneth Oye; Donald Rothchild; and Robert E. Lieber, eds., *Eagle Entangled: U.S. Policy in a Complex World* (New York: Longman, 1979), pp. 34–98.

[60]Barbara Bardes and Robert Oldendick, "Mass and Elite Foreign Policy Opinions," *Public Opinion Quarterly* (Fall 1982), pp. 368–382.

[61]Ibid.

[62]Erwin C. Hargrove, *The Power of the Modern Presidency* (New York: Alfred A. Knopf, 1974), pp. 114–118.

[63]Ibid., p. 115.

[64]See Angus Campbell; Phillip E. Converse; Warren E. Miller; and Donald E. Stokes, *The American Voter* (New York: John Wiley and Sons, 1964), chapter 2.

[65]Hargrove, *The Power of the Modern Presidency*, p. 117.

[66]This discussion is based on Eugene J. Rosi, "Mass and Attentive Opinion on Nuclear Weapons Tests and Fallout, 1954–1963," in Aaron Wildavsky, ed., *The Presidency*, pp. 244–249.

[67]Ibid., p. 249.

[68]"Sense of the House with Respect to the Falkland Islands," *Congressional Record— House* (May 4, 1982), p. H 1739.

[69]"Opinion Roundup: Reagan's Handling of Foreign Policy," *Public Opinion* (April/ May 1982), pp. 35–36.

[70]Ibid.

[71]John E. Mueller, "Presidential Popularity from Truman to Johnson," *American Political Science Review* (March 1970), pp. 18–34.

[72]Nelson Polsby, *Congress and the Presidency* (Englewood Cliffs, N.J.: Prentice-Hall, 1964), p. 25.

[73]Fred I. Greenstein, "The Psychological Functions of the Presidency for Citizens," in Elmer E. Cornwell, ed., *The American Presidency: Vital Center* (Glenview, Ill.: Scott Foresman and Company, 1966), pp. 35–36.

[74]Hargrove, *The Power of the Modern Presidency*, pp. 110–112.

[75]Richard A. Brody and Benjamin I. Page, "Policy Voting and the Electoral Process: The Vietnam War Issue," *American Political Science Review* (September 1972), p. 994.

[76]Vincent A. Mahler, "The United States and the Third World: Dependence, Inter-dependence and the Political Economy of Sugar," unpublished manuscript, Loyola University of Chicago 1982, pp. 24–25. Forthcoming in W. Ladd Hollist and F. LaMond Tullis, eds., *The Global Political Economy of Agriculture.*

[77]This discussion is drawn from various sources including "A Decade of Grain Embargoes," *National Journal* (September 6, 1980), p. 1484; Robert L. Paarlberg, "Lessons of the Grain Embargo," *Foreign Affairs* (Fall 1980), p. 144; and Elizabeth Wehr, "Major Developments of Grain Embargo," *Congressional Quarterly Weekly Report* (January 12, 1980), p. 58.

[78]Michael R. Gordon, "The Grain Embargo—No Great Impact on Either the Farmers or the Soviets," *National Journal* (September 6, 1980), p. 1480.

[79]Paarlberg, "Lessons of the Grain Embargo," p. 161.

[80]Hearings, July 16, 1975, Before the Subcommittee on Multinational Corporations of the Committee on Foreign Relations, U.S. Senate, 94th Congress, 1st Session, part 12 (Washington, D.C.: U.S. Government Printing Office, 1976), p. 239.

[81]Hearings, February 4, 1976, Before the Subcommittee on Multinational Corporations of the Committee on Foreign Relations, U.S. Senate, 94th Congress, 2nd Session, part 14 (Washington, D.C.: U.S. Government Printing Office, 1976), p. 1.

[82]Hearings, July 16, 1975, Before the Subcommittee on Multinational Corporations of the Committee on Foreign Relations, p. 1.

[83]Hearings, July 17, 1975, ibid., part 12, p. 316.

[84]Hearings, June 9, 1975, ibid., part 12, p. 107.

[85]The Bertrand Russell Peace Foundation, *Subversion in Chile: A Case Study in U.S. Corporate Intrigue in the Third World* (Nottingham, Engl.: Russell Press, Ltd., 1972), p. 14.

[86]Hearings, March-April 1973, Before the Subcommittee on Multinational Corporations of the Committee on Foreign Relations, U.S. Senate, 93rd Congress, part 1 (Washington, D.C.: U.S. Government Printing Office, 1973), pp. 41–42.

[87]Ibid., p. 77.

[88]Report to the Committee on Foreign Relations, U.S. Senate, by the Subcommittee on Multinational Corporations, June 21, 1973, 93rd Congress, 1st Session. (Washington, D.C.: U.S. Government Printing Office, 1973), p. 17.

[89]Quoted in Dan Morgan, "Multinationals Show U.S. Administration the Limits of Its Power," *Manchester Guardian* (September 26, 1982), p. 17.

[90]Leroy N. Rieselbach, "The Demography of the Congressional Vote on Foreign Aid, 1938–1958," *American Political Science Review* (1964), pp. 577–588.

[91]See Sanford J. Ungar, "Washington: Jewish and Arab Lobbyists," *The Atlantic* (March 1978), p. 6.

[92]Franck and Weisband, *Foreign Policy by Congress*, p. 186.

[93]" 'Israel Lobby' Loses AWACS Fight," *Congressional Quarterly Guide to Current American Government* (Washington, D.C.: Congressional Quarterly, 1981), p. 85.

[94]Albert R. Hunt, "Some Senators Say They Were Promised White House Favors to Vote for AWACS," *Wall Street Journal* (October 14, 1981), p. 4.

[95]See Richard Whittle, "Special Report: The AWACS Vote: Senate Supports Reagan on AWACS Sale," *Congressional Quarterly Weekly Report* (October 31, 1981), p. 2095.

[96]Quoted in Bill Keller, "Reagan Team May Draw Key Lessons . . . from Difficult Struggle over AWACS," *Congressional Quarterly Weekly Report* (October 31, 1981), p. 2098.

[97]Public Law 90–23, Section 552(4)(b)(1).

[98]David Wise, *The Politics of Lying* (New York: Random House, 1973), pp. 59–60.

[99]Pious, *The American Presidency*, p. 350.

[100]Arthur S. Miller, *Presidential Power in a Nutshell* (St. Paul, Minn.: West Publishing Company, 1977), p. 269.

[101]*United States v. Nixon*, 418 U.S. 683 (1974).

[102]Louis Henkin, " 'A More Effective System' for Foreign Relations: The Constitutional Framework," Commission on the Organization of the Government for the Conduct of Foreign Policy, *Final Report* (Washington, D.C.: U.S. Government Printing Office, 1975), appendix L, p. 15.

[103]Patsy T. Mink, "Institutional Perspective: Misunderstandings, Myths, and Misperceptions: How Congress and the State Department See Each Other," in Thomas M. Franck, ed., *The Tethered Presidency* (New York: New York University Press, 1981), p. 65.

[104]Ibid., p. 66.

[105]These observations are drawn from the excellent essay by Michael J. Glennon, "Investigating Intelligence Activities: The Process of Getting Information for Congress," in Franck, ed., *The Tethered Presidency*, pp. 141–152.

[106]Ibid., p. 149.

[107]*Senate Select Committee v. Nixon*, George W. Calhoun, "Confidentiality and Executive Privilege," in Franck, ed., *The Tethered Presidency*, p. 187.

[108]U.S. Senate, *Congressional Record*, October 9, 1975, S 17957–17965.

[109]Franck and Weisband, *Foreign Policy Congress*, p. 257.

[110]Theodore J. Lowi applies his policy framework to foreign affairs in "Making Democracy Safe for the World: National Politics," in James N. Rosenau, ed., *Domestic Sources of Policy* (New York: Free Press, 1967), pp. 295–331. Also see Randall B. Ripley and Grace A. Franklin, *Congress, the Bureaucracy, and Public Policy* (Homewood, Ill.: The Dorsey Press, 1976); and William Zimmerman, "Issue Area and Foreign-Policy Process: A Research Note in Search of a General Theory," *American Political Science Review* (December 1973), pp. 1204–1212.

[111]Ripley and Franklin, *Congress, the Bureaucracy and Public Policy*, pp. 143–144.

[112]Our analysis in this section is guided by the discussion found in Franck and Weisband, *Foreign Policy by Congress*, pp. 275–286; Pious, *The American Presidency*, pp. 336–338; Theodor Meron, "The Treaty Power: The International Legal Effect of Changes in Obligations Initiated by the Congress," in Franck, ed., *The Tethered Presidency*, pp. 111–123; and "Panama Canal Treaties Spurred Intense Lobby Effort . . . as Supporters, Opponents Sought Senate Votes," *1978 Congressional Quarterly Almanac* (Washington, D.C.: Congressional Quarterly, Inc., 1979), p. 388.

[113]Jimmy Carter, Question-and-Answer Session, Briefing on the Panama Canal Treaties, October 22, 1977, in Denver, Colorado, in *Weekly Compilation of Presidential Documents*, vol. 13, no. 44 (October 31, 1977), p. 1642.

[114]Franck and Weisband, *Foreign Policy by Congress*, p. 198.

[115]Ibid., p. 281.

[116]Pious, *The American Presidency*, p. 338.

SUGGESTED READINGS

Abshire, David M. *Foreign Policy Makers: President vs. Congress.* Beverly Hills, Calif.: Sage, 1979.

Almond, Gabriel. *The American People and Foreign Policy.* New York: Praeger, 1960.

Cheever, Daniel, and Haviland, H. Field. *American Foreign Policy and the Separation of Powers.* Cambridge: Harvard University Press, 1952.

Dahl, Robert A. *Congress and Foreign Policy.* New York: Harcourt, Brace, 1950.

Destler, I. M. *Presidents, Bureaucrats and Foreign Policy.* Princeton, N.J.: Princeton University Press, 1972.

Franck, Richard and Weisband, Edward, eds. *Secrecy and Foreign Policy.* New York: Oxford University Press, 1974.

Franck, Thomas M., *The Tethered Presidency.* New York: New York University Press, 1981.

George, Alexander. *Presidential Decision-Making in Foreign Policy.* Boulder, Colo.: Westview Press, 1979.

Graber, Doris. *Public Opinion, the President, and Foreign Policy.* New York: Holt, Rinehart and Winston, 1968.

Halperin, Morton. *Bureaucratic Politics and Foreign Policy.* Washington, D.C.: Brookings Institution, 1974.

Henkin, Louis. *Foreign Affairs and the Constitution.* Mineola, Minn.: The Foundation Press, 1972.

Hoxie, R. Gordon. *Command Decision and the Presidency.* New York: Readers Digest Press, 1977.

Neuchterlein, Donald E. *National Interests and Presidential Leadership: The Setting of Priorities.* Boulder, Colo.: Westview Press, 1978.

Robinson, James A. *Congress and Foreign Policy-Making.* Homewood, Ill.: The Dorsey Press, 1962.

Rosenau, James. *Public Opinion and Foreign Policy: An Operational Formulation.* New York: Random House, 1961.

Rourke, Francis E. *Bureaucracy and Foreign Policy.* Baltimore: Johns Hopkins University Press, 1972.

Warren, Sidney. *The President as World Leader.* New York: McGraw-Hill, 1967.

Wilcox, Francis, and Franck, Richard, eds. *The Constitution and the Conduct of Foreign Policy.* New York: Praeger, 1976.

CHAPTER SEVEN

Commander-in-Chief: Can the Constitutional Dictator be Checked?

The commander-in-chief role is the most visible of the president's roles and the one in which most executives have exhibited political strength. The role receives the greatest attention from the media, respect from other institutions of government, and concern from students of democracy, because it poses the greatest potential threat to constitutional government. Although scholars and observers of the presidency may differ in their impressions of the overall office of the president, most acknowledge the power of the commander-in-chief. Richard Rose, in labeling the American president "a chief but not an executive," nevertheless acknowledged that, with regard to national security, the president enjoys a unique position as commander-in-chief, a role in which his authority is "unchallenged."[1] Sidney Hyman notes that a president—almost single-handedly—can plunge us into war, and adds, "the decisions of any President have held this same potential since 1790: the cause lies in the functions the constitution allocates to the presidency."[2]

AUTHORITY

It was not the original Framers' intention that the commander-in-chief be as powerful as it has become. Rather, the commander-in-chief role was to be little more than a military title, of the same sort alluded to in the directive accompanying the military commission given to General George Washington in 1783 by the Continental Congress. This commission stated that Washington was "punctually to observe and follow such orders and directives" as he should receive from the Continental Congress. As defined then, the role was dependent on instructions from the Congress. The intended meaning of the role was similar at the Constitutional Convention of 1788. None of the delegates favored a strong commander-in-chief, which becomes evident when one examines the three plans for government presented to the Convention. The New Jersey Plan, which advocated a plural executive, gave the presidency power to "direct all military operations," but it also made clear that no person in the executive body should ". . . take command of any troops, so as personally to conduct any enterprise as General or in any capacity." The Hamiltonian Plan favored a single lifetime executive but did not give him commander-in-chief powers. Instead, the executive was given authority during his lifetime tenure over the "direction of war when authorized or begun." The Virginia Plan was also careful to limit the powers of the executive to ". . . a general authority to execute the National laws," enjoying ". . . the Executive rights vested in Congress by the Confederation."[3] Again no mention was made of the powers of the commander-in-chief. It was the Anti-Federalists, however, who were most outspoken in their opposition to a strong commander-in-chief. As one Anti-Federalist pointed out:

> Who can deny but the *president general* will be a king to all intents and purposes, and one of the most dangerous kind too—a king elected to command a standing army. Thus our laws are to be administered by this *tyrant*.[4]

It was a limited and restricted sense of power for the commander-in-chief that was written into Article II, Section 2 of the Constitution. The words of the document seem direct: the president was to be "Commander in chief of the army and navy of the United States, and of the militia of the several states, when called into the actual service of the United States." Yet the meaning was ambiguous, for it was not obvious what a commander-in-chief could do in times of war and peace. It was necessary, therefore, for various writers to elaborate on what this power entailed. Among the first to do so were the authors of *The Federalist Papers*, in their arguments encouraging adoption of the Constitution. Alexander Hamilton, long an advocate of presidential power, in *Federalist #69* discussed his reasons for restricting the president's military powers. Hamilton said the executive did not enjoy the unlimited authority of an English king, or even the flexibility of command of a state governor. He stressed that this role was a military command, that the president was the "first general and admiral of the Confederacy." According to Hamilton's argument, the primary war-making powers were to belong to Congress, and the president was to respond only to sudden attacks and emergencies.[5]

Hamilton's view reflected the Framers' experience and familiarity with executive power, which encouraged caution regarding the powers of a commander-in-chief. Their past experiences with English kings and crown-appointed governors made them distrustful of power. Their concern about tyranny and distrust of concentrating power in the hands of any one person prompted the Framers to move very deliberately in formulating Article II. However, the Framers were only the first elites to interpret the meaning of the commander-in-chief clause. This clause became the subject of frequent interpretations by Congress, by the Supreme Court, and most important, by the individual presidents themselves.

How presidents view the commander-in-chief role

Over time the wording of the commander-in-chief clause has become a justification for increasing executive power. While Congress and the Supreme Court have contributed to this expansion of power, presidents themselves have been primarily responsible. Table 7-1 indicates that a majority of military engagements (54.2%) occurred during the administrations of those presidents rated as "average" or "below average," but the "great" and "near-great" presidents have been most instrumental in structuring this role. As commanders-in-chief, Presidents Lincoln, Wilson, Franklin D. Roosevelt, Truman, and Johnson had the most forceful impact on this role.

Prior to the Civil War, the frequent uses of military power by our presidents were very limited in scope. The commander-in-chief powers were used in confrontation with pirates, in dispatching troops to protect civil rights or property, and in pursuing bandits across U.S. borders. Possibilities for major armed conflict seemed remote. The few that occurred included

TABLE 7-1   Undeclared military engagements by U.S. forces, 1798–1972

	Military engagements (N = 199)			
Variable	Number	Percent	Number per year	Number per president
Republican	95	47.7	1.40	6.3
Democratic	74	39.2	1.03	6.1
Other	30	13.1	1.07	3.3
Great	36	18.1	.82	7.2
Near great	41	20.6	1.03	6.8
Average	57	28.6	.95	4.8
Below average	38	19.1	1.00	6.6
Failure	13	5.5	1.63	6.5
Not ranked	14	7.1	1.16	4.6
Presidential dominant	92	52.2	1.00	6.5
Modified Pres. dominant	12			
Congressional dominant	89	46.8	1.27	4.6
Modified Cong. dominant	4			
Not classified	2	1.0	.70	2.0

Sources: The presidents' rankings and the historical eras are from Arthur Schlesinger, "Our Presidents: A Rating by 75 Historians," *New York Times Magazine* (July 29, 1962), p. 12 and Roland Egger, *The President of the United States* (New York: McGraw-Hill, 1972), p. 162. A full explanation of these 199 military engagements can be found in *Congressional Record*, 93rd Congress, 1st Session, July 20, 1973, pp. S 14174–84.

naval battles with France (1798–1800), Jefferson's battles with Tripolitan pirates (1801–1805), hostilities in the Caribbean (1814–1825), the Second Barbary War (1815), and Commodore Perry's expeditions to Japan (1853 and 1854). While this period saw two declared wars—the War of 1812 and the Mexican War (1846–1848)—and twenty-six battles each lasting more than thirty days, compared with the years that followed, these confrontations seem of minor consequence. Yet, the pre–Civil War battles did have an effect on the development of the commander-in-chief role. Some sixty-seven of the documented confrontations during this early period took place without a formal declaration of war.[6] Although thirty-three of these incidents did have a congressional statute or treaty as their source of authority, the others relied exclusively on the authority of the commander-in-chief. It is clear that during this period, presidents did not limit their exercise of commander-in-chief powers. Although many presidents acknowledged that Congress held war-making authority, in only half of these cases was Congress consulted or asked for delegations of authority before military actions were initiated. Thus, from the very beginning our presidents began to broadly interpret the commander-in-chief clause.

Lincoln's interpretation

It was not until Abraham Lincoln and the Civil War period, however, that the full potential of the commander-in-chief role was realized. President Lincoln advocated far greater powers for the president than he had tolerated as a congressman. As president, Lincoln now gave a very broad reading to Article II of the Constitution in meeting the domestic crisis at hand. In retrospect, he undertook numerous actions that might reasonably be interpreted to be unconstitutional. During Lincoln's so-called eleven-week dictatorship, he called up 75,000 troops, blockaded Southern ports, and suspended the writ of habeas corpus "at any point or in the vicinity of any military line which is now or which shall be used between the city of Philadelphia and the city of Washington."[7] Lincoln authorized an increase in the Army of some 22,714 officers and an increase in the Navy of 18,000 personnel, and asked for 42,034 other military volunteers over a three-year period. On his own authority Lincoln demanded a draft for 300,000 militiamen. He also issued the emancipation proclamation freeing slaves in the South; this act brought freedom to many but divested slaveowners of property which heretofore had been protected by both statute and Supreme Court decision. Other actions taken by Lincoln included closing the post office to protect it from handling potentially treasonable correspondence, seizing telegraph lines on several occasions, insisting on stringent passport regulations, adding nineteen ships to the Navy, issuing a military code of conduct, suspending the writ of habeas corpus for insurgents and rebels, establishing military commissions, placing the entire state of Kentucky under martial law, and raiding the treasury of unappropriated moneys of up to two million dollars to pay Union agents. One of Lincoln's final actions as commander-in-chief was to issue a proclamation of amnesty and reconstruction for all people in the South.

Abraham Lincoln acted in these instances by executive proclamation and without legislative authorization. When Congress finally did get an opportunity to assess Lincoln's actions, most of them were supported and a few were simply ignored. Congressmen felt compelled to support the president whether his actions had been legal or not. The important consideration for Congress was that Lincoln's actions were "ventured upon under what appeared to be a popular demand and a public necessity."[8] On August 6, 1861, Congress issued the following resolution:

> All the acts, proclamations and orders of the President, respecting the Army and Navy of the United States, and calling out or relating to the militia or volunteers . . . are hereby approved and in all respects made valid . . . as if they had been issued and done under the previous express authority and direction of Congress of the United States.[9]

Lincoln, while admittedly treading heavily on the Constitution, did so under the assumption that the circumstances of the Civil War required decisive action. To Lincoln, preserving the Constitution was not as important as preserving democracy and the Republic. As he stated: "Are all the laws *but one* to go unexecuted, and the Government itself go to pieces lest that one be violated?"[10] Survival of the Union was the important priority for Lincoln, and the Constitution was simply the means to allow him to achieve that end.

Abraham Lincoln also showed the actions available to a president based on two authoritative clauses in the Constitution. The commander-in-chief clause and the clause granting the president power to "take care that the laws be faithfully executed" allowed Lincoln to meet the Civil War crisis. Edward Corwin argues that, through the combination of these two powers, Lincoln created for the first time what is now known as presidential "war power."[11]

The Supreme Court had few opportunities to test the legality of Lincoln's use of his commander-in-chief authority. Those few cases that reached the Court generally supported broad executive power, while limiting it in specific instances. In 1849, for example, the Supreme Court had declared that the propriety of a president's decision concerning whether a military emergency existed could not be judged by the Court. The opinion stated:

> It is said that this power in the President is dangerous to liberty, and may be abused. All power may be abused if placed in unworthy hands. But it would be difficult, we think, to point out any other hands in which this power would be more safe, and at the same time equally effectual.[12]

One year later the Court's reluctance to question presidential power over military affairs became even clearer in the case of *Fleming* v. *Page*. Here the military power of the commander-chief was thought to be all but complete in times of war. As Justice Taney argued in his opinion:

> As commander-in-chief, he [the President] is authorized to direct the movements of the naval and military forces placed by law at his command, and to employ them in the manner he may deem most effectual to harass and conquer and subdue the enemy. He may invade the hostile country, and subject it to the sovereignty and authority of the United States.[13]

Thus, the Supreme Court interpreted the commander-in-chief clause with few implied limitations.

An action by Lincoln challenged in the Supreme Court was his suspension of the writ of habeas corpus. Lincoln did this to prevent John Merryman, an outspoken secessionist, from spreading more dissent. Justice Taney in *Ex Parte Merryman* charged that the president had no right or authority to suspend the writ against a civilian because there was no justifiable need.[14] Consequently, the commander-in-chief power was limited to substantiating a need, which Lincoln had not done. In the *Prize* cases of 1862, however, the Supreme Court did support a broad interpretation of commander-in-chief powers.[15] In these cases four shipowners challenged Lincoln's blockade of Southern ports, charging the president with acting unconstitutionally. The Court rejected their plea and indicated that, while a president could not begin the war or officially declare it, he was ". . . bound to resist force by force. He does not initiate the war, but is bound to accept the challenge without waiting for any special legislative authority." The Court's position was severely criticized by the counsel for the shipowners, who foresaw the destruction of constitutional government resulting from this kind of logic.

> It makes the President, in some sort, the impersonation of the country, and invokes for him the power and right to use all the forces he can command to *"save the life of the nation."* The principle of self-defense is asserted, and all power is claimed for the President. This is to assert that the Constitution contemplated and tacitly provided that the President should be dictator, and all Constitutional Government be at an end, whenever he should think "the life of the nation" is in danger.[16]

Lincoln's move to establish military courts in Indiana, at a time when civilian courts were still functioning, posed a very different problem for the Supreme Court. There appeared to be no need in this instance for executive intervention. As Justice Davis stated in *Ex Parte Milligan*:

> The Constitution of the United States is a law for rulers and people, equally in war and in peace, and covers with the shield of its protection all classes of men, at all times, and under all circumstances. No doctrine, involving more pernicious consequences, was ever invented by the wit of man than that any of its provisions can be suspended during any of the great exigencies of government. Such a doctrine leads directly to anarchy or despotism.[17]

It remains unclear, however, whether *Milligan* has served as an effective check on presidential power during wartime in later years. In analyzing the case, Clinton Rossiter argued:

It cannot be emphasized too strongly that the decision in this case followed the close of the rebellion by a full year, altered not in the slightest degree the extraordinary methods through which that rebellion had been suppressed, and did nothing more than deliver from jail a handful of rascals who in any event would have probably gained their freedom in short order.[18]

As the Civil War period ended, the Court had restricted the president, after the fact, from suspending the writ of habeas corpus and from establishing military courts without cause. And yet during this period the president's general war powers and authority as commander-in-chief were enlarged and legitimated by the Supreme Court.

World Wars I and II

Woodrow Wilson's actions as commander-in-chief during World War I reflected two bases of authority: his mandate in the Constitution and legislative delegation. Legislation such as the Lever Food and Fuel Act of 1917, the Trading with the Enemy Act of 1917, the Selective Service Act of 1918, and the Overman Act of 1918 greatly expanded Wilson's commander-in-chief powers. The Lever Food and Fuel Act, for example, allowed the president to secure the cooperation of the entire government to monitor the use of food and fuel during a crisis and to create new agencies if necessary to assure compliance with this law. The act also permitted the president to license and regulate mining and the storage and importation of goods and to seize and use factories, mines, or plants for the war effort. The Trading with the Enemy Act authorized the president to license trade, determine who could transport and ship goods, and curtail business activities with enemy nations. This law also permitted the president to censor the mails and to monitor the exchange of currency with those nations against which we declared war. The Selective Service Act allowed Wilson to draft personnel for the military, including males aged 18 to 45. But it was the Overman Act that provided Wilson with his most far-reaching powers as commander-in-chief. This legislation allowed the president to shape and organize the bureaucracy as needed for purposes of national security. To best utilize the scarce resources, the president could modify the functions of executive departments, commissions, or agencies during the crisis of World War I. Wilson enjoyed carte blanche authority to abolish any bureau or agency of government or to strengthen an agency by new regulations. This power, however, was to end six months after the conclusion of the war, and the status of governmental agencies was to be restored to their prewar levels.

Woodrow Wilson did not always await enactment of legislation before he acted. Indeed, when Congress resisted Wilson's requests for additional authority, Wilson often proceeded with his plans in spite of Congress. For example, when Wilson asked Congress for the authority to arm merchant vessels in the Atlantic with defensive weapons, and Congress refused, he exerted his own authority and issued the merchant marine with the intended weapons. In 1918, Wilson made his own executive agreements with European nations, committing the United States to providing aid to the anti-Bolsheviks in the Soviet Union. Thus, during this period a very strong commander-in-chief role was affirmed, while at the same time possible checks on this role were weakened, because Congress acted in ways to strengthen the chief commander's power. Clinton Rossiter, in describing the relationship between President Wilson and the Congress, remarked that Wilson, "as a teacher of politics [had] conceived a President who would ignore the rigid theory of the separation of powers and provide Congress with vigorous leadership even in normal times. As a practitioner he was a President much after the model he had drawn."[19]

World War II provided many opportunities for Franklin D. Roosevelt's expansion of the commander-in-chief role. Like Wilson, he increased its powers both through his interpretation of the Constitution's commander-in-chief clause and his requests for added authority from Congress. Various actions taken by Roosevelt as commander-in-chief were of questionable legality. Before World War II began, for example, he deployed troops to Greenland and Iceland in 1941 even though the 1940 Reserve Act and the Selective Service Act of 1940 had prohibited the use of U.S. troops outside the western hemisphere. Roosevelt also deployed renovated ships to Great Britain in exchange for American bases in the famous Fifty Destroyer Deal of 1941. Attorney General Robert Jackson (later a member of the Supreme Court) justified the destroyer pact on the basis of the commander-in-chief clause as well as on the president's authority to control foreign relations as the "sole organ of the Federal Government." Attorney General Jackson went even further by arguing the unusual, and perhaps unconstitutional, view that the destroyer deal was legal under the president's power to "dispose of" United States property. This power clearly is given to Congress according to Article IV, Section 3 of the Constitution.

In one of his most controversial actions of 1941, Franklin Roosevelt delivered his well-known "shoot-on-sight" order to the U.S. Navy. He defended his decision with this advice to the sailors: "When you see a rattlesnake poised to strike, you do not wait until he has struck before you crush him. . . . These Nazi submarines and raiders are the rattlesnakes of the Atlantic. . . . They are a challenge to our sovereignty."[20] Yet these military actions, all taken before U.S. participation in World War II began, were rarely challenged in the courts, which suggests that other decision makers as well as the American people were sympathetic to Roosevelt's expansion of commander-in-chief authority. Moreover, unlike in the period following the presidency of Abraham Lincoln, these new powers added to the commander-in-chief role by Roosevelt were not restricted by his successors after the war was over. For this reason, the war powers exercised by Woodrow Wilson during World War I, as well as those used by Franklin D. Roosevelt established important precedents.

Once World War II began, other actions by Roosevelt as commander-in-chief were legally questionable. On several occasions he seized property on his own authority. Between 1941–1952, Roosevelt and Truman together authorized seventy-nine seizures of private facilities.[21] Roosevelt used the commander-in-chief authority in 1942 to establish a military commission to try saboteurs, and the Supreme Court in *Ex Parte Quirin* unanimously agreed that such a military commission was lawful.[22] The most infamous example of Roosevelt's use of commander-in-chief authority was Executive Order 9066 of 1942, which affected 112,000 Japanese-Americans during the war. This "exclusion order" permitted the secretary of war and designated military commanders to establish military zones in the United States from which Japanese-Americans could be excluded. The intent of this executive order was to protect military equipment from possible sabotage, but its effect was to take property and civil liberties from thousands of U.S. citizens. Though it was controversial, Roosevelt was supported in this action by Congress in a resolution of March 21, 1942, coming one month after the executive order, and by the Supreme Court in the cases of *Hirabayashi* v. *United States* and *Korematsu* v. *United States*.[23]

The commander-in-chief clause was also used by Roosevelt to structure his own military alliances. Forty-six nations, at the end of World War II, signed the Atlantic Charter agreeing not to make a separate peace without the other signatories. Like Woodrow Wilson, Franklin Roosevelt viewed these broad interpretations of the commander-in-chief clause as a means of strengthening his control over public policy. As one observer of the Roosevelt years suggested, the president used this role "as the shield and buckler of his presidential powers and his presidential policies."[24]

Truman

For Harry Truman, the Constitution ceased to be the only source of authority for his powers as commander-in-chief. Although presidents before Truman had felt bound to "gentleman's agreements," executive orders, and treaty obligations, never before had these served as justifications for a president's use of commander-in-chief power. When Truman in 1950 committed thousands of American troops to helping the South Korean government, both the commander-in-chief clause and the United Nations Charter became important sources of justification. Truman stated on June 27, 1950:

> The Security Council called upon all members of the United Nations to render every assistance to the United Nations in the execution of this resolution [a U.N. resolution to North Korea to cease hostilities]. . . .
>
> I know that all members of the United Nations will consider carefully the consequences of this latest aggression in Korea in defiance of the Charter of the United Nations. A return to the rule of force in international affairs would have far-reaching effects. The United States will continue to uphold the rule of law.[25]

Another change introduced by Truman, in contrast with his predecessors, was Truman's willingness to justify a three-year commitment of troops to South Korea on the basis of precedent. While precedent had been cited before to justify military actions, it had not been used to defend such a serious commitment of resources and the invasion of another country's sovereign territory. Our commitment involved about 25,000 troops over the three-year period. Truman believed that references to similar actions by other presidents, whether constitutional or not, would serve to quiet criticism. In a State Department Memorandum presented to the Congress in 1950, Secretary of State Dean Acheson listed eighty-seven confrontations and incidents of military conflict during U.S. history: this documentation was used to support Truman's action. Acheson also stated: "There has never . . . been any serious doubt . . . of the President's constitutional authority to do what he did."[26] The reference to historical cases of military confrontation was rather weak justification, since these had been examples of war making on a very small scale, but nevertheless the logic of Truman's position has been accepted by subsequent presidents, by Congress, and by the Supreme Court.

Truman strengthened the role of commander-in-chief in other ways as well. In 1945 he ordered the atomic bomb dropped on Japan, ushering in the era of nuclear deterrents, and in 1950 instructed the Atomic Energy Commission to continue its program to develop other atomic weapons, including the hydrogen bomb. Truman also used his commander-in-chief authority to preserve civilian supremacy in the face of a serious challenge posed by General Douglas MacArthur. MacArthur, who was serving as supreme commander of the Allied Forces in Korea, began to openly defy Truman's war objectives. Truman saw no option but to relieve MacArthur of his command. Since General MacArthur was popular at home and abroad as a World War II military hero, and given the fact that Truman's popularity was not high at the time, this decision was not an easy one for the president. William Goldsmith has suggested that the ramifications of the confrontation between Truman and MacArthur were very serious: "It is no exaggeration to say that not only the powers of the Commander in Chief, but the entire foundations of constitutional government, were at stake in this crisis."[27]

The major legacy of the Truman years is that presidents since then have followed his use of commander-in-chief power, though with variations. In recent decades, presidents have exercised commander-in-chief powers not so much on the basis of the Constitution as on such justifications as "inherent power," "emergency powers," "open-ended grants of authority from Congress," "national security needs," "executive prerogative," and "prior commitments." Lyndon Johnson, Richard Nixon, and Jimmy Carter all provide examples of presidents who justified strengthening the commander-in-chief in these ways.

Vietnam

The Vietnam War offered Lyndon Johnson an opportunity to exert his commander-in-chief powers without having to explicitly cite the Constitution. Instead, he justified his actions in Vietnam on the basis of the agreements of the Southeast Asia Treaty Organization (SEATO); precedent; the executive's inherent powers; and most important, the grant of authority given him by Congress in the Gulf of Tonkin Resolution. This resolution was passed overwhelmingly by Congress in 1964 with only two opposing votes in the Senate. Later, as public support for the Vietnam War deteriorated, many congressmen would argue that they did not know what actions they had approved when enacting the Gulf of Tonkin Resolution. This (joint) resolution began by suggesting that North Vietnam had violated the United Nations Charter as well as international law in attacking U.S. naval vessels in the Gulf of Tonkin. It then stated that ". . . the Congress approves and supports the determination of the President, as Commander in Chief, to take all necessary measures to repel any armed attack against the forces of the United States and to prevent further aggression." The resolution also justified the use of force according to three sources of authority: the Constitution, the United Nations Charter, and SEATO. Moreover, U.S. commitments to Southeast Asia were mentioned in this resolution: ". . . the United States is, therefore, prepared, as the President determines, to take all necessary steps, including the use of armed force, to assist any member or protocol state of the Southeast Asia Collective Defense Treaty requesting assistance in defense of its freedom." It also made clear that the president would determine when hostilities would end.

Alexander Bickel has raised serious questions about the legality of such a broad delegation from Congress. He pointed out that the Supreme Court had three times earlier invalidated legislative delegations to the executive that did not provide the necessary guidelines for implementation.[28] Bickel's concern was that "delegation without standards short-circuits the lines of responsibility that make the political process meaningful."[29] Bickel admits that Congress enacted the Gulf of Tonkin Resolution partly because public opinion since the Korean War has sustained a united front between Congress and the executive in foreign affairs. Such a situation was achieved by the resolution.

Though the Gulf of Tonkin Resolution went far in legitimizing Johnson's war making, the president believed that he did not need any additional authority to wage the Vietnam War. This view was the essence of Undersecretary of State Nicholas Katzenbach's testimony before a legislative committee chaired by Sen. William Fulbright:

In my judgment, Senator, [LBJ] already had constitutionally that authority. But I would think as a matter of history and precedent it would be extremely difficult, in this kind of situation for a President to exercise that authority on his own when, one, the authority would be disputed, and the fact of the authority would be disputed, and secondly, when he wanted and needed, needed very much, the sense of Congress in this respect. He knew as a constitutional matter that he would have to depend upon the Congress if he were to exercise the policy in that way and he wanted in a sense an indication that the Congress would support that exercise of his authority. He also wanted to avoid the constitutional questions that had come up at the time of Korea.[30]

Furthermore, Lyndon Johnson's defense of his actions in Southeast Asia was related to precedents. Leonard C. Meeker, State Department adviser, argued that, by 1966, there were at least 125 cases in which presidents had ordered military action without first obtaining Congress' authorization.

During the Nixon presidency, the Senate reevaluated the Gulf of Tonkin Resolution and rescinded it in 1970. Nonetheless, when asked about the implications of this action on his war powers, Richard Nixon argued that he still had the authority as commander-in-chief to continue the Vietnam War. He stated:

> The President of the United States has the constitutional right—not only the right, but the responsibility—to use his powers to protect American forces when they are engaged in military actions, and under these circumstances starting at the time that I became President, I have that power and I am exercising that power.[31]

Even when President Nixon expanded the war in Southeast Asia by bombing Cambodia, a neutral country, his justification for flying 3,695 sorties to drop some 105,837 tons of bombs was based on similar grounds. As Nixon argued, "As Commander in Chief, I had no choice but to act to defend those men [U.S. troops]. And as Commander in Chief, if I am faced with that decision again, I will exercise that power to defend these men."[32] In addition, like his predecessors, Nixon defended his Cambodian bombing and the invasions of its sovereign territory on the grounds of precedent, the SEATO Treaty, and his inherent powers as president. In a major address of April 30, 1970, President Nixon made little effort to justify his actions in Cambodia on legal grounds. Rather, he believed it only necessary to "describe" the enemy actions and his response as commander-in-chief; moreover, he cited various war actions taken by Presidents Wilson, Franklin Roosevelt, Eisenhower, and Kennedy.[33]

To provide legal support for his commander-in-chief initiatives, Nixon deferred to William Rehnquist, then assistant attorney general. Rehnquist felt obliged to address three issues: (1) whether the United States could engage in armed hostilities without a declaration of war, (2) whether the president as commander-in-chief has substantive powers, and (3) whether the president's power as commander-in-chief is limited without legislative authorization.[34] He answered the first two questions in the affirmative and the third in the negative. Rehnquist also relied heavily on precedent, on those many instances of "undeclared wars," on the actions of specific presidents, and on Supreme Court cases to justify war making. He noted that even the Supreme Court decision in *Youngstown Sheet and Tube Co. v. Sawyer*, thought by many scholars to limit presidential power, did not truly restrict the president. As Justice Jackson had argued in that case, the Court seemed to be supporting unlimited presidential power. Justice Jackson said:

> We should not use this occasion to circumscribe, much less to contract, the lawful role of the President as Commander-in-Chief. I should indulge the widest latitude of interpretation to sustain his exclusive function to command the instruments of national force, at least when turned against the outside world for the security of our society.[35]

We have seen that during the Vietnam War era, both Lyndon Johnson and Richard Nixon extended the power of the commander-in-chief because they ultimately based their authority on sources other than the Constitution. This kind of rationale for war making deeply disturbed many liberal scholars, including historian Arthur Schlesinger, Jr., who argued the following position:

> Both Johnson and Nixon had indulged in presidential war-making beyond the boldest dreams of their predecessors. Those who had stretched the executive war power to what had seemed its "outer limits" in the past had done so in the face of visible and dire threat to national survival. . . . Johnson and Nixon had surpassed all their predecessors in claiming that inherent and exclusive presidential authority, unaccompanied by emergencies threatening the life of the nation, unaccompanied by the authorization of Congress or the blessing of an international organization, permitted a President to order troops into battle at his unilateral pleasure.[36]

Ford and Carter

The use of military force by Presidents Ford and Carter directly confronted the War Powers Act. Approved in 1973, this legislation resulted from the backlash that followed Johnson's and Nixon's handling of the Vietnam War. Under the act's provisions, the president must inform Congress within forty-eight hours when he commits U.S. troops abroad. He is required to end such action within sixty days unless Congress (1) declares war, (2) specifically authorizes the continued use of troops, (3) grants the president a thirty-day extension (to ninety days), or (4) in the event that Congress is "physically unable to meet" because of an armed attack on the country. However, at any time during the sixty or ninety days the president's use of troops can be terminated by Congress' passing a concurrent resolution. The law also provides for consultation between the president and Congress before troops are committed. (See text of War Powers Resolution pp. 364–365.)

Gerald Ford violated the spirit of the War Powers Act by his intervention in the *Mayaguez* incident. During 1975, the S.S. *Mayaguez*, an American vessel, had been fired upon and then seized by the Cambodian government, who said the ship was gathering intelligence information while in Cambodian waters. Ford immediately responded by sending the Navy, the Marines, and aircraft to invade the Cambodian mainland. Some forty-one Marines were killed in the operation, which freed the ship's thirty-nine crewmen. This incident was so serious that Arthur Schlesinger, Jr., was moved to say that "the President, without Congressional authorization or even consultation, started a small war against the new Cambodian Government."[37] Though Ford was obliged by the War Powers Act to consult with Congress, instead he chose only to report what he had done within the required forty-eight hours. In his report to Congress, Ford refused to recognize that Congress had authority in this matter. He stated: "This operation was ordered and conducted pursuant to the President's constitutional executive power and his authority as Commander in Chief of the United States armed forces."[38]

Congressional leaders were not satisfied with his explanation. Neither Sen. Mike Mansfield, the majority party leader, nor Sen. Hugh Scott, the minority party leader, felt that President Ford had adequately notified them. This incident, therefore, points out the major problem with the War Powers Act; namely, that there seems to be no adequate mechanism in it to *require* the president to consult with the Congress. Section 3 of the War Powers Resolution simply says that the president ". . . in every possible instance shall consult with Congress before introducing United States Armed Forces into hostilities or into situations where imminent involvement in hostilities is clearly indicated by the circumstances. . . ." In Pat Holt's evaluation of this provision, however, he argues that during a national emergency time is critical and no president would be able to consult with Congress at every stage in the decision-making process.[39] Gerald Ford was never willing to accept the authority of the War Powers Act. As he reviewed the six incidents of foreign involvement during his tenure in office (three evacuations from Danang, Phnom Penh, and Saigon in 1975; the *Mayaguez* incident in 1975; and two evacuations from Lebanon in 1976), Ford argued, "I did not concede that the resolution itself was legally binding on the President on Constitutional grounds."[40] He filed reports with Congress for the three 1975 operations, but no written reports were received by Congress for those of 1976. In none of these cases did congressional leaders feel that they had been properly consulted.

It was Henry Kissinger, then secretary of state, who tried to explain to Congress why nothing more had been done to keep its members informed. Testifying before the House International Relations Committee, Rep. Clement J. Zablocki (D.–Wis.) asked Kissinger whether he felt that Congress had been consulted or informed about the Lebanese evacuations. Kissinger declared: "Well, it would be both. But realistically, the time period for consultation would have to be very short, because one would not want too much opportunity for opposition to develop."[41] This answer did not satisfy Congressman Zablocki, who believed that "the executive branch proclivity is toward evasive and selective interpretation of the War Powers Resolution."[42]

Even Jimmy Carter, who entered the presidency committed to reducing the manifestations of its "imperialism," ended his term after using many sources of authority to defend his unilateral actions as commander-in-chief and to evade the intent of the War Powers Act. President Carter, in dealing with Iran, used his authority as commander-in-chief to sever diplomatic relations, to impose diplomatic and economic sanctions, and to invade its territory in the abortive rescue mission to release the American hostages. The rescue attempt on April 24, 1980, was cancelled abruptly on the basis of his executive authority. But in his report to Congress, Carter stated that he had ordered the operation

> pursuant to the President's powers under the Constitution as Chief Executive and as Commander-in-Chief of the United States Armed Forces, expressly rec-

ognized in Section 8(d)(1) of the War Powers Resolution. In carrying out this operation, the United States was acting wholly within its right, in accordance with Article 51 of the United Nations Charter, to protect and rescue its citizens where the government of the territory in which they are located is unable or unwilling to protect them.[43]

This action by President Carter, then, was taken in spite of the War Powers Act, which in fact he used as additional justification. This incident simply illustrated what Sen. Thomas Eagleton (D.–Mo.) had contended was a fundamental problem with this legislation. Eagleton argued that, rather than limiting a president's involvement in foreign confrontations, the act might actually encourage a president to initiate a war during the sixty-day grace period when legislative approval is not required.[44]

Congress and war making

The War Powers Act of 1973 suggests that Congress is trying to oversee and curb the president's awesome powers as commander-in-chief. Yet it is Congress itself that is responsible for much of the expansion in this role, for it more typically acts to support the president as commander-in-chief. The Gulf of Tonkin Resolution is only the most famous example of this kind of legislative delegation. Congress' support of the strong commander-in-chief began as early as 1791 when it granted George Washington the authority he requested to call up additional troops to fight "Indian tribes." In 1792 the Congress granted Washington added authority to organize the militia. In 1795 Washington also received power under the Militia Act to call up the militia ". . . whenever the United States shall be invaded, *or be in imminent danger of invasion* from any foreign nation or Indian tribe." In some instances, statutory delegations to presidents have all but given them, in Edward Corwin's opinion, "a qualified declaration of war." Thus, to Eisenhower Congress granted war authority in January 1955 (before he requested it) to initiate actions to defend Formosa (Taiwan) against threats from Mainland China. According to this statute, Eisenhower has authority to ". . . employ the Armed Forces of the United States for protecting the security of Formosa, the Pescadores, and related positions and territories."[45] This authority was given to Eisenhower even though there was no formal, or even informal, "war" declared.

In the early 1970s the federal courts were asked to review the constitutionality of the president's war powers and Congress' role in war making.[46] In the case of *Massachusetts v. Laird* (1970), the Supreme Court dismissed out of hand the question of the legality of the Vietnam War brought by the Commonwealth of Massachusetts. Justice Douglas dissented however; he argued that this was a legitimate question and that it was time to test the constitutionality of both the war and presidential war powers. In the case of *Orlando v. Laird* (1971), a court of appeal decided that official congressional sanction of a presidential war was not necessary, because the very fact that Congress furnished the materials for war was sufficient reason to show its support without a formal declaration. Here Appellate Court Judge Anderson indicated that Congress and the president took mutual actions, such as the passage of the Tonkin Gulf Resolution and the extension of the Military Selective Service Act, which allowed conscription for the Vietnam War. The inference of support for the war was, according to the judge, sufficient to legitimize war making.

In 1973, in the case of *Holtzman* v. *Schlesinger,* Justice Thurgood Marshall, acting as circuit justice for the Supreme Court (which was not in session at the time), was asked by Rep. Elizabeth Holtzman (D.–N.Y.) and some Air Force officers serving in Southeast Asia to stop air operations over Cambodia because such operations had not been authorized by Congress. Marshall refused to contradict the decision of a court of appeals staying a district court ruling that prohibited the government from engaging in those military actions. But Representative Holtzman tried again, this time by appealing to Justice William O. Douglas. Douglas avoided ruling on the constitutionality of the Vietnam War by arguing that the question should be treated as a death penalty case because the airmen were sent to a "death zone." Based on this logic, he stayed the appellate court's ruling, thereby prohibiting the bombing in Cambodia. Thereupon the solicitor general asked Justice Marshall to stay the order of the district court, which Marshall did after surveying his fellow justices by telephone. Douglas, however, remained opposed to the majority's viewpoint.

Thus, the reluctance of the judiciary to become involved gave added legitimacy to presidential war making. An overview of the commander-in-chief role shows that all presidents enjoy substantial authority to initiate and vigorously pursue military actions abroad. Not only does the Constitution justify an expansive view of presidential war powers, but legislative resolutions and statutes, judicial decisions, and precedents by earlier presidents all legitimize a strong commander-in-chief role.

DECISION MAKING

Since the commander-in-chief is a role with significant authority, one would suspect that decision making is highly centralized, primarily involving only the president and his key advisers. Usually there are relatively few people involved in formulating war policies, in determining strategy and priorities, and in mobilizing support from Congress and the people for those policies. This does not mean that decision making in times of crisis always involves the same actors. To the contrary, decision making during each crisis reflects the president's own personality, needs, and priorities. The National Security Council, in whole or in part, is most consistently relied on by presidents today, but other advisory groups could include the Joint Chiefs of Staff, cabinet members, and ad hoc groups representing the White House staff as well as outside consultants.

During wartime, a primary advisory group is the Joint Chiefs of Staff, composed of representatives of the major military services. Included are the chief of staff of the Army, the chief of Naval Operations, the chief of staff of the Air Force, and the commandant of the Marine Corps. A military chairman appointed by the president presides, after being confirmed by the Senate. The term of the chairman is two years, but it may be extended for one additional term. In the case of war, there is no limit to the number of terms the chairman may serve. The Joint Chiefs are responsible for military planning and operations for the armed forces. They also are supposed to provide a unified command when troops are in the field. As advisers to the president, they counsel him about personnel and materiel needs for the armed forces, and they act as liaison with the UN Military Staff Committee. The chairman of the Joint Chiefs often testifies before Congress in support of military policy. A Joint Staff of nearly four hundred officers appointed by the Joint Chiefs supports their decision making, and this staff can be utilized by the commander-in-chief as he wishes. The staff members, chosen in equal numbers from the Army, Navy, Air Force, and Marine Corps, have three-year terms.

The Joint Chiefs were created in 1942 during World War II, and were formalized as an institution in the National Security Act of 1947. Strong interservice rivalries have beset their operations from the very beginning; moreover, tension exists between the Joint Chiefs and the civilian secretaries (secretary of the Navy, secretary of the Army, secretary of the Air Force). In the past, the service secretaries focused most of their attention on research and development, on military logistics, and on personnel and training requirements. Since 1958, when they were removed from the military chain of command, the secretaries have been excluded from strategy planning. The competition between the president's military and civilian advisers has been so serious that, on October 20, 1975, Sen. Thomas J. McIntyre (Dem.– N.H.) was prompted to introduce legislation in Congress that would have required the Joint Chiefs to keep the civilian secretaries fully informed about military actions. This bill was proposed because the Air Force was secretly bombing Cambodia, in 1969–1970 during the Vietnam War, though the Air Force secretary, Robert Seamans, knew nothing about those military operations.[47]

Recent proposals for reform have focused on the need to strengthen the Joint Chiefs to provide a more coordinated military policy. One plan being considered proposes that a new general staff be created, thus eliminating the dominance of any one service among the Joint Chiefs and thereby forcing greater coordination among the armed services. Former chairman of the Joint Chiefs of Staff, General David C. Jones, has recommended, at the very least, strengthening the role of the chairman by allowing him to remain above interservice rivalries. Jones also suggested eliminating each service's veto over military policy to encourage more interchange among the officers from all the services. He recommended, in addition, the appointment of a deputy to the chairman to aid in the structuring of war plans and joint military exercises. By this change, the chairman could concentrate more time on his important duties and be more available to the president.[48]

The National Security Council (NSC) is a very important advisory group to the president. Since its establishment in 1947, the NSC has become responsible for much of the military, diplomatic, and domestic planning, which previously had been formulated by individual presidents acting in consultation with whomever they included in decision making. Under the NSC, security policy is approached as a coherent program. Another effect of institutionalizing policymaking in the NSC has been to routinize the commander-in-chief role as a peacetime, as well as a wartime, responsibility. In 1949, the NSC was strengthened by a series of amendments to the 1947 National Security Act enabling the secretary of defense to become the primary spokesman for the military services. As a result, the service secretaries and the Joint Chiefs of Staff no longer regularly attend NSC meetings. Under this arrangement, the president, his secretaries of state and defense, the chairman of the newly created National Security Resources Board, and the vice-president became regular members of the NSC. Other officials could be added by the president as needed. Through these structural changes, a mechanism of control and information dissemination was provided. The existence of a strongly organized NSC meant that national security issues would be deliberated by a small network of top administrators, who were also the president's most important cabinet members. Thus, the views of those agencies charged with implementing military policy could influence the commander-in-chief's evaluation of policies at an early stage of decision making.

A much less important component of the commander-in-chief's advisory system is the cabinet. Key members of the cabinet often are included in decision making during times of crisis, but the cabinet as a collectivity never has been engaged in this capacity. For example, during World War I Woodrow Wilson never held a meeting of his cabinet. Presidents usually rely on the secretaries of the Departments of State, Defense, and Treasury, and the attorney general (the so-called inner cabinet). Equally important, however, are those trusted members of the White House staff, who also participate in crisis decision making. On the other hand, members of Congress have much less input in these kinds of deliberations. More often the Congress or selected legislators are consulted by the president for purposes of alerting them to pending decisions or to decisions already made, rather than seeking their advice in formulating such policies. In decision making affecting military policy, therefore, a president usually organizes his advisory system in ad hoc groups, for by this technique a president can surround himself with individuals with whom he feels most comfortable. However, as noted before, while this system permits a president to generate a consensus for his policies, it also can hamper open, uninhibited consideration of all policy options and viewpoints. Having identified the key actors who advise the commander-in-chief, let us analyze their participation in four military decisions: the Korean War, the Cuban missile crisis, the *Mayaguez* incident, and the Iran crisis.

Korea

On June 25, 1950, North Korea invaded South Korea in a move to reunify a country that had been divided since World War II.[49] President Harry Truman, whose administration followed a "containment" policy toward the Soviet Union, viewed this aggression as yet another example of Russian imperialism. Truman was visiting his family in Missouri when he was notified of the North Korean invasion, and he instructed Secretary of State Dean Acheson to request a meeting of the United Nations Security Council. On his return flight to Washington, Truman had decided to meet this Soviet challenge with military force; he ordered General Douglas MacArthur to use air and naval power to reinforce the South Korean army. On June 27, President Truman appraised congressional leaders of the Korean situation, and within days ordered American troops into Korea. The UN Security Council passed one resolution demanding the immediate withdrawal of North Korean forces, which was ignored, and a second resolution—authored by the United States—asking UN member states to render assistance to South Korea. The Congress and public opinion rallied behind the president's action; moreover, he defended his use of military force without legislative authorization on the grounds that this was a "police action" under UN auspices. Because Truman wanted to intervene quickly in Korea, he wished to avoid any lengthy debate in Congress about the constitutional issues.

When U.S. forces arrived in Korea under the command of Douglas MacArthur, they succeeded in driving the North Korean army northward across the 38th parallel. But, as the American forces continued their march north, on November 28, 1950, Communist China attacked the American troops, pushing them down the peninsula. After months of bitter fighting, the war stalemated around the 38th parallel, where eventually a truce was signed. Throughout the Korean War, Dean Acheson, the secretary of state, was Truman's principal adviser. Acheson was always in contact with the president and with others in the advisory system—he set the agenda for discussions, and he, along with the secretary of defense, was the most important spokesman for the administration's policies in Congress. President Truman did not convene the National Security Council, created just three years earlier; rather he relied most heavily on a dozen top-level advisers from the Department of Defense, the Department of State, and the Joint Chiefs of Staff. And when Truman deliberated on the matter of firing General Douglas MacArthur for insubordination, he discussed this issue with only four persons—two Army generals and two members of his cabinet.[50]

The decision by the Truman administration, after the initial assault by American forces in Korea, to reunify the country under a democratic government of South Korea rather than simply restore the status quo at the

38th parallel, is seen by Janis to exemplify "groupthink."[51] Many of Truman's advisers, particularly General MacArthur, believed that the war could be won quickly and that Communist China would not enter the conflict on behalf of North Korea. The American response to the Korean War, therefore, was formulated to a large degree by President Truman, aided by a small ad hoc group of military and civilian advisers. Obviously Congress had no role in the decision-making process. In retrospect, Truman's failure to involve the Congress in policymaking may have served to weaken his political position later, when the war became stalemated and General MacArthur publicly stated that the Truman administration's policies were tantamount to appeasement.

Cuban missile crisis

The Cuban missile crisis brought forth a different cast of decision makers around President John F. Kennedy.[52] On October 16, 1962, Kennedy was informed that Air Force aerial photographs had confirmed that the Soviets were building medium-range ballistic missile bases in Cuba. During the thirteen-day crisis, President Kennedy sought advice from two groups, the thirteen-member Committee on Overhead Reconnaissance and the Executive Committee of the National Security Council (EXCOM), composed of fifteen high-ranking officials whom Kennedy had personally selected. Included in its membership were Secretary of State Rusk, Defense Secretary McNamara, Attorney General Robert Kennedy, Treasury Secretary Dillon, National Security Adviser McGeorge Bundy, and General Maxwell Taylor, chairman of the Joint Chiefs of Staff. EXCOM was convened by Kennedy within three hours after he learned about the missiles, and its deliberations over the next six days illustrate the "multiple advocacy" approach to decision making. Many competing views were represented in EXCOM, and at times President Kennedy was absent from its deliberative sessions in order to allow the fullest exchange of ideas. Its major role was to assess the dangers involved in the various policy options being studied, and military experts were questioned by EXCOM members to assess the feasibility of each alternative. EXCOM also monitored the ships entering Cuban waters, keeping President Kennedy informed of developments and relaying orders to the military commanders on the scene. As Graham Allison points out, this was the first time that military officers "received repeated orders about the details of their military operations directly from political leaders."[53]

EXCOM's discussions were held in strict secrecy; in fact Kennedy on October 19 resumed his political campaigning for the upcoming midterm congressional elections by visiting Cleveland, Chicago, and Springfield, Illinois. These campaign trips were undertaken to allay suspicions in the press that something important was happening at the White House. The political advisers to President Kennedy, and not the military, therefore dominated the decision-making process. It was EXCOM's decision to institute a blockade of Soviet shipping to Cuba, but this recommendation was by no means based on a consensus. Dean Acheson, the former secretary of state who was invited to attend these proceedings, Secretary of State Dean Rusk, CIA Director McCone, and Assistant Secretary of Defense Paul Nitze all favored an air attack on the missile bases instead. The blockade strategy was chosen as a compromise solution by the group, and was supported by President Kennedy, Robert Kennedy (the president's brother), and Special-Counsel Theodore Sorenson. On October 22, 1962, President Kennedy in a radio and television broadcast told the American people about the Soviet military buildup in Cuba and his decision to impose "a strict quarantine on all offensive military equipment under shipment to Cuba"; ships with such cargo would be turned back by the Navy. For six tense days Kennedy stood firm and waited for a reaction from Nikita Khrushchev, the Soviet premier; Khrushchev then tried to negotiate with Kennedy by proposing that the Soviet Union would withdraw its missile bases from Cuba in return for our removing NATO missiles from Greece and Turkey. Kennedy refused to yield, and rather openly began to deploy American forces around the globe, in an attempt to convince the Soviets that he was deadly serious. On October 28, Khruschev responded to President Kennedy by ordering work on the Cuban missile bases ended, and the Cuban missile crisis was over.

During the Cuban missile crisis, President Kennedy was determined to meet the Soviet challenge to the United States. Though he was firm, Kennedy wanted to avoid an outright military confrontation and to allow the Soviet leader a face-saving way out of the dilemma. There was too little time available to use diplomatic means to resolve this conflict. On the other hand, the option of mounting an air strike on the Cuban missile bases could pose serious problems: Soviet technicians in Cuba might be killed; it was unclear whether our Air Force could destroy the missile bases successfully; the advocates of an air strike also contemplated landing Marines in Cuba; and there was the possibility that the Soviet Union might intervene elsewhere, such as in Berlin.

While these questions were being explored by the NSC Executive Committee, Congress played no role in the decision-making process. President Kennedy did consult with the party leadership in Congress as EXCOM was preparing its response to the Soviets, and when the blockade was announced the Republicans in Congress were generally supportive. Some Democrats argued, however, that Kennedy's action did not go far enough. Though the revelations about Soviet missile bases in Cuba were a surprise, rumors had been circulating beforehand about a Soviet military buildup in Cuba. In response to the rumors, in September 1962, Congress had passed a resolution citing the Monroe Doctrine, stating that the United States was determined to prevent, by "use of arms" if necessary, foreign intervention in Cuba. Congress' purpose was twofold: to warn the Soviet Union and to strengthen the resolve of the Kennedy administration to confront this challenge to our national security.

The Mayaguez incident

In the *Mayaguez* crisis, which lasted three days, President Ford relied primarily on the National Security Council to devise a strategy to rescue the crew of the *Mayaguez*, which had been seized by the Cambodian navy on May 12, 1975. Nine hours after the seizure President Ford convened the National Security Council. Among the nine advisers in attendance at the first NSC meeting were Secretary of State Henry Kissinger, Secretary of Defense James Schlesinger, CIA Director William Colby, Vice-President Nelson Rockefeller, and General David C. Jones, acting chairman of the Joint Chiefs of Staff.[54] Ford and the NSC were determined to control the decision-making process, despite Congress' efforts during this period to wrest the initiative in foreign affairs from the president. Because of the executive's predominance, Congress once again played virtually no role in the decision to rescue the crew of the *Mayaguez*.

At its first meeting the NSC tried to determine what the motives of the Cambodian government were; the ship had been seized because Cambodia believed it to be engaged in intelligence activities. The use of economic, military, and diplomatic sanctions was discussed, and the meeting concluded with all members agreeing that rescue of the crew was necessary, and that it should be done in such a way to clearly indicate that the United States intended to act quickly and firmly to protect its interests. President Ford and the NSC also decided to protest the seizure and to demand that the ship be returned. The NSC met twice on May 13, 1975, and plans for military action were seriously entertained after it was reported that Cambodia had not responded to our diplomatic protests. Secretary of State Henry Kissinger vigorously urged the use of force to free the ship, and President Ford directed the aircraft carrier *Hancock* to enter Cambodian waters. Because Section 3 of the War Powers Act encouraged the president to consult with Congress before he commits troops in a military action, President Ford met with selected members of Congress on four different occasions. These reporting sessions took the form of informal and formal briefings; the White House staff kept about twenty-one representatives and senators informed, including those legislators who served on the Senate Foreign Relations Committee and the House International Relations Committee.

A final NSC meeting took place on May 14, and at this time the details of the rescue mission were reviewed and approved by President Ford. The actual military operation had been planned by the Joint Chiefs of Staff. It was General Jones who presented the final military plan, which included air strikes, helicopter combat assaults, and a boarding party composed of Marines. After approving this plan, President Ford again briefed the leaders of Congress. However, in retrospect, the role of Congress in the *Mayaguez* incident was minimal. Senate Majority Party Leader Mike Mansfield (D.– Mont.) said: "I was not consulted. I was notified after the fact about what the administration had already decided to do. . . ."[55] But Ron Nessen, the White House press secretary, viewed the situation differently; he felt that

Congress' acknowledgment of what had happened was sufficient evidence to indicate its support for President Ford's actions. Within three hours after the Marines had landed in Cambodia, the crew was returned to the *Maya-guez* and, though 41 Americans had been killed in this military operation, the rescue was proclaimed a success by administration spokesmen and the press. And as a result, President Ford's popularity in the Gallup Polls rose from 40 to 52 percent approval.

Iran crisis

The Iran crisis occurred during the term of Jimmy Carter, whose attempt to rescue the Americans held hostage in Iran ended in failure.[56] On November 4, 1979, Iranian student militants, inspired by their country's leader—Ayatollah Khomeini—seized the American Embassy in Teheran, holding sixty-two Americans hostage. Though Khomeini allowed a few hostages to be released weeks later, it was 444 days before all the Americans were freed. The takeover of the embassy followed in the wake of a successful revolution staged by Islamic extremists under the leadership of Khomeini, which toppled the U.S.-backed government of the Shah of Iran. The embassy takeover was precipitated when the ousted Shah, who was suffering from cancer, visited the United States for medical treatment. That action by the militants, however, stimulated unified public outcry in the United States, and President Carter's popularity increased from 29 to 61 percent within one month. President Carter stopped the importation of Iranian oil and froze the assets of the Iranian government in U.S. banks; the House of Representatives voted 379 to 0 to end military and economic aid to Iran; and in some U.S. communities Iranian students were assaulted.

In dealing with the Iran crisis, President Carter relied on various ad hoc groups of advisers. Although he did meet formally with the National Security Council, the more important advisory group monitoring events in Iran was the Special Coordinating Committee. This body was convened immediately after the Shah was overthrown. The Special Coordinating Committee was chaired by National Security Adviser Zbigniew Brzezinski and included most of the NSC membership, but it also consulted with other top-level officials as the need arose. Therefore, President Carter's style of decision making hinged on his desire to hear differing viewpoints expressed by the various groups of advisers. It has been suggested that one drawback in the Carter mode of operations was that he may have received too much advice and structured too few guidelines for his advisers to follow in their deliberations. For example, Ledeen and Lewis contend that, had Carter clarified his objectives to the NSC and the Departments of State and Defense, he would have received more support from those agencies than he did.[57] As a result, the Carter administration sent the world mixed signals concerning its policies toward Iran.

However, when President Carter decided to try to rescue the American hostages in Iran, he abandoned his earlier decision-making style. By May

2, 1980, an elite, all-volunteer, team of military commandoes had landed in Iran to rescue the hostages from the embassy compound. The attempt was a disaster. It ended 250 miles from Teheran, at the desert staging area, because three of the eight helicopters assigned to the mission developed mechanical malfunctions, rendering them useless. President Carter immediately cancelled the mission and assumed all responsibility. In a televised broadcast he said: "It was my decision to attempt the rescue operation. It was my decision to cancel it when problems developed. The responsibility is fully my own." The rescue attempt had been planned, Carter said, because the situation in Iran had become very tense and volatile in recent days, bloodshed had occurred among the rival factions of students holding the hostages, and concern for the safety of the Americans was mounting.

By April 1980 President Carter became convinced of the necessity to try the rescue attempt, but the preparations were kept in the strictest confidence. The Joint Chiefs of Staff, who heretofore had had little role to play in the diplomatic maneuvers between the United States and Iran, were responsible for military planning. On the other hand; very few civilian officials knew about this secret mission; advisers who did know included Vice-President Walter Mondale, Defense Secretary Harold Brown, Secretary of State Cyrus Vance, Deputy Secretary of State Warren Christopher, National Security Adviser Zbigniew Brzezinski, CIA Director Stansfield Turner, and White House Chief of Staff Hamilton Jordan. The secrecy with which the rescue mission was organized is underscored by the fact that, although Secretary of State Vance and National Security Adviser Brzezinski disagreed about using military intervention, their dispute was not revealed to the press until after the rescue aborted. Thereupon Cyrus Vance resigned from the Carter administration and was replaced with Sen. Edmund Muskie (D.–Me.). Congress had known nothing about the plans, nor had President Carter consulted with congressional leaders. Though some representatives and senators were concerned that his action violated the intent of the War Powers Act, President Carter insisted that it was undertaken as an act of mercy, not as an act of war. In the end, most legislators of both political parties supported the president's bold strategy for freeing the Americans.

Summary

These four cases indicate that the commander-in-chief relies on relatively small groups of advisers to formulate military policy. But each president organizes a slightly different collection of advisers: Truman did not convene the NSC; President Ford formally consulted the NSC; and Kennedy and Carter included members of the NSC in the ad hoc advisory groups they created. It is clear that Congress plays no role in formulating military policy during a crisis, though it may serve to legitimize the president's actions afterward. When military crises involve the use of force, the Joint Chiefs of Staff, or at least the chairman of the Joint Chiefs, are involved in decision making. However, in these instances the civilian advisers, particularly those from the Departments of State and Defense, seem to be more important to the president when he seeks advice on "political" issues and when overall national security priorities are evaluated.

PUBLIC INPUTS

When the United States goes to war, the nation tends to unify behind the president's leadership. People generally defer to the commander-in-chief's judgment regarding war priorities and strategy, but Americans want to win those wars in which they are engaged. During the past four decades, the United States has fought in three major military confrontations, two of which (Korea and Vietnam) were "undeclared." Public opinion data reveal that the collective reactions to Korea and to Vietnam were quite similar, and somewhat distinct from our reaction to World War II. We have less data about public opinion during World War II because the technology of opinion polling was less sophisticated and fewer surveys were taken during that period. Available opinion data do suggest, however, that World War II was a "popular" war and that Americans quickly identified with the war objectives enunciated by President Franklin D. Roosevelt.[58]

World War II

As already noted in the discussion of foreign policy, a strong "isolationist" sentiment characterized public opinion before our entrance into World War II. The American Institute of Public Opinion (Gallup) surveys taken in 1937 and in 1939 showed that 60 percent of the respondents viewed U.S. involvement in World War I as being a mistake. By January 1941, when Germany occupied most of Western Europe, this viewpoint about World War I was held by only 39 percent of the respondents, and a plurality (42%) now believed that World War I was justified. However, no fewer than 79 percent of the adults surveyed in five polls between March 1939 and October 1941 expressed the view that this nation should stay out of the coming war between the Allies and the Axis powers. As the position of the Allied nations deteriorated, however, Rita James Simon maintains that public opinion data

> . . . show a consistent trend in the direction of support for France and Britain, and then after the French defeat, for Britain alone. But even as of May 1941, seven months before Pearl Harbor, and one year after the British had been fighting alone, 39 percent believed that above any other consideration, the United States should not risk getting involved in the war.[59]

Once the United States entered World War II, the belief was widespread that we would win the war, and, despite Japan's surprise attack on Pearl Harbor, the American people felt in 1941 that Germany was our major enemy and not Japan. Japan did not become the primary antagonist in the public's mind until September 1943. The polls seem to indicate, therefore, that the public was following Roosevelt's choice of priorities when he argued that the war in Europe, and not the war in the Pacific, should be our foremost priority. Similarly, public opinion supported Roosevelt's demand for Germany's "unconditional surrender," and the American people seem to have been influenced by the stories and rumors that circulated about German atrocities and concentration camps. In Fall 1943 adult Americans were polled on this question: "Suppose the German army gets rid of Hitler, gives up all the territories Germany has conquered, and offers to make peace. If that happens, we should. . . ." Only 24 percent favored making peace, whereas 70 percent wanted to continue the fight until Germany was crushed. One month before the invasion of Normandy by Allied Forces, 82 percent wanted Germany's unconditional surrender before the war ended.

An equally high number (84%) expressed similar terms for making peace with Japan only two months before V-J Day in 1945. When President Truman ordered atomic bombs dropped on the Japanese cities of Nagasaki and Hiroshima, 85 percent of Americans surveyed approved of this action. This high level of support for dropping the atomic bombs may have reflected the intensity of anti-Japanese feelings in the United States at the time. Rita James Simon makes this observation about public opinion toward both Germany and Japan:

> During the war the American public favored harsh treatment toward its enemies, in large measure held the citizenry of the two major powers involved responsible for their government's behavior, and supported the verdicts handed down at Nuremberg against the leaders of the Nazi regime.[60]

As the end of World War II approached, over two-thirds of Americans favored strict supervision of the Axis powers. More extreme were the views held by one-third of the respondents that Germany should be destroyed as a political entity and the attitudes expressed by 14 percent of those surveyed that all Japanese should be killed. Resentment against Japan extended to Japanese-Americans who were subject to relocation during the War.

In a survey taken one year after Pearl Harbor, 49 percent of the West Coast residents polled said that they would not hire Japanese-American servants to work in their homes after the war was over. In January 1945 another poll found that more than 60 percent of Americans believed that Japanese-Americans should not have the same opportunity as white people for employment.

Many aspects of public opinion during World War II were not studied by the surveys, but issues that were analyzed indicate overwhelming support by the citizenry for the nation's war objectives and for Franklin D. Roosevelt's leadership. Moreover, it appears that the desire of Americans to win World War II never weakened during the course of that confrontation.

Korea and Vietnam

In contrast, the survey data indicate that the public's support for the Korean and Vietnam Wars was not so consistent. Both conflicts began with high levels of public approval, with large majorities backing our early involvement in both Korea and Vietnam. But support for both wars sharply declined over time. John Mueller, who studied public opinion during both conflicts, argued: "While support for the war in Vietnam finally dropped below those levels found during Korea, it did so only after the war had gone on considerably longer and only after American casualties had far surpassed those of the earlier war."[61] His data, therefore, contradict the commonly held view that Vietnam was a less popular war than the Korean conflict.

When Truman sent American troops in reaction to the North Korean invasion of South Korea, a Gallup Poll in July 1950 found that 77 percent approved that decision in spite of the view held by 43 percent that this action would "lead to another world war." Public support remained high during the Fall of 1950, when North Korean troops were stopped by American forces. Mueller offers the hypothesis that public support was linked to our feeling that the Korean War would not last long. When Communist China entered the war, support for the Korean War dropped 25 percentage points. Thereafter very little decline in the level of public approval occurred. Given this trend, Mueller discounts any notion that public opinion during wartime is subject to discontinuous "moods." He states:

> Thus, although there seems to have been an important shift of opinion on the war after one major event, events thereafter had comparatively little impact on support for the Korean War. The Chinese intervention seemed to shake from the support ranks the tenuous and those who felt they could support only a short war. The war was then left with a relatively hard core of support that remained generally constant for the duration, despite changes of fortune and climbing casualty figures.[62]

Unlike the Korean War, the war in Vietnam began more gradually. Prior to our military buildup beginning in 1965, the public was largely ignorant of the conflict in Southeast Asia. Moreover, during the Vietnam War there was no spectacular event equivalent to the entrance of China into the Korean War. When Lyndon Johnson committed U.S. troops to the Vietnam War, however, public support for our war policy rose significantly and remained high well into 1966. As with Korea, Mueller argues that wartime events had little effect on public opinion toward Vietnam. But the perception that the war in Vietnam would not be won easily, coupled with increased loss of American lives, caused support for this war to erode beginning about the middle of 1966. Not until 1969, however, had support for the Vietnam War dropped to the low levels recorded during the Korean War, and by now Vietnam had been going on for one year longer. Mueller discounts the role of the anti-War militants in shaping public opinion, arguing that "while the opposition to the war in Vietnam may have been more vocal than that in Korea, it was not more extensive."[63]

A similar argument is made by Converse and Schuman, who also studied public opinion during this period. Writing in 1970, they tried to evaluate President Nixon's claim that a "silent majority" supported his war policies.[64]

They focused on a series of Gallup Polls that asked the following question: "In view of the developments since we entered the fighting do you think the United States made a mistake in sending troops to fight in Vietnam?" The majority tended to support our Vietnam policy during 1965–1966, but by 1967–1968 most Americans surveyed believed that our involvement in Vietnam was a mistake. There was also a decline of confidence in President Johnson's handling of the war. When Richard Nixon assumed the presidency in 1969, public support for his leadership in the war increased to almost the 1965 level achieved by Johnson. Nixon's announcement in November 1969 that he intended to reduce our military commitment to Vietnam undoubtedly was responsible for his strength in the polls. By 1970, however, Converse and Schuman concluded that Nixon "stood squarely aligned with several majorities: those regretting American involvement in Vietnam, those wanting to reduce the nation's commitment there and the large majority rejecting complete withdrawal as an alternative."[65]

These inconsistent strains in public opinion indicate that the public's attitudes about Vietnam were not crystallized by this time. The sporadic fluctuation in public opinion was illustrated by the attitudes toward ceasing the bombing of North Vietnam. In March 1968, only 40 percent agreed that we should stop our bombing on the condition that this action would prompt North Vietnam to begin peace negotiations. Shortly thereafter, President Johnson announced his decision to stop the bombing, and now almost two-thirds of adult Americans approved of that action. Converse and Schuman conclude, "It is safe to assume that the shift of some 25 percent in one month was largely due to the President's speech."[66] However, when it became clear that nothing had been accomplished by this bombing pause, public support for Johnson's leadership of the war again waned. Similar temporary surges in public approval accompanied Nixon's November 1969 speech promising a reduced military commitment and Nixon's expansion of the war by sending troops into Cambodia in 1970. This pattern, therefore, affirms the tendency for Americans to support the president, argue Converse and Schuman, "after any new initiative, whether it is in the direction of escalation or a reduction of commitment."[67]

Converse and Schuman also analyzed the nature of dissent during the Vietnam War. Whereas moral outrage typified the attitude of a small number of highly educated and articulate anti-War dissenters, opposition to the war by a larger minority was based on more practical considerations. "Most disenchantment with the war seems pragmatic and can be summed up in the attitude that 'we have not won and have little prospect of doing so.' "[68] Thus, simple war-weariness explains the opposition to Vietnam by most citizens and, like Mueller, these authors suggest that the news commentators failed to differentiate between these differing strains of anti-Vietnam War thinking. According to Converse and Schuman, the larger minority in opposition to Vietnam—whose position was more pragmatic in nature—could have been persuaded to support the war effort had the anti-War militants turned to violence or extremist tactics to publicize their cause.

Thus, they cautioned that "the net effect of vigorous protest in the streets has been to shift mass opinion toward renewed support of the President."[69]

Most important for consideration here is the degree to which public opinion during wartime bolsters or undermines a president's popularity. It is commonly assumed that both Truman and Johnson were hurt politically by these wars, and Lyndon Johnson, in fact, attributed a 20 percent drop in his approval ratings to the Vietnam War. But Mueller finds that, although the Korean War had a negative impact on Truman's popularity, the Vietnam War had very little independent effect on Johnson's ratings.[70] Mueller estimated that the Korean War cost Truman about 18 percentage points in his approval ratings, and attributed this decline to Truman's inability to keep his war policies above partisan politics. The Republican party became highly critical of Truman, and it appeared that Truman was restraining the military's conduct of the war. This is the reason his firing of General Douglas MacArthur had such a negative effect on President Truman's popularity. In contrast, Lyndon Johnson attracted bipartisan support for his conduct of the Vietnam War, and was perceived as fully backing his field generals. Moreover, the Korean War took place during a period of relative domestic stability whereas the Vietnam War coincided with a time of social unrest and urban rioting. Mueller realistically asserts that the decline of Johnson's popularity might have been due more to domestic conditions rather than to the Vietnam War.

In looking at these findings, we see that the measurement and evaluation of public opinion during wartime is a complicated problem, for the attitudes of citizens are not stable or rigid. The data collected during the wars in Korea and Vietnam do suggest, however, that public opinion rallies behind a president's leadership when war begins, though the levels of public support sink as war-weariness sets in. For both Korea and Vietnam, the level of public support for war is best predicted by the casualty rate. The public seems to desire a quick victory in war; if this does not come easily, then we tire of a prolonged conflict. When Richard Nixon succeeded to the presidency after Johnson, his war policies generated increased public approval because many people thought his approach would lead either to a victory or to a withdrawal from Vietnam. But as the war continued to stagnate, Nixon's popularity also fell. Finally, it appears that public support for a president's war policies is strengthened when the American people perceive that a true communist threat exists or that antiwar critics are using undemocratic or extremist tactics to end military commitments.

EXPERTISE

The commander-in-chief enjoys a relatively unassailable position because of the president's access to information and his ability to monopolize it. When compared with Congress, for example, the imbalance in information gathering has always favored the executive branch. In 1971, the executive branch was spending about $2 billion a year to operate 5,400 computers in forty-four military and nonmilitary agencies, whereas Congress was spending no more than $2 million operating three computers, used mainly for its housekeeping and administrative work. The president is at the very center of what Wise and Ross refer to as the "invisible government," which "gathers intelligence, conducts espionage, and plans and executes secret operations all over the globe."[71]

The commander-in-chief monopolizes information by his constant reliance on information-gathering agencies in the federal bureaucracy. Presidents since Franklin D. Roosevelt have used their influence to obtain political intelligence from agency sources. The Federal Bureau of Investigation has been a primary agency fulfilling this function. As of 1975, for example, the FBI had gathered enough information to maintain 500,000 domestic intelligence files on U.S. citizens. Between 1940 and 1966, the FBI opened 130,000 first-class letters.[72] Moreover, the FBI runs an extensive counterintelligence program. For the president, the FBI has supplied information on the political activities of members of Congress and on lobbying activities by individuals and groups. Franklin D. Roosevelt had the FBI record the names of all citizens who sent telegrams opposing the government's national defense policies as well as those who supported the isolationist proposals made by Charles Lindbergh. President Truman received information from the FBI on labor union negotiations and on various journalists who actively opposed his policies. Eisenhower sought information from the FBI about individuals who had filed a suit to stop atomic energy testing and about Robert Welch, the founder of the right-wing John Birch Society (which accused Eisenhower of being a "fellow traveler" of the Communist party). John F. Kennedy used FBI wiretaps to gain information on a lobbyist, a staff member in Congress, and various officials in his own administration. Lyndon Johnson asked the FBI to keep a watch over the Goldwater staff and some of the leading critics of his policies both within and outside government. President Nixon requested information from FBI sources about U.S. citizens, including a justice on the Supreme Court. The record shows, therefore, that presidents of both political parties have used domestic surveillance to strengthen their political positions against potential opponents. Significantly, most of these cases have been exposed after the president involved had left office, which implies the extreme secrecy with which these activities were carried out.

In addition to the FBI, a commander-in-chief regularly relies on information from the military intelligence agencies, the Central Intelligence Agency, the Office of Management and Budget, the National Security Council, and various ad hoc organizations. Military intelligence is related directly to a president's responsibilities as commander-in-chief. From Army Intelligence, the Office of Naval Intelligence, and Air Force Intelligence the president obtains technical information on weapons systems of foreign nations and counterintelligence information concerning treason, sabotage, or espionage. He also receives from military sources relevant information on foreign attachés, enemy targets, and mapping data. The highly secret National

Security Agency and the National Reconnaissance Office were created by executive order to monitor communications and satellite intelligence. These kinds of data obtained by the intelligence agencies have always been privileged information, known only to a relatively few persons besides the president.

The Central Intelligence Agency is an important source of information for the commander-in-chief. The National Security Act of 1947 created the CIA and gave it the responsibility to advise the National Security Council on intelligence and espionage activities affecting our national security. It also performs such other duties as the NSC shall require. Operating from embassies in foreign capitals, CIA agents keep in contact with Washington. In 1976 a Senate committee investigating the CIA determined that, during the twenty-year period (1953–1973), it had opened and photographed approximately a quarter of a million first-class letters, which constituted an index file on 1.5 million persons. In addition to these information-gathering functions, the CIA has been involved in covert foreign operations in every corner of the world (interference in Cuba, Chile, and Angola are just a few examples).

Criticism of CIA support for right-wing dictatorships and revelations of CIA monitoring of domestic protest groups led to investigations by Congress and the executive. In 1974 Congress enacted legislation requiring the president to report any CIA covert operation to the Senate Foreign Relations Committee, the House Foreign Affairs Committee, and other committees with oversight jurisdiction. So many complaints about the CIA surfaced that President Ford created a presidential commission, chaired by Vice-President Nelson Rockefeller, to study those charges; its report recommended that the CIA be limited to foreign intelligence activities, prohibited from doing domestic surveillance, and scrutinized more closely by the president and Congress. In 1976, CIA covert activities were also investigated by the Senate Select Committee to Study Governmental Operations with Respect to Intelligence Activities (the Church Committee) and the House Select Committee on Intelligence (the Pike Committee). The two-volume report by the Church Committee detailed a long list of abuses by the CIA: invasions of privacy, harassment of U.S. citizens, interference with domestic protest demonstrations, involvement in assassination plots, attempts to overthrow foreign governments, and violations of presidential directives and statutory law. President Carter proposed a new charter for the CIA and other intelligence agencies, but that legislation was not considered by Congress before his term ended.[73]

Under the Reagan administration the CIA was to retain its foreign intelligence function while strengthening its role in domestic information gathering. Moreover, President Reagan proposed to strengthen the CIA by making it a criminal offense to disclose national security information or to reveal the identity of CIA agents. The Reagan administration also wanted to exempt the CIA from the Freedom of Information Act in order to reduce the number of people, including citizens, who are able to share the data collected by the CIA.[74] This CIA exemption from the Freedom of Information Act took effect on June 13, 1982.

Still other permanent and ad hoc agencies of government supply confidential information to the president: the Internal Revenue Service, the Atomic Energy Commission, the State Department's Bureau of Intelligence and Research, and the Defense Intelligence Agency. A president can also obtain information from the hundreds of agencies concerned mainly with domestic policymaking, such as the Drug Enforcement Administration and the U.S. Postal Service. By 1967, in fact, so much information was coming to the president that the Interdivision Information Unit was created to coordinate the intelligence data from the various agencies of government. In 1970, this unit received 42,000 intelligence reports for that year on civil disorders from the FBI, U.S. Attorneys, the Bureau of Narcotics, and the Alcohol, Tobacco and Firearms Division of the Department of Treasury.[75]

On occasion, however, government agencies limit information to the president in order to enhance their own power and importance. The FBI, for example, had kept information secret from the executive in 1946, when it discovered that there were about one hundred persons who were part of a "Government Communist Underground" movement.[76] During the Bay of Pigs invasion, John Kennedy was distressed by the lack of information provided to him by the Joint Chiefs of Staff and the CIA. Because they were not being candid with the president, these groups were accused of trying to influence executive decision making. Moreover, at times the president's reliance on key advisers for information can obscure his ability to make meaningful decisions as commander-in-chief. As secretary of defense to Presidents Kennedy and Johnson, Robert McNamara is credited with asserting civilian control over the armed services and for reducing the degree of interservice rivalries. However, McNamara's expertise also had the effect of protecting the Joint Chiefs of Staff, because his reliance on statistics and systems analysis prevented any serious reevaluation of strategy or priorities. According to David Halberstam, this approach had disastrous effects on our ability to assess the military policy in Vietnam. He states:

> It was convenient for McNamara to stick to these statistics, since they were not only the thing he knew best, but more important, by holding to them he did not get into a fight with his generals over the failure of the existing policy, and thus perhaps have to confront the pressure for a new, expanded policy.[77]

Wartime censorship

In wartime a commander-in-chief has access to emergency statutes such as the Espionage Acts of 1917–1918 and the Internal Security Act of 1950. This kind of legislation allows the president to control information pertaining to the national defense. The Espionage Act prohibited the public from collecting data about military installations, and also disallowed the transfer of documents to unauthorized persons. The Trading with the Enemy Act of 1917 authorized censorship of all communications in and outside the

United States, and the Sedition Act of 1918, which expanded the Espionage Act of 1917, made it a crime to write or publish "any disloyal, profane, scurrilous or abusive language about the form of government of the United States or the Constitution, military or naval forces, flag, or the uniform" or to use language intended to bring these institutions "into contempt, scorn, contumely, or disrepute." In 1941, the First War Powers Act was enacted by Congress to allow the president to censor the mails, telegraph, telephone, and the wireless. This act was accompanied by the creation of the first Office of Censorship (established by Roosevelt) to enforce that law.

During the Eisenhower administration, a censorship code was drafted to apply to the major wire services and newspapers in times of crisis. This code was specifically designed to prevent our giving publicity to the accomplishments of enemy forces.[78] This tradition of information control was extended in 1972 by President Nixon, whose Executive Order 11652 established a unit within the Department of Defense to screen the release of information to the public. Later its name was changed to the War Time Information Security Program, due to public opposition to the term *censorship*.

Often, however, a president does not have to formally censor the media to suppress vital information. Several instances have occurred in which presidents persuaded the press to delay stories or to not print them at all. Arthur Miller recounts four cases.[79] In the 1950s, newsmen from the *Washington Post* and the *New York Times* apparently knew well in advance that the government was using U-2 spy planes to photograph the Soviet Union. The news editors had been persuaded by Eisenhower's concern that publicizing the story about our U-2 planes could jeopardize future reconnaissance flights over the Soviet Union. Nothing about these activities was printed in the newspapers until a Soviet SAM missile shot down U-2 pilot Gary Powers on May 1, 1960. In 1961, at the request of the Kennedy administration, the *New York Times* and the *New Republic* decided against publishing a story about the ill-fated Bay of Pigs invasion of Cuba. The *New Republic* article had been written by Karl Meyer, but editor Gilbert Harrison decided, after sending an advance copy to the White House, against releasing the story.[80]

Another instance of suppression of a news story in the face of pressure from the president occurred in 1975. When the CIA and the Howard Hughes Corporation attempted to find and raise a Soviet submarine that had sunk in the Pacific Ocean, both the *New York Times* and the *Washington Post*, after learning the story, refused to print it after William Colby, then CIA director, requested that it be withheld. Other newspapers and magazines (*Los Angeles Times*, *Time*, and *Newsweek*) also refused to print the story. However, after columnist Jack Anderson broke the silence on March 18, 1975, the other publications felt free to print the story. A final example of presidential influence over the press took place during the Vietnam War. It was Seymour Hersh, a *New York Times* reporter, who printed the story of the My Lai massacre. Before its release, however, the Johnson administration tried to discourage the publication of this war atrocity. The *Washington Post* and

Newsweek agreed with the administration and refused to publish its stories by Martha Gellhorn, whose account was especially graphic and horrible.

As commander-in-chief the president can control information by simple distortion—by releasing false information to the public to safeguard actual material which might embarrass him or undermine national security. In his book, *The Politics of Lying*, David Wise argues that the "credibility gap" was not invented by Lyndon Johnson, for such tactics have been used by virtually all our presidents. Andrew Jackson, for example, misled the public when he explained how generous his policy was toward Native Americans while, at the same time, he crushed the Seminole tribe and involved the United States in the Black Hawk War of 1832. President James K. Polk in 1846 accused Mexico of aggressive actions on American soil when, in fact, the clash between Mexican and American troops had taken place in disputed territory. And in preparing for war, Franklin D. Roosevelt deliberately lied to the American people. Speaking to a Boston audience before the 1940 election, Roosevelt promised that no Americans would be sent into combat. Another instance of blatant deception during the Vietnam War, involved government lying by issuing exaggerated "body counts" of American and Viet Cong casualties. In 1960 government figures indicated that there were no American deaths but that there were 5,667 Vietcong casualties. In 1964 the U.S. death toll rose to 146 while Vietcong deaths were numbered at 16,285; by 1966 the U.S. casualty number was said to be 3,523 while we claimed to have killed 40,149 Vietcong.[81]

During peacetime the commander-in-chief can maintain his control over information by using classification systems. President Franklin D. Roosevelt's 1940 Executive Order 8381 is considered to be the first directive to classify military information and data, although the first extensive security classification system was established by the Eisenhower administration. Executive Order 10501, by President Eisenhower, on November 5, 1953, remained in force for twenty years. Known as the "bible of security stamping," it restricted the number of agencies that could classify information and tried to limit excessive use of classification, which at the time numbered approximately 470 million pages of documents covering the years 1939–1954.[82] The Eisenhower directive established a three-level classification system primarily intended to cover national security information: "top secret," "secret," and "confidential." However, though the Eisenhower administration tried to limit the use of classifications, its system has been utilized to create more and more elaborate and complex schemes to restrict information use. As one commentator argued:

> So much has been classified and so little declassified since World War II that even the government itself has been compelled to find ways of circumventing the rules by either leaking classified information to newsmen or including such material in public statements. The government also devised legal means for granting limited public access to classified material.[83]

Steven Garfinkel, director of the Information Security Oversight Office, recently estimated that approximately 300,000 government documents are classified each year.[84] The trend to classify information since World War II has been increasing, and the reasons given for classification today have very little to do with the national security. As James C. Thomson, Jr. observes:

> Most of what is concealed through classification is anything whose revelation might be politically embarrassing to the Administration in power, or to individual officials, in terms of The Enemy at home: the opposition party, the Congress, the press and thereby the wider voting public.[85]

Martin Shapiro echoes these sentiments when he asserts: "The praiseworthy slogan of Defense Secretary McNamara—'when in doubt, underclassify'—has little effect when there is absolutely no penalty to prevent secrecy from being used to insure individual job security rather than national military security."[86]

Loyalty-security programs

The government's control over information use extends to its employees as well. There are now about twenty different statutes that penalize agency employees who disclose information. These laws cover personnel of the FBI, the CIA, the IRS, and the Federal Home Loan Bank Board. The president is one of the few decision makers privy to most of these data, however. It was President Harry Truman, in Executive Order 9835 of 1947, who first established a loyalty-security program within his administration. The purpose was to uncover instances of treason, sedition, sabotage, and espionage, although Truman resorted to this technique reluctantly. Conservatives and Republicans in Congress had argued that "fellow travelers" and subversives had infiltrated governmental agencies. These charges were the beginnings of the Red Scare and McCarthyism in the early 1950s.[87]

In addition, the commander-in-chief can authorize illegal intelligence activities to uncover leaks of information to outsiders, such as the press. Richard Nixon approved the so-called Huston Plan in 1970. In a plan that markedly expanded domestic surveillance, he authorized the intelligence community to wiretap illegally and to open first-class mail as well as monitor the activities of student radicals. About seventeen wiretaps were made on executive officials and news reporters between 1969 and 1971, a tactic that provided Nixon with political information and access to the names of individuals who opposed his policies.

Thus, the commander-in-chief has the power to suppress the public's "right to know," Congress' "need to know," and the bureaucracy's "desire to know." Expertise, data manipulation, and classification and censorship techniques provide the president as commander-in-chief with sources of power unavailable to him in his weaker roles.

CRISIS

Today we live in an age of potential "total war." When such conflicts as World War I and World War II were fought, they required a total commitment of the nation's human and material resources as the economy shifted from domestic to wartime production. "Total war" efforts also may require the suppression of civil liberties, such as free speech, free press, and due process, in order to maintain a united front against the enemy, as well as to sustain national morale. Extreme measures are justified by wars that seemingly threaten the country's survival, and in these circumstances a president's actions, even when dictatorial, are rarely challenged by the Congress, the Supreme Court, or public opinion. In discussing Lincoln's actions during the Civil War before Congress was convened in special session, we noted the extremity of his decisions, such as his elimination of the right to habeas corpus. But the most far-reaching manifestations of "total war" have taken place in the twentieth century.

In 1918 Woodrow Wilson believed the war effort necessitated assuming control of all telegraph and telephone lines to set rate schedules. The following year the Supreme Court, in the case of *Northern Pacific Railroad Co. v. North Dakota ex rel William Langer,* validated Wilson's actions.[88] Wilson also relied on extensive delegations from Congress to manage the domestic economy; namely, legislation allowing him to

> . . . operate the railroads and water systems, to regulate or commandeer all ship-building facilities in the United States, to regulate and prohibit exports, to raise an army by conscription, to allocate priorities in transportation, to regulate the conduct of resident enemy aliens, to take over and operate the telegraph and telephone systems, to redistribute functions among the executive agencies of the federal government, to control the foreign language press, and to censor all communications to and from foreign countries.[89]

To implement these many objectives, the War and Navy Departments had direct responsibility for the military effort of World War I. Functioning within the War Department, for example, were the Red Cross, the Army Air Service, the Army War College, the Army Tank Corps, the General Staff Corps, and military training centers. The Navigation Bureau, Naval Ordinance, the Coast Guard and Marine Corps, a Yards and Docks Bureau, and general Naval Operations all functioned within the Navy Department.

The civilian resources that were converted to wartime use were administered by various boards and commissions. A 6-member Council of National Defense, organized in 1916 with a 408-member staff, coordinated and provided for overall military needs using available civilian resources. Its subcommittees were divided by region, by subject, and by craft, and executed decisions affecting all types of material, from food to munitions. The War Finance Corporation, created in 1918, was a government-owned company aiding war contractors to obtain loans from banks; it also assisted farmers' efforts to persuade the Federal Reserve Board to extend low interest credit to the agricultural sector. The War Industries Board was founded in 1917 to procure raw materials from private sources for the war effort. Particularly vital to the war effort was its procurement of rubber, manganese, wool, leather goods, pulp, and paper. The War Trade Board controlled the flow of exports and imports; licenses were issued by this board to any agencies involved in foreign trade. Among the other boards and commissions with wartime responsibilities were the U.S. Shipping Board, the Emergency Fleet Corporation, the General Munitions Board, and the National War Labor Board.

During World War II, one of the broadest delegations of power granted any president was that provided under the Lend-Lease Act of 1941. This legislation had implications both for our foreign relations and for the domestic economy. It allowed Franklin D. Roosevelt to select those countries he deemed essential to our defense and to extend to them millions of dollars worth of goods and services on credit for their purchase. The items included "anything from butter to battleships." The president could " 'sell, transfer, exchange, lease or otherwise dispose of the same to any government whose defense the President deemed vital' to that of the United States, and on any terms he deemed 'satisfactory.' " Pursuant to this law, FDR could increase the manufacture of military materiel, and could repair, recondition, test, or inspect any defense article destined for another government. Convoying of vessels was the only action prohibited by the act. Roosevelt also was given the authority under the Lend-Lease Act to determine the type of repayment provisions to be applied to assisted countries. Lend-Lease was described as the "king-link in the chain of international cooperation for victory," but Congress had some concerns. Most important was Congress' worry that the president might engage in a postwar agreement with another nation committing this country to a policy that did not have Congress' approval. This concern was voiced in 1943 and in 1944, when Congress amended the Lend-Lease program to provide that no president could commit the nation to a postwar policy that was in opposition to "constitutional procedure." In 1945, an amendment was attached to this act to prevent the president from entering into postwar agreements to reconstruct or rehabilitate any other nation.

Lend-Lease was a watershed in the practice of granting extensive authority to the president by statute. As one critic of the Roosevelt years remarked, this law "delegated to the President the power to fight wars by deputy; to all intents and purposes, it was a qualified declaration of war."[90] Despite these criticisms, Lend-Lease helped to structure an industrial base during wartime. A total of $47.9 billion was lent to some thirty-eight countries, and such major automobile firms as Ford, Chrysler, Packard, and General Motors built bombers and tanks during the war. By this effort, their production facilities were expanded for later peacetime uses. In addition, the primary aircraft industry, ammunition plants, naval yards, piers, and machine tool companies were all financially aided by Lend-Lease. As a result of this program, moreover, food supplies were increased in 1941 so that 347 million pounds of meat could be shipped to recipient nations; overall, U.S. meat production increased by 511 million pounds.[91]

Although Congress had been most cooperative with Roosevelt during his first term of office, FDR was impatient when his efforts to deal with the domestic crisis were frustrated by the legislative branch. On one occasion Congress was confronted by Roosevelt, who threatened to use his commander-in-chief authority without Congress' consent. During the legislative debate over repealing a provision of the Emergency Price Control Act of February 2, 1942, Roosevelt told Congress that, should it fail to modify that legislation, he would act contrary to the law anyway. This legislation was designed to prohibit food product price ceilings until crop prices had advanced 16 percent above parity. In addressing Congress, demanding the repeal of this provision, Roosevelt argued:

> I ask the Congress to take this action by the first of October. Inaction on your part by that date will leave me with an inescapable responsibility to the people of this country to see to it that the war effort is not longer imperiled by threat of economic chaos.
>
> In the event that the Congress should fail to act, and act adequately, I shall accept the responsibility and I will act.
>
> The president has the power, under the Constitution and Congressional acts, to take measures necessary to avert a disaster which would interfere with the winning of the war. . . .[92]

Whether the president did or did not have the authority as commander-in-chief to implement this legislation without Congress' approval is less compelling an issue than Roosevelt's attitude toward the legislative branch. That he would disregard Congress' responsibility for policymaking troubled Clinton Rossiter greatly. He observed:

> The man charged by the Constitution to "take care that the laws be faithfully executed" announced to the makers of one of those laws, a law which he himself had approved, that he was about to act in direct disregard of its terms if they didn't repeal it immediately.[93]

Here was an instance in which the commander-in-chief's power nearly inflicted serious damage on the separation of powers principle.

As commander-in-chief, Franklin D. Roosevelt also seized private property on many occasions, for example when labor/management disputes threatened wartime production. During the years 1941–1952, which spanned the Roosevelt and Truman administrations, there were seventy-nine seizures of private facilities. Roosevelt took over North American Aviation, Inc., the Federal Shipbuilding and Drydock facility, and Air Associates, Inc. in 1941; the General Cable Company in New Jersey and the S. A. Woods Machine Company in Boston in 1942; and the Western Electric Company in Baltimore, Leather Manufactures, a Massachusetts firm, and Atlantic Basin Iron Works of Brooklyn, New York in 1943. In 1944, there were about eighteen seizures, including Roosevelt's well known takeover of the Montgomery Ward Company. The Chicago branch of Wards had refused to obey a War Labor Board order governing collective bargaining representation for its employees. This dispute arose over the issues of unionization, arbitration of employee grievances, and seniority. On April 23, 1944, the president persuaded the union, which had called a strike earlier in the month, to return to work, but Wards refused to comply with Roosevelt's request. Thus, the president instructed the secretary of commerce to seize the Chicago plant. Wards refused to recognize the government seizure, and in December 1944, after the company's continued defiance of War Labor Board directives, President Roosevelt ordered seized all Montgomery Ward's property throughout the country.

In Congress a Select Committee to Investigate Seizure of the Property of Montgomery Ward and Co. concluded that Roosevelt's seizure "was not only within the constitutional power but was the plain duty of the President."[94] The dispute then went to a court of appeals, which upheld the seizure on statutory grounds and indicated its disapproval of a lower court's decision denying the president's use of seizure power.[95] In its arguments, the court of appeals supported the constitutionality of the War Labor Disputes Act, which granted the president, as commander-in-chief, seizure power over all U.S. plants and property whether engaged directly in war production or not.

Like Woodrow Wilson, Franklin Roosevelt controlled the economy through various agencies of government, both temporary and permanent. About twenty-nine such agencies came under the president's direct control for this purpose, including the War Department, the War Resources Board, the National War Labor Board, the War Production Board, the Office of War Mobilization, the Office of Censorship, the Office of War Information, the War Relocation Authority, the Works Progress Administration, the National Youth Administration, the War Food Administration, and the War Manpower Commission. One of the most important agencies was the twelve-member National War Labor Board; it decided some 362,000 employee/management disputes affecting 24,000,000 employees during the years 1942–1944.

The exigencies of "total war" also permitted Roosevelt to subvert civil liberties and normal due process procedures during World War II. For example, FDR established a military commission to try a number of saboteurs who had landed in submarines off the coasts of Florida and Long Island. Nothing in the Constitution addresses this wartime contingency but, as noted earlier, the Supreme Court in *Ex Parte Quirin* upheld FDR's power. The most extensive violations of civil liberties, however, affected the Territory of Hawaii and Japanese-Americans living on the West Coast of the United States.

Martial law in Hawaii

Franklin D. Roosevelt imposed a state of martial law in the Territory of Hawaii following the Japanese attack on Pearl Harbor on December 7, 1941. Because of the fear that the Japanese would return to Hawaii with landing forces, aided by Japanese residents there, General Short, acting on the authority of the president, imposed martial law.[96] At first Hawaii's governor was reluctant to forego his leadership to the Army but, after talking to the president, he was convinced that the situation at hand made it difficult to question the judgment of the military. Martial law was invoked on December 8; civilian courts were closed and replaced by a military judiciary. Suspects were arrested, including 370 Japanese residents, 98 German aliens, and 14 Italian aliens. Other actions taken under martial law included surrounding the Japanese consulate with military troops, collecting all explosives from the island, and suspending the writ of habeas corpus. With the exception of judicial matters, however, the rest of Hawaii's local government functioned fairly routinely except that the military governor oversaw its operations. Elections took place, and the legislature met regularly and disposed of its business in spite of the three-year-long imposition of martial law.

Civil liberties in Hawaii were endangered during this time, however. The territorial courts were opened only for a brief period to allow them to process those cases pending before December 7. The military courts conducted the majority of cases, by means of a military commission and a series of provost courts. The military commission, composed of both civilians and army officers, tried all cases in which possible punishment involved penalties exceeding a $5,000 fine and five years in prison. The provost courts, made up of individual military judges, heard lesser cases. During the period of martial law, the military commission tried eight cases, including charges of murder, espionage, and robbery, while the provost courts heard nearly 19,000 cases in the first six months of their operations.

The most irritating aspects of the martial law for U.S. citizens were the incessant searches and seizures, the arrests and detentions of citizens, the trials for criminal offenses held without juries, and the suspension of habeas corpus. In 1942 the new territorial governor, Ingram M. Stainback, tried to have martial law rescinded, but was opposed by the powerful Chamber of Commerce and the American Legion in Hawaii. At this time, however, the Roosevelt administration decided to retain the military governor there but agreed to return some eighteen governmental functions to civilian authorities. Thus, the Office of the Military Governor continued to function until 1944, when it became known as the Office of Internal Security. On October 24, 1944, martial law was terminated, and habeas corpus was reinstated in Hawaii. However, the islands remained a "military area" and special security arrangements were applied to segments of its civilian population.

Several attempts were made to test the constitutionality of martial law in Hawaii. The most important case involved Lloyd C. Duncan, who challenged the provost court system. He charged that military courts did not have the authority to make judgments in civilian cases if the civil courts were able to function in a normal way. On February 25, 1946, the Supreme Court reviewed the legality of Hawaiian martial law, and in the case of *Duncan* v. *Kahanamoku Sheriff* declared that the imposition of martial law had exceeded the authority of the Hawaiian Organic Act. In a 6 to 2 decision, Justice Black for the majority charged that

> our system of government clearly is the antithesis of total military rule and the founders of this country are not likely to have contemplated complete military dominance within the limits of a territory made part of this country and not recently taken from an enemy. They were opposed to governments that placed in the hands of one man the power to make, interpret and enforce the laws.[97]

Relocating Japanese-Americans

Perhaps even more extreme than imposition of martial law in Hawaii was the violation of civil liberties affecting Japanese-American citizens on the mainland. Their trying experiences reveal how the Congress, the president, and the Supreme Court are able to rationalize the serious abuse of civil liberties and freedoms in the face of a war crisis. On February 19, 1942, Franklin Roosevelt issued Executive Order 9066 to deal with the potential danger of Japanese sabotage on our West Coast. The executive ordered the forceful removal of some 112,000 Japanese-Americans from their homes. Most of these residents were native-born citizens. Military zones were established along the West Coast to protect military installations. Each Japanese-American family was removed from these zones and sent to "relocation centers" in the desert areas of California, Arizona, Idaho, Utah, Colorado, and Wyoming. Congress supported FDR's action by passing, on March 21, 1942, a resolution making it a misdemeanor against the United States "to knowingly enter, remain in, or leave prescribed military areas" against the orders of the secretary of war and the military officers in charge. Those who defend this harsh treatment of the Japanese-Americans argue that their concentration on the West Coast was feared by the rest of the population who believed the Japanese-Americans' location in strategic areas and cultural and traditional ties to Japan were dangerous to U.S. security.

Executive Order 9066 and Congress' action were challenged in suits taken to the Supreme Court, as mentioned earlier. The Court decided these cases in June 1943 (*Hirabayashi* v. *U.S.*) and in December 1944 (*Korematsu* v. *United States*). In the first case, the Supreme Court supported the president's power to remove the Japanese-Americans. Specifically approved was a curfew that limited these people's movement in the military zones established on the West Coast. The manner in which the curfew issue had been presented to the Court, as part of presidential war power, made it very difficult for any justice to declare it unconstitutional, despite arguments by some members of the Supreme Court that it represented clear discrimination against Japanese-Americans. Justice Stone defended this action in time of war:

> We cannot close our eyes to the fact, demonstrated by experience, that in time of war residents having ethnic affiliations with an invading enemy may be a greater source of danger than those of a different ancestry. Nor can we deny that Congress, and the military authorities acting with its authorization, have constitutional power to appraise the danger in the light of facts of public notoriety.

In the Korematsu decision that followed in 1944, the question raised concerned the authority to implement an exclusionary order housing the Japanese-Americans in internment camps in the Rocky Mountain states for the duration of the War. In a 6 to 3 decision, the majority of justices upheld the commander-in-chief, arguing that the exclusionary order was a legitimate outgrowth of presidential and congressional authority. In the dissenting opinions were charges of discrimination and accounts of hardships suffered by the interned Japanese-Americans, but Justice Black, writing for the majority, ignored these pleas and argued: ". . . hardships are a part of war, and war is an aggregation of hardships. Citizenship has its responsibilities as well as its privileges, and in time of war the burden is always heavier."[98]

The Japanese-American cases serve as some of the clearest indexes of the real power potential of a commander-in-chief during wartime. Here the Supreme Court rejected its traditional role of protecting minority rights to support a wartime president, who was committing an act of racism against U.S. citizens. Added evidence for this interpretation is found in the fact that, though the United States had declared war against Germany and Italy as well as Japan, German- or Italian-Americans were not treated in the same manner. As Justice Murphy stated:

> No adequate reason is given for the failure to treat these Japanese Americans on an individual basis by holding investigations and hearings to separate the loyal from the disloyal, as was done in the case of persons of German and Italian ancestry.

Truman's steel seizure

One possible exception to the tendency to allow extraordinary powers for the commander-in-chief involves Harry Truman's seizure of the steel mills during the Korean War. 86 steel companies were seized by Truman under his authority as commander-in-chief on April 8, 1952, but the Supreme Court later that year, in the case of *Youngstown Sheet and Tube Company* v. *Sawyer,* stated that the President had over-extended his power and violated the separation of powers. By a 6–3 vote the Court refused to allow the commander-in-chief to take control of private property for war purposes. Congress, the court reasoned, had already provided the means to resolve the steel strike. According to Truman, a threatened steel strike posed a national crisis. He argued that steel production for the war effort was absolutely essential. But the Supreme Court said that presidential power in times of crisis cannot go so far as to undermine Congress' authority. The court reasoned that Truman should have relied on the Taft-Hartley Act in this situation.[99]

Defenders of presidential power during emergencies criticized the Supreme Court in this case for being too rigid.[100] Even some Justices who voted with the majority were careful to indicate that this decision was limited in scope. As Justice Clark suggested:

> In my view . . . the Constitution does grant to the president extensive authority in times of grave and imperative national emergency. In fact, to my thinking, such a grant may well be necessary to the very existence of the Constitution itself.

Given this degree of ambiguity, perhaps the decision rendered in *Youngstown* is not a clear repudiation of commander-in-chief powers during crisis. Glendon Schubert is one scholar who argues this position.

> It would be highly misleading to tout this case as holding against the President's right to exercise implied ("inherent," "residual," "prerogative") constitutional powers. On the contrary, a majority of the Court explicitly affirmed their acceptance of the theory of implied presidential powers; two members of the Court expressly reserved the question; and only two held against such a theory, and then only insofar as it would justify the President's action in this particular case.[101]

Since the *Youngstown* case there have been relatively few instances when the Supreme Court has limited the president's use of commander-in-chief authority. Two such cases occurred during the Nixon presidency. In *U.S. v. District Court for the Eastern District of Michigan* the president defended wiretapping done without search warrants in the name of national security.[102] The Supreme Court rejected Nixon's justification and argued that warrant procedures were absolutely essential to the process of justice, particularly when domestic organizations were involved. The more important case of *U.S. v. Nixon*, mentioned previously, found the Supreme Court requiring President Nixon to release the Watergate tapes and transcripts. Nixon had refused to supply those materials, invoking executive privilege, on the grounds that their revelations would hurt national security. The Court was not sympathetic to his arguments, though it admitted that "executive privilege" could extend to legitimate matters of national security. As these two cases suggest, the power of the president as commander-in-chief sometimes goes beyond reasonable limits. This entire issue was studied by the Congress during its debate over our involvement in Vietnam.

In 1973 a Special Senate Committee on the Termination of the National Emergency discovered that, as a result of four executive proclamations (Franklin Roosevelt's in 1933, Truman's in 1950, and Nixon's in 1970 and 1971), there were 470 emergency statutes granting extraordinary powers to the president. These statutes allowed him ". . . the right to seize property, organize and control the means of production, seize commodities, assign military forces abroad, call reserve forces amounting to 2.5 million men to duty, institute martial law, seize and control all means of transportation, regulate all private enterprise, and restrict travel."[103] Even though the emergencies that resulted in these statutes, such as the Korean War, had long passed, the president still held these powers. As a consequence, Congress enacted legislation to rescind those emergency powers and the National

Emergencies Act was signed into law by Gerald Ford in 1976. (The National Emergencies Act is excerpted on pp. 00–00.) Though Congress' action in this instance shows that it can be an effective check on executive power, it is also true that Congress had willingly delegated such emergency powers to the president in the first place.

CAN THE COMMANDER-IN-CHIEF BE CHECKED?

Nineteenth-century presidents were more cautious than contemporary ones in the ways they used war powers, but the commander-in-chief role always has been the most potentially powerful one. It was Abraham Lincoln, as a congressman, who warned the nation: "Allow the President to invade a neighboring nation, whenever he shall deem it necessary to repel an invasion . . . and you allow him to make war at pleasure. Study to see if you can fix any limit to his power in this respect."[104]

By broadly interpreting their war powers, presidents have made it even more difficult than Lincoln had anticipated for Congress or public opinion to limit the commander-in-chief. In the early years of the Republic no president claimed an "inherent right" or plenary authority to justify war making, nor did they seek extraconstitutional grounds for using force. Fundamental to the issue of accountability is the fact that contemporary presidents now defend their use of war powers on numerous grounds. Regarding Richard Nixon in 1973 Arthur Schlesinger, Jr., observed:

> Today President Nixon has equipped himself with so expansive a theory of the powers of the Commander in Chief, and so elastic a theory of defensive war, that he can freely, on his own initiative, without a national emergency, as a routine employment of Presidential power, go to war against any country containing any troops that might in any conceivable circumstance be used in an attack on American forces.[105]

Congress should be the most effective check on the commander-in-chief by virtue of its power to "declare" war and to appropriate funds. But only on a few occasions has Congress exerted its authority: when it tried to hold President Tyler accountable for wanting to annex Texas, when it debated President Polk's request for a declaration of war against Mexico, and when it attempted to influence President Lincoln's conduct of the Civil War. Despite President Nixon's intentions to the contrary, the Vietnam War was terminated by Congress' enactment of legislation prohibiting the use of funds for military purposes in that region. But this conclusion of the conflict in Southeast Asia came about ten years after massive involvement there began. On the other hand, Congress has shown its willingness to expand the president's authority as commander-in-chief. Its enactment of the 1964 Gulf of Tonkin Resolution was not a unique event but rather one indicative of a more general pattern. According to Louis Koenig,

> Congress seldom has objected to the action of the President, as commander-in-chief, in sending abroad and maintaining the armed forces without its prior

concurrence. The instances of objection are important, but the otherwise general consent has tacitly established the rule of practice.[106]

The enactment of the War Powers Act of 1973 assures that a future president's use of troops will precipitate a congressional debate, because such military involvement cannot continue beyond sixty or ninety days without Congress' approval. Nevertheless, the Act's provisions for executive/legislative consultations before a president commits troops were successfully sidestepped by Gerald Ford and Jimmy Carter. Significantly, its provision allowing the commander-in-chief to use military force for sixty days without explicit legislative authorization legitimizes a war-making power that heretofore had been based on customary practice and precedent. Moreover, the fact that a president may continue a military action beyond the two- or three-month period without a formal "declaration" of war (only a concurrent resolution is required) suggests that Congress wants the commander-in-chief to enjoy the ability to respond quickly to international crises. The same rationale influenced the Framers when at the Constitutional Convention they rejected giving Congress the power to "make" war in favor of the authority to "declare" war; by that change in language, the commander-in-chief was empowered to respond to emergencies and to dire threats to the nation's security. It remains to be seen whether the War Powers Act will curb a president's inclination to make war.

Nor has the Supreme Court acted to restrain the commander-in-chief. As Robert Dahl once argued, the Supreme Court will not stand against a source of political power.[107] With the possible exception of the *Youngstown* case, therefore, the Court has never interfered with the president's interpretation of his war powers. This is especially obvious when the executive and legislative branches agree about military policy, as was illustrated by the *Hirabayashi* and *Korematsu* cases. The Supreme Court's refusal to hear challenges of the legality of the Vietnam War legitimized presidential war making without a declaration. Philippa Strum argued that, since the Supreme Court did not label war making in Vietnam a "political question," the Court's posture shows its ". . . unwillingness to establish the rule that a President could not be stopped from involving the country in a war."[108] Nonetheless, the Court's action in *Massachusetts v. Laird* may discourage further appeals to the courts on this issue.

As Ronald Reagan moved to involve the United States in aiding the government in El Salvador in opposing communist and right-wing forces, no real answer had been found to the problem of restraining the commander-in-chief. Arthur Schlesinger, Jr., rightly accuses modern presidents of having ". . . neglected the collection of consent, removed significant executive decisions from the political process, and departed considerably from the principles, if somewhat less from the practice, of the early republic."[109] The commander-in-chief role is the president's most powerful one, and the one presenting the most serious challenge to constitutional government and democratic politics.

War Powers Resolution
Public Law 93–148
November 7, 1973
(Excerpts)

Purpose and policy

Sec. 2. (a) It is the purpose of this joint resolution to fulfill the intent of the framers of the Constitution of the United States and insure that the collective judgment of both the Congress and the President will apply to the introduction of United States Armed Forces into hostilities, or into situations where imminent involvement in hostilities is clearly indicated by the circumstances, and to the continued use of such forces in hostilities or in such situations.

(b) Under article I, section 8, of the Constitution, it is specifically provided that the Congress shall have the power to make all laws necessary and proper for carrying into execution, not only its own powers but also all other powers vested by the Constitution in the Government of the United States, or in any department or officer thereof.

(c) The constitutional powers of the President as Commander-in-Chief to introduce United States Armed Forces into hostilities, or into situations where imminent involvement in hostilities is clearly indicated by the circumstances, are exercised only pursuant to (1) a declaration of war, (2) specific statutory authorization, or (3) a national emergency created by attack upon the United States, its territories or possessions, or its armed forces.

Consultation

Sec. 3. The President in every possible instance shall consult with Congress before introducing United States Armed Forces into hostilities or into situations where imminent involvement in hostilities is clearly indicated by the circumstances, and after every such introduction shall consult regularly with the Congress until United States Armed Forces are no longer engaged in hostilities or have been removed from such situations.

Reporting

Sec. 4. (a) In the absence of a declaration of war, in any case in which United States Armed Forces are introduced—

(1) into hostilities or into situations where imminent involvement in hostilities is clearly indicated by the circumstances;

(2) into the territory, airspace or waters of a foreign nation, while equipped for combat, except for deployments which relate solely to supply, replacement, repair, or training of such forces; or

(3) in numbers which substantially enlarge United States Armed Forces equipped for combat already located in a foreign nation;

the President shall submit within 48 hours to the Speaker of the House of Representatives and to the President pro tempore of the Senate a report, in writing, setting forth—

(A) the circumstances necessitating the introduction of United States Armed Forces;

(B) the constitutional and legislative authority under which such introduction took place; and

(C) the estimated scope and duration of the hostilities or involvement.

(b) The President shall provide such other information as the Congress may request in the fulfillment of its constitutional responsibilities with respect to committing the Nation to war and to the use of United States Armed Forces abroad.

(c) Whenever United States Armed Forces are introduced into hostilities or into any situation described in subsection (a) of this section, the President shall, so long as such armed forces continue to be engaged in such hostilities or situation, report to the Congress periodically on the status of such hostilities or situation as well as on the scope and duration of such hostilities or situation, but in no event shall he report to the Congress less often than once every six months . . .

Congressional action

Sec. 5. (b) Within sixty calendar days after a report is submitted or is required to be submitted pursuant to section 4(a)(1), whichever is earlier, the President shall terminate any use of United States Armed Forces with respect to which such report was submitted (or required to be submitted), unless the Congress (1) has declared war or has enacted a specific authorization for such use of United States Armed Forces, (2) has extended by law such sixty-day period, or (3) is physically unable to meet as a result of an armed attack upon the United States. Such sixty-day period shall be extended for not more than an additional thirty days if the President determines and certifies to the Congress in writing that unavoidable military necessity respecting the safety of United States Armed Forces requires the continued use of such armed forces in the course of bringing about a prompt removal of such forces.

(c) Notwithstanding subsection (b), at any time that United States Armed Forces are engaged in hostilities outside the territory of the United States, its possessions and territories without a declaration of war or specific statutory authorization, such forces shall be removed by the President if the Congress so directs by concurrent resolution . . .

Interpretation of joint resolution

Sec. 8. (a) Authority to introduce United States Armed Forces into hostilities or into situations wherein involvement in hostilities is clearly indicated by the circumstances shall not be inferred—

(1) from any provision of law (whether or not in effect before the date of the enactment of this joint resolution), including any provision contained in any appropriation Act, unless such provision specifically authorizes the introduction of United States Armed Forces into hostilities or into such situations and states that it is intended to constitute specific statutory authorization within the meaning of this joint resolution; or

(2) from any treaty heretofore or hereafter ratified unless such treaty is implemented by legislation specifically authorizing the introduction of United States Armed Forces into hostilities or into such situations and stating that it is intended to constitute specific statutory authorization within the meaning of this joint resolution.

Sec. 8. (d) Nothing in this joint resolution—

(1) is intended to alter the constitutional authority of the Congress or of the President, or the provisions of existing treaties; or

(2) shall be construed as granting any authority to the President with respect to the introduction of United States Armed Forces into hostilities or into situations wherein involvement in hostilities is clearly indicated by the circumstances which authority he would not have had in the absence of this joint resolution . . .

National Emergencies Act
Public Law 94–412
September 14, 1976
(Excerpts)

Terminating existing declared emergencies

Sec. 101. (a) All powers and authorities possessed by the President, any other officer or employee of the Federal Government, or any executive agency, as defined in section 105 of title 5, United States Code, as a result of the existence of any declaration of national emergency in effect on the date of enactment of this Act are terminated two years from the date such enactment. Such termination shall not affect—

(1) any action taken or proceeding pending not finally concluded or determined on such date;

(2) any action or proceeding based on any act committed prior to such date; or

(3) any rights or duties that matured or penalties that were incurred prior to such date.

(b) For the purpose of this section, the words "any national emergency in effect" means a general declaration of emergency made by the President.

Declarations of future national emergencies

Sec. 201. (a) With respect to Acts of Congress authorizing the exercise, during the period of a national emergency, of any special or extraordinary power, the President is authorized to declare such national emergency. Such proclamation shall immediately be transmitted to the Congress and published in the Federal Register.

(b) Any provisions of law conferring powers and authorities to be exercised during a national emergency shall be effective and remain in effect (1) only when the President (in accordance with subsection (a) of this section), specifically declares a national emergency, and (2) only in accordance with this Act. No law enacted after the date of enactment of this Act shall supersede this title unless it does so in specific terms, referring to this title, and declaring that the new law supersedes the provisions of this title.

Sec. 202. (a) Any national emergency declared by the President in accordance with this title shall terminate if—

(1) Congress terminates the emergency by concurrent resolution; or

(2) the President issues a proclamation terminating the emergency . . .

Publication of Executive Orders and transmittal to congress

Sec. 301. When the President declares a national emergency, no powers or authorities made available by statute for use in the event of an emergency shall be exercised unless and until the President specifies the provisions of law under which he proposes that he, or other officers will act. Such specification may be made either in the declaration of a national emergency, or by one or more contemporaneous or subsequent Executive orders published in the Federal Register and transmitted to the Congress.

NOTES

[1]Richard Rose, "The President: A Chief But Not an Executive," *Presidential Studies Quarterly* (Winter 1977), p. 9.

[2]Sidney Hyman, *The American Presidency* (New York: Harper and Brothers, 1954), p. 10.

[3]Winton U. Solberg, *The Federal Convention and the Formation of the Union of the American States* (Indianapolis: Bobbs-Merrill Company, 1958), pp. 78, 133, 148.

[4]Morton Borden, ed., *The AntiFederalist Papers* (East Lansing: Michigan State University, 1965), no. 74, p. 212.

[5]The following works elaborate on this argument: Raoul Berger, "War Making by the President," *University of Pennsylvania Law Review* (1972), pp. 29–86; Charles Lofgren, "War Making Under the Constitution: The Original Understanding," *Yale Law Journal* (1972), pp. 672–702; William Van Alstyne, "Congress, the President, and the Power to Declare War: A Requiem for Vietnam," *University of Pennsylvania Law Review* (1972), pp. 1–28.

[6]See a complete listing of 192 U.S. military engagements taking place during 1798–1970 without a formal declaration of war in J. Terry Everson, "War Powers Legislation," *West Virginia Law Review* (August/November 1971), pp. 53–119.

[7]Dorothy Schaffter and Dorothy M. Mathews, *The Powers of the President as Commander in Chief of the Army and Navy of the United States;* United States, 84th Congress, 2nd Session, House Document no. 443 (New York: DaCapo Press, 1974), p. 4.

[8]J. Malcolm Smith and Stephen Jurika, Jr., *The President and National Security: His Role as Commander-in-Chief* (Dubuque, Iowa: Kendall/Hunt Publishing Company, 1972), p. 12.

[9]Ibid.

[10]Edward S. Corwin, *Total War and the Constitution* (New York: Alfred A. Knopf, 1947), p. 17.

[11]Ibid., p. 16.

[12]*Luther* v. *Borden,* 48 US (7 How.) 44 (1849).

[13]*Fleming* v. *Page,* 9 How. 615 (1850).

[14]*Ex Parte Merryman,* 17 Fed. Cas. 144 (1861).

[15]The *Prize* Cases, 67 US (2 Black) 635 (1862).

[16]Ibid.

[17]*Ex Parte Milligan,* 71 US (4 Wallace) 2 (1866).

[18]Clinton Rossiter, *The Supreme Court and the Commander in Chief* (New York: Cornell University Press, 1951), p. 34.

[19]Clinton Rossiter, *Constitutional Dictatorship: Crisis Government in the Modern Democracy* (Princeton, N.J.: Princeton University Press, 1948), p. 244.

[20]"U.S. Destroyer *Greer* Sunk by German Submarine," radio broadcast, September 11, 1941, in Wilfred Funk, ed., *Roosevelt's Foreign Policy, 1933–1941: Franklin D. Roosevelt's Unedited Speeches and Messages* (New York: Wilfred Funk, Inc., 1942), pp. 470–475.

[21]Schaffter and Mathews, *The Power of the President as Commander in Chief of the Army and Navy of the United States,* p. 9.

[22]*Ex Parte Quirin,* 317 US 1 (1942).

[23]*Hirabayashi* v. *United States,* 320 US 81 (1943); *Korematsu* v. *United States,* 323 US 214 (1944).

[24]William Emerson, "Franklin Roosevelt as Commander-In-Chief in World War II," *Military Affairs* (1958), p. 206.

[25]"Statement on Korea," *The New York Times* (June 28, 1950), p. 1, col. 6.

[26]Dean Acheson, *Present at the Creation: My Years in the State Department* (New York: Norton, 1969), pp. 414–415.

[27]William M. Goldsmith, *The Growth of Presidential Power: A Documented History,* vol. 3 (New York: Chelsea House Publishers, 1974), p. 1819.

[28]*Schechter Poultry Corp.* v. *U.S.,* 295 US 495 (1935); *Panama Refining Co.* v. *Ryan,* 293 US 388 (1935); *Kent* v. *Dulles,* 357 US 116 (1958).

[29]Alexander Bickel, "Congress, the President and the Power to Wage War," *Chicago Kent Law Review* (Fall/Winter 1971), p. 137.

[30]See U.S. Congress, Senate, *U.S. Commitments to Foreign Powers,* Hearings before

the Foreign Relations committee, 90th Congress, 1st Session, 1967, pp. 79–83, 141.

[31]"A Conversation With the President About Foreign Policy," *Public Papers of the Presidents of the United States: Richard Nixon; Containing the Public Messages, Speeches and Statements of the President, 1970* (Washington, D.C.: U.S. Government Printing Office, 1971), p. 546.

[32]Arthur M. Schlesinger, Jr., *The Imperial Presidency* (Boston: Houghton Mifflin, 1973), pp. 187–188.

[33]"Address to the Nation on the Situation in Southeast Asia," April 30, 1970, *Public Papers of the Presidents of the United States: Richard Nixon*, pp. 405–410.

[34]William H. Rehnquist, "The Constitutional Issues—Administration Position," *New York University Law Review* (June 1970), pp. 628–639.

[35]*Youngstown Sheet and Tube Co. v. Sawyer*, 343 US 579 (1952).

[36]Schlesinger, *The Imperial Presidency*, p. 193.

[37]Arthur M. Schlesinger, Jr., "Is the Presidency Too Powerful?" *Reader's Digest* (December 1975), p. 88.

[38]Cited in Theodore J. Lowi, *American Government: Incomplete Conquest* (Hinsdale, Ill.: Dryden Press, 1976), p. 400.

[39]Pat M. Holt, *The War Powers Resolution: The Role of Congress in U.S. Armed Intervention* (Washington, D.C.: American Enterprise Institute for Public Policy Research, 1978), p. 26.

[40]Cited in Milton C. Cummings, Jr. and David Wise, *Democracy Under Pressure* (New York: Harcourt Brace Jovanovich, 1981), p. 362.

[41]U.S. Congress, House of Representatives, *Report of Secretary of State Kissinger on His Visits to Latin America, Western Europe, and Africa*, Hearings before the Committee on International Relations, 94th Congress, 2nd Session, 1976, p. 13.

[42]U.S. Congress, House of Representatives, *War Powers: A Test of Compliance Relative to the Danang Sealift, the Evacuation of Phnom Penh, the Evacuation of Saigon, and the Mayaguez Incident*, Hearings before the Subcommittee on International Security and Scientific Affairs of the Committee on International Relations, 94th Congress, 1st Session, 1975, p. vi.

[43]"Rescue Attempt for American Hostages in Iran," Letter to the Speaker of the House and the President Pro Tempore of the Senate, reporting on the operation, *Weekly Compilation of Presidential Documents*, vol. 16, no. 18 (Washington, D.C.: Office of the Federal Register, National Archives, May 5, 1980), pp. 777–779.

[44]Goldsmith, *The Growth of Presidential Power: A Documented History*, vol. 3, p. 2136.

[45]Corwin, *Total War and the Constitution*, p. 29.

[46]*Massachusetts v. Laird*, 400 US 886 (1970); *Orlando v. Laird*, 443 F 2d 1039 (1971); *Holtzman v. Schlesinger*, 414 U.S. 1304–1326 (1973).

[47]"Introduction of Bills and Joint Resolutions," *Congressional Record*, 94th Congress, 1st Session, vol. 121, part 26 (October 20, 1975), p. 33067.

[48]Drew Middleton, "Debate over Joint Chiefs is Widening," *New York Times* (March 1, 1982), p. 8.

[49]This discussion is based on Glenn D. Paige, *The Korean Decision* (New York: The Free Press, 1968).

[50]Sidney Warren, *The President as World Leader* (New York: McGraw-Hill, 1964), p. 343. Those consulted were Generals Marshall and Bradley and Secretaries Acheson and Harriman.

[51]See Irving L. Janis, *Victims of Groupthink: A Psychological Study of Foreign Policy Decisions and Fiascoes* (Boston: Houghton Mifflin, 1972), p. 57.

[52]Graham T. Allison, *Essence of Decision: Explaining the Cuban Missile Crisis* (Boston: Little, Brown and Company, 1971). Our discussion is based on this excellent case study.

[53]Ibid., p. 128.

[54]Our explanation of the *Mayaguez* incident is based on the information in Richard

G. Head; Frisco W. Short; and Robert C. McFarlane, *Crisis Resolution: Presidential Decision Making in the Mayaguez and Korean Confrontations* (Boulder, Colo.: Westview Press, 1978), pp. 101–148.

[55]"Ford Backed in Congress on Military Action Against Cambodia," *New York Times* (May 15, 1975), p. 18.

[56]Two studies of our involvement in the Iran crisis are Barry Rubin, *Paved With Good Intentions: The American Experience and Iran* (New York: Oxford University Press, 1980); Michael Ledeen and William Lewis, *Debacle: The American Failure in Iran* (New York: Knopf, 1981).

[57]Ledeen and Lewis, *Debacle: The American Failure in Iran*, p. 234.

[58]Rita James Simon, *Public Opinion in America: 1936–1970* (Chicago: Rand McNally, 1974), p. 150. Our discussion of public opinion during World War II is based on Simon's analysis on pages 123–147. In three surveys asking Americans whether our entry into World War II had been a mistake, overwhelming majorities said "no" in 1946 (77%), in 1947 (66%), and in 1948 (78%).

[59]Ibid., p. 128.

[60]Ibid., p. 196.

[61]John E. Mueller, "Trends in Popular Support for the Wars in Korea and Vietnam," *American Political Science Review* (June 1971), p. 371.

[62]Ibid., p. 361.

[63]Ibid., p. 371.

[64]Philip E. Converse and Howard Schuman, " 'Silent Majorities' and the Vietnam War," *Scientific American* (June 1970), pp. 17–25.

[65]Ibid., p. 20.

[66]Ibid., p. 21.

[67]Ibid.

[68]Ibid., p. 24.

[69]Ibid.

[70]John E. Mueller, "Presidential Popularity from Truman to Johnson," *American Political Science Review* (March 1970), pp. 18–34.

[71]David Wise and Thomas B. Ross, *The Invisible Government* (New York: Random House, 1964), p. 3.

[72]U.S. Congress, Senate, "Intelligence Activities and the Rights of Americans," book 2, *Final Report of the Select Committee to Study Governmental Operations with Respect to Intelligence Activities*, 94th Congress, 2nd Session, report no. 94–755, April 26, 1976, p. 6.

[73]Ibid.

[74]Dom Bonafede, "Press Leaks: Reagan Not First to be Concerned," *Today* (March 12, 1982), p. 4.

[75]"Intelligence Activities and the Rights of Americans," p. 80.

[76]Ibid., p. 56.

[77]David Halberstam, *The Best and the Brightest* (New York: Random House, 1972), p. 256.

[78]David Wise, *The Politics of Lying: Government Deception, Secrecy and Power* (New York: Vintage Books, 1973), p. 203.

[79]Arthur S. Miller, *Presidential Power in a Nutshell* (St. Paul: West Publishing Company, 1977), pp. 281–284.

[80]James J. Kilpatrick, "The Right to Know the Whole Story," *Indianapolis Star* (March 16 1982), p. 8.

[81]See George McTurnan Kahin and John W. Lewis, *The United States in Vietnam* (New York: Delta, 1969), p. 188.

[82]Norman Dorsen and Stephen Gillers, *None of Your Business: Government Secrecy in America* (New York: Penguin, 1975), p. 71.

[83]Carol M. Barker and Matthew H. Fox, *Classified Files: The Yellowing Pages* (New York: Twentieth Century Fund, 1972), pp. 15–16.

[84]"Administration Asks Secret Data Rules," *Chicago Tribune* (October 22, 1981), sec. 1, p. 16.

[85]James C. Thomson, Jr., "Government and Press: Good News About a Bad Marriage," *New York Times Magazine* (November 25, 1973), p. 56.

[86]Martin Shapiro, ed., *The Pentagon Papers and the Courts* (San Francisco: Chandler Publishing Company, 1972), p. 53.

[87]Howard Simons and Joseph A. Califano, Jr., eds., *The Media and the Law* (New York: Praeger, 1976), p. 98.

[88]*Northern Pacific Railroad Co. v. North Dakota ex rel William Langer,* 250 US 135 (1919).

[89]Rossiter, *Constitutional Dictatorship,* p. 243. For an elaboration on the specific statutes alluded to here, see Clarence A. Berdahl, *War Powers of the Executive in the United States* (New York: Johnson Reprint Corp., 1970).

[90]Schaffter and Mathews, *The Power of the President as Commander in Chief of the Army and Navy of the United States,* p. 25.

[91]Edward R. Stettinius, Jr., *Lend-Lease—Weapon for Victory* (New York: Macmillan Company, 1944), p. 101.

[92]Clinton Rossiter, *The American Presidency,* 2nd ed. (New York: Harcourt, Brace, and World, 1960), p. 147.

[93]Rossiter, *Constitutional Dictatorship,* p. 269.

[94]H.R. Rep. No. 1904, 78th Congress, 2nd Session 25 (1944).

[95]*U.S. v. Montgomery Ward and Co.,* 150 F 2d 369 (C.A. 7th. Cir. 1945).

[96]This narrative on martial law in Hawaii is drawn largely from Gwenfread Allen, *Hawaii's War Years* (Honolulu: University of Hawaii Press, 1950).

[97]*Duncan v. Kahanamoku Sheriff,* 327 US 304 (1946).

[98]*Hirabayashi v. U.S.,* 320 US 81 (1943); *Korematsu v. United States,* 323 US 214 (1944).

[99] *Youngstown Sheet and Tube Company v. Sawyer,* 343 US 579 (1952).

[100]See for example John P. Roche, "Executive Power and Domestic Emergency: The Quest for Prerogative," *Western Political Quarterly* (December 1952), pp. 592–618; G. A. Schubert, Jr., "The Steel Case: Presidential Responsibility and Judicial Irresponsibility," *Western Political Quarterly* (March 1953), pp. 61–77.

[101]Glendon A. Schubert, Jr., *The Presidency in the Courts* (Minneapolis: University of Minnesota Press, 1957), p. 284.

[102]*U.S. v. District Court for the Eastern District of Michigan,* 407 US 297 (1972).

[103]"Committee Lists 'Unlimited' Presidential Powers," *Congressional Quarterly Weekly Report* (October 13, 1973), p. 2732.

[104]A. Lincoln to Herndon, February 15, 1848, in Roy P. Basler, ed., *The Collected Works of Abraham Lincoln* (New Brunswick, N.J.: Rutgers University Press, 1953), pp. 451–452.

[105]Arthur Schlesinger, Jr., "Presidential War: 'See If You Can Fix Any Limit to His Power,' " *New York Times Magazine* (January 7, 1973), p. 26.

[106]Louis W. Koenig, *The Presidency and the Crisis: Powers of the Office From the Invasion of Poland to Pearl Harbor* (New York: King's Crown Press, 1944), p. 46.

[107]See Robert A. Dahl, "Decision-Making in a Democracy: The Supreme Court as a National Policy-Maker," *Journal of Public Law* (1957), pp. 279–295.

[108]Philippa Strum, *The Supreme Court and 'Political' Questions: A Study in Judicial Evasion* (University: University of Alabama Press, 1974), pp. 144–145. See also note 46, above.

[109]Arthur M. Schlesinger, Jr., "Who Makes War—and How," *American Bar Association Journal* (January 1977), p. 79.

SUGGESTED READINGS

Allison, Graham T. *The Essence of Decision: Explaining the Cuban Missile Crisis.* Boston: Little, Brown, 1971.

Austin, Anthony. *The President's War: The Story of the Tonkin Gulf Resolution and How the Nation Was Trapped in Vietnam.* Philadelphia: Lippincott, 1971.

Barnett, Richard. *The Roots of War.* New York: Atheneum, 1972.

Chomsky, Noam. *American Power and the New Mandarins.* New York: Pantheon, 1969.

Clark, Keith, and Legere, Laurence. *The President and the Management of National Security.* New York: Praeger, 1968.

Eagleton, Thomas. *War and Presidential Power.* New York: Liveright, 1974.

Ellsberg, Daniel. *Papers on the War.* New York: Simon and Schuster, 1972.

Halberstam, David. *The Best and the Brightest.* New York: Random House, 1969.

Hassler, W. W., Jr. *The President as Commander in Chief.* Reading, Mass.: Addison-Wesley, 1971.

Head, Richard G.; Short, Frisco W.; and McFarlane, Robert C. *Crisis Resolution: Presidential Decision Making in Mayaquez and Korean Confrontations.* Boulder, Colo.: Westview Press, 1978.

Javits, Jacob. *Who Makes War?* New York: Morrow, 1973.

Koenig, Louis W. *The Presidency and the Crisis: Powers of the Office From the Invasion of Poland to Pearl Harbor.* New York: King's Crown Press, 1944.

Mueller, John E. *War, Presidents and Public Opinion.* New York: Wiley, 1973.

Neustadt, Richard. *Alliance Politics.* New York: Columbia University Press, 1970.

Paige, Glen P. *The Korean Decision: June 24–30, 1950.* New York: The Free Press, 1968.

Rossiter, Clinton. *Constitutional Dictatorship: Crisis Government in Modern Democracy.* Princeton, N.J.: Princeton University Press, 1948.

Rossiter, Clinton, with Longaker, Richard P. *The Supreme Court and the Commander-in-Chief.* Expanded ed. Ithaca, N.Y.: Cornell University Press, 1976.

Schaffter, Dorothy, and Mathews, Dorothy M. *The Powers of the President as Commander in Chief of the Army and Navy of the United States.* United States 84th Congress, 2nd Session. House Document no. 443. New York: DaCapo Press, 1974.

Smith, J. Malcolm, and Jurika, Stephen, Jr. *The President and National Security: His Role As Commander-in-Chief.* Dubuque, Iowa: Kendall/Hunt Publishing Company, 1972.

CHAPTER EIGHT

The Man or the Office: What Makes the President a Leader?

A relatively new approach to studying presidential power is to focus on the personality of the president as a clue in determining his performance in office. The assumption is that personal experiences during childhood and adolescence have a profound impact on a person's personality development and on adult behavior. Even if one accepts the validity of this proposition, however, a problem arises: during an election campaign most voters, including seasoned journalists who follow presidential elections, tend to concentrate on the candidates' campaign strategies, policy statements, and various commitments made to voter groups rather than on the makeup or stability of their personalities. An exception occurred in 1972 when it was discovered that Sen. Thomas Eagleton (D.–Mo.) had undergone therapy for a form of mental illness. Public concern about Eagleton's mental well-being forced presidential candidate George McGovern to replace him with Sargent Shriver as the Democratic candidate for vice-president. Apart from this kind of sensational revelation, it seems highly unlikely that we could structure an electoral system geared to finding those presidential candidates with certain personality attributes deemed "optimal" for the presidency. Thus, in large measure, a person brings to the presidency a variety of experiences, values, and psychological needs that go unrecognized by the citizenry. This was obviously the case with Richard M. Nixon: he was able to overcome a negative image ("Tricky Dick") and become known as the "new" Richard Nixon, who then proceeded to defeat Hubert Humphrey in the 1968 presidential election.

ACTIVES OR PASSIVES

For many years political scientists have differentiated between more "active" and more "passive" presidents. Usually this distinction is made by contrasting the views of the presidency held by Theodore Roosevelt and William Howard Taft. Teddy Roosevelt's activist presidency is characterized by his "stewardship" theory. Roosevelt argued:

> The most important factor in getting the right spirit in my Administration, next to the insistence upon courage, honesty, and a genuine democracy of desire to serve the plain people, was my insistence upon the theory that the executive power was limited only by specific restrictions and prohibitions appearing in the Constitution or imposed by the Congress under its Constitutional powers. My view was that every executive officer . . . was a steward of the people bound actively and affirmatively to do all he could for the people, and not to content himself with the negative merit of keeping his talents undamaged in a napkin. I declined to adopt the view that what was imperatively necessary for the Nation could not be done by the President unless he could find some specific authorization to do it. My belief was that it was not only his right but his duty to do anything that the needs of the Nation demanded unless such action was forbidden by the Constitution or the laws.[1]

On the other hand, consider this argument by William Howard Taft:

> The true view of the Executive function is, as I conceive it, that the President can exercise no power which cannot be fairly and reasonably traced to some specific grant of power or justly implied and indicated within such express grant as proper and necessary to its exercise. Such specific grant must be either in the Federal Constitution or in an act of Congress passed in pursuance thereof. There is no undefined residuum of power which he can exercise because it seems to him to be in the public interest. . . . The grants of Executive power are necessarily in general terms in order not to embarrass the Executive within the field of action plainly marked for him, but his jurisdiction must be justified and vindicated by affirmative constitutional or statutory provision, or it does not exist.[2]

It may seem that Roosevelt and Taft were talking about one another, and in fact their divergent views of the presidency led to a serious breakdown in their friendship. Their statements indicate, moreover, just how powerful the force of personality can be in affecting one's use of presidential power. Roosevelt's view of the presidency is almost open-ended; he says that the president can do anything unless it is explicitly denied to him by the Constitution or the laws. Taft held a narrower view of the office, for he believed that the president could do no more than what was specifically allowed him in the Constitution or by statutes. The tension personified in the Roosevelt–Taft debate can be found throughout American history, and its persistence led various political scientists to try to evaluate presidential personality on this basis (see table 8-1).

Erwin Hargrove, for example, contrasted "Presidents of Action" and "Presidents of Restraint."[3] Presidents in the first category—such as Theo-

TABLE 8-1　Personality and power: Classifications of presidents

President	Barber	Burns	Hyman	Hargrove
Washington	passive-negative	Hamiltonian		
Adams	active-negative	Madisonian	Cleveland	
Jefferson	active-positive	Jeffersonian	Lincoln	
Madison	passive-positive			
Monroe				
J. Q. Adams			Cleveland	
Jackson		Jeffersonian	Lincoln	
Van Buren			Cleveland	
W. Harrison			Buchanan	
Tyler				
Polk			Lincoln	
Taylor				
Fillmore			Buchanan	
Pierce			Buchanan	
Buchanan			Buchanan	
Lincoln		Hamiltonian		
Johnson			Cleveland	
Grant			Buchanan	
Hayes			Cleveland	
Garfield			Buchanan	
Arthur			Buchanan	
Cleveland			Cleveland	
B. Harrison				
McKinley			Buchanan	
T. Roosevelt		Hamiltonian	Lincoln	Action
Taft	passive-positive	Madisonian	Buchanan	Restraint
Wilson	active-negative	Jeffersonian	Lincoln	Action
Harding	passive-positive		Buchanan	
Coolidge	passive-negative		Buchanan	
Hoover	active-negative		Buchanan	Restraint
F. D. Roosevelt	active-positive	Hamiltonian	Lincoln	Action
Truman	active-positive		Lincoln	Action
Eisenhower	passive-negative		Buchanan	
Kennedy	active-positive		Cleveland	Action
Johnson	active-negative			Action
Nixon	active-negative			
Ford	active-positive			
Carter	active-positive			
Reagan	passive-positive			

Sources: James David Barber, *The Presidential Character* (Englewood Cliffs, N. J. Prentice-Hall, 1977); James MacGregor Burns, *Presidential Government* (Boston: Houghton Mifflin, 1973); Erwin C. Hargrove, *Presidential Leadership: Personality and Political Style* (New York: Macmillan, 1966); Sidney Hyman, "What Is the President's True Role?" *New York Times Magazine* (September 7, 1958). Barber's classification of Reagan is found in "Carter and Reagan: Clues to their Character," *U.S. News and World Report* (October 27, 1980), pp. 30, 33.

dore Roosevelt, Harry Truman, and John Kennedy—greatly expanded presidential power: "Each was a political artist whose deepest needs and talents were served by a political career." William Howard Taft and Herbert Hoover, Hargrove's "Presidents of Restraint," were nonpolitical technicians: "They did not put a high value on personal or presidential power, and in the course of their careers they did not develop political skills."

An earlier typology by Sidney Hyman, delineated a leadership style between the activist and passive extremes. Hyman classified the presidents according to what he called Buchanan, Lincoln, and Cleveland models.[4] Presidents in the same category as James Buchanan, including William McKinley and Calvin Coolidge, reject the notion of a president as political leader of the nation; rather, they are purely administrative officers who stress the need to be efficient, honest, and decorous. They fail to exert leadership over Congress and do not make demands on the people, and the last thing they would ever do is rally the nation during a crisis. Polar opposite to these presidents are the Abraham Lincoln types. Thomas Jefferson, Woodrow Wilson, and Franklin D. Roosevelt, among others, were more political than legalistic in their approach; they loved the taste of political battle and saw partisan conflict as natural and creative. Such presidents, in addition, were strong-willed, bent on innovation, and assumed full responsibility for their actions. Somewhere between the Buchanan and Lincoln types, according to Hyman, lies the Cleveland model. Characterized by Grover Cleveland and Dwight Eisenhower, these presidents are primarily administrators, but they also are political in a minor way. They are political leaders insofar as they talk about innovation but refrain from any meaningful action; instead, they are defensive-oriented and come to rely on the veto power.

Research by James MacGregor Burns also postulates three models of the presidency based on leadership style: Hamiltonian, Jeffersonian, and Madisonian.[5] In Burns's view, the Hamiltonian model (named after George Washington's secretary of the treasury) stresses the use of personal leadership within the checks and balances system. This style emphasizes the heroic leader, who exploits opportunity, manipulation, and political pressure to increase executive power. The less activist Madisonian model, first adopted by President John Adams, adheres to the Framers' outline of government, because minority rights are deemed more important than majority rule. For this reason, Burns argues that the Madisonian model leads to "deadlock"—an inability to govern. The Jeffersonian model, on the other hand, bases presidential power in a strong political party organization. The style of Thomas Jefferson implies effective majoritarianism under strong presidential leadership, a vigorous two-party system, and greater concern for democratic and egalitarian values. James MacGregor Burns concludes that "the Hamiltonian model was perhaps a more resourceful and flexible kind of government, the Madisonian more stable and prudent, and the Jeffersonian more democratic and potentially more powerful."[6]

Hargrove, Hyman, and Burns agree that each president can adopt a more active or a more passive attitude toward his responsibilities, and this points to one enduring relationship between personality and power use. Hargrove's "Presidents of Action" in most instances are called Lincoln types by Hyman; most of Hyman's Lincoln-type presidents are considered Jeffersonians or Hamiltonians by James MacGregor Burns. In terms of the way these scholars have classified the various presidents, moreover, Republicans tend to be more passive than Democrats in their use of presidential power. A major reason for this, we would add, is that historically the Democratic party has been more representative of the have-nots (the poor, the working classes, and minority groups), with the result that Democratic presidents were elected on platforms dedicated to modifying the system of established privilege. On the other hand, more passive presidents affirm the status quo. First, as Republicans they probably were less concerned about far-reaching social reforms; second, their very inaction permitted Congress to exert more influence over policymaking. Many observers argue, furthermore, that Congress overrepresents conservative values, localism, and special interests, all of which tend to affirm the status quo.

PRESIDENTIAL PERSONALITY

The study of presidential personality gained a new dimension with the first publication in 1972 of James David Barber's *The Presidential Character*, based on the so-called psychobiographical or psychohistorical approach.[7] Before this research appeared, the relationship between presidential power and personality seemed to be more straightforward. Writing in the 1960s, for example, Erwin Hargrove had argued that a degree of personal insecurity was needed for effective political leadership. He stated:

> In the heyday of Lyndon Johnson [I] developed the thesis that personal insecurity and political skill were linked. The creative politician was depicted as the man who required attention and needed to dominate and therefore had developed skills of self-dramatization and persuasion that would serve those needs. The thesis was applied to American Presidents. The two Roosevelts and Wilson were pictured as men in need of attention and power, and skill and creativity were related to a perpetual striving to serve these goals. Presidents lacking such needs were also seen as lacking in abilities, for instance Taft, Hoover, and Eisenhower. They were pictured as almost too healthy to be good leaders.[8]

Public reaction to President Johnson's conduct of the Vietnam War, coupled with James David Barber's counterthesis that personal insecurity leads to aberrant behavior during crises, led Hargrove to reassess his earlier position. This Hargrove does by trying to formulate a psychological profile of those presidents having a "democratic character."[9]

Barber's fourfold classification is based on two dimensions: one pertains to the degree of activity (active or passive) and the other measures the degree of satisfaction (positive or negative). The "active-positive" president, whom Barber prefers, is self-confident and actively pursues important goals:

"He sees himself as developing over time toward relatively well-defined personal goals—growing toward his image of himself as he might yet be. There is an emphasis on rational mastery, on using the brain to move the feet."[10] In contrast, the "active-negative" president views life as "a hard struggle to achieve and hold power." Such a person finds little satisfaction because he strives to overcome feelings of personal inadequacy: "The activity has a compulsive quality, as if the man were trying to make up for something or to escape from anxiety into hard work."[11]

The "passive-positive" president also lacks self-confidence, but seeks to neutralize a hostile environment by eliciting affection or acceptance from other people. Barber observes: "This is the receptive, compliant, other-directed character whose life is a search for affection as a reward for being agreeable and cooperative rather than personally assertive."[12] Finally, the "passive-negative" president assumes office out of a sense of duty. For this reason he does not enjoy his work and contributes little to the office. Barber summarizes the impact of "passive-negatives" on the presidency in this way:

> Passive-negative types are in politics because they think they ought to be. . . . Their tendency is to withdraw, to escape from the conflict and uncertainty of politics by emphasizing vague principles (especially prohibitions) and procedural arrangements. They become guardians of the right and proper way, above the sordid politicking of lesser men.[13]

A danger resulting from both "passive-positive" (Taft, Harding) and "passive-negative" (Coolidge, Eisenhower) presidents is that they allow the nation to drift, and ignore pressing social problems. Hargrove, Burns, and Hyman would probably agree with this assessment; unlike those scholars, however, Barber raises the more serious concern that "active-negative" presidents can be dangerous, because they tend to overreact to situations and continue ineffectual policies long after they have been repudiated. The proponents of the "textbook presidency" never really considered this possibility, so this aspect of Barber's analysis is compatible with the "revisionist" argument that surfaced during the 1970s (see Introduction). It is no coincidence that Barber classifies Franklin D. Roosevelt, Harry Truman, John Kennedy, as well as Thomas Jefferson, as "active-positives," and Herbert Hoover, Lyndon Johnson, and Richard Nixon as "active-negatives." His major departure from conventional wisdom pertains to Woodrow Wilson; though ranked "great" by the historians, Barber calls him an "active-negative." The preferred presidential "character," argues Barber, is the "active-positive" because such presidents "display virtues of omission: they avoided both obsession and lassitude. Yet they also display personal strengths specially attuned to the Presidency, strengths which enabled them to make of that office an engine of progress."[14] "Active-negative" presidents, on the other hand, can be identified with major public policy blunders. The following sections examine the psychological makeups of Wilson, Hoover, Johnson, and Nixon, each of whom may have done serious political harm to the nation.

Wilson

Woodrow Wilson's personalized conflict with Sen. Henry Cabot Lodge over Senate ratification of the League of Nations would seem to be a classic manifestation of ego-defensive behavior. An early study of President Wilson by Bullitt and Freud argued that the president's difficulties with Senator Lodge resulted from Wilson's relationship with his own father.[15] His father had been a Presbyterian minister, an overpowering man who dominated Woodrow; Wilson therefore came to view his relationship with other people in terms only of submission or domination. When faced with Lodge's intransigence, consequently, Wilson became rigid, refused to compromise, and thus the League of Nations was defeated. A later analysis of this episode by George and George also emphasized Wilson's childhood experiences coupled with his strict religious training.[16]

James David Barber's account of Wilson's childhood is consistent with the latter assessment. He sees three important themes emerging from Woodrow Wilson's religious background: "God judges man by standards of perfection, to which man must aspire; life is a constant struggle of good against evil; there is no room for compromise in that struggle." Barber agrees that Wilson's father dominated in their relationship, and always blamed Woodrow for not living up to his high expectations. Though frustrated, Wilson did not express anger toward his parents who also gave him love and protection; instead Wilson turned against himself and developed "that sense of fundamental inferiority which was to haunt and depress him throughout his life."[17] Barber's account, therefore, assumes the saliency of the president's psychological attributes rather than pervasive political conditions— such as an "isolationist" sentiment in America—for the League's defeat in the Senate.

This entire line of inquiry into Woodrow Wilson's difficulties, however, has been questioned by other scholars. Weinstein, Anderson, and Link relate President Wilson's problems to physiological causes; that is, his series of strokes.[18] In an earlier appraisal, historian Arthur Link was particularly disturbed by the thesis advanced by Bullitt and Freud. He pointed out that "for a mentally unbalanced person, Wilson had a remarkable career. Somehow he managed to make distinguished contributions to the four separate fields of scholarship, higher education, domestic politics, and diplomacy."[19]

Hoover

Barber links Herbert Hoover's feelings of personal inadequacy to his early childhood experiences.

> The motive force in Hoover's life collected itself over the years of his childhood. The child who loses his father at age six and his mother at age eight is scarred by that, no matter how many relatives try to fill the void. But besides that, Herbert had an unsettled childhood . . . he was sent at critical times from one relation to another, where he was expected to perform whatever they wanted done. . . . I think he experienced a sense of powerlessness, an inability to guide his own fate, a vulnerability to sudden, externally imposed, radical changes in his life.[20]

The most serious threat to Hoover's presidency was, of course, the Great Depression. Barber faults Hoover on his inability to cope with this national disaster: Hoover could not rally the nation during these hard times because he lacked confidence and inspiration. According to Barber, Hoover had adjusted to his childhood insecurities by adopting a view of the world that stressed its "regularity." When the stock market crashed in 1929 he simply tried to deny its existence by affirming that all was well and that prosperity was just around the corner. As economic conditions worsened and criticisms of his policies increased, Barber says that Hoover "stood firm" and saw himself as a "martyr." Hoover proceeded to veto numerous relief bills and commanded the Army to disperse the "Bonus Expeditionary Force"— veterans who camped in Washington, D.C., to demand payment of their bonuses. By Barber's account, Hoover's inflexibility in the face of the Great Depression and its dire consequences is a manifestation of ego-defensive behavior; Hoover simply could not act without damaging his weak self-esteem.

Barber's assessment of President Hoover is criticized by scholars who emphasize political factors. Erwin Hargrove, as noted earlier, once argued that Hoover was too healthy to be an effective leader.[21] What motivated Hoover in this instance, says Hargrove, "may also have been an ideological rigidity that was always present but was intensified by crisis."[22] This same argument is forcefully made by Alexander George who reproves Barber for underestimating the power of ideological commitments; George points to Hoover's long-standing defense of capitalism and individualism as the reason why he could not promote welfarism. "Certainly Hoover was stubborn on the matter of a public dole, but he appears to have been strongly opposed to it from the beginning—before attacks on his politics posed threats to his power and rectitude—because he found the idea peculiarly antithetical to his political philosophy."[23]

Johnson

For Lyndon Johnson the Vietnam War became a political disaster because it became an obsession. Even more than Wilson or Hoover, Lyndon Johnson took his tragic fate personally. Barber quotes Johnson as saying, "I am not going to lose Vietnam. I am not going to be the President who saw Southeast Asia go the way China went."[24] The origins of Johnson's insecurities Barber traces to LBJ's childhood, and his domineering mother whose "everlasting persistence in loving and shoving Lyndon gave him a sense of special destiny." At the same time Johnson identified with a "rough, tough macho" image. "From very early on, Lyndon Johnson lived two great expectations, that he achieve beyond what any of his peers could do and that he perform like a Texas-type male."[25] Barber relates that Johnson even made analogies between Vietnam and the heroic stand at the Alamo. Because the Vietnam War was Johnson's war, the frustrations and disappointments in winning a victory there were internalized, and Johnson came to view the anti-War critics as personal enemies. Those who criticized his policies were challenging his worth. As the war deteriorated, President Johnson dismissed all but the most loyal advisers on his staff.

In the end, faced with an eroding political base, Lyndon Johnson declined to seek reelection in 1968. According to James David Barber, President Johnson believed that "if he went away the war would go away, or at least that negotiations could begin in earnest."

Barber's characterization of Lyndon Johnson is generally supported by Erwin Hargrove, who points out Johnson's "strong desire to do good" coupled with "a compulsion to rule others." Johnson's compulsion was rooted in an insecurity which, according to Hargrove's analysis, had two dimensions:

> There was the cultural insecurity of being from Texas, of not having gone to Harvard and feeling ill at ease with intellectuals and Eastern "establishment" figures. But there was also a much deeper uneasiness that showed in his sensitiveness to criticism and the demand for absolute loyalty from subordinates and associates.[26]

Hargrove agrees with Barber that President Johnson's defensiveness and rigidity adversely affected his conduct of the Vietnam War—apart from the rightness or wrongness of that policy.

Nixon

Richard Nixon, observes Hargrove, "seems to have many of the same self-defeating traits that plagued Lyndon Johnson."[27] In 1971, James David Barber predicted the decline of the Nixon presidency:

> The primary danger of the Nixon Presidency is that the frustrations and erosions of self he experiences will accumulate and that the process of rigidification, triggered by a serious threat to his power and his moral confidence, will show him a way to rescue, as he sees it, his Presidential heroism.[28]

Seen in retrospect, there are incidents in Nixon's political career in which his deepest insecurities came rushing to the surface. In his memoirs, *Six Crises*, Nixon revealed how he identified political problems as major personal crises. Such episodes, it now appears, were moments of intense decision making for Richard Nixon; similarly, Hargrove argues that Nixon's decisions to invade Cambodia in 1970 and in 1971 were made in "a self-induced crisis atmosphere." Hargrove does not dismiss entirely the notion that Nixon's war policies simply reflected his view of the national interest, but asserts that Nixon invested "these ideas with a particularly intense personal theme of concern about his own strength and will."[29]

Barber claims that Richard Nixon did not enjoy a happy childhood. His family suffered economic hardship, with the result that "Nixon brought a persistent bent toward life as painful, difficult, and . . . uncertain."[30] Nixon also learned that obstacles could be overcome by hard work and perseverance; this led to his preoccupation with developing the skills of self-management. In the main, argues Barber, Nixon's political career cannot be explained in terms of ideology or philosophy but by psychology; namely, "the struggle to control aggression, and the pursuit of power, prestige, and status." Hargrove adds that Nixon wanted "to be regarded as an event-making man, like Wilson, Churchill, or de Gaulle, whose presence will make a difference in history."

But it did not turn out that way. In his second term, President Nixon was determined to reverse the New Deal, argues Hargrove, "in a unilateral way outside of the normal canons of political compromise."[31] More than any other recent president, Nixon focused on his bureaucracy—he surrounded himself with strong but loyal men—and virtually ignored the Congress. Richard Nathan suggests that Nixon exploited his administrative powers precisely because he had so little influence with the Democratic-controlled Congress.

> Few of the President's domestic initiatives succeeded. . . . Gradually the strategy shifted. Ehrlichman . . . replaced Moynihan and Burns . . . as the dominant White House assistant for domestic affairs. New structures were established. . . . Along with these personnel and organizational changes came a decided shift in approach. More attention was paid to opportunities to achieve policy aims through administrative action as opposed to legislative change, the former to be accomplished by taking advantage of the wide discretion available to federal officials under many existing laws.[32]

Watergate was the natural result of President Nixon's isolation and feelings of being threatened by political opponents. He had authorized or encouraged his aides to use extraordinary means, some illegal, to prevent news leaks, to intimidate adversaries, and to bolster his sinking reputation.

PERSONALITY AND POWER

Given the apparent validity of James David Barber's thesis regarding Lyndon Johnson and Richard Nixon, students of the presidency must always consider the conditions under which aberrant behavior by a president can be most damaging. Two relationships arise between Barber's assessment of the "active-negative" president and our framework of analysis. First, "active-negatives" are especially dangerous during times of crisis, and we have shown that crisis—as a determinant of presidential power—has the effect of expanding the scope of executive authority while, at the same time, increasing the dependence of citizens and other decision makers on the president. Second, we further hypothesize that a president's personality gains saliency to the extent that it is allowed extraordinary room to shape policy without being constrained by external forces. This latitude is most likely to occur in the roles of commander-in-chief and chief diplomat, and to a lesser degree, in the role of chief executive.

On the other hand, it is difficult to see any relationship between Barber's typology and effective presidential leadership. The skills required to be effective in such roles as legislative leader or opinion/party leader derive from personality attributes, such as charisma, rhetorical ability, and political acumen. Presumably these qualities would not be so well developed among "passive-positives" or "passive-negatives." Such a relationship, however, simply is not obvious in many cases. Harry Truman was an ineffectual legislative leader, and his low standing in the opinion polls caused him not to seek reelection in 1952. Nor was John F. Kennedy very effective in dealing with the Congress. Moreover, there are few "active-positives" among our "great" presidents: Thomas Jefferson and Franklin D. Roosevelt were "active-positives," but George Washington was a "passive-negative" and Woodrow Wilson, as noted, was an "active-negative." Barber did not categorize Abraham Lincoln, but Erwin Hargrove doubts that he would be considered an "active-positive."[33] It is likely that Abraham Lincoln was another "active-negative" president.

A fundamental problem with Barber's approach is that any attempt to employ psychoanalytical theory based upon such materials as autobiographies or biographies, personal correspondence and memoirs, and public actions and speeches can be misleading. Often-times it is difficult for psychiatrists to agree on the mental state of the patients they personally interview for long hours. To try to uncover the parameters of somebody's character using historical sources seems an overwhelming task. There are legitimate disagreements about the motivations for Wilson's battle with Lodge or Hoover's intransigence when faced with the Great Depression. Similar questions can be raised about James David Barber's early prognoses regarding Jimmy Carter and Ronald Reagan. To conclude this examination of the presidency, we will analyze the Carter and Reagan presidencies in terms of their personality styles as well as in terms of the five variables that underlie presidential power. More can be learned about Carter and Reagan, we assert, by studying authority, decision making, public inputs, expertise, and crisis rather than the superficial differences in their character.

Carter

Jimmy Carter read Barber's *The Presidential Character* and James David Barber read Carter's *Why Not the Best?* (written in 1975).[34] Barber denies that he was unduly influenced by any relationship with Jimmy Carter, but he unequivocally sees Carter as a well-adjusted person. Jimmy Carter, says Barber, "is, has been, and will be an extraordinary, energetic person and politician, up-and-at-'em, day after day, often right past the lunch hour and into that afternoon period when your average politician wants a drink." Moreover, Barber predicted that Carter would enjoy his tenure as president: "I believe he will also turn out to be a pleasured President, finding, as did FDR and HST and JFK, that life in the Oval Office can be fun—is, on the average."[35] During the 1980 presidential campaign Jimmy Carter tried to project a self-assured image to the mass media, particularly when he was the favorite in the public opinion polls. Carter exhibited a more aggressive nature toward his political opponents when he fell behind in the polls.[36]

Few commentators have denied Carter's capable intellect. Historian Arthur Link described him as a "managerial type: He believes that all problems can be solved by intelligence. He was educated as an engineer, and he clearly believes that when a difficult problem arises, you sit down and solve it."[37] In addition, Barber predicted that, like John Kennedy or FDR, President Carter's difficulties would stem from "an excess of an active-positive virtue: the thirst for results," but doubted that Carter would persist "in an obviously losing line of action."[38] Nor was Carter likely to engage in volatile behavior, a characteristic of presidents who lack inner strength. As a former member of the Carter administration observed, when Carter was faced with questions of ". . . life and death, of nuclear war and human destruction . . . he would act on them calmly, with self-knowledge, free of interior demons that might tempt him to act rashly or to prove at terrible cost that he was a man."[39]

Other scholars question Barber's analysis of Jimmy Carter. Some suggest that, in fact, Carter is an insecure person whose pride and moralistic, overweening sense of superiority make it difficult for him to deal with other people.[40] Some historians already have judged Jimmy Carter to be among the ten worst presidents in our history. By any standard, his four years in office had few successes, and his massive defeat by Ronald Reagan in 1980 marked the first time in the twentieth century that a Democratic incumbent lost reelection. Our assessment indicates that Carter's problems resulted more from adverse political conditions and his inexperience than from psychological variables. Carter's personality no doubt affected his style of governing, but his character makeup had less to do with his performance in office.

President Carter had his greatest impact in military and foreign affairs, in which he enjoyed the formal authority to act, the ability to control decision making, and some vision in terms of his objective. In negotiating the Camp David agreements between Israel and Egypt, Carter's role was pivotal. He took a personal interest in both President Sadat and Prime Minister Begin, but allowed them a free hand to negotiate when the discussions began in 1977. When deadlocks occurred, however, Carter made personal appeals to Sadat to continue the dialog. After nearly a year of frustrating negotiations and many disagreements, the discussions among Carter, Sadat, and Begin resulted in a framework for peace between the two Middle Eastern nations. This victory was extremely important to the Carter presidency. Betty Glad observes:

> Camp David did miracles for the Carter presidency. Prior to the summit, he had suffered a steady decline in the polls, and many people, including members of his own party, were beginning to question the effectiveness of his leadership. . . . Suddenly his former critics, both within and outside his party, were hailing him as a hero and statesman.[41]

In foreign affairs, President Carter negotiated some 32 treaties and 841 executive agreements during his term. Of these, one of the most controversial was his decision to "recognize" the People's Republic of China and to end a mutual defense treaty with Taiwan. His decision was challenged in court, but the Supreme Court's ruling, remanding the case back to a district court with instructions to dismiss, in effect legitimized the president's authority in this matter. Carter's most difficult problem in the international arena was, of course, the crisis in Iran. In various ways Carter mobilized his formal authority against Iran after the seizure of American hostages there. He severed diplomatic relations with Iran, imposed diplomatic and economic sanctions, and authorized the abortive rescue mission. Another trouble spot was Afghanistan. When Soviet troops occupied that country, President Carter pressured other nations not to participate in the 1980 Olympics, which were to be held in Moscow. He was able to persuade sixty-two countries not to send athletes to the Olympics, including Japan and West Germany, although eighty-one other nations joined in the games.

In making his decisions Jimmy Carter probably received too much advice without knowing how to use such varied input. During the Iranian crisis, for example, he received information from ad hoc groups as well as from his inner-circle advisers. In planning the rescue mission, however, he listened only to the Joint Chiefs of Staff, the defense secretary, the secretary of state, the CIA director, and his White House chief of staff. Moreover, though President Carter immersed himself in the details of government management, he was unable to set domestic priorities for his administration and virtually lost control over his agency heads. In formulating his 1977 welfare reform proposals, for example, Carter delegated much discretion to HEW Secretary Joseph Califano. Although he instructed his own staff not to get involved in that question, the Department of Labor—which had an interest in this area—began to interfere, causing conflict within the Carter administration. Yet President Carter did not quell these rivalries; he seemed too preoccupied with the technical and fiscal details of welfare reform. He wanted comprehensive welfare reform without great expense, but he gave little guidance to his advisers in formulating such a policy. As Lynn and Whiteman have pointed out, in this situation

> Carter . . . was relatively passive and inflexible. Once he had decided on the process he wanted followed, he took little personal interest in following through and showed little resilience when his advisers ran into difficulties or sought his help.[42]

A major handicap of Carter's advisory network arose from his own inexperience and the lack of expertise by his key aides. Jimmy Carter, like most contemporary presidents, recruited advisers from among those activists who labored in his presidential campaign. Few of those individuals were knowledgeable about Washington politics, nor could they deal with Congress. Eventually Carter learned from his early mistakes. He greatly improved his decision-making apparatus, but he could never erase completely the reputation he had gained as an indecisive novice, confused over policy. For example, at first he wanted a cabinet-controlled government, but later learned that he was losing control under that system. Next he tried to reassert personal control over decision making but, in the process, had to replace members of his cabinet.

As chief executive, however, President Carter deserves credit for novel proposals aimed at strengthening his managerial control. In 1978 he proposed a reorganization plan, which Congress approved, eliminating the Civil Service Commission in favor of an Office of Personnel Management. These changes, as noted, were supposed to facilitate mobility among high-level civil servants, to make them more responsive to the president, and to tie their salaries to performance standards. Carter also increased the size of the federal judiciary when Congress enacted his Omnibus Judgeship Act of 1978, creating 117 new district court judgeships and 35 new positions on the courts of appeals. In filling these positions, moreover, Carter encouraged the use of state selection commissions to recommend qualified candidates. In addition to gaining more freedom from political and professional influences over the appointment process, Carter wanted to actively recruit minorities and women as judges.

Carter's legislative leadership over Congress was severely limited by his ignorance of the lawmaking process and his seeming unwillingness to compromise or to exploit patronage powers to achieve his ends. Frank Moore, his chief liaison with Congress, was equally unfamiliar about the legislative process. Much valuable time was lost while Carter and his staff learned about Washington politics. President Carter, consequently, failed to take advantage of his "honeymoon" period to define a policy agenda for Congress and then aggressively promote it. Instead, political mistakes marred his early years in office. For example, Carter offended congressional leaders in his own party when he eliminated nineteen water projects from his 1978 budget without consulting those congressmen affected. Though it was at the heart of his early economic recovery program, Carter suddenly withdrew his tax rebate proposal from congressional review without notifying his staunchest allies in the Congress. For this indelicate action, he was forced to apologize to those legislators.

Relatively few proposals enacted by Congress bore Carter's leadership imprint. As noted earlier, Carter's best year was only 3.3 percent better than Lyndon Johnson's worst year in terms of legislative victories on key votes in Congress. The National Energy Act of 1978 was enacted without Carter's proposal for a crude oil and industrial oil tax. Although Congress had no role in negotiating the Panama Canal Treaties, President Carter gained little political leverage from his assumed expertise in this matter. In fact, our analysis showed that Carter's leadership was eroded because legitimate differences of opinion over the language of the treaties emerged in the Senate. The result was that the Senate added important amendments to those agreements.

The fundamental political weakness underlying Carter's lackluster performance may have been his ineffectual role as opinion/party leader. Because he narrowly defeated Gerald Ford in 1976, Carter carried into office few

Democratic congressmen who were beholden to him. The fact that he gained the party's nomination without courting its leadership in Congress, or even at the state and local levels, deprived him of a strong political base. The image of quiet strength, which Jimmy Carter cultivated during the election campaign, quickly faded during his presidency, and throughout his term Carter was saddled with the reputation of being weak and indecisive. As a person, the public liked Jimmy Carter but Americans did not respect him as a leader. President Carter's highest approval rating was 75 percent and his lowest was 21 percent; like other presidents, he followed the pattern of steadily losing popularity with each year in office. Opinion polls indicate that during 1980 the public's perception of the Carter presidency was consistently negative; in the 1980 presidential election the American people voted against Carter rather than for Ronald Reagan.

Carter's popularity rose after the Camp David accords (for which he was nominated for a Nobel Peace Prize) and after the Iran embassy takeover, but the effects of these episodes were only temporary. Carter was unable to fully capitalize on them. The fact that Americans were held hostage in Iran for 444 days served to reinforce the public's view that Carter's leadership had crippled America's position in the world community, a theme later exploited by Ronald Reagan in the election campaign. In three other instances, the public and other decision makers refused to recognize the existence of a "crisis" and thus failed to rally around Carter's leadership. First, Congress did not quickly ratify the Panama Canal Treaties though the president said that its delay would endanger our relations with Latin America. Second, when Carter called the energy crisis the "moral equivalent of war," a June 1979 Gallup Poll showed that only 37 percent of the public thought the energy problem was one of the most important problems facing America.[43] Finally, regarding the Soviet invasion of Afghanistan, Carter referred to this matter as "the most serious threat to peace since World War II" in his State of the Union Message. Congress agreed that the United States should boycott the 1980 summer Olympics in Moscow, and Carter proceeded to embargo grain shipments to the Soviet Union, yet he failed to win much support from our allies in Western Europe or from the public in general. Rather, he incurred the hostility of the American farm community, which suffered financially as a result of the grain embargo.

Various commentators, as noted, observed that special interests seemed to gain importance during Carter's tenure. Although this development can be attributed to many factors—including the growth in the number of Political Action Committees, which raise money for congressional elections—the overall effect was to further weaken Carter's leadership, especially in Congress. In 1978, for example, the sugar beet industry lobbied against U.S. ratification of the International Sugar Agreement until President Carter agreed to increase domestic subsidies for that commodity. Many presidents are frustrated by special interest lobbies, but Jimmy Carter's position was especially precarious; he was unable to mobilize his party organization or public opinion as countervailing powers against those interest groups or single-issue causes. Opposition by industry representatives to Carter's energy package was a chief reason for the defeat of its major provisions in Congress. Opposition of the same nature affected Carter's attempt to ease shoe import quotas. In evaluating this question, he conferred with thirty-six governors, the AFL-CIO, congressmen, shoe manufacturers, consumer groups, retailers, the chairman of the Federal Reserve Board, his national security adviser, and the Economic Policy Group, which was composed of representatives from the Departments of State, Treasury, HUD, Labor, Commerce, Agriculture, OMB, and the Council of Economic Advisers. In the end, according to David Edwards, Carter's decision "was a compromise between the free trade position he advocated in the abstract, and intense special-interest pressures he felt in the concrete."[44]

In summary, President Carter was able to exert influence in policy areas in which he enjoyed formal authority and dominated the decision-making process, as commander-in-chief and chief diplomat. Given his weak political position, the relative inexperience of his staff, and the failure of public opinion to rally behind his leadership—even during alleged crises, Carter's impact on the roles of chief executive, legislative leader, and opinion/party leader was modest indeed. The contrast with Ronald Reagan is especially great in these weaker roles, because Reagan—at least during his first year— exploited his political advantages to score impressive policy victories, particularly in Congress.

Reagan

Ronald Reagan poses another problem for James David Barber's typology; Reagan has been called a "passive-positive," the kind of president embodied in William Howard Taft and Warren G. Harding. In 1980, Barber argued that Reagan "is likely to try to please people."

> His political life centers on collecting affection from his environment. He wants to be at the center of a friendly crew of colleagues who are appreciative of him and like him. The man, after all, is an actor who wants to please his audiences. He has spent his lifetime trying to do that. Even as a young man, he tried to please his family and his friends. He always was reputed to be a nice, friendly, cheerful, optimistic sort of guy.[45]

While the final assessment of Reagan's presidency has yet to be written, evaluations of his first year in office indicated that he was very effective. Norman Ornstein, for example, argues that Reagan dominated the legislative agenda of Congress during 1981 "in a fashion comparable only to the first years of Franklin Roosevelt and of Lyndon Johnson."[46] Far from being a "passive" president, moreover, one suspects that Ronald Reagan is actually an activist, though certainly he is a conservative and not a liberal one. After reviewing Reagan's first 200 days in office, Hedley Donovan concluded:

> Ronald Reagan, age 70, . . . has neatly stood on its head a cherished assumption of most students of the presidency. That is the assumption that vigorous, ebullient presidential leadership will just naturally be devoted to expanding the role of the

federal government (and the Chief Magistrate) in our national life, and that any President of contrary outlook will necessarily be a cold, crabbed type, or at best likably lazy.[47]

President Reagan's effectiveness declined after his first year in office, but for many of the same political reasons for which he was initially successful. Unlike Jimmy Carter, Ronald Reagan gave budgetary policies top priority and paid much less attention to foreign affairs. On occasion he did exercise the prerogatives available to a commander-in-chief and chief diplomat. Reagan's greatest achievement was U.S. mediation in Lebanon between Israel and the Palestine Liberation Organization in 1982, which allowed the besieged PLO troops to safely evacuate Beirut and began the process of Israeli withdrawal. To keep order in Lebanon while negotiations between Israel and Lebanon continued, President Reagan sent U.S. Marines into that country as a peace-keeping force. In August 1981, American aircraft shot down Libyan fighters after being provoked, though this decision was made by Reagan's advisers while he slept. Another policy dispute affecting the Middle East was President Reagan's decision to sell AWACS radar planes to Saudi Arabia against Israel's objections. This agreement survived a veto attempt by Congress.

Ronald Reagan used his bargaining power as chief diplomat in trade negotiations with Japan. These talks were aimed at obtaining voluntary agreement from Japan not to increase exports of Japanese automobiles to the United States. The 1982 Falklands War between Great Britain and Argentina precipitated an international crisis to be faced by the Reagan administration. Reagan dispatched Secretary of State Alexander Haig to try to negotiate a settlement. Haig was unsuccessful, and as the English naval fleet sailed to the Falkland Islands, the president supplied the British with intelligence information and permitted their ships to use American repair and refueling facilities.

While these episodes illustrate the use of presidential power, Reagan's critics argue that his administration had no coherent foreign policy. The only consistent policy was Reagan's "get-tough" attitude toward the Soviet Union. In 1980 Reagan campaigned that the United States was losing its military superiority relative to the Russians; as president, he has proposed greater defense spending, and maintained a firm posture towards the Soviets. In reaction to the imposition of martial law in Poland by the Soviet-backed government there, Reagan imposed trade sanctions; he forbade American companies from selling the Russians equipment needed for the construction of their gas pipeline to western Europe, and he pressured our European allies to honor that boycott.

As chief executive, President Reagan asserted control over his key agencies by staffing them with appointees who were loyal to him and who shared his conservative viewpoint. Reagan wasted no time replacing Jimmy Carter's political appointees. But in general Reagan is not personally involved in the formulation of policy and he delegates substantial responsibility to his aides to handle the details of policy implementation. According to Edwin Meese, ". . . the President is at the top of the pyramid . . . once a policy decision is made, President Reagan does not believe he has to supervise every detail of its implementation."[48] By this method of operation, Reagan gives himself more time to focus on his top priorities, but one major disadvantage is that delegation of responsibility can lead to disagreements among his advisers. As Lou Cannon suggests, Reagan was offended by "acrimony and discord,"[49] but unlike Nixon he did not view such rivalries as disloyalty to the president. When disagreements emerged among Secretary of State Alexander Haig, Defense Secretary Caspar Weinberger, and former National Security Adviser Richard Allen, Haig was seen to be the cause of much friction. As a consequence, Haig was encouraged to resign, and Reagan replaced him with George Schultz, a person who brought harmony to the cabinet and inner staff.

A cogent example of Reagan's approach to decision making involved the MX missile. In 1981 Reagan delegated this matter to Defense Secretary Caspar Weinberger, who immediately appointed a fifteen-member panel chaired by Charles Townes, a recognized physicist from the University of California. Though Weinberger favored an airborne delivery system for the MX missile, the Townes Committee recommended building one hundred MX missiles in one hundred existing shelters and missile silos.[50] The committee made this recommendation even though a majority were not convinced that a land-based system would survive a nuclear attack. Other policymakers, such as Alexander Haig, also favored the land-based scheme, so Weinberger found himself isolated from Reagan's advisers in opposing that plan. However, though Weinberger failed to gain acceptance of his alternative, he did succeed in keeping the reservations of the Townes Committee report secret and in delaying the decision for one year. President Reagan approved Weinberger's recommendation to postpone the basing decision, mainly because strong opposition to a land-based MX missile system developed among Western governors and the leadership of the Mormon Church. Nonetheless, though Reagan sided with Weinberger, he knew virtually nothing about the details of that decision and nothing of the options that had been considered. When confronted by the press on October 2, 1981, concerning the matter, Reagan repeatedly deferred to Weinberger. As Lou Cannon described the situation,

> What Reagan did not know was that his delegated decision had in fact been made after a one-sided scrutiny which had frustrated and dismayed the administration experts most knowledgeable about the MX. He did not care to know.[51]

Reagan's decision-making style partly explains his mismanagement of the decision to sell AWACS planes to Saudi Arabia. Rather than listen to the advice of Secretary of State Haig, who had been negotiating with Israel on arms sales, President Reagan once again conferred only with his defense secretary. The AWACS sale was not high on Reagan's priority list, because his major concerns focused on budgetary and tax matters. None of Reagan's top aides understood the intricacies of Middle East politics. When the sale was announced, however, determined opposition by the American Israel Public Affairs Committee emerged; AIPAC gained the support of 54 senators and 224 representatives, who signed a letter to President Reagan opposing that sale. Reagan did not become personally involved in the issue until the last few weeks, and to secure final victory he had to resort to, what I. M. Destler called, the "argument from weakness: you cannot afford to destroy me, your only president."[52] Reagan won, but it was a Pyrrhic victory.

These case studies seem to imply that Reagan's reliance on cabinet government, his delegation of responsibility to key advisers, and his inattention to the details of policy implementation are indicative of a "passive"-type president. Such an assessment, however, would not accurately portray his dealings as legislative leader. Though he faced a Republican-controlled Senate and a House of Representatives with a Democratic majority, compared with Jimmy Carter, whose political party held both chambers, Reagan enjoyed one of the most successful "honeymoon" periods of any contemporary president. Ronald Reagan's experience as governor of California, where he faced a Democratic-controlled state legislature, taught him that compromise with the opposition was essential to achieve policy goals. During his second year President Reagan adopted a more "bipartisan" strategy when promoting his budgetary proposals in Congress. Arguing that his election constituted a mandate to establish new domestic priorities for the nation, Reagan focused on the budget as the means to implement his programs. For example, in his first year Reagan asked (in his fiscal year 1982 budget) to spend twenty-five cents of each tax dollar for the military and defense, while for the next two years he earmarked twenty-nine cents of every tax dollar for military expenditures.[53] On the other hand, unemployment benefits were reduced and Medicare patients were asked to pay a larger share of their own medical expenses. Military spending substituted for public service jobs and educational benefits under Social Security. Reagan also talked about altering federal and state responsibilities by shifting fiscal burdens from the national government to the states. In his 1982 budget, Reagan proposed consolidating ninety grant-in-aid programs into four block grants; eventually, Congress agreed to consolidate seventy-seven programs into nine block grants.[54]

Reagan's liaison with the Congress during his first year—unlike his approach to administration—proceeded at a feverish pace, as Cannon observes:

> In his first 100 days Reagan held 69 meetings with congressmen in which 467 members participated. He went to Capitol Hill for meetings with congressional leaders and twice addressed the nation from the Capitol, including a memorable April 28 speech which marked his recovery from wounds suffered in an assassination attempt less than a month earlier.[55]

In contrast with Jimmy Carter, Reagan was effective during 1981 because he monopolized Congress' agenda; he made specific demands and concentrated his energies on reducing social-welfare expenditures, increasing military spending, and enacting the largest income tax cut in U.S. history. The public seemed to understand Reagan's domestic priorities, and he launched a massive lobbying campaign to convince Congress. Every possible technique was used: personal visits, telephone calls, mailgrams and letters, and legislative liaison. Reagan's effectiveness was enhanced by the Office of Congressional Relations and its director, Max Friedersdorf, who was an expert in his own right. President Reagan understood Congress. Allen Schick—in describing Reagan's 1981 liaison activities—was moved to conclude that Reagan

> succeeded in spacing the major budget battles throughout the year. He did not have to yield on a budget issue to win a member's vote on another matter pending before Congress. Reagan demanded one thing from Congress at a time. When he spoke on national television, there could be no doubt as to what he wanted Congress to do. He did not clutter the legislative calendar with peripheral issues. As a conservative bent on scaling down the federal government, President Reagan did not have an ambitious legislative program; he wanted Congress to legislate less.[56]

The early budget successes were engineered by OMB Director David Stockman, whose expertise on budgetary matters overwhelmed the opposition legislators. Stockman dominated the discussions of statistical trends, economic projections, and budgetary estimates during congressional hearings. Apart from the failure of economic recovery during 1981 and 1982, strident criticism of "supply-side" economics, which had influenced Reagan's thinking at the start of his term, accompanied Stockman's public admission that such policies were based on doubtful economic assumptions. Also important to Reagan's legislative leadership was the fact that the Republican party controlled the Senate for the first time since 1953. Senate Republicans were especially united behind Reagan's leadership during 1981, giving the president more leverage in dealing with the Democratic-controlled House of Representatives. For example, although the House disapproved the sale of AWACS planes to Saudi Arabia, the Senate failed to sustain that "legislative veto" and the sale was not halted.

In two domestic emergencies, Congress was a willing ally in Reagan's use of presidential power. In September 1982, in the face of a threatened nationwide railroad strike, Congress quickly responded to Reagan's initiative that the striking engineers be ordered back to work. A year earlier, President Reagan had used his executive authority to end the strike by the Professional Air Traffic Controllers Organization (PATCO) by firing more than 11,000 air traffic controllers; the final administration victory came when the Federal Labor Relations Authority revoked PATCO's authority to represent those workers.

Just as Jimmy Carter's fundamental weakness was his lack of a strong political base from which to act, Reagan's initial popularity gave him momentum in pressuring Congress to accept his domestic agenda. Reagan soundly defeated Jimmy Carter, and interpreted the election as a "mandate" for his conservative policies. His political strength was augmented by Republican gains in the House of Representatives and his party's control of the Senate. Many Democrats, particularly in the House, hesitated to oppose such a popular president but, more important, they could not offer serious alternatives to President Reagan's budgetary policies. Unlike Jimmy Carter, President Reagan did enjoy a "honeymoon" period, during which criticisms of his programs were muted and most Americans, including Democrats, believed that he should be given an opportunity to act decisively to reduce inflation, stimulate economic growth, and balance the budget.

However, President Reagan's failure to improve the economy, and the perception that he was indifferent to an unemployment rate that exceeded 10 percent (a post-Depression record), seemed to be major factors crippling his administration. Compared with presidents since FDR, Ronald Reagan suffered the most rapid decline in his public "approval" ratings. By January 1983—midway in his term—a *New York Times*-CBS Poll showed that only 41 percent of respondents approved of the way Reagan was handling his job as president.[57] Moreover, even fewer respondents approved of his handling of the economy (35%) or foreign affairs (39%). On the other hand, 60 percent of respondents felt that, as a person, Ronald Reagan was very competent.

Reagan's slide in public opinion seriously hurt the Republican party in the 1982 midterm elections. The Republicans, while keeping control of the Senate, lost twenty-six seats in the House of Representatives. With Reagan's popularity sinking and fewer Republican allies in Congress, Democrats began to view President Reagan as politically vulnerable in 1984. Criticisms of Reagan's policies by the media, Democratic presidential hopefuls, representatives of special interests and voter blocs, and even fellow Republicans in the Congress have increased.

Most observers acknowledged Ronald Reagan's superb use of the media during 1981, and judged him to be the most effective opinion/party leader since John F. Kennedy. Reagan's subsequent loss of credibility was related less to his mode of decision making or personal style than to a disintegration in his political coalition. A stagnant economy is forcing growing numbers of blue-collar workers into unemployment; the elderly are concerned about cuts in their Social Security payments; many people fear a renewed arms race and the dangers of a nuclear confrontation with the Soviets; and even the conservative wing is disheartened by President Reagan's failure to balance the budget and neglect of social issues such as abortion and school prayer. Whether Ronald Reagan is driven from office or succeeds in winning reelection depends on how he contends with these changes in the political climate. More than personality alone, the key to assessing Reagan's successes and failures as president will rest on his decision to either abandon or moderate his policies to bolster his public esteem or to stay committed to a rigid ideological position in spite of the political costs.

CONCLUSION

The emerging literature on presidential personality does not draw a clear picture of which psychological attributes lead to effective leadership. It may be that psychoanalytical studies of presidents somehow trivialize the deeper meaning of a person's character, especially when one tries to explain a range of behavior by means of a few, neatly defined categories. It is unlikely that personality is formed by any single causal factor. Moreover, a political career sensitizes all presidents to the exigencies of partisan politics, the pressure to win elections, and the obligation to honor commitments to supporters, special interests, and voter blocs. Nor can one depreciate the importance political ideology has in shaping a president's priorities.

Our sketches of Jimmy Carter and Ronald Reagan suggest that presidents do develop personal styles of decision making: whereas Carter gave much attention to the details of public policy, Reagan delegated much responsibility to his advisers. In addition, while Ronald Reagan articulated a commitment to conservative policies, Jimmy Carter's general liberalism was less a product of ideological rigidity. In fact, Carter's loss of political support was related to his failure to formulate coherent public policies: it appeared to many observers that he simply tried to satisfy the various segments of his political constituency—though in many cases those demands could not be easily reconciled. Thus, if Carter's political decline reflected a lack of purpose, Reagan's difficulties stemmed partly from his unwillingness to abandon economic programs that were not working. Both Carter and Reagan, therefore, lost power in the roles of legislative leader and opinion/party leader; on the other hand, each could point to successes in military policy and foreign affairs.

At this juncture the most one can say about personality and presidential power is that, although certain personal attributes (whether based on high self-esteem or insecurity) may be a necessary condition for political leadership, they are not a *sufficient* condition. Presidential power is a function both of personality and of political resources. And because the research on presidential character does not satisfactorily explain why a president is more or less effective in the various roles, we have stressed those political resources available to a president in each role. Regardless of their psychological makeup, more can be learned about Jimmy Carter, Ronald Reagan, or any other president, by studying their use of power in terms of authority, decision making, public inputs, expertise, and crisis.

NOTES

[1]Theodore Roosevelt, *An Autobiography* (New York: Charles Scribner's Sons, 1929), p. 357.

[2]William Howard Taft, *Our Chief Magistrate and His Powers* (New York: Columbia University Press, 1916), pp. 139–140.

[3]Erwin C. Hargrove, *Presidential Leadership* (New York: Macmillan, 1966), p. 1.

[4]Sidney Hyman, "What Is the President's True Role?" *New York Times* (September 7, 1958).

[5]James MacGregor Burns, *Presidential Government* (Boston: Houghton Mifflin, 1973).

[6]Ibid., p. 29.

[7]James David Barber, *The Presidential Character: Predicting Performance in the White House*, 2nd ed. (Englewood Cliffs, N.J. Prentice-Hall, 1977).

[8]Hargrove, "The Crisis of the Contemporary Presidency," in Barber, ed., *Choosing the President*, (Englewood Cliffs, N.J. Prentice-Hall, 1974), p. 17

[9]Ibid., pp. 19–21, 30–33.

[10]Barber, *The Presidential Character*, 2nd ed. p. 12.

[11]Ibid.

[12]Ibid., p. 13.

[13]Ibid.

[14]Ibid., p. 210.

[15]Sigmund Freud and William C. Bullitt, *Thomas Woodrow Wilson: A Psychological Study* (Boston: Houghton Mifflin, 1967).

[16]Alexander L. George and Juliette L. George, *Woodrow Wilson and Colonel House: A Personality Study* (New York: John Day, 1956).

[17]Barber, *The Presidential Character*, 2nd ed. pp. 109, 116.

[18]Edwin A. Weinstein; James W. Anderson; and Arthur S. Link, "Woodrow Wilson's Personality: A Reappraisal," *Political Science Quarterly* (Winter 1978), pp. 585–598.

[19]Arthur S. Link, "The Case for Woodrow Wilson," *Harper's Magazine* (April 1967), p. 93.

[20]Barber, *The Presidential Character*, 2nd ed. pp. 128–129.

[21]Erwin C. Hargrove, "The Crisis of the Contemporary Presidency," in Barber, ed., *Choosing the President*, p. 17.

[22]Erwin C. Hargrove, *The Power of the Modern Presidency* (New York: Alfred A. Knopf, 1974), p. 75.

[23]Alexander L. George, "Assessing Presidential Character," *World Politics* (January 1974), p. 75.

[24]Barber, *The Presidential Character*, 2nd ed. p. 51.

[25]Ibid., pp. 132, 140.

[26]Hargrove, "The Crisis of the Contemporary Presidency," in Barber, ed., *Choosing the President*, p. 18.

[27]Hargrove, *The Power of the Modern Presidency*, p. 45.

[28]Barber, *The Presidential Character*, 2nd ed. p. 418.

[29]Cited in Hargrove, *The Power of the Modern Presidency*, p. 45.

[30]Barber, *The Presidential Character*, 2nd ed. p. 401.

[31]Hargrove, *The Power of the Modern Presidency*, p. 48.

[32]Richard P. Nathan, *The Plot That Failed: Nixon and the Administrative Presidency* (New York: John Wiley and Sons, 1975), p. 7.

[33]Hargrove, *The Power of the Modern Presidency*, p. 77.

[34]Jimmy Carter, *Why Not the Best?* (Nashville, Tenn.: Broadman Press, 1975).

[35]Barber, *The Presidential Character*, 2nd ed. p. 535.

[36]Charles Funderburk, *Presidents and Politics: The Limits of Power* (Monterey, Calif.: Brooks/Cole, 1982), p. 309.

[37]Cited in Haynes Johnson, *In the Absence of Power: Governing America* (New York: The Viking Press, 1980), p. 301.

[38]Barber, *The Presidential Character*, 2nd ed. p. 536.

[39]James Fallows, "The Passionless Presidency," in Peter Woll, ed., *Behind the Scenes in American Government: Personality and Politics*, 3rd ed. (Boston: Little, Brown, 1981), p. 141.

[40]See Betty Glad, *Jimmy Carter: In Search of the Great White House* (New York: W. W. Norton, 1980); Bruce Mazlish and Edwin Diamond, *Jimmy Carter: An Interpretive Biography* (New York: Simon and Schuster, 1979); Lloyd deMause and Henry Ebel,

eds., *Jimmy Carter and American Fantasy* (New York: Two Continents/Psychohistory Press, 1977).

[41]Glad, *Jimmy Carter: In Search of the Great White House*, p. 433.

[42]Laurence E. Lynn, Jr. and David deF. Whiteman, *The President as Policymaker: Jimmy Carter and Welfare Reform* (Philadelphia: Temple University Press, 1981), p. 275.

[43]George Gallup, "Public Concern Is Growing Over Energy Crisis," *Washington Post* (September 2, 1979), p. A12.

[44]David V. Edwards, *The American Political Experience* (Englewood Cliffs, N.J. Prentice-Hall, 1982), p. 497.

[45]Quoted in "Carter and Reagan: Clues to their Character," *U.S. News and World Report* (October 27, 1980), p. 30.

[46]Norman J. Ornstein, ed., *President and Congress, Assessing Reagan's First Year* (Washington, D.C.: American Enterprise Institute for Public Policy Research, 1982), p. 1. All the essays in this edition document Reagan's extraordinarily successful first-year achievements, but the various contributors also agreed that Reagan would have more difficulties with Congress in his later years.

[47]Hedley Donovan, "Reagan's First 200 Days," *Fortune* (September 21, 1981), pp. 63–72.

[48]"The Power Brokers Around the President," *U.S. News and World Report* (February 9, 1981), pp. 19–22.

[49]Lou Cannon, *Reagan* (New York: G. P. Putnam's Sons, 1982), p. 376.

[50]Ibid., p. 391.

[51]Ibid., p. 393.

[52]I. M. Destler, "Reagan, Congress and Foreign Policy in 1981," in Norman J. Ornstein, ed., *President and Congress: Assessing Reagan's First Year*, p. 76.

[53]See *The United States Budget in Brief—FY 1982* (Washington, D.C.: Executive Office of the President, Office of Management and Budget, 1981), cover page; *The United States Budget in Brief—FY 1983* (Washington, D.C.: Executive Office of the President, Office of Management and Budget, 1982), cover page; Dale Tate, "Fiscal 1984 Budget: Reagan Foresees Triple-Digit '84–88 Deficits," *Congressional Quarterly Weekly Report* (February 5, 1983), p. 247.

[54]John L. Palmer and Isabel V. Sawhill, *The Reagan Experiment* (Washington, D.C.: The Urban Institute Press, 1982), p. 16.

[55]Cannon, *Reagan*, p. 333.

[56]Allen Schick, "How the Budget Was Won and Lost," in Ornstein, ed., *President and Congress: Assessing Reagan's First Year*, p. 28.

[57]"New York Times/CBS News Poll, January 16–19, 1983," *New York Times* (January 25, 1983), p. 13.

SUGGESTED READINGS

Barber, James David. *The Presidential Character: Predicting Performance in the White House.* 2nd ed. Englewood Cliffs, N.J. Prentice-Hall, 1977.

Buchanan, Bruce. *The Presidential Experience: What the Office Does to the Man.* Englewood Cliffs, N.J. Prentice-Hall, 1978.

Burns, James MacGregor. *Roosevelt: The Lion and the Fox.* New York: Harcourt Brace and World, 1956.

Carter, Jimmy. *Why Not the Best?* Nashville, Tenn.: Broadman Press, 1975.

deMause, Lloyd, and Ebel, Henry, eds. *Jimmy Carter and American Fantasy.* New York: Two Continents/Psychohistory Press, 1977.

Freud, Sigmund, and Bullitt, William C. *Thomas Woodrow Wilson: A Psychological Study.* Boston: Houghton Mifflin, 1967.

George, Alexander L., and George, Juliette L. *Woodrow Wilson and Colonel House: A Personality Study.* New York: Dover Publications, Inc., 1964.

Glad, Betty. *Jimmy Carter: In Search of the Great White House.* New York: W. W. Norton, 1980.

Greenstein, Fred I. *Personality and Politics: Problems of Evidence, Inference and Conceptualization.* Chicago: Markham, 1969.

Greenstein, Fred I., and Lerner, M. *Sourcebook for the Study of Personality and Politics.* Chicago: Markham, 1971.

Hargrove, Erwin C. *Presidential Leadership, Personality and Political Style.* New York: Macmillan, 1966.

Kearns, Doris. *Lyndon Johnson and The American Dream.* New York: New American Library (Signet), 1977.

Lasswell, Harold D. *Psychopathology and Politics.* New York: Viking Press, 1960.

Mazlish, Bruce. *In Search of Nixon: A Psychohistorical Inquiry.* Baltimore: Penguin Books, 1973.

Mazlish, Bruce, and Diamond, Edwin. *Jimmy Carter: An Interpretive Biography.* New York: Simon and Schuster, 1979.

Nixon Richard M. *Six Crises.* New York: Pyramid Books, 1968.

Smith, Hedrich, Adam Clymer, Leonard Silk, Robert Lindsey, and Richard Burt. *Reagan the Man, the President.* New York: Macmillan, 1981.

Stoessinger, John G. *Crusaders and Pragmatists: Movers of Modern American Foreign Policy.* New York: W. W. Norton, 1979.

Wicker, Tom. *JFK and LBJ: The Influence of Personality upon Politics.* Baltimore: Penguin Books, 1969.

APPENDIX A

The Constitution: Provisions on the Presidency

Article II

Section 1. The executive power shall be vested in a President of the United States of America. He shall hold his office during the term of four years, and, together with the Vice President, chosen for the same term, be elected as follows:

Each State shall appoint, in such manner as the legislature thereof may direct, a number of electors, equal to the whole number of senators and representatives to which the State may be entitled in the Congress: but no senator or representative, or person holding an office of trust or profit under the United States, shall be appointed an elector.

The electors shall meet in their respective States, and vote by ballot for two persons, of whom one at least shall not be an inhabitant of the same State with themselves. And they shall make a list of all the persons voted for, and of the number of votes for each; which list they shall sign and certify, and transmit sealed to the seat of the government of the United States, directed to the president of the Senate. The president of the Senate shall, in the presence of the Senate and House of Representatives, open all the certificates, and the votes shall then be counted. The person having the greatest number of votes shall be the President, if such number be a majority of the whole number of electors appointed; and if there be more than one who have such majority, and have an equal number of votes, then the House of Representatives shall immediately choose by ballot one of them for President; and if no person have a majority, then from the five highest on the list the said House shall in like manner choose the President. But in choosing the President, the votes shall be taken by States, the representation from each State having one vote; a quorum for this purpose shall consist of a member or members from two thirds of the States, and a majority of all the States shall be necessary to a choice. In every case, after the choice of the President, the person having the greatest number of votes of the electors shall be the Vice President. But if there should remain two or more who have equal votes, the Senate shall choose from them by ballot the Vice President.[1]

The Congress may determine the time of choosing the electors, and the day on which they shall give their votes; which day shall be the same throughout the United States.

No person except a natural born citizen, or a citizen of the United States, at the time of the adoption of this Constitution, shall be eligible to the office of President;

neither shall any person be eligible to that office who shall not have attained to the age of thirty-five years, and been fourteen years a resident within the United States.

In case of the removal of the President from office, or of his death, resignation, or inability to discharge the powers and duties of the said office, the same shall devolve on the Vice President, and the Congress may by law provide for the case of removal, death, resignation or inability, both of the President and Vice President, declaring what officer shall then act as President, and such officer shall act accordingly, until the disability be removed or a President shall be elected.[2]

The President shall, at stated times, receive for his services a compensation, which shall neither be increased nor diminished during the period for which he shall have been elected, and he shall not receive within that period any other emolument from the United States, or any of them.

Before he enter on the execution of his office, he shall take the following oath or affirmation: "I do solemnly swear (or affirm) that I will faithfully execute the office of President of the United States, and will to the best of my ability, preserve, protect and defend the Constitution of the United States."

Section 2. The President shall be Commander in Chief of the army and navy of the United States, and of the militia of the several States, when called into the actual service of the United States; he may require the opinion, in writing, of the principal officer in each of the executive departments, upon any subject relating to the duties of their respective offices, and he shall have power to grant reprieves and pardons for offenses against the United States, except in cases of impeachment.

He shall have power, by and with the advice and consent of the Senate, to make treaties, provided two thirds of the senators present concur; and he shall nominate, and by and with the advice and consent of the Senate, shall appoint ambassadors, other public ministers and consuls, judges of the Supreme Court, and all other officers of the United States, whose appointments are not herein otherwise provided for, and which shall be established by law: but the Congress may by law vest the appointment of such inferior officers, as they think proper, in the President alone, in the courts of law, or in the heads of departments.

The President shall have power to fill up all vacancies that may happen during the recess of the Senate, by granting commissions which shall expire at the end of their next session.

Section 3. He shall from time to time give to the Congress information of the state of the Union, and recommend to their consideration such measures as he shall judge necessary and expedient; he may, on extraordinary occasions, convene both Houses, or either of them, and in case of disagreement between them with respect to the time of adjournment, he may adjourn them to such time as he shall think proper; he shall receive ambassadors and other public ministers; he shall take care that the laws be faithfully executed, and shall commission all the officers of the United States.

Section 4. The President, Vice President, and all civil officers of the United States, shall be removed from office on impeachment for, and conviction of, treason, bribery, or other high crimes and misdemeanors.

Article I

Section 3. . . . . The Vice President of the United States shall be President of the Senate, but shall have no vote, unless they be equally divided.

The Senate shall choose their other officers, and also a president *pro tempore*, in the absence of the Vice President, or when he shall exercise the office of the President of the United States.

The Senate shall have the sole power to try all impeachments. When sitting for that purpose, they shall be on oath or affirmation. When the President of the United States is tried, the chief justice shall preside: and no person shall be convicted without the concurrence of two thirds of the members present.

Judgment in cases of impeachment shall not extend further than to removal from office, and disqualifications to hold and enjoy any office of honor, trust or profit under the United States: but the party convicted shall nevertheless be liable and subject to indictment, trial, judgment and punishment, according to law.

Section 7. . . . Every bill which shall have passed the House of Representatives and the Senate, shall, before it becomes a law, be presented to the President of the United States; if he approves he shall sign it, but if not he shall return it, with his objections to that House in which it shall have originated, who shall enter the objections at large on their journal, and proceed to reconsider it. If after such reconsideration two thirds of that House shall agree to pass the bill, it shall be sent, together with the objections, to the other House, by which it shall likewise be reconsidered, and if approved by two thirds of that House, it shall become a law. But in all such cases the votes of both Houses shall be determined by yeas and nays, and the names of the persons voting for and against the bill shall be entered on the journal of each House respectively. If any bill shall not be returned by the President within ten days (Sundays excepted) after it shall have been presented to him, the same shall be a law, in like manner as if he had signed it, unless the Congress by their adjournment prevent its return, in which case it shall not be a law.

Every order, resolution, or vote to which the concurrence of the Senate and the House of Representatives may be necessary (except on a question of adjournment) shall be presented to the President of the United States; and before the same shall take effect, shall be approved by him, or being disapproved by him, shall be repassed by two thirds of the Senate and House of Representatives, according to the rules and limitations prescribed in the case of a bill.

Section 9. . . . The privilege of the writ of *habeas corpus* shall not be suspended, unless when in cases of rebellion or invasion the public safety may require it.

Article IV

Section 4. The United States shall guarantee to every State in this Union a republican form of government, and shall protect each of them against invasion; and on application of the legislature, or of the executive (when the legislature cannot be convened) against domestic violence.

Amendment XII

Adopted September 25, 1804

The electors shall meet in their respective States, and vote by ballot for President and Vice President, one of whom, at least, shall not be an inhabitant of the same State with themselves; they shall name in their ballots the person voted for as President, and in distinct ballots the person voted for as Vice President and they shall make distinct lists of all persons voted for as President and of all persons voted for as Vice President, and of the number of votes for each, which lists they shall sign and certify, and transmit sealed to the seat of the government of the United States, directed to the President of the Senate; The President of the Senate shall, in the presence of the Senate and House of Representatives, open all the certificates and the votes shall then be counted; The person having the greatest number of votes for President, shall be the President, if such number be a majority of the whole number of electors appointed; and if no person have such majority, then from the persons having the highest numbers not exceeding three on the list of those voted for as President, the House of Representatives shall choose immediately, by ballot, the President. But in choosing the President, the votes shall be taken by States, the representation from each State having one vote; a quorum for this purpose shall consist of a member or members from two thirds of the States, and a majority of all the States shall be necessary to a choice. And if the House of Representatives shall not choose a President whenever the right of choice shall devolve upon them, before the fourth day of March next following, then the Vice President shall act as President, as in the case of the death or other constitutional disability of the President. The person having the greatest number of votes as Vice President shall be the Vice President, if such number be a majority of the whole number of electors appointed, and if no person have a majority, then from the two highest numbers on the list, the Senate shall choose the Vice President; a quorum for the purpose shall consist of two thirds of the whole number of Senators, and a majority of the whole number shall be necessary to a choice. But no person constitutionally ineligible to the office of President shall be eligible to that of Vice President of the United States.

Amendment XX
Adopted January 23, 1933

Section 1. The terms of the President and Vice President shall end at noon on the 20th day of January, and the terms of Senators and Representatives at noon on the 3rd day of January, of the years in which such terms would have ended if this article had not been ratified; and the terms of their successors shall then begin.

Section 2. The Congress shall assemble at least once in every year, and such meeting shall begin at noon on the 3rd day of January, unless they shall by law appoint a different day.

Section 3. If, at the time fixed for the beginning of the term of the President, the President-elect shall have died, the Vice President-elect shall become President. If a President shall not have been chosen before the time fixed for the beginning of his term, or if the President-elect shall have failed to qualify, then the Vice President-elect shall act as President until a President shall have qualified; and the Congress may by law provide for the case wherein neither a President-elect nor a Vice President-elect shall have qualified, declaring who shall then act as President, or the manner in which one who is to act shall be selected, and such person shall act accordingly until a President or Vice President shall have qualified.

Section 4. The Congress may by law provide for the case of the death of any of the persons from whom the House of Representatives may choose a President whenever the right of choice shall have devolved upon them, and for the case of the death of any of the persons from whom the Senate may choose a Vice President whenever the right of choice shall have devolved upon them.

Section 5. Sections 1 and 2 shall take effect on the 15th day of October following the ratification of this article.

Section 6. This article shall be inoperative unless it shall have been ratified as an amendment to the Constitution by the legislatures of three fourths of the several States within seven years from the date of its submission.

Amendment XXII
Adopted February 26, 1951

No person shall be elected to the office of the President more than twice, and no person who has held the office of the President, or acted as President, for more than two years of a term to which some other person was elected President shall be elected to the office of the President more than once.

But this article shall not apply to any person holding the office of President when this article was proposed by the Congress, and shall not prevent any person who may be holding the office of President, or acting as President, during the term within which this article becomes operative from holding the office of President or acting as President during the remainder of such term.

This article shall be inoperative unless it shall have been ratified as an amendment to the Constitution by the legislatures of three fourths of the several States within seven years from the date of its submission to the States by the Congress.

Amendment XXIII
Adopted March 29, 1961

Section 1. The District constituting the seat of Government of the United States shall appoint in such manner as the Congress may direct:

A number of electors of President and Vice President equal to the whole number of Senators and Representatives in Congress to which the District would be entitled if it were a State, but in no event more than the least populous State; they shall be in addition to those appointed by the States, but they shall be considered, for the purposes of the election of President and Vice President, to be electors appointed by a State; and they shall meet in the District and perform such duties as provided by the twelfth article of amendment.

Section 2. The Congress shall have power to enforce this article by appropriate legislation.

Amendment XXV
Adopted February 10, 1967

Section 1. In case of the removal of the President from office or of his death or resignation, the Vice President shall become President.

Section 2. Whenever there is a vacancy in the office of the Vice President, the President shall nominate a Vice President who shall take office upon confirmation by a majority vote of both Houses of Congress.

Section 3. Whenever the President transmits to the President *pro tempore* of the Senate and the Speaker of the House of Representatives his written declaration that he is unable to discharge the powers and duties of his office, and until he transmits to them a written declaration to the contrary, such powers and duties shall be discharged by the Vice President as Acting President.

Section 4. Whenever the Vice President and a majority of either the principal officers of the executive department or of such other body as Congress may by law provide, transmit to the President *pro tempore* of the Senate and the Speaker of the House of Representatives their written declaration that the President is unable to discharge the powers and duties of his office, the Vice President shall immediately assume the powers and duties of the office as Acting President.

Thereafter, when the President transmits to the President *pro tempore* of the Senate and the Speaker of the House of Representatives his written declaration that no inability exists, he shall resume the powers and duties of his office unless the Vice President and a majority of either the principal officers of the executive department or of such other body as Congress may by law provide, transmit within four days to the President *pro tempore* of the Senate and the Speaker of the House of Representatives their written declaration that the President is unable to discharge the powers and duties of his office. Thereupon Congress shall decide the issue, assembling within forty-eight hours for that purpose if not in session. If the Congress, within twenty-one days after receipt of the latter written declaration, or, if Congress is not in session, within twenty-one days after Congress is required to assemble, determines by two thirds vote of both Houses that the President is unable to discharge the powers and duties of his office, the Vice President shall continue to discharge the same as Acting President; otherwise, the President shall resume the powers and duties of his office.

Amendment XXVI
Adopted June 30, 1971

Section 1. The right of citizens of the United States, who are 18 years of age or older, to vote shall not be denied or abridged by the United States or by any state on account of age.

Section 2. The Congress shall have power to enforce this article by appropriate legislation.

NOTES

[1] Superseded by the Twelfth Amendment
[2] See the Twenty-Fifth Amendment

APPENDIX B

Presidential Elections, 1789–1980

Year	Candidate	Political party	Electoral votes	Popular votes
1789	George Washington[1]		69	
	John Adams		34	
	John Jay		9	
	Others		26	
	(Electoral votes not cast)		12	
1792	George Washington[1]	Federalist	132	
	John Adams	Federalist	77	
	George Clinton	Democratic-Republican	50	
	Thomas Jefferson		4	
	Aaron Burr		1	
1796	John Adams[1]	Federalist	71	
	Thomas Jefferson	Democratic-Republican	68	
	Thomas Pinckney	Federalist	59	
	Aaron Burr	Anti-Federalist	30	
	Others		48	
1800	Thomas Jefferson[1]	Democratic-Republican	73[2]	
	Aaron Burr	Democratic-Republican	73[2]	
	John Adams	Federalist	65	
	C. C. Pinckney	Federalist	64	
	John Jay	Federalist	1	
1804	Thomas Jefferson	Democratic-Republican	162	
	C. C. Pinckney	Federalist	14	
1808	James Madison	Democratic-Republican	122	
	C. C. Pinckney	Federalist	47	
	George Clinton	Independent-Rep.	6	
	(Electoral votes not cast)		1	

Year	Candidate	Political party	Electoral votes	Popular votes
1812	James Madison	Democratic-Republican	128	
	De Witt Clinton	Fusion	89	
	(Electoral votes not cast)		1	
1816	James Monroe	Republican	183	
	Rufus King	Federalist	34	
	(Electoral votes not cast)		4	
1820	James Monroe	Republican	231	
	John Q. Adams	Independent-Rep.	1	
	(Electoral votes not cast)		3	
1824	John Q. Adams		84[2]	108,740
	Andrew Jackson		99[2]	153,544
	Henry Clay		37	47,136
	W. H. Crawford		41	46,618
1828	Andrew Jackson	Democratic	178	647,286
	John Q. Adams	National Republican	83	508,064
1832	Andrew Jackson	Democratic	219	687,502
	Henry Clay	National Republican	49	530,189
	Others		18	
	(Electoral votes not cast)		2	
1836	Martin Van Buren	Democratic	170	765,483
	William H. Harrison	Whig	73 ⎱	
	Hugh L. White	Whig	26 ⎰	739,795[3]
	Daniel Webster	Whig	14	
	Others		11	
1840	William H. Harrison	Whig	234	1,274,624
	Martin Van Buren	Democratic	60	1,127,781
1844	James K. Polk	Democratic	170	1,338,464
	Henry Clay	Whig	105	1,300,097
	Others		—	62,300
1848	Zachary Taylor	Whig	163	1,360,967
	Lewis Cass	Democratic	127	1,222,342
	Martin Van Buren	Free Soil	—	291,263
1852	Franklin Pierce	Democratic	254	1,601,117
	Winfield Scott	Whig	42	1,385,453
	John P. Hale	Free Soil	—	155,825
1856	James Buchanan	Democratic	174	1,832,955
	John C. Fremont	Republican	114	1,339,932
	Millard Fillmore	American	8	871,731

Year	Candidate	Political party	Electoral votes	Popular votes
1860	Abraham Lincoln	Republican	180	1,865,593
	J. C. Breckinridge	Democratic (S)	72	848,356
	Stephen A. Douglas	Democratic	12	1,382,713
	John Bell	Constitutional Union	39	592,906
1864	Abraham Lincoln	Republican	212	2,206,938
	George B. McClellan	Democratic	21	1,803,787
	(Electoral votes not cast)		81	
1868	Ulysses S. Grant	Republican	214	3,013,421
	Horatio Seymour	Democratic	80	2,706,829
	(Electoral votes not cast)		23	
1872	Ulysses S. Grant	Republican	286	3,596,745
	Horace Greeley	Democratic	—	2,843,446
	Others		63	
	(Electoral votes not cast)		17	
1876	Rutherford B. Hayes	Republican	185	4,036,572
	Samuel J. Tilden	Democratic	184	4,284,020
			—	81,737
1880	James A. Garfield	Republican	214	4,453,295
	Winfield S. Hancock	Democratic	155	4,414,082
	Others		—	318,883
1884	Grover Cleveland	Democratic	219	4,879,507
	James G. Blaine	Republican	182	4,850,293
	Others		—	325,739
1888	Benjamin Harrison	Republican	233	5,447,129
	Grover Cleveland	Democratic	168	5,537,857
	Others		—	396,441
1892	Grover Cleveland	Democratic	277	5,555,426
	Benjamin Harrison	Republican	145	5,182,690
	James B. Weaver	People's	22	1,029,846
	Others		—	285,297
1896	William McKinley	Republican	271	7,102,246
	William J. Bryan	Democratic	176	6,492,559
	Others		—	315,398
1900	William McKinley	Republican	292	7,218,491
	William J. Bryan	Democratic	155	6,356,734
	Others		—	386,840
1904	Theodore Roosevelt	Republican	336	7,628,461
	Alton B. Parker	Democratic	140	5,084,223
	Eugene V. Debs	Socialist	—	402,283
	Others		—	406,968

Year	Candidate	Political party	Electoral votes	Popular votes
1908	William H. Taft	Republican	321	7,675,320
	William J. Bryan	Democratic	162	6,412,294
	Eugene V. Debs	Socialist	—	420,793
	Others		—	379,833
1912	Woodrow Wilson	Democratic	435	6,296,547
	Theodore Roosevelt	Progressive	88	4,118,571
	William H. Taft	Republican	8	3,486,720
	Eugene V. Debs	Socialist	—	900,672
	Others		—	235,025
1916	Woodrow Wilson	Democratic	277	9,127,695
	Charles E. Hughes	Republican	254	8,533,507
	Others		—	819,022
1920	Warren G. Harding	Republican	404	16,143,047
	James M. Cox	Democratic	127	9,130,328
	Eugene V. Debs	Socialist	—	919,799
	Others		—	534,534
1924	Calvin Coolidge	Republican	382	15,718,211
	John W. Davis	Democratic	136	8,385,283
	Robert M. LaFollette	Progressive	13	4,831,289
	Others		—	154,301
1928	Herbert C. Hoover	Republican	444	21,391,993
	Alfred E. Smith	Democratic	87	15,016,169
	Others		—	330,725
1932	Franklin D. Roosevelt	Democratic	472	22,809,638
	Herbert C. Hoover	Republican	59	15,758,901
	Norman Thomas	Socialist	—	881,951
	Others		—	271,355
1936	Franklin D. Roosevelt	Democratic	523	27,752,869
	Alfred M. Landon	Republican	8	16,674,665
	William Lemke	Union	—	882,479
	Others		—	318,503
1940	Franklin D. Roosevelt	Democratic	449	27,307,819
	Wendell L. Willkie	Republican	82	22,321,018
	Others		—	218,512
1944	Franklin D. Roosevelt	Democratic	432	25,606,585
	Thomas E. Dewey	Republican	99	22,014,745
	Others		—	200,612
1948	Harry S. Truman	Democratic	303	24,179,345
	Thomas E. Dewey	Republican	189	21,991,291
	J. Strom Thurmond	States' Rights	39	1,176,125
	Henry A. Wallace	Progressive	—	1,157,326
	Others		—	286,327

Year	Candidate	Political party	Electoral votes	Popular votes
1952	Dwight D. Eisenhower	Republican	442	33,936,234
	Adlai E. Stevenson	Democratic	89	27,314,992
	Others		—	290,959
1956	Dwight D. Eisenhower	Republican	457	35,590,472
	Adlai E. Stevenson	Democratic	73[4]	26,022,752
	Others		—	197,565
1960	John F. Kennedy	Democratic	303[5]	34,226,731
	Richard M. Nixon	Republican	219	34,108,157
	Others		—	197,029
1964	Lyndon B. Johnson	Democratic	486	43,129,566
	Barry M. Goldwater	Republican	52	27,178,188
	Others		—	101,206
1968	Richard M. Nixon	Republican	301	31,785,480
	Hubert H. Humphrey	Democratic	191	31,275,166
	George C. Wallace	American Independent	46	9,906,473
	Others		—	218,347
1972	Richard M. Nixon	Republican	520	47,169,911
	George S. McGovern	Democratic	17	29,170,383
	John G. Schmitz	American Independent	—	1,099,482
	Others		1[6]	278,778
1976	Jimmy Carter	Democratic	297	40,830,763
	Gerald R. Ford, Jr.	Republican	240	39,147,793
	Eugene J. McCarthy	Independent	—	756,691
	Others		1[7]	820,642
1980	Ronald Reagan	Republican	489	43,904,153
	Jimmy Carter	Democratic	49	35,483,883
	John Anderson	Independent	—	5,720,060
	Ed Clark	Libertarian	—	921,299
	Barry Commoner	Citizens	—	234,294
	Others		—	251,532

Source: U.S. Department of Commerce, *Historical Statistics of the United States, Colonial Times to 1970*, Part II (Washington, D.C.: U.S. Government Printing Office, 1975), pp. 1073–1074: Richard M. Scammon and Alice V. McGillivray, eds., *American Votes 14* (Washington, D.C.: Congressional Quarterly, 1981), pp. 14–19.

[1] Prior to the 1804 election, each Elector cast two votes; the person getting the highest number—if a majority—was elected President and the person with the second-highest number—if a majority—was elected Vice President.

[2] Since no candidate received the majority of Electoral Votes, this election was decided in the House of Representatives.

[3] The Whig tickets were pledged to different candidates in the various states.

[4] One Democratic Elector voted for Walter Jones.

[5] Fifteen Democratic Electors voted for Senator Harry F. Byrd, Democrat of Virginia.

[6] One Republican Elector voted for John Hospers, Libertarian Party candidate.

[7] One Republican Elector voted for Ronald Reagan.

Name Index

Subject Index